LOCAL EXPLORER

CORNWALL

& PLYMOUTH

www.philips-maps.co.uk

Published by Philip's, a division of
Octopus Publishing Group Ltd
www.octopusbooks.co.uk
Carmelite House, 50 Victoria Embankment
London EC4Y 0DZ
An Hachette UK Company,
www.hachette.co.uk

First edition 2022
COREA

ISBN 978-1-84907-599-2

© Philip's 2022

Photographic acknowledgements:
Alamy Stock Photo: /christopher jones X top right. /James Hughes IX bottom.
Dreamstime.com: /Mick Blakey VIII top; / Simone Van Den Berg VIII right; /Gary Perkin VIII bottom; /Ariadna De Raadt IX top; / Pbnash1964 X top left; /Tomas Marek X centre.
iStock: ianwool front cover.

Printed in China

CONTENTS

II	Key to map pages
IV	Route planning
VIII	Best places to visit
1	Key to map symbols
2	**Street maps** at 1¾ inches to 1 mile
104	**Street maps** at 3½ inches to 1 mile
148	**Street map of Plymouth city centre** at 7 inches to 1 mile
150	**Index** of towns, villages, streets, hospitals, industrial estates, railway stations, schools, shopping centres, universities and places of interest

T0329504

Key to map pages

80	**Map pages at** 1¾ inches to 1 mile
112	**Map pages at** 3½ inches to 1 mile
148	**Map pages at** 7 inches to 1 mile

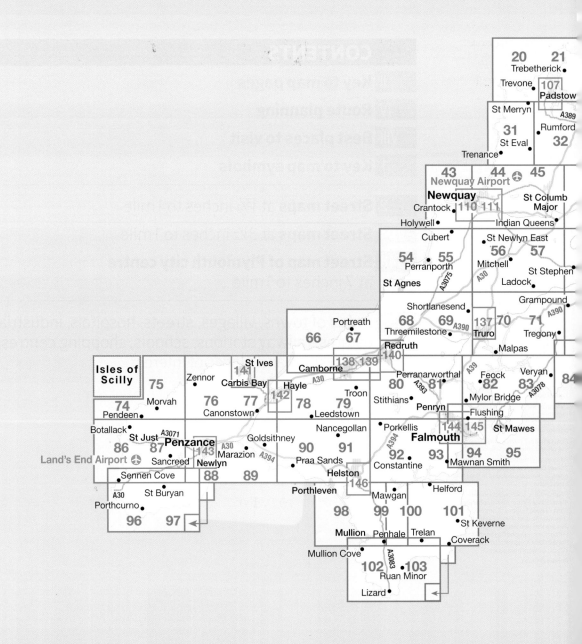

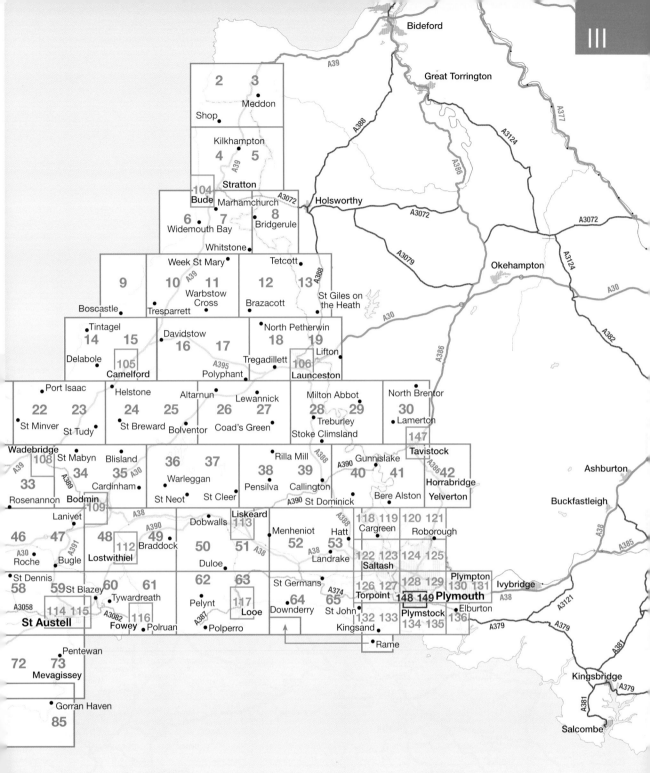

Bideford

Great Torrington

2 **3**
Meddon
Shop

Kilkhampton
4 **5**
Stratton
104
Bude Marhamchurch
6 **7** **8**
Widemouth Bay Bridgerule
Whitstone

Holsworthy

Okehampton

Week St Mary Tetcott
9 **10** **11** **12** **13**
Warbstow St Giles on
Boscastle Cross the Heath
Tresparrett Brazacott

North Petherwin
Tintagel Davidstow **18** **19**
14 **15** **16** **17** Lifton
Tregadillett **106**
Delabole Polyphant Launceston
105
Camelford

Port Isaac Helstone Altarnun Lewannick Milton Abbot North Brentor
22 **23** **24** **25** **26** **27** **28** **29** **30**
St Minver St Breward Coad's Green Treburley Lamerton
St Tudy Bolventor Stoke Climsland
147
Tavistock

Ashburton
Wadebridge Rilla Mill Gunnislake
108 St Mabyn Blisland **36** **37** **38** **39** **40** **41** **42**
34 **35** Warleggan Pensilva Callington Bere Alston Horrabridge
33 Cardinham St Neot St Cleer St Dominick Yelverton
Rosenannon Bodmin Buckfastleigh
109
Lanivet **118** **119** **120** **121**
46 **47** Dobwalls Menheniot Cargreen Roborough
48 **49** **113** Hatt
112 Braddock **50** **51** **52** **53**
Roche Bugle Lostwithiel Duloe Landrake **122** **123** **124** **125**
Saltash
St Dennis Torpoint Plympton
58 **59** **60** **61** **62** **63** St Germans **126** **127** **128** **129** **130** **131** Ivybridge
St Blazey **65**
Tywardreath Pelynt **117** **64** St John **148 149** Plymouth
114 115 Looe Downderry **132** **133** Plymstock Elburton
St Austell Fowey Polruan Kingsand **134** **135** **136**
Polperro Rame

72 **73** Pentewan
Mevagissey Kingsbridge

Gorran Haven
85
Salcombe

Scale
0   5   10   15   20   25 km
0   5   10   15 miles

Route planning

Scale

0   5   10 km
0   1   2   3   4   5   6 miles

ISLES OF SCILLY

St Helens
White Island
Bryher
St Martin's 47
New Grimsby
Higher Town
Bryher
Tresco
Samson
Crow Sound
Eastern Isles
North West Passage
The Road
Newford 51
Maypole
A3110
Hugh Town
St Mary's
Crim Rocks
Old Town
ST MARY'S
Broad Sound
Annet
St Mary's Sound
Gugh
PENZANCE 2:40 (Apr–Nov)
St Agnes
Smith Sound
St Agnes
Bishop Rock

Godrevy Island
St Agnes
192
Porthtowan
Portreath
B3301
Three Blacky
Mawla
A3047
St D
Redru
Roscroggan
Illogan
Kehelland
A30
A3047
Tuckingmill
Pool 225
Cambro
Redru
Gwithian
B3301
Roseworthy
CAMBORNE
Carnkie
Four Lanes
Lanr
St Ives Bay
Connor Downs
Barripper
Troon
Penhalvaen
St Ives
Halsetown
Phillack
Copperhouse
Carnhell Green
Praze-an-Beeble
Penmarth
252
Stithi
Carbis Bay
Lelant
Hayle
Crowan
Burras
Res.
Zennor
Towednack 247
Cripplesease
B3306
Nancledra
Canon's Town
St Erth
Leedstown
Drym
B3302
Nancegollan
Carnkie
Porkellis
Sewor
Porthmeor
B3306
Newmill
Hayle
Townshend
Godolphin Cross
Wendron
9
Morvah
Bojewyan
252
Madron
Ludgvan
Crowlas
Relubbus
Trescowe
Crowntown
Pendeen
Higher Boscaswell
Gulval
B3280
A394
Trewellard
B3311
B3309
St Hilary
Goldsithney
Crowntown
Botallack
Carnyorth
Heamoor
A3071
Chyandour
Marazion
Germoe
Sithney
Trewennack
St Just
Newbridge
Penzance
Perranuthnoe
Ashton
Breage
A394
The Brisons
Bosavern
Res.
Tredavoe
Praa Sands
A394
Helston
Kelynack
224
Sancreed
Newlyn
Rinsey
Whitesand Bay
LAND'S END
Brane
Paul
Crows-an-wra
Catchall
Mousehole
Gweek
Sennen Cove
A30
Kerris
B3283
St Buryan
Trewoofe
Lamorna
MOUNT'S BAY
Porthleven
The Loe
A3083
Garras
Sennen
B3315
Polgigga
B3315
Boskenna
Lamorna Cove
Bérepper
Maw
Treen
Porthcurno
Gunwalloe
Cury
Cross Lanes
St Levan
ISLES OF SCILLY (Mar–Nov)
10
Mullion
B3296
Penhale
Mullion Cove
A3083
Mullion Cove
Predannack Wollas
St Ruan
Grade
Kynance Cove
Lizard

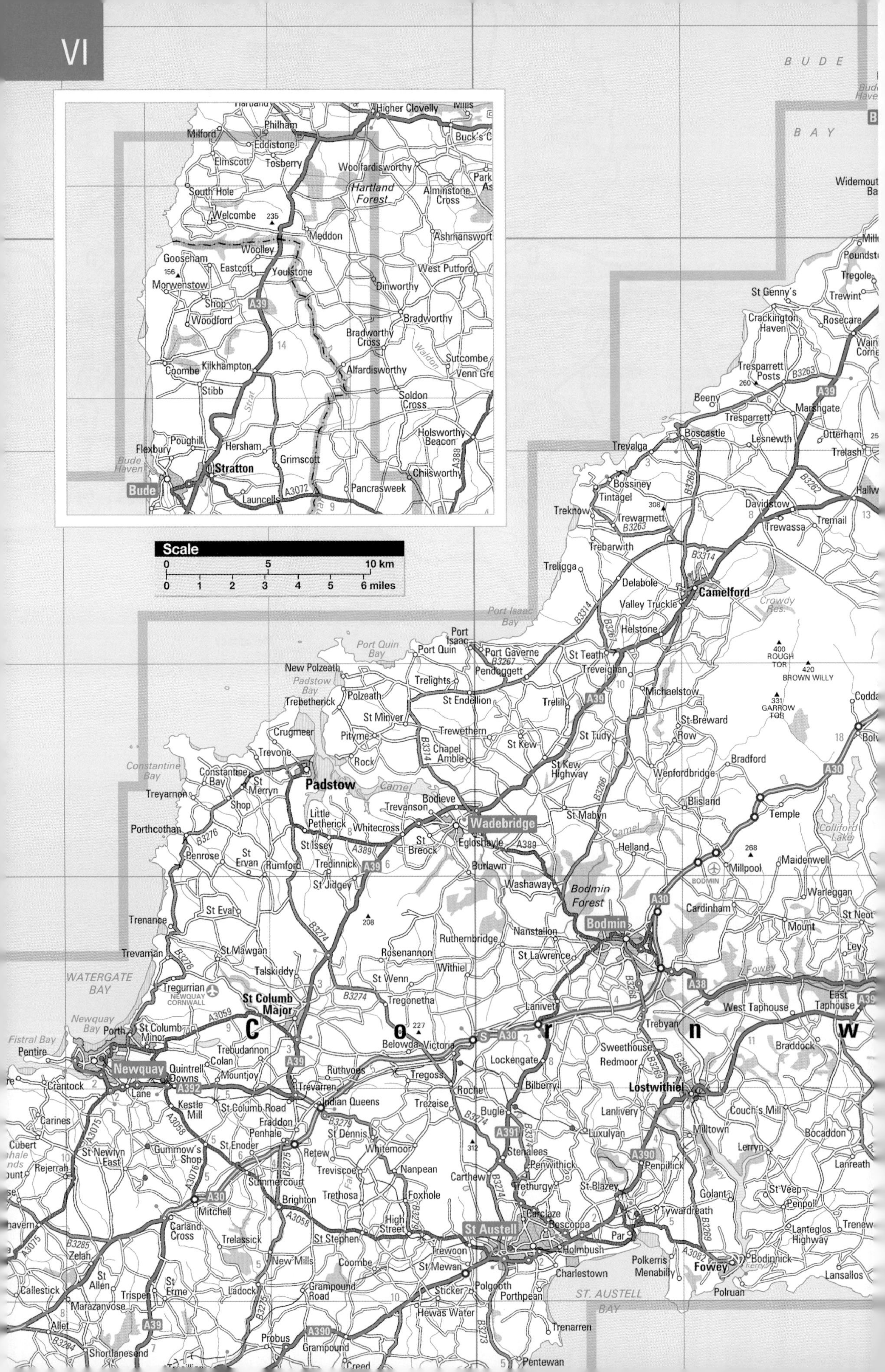

BUDE
BAY
Bude
Stratton
Launcells
Higher Clovelly
Philham
Milford
Eddistone
Elmscott
Tosberry
Woolfardisworthy
Hartland
Forest
Alminstone
Cross
Buck's C
South Hole
Welcombe
235
Meddon
Ashmansworthy
Woolley
Gooseham
Eastcott
Youlstone
West Putford
156
Morwenstow
Dinworthy
Shop
A39
Woodford
Bradworthy
Bradworthy
Cross
14
Waldon
Sutcombe
Alfardisworthy
Venn Gr
Coombe
Kilkhampton
Stibb
Soldon
Cross
Strat
Holsworthy
Beacon
Poughill
Flexbury
Hersham
Grimscott
A388
Bude
Haven
Chilsworthy
A3072
Pancrasweek
9
Scale
0
5
10 km
0
1
2
3
4
5
6 miles
Widemouth
St Genny's
Tregole
Trewint
Crackington
Haven
Rosecare
Tresparrett
Posts
260
B3263
Beeny
Tresparrett
Marshgate
Boscastle
Otterham
Lesnewth
Trelash
Trevalga
Bossiney
Tintagel
B3266
B3262
308
Trewarmett
Davidstow
Treknow
B3263
Trewassa
Tremail
Hallworthy
13
Trebarwith
B3314
Treligga
Delabole
Camelford
Valley Truckle
Crowdy
Res.
Port Isaac
Bay
B3314
B3267
Helstone
Port
Isaac
Port Quin
Bay
Port Quin
Port Gaverne
B3267
St Teath
400
ROUGH
TOR
420
BROWN WILLY
New Polzeath
Pendoggett
Treveighan
Padstow
Bay
Trelights
10
Michaelstow
331
GARROW
TOR
Trebetherick
Polzeath
St Endellion
Trelill
A39
St Minver
St Breward
Crugmeer
Pityme
Trewethern
St Tudy
Row
18
Trevone
B3314
Chapel
Amble
St Kew
Rock
St Kew
Highway
Constantine
Bay
Constantine
Bay
St
Merryn
Padstow
Camel
Wenfordbridge
Bradford
A30
Treyarnon
Shop
Bodieve
B3266
Blisland
Trevanson
Little
Petherick
Wadebridge
Temple
Porthcothan
Whitecross
St Mabyn
Colliford
Lake
B3276
St Issey
St
Breock
Egloshayle
A389
Camel
Helland
268
Maidenwell
Penrose
St
Ervan
Rumford
Tredinnick
A39
6
Burlawn
Millpool
St Jidgey
Washaway
BODMIN
Bodmin
Forest
Warleggan
St Eval
208
Cardinham
Trenance
St Neot
B3274
Nanstallon
Bodmin
Mount
Ruthernbridge
Trevarrian
St Mawgan
Rosenannon
St Lawrence
B3276
WATERGATE
BAY
Talskiddy
Withiel
St Wenn
Fowey
A38
Tregurrian
NEWQUAY
CORNWALL
St Columb
Major
B3274
Tregonetha
B3268
East
Taphouse
West Taphouse
Lanivet
Newquay
Bay
Porth
St Columb
Minor
A3059
227
Trebyan
Fistral Bay
Pentire
Trebudannon
Belowda
Victoria
A30
Sweethouse
Braddock
C
o
r
n
w
Colan
Lockengate
Redmoor
Newquay
Quintrell
Downs
Mountjoy
A39
Ruthvoes
Tregoss
B3268
B3269
Crantock
A392
Trevarren
Roche
Bilberry
Lostwithiel
Lane
Kestle
Mill
St Columb Road
Indian Queens
Trezaise
Bugle
Lanlivery
Couch's Mill
Carines
Fraddon
B3279
St Dennis
B3274
A391
Luxulyan
Milltown
Bocaddon
Penhale
Cubert
St Newlyn
East
A3058
Gummow's
Shop
St Enoder
Retew
Whitemoor
312
Stenalees
Lerryn
A3075
Rejerrah
Treviscoe
Nanpean
Penwithick
A390
Penpillick
Lanreath
A3076
Summercourt
Carthew
Trethurgy
St Blazey
Golant
St Veep
Mitchell
A30
Brighton
Trethosa
Foxhole
B3274
Carclaze
Tywardreath
Penpoll
Carland
Cross
A3058
High
Street
B3279
St Austell
Boscoppa
Par
Trenewan
Lanteglos
Highway
Trelassick
St Stephen
Trewoon
Holmbush
B3269
Zelah
B3285
New Mills
Coombe
St Mewan
Polkerris
A3082
Bodinnick
St
Allen
Menabilly
Fowey
Lansallos
Callestick
St
Erme
Ladock
Grampound
Road
Sticker
Polgooth
Charlestown
Polruan
Trispen
Porthpean
ST. AUSTELL
BAY
Marazanvose
B3275
Hewas Water
A39
Allet
B3273
Trenarren
B3284
Probus
A390
Shortlanesend
Grampound
Creed
Pentewan

Best places to visit

▼ St Ives Harbour

▲ Minack Theatre

Outdoors

Bodmin Moor Cornwall's largest Area of Outstanding Natural Beauty, covers an area of 80 square miles and includes Brown Willy, Cornwall's highest point. Criss-crossed with footpaths, it is an ideal spot for walkers. South of the A30 that bisects the heather-covered moor is **Siblyback Lake**, a popular location for water sports, bird watching and camping. *Siblyback Lake, Common Moor* ⌨ www.swlakestrust.org.uk **37 E5**

Chysauster Ancient Village A fine example of an Iron Age village with stone houses made up of rooms arranged around an open courtyard, a design unique to western Cornwall and the Isles of Scilly. Walk around the remains to get a sense of what life was like thousands of years ago. *Newmill* ⌨ www.english-heritage.org.uk **76 D2**

Cornwall and West Devon Mining Landscape A World Heritage Site – designated by UNESCO as being of Outstanding Universal Value and to be protected for future generations – because of how the landscape was shaped by the metal mining so vital to the Industrial Revolution and beyond. There are ten areas within the Site, spanning areas from the St Just Mining District near Land's End to the Caradon Mining District on Bodmin Moor. ⌨ www.cornishmining. org.uk

▶ *The King Arthur statue, Tintagel*

Eden Project Featuring two enormous covered domes, each containing thousands of plants. The Rainforest Biome is the largest indoor rainforest in the world and includes a canopy walkway above the trees. The Mediterranean Biome showcases plants from places such as South Africa, California and Australia, and there is also a 30-acre Outdoor Garden to explore. There are summer concerts, workshops, activity days, regular performance and storytelling events, plus permanent and temporary art exhibitions. *Bodelva, St Austell* ⌨ www.edenproject.com **115 D7**

Glendurgan Garden Set over 30 acres, Glendurgan Garden is made up of three valleys, which enjoy a mild climate, and has rare trees and shrubs from around the world, including a gigantic tulip tree. The laurel maze – complete with viewing platform – is a great hit with children. Walk down through the garden to the tiny hamlet of Durgan on the Helford River. *Mawnan Smith* ⌨ www.nationaltrust.org.uk **93 D2**

Hurlers Stone Circles A few miles north of Liskeard are the three large late Neolithic or Early Bronze Age stone circles grouped in a line and said to be the men turned to stone for playing hurling on a Sunday. *Minions* ⌨ www.english-heritage.org.uk **38 A6**

Isles of Scilly An archipelago lying some 25 nautical miles off Land's End, the Scilly Isles comprise around 140 islands and rocky islets. Only five islands are inhabited with the largest being St Mary's. The climate is said to be

so mild there are only two seasons – spring and summer. The fastest way to get to there is by helicopter from Penzance to either St Mary's or Tresco islands. Alternatively, opt for a fixed-wing plane flight from Land's End (year round, 20 minutes), Exeter (March to October, 30 minutes) and Newquay (from May, 30 minutes) Airports. Or catch the passenger ferry from Penzance Harbour to St Mary's, sailing time 2 hours 45 minutes. This operates once a day from March to November. **Tresco Abbey Garden** is established in the ruins of a 19th-century Benedictine abbey, this lush garden is home to 20,000 plants from countries across the world's Mediterranean climate zones. The Valhalla Museum within the garden has a collection of ships' figureheads. ⌨ www.visitislesofscilly.com *Tresco* ⌨ www.tresco.co.uk **74**

Land's End This famous landmark is the most westerly point of the English mainland with views out to sea including the Longships and Wolf Rock lighthouses and, on a clear day, the Isles of Scilly on the horizon. There's a tourist complex with family attractions, restaurants, a shopping village and hotel. A short walk over the cliffs is Sennen Cove, a wide, sandy beach. **96 A6**

Lizard Point British mainland's most southerly point and famed for its rare flora, Lizard Point has dramatic clifftop walks and views. Visit the Lizard Lighthouse Heritage Centre for a tour of the lighthouse and interactive exhibits on its workings, navigation and life as a lighthouse keeper. A short walk away, at Bass Point, is the radio station where inventor Guglielmo Marconi conducted his ground-breaking wireless experiments. *Lizard Lighthouse Heritage Centre, Lighthouse Rd* ⌨ www.trinityhouse.co.uk **102 F1** • **Lizard Wireless Station**, *Bass Point* ⌨ www.english-heritage.org.uk **103 A1**

Lost Gardens of Heligan After decades of neglect, these bramble-shrouded gardens, that had disappeared from view, were extensively restored and form Europe's biggest restored gardens, covering 200 acres. Visit the Victorian Productive Garden to see the Walled Flower Garden, Kitchen Garden and Melon Yard. The Pleasure Grounds include Maori-carved tree ferns and an Italian Garden. The Jungle is a flourishing mass of tropical plants including bamboo, palms and banana. There are also 60 acres of woodland to be discovered along the Woodland Walk. *Pentewan* ⌨ www.heligan.com **73 B5**

Minack Theatre This world-famous open-air theatre is built on a steep granite cliffside overlooking Porthcurno Bay. There are over 200 live performances, come rain or shine – including plays, opera, ballet, music and children's events – from April to October each year. Visit all year round to enjoy the sub-tropical gardens, featuring rare plants from around the world, and explore the theatre, including backstage. *Porthcurno* ⌨ www.minack.com **96 E3**

Mount Edgcumbe House & Country Park Mount Edgcumbe House is the former home of the Earls of Mount Edgcumbe, within an 865-acre country park on the Rame Peninsula which includes the villages of Cawsand and Kingsand. The Park has several formal gardens, among them the colourful Regency-era Italian Garden and the more recently created New Zealand Garden, the National Camellia Collection and numerous coastal and woodland walks. *Cremyll* ⌨ www.mountedgcumbe.gov. uk **133 E6**

St Michael's Mount Walk across the cobbled causeway at low tide or take short boat ride to this historic rocky island. Visit the 14th-century church and the castle, still lived in by the St Aubyn family, which

features an eclectic collection of objects including a piece of Napoleon's uniform worn at the Battle of Waterloo. Head up to the gun batteries at the summit of the island for views out to sea and the mainland and to look down over the terraced gardens. *Marazion* ⌨ www. stmichaelsmount.co.uk **89 B4**

Tintagel The Old Post Office is a 14th-century stone building, with a distinctive undulating roof, originally built as a farmhouse. There are five furnished rooms to view and a display of Victorian postal equipment, plus a colourful cottage garden outside. Tintagel Castle, long associated with King Arthur, is perched high on the rugged coast. Cross the spectacular footbridge to the island to walk among the castle ruins and visit the beach below the castle for a stroll or paddle. **Old Post Office**, *Fore St* ⌨ www.nationaltrust.org.uk • **Tintagel Castle**, *Castle Rd* ⌨ www.english-heritage.org.uk **14 C7**

Trebah Garden One of the 'Great Gardens of Cornwall', Trebah has 26 acres of lush sub-tropical planting, including three acres of hydrangeas. Four miles of footpaths meander through the steep valley, leading down to a private beach, Polgwidden Cove, on the Helford River where there is café. There's an outdoor theatre which stages performances from stand-up comedy to theatre and music. *Mawnan Smith, Falmouth* ⌨ www.trebahgarden.co.uk **93 C2**

Trelissick Sitting on its own peninsula, with glorious views over the Fal River, this tranquil garden covers more than 30 acres. The main lawn features

exotic borders and a magnificent Japanese red cedar. There are summerhouses dotted around the garden, an orchard and the tennis lawn, which offers stunning views. The wider estate has parkland and woodlands to explore, via two paths that wind their way through the trees. An art gallery run by Cornwall Crafts Association sells work by local artists. *Feock* 🖥 www.nationaltrust.org.uk **82 D6**

Trengwainton Garden

Enjoying a uniquely warm microclimate, Trengwainton is full of exotic plants that thrive. Five sections of the ten-section walled gardens are full of tender plants from around the world; the other five make up a kitchen garden built to the dimensions of Noah's Ark. There is an award-winning collection of rhododendrons, magnolias and camellias and two giant tree fern glades. Walk to the top of the garden for views of Mount's Bay and the Lizard. *Madron* 🖥 www.nationaltrust.org.uk **88 A6**

Trethevy Quoit

Dating to the Neolithic period, around 3500–2500 BC, this is an especially well-preserved example of a portal dolmen – a monument thought to honour the dead. It stands 2.7 metres (9 feet) high and is made up of five standing stones and a massive capstone, weighing about 20 tonnes. *Off B3254 near Darite* 🖥 www.english-heritage.org.uk **38 A3**

Towns & villages

Bodmin Former county town of Cornwall, Bodmin has a number of attractions, including the **Bodmin & Wenford Railway**, Cornwall's only full-size railway operated by steam locomotives. Originally built in 1779, **Bodmin Jail** was based on the ideals of prison reformer John Howard, and one of the first to have individual cells. Delve into its history, including the 55 prisoners executed within its walls, among them William Hampton, the last man hanged in Cornwall. There is also a hotel within the building. *Bodmin General Station* 🖥 www.bodminrailway.co.uk •

Bodmin Jail, *Berrycoombe Road* 🖥 www.bodminjail.org **109**

Boscastle A picturesque village with a tiny harbour. The National Trust owns most of the land in and around Boscastle and there are numerous walks. Opt for a gentle stroll around the medieval harbour, explore the cliffs above Boscastle or head inland across the Valency Valley. The fascinating **Museum of Witchcraft and Magic** is one of the world's biggest collections of items relating to magical practice and the occult. The extensive library of books on the subject can be visited by appointment. **Boscastle** 🖥 www.nationaltrust.org.uk • **The Museum of Witchcraft and Magic**, *The Harbour* 🖥 www.museumofwitchcraftandmagic.co.uk **9 C1**

Bude A good range of accommodation, shops, restaurants ad activities. Join the South West Coast Path for clifftop walks or head to one of several sandy beaches for swimming or surfing. Bude Sea Pool, cut into the rock at Summerleaze Beach, offers swimming safe from Atlantic waves. There is an annual Jazz Festival in late summer. **104**

Falmouth The deep harbour makes it popular as a yachting centre and it has many lovely beaches, including Gyllyngvase Beach, under 10 minutes' walk from the town centre. Trace the history of **Pendennis Castle** from its beginnings as one of Henry VIII's artillery forts to its role in World War II. Falmouth is home to the **National Maritime Museum Cornwall**. The Main Hall displays a hanging flotilla of small boats. There is a RNLI Rescue Zone and a Boat Building Workshop, a living exhibit. **Pendennis Castle**, *Pendennis Point* 🖥 www.english-heritage.org.uk • **National Maritime Museum**, *Discovery Quay* 🖥 www.nmmc.co.uk **145**

Launceston An array of independent shops line the narrow streets of this ancient market town, once the capital of Cornwall. In summer, take a trip into the countryside on

a narrow-gauge steam train hauled by a restored Victorian locomotive. Visit Launceston Castle, a Norman motte and bailey castle that towers above the town. **Launceston Steam Railway**, *St Thomas Rd* 🖥 www.launcestonsr.co.uk • **Launceston Castle**, *Castle Lodge* 🖥 www.english-heritage.org.uk **106**

Liskeard A market town with a 15th-century church, museum and Stuart House Arts and Heritage Centre, a late medieval town house. **St Martin's Church**, *Church Gate* 🖥 www.stmartchurchliskeard.co.uk • **Liskeard & District Museum**, *Pike St* 🖥 www.liskeardmuseum.com • **Stuart House Arts and Heritage Centre**, *Barras St* **113**

Looe A picturesque port with seven-arched, stone-built Looe Bridge connecting the East and West towns. The **Old Guildhall Museum & Gaol** features smuggling memorabilia and model boats among its exhibits and **Looe Harbour Heritage Centre** explores the maritime history of Looe. There's a sandy beach and the South West Coast Path passes through the town. **Old Guildhall Museum & Gaol**, *Higher Market St* 🖥 www.looemuseum.co.uk • **Looe Harbour Heritage Centre**, *The Quay, West Looe* 🖥 www.looeharbourheritagecentre.co.uk **117**

Newquay Newquay's sandy beaches are a big draw for holiday makers and surfers. **Newquay Zoo** has creatures ranging from armadillos to zebra all homed in enclosures designed to replicate their natural habitat. There are also gardens and outdoor play areas. Get close to marine life at **Blue Reef Aquarium** with its amazing underwater tunnel that runs through the ocean tank, allowing visitors to see the coral reef and its inhabitants, including sharks, turtles and pufferfish. **Newquay Zoo**, *Trenance Gardens* 🖥 www.newquayzoo.org.uk • **Blue Reef Aquarium**, *Towan Promenade* 🖥 www.bluereefaquarium.co.uk **110**

▲ *Truro Cathedral*

Padstow Centred around a working harbour and at the head of the Camel River, this is one of Cornwall's most popular spots. There are plenty of cafés, inns and benches at the quayside to sit and watch the activity. For beaches, make the short ferry journey across the river to Rock or walk along the Coast Path to St George's Cove. **107**

Penzance Head to **Penlee House Gallery & Museum** to learn about the history of west Cornwall and discover the works of Cornish Newlyn School and Lamorna artists. If the weather is good, swim at **Jubilee Pool**, a celebrated Art Deco saltwater lido and one of the few remaining from the 1930s. Wander down Chapel St to admire the façade of the unusual **Egyptian House**, built in the style of Egyptian Revival architecture and owned by the Landmark Trust. **Penlee House Gallery & Museum**, *Morrab Rd* 🖥 www.penleehouse.org.uk • **Jubilee Pool**, *Battery Rd* 🖥 www.jubileepool.co.uk • **Egyptian House**, *Chapel St* 🖥 www.landmarktrust.org.uk **143**

St Ives A popular and picturesque harbour and seaside town. Visit **Tate St Ives** for views across the Atlantic and its collection of 20th-century art plus a changing

programme of exhibitions. Renowned sculptor Barbara Hepworth was a long-time St Ives resident and her work is celebrated at the **Barbara Hepworth Museum and Sculpture Garden**, once her own home and studio. Most of the statues in the garden remain in the positions she herself chose. **Tate St Ives**, *Porthmeor Beach* • **Barbara Hepworth Museum**, *Barnoon Hill* 🖥 www.tate.org.uk **141 B6**

Truro Truro is Cornwall's only city and the most southerly in the UK. Visit the **Royal Cornwall Museum**, which aims to celebrate Cornish art, heritage and culture. There are permanent exhibits of ancient Egyptian, Greek and Roman objects. The Courtney Library has a collection of rare books and manuscripts. The spires of **Truro Cathedral**, built between 1880 and 1910, soar above the city's skyline. Take advantage of free entry to admire the beautiful stained-glass rose windows and brass eagle lectern. **Royal Cornwall Museum**, *River St* 🖥 www.royalcornwallmuseum.org.uk • **Truro Cathedral**, *High Cross* 🖥 www.trurocathedral.org.uk **137**

Plymouth Attractions are plentiful in this city, with its rich maritime heritage. See the famous **Mayflower Steps** that mark the departure point for the Pilgrims on the Mayflower in 1620 and follow that with a trip to the **Mayflower Museum** to learn more about them and their voyage to the New World. Take to the water to kayak, sail or learn to scuba dive or enjoy the sea air on a leisurely cruise around the harbour or up the Tamar River. Explore the historic cobbled streets of the Barbican and Sutton Harbour, home to the **National Marine Aquarium**, which is the UK's largest. Visit **Plymouth Gin Distillery**, the oldest in England,

for a guided tour and tasting. To learn more about Plymouth past and present pay a visit to **The Box**, a major museum, gallery and archive. **Mayflower Steps**, The Barbican • **Mayflower Museum**, *The Barbican* 🖥 www.visitplymouth.co.uk • **National Marine Aquarium**, *Rope Walk* 🖥 www.national-aquarium.co.uk • **Plymouth Gin Distillery**, *Southside St* 🖥 www.plymouth.gin.com • **The Box**, *Tavistock Place* 🖥 www.theboxplymouth.com **148–149**

▶ *Smeaton's Tower on Plymouth Hoe*

▲ The narrow-gauge railway at Lappa Valley

◀ Restormel Castle

Buildings

Antony House Home to the Carew Pole family for over 600 years and still lived in by the family, 18th-century Antony House, with its grey Pentewan-stone exterior, houses an impressive collection of tapestries, furniture and portraits. The gardens, designed by Humphrey Repton, include a National Collection of daylilies, topiary, statuary and sculptures. *Ferry Lane, near Torpoint* 💻 www.nationaltrust.org.uk **126 D5**

Cotehele A Tudor house, with a superb collection of tapestries, armour, brass and furniture, set in extensive grounds and woodlands with riverside walks. There are formal terraced gardens and two orchards, while the Valley Garden, with its domed dovecote, leads down to the Tamar River. Prospect Tower, a triangular 18th-century folly, offers views over the countryside. Cotehele Quay has a free museum on the Tamar, a gallery and tearoom. A short walk from Cotehele is Cotehele Mill, a working Victorian mill. *St Dominick, Saltash* 💻 www.nationaltrust.org.uk **40 F3**

Godolphin The house at Godolphin is over 700 years old and open to tour in the first week of each month. The 16th-century garden is considered one of the most important historic gardens in Europe, with informal planting set among paths. Covering 550 acres, the Godolphin estate has a number of walks, including one up Godolphin Hill for great views, and encompasses the derelict workings of the Godolphin family mine, bluebell woods and Bronze Age archaeological remains. *Godolphin Cross* 💻 www.nationaltrust.org.uk **90 E6**

Lanhydrock The house has 54 rooms open to view and shows the contrast between life 'below stairs' in the kitchen and the comforts of 'upstairs' life. There are extensive gardens with colourful herbaceous borders and a parterre. Hire a bicycle to try one of the off-road cycle tracks on the 900-acre estate or set off on a circular walk to enjoy the countryside at a more leisurely pace. *Bodmin* 💻 www.nationaltrust.org.uk **48 D6**

Pencarrow House & Gardens Home of the Molesworth-St Aubyns for nearly 500 years, take a guided tour

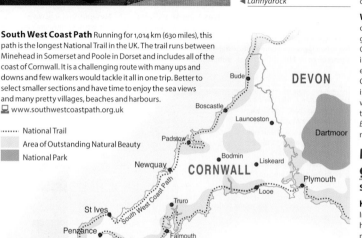

◀ Lanhydrock

of the Grade II*-listed house or explore the gardens – children admitted free to the gardens – which encompass formal landscaping and woodland. Highlights include an Iron Age fort and sunken Italian garden. *Pencarrow* 💻 www.pencarrow.co.uk **34 D6**

Restormel Castle Built on an earlier Norman mound, this ruined castle is striking because of its perfectly circular design. Built in the 13th century, it is surrounded by lovely countryside and a good spot for a picnic before exploring the remains of the castle's rooms and climbing the staircase from the courtyard for the views. *Off Restormel Rd, Lostwithiel* 💻 www.english-heritage.org.uk **112 C5**

Trerice The Elizabethan manor house has a collection of over a thousand pieces including a 300-year-old longcase clock and an enormous table. Although small, the lovely garden is varied and has an Elizabethan knot garden, inspired by the decorative plaster ceiling in the Great Chamber that overlooks it, an apple orchard, wild meadow and mowhay (a maze). *Kestle Mill, Newquay* 💻 www.nationaltrust.org.uk **44 D1**

Wheal Coates Perched on cliffs covered with heather and gorse are what remains of Wheal Coates mine, opened in 1802, including the iconic Towanroath engine house which is now a Grade II-listed building. There is a way-marked short circular walk along the Coastal Path and through the mine buildings. *Beacon Drive, St Agnes* 💻 www.nationaltrust.org.uk **54 B1**

Museums & galleries

See also St Ives

King Edward Mine Museum Informative guides reveal the history of Cornish mining at this museum, the oldest complete mine site in Cornwall, and demonstrate how the mined tin was processed using the original equipment, much of which is still in working order. As well as the indoor exhibitions, there is a trail to follow around the mine site. *Troon, Camborne* 💻 www.kingedwardmine.co.uk **79 E5**

Wheal Martyn Clay Works This museum dedicated to china clay mining – Cornwall's biggest mining industry – is located within two former Victorian clay works, one of which is preserved in a working state. There is a unique collection of working mining machinery. Visit the interactive Discovery Centre and explore woodland walks and historic trails. *Carthew, St Austell* 💻 www.wheal-martyn.com **59 B6**

Family activities

See also Land's End

Cornish Seal Sanctuary The sanctuary rescues and rehabilitates grey seal pups and other marine animals before releasing them back into their natural environment, as well as providing a permanent home for those that can't be returned to the wild. The site has underwater viewing areas, sea pools and a hospital, and there are daily talks and feed times. Animals that can be visited include penguins, beavers and sea lions, goats, sheep and ponies. *Gweek* 💻 www.sealifetrust.org **92 C1**

Flambards Enjoy family fun at this theme park, from taking a spin on the Hornet Rollercoaster to spotting dinosaurs aboard the Dino Express. Indoor attractions include a life-size replica Victorian village and a London street during the Blitz. It has extensive gardens with picnic spots. *Clodgey Lane, Helston* 💻 www.flambards.co.uk **146 D4**

Lappa Valley For a family day out, climb aboard a narrow-gauge steam train for a journey through the countryside to Lappa Valley, a 35-acre site, with activities that include a boating lake with canoes and pedalo boats, crazy golf, several play areas, two miniature railways and woodland walks. *St Newlyn East* 💻 www.lappavalley.co.uk **56 C8**

South West Coast Path Running for 1,014 km (630 miles), this path is the longest National Trail in the UK. The trail runs between Minehead in Somerset and Poole in Dorset and includes all of the coast of Cornwall. It is a challenging route with many ups and downs and few walkers would tackle it all in one trip. Better to select smaller sections and have time to enjoy the sea views and many pretty villages, beaches and harbours. 💻 www.southwestcoastpath.org.uk

········ National Trail
▨ Area of Outstanding Natural Beauty
▨ National Park

Isles of Scilly

DEVON

Bude
Boscastle
Launceston
Padstow
Dartmoor
Newquay
Bodmin
Liskeard
CORNWALL
Truro
Plymouth
Looe
St Ives
Falmouth
Penzance

Key to map symbols

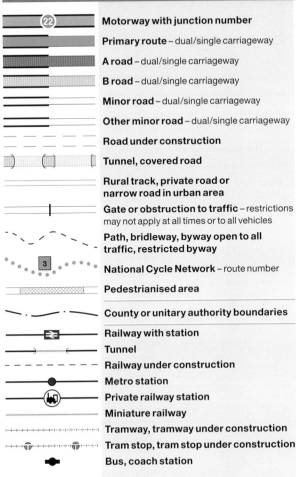

Motorway with junction number

Primary route – dual/single carriageway

A road – dual/single carriageway

B road – dual/single carriageway

Minor road – dual/single carriageway

Other minor road – dual/single carriageway

Road under construction

Tunnel, covered road

Rural track, private road or narrow road in urban area

Gate or obstruction to traffic – restrictions may not apply at all times or to all vehicles

Path, bridleway, byway open to all traffic, restricted byway

National Cycle Network – route number

Pedestrianised area

County or unitary authority boundaries

Railway with station

Tunnel

Railway under construction

Metro station

Private railway station

Miniature railway

Tramway, tramway under construction

Tram stop, tram stop under construction

Bus, coach station

Ambulance station

Coastguard station

Fire station

Police station

Accident and Emergency entrance to hospital

H Hospital

+ Place of worship

i Information centre

Shopping centre, parking

P&R **PO** Park and Ride, Post Office

Camping site, caravan site

Golf course, picnic site

Church ROMAN FORT Non-Roman antiquity, Roman antiquity

Univ Important buildings, schools, colleges, universities and hospitals

Woods, built-up area

River Medway Water name

River, weir

Stream

Canal, lock, tunnel

Water

Tidal water

58 **87** Adjoining page indicators and overlap bands – the colour of the arrow and band indicates the scale of the adjoining or overlapping page (see scales below)

246

The dark grey border on the inside edge of some pages indicates that the mapping does not continue onto the adjacent page

The small numbers around the edges of the maps identify the 1-kilometre National Grid lines

Abbreviations

Acad	**Academy**	Meml	**Memorial**
Allot Gdns	**Allotments**	Mon	**Monument**
Cemy	**Cemetery**	Mus	**Museum**
C Ctr	**Civic centre**	Obsy	**Observatory**
CH	**Club house**	Pal	**Royal palace**
Coll	**College**	PH	**Public house**
Crem	**Crematorium**	Recn Gd	**Recreation ground**
Ent	**Enterprise**	Resr	**Reservoir**
Ex H	**Exhibition hall**	Ret Pk	**Retail park**
Ind Est	**Industrial Estate**	Sch	**School**
IRB Sta	**Inshore rescue boat station**	Sh Ctr	**Shopping centre**
Inst	**Institute**	TH	**Town hall / house**
Ct	**Law court**	Trad Est	**Trading estate**
L Ctr	**Leisure centre**	Univ	**University**
LC	**Level crossing**	W Twr	**Water tower**
Liby	**Library**	Wks	**Works**
Mkt	**Market**	YH	**Youth hostel**

Enlarged maps only

Railway or bus station building

Place of interest

Parkland

The map scale on the pages numbered in green is 1¾ inches to 1 mile
2.76 cm to 1 km • 1 : 36 206

0	½ mile	1 mile	1½ miles	2 miles
0	500m	1 km	1½ km	2km

The map scale on the pages numbered in blue is 3½ inches to 1 mile
5.52 cm to 1 km • 1 : 18 103

0	¼ mile	½ mile	¾ mile	1 mile
0	250m	500m	750m	1km

The map scale on the pages numbered in red is 7 inches to 1 mile
11.04 cm to 1 km • 1 : 9051

0	220yds	440yds	660yds	½ mile
0	125m	250m	375m	500m

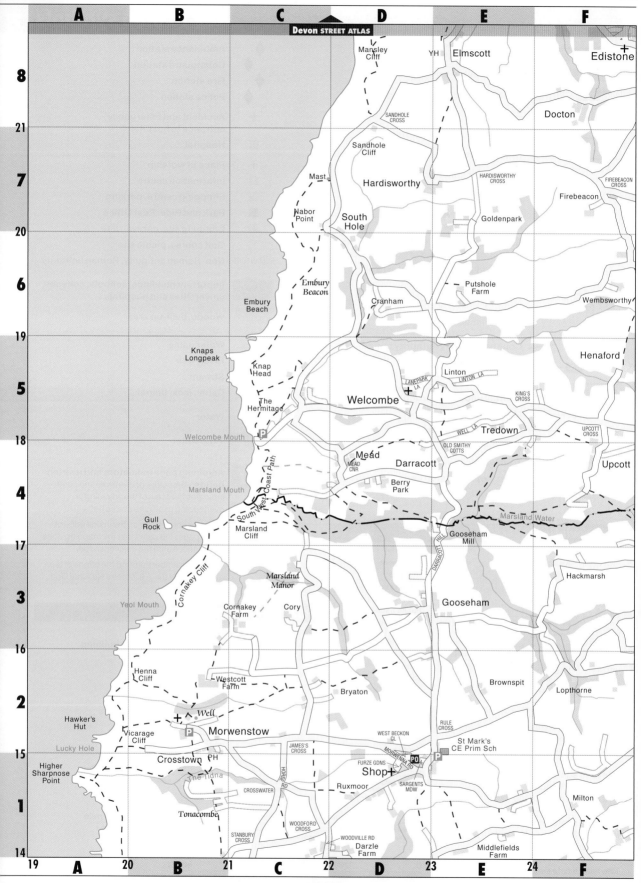

A   B   C   D   E   F

8
21
7
20
6
19
5
18
4
17
3
16
2
15
1
14

19   A   20   B   21   C   22   D   23   E   24   F

Edistone

Elmscott
Mansley Cliff
YH
Docton
SANDHOLE CROSS
Sandhole Cliff
HARDISWORTHY CROSS
FIREBEACON CROSS
Mast
Hardisworthy
Firebeacon
Nabor Point
South Hole
Goldenpark
Wembsworthy
Embury Beacon
Putshole Farm
Embury Beach
Cranham
Henaford
Knaps Longpeak
Linton
LINTON LA
Knap Head
LANEPARK LA
KING'S CROSS
Welcombe
The Hermitage
WELL LA
Tredown
UPCOTT CROSS
Welcombe Mouth
P
OLD SMITHY COTTS
Mead
MEAD CNR
Darracott
Upcott
Marsland Mouth
South West Coast Path
Berry Park
Marsland Water
Gull Rock
Marsland Cliff
Gooseham Mill
DARRACOTT HILL
Yeol Mouth
Cornakey Cliff
Marsland Manor
Hackmarsh
Cornakey Farm
Cory
Gooseham
Henna Cliff
Westcott Farm
Brownspit
Lopthorne
Bryaton
Hawker's Hut
Well
RULE CROSS
Vicarage Cliff
P
Morwenstow
WEST BECKON CL
St Mark's CE Prim Sch
Lucky Hole
Crosstown
PH
JAMES'S CROSS
MORWENNA RD
PO
P
Higher Sharpnose Point
The Tidna
FURZE GDNS
Shop
HOBB RD
Milton
CROSSWATER
Ruxmoor
SARGENTS MDW
Tonacombe
STANBURY CROSS
WOODFORD CROSS
WOODVILLE RD
Darzle Farm
Middlefields Farm

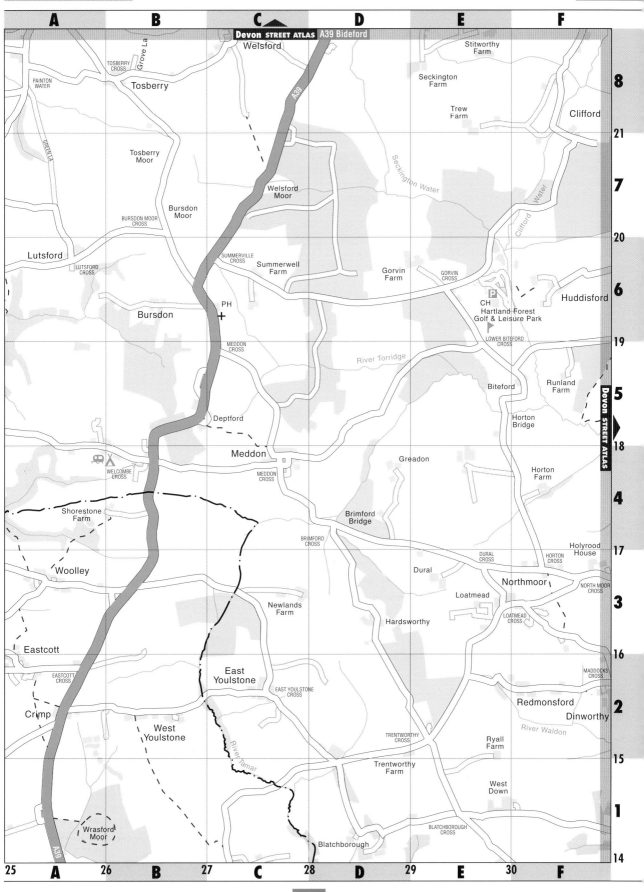

Scale: 1¾ inches to 1 mile

0   ¼   ½ mile
0   250m 500m 750m 1 km

Welsford

Tosberry Cross
Grove La
PAINTON WATER
Tosberry
GREEN LA
Tosberry Moor
BURSDON MOOR CROSS
Bursdon Moor
Bursdon Moor Cross
Lutsford
LUTSFORD CROSS
Bursdon
PH
SUMMERVILLE CROSS
Welsford Moor
Summerwell Farm
Stitworthy Farm
Seckington Farm
Trew Farm
Clifford
Seckington Water
Clifford Water
Gorvin Farm
Gorvin Cross
Huddisford
P
CH
Hartland Forest Golf & Leisure Park
LOWER BITEFORD CROSS
MEDDON CROSS
River Torridge
Deptford
Meddon
MEDDON CROSS
WELCOMBE CROSS
Shorestone Farm
Brimford Bridge
BRIMFORD CROSS
Greadon
Biteford
Runland Farm
Horton Bridge
Horton Farm
Holyrood House
DURAL CROSS
HORTON CROSS
Woolley
Newlands Farm
Dural
Hardsworthy
Loatmead
Northmoor
NORTH MOOR CROSS
LOATMEAD CROSS
Eastcott
EASTCOTT CROSS
East Youlstone
EAST YOULSTONE CROSS
MADDOCKS CROSS
Redmonsford
Dinworthy
River Waldon
Crimp
West Youlstone
River Tamar
TRENTWORTHY CROSS
Ryall Farm
Trentworthy Farm
West Down
Wrasford Moor
Blatchborough
BLATCHBOROUGH CROSS

8
21
7
20
6
19
5
18
4
17
3
16
2
15
1
14

A 25 26 B 27 C 28 D 29 E 30 F

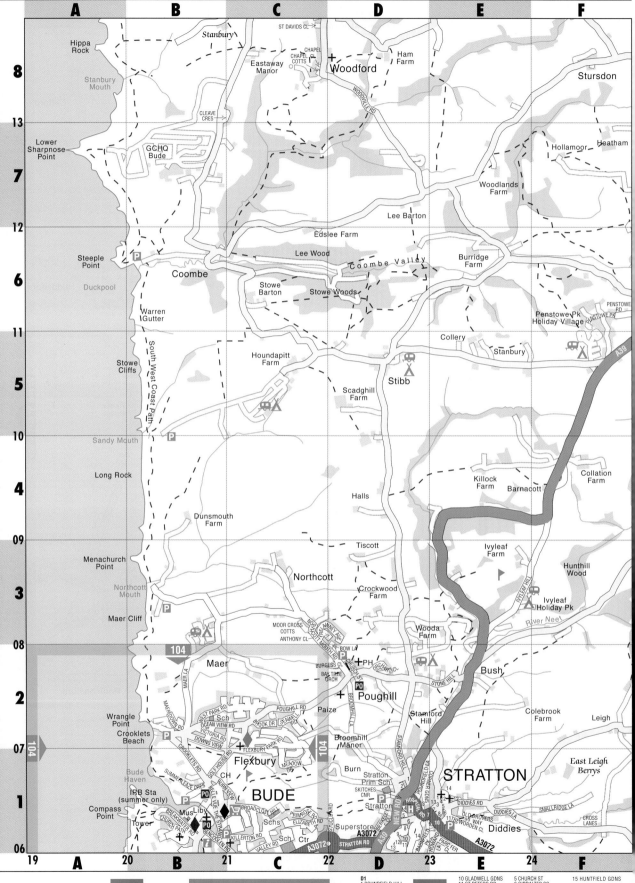

Scale: 1¾ inches to 1 mile

For full street detail of the highlighted area see page 104.

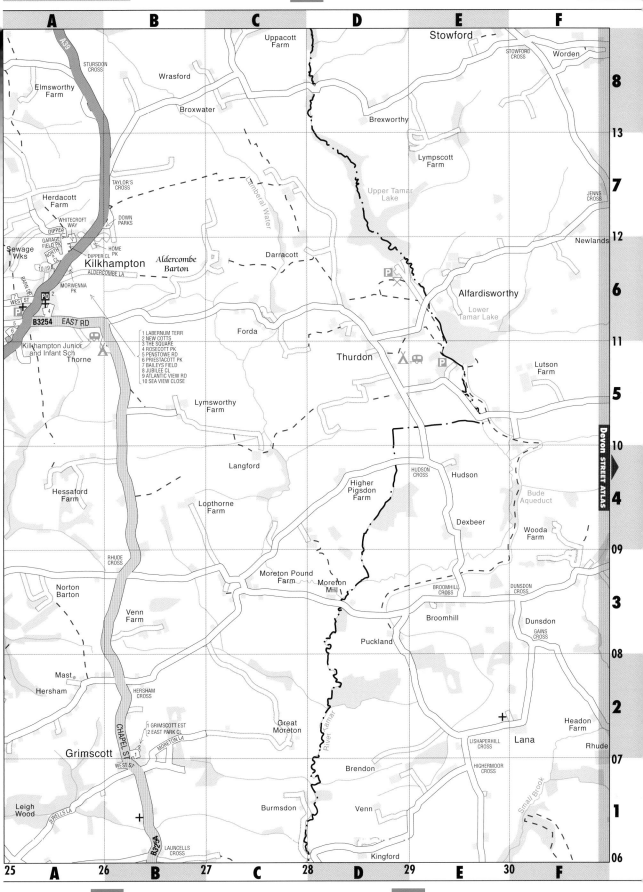

A   B   C   D   E   F

8

13

7

12

6

11

5

10

4

09

3

08

2

07

1

06

Stowford

STOWFORD CROSS

Worden

Uppacott Farm

Wrasford

STURSDON CROSS

Elmsworthy Farm

A39

Broxwater

Brexworthy

Lympscott Farm

JENNS CROSS

TAYLOR'S CROSS

Herdacott Farm

DOWN PARKS

Upper Tamar Lake

Newlands

WHITECROFT WAY

DIPPER

GARAGE FIELD PK

NORTH CL

HOME PK

Alardisworthy

Sewage Wks

WEST ST

10/9

DIPPER CL

Kilkhampton

Aldercombe Barton

Darracott

Lower Tamar Lake

MORWENNA PK

ALDERCOMBE LA

PO 2

B3254   EAST RD

Forda

Thurdon

Lutson Farm

1 LABERNUM TERR
2 NEW COTTS
3 THE SQUARE
4 ROSECOTT PK
5 PENSTOWE RD
6 PRIESTACOTT PK
7 BAILEYS FIELD
8 JUBILEE CL
9 ATLANTIC VIEW RD
10 SEA VIEW CLOSE

Kilkhampton Junior and Infant Sch

Thorne

Lymsworthy Farm

Langford

Hudson

HUDSON CROSS

Higher Pigsdon Farm

Hessaford Farm

Lopthorne Farm

Dexbeer

Wooda Farm

Bude Aqueduct

RHUDE CROSS

Moreton Pound Farm

Moreton Mill

BROOMHILL CROSS

DUNSDON CROSS

Norton Barton

Venn Farm

Puckland

Broomhill

Dunsden

GAINS CROSS

Mast

Hersham

HERSHAM CROSS

Great Moreton

River Tamar

LISHAPERHILL CROSS

Lana

Headon Farm

1 GRIMSCOTT EST
2 EAST PARK CL

Grimscott

CHAPEL ST

MORETON LA

Rhude

WEST ST

Brendon

HIGHERMOOR CROSS

Small Brook

Leigh Wood

JEWELLS LA

B3254

LAUNCELLS CROSS

Burmsdon

Venn

Kingford

Devon STREET ATLAS

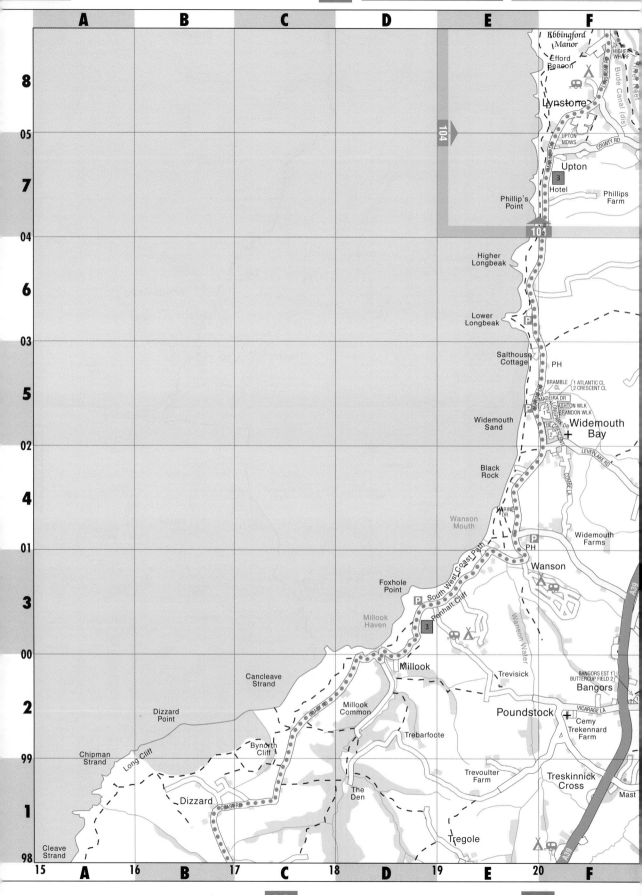

For full street detail of the highlighted area see page 104.

Scale: 1¾ inches to 1 mile

0	¼	½ mile

0	250m	500m	750m	1 km

Ebbingford Manor

HIGHER WHARF

Efford Beacon

Lynstone

River Neet

Bude Canal (dis)

UPTON MDWS

LANGSTONE RD

COUNTY RD

Upton

3

Hotel

Phillips Farm

Phillip's Point

104

Higher Longbeak

Lower Longbeak

P

Salthouse Cottage

PH

BRAMBLE CL

1 ATLANTIC CL
2 CRESCENT CL

MADEIRA DR

ASHTON WLK

BRANDON WLK

P

Widemouth Sand

THE CRESCENT

LONGBEAK DR

MARINE DR

Widemouth Bay

Black Rock

LEVERLAKE RD

COMBE LA

Wanson Mouth

MARINE DR

Widemouth Farms

P

PH

Wanson

Foxhole Point

South West Coast Path

P

Penhalt Cliff

Millook Haven

3

Wanson Water

Trevisick

BANGORS EST 1
BUTTERCUP FIELD 2

Bangors

Cancleave Strand

Millook

Millook Common

CRACKINGTON RD

Trebarfoote

Poundstock

VICARAGE LA

Cemy Trekennard Farm

Dizzard Point

Bynorth Cliff

Trevoulter Farm

Treskinnick Cross

Chipman Strand

Long Cliff

Dizzard

COAST RD

The Den

Trevoulter Farm

Mast

Cleave Strand

Tregole

A39

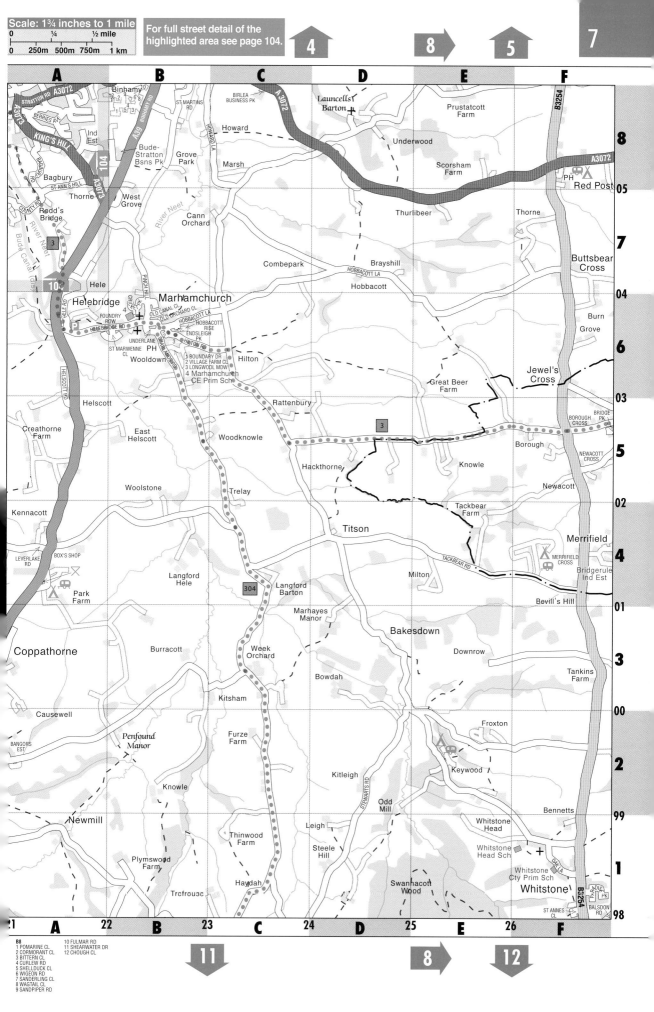

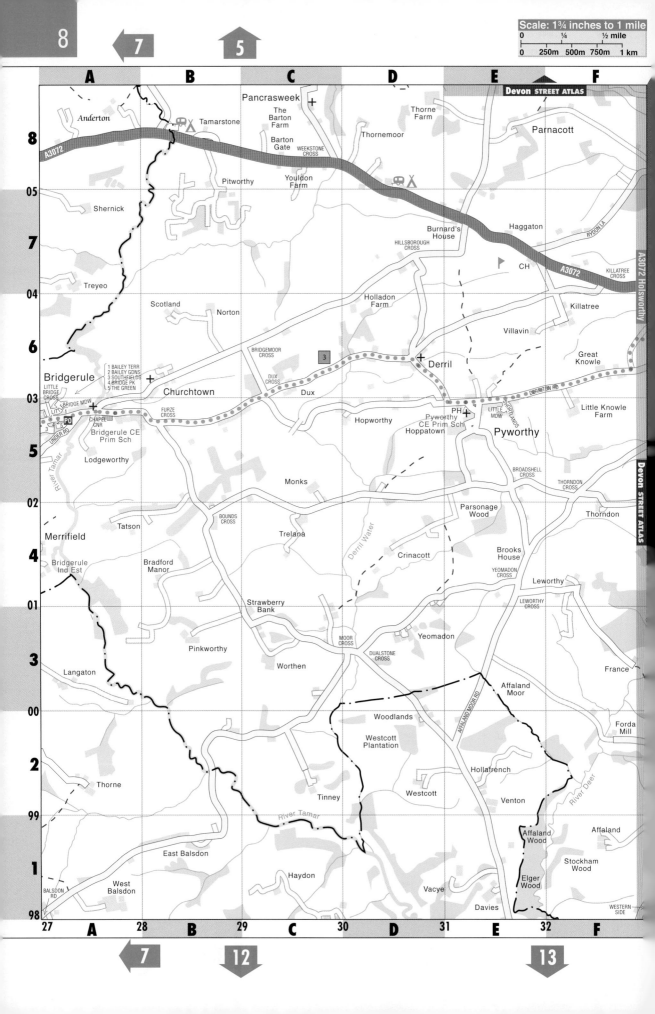

Scale: 1¾ inches to 1 mile

0   ¼   ½ mile

0   250m 500m 750m 1 km

A **B** **C** **D** **E** **F**

8

97

Cambeak

7

96

6

Voter
Run

95

High
Cliff

5

Rusey
Beach

94

Rusey
Cliff

Buckator

4

Gull
Rock

Beeny
Sisters

93

Fire Beacon
Point

Seals
Hole

South West Coast Path

Beeny

3

Beeny
Cliff

Trebyla
Farm

B3263

92

Pentargon

Hillsborough

Tremorle

Mus of
Witchcraft

Trewannett

Penally
Point

Penally
Hill

Penally
TERR

VALENCY
ROW

Penally
House

2

Meachard

Harbour

THE HARBOUR

PENALLY HILL

PENALLY
CT

Tresuck

Newmills

River Valency

Willapark

NEW RD

WATER LA

Visitor
Ctr

MARINE
TERR

Trafalgar
Farm

91

Forrabury

Mast

Boscastle
Com Prim Sch
FORE
ST

Home
Farm

MINSTER RD

Short
Island

Grower Rock

UNDER RD

GREEN LA

B3263
PO

Trebiffin

Firebeacon
Hill

Boscastle

CAMBELL RD

POTTERS

Trewold

Ladies
Window

1 2
3 4
5 6
7
8 9

HIGH ST

B3266

Long
Island

Welltown
Manor

TINTAGEL RD

BARN PARK RD

PARADISE RD

GIBBON

Mount
Pleasant

1

Trevalga

WILLAPARK
VIEW

Paradise
House

B3266

B3263

90

07   **A**   08   **B**   09   **C**   10   **D**   11   **E**   12   **F**

C1
1 PENTARGON RD
2 EGLOS VIEW
3 TREFLEUR CL
4 LANGFORDS MDW
5 FORRABURY HILL
6 CLOVER LANE CL
7 WHITE SMOCK MDW
8 DOCTORS HILL
9 GUNPOOL LA

10 DUNN ST

C2
1 HOLLOWELL HO
2 BRIDGE WLK
3 THE OLD MILL

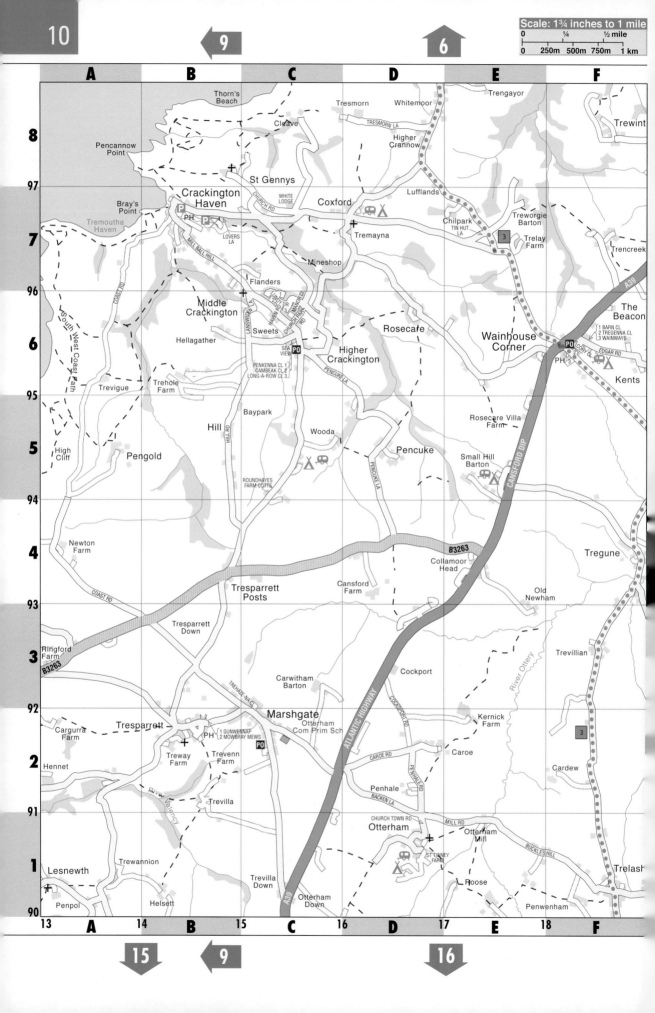

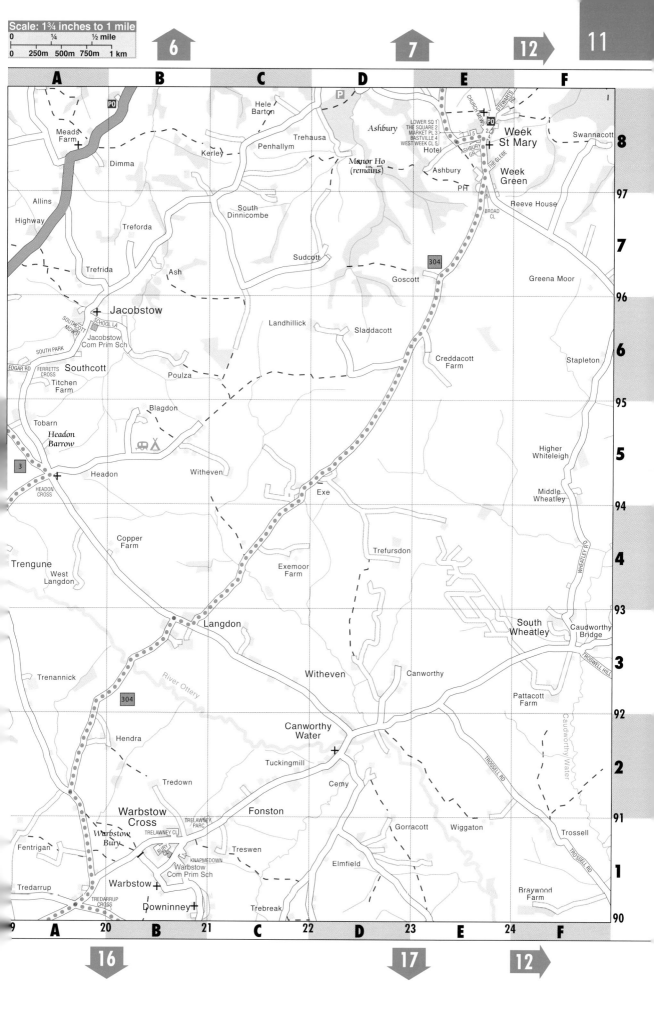

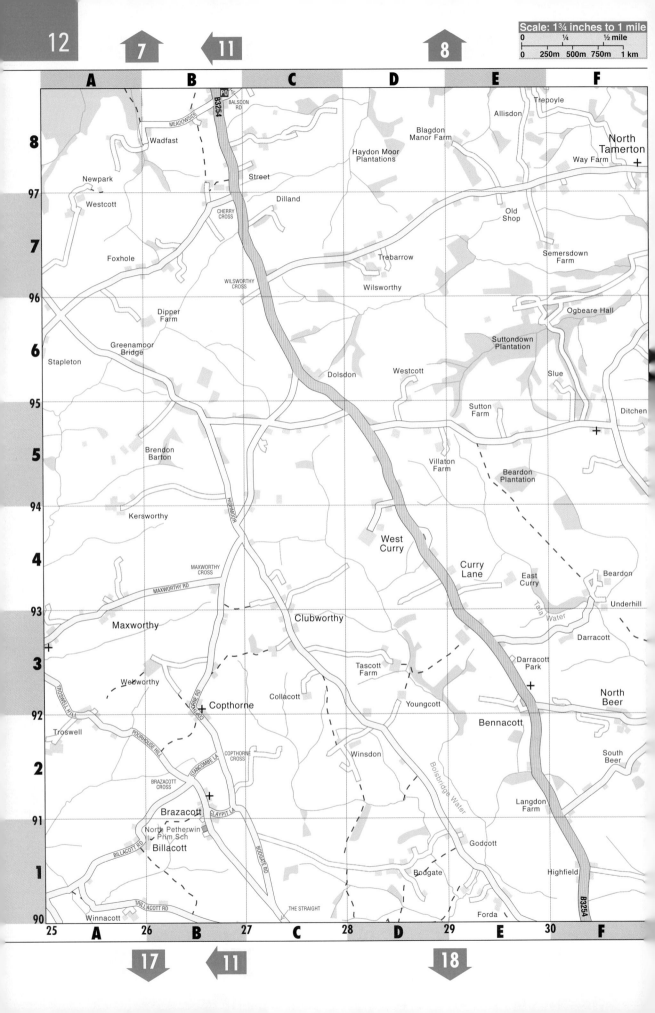

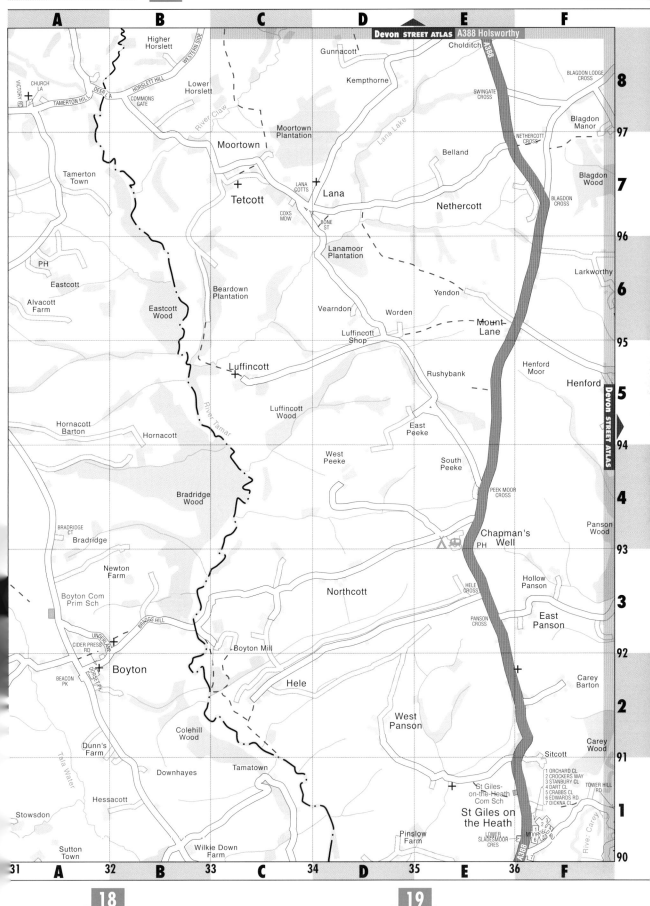

Scale: 1¾ inches to 1 mile

0   ¼   ½ mile

0   250m   500m   750m   1 km

8

Devon STREET ATLAS

A388

A B C D E F

8 7 97 7 96 6 95 5 94 4 93 3 92 2 91 1 90

Row 8:
CHURCH LA
VICTORY RD
TAMERTON HILL
DEEP LA
Higher Horslett
WESTERN SIDE
HORSLETT HILL
Lower Horslett
COMMONS GATE
Gunnacott
Kempthorne
Choldich
A388
SWINGATE CROSS
BLAGDON LODGE CROSS

97 / Row 7:
River Claw
Moortown Plantation
Moortown
NETHERCOTT CROSS
Blagdon Manor

Row 7:
Tamerton Town
Tetcott
LANA COTTS
COXS MDW
Lana
BONE ST
Belland
Nethercott
Blagdon Cross
BLAGDON CROSS
Blagdon Wood

Row 6:
PH
Eastcott
Beardown Plantation
Lanamoor Plantation
Yendon
Larkworthy

95 / Row 5:
Alvacott Farm
Eastcott Wood
Vearndon
Worden
Luffincott Shop
Mount Lane

Row 5:
Luffincott
River Tamar
Rushybank
Henford Moor
Henford

94:
Hornacott Barton
Hornacott
Luffincott Wood
East Peeke
South Peeke

Row 4:
Bradridge Wood
West Peeke
PEEK MOOR CROSS
Panson Wood

93:
BRADRIDGE CT
Bradridge
Chapman's Well
PH
HELE CROSS
Hollow Panson

Row 3:
Newton Farm
BRAGGS HILL
Northcott
PANSON CROSS
East Panson

92:
Boyton Com Prim Sch
UNDERLANE
CIDER PRESS RD
Boyton Mill

Row 2:
BEACON PK
DORSET PK
Boyton
Hele
West Panson
Carey Barton
Carey Wood

91:
Tala Water
Colehill Wood
Tamatown
Sitcott
1 ORCHARD CL
2 CROCKERS WAY
3 STANBURY CL
4 DART CL
5 CRABBS CL
6 EDWARDS RD
7 DICKNA CL
TOWER HILL RD

Row 1:
Dunn's Farm
Downhayes
St Giles-on-the-Heath Com Sch
St Giles on the Heath
LOWER SLADESMOOR CRES
River Carey

90:
Stowsdon
Hessacott
Sutton Town
Wilkie Down Farm
Pinslow Farm
A388

18

19

Scale: 1¾ inches to 1 mile
0   ¼   ½ mile
0 250m 500m 750m 1 km

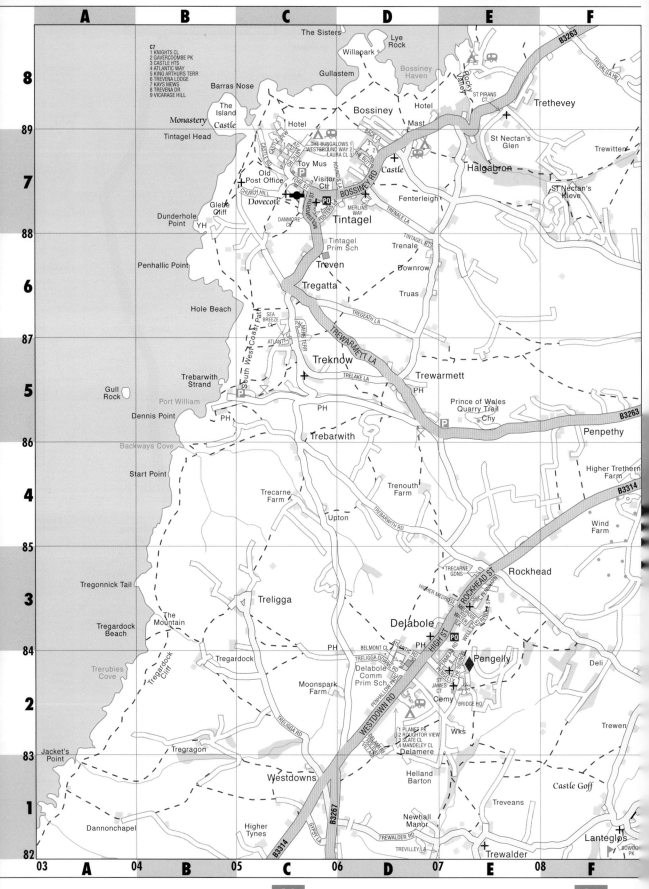

C7
1 KNIGHTS CL
2 GAVERCOOMBE PK
3 CASTLE HTS
4 ATLANTIC WAY
5 KING ARTHURS TERR
6 TREVENA LODGE
7 KAYS MEWS
8 TREVENA DR
9 VICARAGE HILL

The Sisters

Lye Rock

Willapark

Gullastem

Bossiney Haven

B3263

TREVALGA HILL

Barras Nose

Bossiney

Hotel

Mast

Rocky Valley

St Pirans Ct

Trethevey

Trewitten

The Island

Castle

Monastery

Tintagel Head

The Bungalows
Westground Way
Laura Cl

Hotel

Castle

St Nectan's Glen

Halgabron

St Nectan's Kieve

Toy Mus

Old Post Office

Visitor Ctr

PO

Dovecote

Bossiney Rd

Fenterleigh

Glebe Cliff

Church Hill

Danmore Ct

Trevena Rd

Fosters

Tintagel

Merlins Way

Trenale La

Dunderhole Point

YH

Tintagel Prim Sch

Treven

Tintagel Hts

Trenale

Downrow

Penhallic Point

Tregatta

Truas

South West Coast Path

Hole Beach

Sea Breeze Cl

Palmers Terr

Atlantic

Tregeath La

Trewarmett La

Gull Rock

Port William

Treknow

Trelake La

Trewarmett

PH

Dennis Point

PH

Prince of Wales Quarry Trail
Chy

B3263

Penpethy

Backways Cove

Trebarwith

PH

Start Point

PH

P

Higher Trethern Farm

B3314

Trecarne Farm

Trenouth Farm

Trebarwith Rd

Upton

Wind Farm

Tregonnick Tail

Trecarne Gdns

Higher Medrose

Rockhead St

Rockhead

Treligga

The Mountain

Delabole

Pengelly

Deli

Tregardock Beach

High St

PH

PO

Tregardock

Belmont Cl

Atlantic Rd

Trerubies Cove

Tregardock Cliff

Treligga Downs Rd

Delabole Comm Prim Sch

St James Ct

Cemy

Bridge Ho

Trewen

Moonspark Farm

Penhallow Park

Wks

1 Planet Pk
2 Roughtor View
3 Slate Cl
4 Mandeley Cl

Delamere

Castle Goff

Tregragon

Westdown Rd

Delabole Village

Helland Barton

Treveans

Jacket's Point

Treligga Rd

Lanteglos

Bowoo Pk

Dannonchapel

Higher Tynes

B3314

Gypsy La

B3267

Newhall Manor

Trewalder Rd

Trevilley La

Trewalder

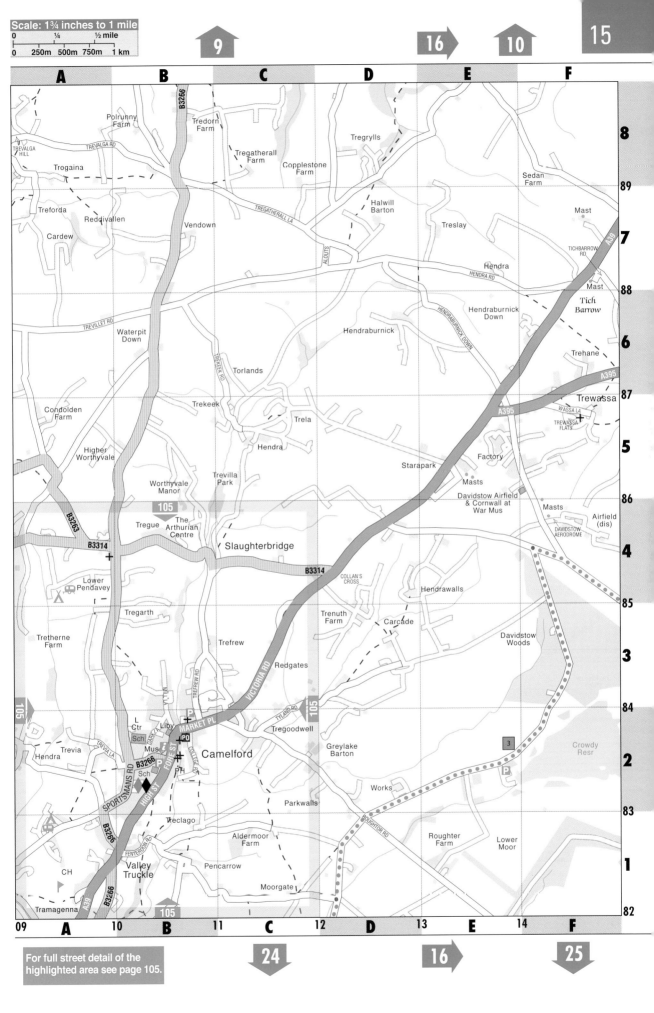

A   B   C   D   E   F

8

89

TREVALGA HILL
TREVALGA RD
Polrunny Farm
Tredorn Farm
Tregatherall Farm
Tregrylls
Copplestone Farm
Sedan Farm
Trogaina
Treforda
Reddivallen
Cardew
Vendown
TREGATHERALL LA
Halwill Barton
Treslay
Mast
A39
TICHBARROW RD

7

88

6

Mast

Tich Barrow

Trehane

A395

Trewassa

WASSA LA

TREWASSA FLATS

87

5

B3263
TREVILLET RD
Waterpit Down
TREKEEK RD
ALOUTS
Hendra
HENDRA RD
Hendraburnick
HENDRABURNICK DOWN
Hendraburnick Down
A395
Starapark
Factory
Masts

86

Condolden Farm
Torlands
Trekeek
Trela
Hendra
Higher Worthyvale
Trevilla Park
Worthyvale Manor
105
Tregue
The Arthurian Centre
Slaughterbridge
Davidstow Airfield & Cornwall at War Mus
Masts
Airfield (dis)
DAVIDSTOW AERODROME

4

B3314

B3314
COLLAN'S CROSS

85

Lower Pendavey
Tregarth
Trenuth Farm
Carcade
Hendrawalls
Davidstow Woods

3

84

Tretherne Farm
Trefrew
VICTORIA RD
Redgates
105
Tregoodwell
TYLAND RD
3

Hendra
TREVIA LA
Trevia
MILL LA
TREFREW RD
L Ctr
Liby
MARKET PL
Camelford
Greylake Barton
Crowdy Resr

2

B3266
Sch
Mus
COLLEGE RD
FORE ST
PO
PH
Works
P

83

SPORTSMANS RD
Sch
HIGH ST
Treclago
Parkwalls
ROUGHTOR RD
Roughter Farm
Lower Moor

B3266
FENTEROON RD
Aldermoor Farm
Pencarrow

1

CH
Valley Truckle
Moorgate

A39
B3266
105

82

09   A   10   B   11   C   12   D   13   E   14   F

Tramagenna

For full street detail of the highlighted area see page 105.

Scale: 1¾ inches to 1 mile

0   0½   0¼ mile

0   250m   500m   750m   1 km

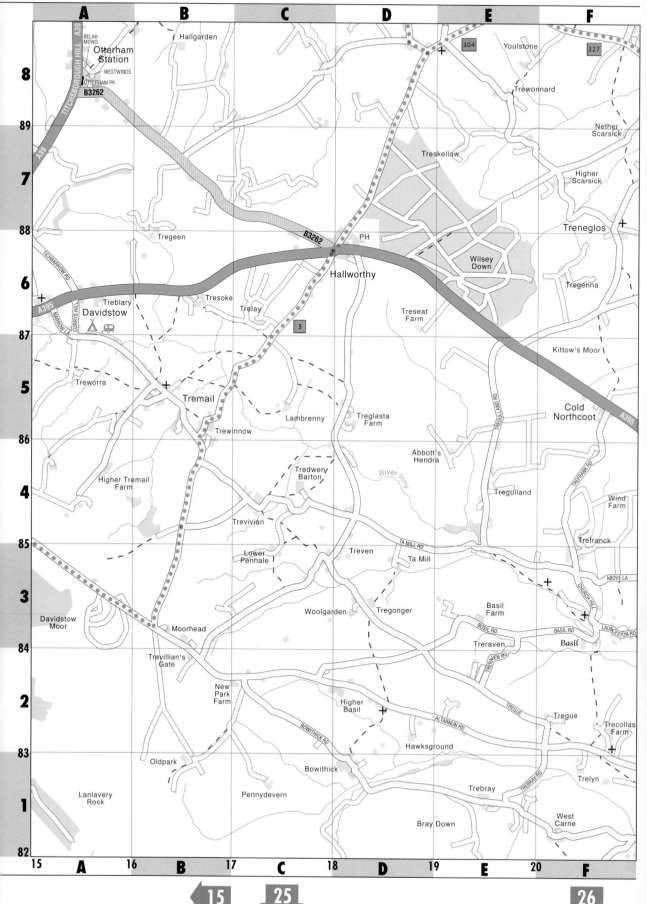

A   B   C   D   E   F

BELAH MDWS
Hallgarden
Otterham Station
WESTWINDS
OTTERHAM PK
TICHBARROW HILL
B3262
A39
Tregeen
B3262
PH
304
Youlstone
327
Treskellow
Trewonnard
Nether Scarsick
Higher Scarsick
Treneglos
TICHBARROW RD
A39
A395
CURRY'S HILL
NARROW LA
Treblary
Davidstow
Tresoke
Trelay
Hallworthy
Wilsey Down
Treseat Farm
Tregenna
3
Treworra
Tremail
Trewinnow
Lambrenny
Treglasta Farm
Abbott's Hendra
Kittow's Moor
TREGULLAND RD
Cold Northcoot
A395
Higher Tremail Farm
River Inny
Tregulland
Wind Farm
Trevivian
Tredwen Barton
TA MILL RD
Treven
Ta Mill
Tregonger
Trefranck
TREFRANK RD
ABOVE LA
Lower Penhale
Woolgarden
Basil Farm
CHURCH HILL
LAUNCESTON RD
Davidstow Moor
Moorhead
BOSIL RD
Treraven
BASIL RD
Basil
Trevillian's Gate
TREVEN RD
New Park Farm
Higher Basil
ALTARNUN RD
TREGUE
Tregue
Trecollas Farm
BOWITHICK RD
Hawksground
Oldpark
Bowithick
TREBRAY RD
Trelyn
Lanlavery Rock
Pennydevern
Trebray
West Carne
Bray Down

82

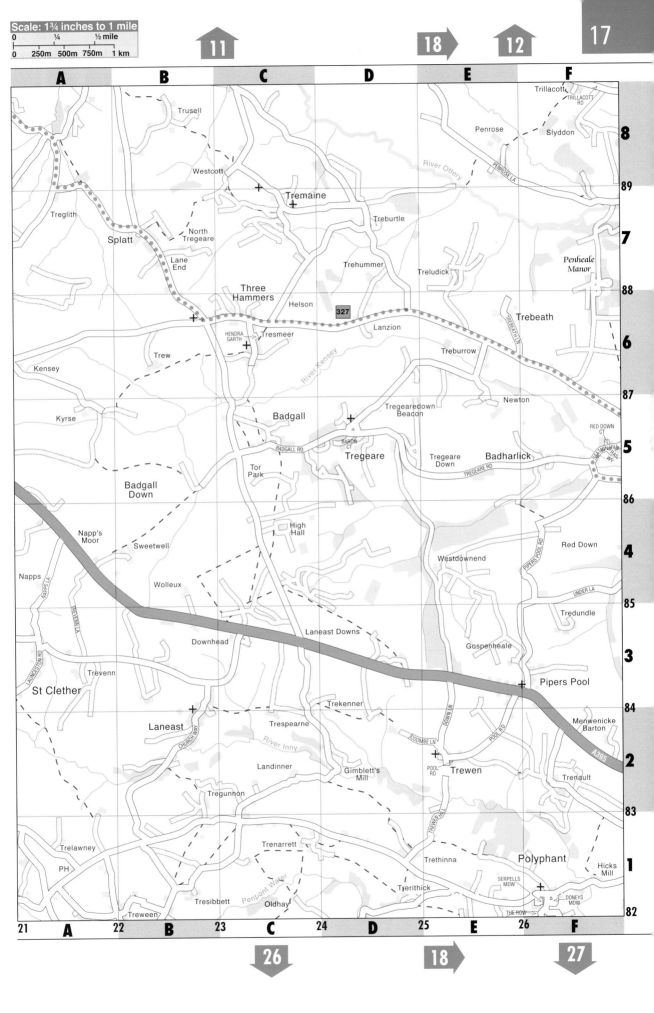

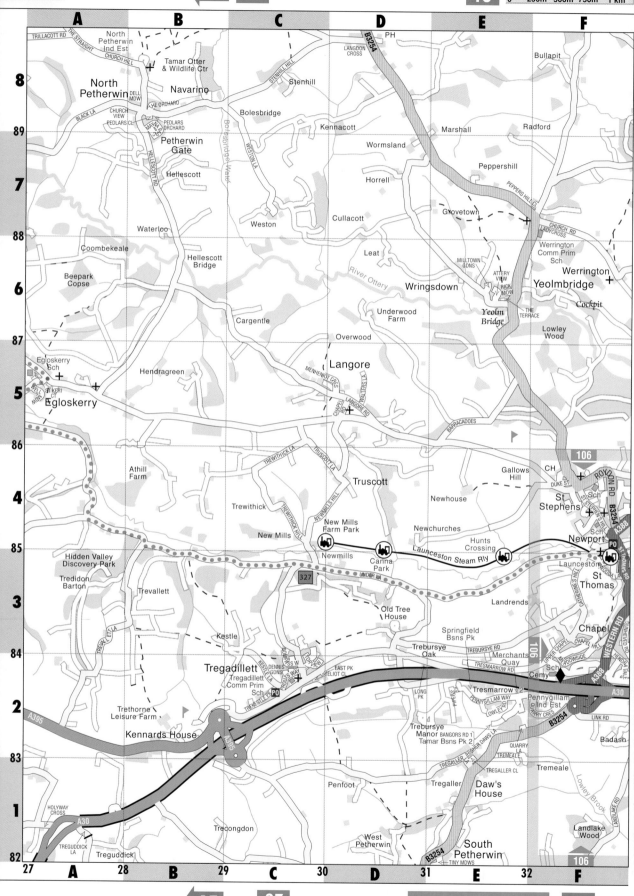

Scale: 1¾ inches to 1 mile
0   ¼   ½ mile
0   250m 500m 750m 1 km

A   B   C   D   E   F

TRILLACOTT RD
THE STRAIGHT
North Petherwin Ind Est
CHURCH HILL
Tamar Otter & Wildlife Ctr
Navarino
B3254
PH
LANGDON CROSS
Bullapit

North Petherwin
DELL MDW
THE ORCHARD
Stenhill Hill
Stenhill
Radford

8

BLACK LA
CHURCH VIEW
PEDLARS CL
PEDLARS ORCHARD
MAIN RD
Petherwin Gate
Bolesbridge
Kennacott
Marshall

89

HELLESCOTT RD
Hellescott
WESTON LA
Wormsland
Peppershill

7

Waterloo
Weston
Cullacott
Grovetown
PEPPERS HILL CL
CHURCH RD
LADYCROSS
Werrington Comm Prim Sch

88

Coombekeale
Hellescott Bridge
Leat
Wringsdown
MILLTOWN GDNS
ATTERY VIEW
RICK MDW
Werrington
Yeolmbridge
Cockpit

6

BOTESBRIDGE WATER
RIVER OTTERY
Beepark Copse
Cargentle
Underwood Farm
Yeolm Bridge
THE TERRACE
Lowley Wood

87

Overwood

Egloskerry Sch
BELL MDW
ST KERI CT
Hendragreen
Langore
MENHENIOT CRES
WATERS LA
LANGORE RD
Gallows Hill
Werrington
106

5

Egloskerry
CHAPEL
BARRACADOES
CH
ROYDON RD
DUKE ST

86

Athill Farm
TREWITHICK LA
TRUSCOTT LA
Truscott
St Stephens
A388
ST STEPHENS HILL

4

Trewithick
NEWMILLS HILL
TREWITHICK HILL
New Mills Farm Park
Newhouse
Newchurches
Newport
Sch
PO

85

Hidden Valley Discovery Park
New Mills
Newmills
Canna Park
Launceston Steam Rly
Hunts Crossing
Launceston Hill
St Thomas
CATHERINE'S HILL

Tredidon Barton
UNDER RD
327
Old Tree House
Landrends
ST THOMAS RD

3

Trevallett
Kestle
Springfield Bsns Pk
Trebursye Oak
Merchants Quay
Chapel
WESTERN RD
CHAPEL HILL

TREWEN ET LA
DENNIS GDNS
COMPASS WAY
TOR LA
EAST PK
ELIOT CL
TREBURSYE RD
TRESMARROW RD
106
UPPER CHAPEL
MEADOWSIDE
A388

84

Tregadillett
TREMSTILE LA
KESTLE LA
PO
LONG PK
Tresmarrow
Cemy
A30

2

A395
Tregadillett Comm Prim Sch
LOWLEY RD
PENNYGILLAM WAY
PENNYGILLAM
Pennygillam Ind Est
QUARRY CRES
B3254
LINK RD
Badash

Trethorne Leisure Farm
Treburtsye Manor
BANGORS RD 1
Tamar Bsns Pk 2
QUARRY
TREMEALE
Tremeale

83

Kennards House
A395
A30
Penfoot
Tregaller
HIGHER DAWS LA
TREGALLER CL
Daw's House
LOWLEY BROOK
LANDLAKE RD

1

HOLYWAY CROSS
A30
West Petherwin
South Petherwin
B3254
TINY MDWS
Landlake Wood
106

82

TREGUDDICK LA
Treguddick
Trecongdon

27   A   28   B   29   C   30   D   31   E   32   F

For full street detail of the highlighted area see page 106.

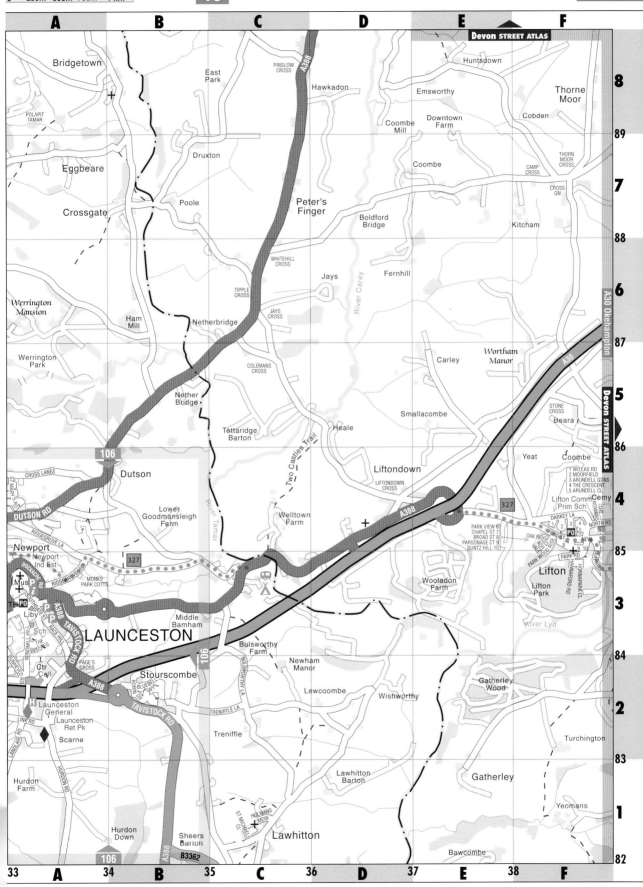

13

Devon STREET ATLAS

A30 Okehampton

Devon STREET ATLAS

8
89
7
88
6
87
5
86
4
85
3
84
2
83
1
82

A B C D E F

Bridgetown

POLAPIT TAMAR

Eggbeare

Crossgate

East Park

Druxton

Poole

Pinslow Cross

Hawkadon

Peter's Finger

WHITEHILL CROSS

Jays

TIPPLE CROSS

Netherbridge

Nether Bridge

JAYS CROSS

COLEMANS CROSS

Tettaridge Barton

Two Castles Trail

Heale

Huntsdown

Emsworthy

Coombe Mill

Downtown Farm

Coombe

Boldford Bridge

Fernhill

River Carey

Thorne Moor

Cobden

THORN MOOR CROSS

CAMP CROSS

CROSS GN

Kitcham

Carley

Wortham Manor

Smallacombe

Liftondown

LIFTONDOWN CROSS

STONE CROSS

Beara

Yeat

Coombe

1 WILLAS RD
2 MOORFIELD
3 ARUNDELL GDNS
4 THE CRESCENT
5 ARUNDELL CL

Lifton Comm Prim Sch

Cemy

THE ROWANS

NORTH RD

DARKEY LA

PARK VIEW 6
CHAPEL ST 7
BROAD ST 8
PARSONAGE CT 9
DUNTZ HILL 10

OAK RIDGE

PARK WOOD RISE

PO

NEW RD

HANNAFORD RD

Lifton

Lifton Park

River Lyd

Werrington Mansion

Ham Mill

Werrington Park

106

Dutson

Lower Goodmansleigh Farm

327

River Tamar

Welltown Farm

Wooladon Farm

Gatherly Wood

CROSS LANES

ST MARY'S RD

DUTSON RD

RIDGEGROVE LA

Newport

Newport Ind Est

327

RIDGEGROVE LA

MONKS PARK COTTS

Mus

P

TH PO

Liby

Sch

THE BEECHES

Ctr Coll

A388

TAVISTOCK RD

RACE HILL

WINDMILL HILL

DUNHEVED RD

LANDLAKE RD

LINK RD

H

Launceston General

Launceston Ret Pk

Scarne

Hurdon Farm

HURDON RD

Hurdon Down

106

A388

B3362

Sheers Barton

LAUNCESTON

PAGE'S CROSS

Middle Bamham

Stourscombe

106

BLUEBELL

ROBIN DR

BULSWORTHY LA

TRENIFFLE LA

Bulsworthy Farm

Newham Manor

Lewcoombe

Treniffle

ST MICHAELS MDW

HOLMANS MDW

St Michaels Ch

Lawhitton

Wishworthy

Lawhitton Barton

Gatherley

Bawcombe

Turchington

Yeomans

33 34 35 36 37 38

A B C D E F

For full street detail of the highlighted area see page 106.

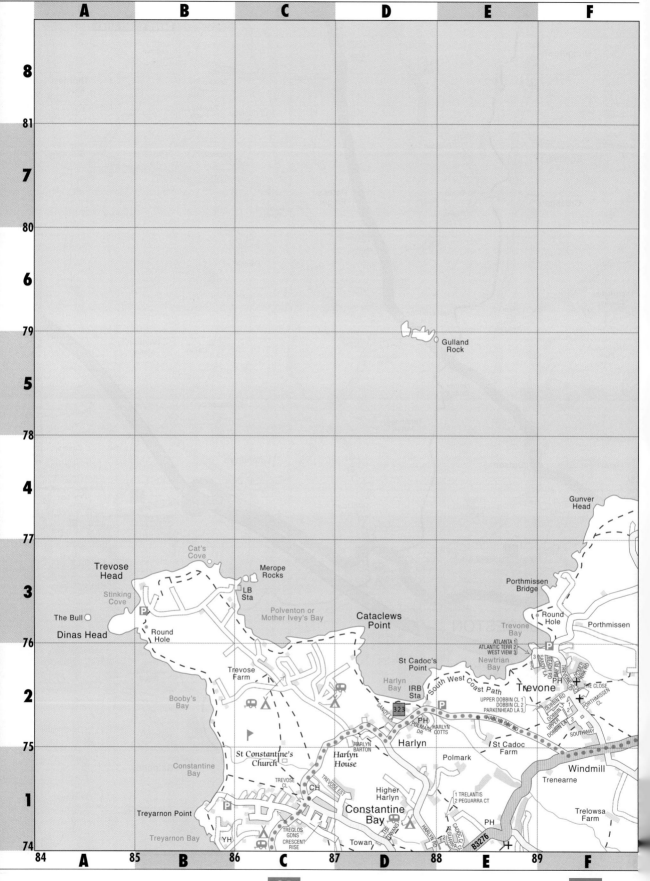

A B C D E F

8
81
7
80
6
79
5
78
4
77
3
76
2
75
1
74

Gulland Rock

Gunver Head

Trevose Head

Cat's Cove

Merope Rocks

Stinking Cove

Porthmissen Bridge

Round Hole

Porthmissen

The Bull

Dinas Head

Round Hole

LB Sta

Polventon or Mother Ivey's Bay

Cataclews Point

Trevone Bay

ATLANTA 1
ATLANTIC TERR 2
WEST VIEW 3

Trevose Farm

St Cadoc's Point

Newtrian Bay

BEECH RD
SANDY LA

Trevone

THE CLOSE

Booby's Bay

Harlyn Bay

IRB Sta

South West Coast Path

UPPER DOBBIN CL 1
DOBBIN CL 2
PARKENHEAD LA 3

DOBBIN RD

FORTHMISSEN CL

SANDY LA

323

PH

UPPER DOBBIN LA

SOUTHWAY

POLMARK DR

HARLYN COTTS

HARLYN BAY RD

Harlyn

St Cadoc Farm

Constantine Bay

St Constantine's Church

HARLYN BARTON

Harlyn House

Polmark

Windmill

Trenearne

TREVOSE CL

TREVOSE EST

CH

Higher Harlyn

1 TRELANTIS
2 PEGUARRA CT

Trelowsa Farm

Treyarnon Point

Constantine Bay

THE DRANS

HARLYN RD

CADOC CL
PEGUARRA

PH

Treyarnon Bay

YH

TREGLOS GDNS
CRESCENT RISE

Towan

B3276

84   85   86   87   88   89

A B C D E F

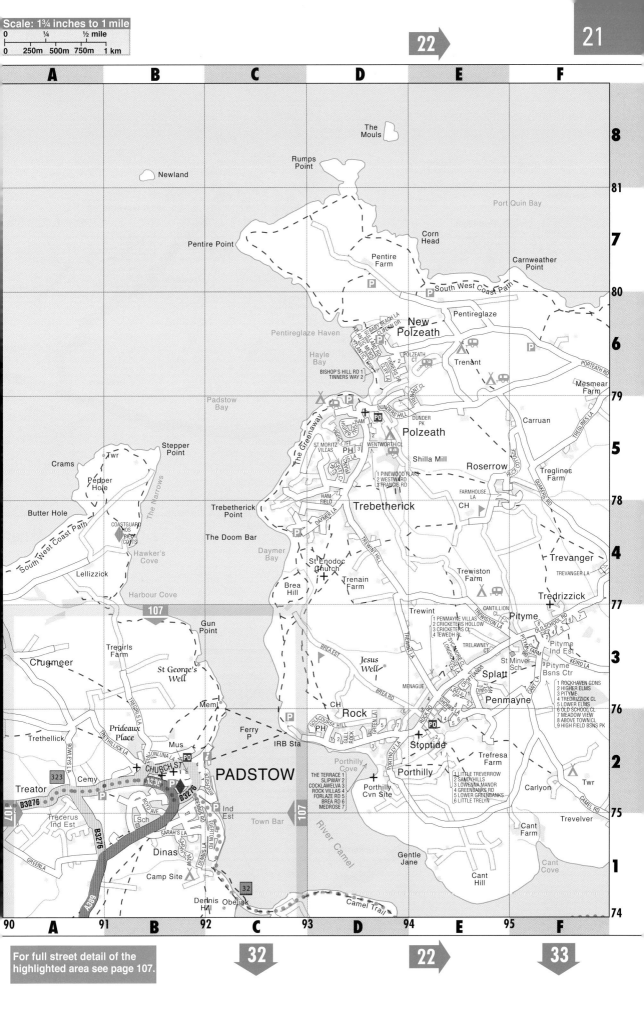

A   B   C   D   E   F

8

81

Port Quin Bay

7

The Mouls

Newland

Rumps
Point

Corn
Head

Pentire Point

Carnweather
Point

Pentire
Farm

South West Coast Path

80

Pentireglaze

6

New
Polzeath

BABY BEACH LA
CLIFTON DR
ATLANTIC MEWS
ATLANTIC TER
POLZEATH
CT
CLIFF LA
CLIFF DR
TREVANT CL

Trenant

Mesmear
Farm

Pentireglaze Haven

Hayle
Bay

BISHOP'S HILL RD 1
TINNERS WAY 2

79

Padstow
Bay

PO

DUNDERS HILL
DUNDER
PK

Polzeath

Carruan

Tregirls
Farm

The Greenaway

ST MORITZ
VILLAS
HIGH CT
TEE
 PH
ST MORITZ LA

SAM

WENTWORTH CL

Shilla Mill

Roserrow

Treglines
Farm

Crams

Twr

Stepper
Point

5

Pepper
Hole

The Narrows

1 PINEWOOD FLATS
2 WESTWARD
3 FRANCIS RD

FARMHOUSE
LA
CH

78

Butter Hole

Trebetherick
Point

HAM
FIELD

DAYMER LA

Trebetherick

South West Coast Path

COASTGUARD
HOS
PILOT
COTTS

Hawker's
Cove

The Doom Bar

Daymer
Bay

TREWINT HILL

Trewiston
Farm

Trevanger

TREVANGER LA

4

Lellizzick

St Enodoc
Church

Trenain
Farm

Tredrizzick

Harbour Cove

Brea
Hill

Trewint

77

Pityme

107

Gun
Point

1 PENMAYNE VILLAS
2 CRICKETERS HOLLOW
3 CRICKETERS CL
4 TEWEDH PL

TREWISTON LA
CANTILLION
CL

OLD SCHOOL RD

Crugmeer

BREA EST

Jesus
Well

TRELAWNEY
CT

PITYME
FARM
RD

St Minver
Sch

Pityme
Ind Est

KEIRO LA

Pityme
Bsns Ctr

St George's
Well

TREWINT LA

STANDREW LA
LONGMORE LA

Splatt

9

3

TREGIRLS LA

BREA RD

CROFTLANDS

MENAGUE

Penmayne

1 ROCKHAVEN GDNS
2 HIGHER ELMS
3 PITYME
4 TREDRIZZICK CL
5 LOWER ELMS
6 OLD SCHOOL CL
7 MEADOW VIEW
8 ABOVE TOWN CL
9 HIGH FIELD BSNS PK

Trethellick

Prideaux
Place

Mem

Ferry
P

CH

Rock

PH

GULL
ROCK

GREEN LA

SHORES LA

ROCK RD

PO

Stoptide

Trefresa
Farm

76

BOWLERS LA

TREGIRLS LA

TRETHELLICK LA

Mus

IRB Sta

GOLF
COURSE HILL

ROCK RD

Porthilly
Cove

Porthilly

Twr

PADSTOW

CHURCH ST

A389

ONLUNA LA

PO

Treator

323

Cemy

A389

B3276

BUSHPILL
DENNIS RD

Porthilly
Cvn Site

THE TERRACE 1
SLIPWAY 2
COCKLAWELVA 3
ROCK VILLAS 4
FORLAZE RD 5
BREA RD 6
MEDROSE 7

1 LITTLE TREVERROW
2 SANDYHILLS
3 LOWENNA MANOR
4 GREENBANKS RD
5 LOWER GREENBANKS
6 LITTLE TRELYN

Carlyon

2

B3276

Town Bar

River Camel

Cant
Farm

Trevelver

107

Trecerus
Ind Est

Sch

SARAH'S LA

EGERTON RD

BOLD AVE

Ind
Est

Gentle
Jane

75

B3276

GREENLA

A389

Dinas

Camp Site

Cant
Hill

Cant
Cove

1

Dennis
Hill

Obelisk

32

Camel Trail

74

90   A   91   B   92   C   93   D   94   E   95   F

32

22

33

For full street detail of the
highlighted area see page 107.

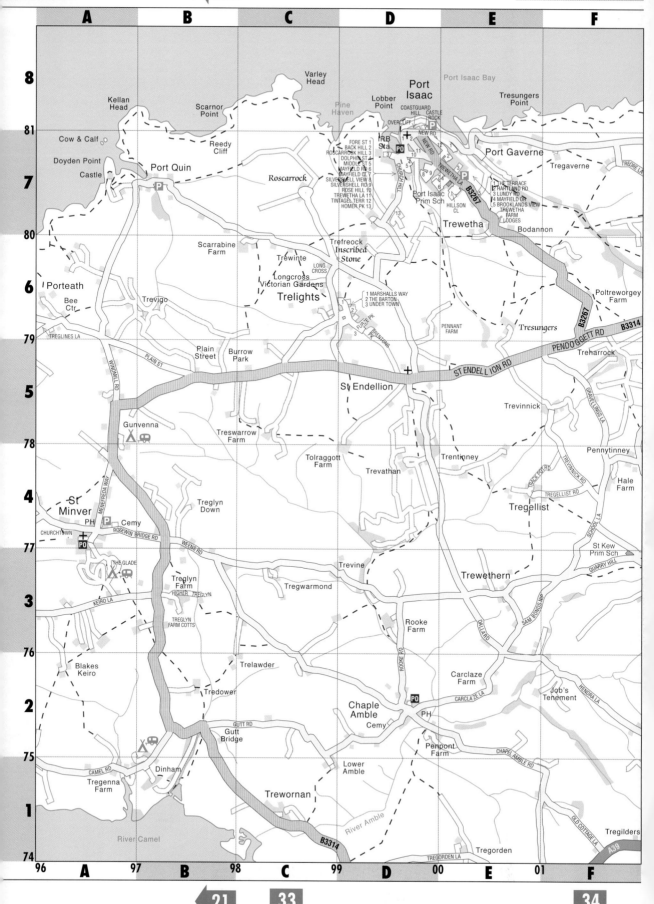

Scale: 1¾ inches to 1 mile

0 ¼ ½ mile

0 250m 500m 750m 1 km

A **B** **C** **D** **E** **F**

8

Varley Head

Port Isaac Bay

Port Isaac

Tresungers Point

81

Kellan Head

Scarnor Point

Pine Haven

Lobber Point

COASTGUARD HILL

CASTLE ROCK

OVERCLIFF

NEW RD

Port Gaverne

Tregaverne

TREORE LA

Cow & Calf

Reedy Cliff

Port Quin

Roscarrock

FORE ST 1
BACK HILL 2
ROSCARROCK HILL 3
DOLPHIN ST 4
MIDDLE ST 5
MAYFIELD RD 6
MAYFIELD CL 7
SILVERSHELL VIEW 8
SILVERSHELL RD 9
ROSE HILL 10
TREWETHA LA 11
TINTAGEL TERR 12
HOMER PK 13

7

Doyden Point Castle

CHURCH HILL

Port Isaac Prim Sch

HILLSON CL

TREWETHA LA

B3267

1 THE TERRACE
2 HARTLAND RD
3 LUNDY RD
4 MAYFIELD DR
5 BROOKLANDS VIEW

TREWETHA FARM LODGES

Trewetha

Bodannon

80

Scarrabine Farm

Trefreock Inscribed Stone

Trewinte

LONG CROSS

Poltreworgey Farm

B3267

6

Porteath

Bee Ctr

Trevigo

Longcross Victorian Gardens

Trelights

1 MARSHALLS WAY
2 THE BARTON
3 UNDER TOWN

FURZE PK

BREAKONS PK

PENNANT FARM

Tresungers

B3314

PENDOGGETT RD

79

TREGLINES LA

PLAIN ST

Plain Street

Burrow Park

ST ENDELLION RD

Treharrock

GRAVEL LINGS LA

5

WINDMILL RD

St Endellion

Trevinnick

78

Gunvenna

Treswarrow Farm

Tolraggott Farm

Trevathan

Trentinney

TRACK POT RD

TREVINNICK RD

Pennytinney

4

St Minver

Treglyn Down

Trewethern

Tregellist

Hale Farm

TREGELLIST RD

SCHOOL LA

MENEFREDA WAY

PH

Cemy

ROSEWIN BRIDGE RD

St Kew Prim Sch

QUARRY HILL

CHURCHTOWN

WEENS RD

Trevine

77

THE GLADE

KEIRO LA

Treglyn Farm

HIGHER TREGLYN

Tregwarmond

Trewethern

DALLARD

3

TREGLYN FARM COTTS

Rooke Farm

SAM BONDS HP

76

Blakes Keiro

Trelawder

Carclaze Farm

Job's Tenement

HENDRA LA

2

Tredower

GUTT RD

Gutt Bridge

ROOKE RD

Chaple Amble

Cemy

CARCLA ZE LA

PH

Penpont Farm

CHAPEL AMBLE RD

75

CAMEL RD

Dinham

Lower Amble

Tregenna Farm

OLD COTTAGE LA

Tregilders

1

Trewornan

River Amble

74

River Camel

B3314

Tregorden

A39

TREGORDEN LA

96 **A** **97** **B** **98** **C** **99** **D** **00** **E** **01** **F**

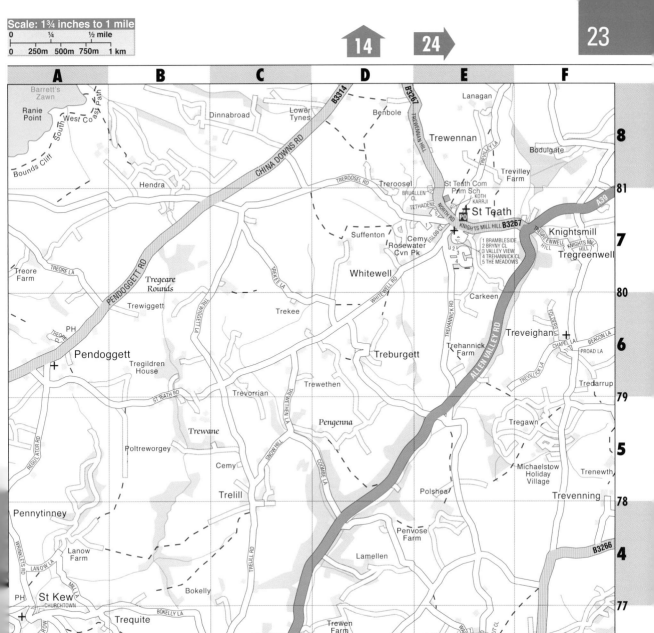

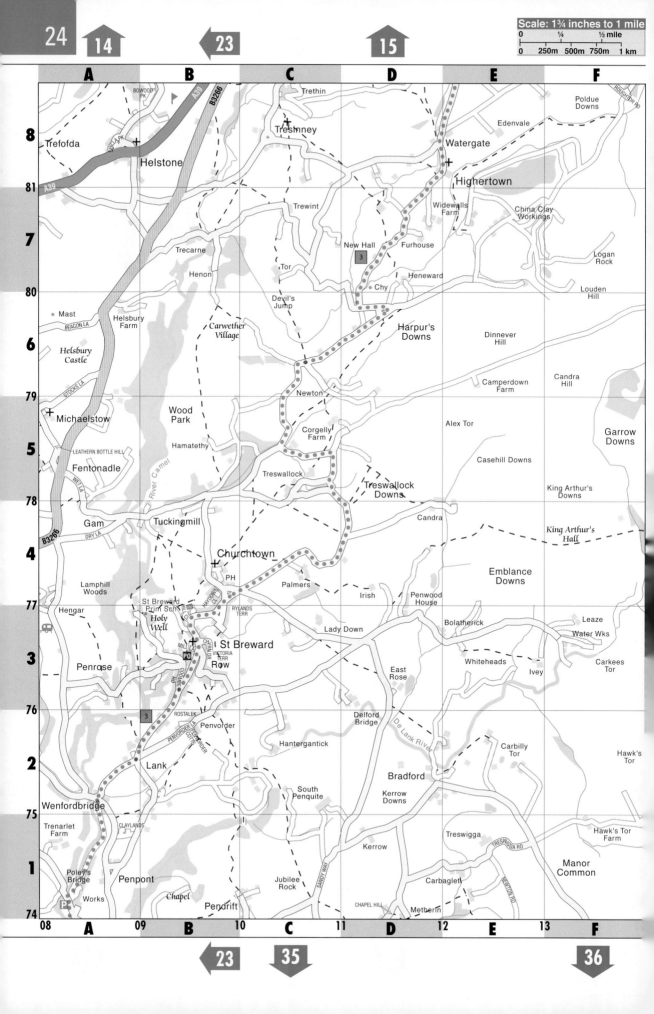

Scale: 1¾ inches to 1 mile

0   ¼   ½ mile

0 250m 500m 750m 1 km

A   **B**   **C**   **D**   **E**   **F**

BOWOOD PK

Trethin

Poldue Downs

Tresinney

Edenvale

8

Trefofda

Helstone

Watergate

Highertown

81

A39

Trewint

Widewalls Farm

China Clay Workings

7

Trecarne

Tor

New Hall
3

Furhouse

Logan Rock

Henon

Devil's Jump

Chy

Heneward

Louden Hill

80

Mast

Carwether Village

Harpur's Downs

Dinnever Hill

BEACON LA

Helsbury Farm

Candra Hill

6

Helsbury Castle

Newton

Camperdown Farm

STOCKS LA

79

Michaelstow

Wood Park

Alex Tor

Garrow Downs

Hamatethy

Corgelly Farm

Casehill Downs

5

LEATHERN BOTTLE HILL

Fentonadle

Treswallock

King Arthur's Downs

WET LA

River Camel

Treswallock Downs

78

Candra

King Arthur's Hall

B3266

Gam

Tuckingmill

DRY LA

4

Churchtown

Emblance Downs

PH

Palmers

Lamphill Woods

St Breward Prim Sch

Irish

Penwood House

77

Hengar

HAYDOWN CL

RYLANDS TERR

Holy Well

Lady Down

Bolatherick

Leaze

Water Wks

3

MILL LA

CHILLA DR

St Breward

VICTORIA TERR

Whiteheads

Ivey

Carkees Tor

PO

Row

Penrose

PH

East Rose

76

3

ROSTALEK

Penvorder

Delford Bridge

De Lank River

Carbilly Tor

Hawk's Tor

PENVORDER LA

PENVORDER COTTS

Hantergantick

2

Lank

Bradford

Kerrow Downs

Treswigga

TRESWIGGA RD

Hawk's Tor Farm

Wenfordbridge

CLAYLANDS

South Penquite

Kerrow

NEWTON RD

75

Trenarlet Farm

Manor Common

1

Poley's Bridge

Penpont

Jubilee Rock

SANDY WAY

Carbilly

Chapel

Pendrift

CHAPEL HILL

Metherin

P

Works

74

08   **A**   **09**   **B**   **10**   **C**   **11**   **D**   **12**   **E**   **13**   **F**

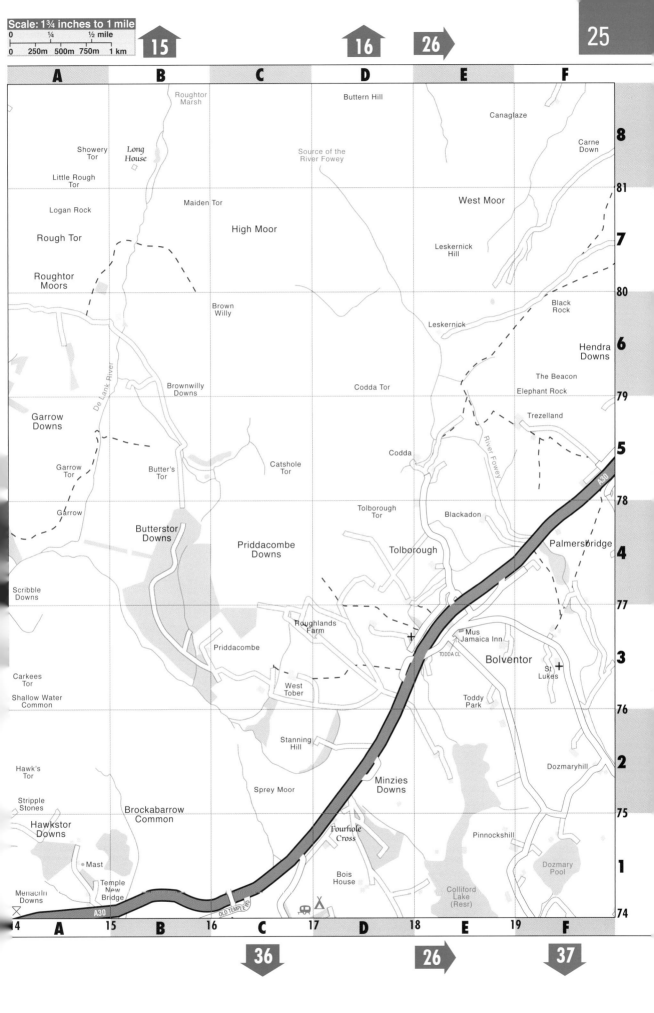

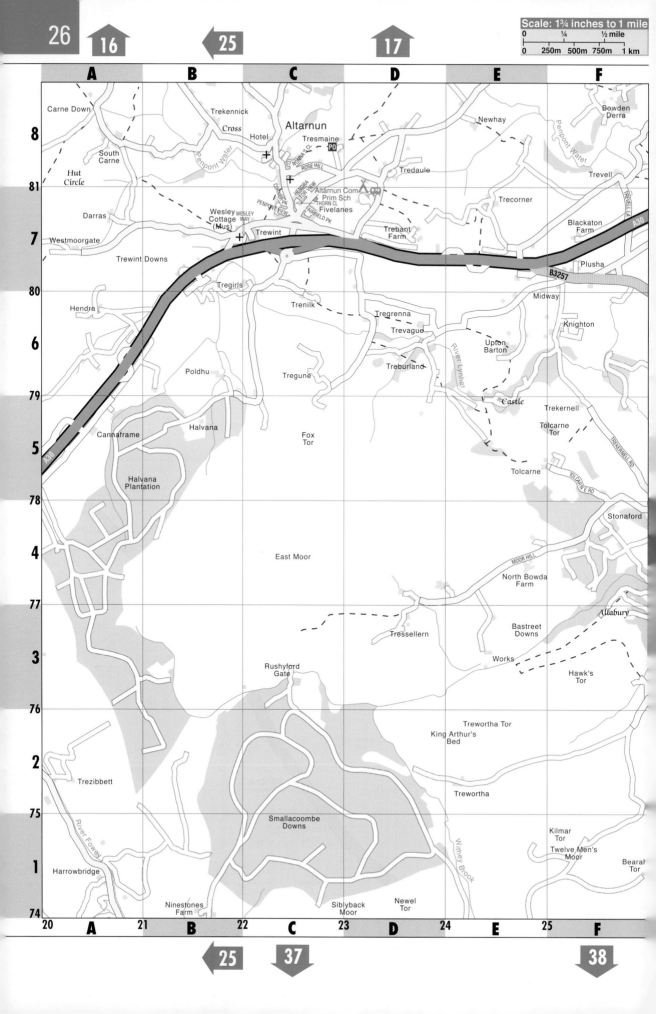

A   B   C   D   E   F

Carne Down

Trekennick
Cross
Hotel   Altarnun
8   Tresmaine   Newhay   Bowden
        South   PO   Derra
        Carne   ST NONNA'S CL
81   ROSE HILL   Tredaule   Trevell
    Hut   HENDRA
    Circle   TOR VIEW   Altarnun Com
Darras   Wesley   THORN CL Prim Sch   Trecorner
                Cottage WESLEY   FAIRFIELD PK Fivelanes   Blackaton
                (Mus)   WAY   Farm
7   Westmoorgate   Trewint   Trebant   Plusha
                                          Farm
        Trewint Downs   B3257
                    Tregirls
80   Midway
    Hendra   Trenilk
                                      Tregrenna   Knighton
6   Trevague
                        Tregune   Treburland   Upton
                                              Barton
        Poldhu   Trekernell
79   Castle   Tolcarne
                                                             Tor
        Cannaframe Halvana   Fox
5   Tor   Tolcarne
        Halvana
        Plantation   Stonaford
78

4   East Moor   North Bowda
                                                        Farm
                                                                      Allabury
77   Bastreet
                         Tressellern   Downs   Hawk's
3   Works   Tor
                    Rushyford
                    Gate   Trewortha Tor
76   King Arthur's
                                                          Bed
2   Trezibbett   Trewortha
                                  Smallacoombe
75   Downs   Kilmar
                                                                   Tor
                                                                   Twelve Men's
1   Harrowbridge   Moor
                         Ninestones   Siblyback   Newel   Bearah
74   Farm   Moor   Tor   Tor

20   A   21   B   22   C   23   D   24   E   25   F

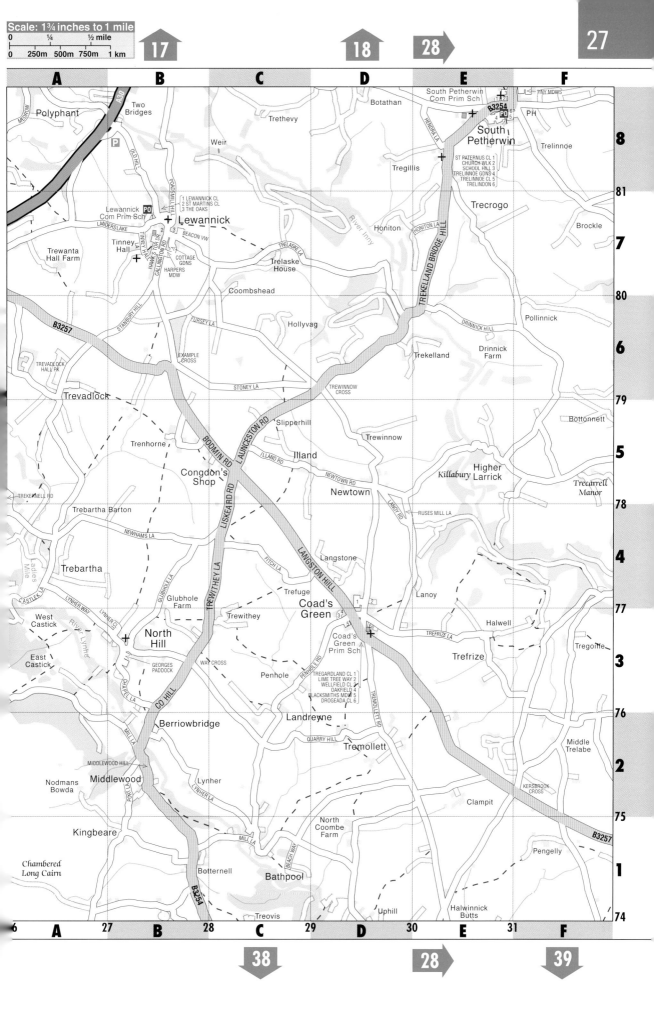

A   B   C   D   E   F

Polyphant
Two Bridges
Weir
Trethevy
Botathan
South Petherwin Com Prim Sch
B3254
PH
TINY MDWS
Trelinnoe
South Petherwin
1 ST PATERNUS CL 1
CHURCH WLK 2
SCHOOL HILL 3
TRELINNOE GDNS 4
TRELINNOE CL 5
TRELINDON 6

8

1 LEWANNICK CL
2 ST MARTINS CL
3 THE OAKS
Lewannick Com Prim Sch
PO
Lewannick
Tregillis
Honiton
Trecrogo
Brockle

81

LMIDERSLAKE
BEACON VW
Trelaske La
7

Trewanta Hall Farm
Tinney Hall
HAWK'S TOR DR
CALLINGTON RD
COTTAGE GDNS
HARPERS MDW
Trelaske House
Coombshead
TREKELLAND BRIDGE HILL
DRINNICK HILL
Pollinnick
80

B3257
STANBURY HILL
FURSEY LA
Hollyvag
Trekelland
Drinnick Farm
6

TREVADLOCK HALL PK
EXAMPLE CROSS
STONEY LA
TREWINNOW CROSS
79

Trevadlock
BODMIN RD
LAUNCESTON RD
Slipperhill
Trewinnow
Bottonnett

Trenhorne
ILLAND RD
Illand
NEWTOWN RD
Higher Larrick
Killabury
Trecarrell Manor
5

Congdon's Shop
Newtown
LANOY RD
RUSES MILL LA
78

TREKERNELL RD
Trebartha Barton
NEWHAMS LA
LISKEARD RD
4

Trebartha
TREWITHEY LA
FITCH LA
LANGSTON HILL
Langstone
Lanoy
Halwell
TREFRIZE LA
Tregoille
77

Ladies Mile
CASTLE LA
LYNHER WAY
LYNHER CL
GLUBHOLE LA
Glubhole Farm
Trewithey
Trefuge
Coad's Green
Trefrize
3

West Castick
River Lynher
North Hill
CO HILL
GEORGES PADDOCK
WAY CROSS
Coad's Green Prim Sch
TREGARDLAND CL 1
LIME TREE WAY 2
WELLFIELD CL 3
OAKFIELD 4
BLACKSMITHS MDW 5
DROGEADA CL 6
TREMOLLETT RD

East Castick
CHAPEL LA
Penhole
PENHOLE RD
Landreyne
76

MILL LA
Berriowbridge
QUARRY HILL
Tremollett
Middle Trelabe
2

MIDDLEWOOD HILL
PORT LA
Lynher
LYNHER LA
KERSBROOK CROSS
Clampit
75

Nodmans Bowda
Middlewood
North Coombe Farm
B3257
B3254
Pengelly

Kingbeare
MILL LA
BEACH WAY
1

Chambered Long Cairn
Botternell
Bathpool
Uphill
Halwinnick Butts

Treovis

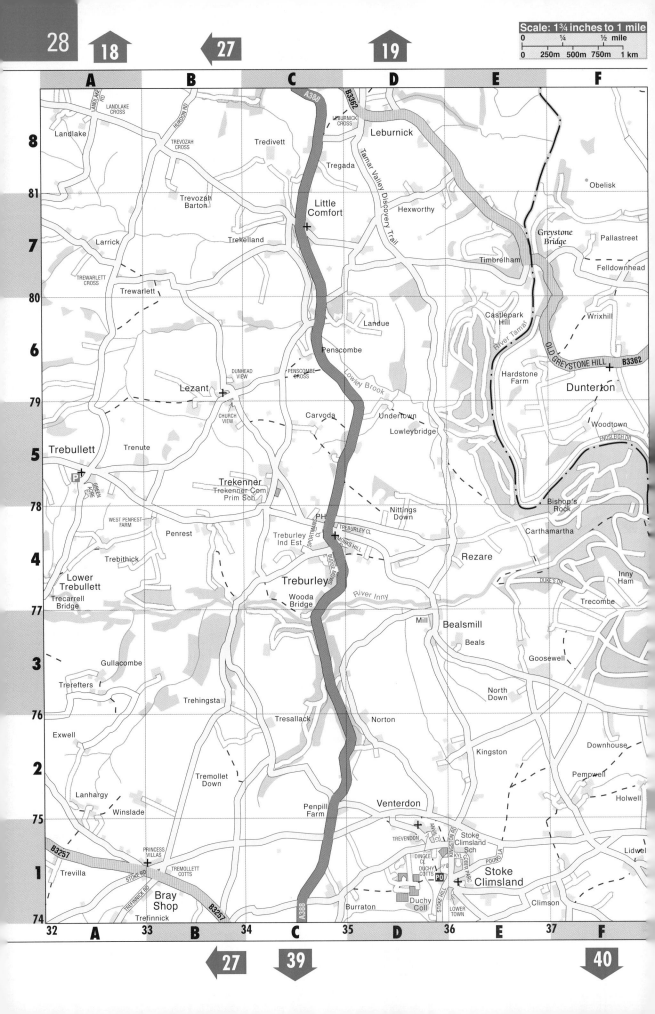

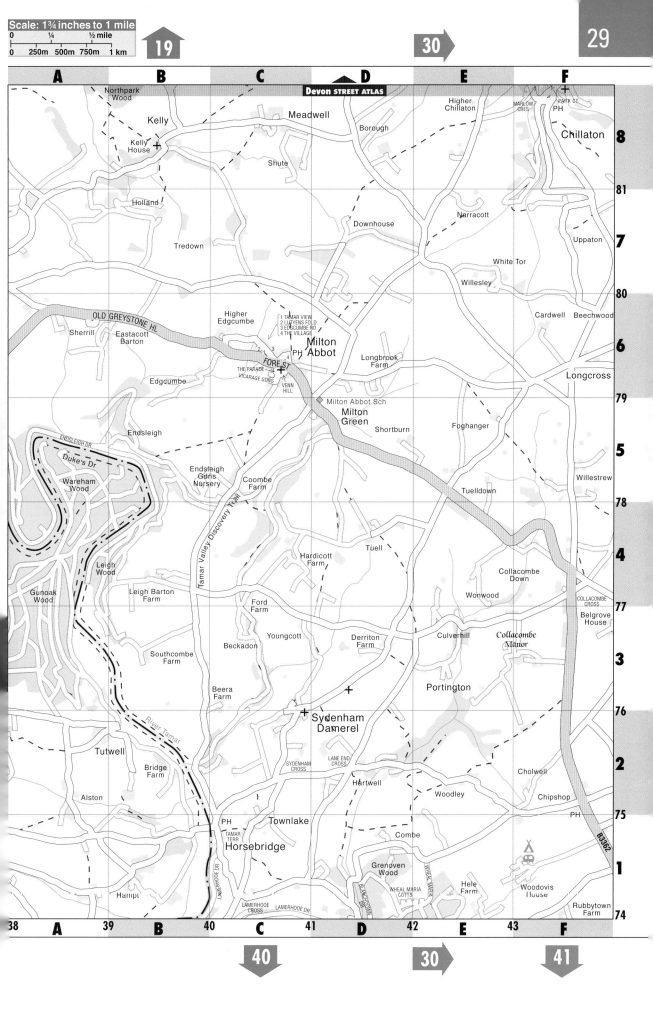

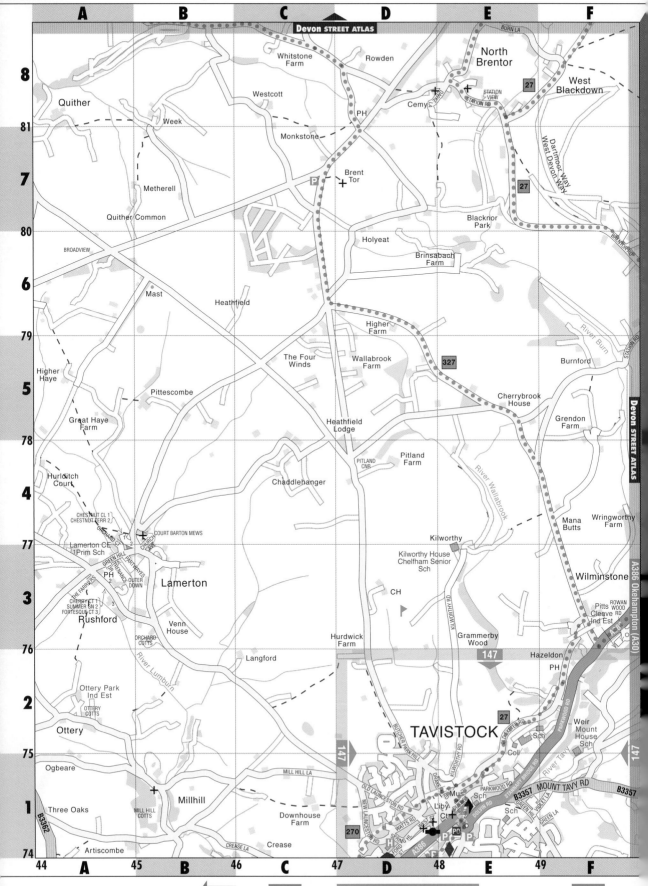

29

Scale: 1¾ inches to 1 mile

0   ¼   ½ mile
0   250m   500m   750m   1 km

Devon STREET ATLAS

8

North Brentor

Whitstone Farm

Rowden

West Blackdown

Quither

Westcott

BURN LA

27

STATION VIEW

Cemy

STATION RD

PH

81

Week

Monkstone

Brent Tor

Dartmoor Way West Devon Way

27

7

P

Metherell

Quither Common

Blacknor Park

80

BROADVIEW

Holyeat

Brinsabach Farm

BRENTOR RD

6

Mast

Heathfield

Higher Farm

River Burn

STATION RD

79

The Four Winds

Wallabrook Farm

327

Burnford

Higher Haye

Pittescombe

Cherrybrook House

Grendon Farm

5

Great Haye Farm

Heathfield Lodge

78

Hurlditch Court

Pitland Cnr

Pitland Farm

River Wallabrook

Mana Butts

Wringworthy Farm

4

CHESTNUT CL 1
CHESTNUT TERR 2

ORCHARD CT

Chaddlehanger

Court Barton Mews

Kilworthy

77

Lamerton CE Prim Sch

CHURCH CLOSE

GREEN HILL

PARTWAYES

Kilworthy House
Chelfham Senior Sch

Wilminstone

THE FARRERS

PH

OUTER DOWN

Lamerton

KILWORTHY RD

Pitts Cleave Ind Est

ROWAN WOOD RD

A386 Okehampton (A30)

3

CHERRY CT 1
SUMMER GN 2
FORTESQUE CT 3

Venn House

CH

Grammerby Wood

Hazeldon

PH

Rushford

ORCHARD COTTS

76

Langford

Hurdwick Farm

147

Ottery Park Ind Est

River Lumburn

BUTCHER PARK HILL

TAVISTOCK

27

Sch

Weir Mount House Sch

2

OTTERY COTTS

Ottery

147

PARKWOOD RD

River Tav

147

75

Ogbeare

MILL HILL LA

Coll

Three Oaks

B3362

Millhill

MILL HILL COTTS

Downhouse Farm

OLD LAUNCESTON RD

NEW LAUNCESTON RD

Mus

Liby
Ct

PARKWOOD RD

Sch

MOUNT TAVY RD

B3357

1

GREEN HILL

VIOLET LA

GREEN LA

74

Artiscombe

CREASE LA

Crease

270

WATTS RD

H

SPRING HILL

A386

DUKE ST

PO

Devon STREET ATLAS

44   A   **45**   B   **46**   C   **47**   D   **48**   E   **49**   F

29   41   42

For full street detail of the highlighted area see page 147.

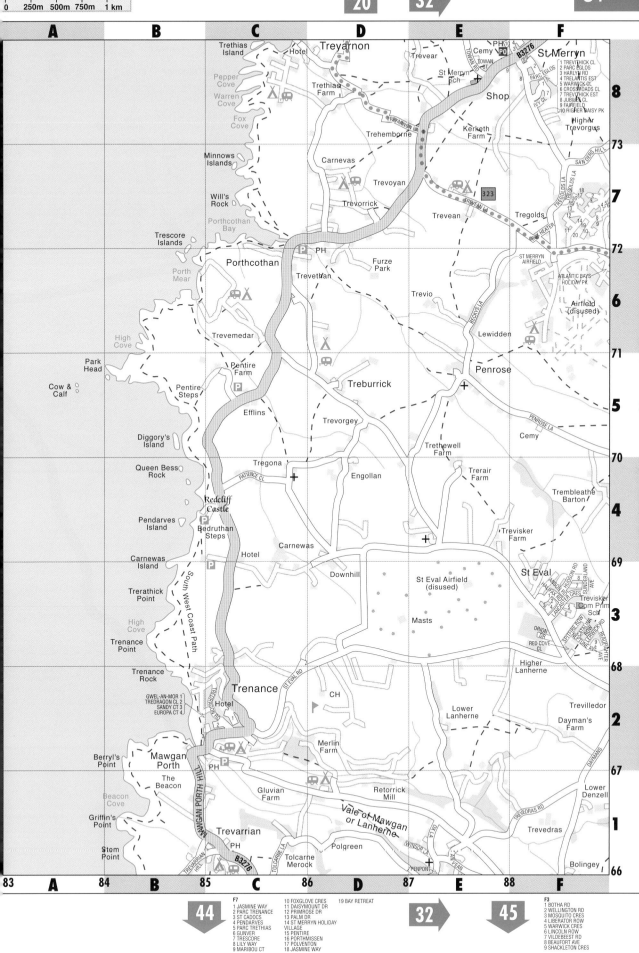

F7
1 JASMINE WAY
2 PARC TRENANCE
3 ST CADOCS
4 PENDARVES
5 PARC TRETHIAS
6 GUNVER
7 TRESCORE
8 LILY WAY
9 MARIBOU CT
10 FOXGLOVE CRES
11 DAISYMOUNT DR
12 PRIMROSE DR
13 PALM DR
14 ST MERRYN HOLIDAY
   VILLAGE
15 PENTIRE
16 PORTHMISSEN
17 POLVENTON
18 JASMINE WAY
19 BAY RETREAT

F3
1 BOTHA RD
2 WELLINGTON RD
3 MOSQUITO CRES
4 LIBERATOR ROW
5 WARWICK CRES
6 LINCOLN ROW
7 VILDEBEEST RD
8 BEAUFORT AVE
9 SHACKLETON CRES

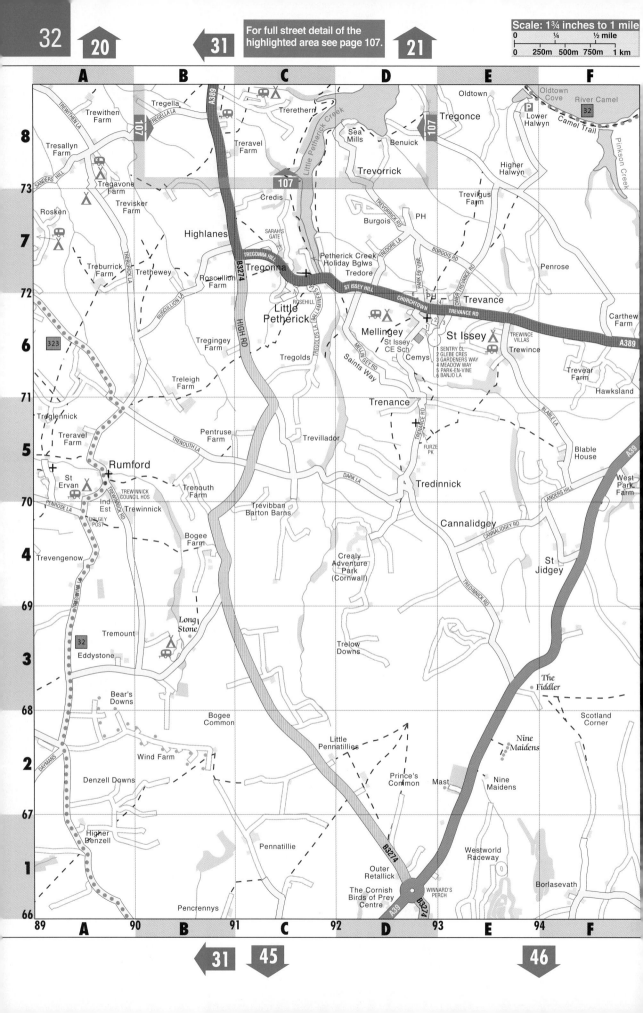

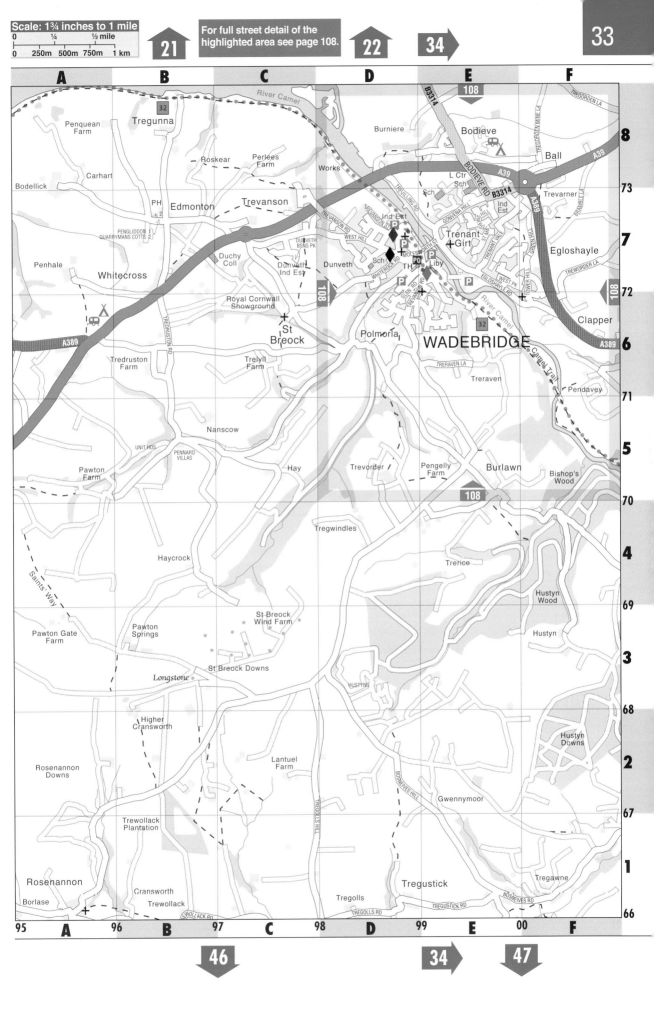

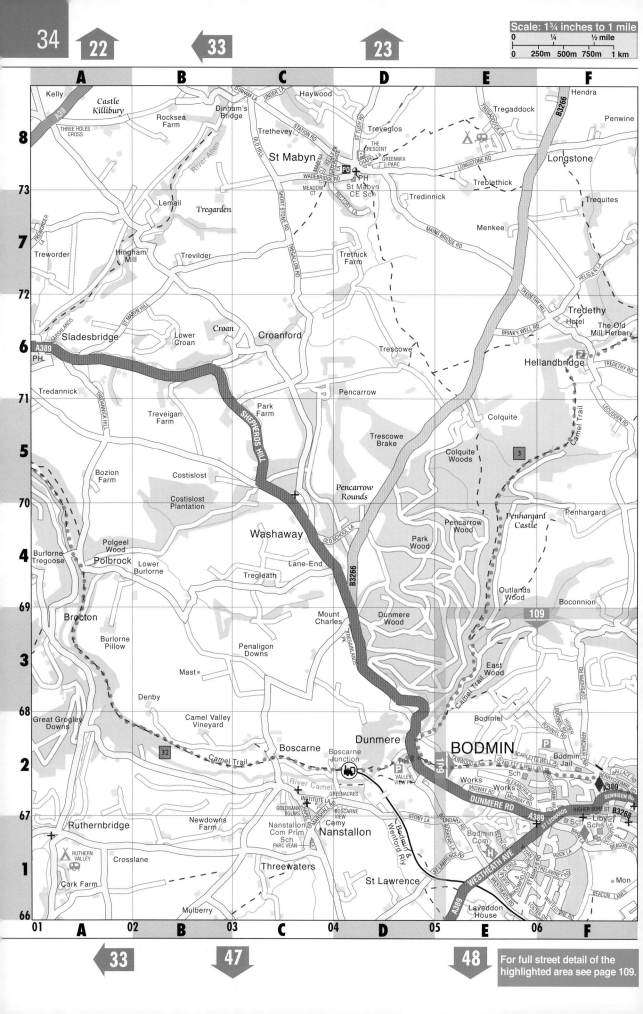

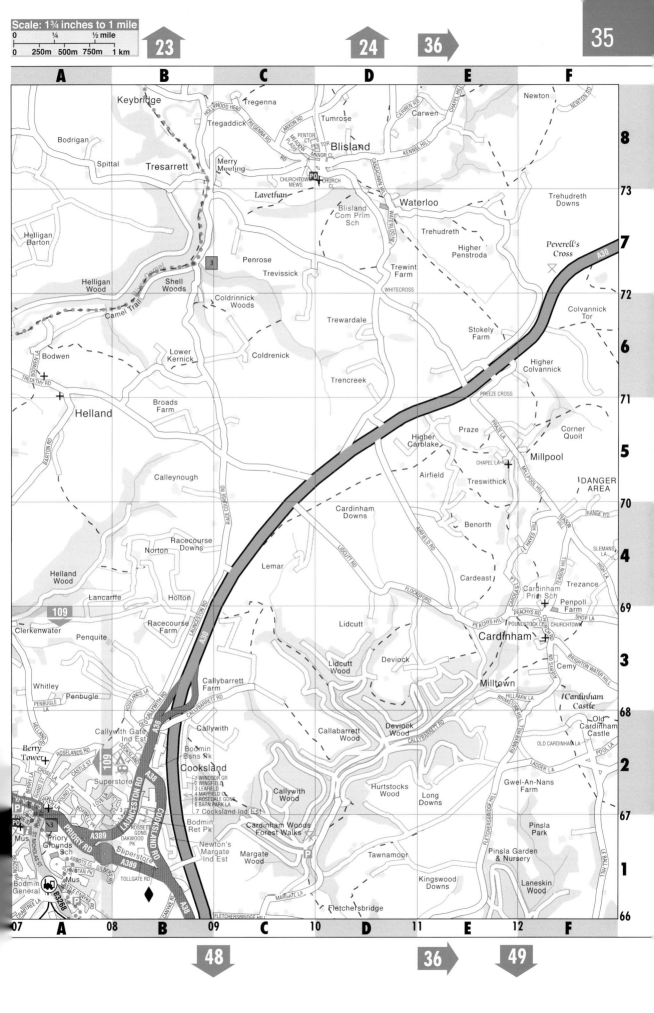

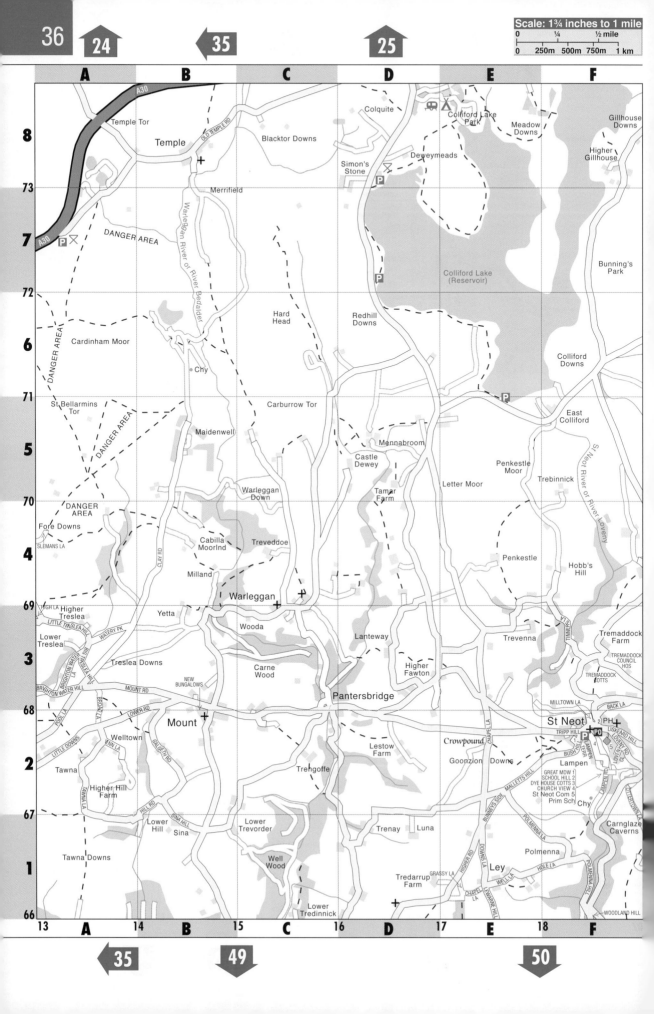

A   B   C   D   E   F

Ninestones Farm

Hill Tor

Siblyback Moor

Gillhouse Downs

Harrowbridge Hill Farm

Carkeet

8

Browngelly Downs

Higher Langdon

73

Brown Gelly

Lower Langdon

Siblyback

7

72

Lord's Park Farm

Westerlake Farm

Sparretts Farm

Craddock Moor

6

New Closes

Furswain

Tregarrick Tor

Trewalla Farm

71

Lamelgate

Siblyback Lake (Resr)

Redhill Downs

Draynes Common

North Trekeive

Crylla Farm

5

Whitebarrow Downs

Chy

Great Gimble

Whitebarrow Farm

WHITEBARROW COTTS

Wortha

Trekeivesteps

70

Mutton's Downs

River Fowey

Common Moor

4

East Northwood

Draynes

DAVY'S ROW

THE CRESCENT

THE BRAKE

Carpuan

TRECARNE VIEW 1
PENHALE CL 2
KILMAR CL 3
LANYON CT 4
KILMAR WAY 5
TRETHEVY CL 6
MEADOW TERR 7
TREMAR LA 8
WESLEY TERR 9
CHURCH VIEW 10
THE GLEBE 11
PENHALE LA 12

69

Berry Down

Lower Bowden

Golitha Falls National Nature Reserve

Golitha Falls

Redgate

King Doniert's Stone

Trecarne House

3

Trenant

Hendergrove

Treworrick

CARADON VIEW

HOCKINGS HO

SYMONS ROW

St Cleer

68

Wenmouth Cross

Treverbyn

EARTA

MOB LA

Lampretten House

2

Wenmouth

Treverbyn Mill

Trengale

Great Fursnewth

Treweatha

Trethinnick Farm

67

Killatown

Bokenna Wood

Little Pellagenna

Treleathick

AMBROSE LACEHILL

POLVENTON HILL

TOTTERDOWN LA

KILLATOWN HILL

BURNTHOUSE

Treworgey Manor

1

Polventon

Ashford Bridge

BOKENNA ONONO

AWETT RD

Venton Veor

66

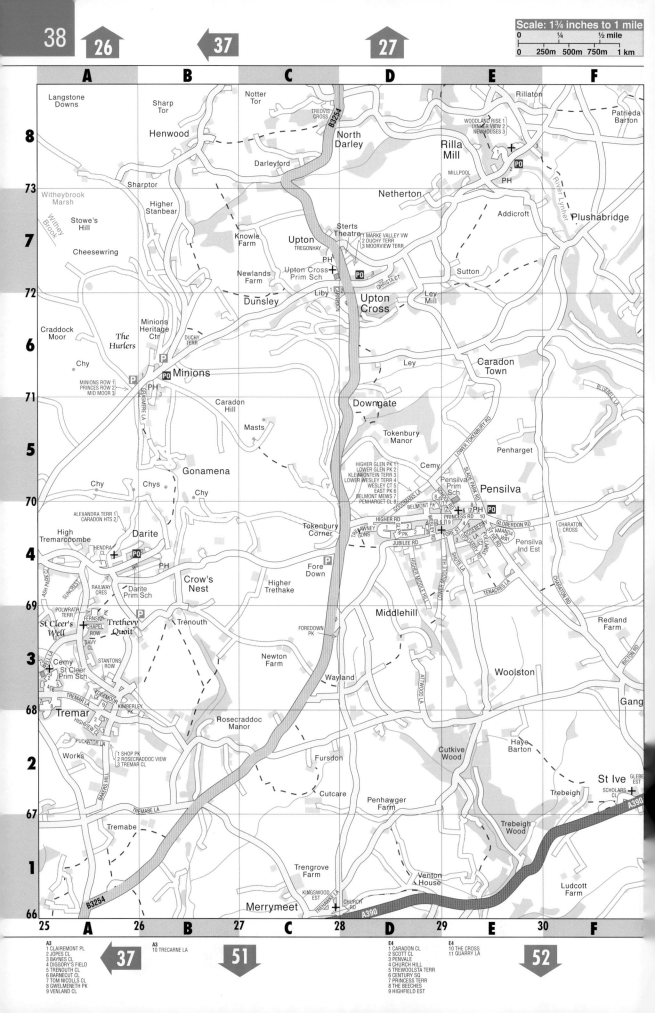

A   B   C   D   E   F

8

73

7

72

6

71

5

70

4

69

3

68

2

67

1

66

Langstone Downs

Sharp Tor

Notter Tor

TREOVIS CROSS

B3254

North Darley

Rillaton

WOODLAND RISE 1
LYNHER VIEW 2
NEWHOUSES 3

Patrieda Barton

Henwood

Darleyford

Rilla Mill

PO

River Lynher

MILLPOOL

PH

Netherton

Plushabridge

Sharptor

Higher Stanbear

Witheybrook Marsh

Stowe's Hill

Cheesewring

Withey Brook

Knowle Farm

Upton

Sterts Theatre

MARKE VALLEY VW 1
DUCHY TERR 2
MOORVIEW TERR 3

Addicroft

TREGONHAY

PH

Upton Cross Prim Sch

CHRISTA CT

Sutton

Newlands Farm

PO

Ley Mill

Dunsley

Liby

Upton Cross

Craddock Moor

The Hurlers

Minions Heritage Ctr

DUCHY TERR

Ley

Caradon Town

Chy

P

P

Minions

MINIONS ROW 1
PRINCES ROW 2
MID MOOR 3

PH

GRASMERE LA

Caradon Hill

Downgate

BLUEBELL LA

Masts

Tokenbury Manor

Penharget

Chy

Chys

Chy

Gonamena

HIGHER GLEN PK 1
LOWER GLEN PK 2
KLEINFONTEIN TERR 3
LOWER WESLEY TERR 4
WESLEY CT 5
EAST PK 6
BELMONT MEWS 7
PENHARGET CL 8

Cemy

Pensilva Prim Sch

LOWER TOKENBURY RD

Pensilva

ALEXANDRA TERR 1
CARADON HTS 2

Darite

HENDRA CL

PO

BELMONT PK

PRINCESS RD

PO

GLOBERDON RD

CHARATON CROSS

High Tremarcoombe

PH

Tokenbury Corner

SLADE PARK RD

SCHOOL LA

Pensilva Ind Est

ASH PARK CL

SUNCREST

RAILWAY CRES

Darite Prim Sch

Crow's Nest

TREPAWNEY GDNS

HIGHER RD

JUBILEE RD

Fore Down

Higher Trethake

GOODMANS LA

WESLEY RD

GOOSEBERRY LA

ST IVE RD

POLLARDS

AMANDA WAY

CHARATON RD

POLWRATH TERR

FERNSIDE

CHAPEL ROW

Trethevy Quoit

Trenouth

Foredown PK

FOREDOWN PK

Middlehill

HIGHER MIDDLE HILL

LOWER MIDDLE HILL

TENACRES LA

Redland Farm

St Cleer's Well

DAVY CL

Newton Farm

Wayland

Woolston

BICTON RD

Cemy

St Cleer Prim Sch

STANTONS ROW

Rosecraddoc Manor

ATTWOOD LA

Gang

WELL LA

EDGEMOOR CL

KIMBERLEY PK

Tremar

HIGHVIEW CL

PUCKATOR LA

Works

1 SHOP PK
2 ROSECRADDOC VIEW
3 TREMAR CL

Fursdon

Cutkive Wood

Haye Barton

GLEBE EST

St Ive

Trebeigh

SCHOLARS CL

BAKERS HILL

TREMABE LA

Cutcare

Penhawger Farm

Trebeigh Wood

A390

Tremabe

Trengrove Farm

Venton House

Ludcott Farm

B3254

Merrymeet

KINGSWOOD EST

TREHAWKE LA

CHURCH RD

A390

25   A   26   B   27   C   28   D   29   E   30   F

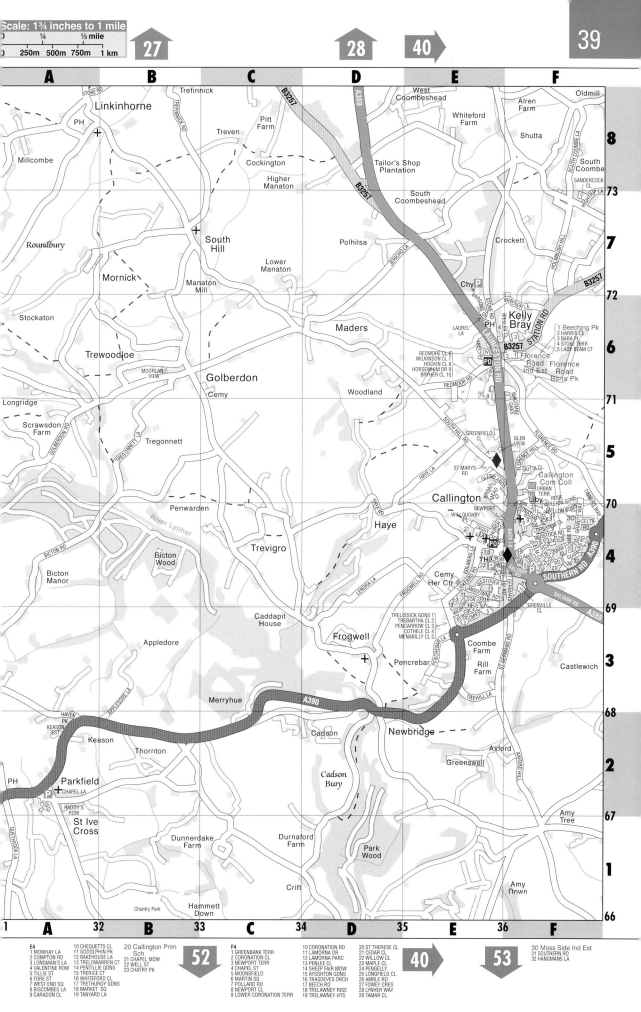

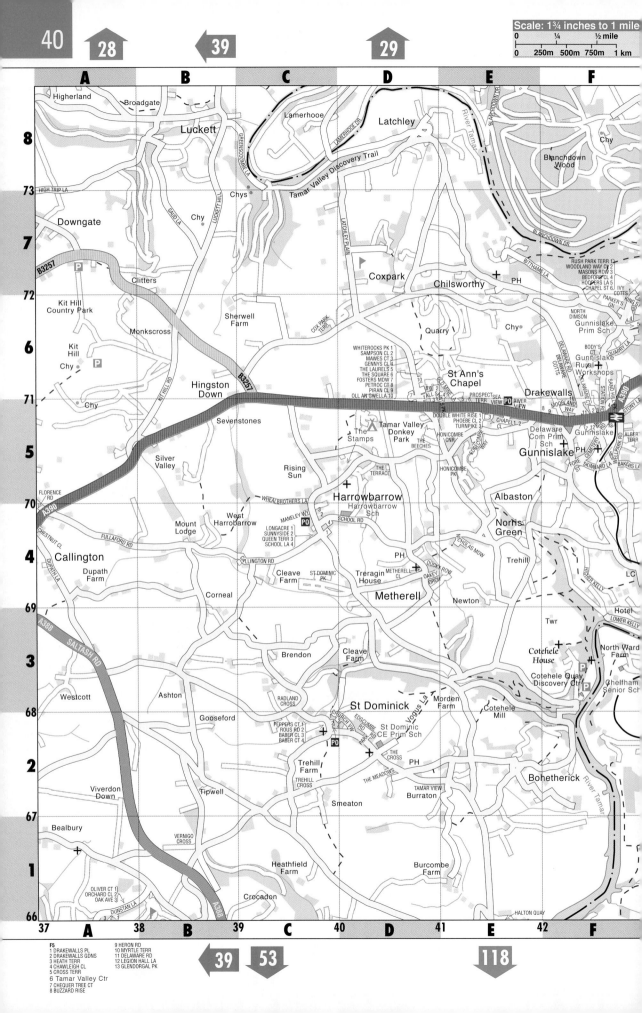

A   B   C   D   E   F

Higherland
Broadgate
Luckett
Lamerhooe
Latchley
River Tamar
Blanchdown Wood
Chy

8

73   HIGH TRIP LA

Downgate

GREENSCOMBE LA
LUCKETT HILL
SAUD LA
Chys
Chy
Tamar Valley Discovery Trail
LATCHLEY PLAIN
Coxpark
Chilsworthy
PH
RUSH PARK TERR 1
WOODLAND WAY CL 2
MASONS ROW 3
BEDFORD CL 4
HOOPERS LA 5
CHAPEL ST 6
IVY COTTS
KING'S
PARKER'S

7

B3257
P
Clitters
Monkscross
Kit Hill Country Park
Kit Hill
Chy
P
Sherwell Farm
COX PARK TERR
Quarry
Chy
NORTH DIMSON
Gunnislake Prim Sch
BODY'S CTT
Gunnislake Rural Workshops
QUARRY LA
DELAWARE RD COTTS
SAND HILL

72

6

Chy   B3257
Hingston Down
WHITEROCKS PK 1
SAMPSON CL 2
MAWES CT 3
GENNYS CL 4
THE LAURELS 5
THE SQUARE 6
FOSTERS MDW 7
PETROC CT 8
PIRAN CL 9
OLL AN GWELLA 10
St Ann's Chapel
OLD MINE
ALL SAINTS WY
PROSPECT TERR
SEA VIEW
PO
RIVER VIEW
Drakewalls
STATION RD
A390
MOORLAND WAY
DELAWARE RD

71

KIT HILL RD
Sevenstones
DOUBLE WHITE RISE 1
PHOEBE CL 2
TURNPIKE
CHAPEL 1 2
CL
Delaware Com Prim Sch
Gunnislake
STONY LA
ALBER TERR
PARK RD
BAKERS LA

FLORENCE RD
A390
Silver Valley
Rising Sun
The Stamps
Tamar Valley Donkey Park
THE BEECHES
HONICOMBE CNR
KELOCOMBE WAY
HONICOMBE WAY
HONICOMBE PK
FORE
Gunnislake
PH
SKINNARD LA
CEMETERY

5

70   CHESTNUT CL
West Harrobarrow
WHEAT BROTHERS LA
MANELEY WY
LONGACRE 1
SUNNYSIDE 2
QUEEN TERR 3
SCHOOL LA 4
PO
Harrowbarrow
Harrowbarrow Sch
SCHOOL RD
THE TERRACE
Albaston
Norris Green

DUPATH LA
Mount Lodge
FULLAFORD RD
CALLINGTON RD
Cleave Farm
ST DOMINIC PK
Treragin House
METHERELL CL
OAKEY ORCH
DUCKY ROW
PH
Trehill

4   Callington
Dupath Farm
Corneal
Metherell
Newton
LC
Hotel

69
A388
SALTASH RD
Brendon
Cleave Farm
LYDCOTT MDW
Twr
Cotehele House
LOWER KELLY
North Ward Farm

3   Westcott
Ashton
RADLAND CROSS
St Dominick
Morden Farm
Cotehele Mill
Cotehele Quay Discovery Ctr
P
P
Chelfham Senior Sch

68   Gooseford
PEPPERS CT 1
ROUS RD 2
BABER CL 3
BABER CT 4
CHURCH VW
EDGCUMBE RD
St Dominic CE Prim Sch
VOGUS LA
PARK RD
THE CROSS
PH

2   Viverdon Down
Tipwell
Trehill Farm
PO
TREHILL CROSS
THE MEADOWS
Smeaton
Burraton
TAMAR VIEW
Bohetherick
River Tamar

67   Bealbury

1
VERNIGO CROSS
Heathfield Farm
Burcombe Farm

66
37
OLIVER CT 1
ORCHARD CL 2
OAK AVE 3
DUNSTAN LA
A388
Crocadon
HALTON QUAY

A   38   B   39   C   40   D   41   E   42   F

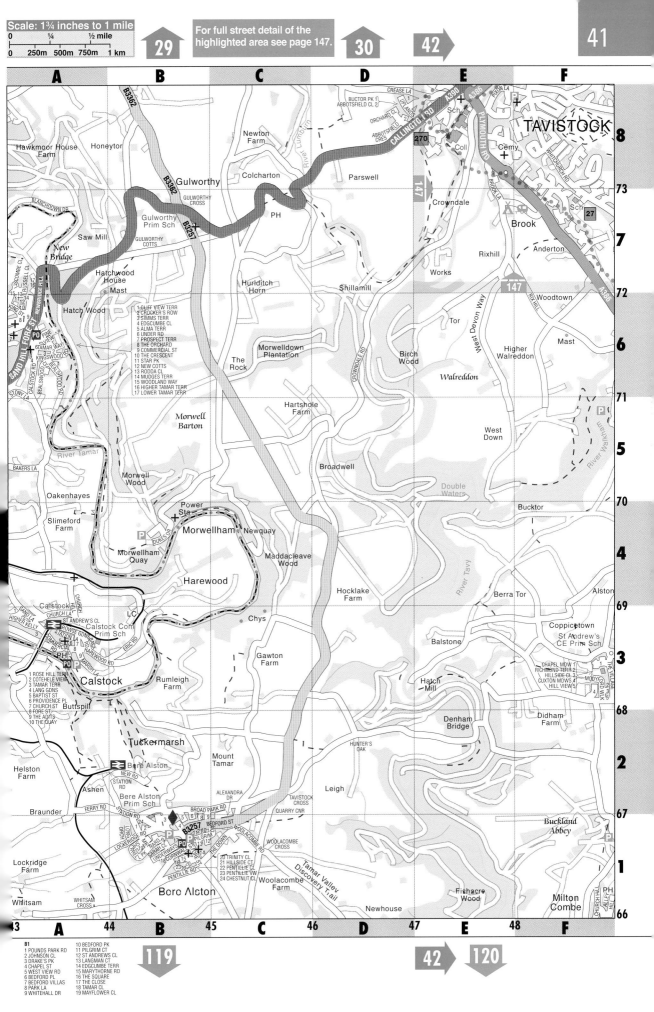

For full street detail of the highlighted area see page 147.

A   B   C   D   E   F

TAVISTOCK

Hawkmoor House Farm
Honeytor
Newton Farm
BUCTOR PK 1
ABBOTSFIELD CL 2
CREASE LA
ORCHARD CL
ABBOTSFIELD CRES
Sch
Coll
Cemy

Gulworthy
Colcharton
Parswell
Crowndale
Brook

B3362
B3362
Gulworthy Cross
GULWORTHY CROSS
Gulworthy Prim Sch
Gulworthy Cotts
B3257
PH
Rixhill
Anderton
Works

Saw Mill
New Bridge
Hatchwood House
Mast
Hurlditch Horn
Shillamill
Higher Walreddon
Mast

Hatch Wood
Tor
Woodtown

SAND HILL • FORE ST
NEWBRIDGE HILL
PO
PINE
TAMAR WAY
KINGSWOOD
BEALSWOOD RD
BEALSWOOD CL
CALSTOCK RD
STONY LA
KINGS
RUSSELL CL
GROSCOMBE DR
BLANCHDOWN DR

1 CLIFF VIEW TERR
2 CROCKER'S ROW
3 SIMMS TERR
4 EDGCUMBE CL
5 ALMA TERR
6 UNDER RD
7 PROSPECT TERR
8 THE ORCHARD
9 COMMERCIAL ST
10 THE CRESCENT
11 STAR PK
12 NEW COTTS
13 RODDA CL
14 MUDGES TERR
15 WOODLAND WAY
16 HIGHER TAMAR TERR
17 LOWER TAMAR TERR

The Rock
Morwelldown Plantation
Birch Wood
Walreddon
CROWNDALE RD
West Devon Way
RIV HILL
147

Morwell Barton
Hartshole Farm
West Down

River Tamar
BAKERS LA
Morwell Wood
Broadwell
Double Waters
Bucktor
River Walkham

Oakenhayes
Slimeford Farm
Power Sta
Morwellham
Newquay
Maddacleave Wood
P
DUKES DR
Morwellham Quay
Harewood
Hocklake Farm
Berra Tor
Alston

Calstock
CHURCH HILL
CHURCH LA
STATION RD
ROWSE GDNS
COMMERCIAL RD
HAREWOOD RD
ERIC RD
MARSH LA
LC
St Andrew's CL
Calstock Com Prim Sch
Chys
Gawton Farm
Balstone
Hatch Mill
Coppicetown
St Andrew's CE Prim Sch
CHAPEL MDW
RICHMOND TERR 2
HILLSIDE CL 3
CUXTON MDWS 4
HILL VIEW 5
MOODY'S
THE VILLAGE
PARK WLK

1 ROSE HILL TERR
2 COTEHELE VIEW
3 TAMAR TERR
4 LANG GDNS
5 BAPTIST ST
6 PROVIDENCE PL
7 CHURCH ST
8 FORE ST
9 THE ADITS
10 THE QUAY

PH
PO
Buttspill
Rumleigh Farm
Didham Farm
Denham Bridge

Tuckermarsh

Helston Farm
Bere Alston
NEW RD
STATION RD
Ashen
Bere Alston Prim Sch
ALEXANDRA DR
Mount Tamar
Leigh
HUNTER'S OAK
Buckland Abbey

Braunder
FERRY RD
STATION RD
BROAD PARK RD
BEDFORD ST
PILGRIM
BEDFORD ST
WOOLACOMBE RD
THE DOWN
B3257
Woolacombe Cross
TAVISTOCK CROSS
QUARRY CNR
Fishacre Wood

Lockridge Farm
LOCKERIDGE RD
LONG RD
ORCH
PILGRIM CT
PENTILLIE RD
UNDERWAY
CORNWALL
Bere Alston
Woolacombe Farm
Tamar Valley Discovery Trail
Newhouse
Milton Combe
CHURCH HILL
PH
ALLEY

20 TRINITY CL
21 HILLSIDE CL
22 PENTILLIE CL
23 PENTILLIE VW
24 CHESTNUT CL

Whitsam
WHITSAM CROSS

43   44   45   46   47   48

A   B   C   D   E   F

B1
1 POUNDS PARK RD
2 JOHNSON CL
3 DRAKE'S PK
4 CHAPEL ST
5 WEST VIEW RD
6 BEDFORD PL
7 BEDFORD VILLAS
8 PARK LA
9 WHITEHALL DR
10 BEDFORD PK
11 PILGRIM CT
12 ST ANDREWS CL
13 LANGMAN CT
14 EDGCUMBE TERR
15 MARYTHORNE RD
16 THE SQUARE
17 THE CLOSE
18 TAMAR CL
19 MAYFLOWER CL

8
73
7
72
6
71
5
70
4
69
3
68
2
67
1
66

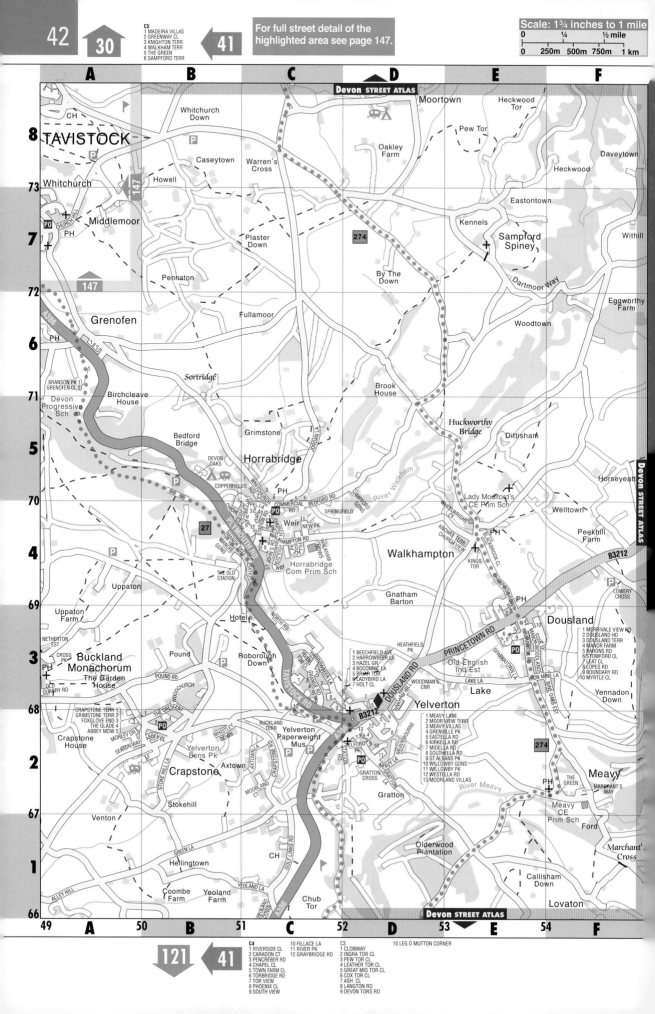

42 30 C5
1 MADEIRA VILLAS
2 GREENWAY CL
3 KNIGHTON TERR
4 WALKHAM TERR
5 THE GREEN
6 SAMPFORD TERR
41

For full street detail of the highlighted area see page 147.

Scale: 1¾ inches to 1 mile
0   ¼   ½ mile
0   250m   500m   750m   1 km

121 41

C4
1 RIVERSIDE CL
2 CARADON CT
3 PENCREBER RD
4 CHAPEL CL
5 TOWN FARM CL
6 TORBRIDGE RD
7 TOR VIEW
8 PHOENIX CL
9 SOUTH VIEW
10 FILLACE LA
11 RIVER PK
12 GRAYBRIDGE RD

C3
1 CLONWAY
2 INGRA TOR CL
3 PEW TOR CL
4 LEATHER TOR CL
5 GREAT MIS TOR CL
6 COX TOR CL
7 ASH CL
8 LANGTON RD
9 DEVON TORS RD

10 LEG O MUTTON CORNER

A   B   C   D   E   F

8

65

7

64

6

63

Towan Head

110

Gazzle

5

Hotel

Fistral
Bay

Fistral
Beach

HEADLAND RD

DANE RD

LB
Sta

62

NEWQUAY

South West Coast Path

CH

Cemy

FORE ST

ST GEORGE'S RD

PO

4

The
Goose

PH

ESPLANADE
RD

ESPLANADE RD

PENTIRE RD

Pentire

PENTIRE AVE

MOUNT
WISE

CRANTOCK RD

Pentire
Point East

TRET CARADO

CHANNEL RD

CHYNANCE DR

Pentire
Point West

Ferry P
(summer only)

PENTIRE CRES

PENMERE DR

TREVEAN WAY

A392

61

The
Chick

Porth
Joke

Vugga
Cove

Crantock
Beach

110

Crantock

Penpol

South West Coast Path

PENPOL HILL

The
Gannel

Kelsey
Head

Hotel

PH

West
Pentire

GREEN LA

GUSTORY RD

OSPORTH HILL

PENPOL HILL

Trevella

Treringey

3

WEST PENTIRE RD

PO

HALWYN AVE

TREVELVER RD

Cave

South West Coast Path

TREAGO RD

PENTIRE GN

LANE

HALWYN RD

60

Treago
Farm

ST
CARANTOC
WAY

Trevella
Park

Holywell
Bay

The
Kelseys

Wheelgate
House Sch

Trevowah

2

Carter's or
Gull Rocks

Holywell
Beach

Cubert
Common

Carines

110

Penhale
Point

Dunes

Lewannick

Treworgans

Carevick

Treworthal

59

Holywell

COMMONS RD

LEWANNICK RD

CH

Trevornick

Tresean

WESLEY RD

Carevick

1

Penhale
Camp

TREGUTH
CL

RHUBARB HILL

PH

GOLDEN DR

Holywell Bay
Fun Park

Trevail

Cubert
C P Sch

Trenissick

Cave

CAMP RD

GULL HILL RD

CENTRY RD

HOLYWELL RD

SEA VIEW LA

TREVAIL
COTTS

HOLYWELL RD

CHYNOWEN
PARC

CHYNOWEN LA

PH

A3075

Hoblyn's
Cove

Ligger
Point

DANGER
AREA

58

75   A   76   B   77   C   78   D   79   E   80   F

55

44

For full street detail of the
highlighted area see page
110.

A B C D E F

Strasse Cliff
South West Coast Path
Tolcarne La
B3276
Cemy
Long La
Newquay Airport

8

Watergate Bay

Tregarrian Hill
TREGURRIAN HILL
Tregurrian
Penvose Farm
Newquay Cornwall Airport

65

Hotel
P P
BEECHCOMBERS
Marbein Cotts
New Rd

7

Mast

Tregurrian or Watergate Beach
WATERGATE RD

64

Trebelsue Farm
Twr
Lime Cl

Zacry's Islands
THE WILLOWS 1
COASTLINE CT 2
TREVELGUE CT 3
HIGH ATLANTIC 4
SPINDRIFT 5
ISLAND POINT 6

Higher Trewince
Aerohub Business Park

6

Trevelgue
Trevelgue Head
Flory Island
Hotel
TREVELGUE RD
Tregustick Farm
Water Tower

Whipsiderry
WHIPSIDERRY RD
ALEXANDRA RD
A3059

63
110 111

Caves
Lusty Glaze
PORTH WAY
Porth
PARKENBUTTS
Penrose
Tregenna
CH
Treloy
Treissac Farm

5

Newquay Bay
NARROWCLIFF
HENVER RD
St Columb Minor
PRIORY RD
Coll
PRIORY HTS
CALSHOT CL
LEANDER CL
Cemy
RIALTON RD
Rialton Barton
32
Melancoose
Porth Resr
Trebarber

Caves
Aquarium
P
CHESTER
GLAMIS RD
HALGROVE RD
B3276
Newquay Tretherras Sch
PARKLANDS
A3058
A3059
RIALTON RD

62

Liby
Newquay
Acad
Sports Ctr
Gusti Veor
East Penhill
Colan

4

Acad
MOUNT WISE
TREWHELA RD
TRENANCE
L Pk
TREVENSON RD
TRERICE DR
NEWQUAY
QUINTRELL RD
Trewollack Farm
Lowertown

Trenance
A3058
TRENANCE LA
RAWLEY LA
TREVEMPER RD
Sch
LC
BLISTRA RD
Gusti Vean
Sch
CHAPEL LA
111
Bejowan
Lady Nance

61

A392 GANNEL RD
Treninnick
MELLANVRANE LA
DALE RD
Trencreek
LC
Chapel
Quintrell Downs
QUINTRELL CL

3

Treloggan Ind Est
POLWHELE RD
Lane
LC
QUINTRELL DOWNS
AVON HILL
Quintrell Downs
QUINTRELL GDNS
PH
EAST RD

Superstore
WEST RD
A3058
WILLOW WAY
BRIDLE WAY

Treringey Round
TREVEMPER RD
A392
PH
Trevithick Manor
Manuels
Trethiggy Farm
PH

60

Trevemper
A3075
Higher Trevilley
32
Trevilley Court Farm
Legonna
Coswarth

Penhallow
River Gannel
TAYLORS LA
Kestle Mill
Kestle

2

Rosecliston Park
Gwills
111
TRERICE HOLDINGS
Trevarthian
Trevean
Tregonning

59
110

Sewage Works
DairyLand Farm World

Polgreen
Trerice
Tresillian House
A3058

1

A3075
Trerew Farm
Tregair Farm
Trewerry Mill

58

81 A 82 B 83 C 84 D 85 E 86 F

For full street detail of the highlighted area see pages 110 and 111. 43 56

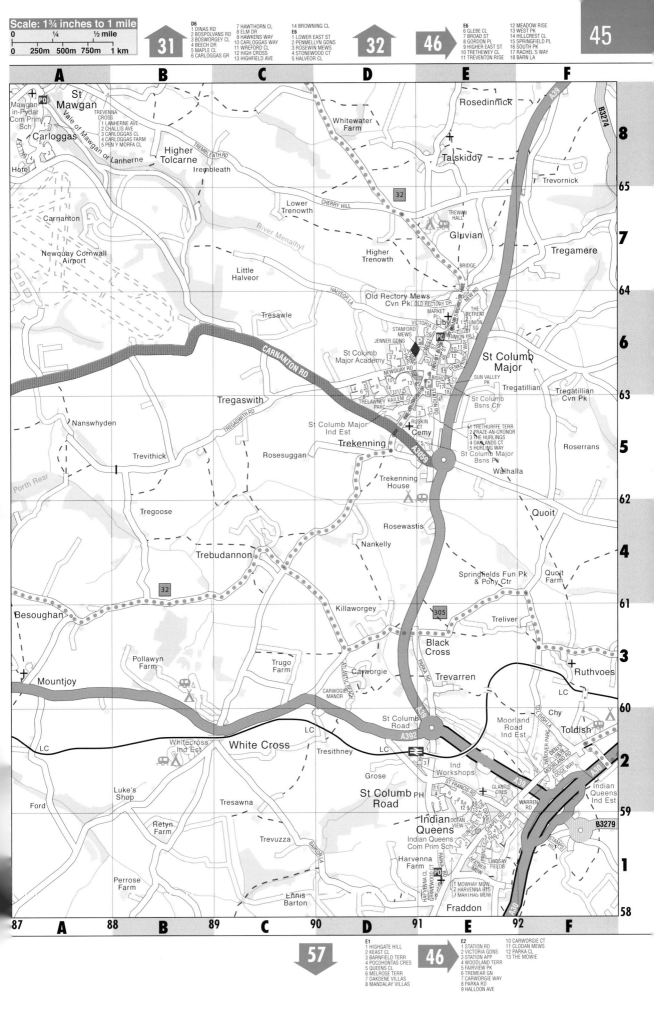

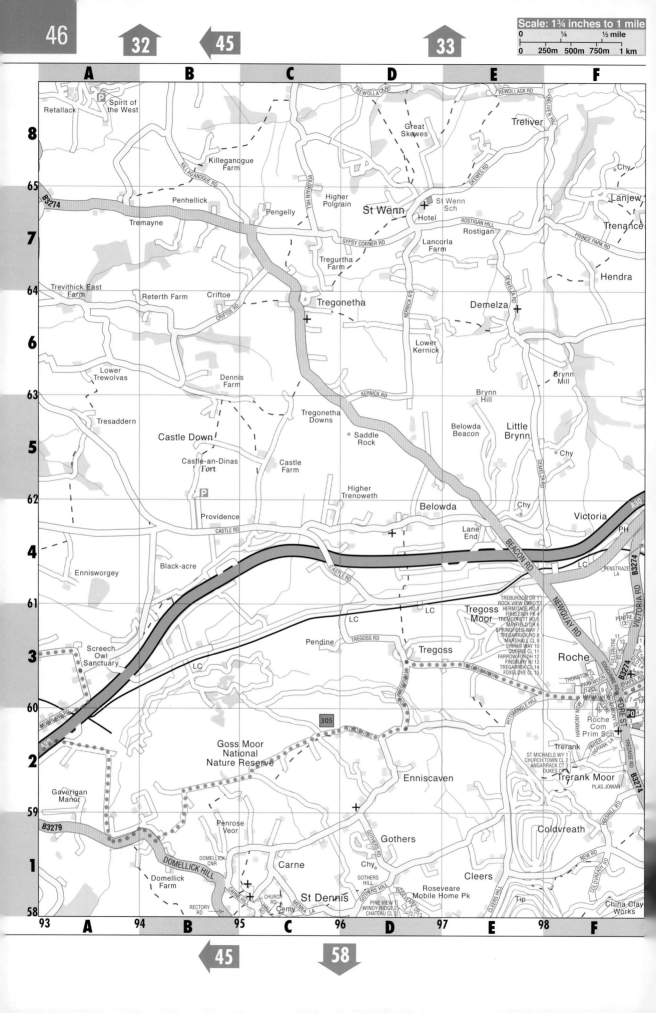

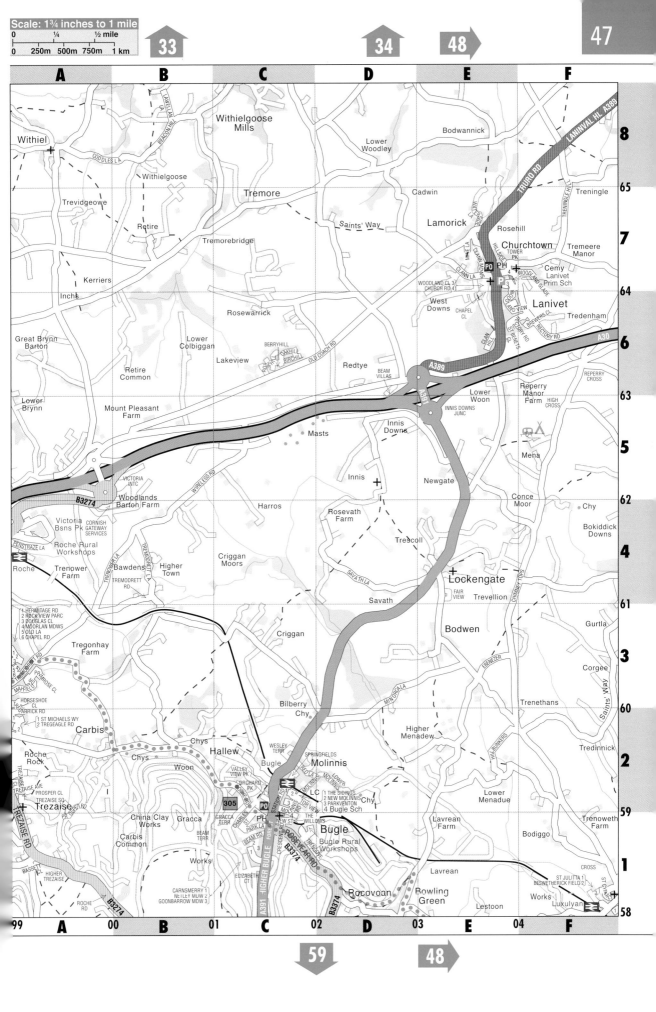

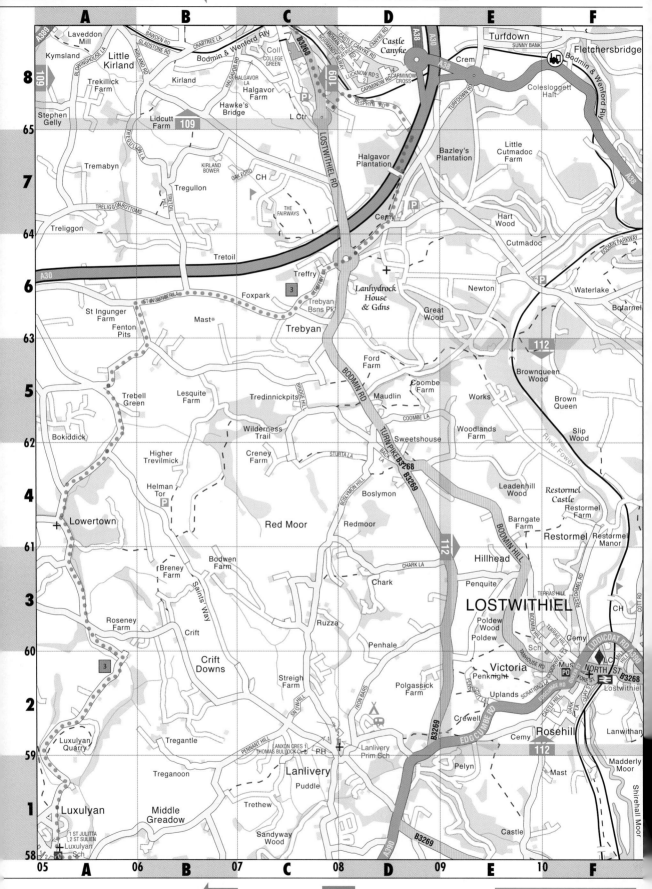

Laveddon Mill
Kymsland
Little Kirland
Trekillick Farm
Kirland
Stephen Gelly
Tremabyn
Lidcutt Farm
Kirland Bower
Oak Ford
CH
Halgavor Farm
Hawke's Bridge
Coll
College Green
Bodmin & Wenford Rly
Treliggow Bottoms
Tregullon
Treligron
Tretoil
THE FAIRWAYS
Treffry
Foxpark
Halgavor Plantation
L Ctr
Cemy
Turfdown
Fletchersbridge
Sunny Bank
Crem
Colesloggett Halt
Castle Canyke
Bazley's Plantation
Little Cutmadoc Farm
Hart Wood
Cutmadoc
Waterlake
Botarnel
Bodmin & Wenford Rly
Bodmin Parkway
St Ingunger Farm
Fenton Pits
Mast
Trebyan Bsns Pk
Trebyan
Ford Farm
Lanhydrock House & Gdns
Great Wood
Newton
112
Brownqueen Wood
Brown Queen
Slip Wood
Trebell Green
Lesquite Farm
Tredinnickpits La
Maudlin
Coombe Farm
COOMBE LA
Works
Woodlands Farm
River Fowey
Bokiddick
Higher Trevilmick
Wilderness Trail
Creney Farm
STURTA LA
Sweetshouse
BACK LA
Leadenhill Wood
Restormel Castle
Restormel Farm
Helman Tor
Boslymon
BOSLYMON HILL
Barngate Farm
Restormel
Restormel Manor
Lowertown
Boslymon
Redmoor
Red Moor
112
Bodmin Hill
Hillhead
Breney Farm
Bodwen Farm
Saints' Way
Chark
CHARK LA
Penquite
TERRAS HILL
LOSTWITHIEL
Roseney Farm
Crift
Ruzza
Penhale
Poldew Wood
Poldew
Sch
PARHOUSE RD
Victoria
Penknight
3
Crift Downs
Streigh Farm
Polgassick Farm
Uplands
Crewell
Cemy
Rosehill
Lanwithan
112
Luxulyan Quarry
Tregantle
PENHART HILL
LANXON CRES
THOMAS BULLOCK CL
PH
Lanlivery Prim Sch
IRON BARS
B3269
Pelyn
Mast
Madderly Moor
Shirehall Moor
Luxulyan
Treganoon
Trethew
Lanlivery
Puddle
Castle
1 ST JULITTA
2 ST SULIEN
Luxulyan Sch
Middle Greadow
Sandyway Wood

For full street detail of the highlighted area see pages 109 and 112.

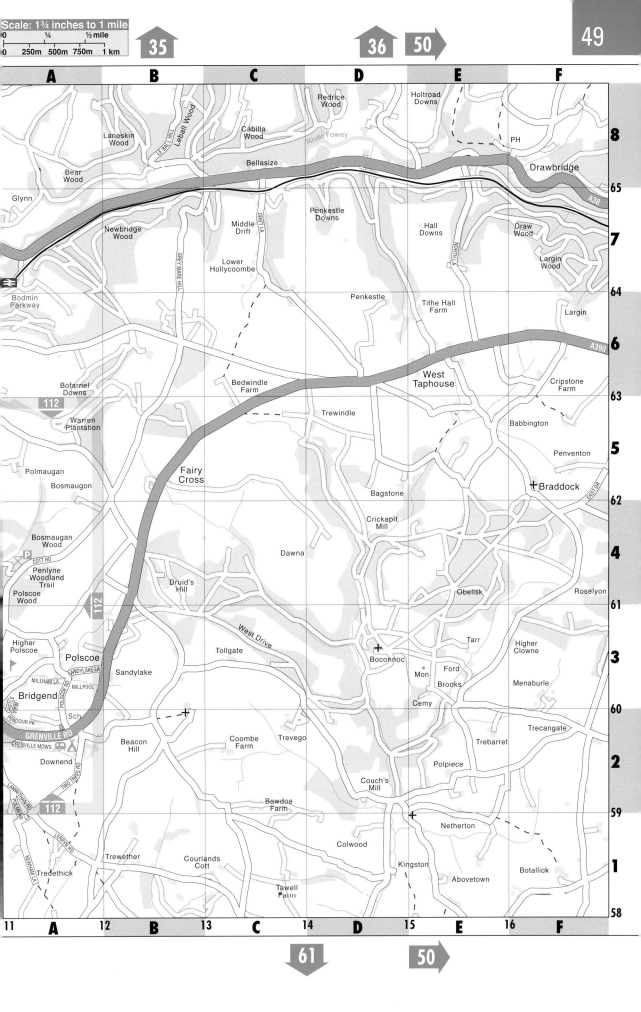

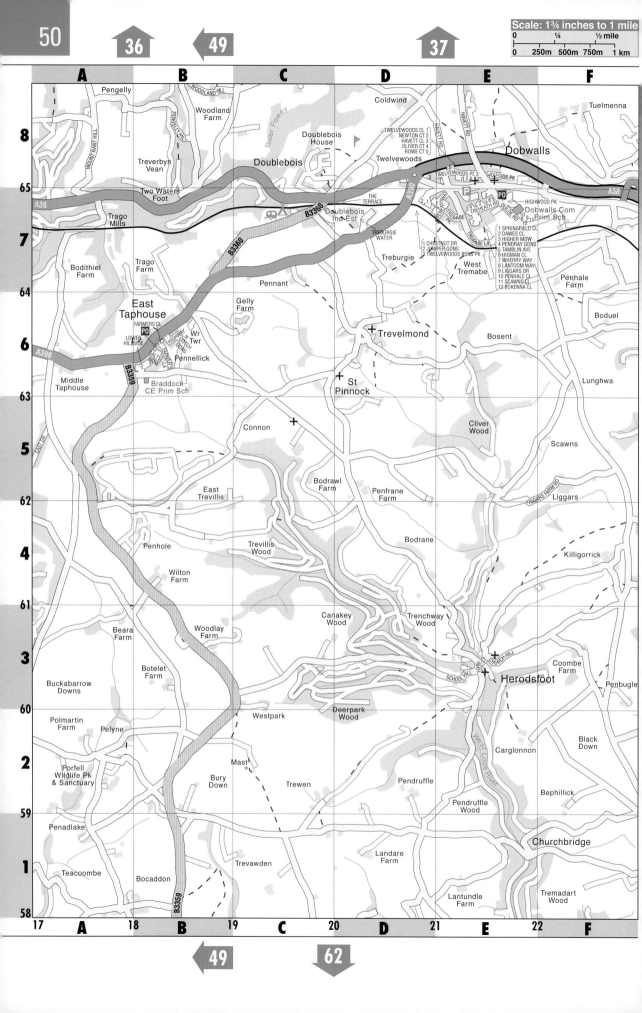

A   B   C   D   E   F

8

65

7

64

6

63

5

62

4

61

3

60

2

59

1

58

Pengelly

Woodland Farm

WOODLAND HILL

River Fowey

Coldwind

Tuelmenna

Treverbyn Vean

Doublebois House

Doublebois

TWELVEWOODS CL 1
NEWTON CT 2
HAVETT CL 3
OLIVER CT 4
ROWE CT 5

Twelvewoods

Dobwalls

HAVETT RD

Two Waters Foot

A38

TWELVEWOODS PL 1
3   2

BRACESIDE PK

A38

Trago Mills

B3360

THE TERRACE

Doublebois Ind Est

A390

TREBARWITH

TREBABE

HIGHWOOD PK

P

PO

Dobwalls Com Prim Sch

TREHEATH RD

DULOE RD

1 SPRINGFIELD CL
2 DAWES CL
3 HIGHER MDW
4 PENDRAY GDNS
5 TAMBLIN AVE
6 HIGMAN CL
7 WHERRY WAY
8 LANTOOM WAY
9 LIGGARS DR
10 PENHALE CL
11 SCAWNS CL
12 BOKENNA CL

Bodithiel Farm

B3360

Trago Farm

TREBURGIE WATER

Treburgie

1 CHESTNUT DR
2 JUNIPER GDNS
3 TWELVEWOODS BSNS PK

TREBABE LA

West Tremabe

Penhale Farm

Pennant

Gelly Farm

Trevelmond

Bosent

Boduel

East Taphouse

FARMERS CL

PO

Wr Twr

HIGHWAY GOTCH GDNS

SALTERS MDW

Pennellick

PLOVERS

St Pinnock

Cliver Wood

Lunghwa

Scawns

B3359

LOWER HILLSIDE

Braddock CE Prim Sch

Middle Taphouse

Connon

Bodrawl Farm

Penfrane Farm

Liggars

LIGGARS PARK RD

EAST DR

East Trevillis

Trevillis Wood

Bodrane

Killigorrick

Penhole

Wilton Farm

Canakey Wood

Trenchway Wood

Beara Farm

Woodlay Farm

SCHOOL HILL

FORE ST

CHURCH HILL

Herodsfoot

Coombe Farm

Penbugle

Botelet Farm

Buckabarrow Downs

Westpark

Deerpark Wood

West Looe River

Carglonnon

Black Down

Polmartin Farm

Pelyne

Mast

Bury Down

Trewen

Pendruffle

Pendruffle Wood

Bephillick

Porfell Wildlife Pk & Sanctuary

Penadlake

Churchbridge

Teacoombe

B3359

Bocaddon

Trevawden

Landare Farm

Lantundle Farm

Tremadart Wood

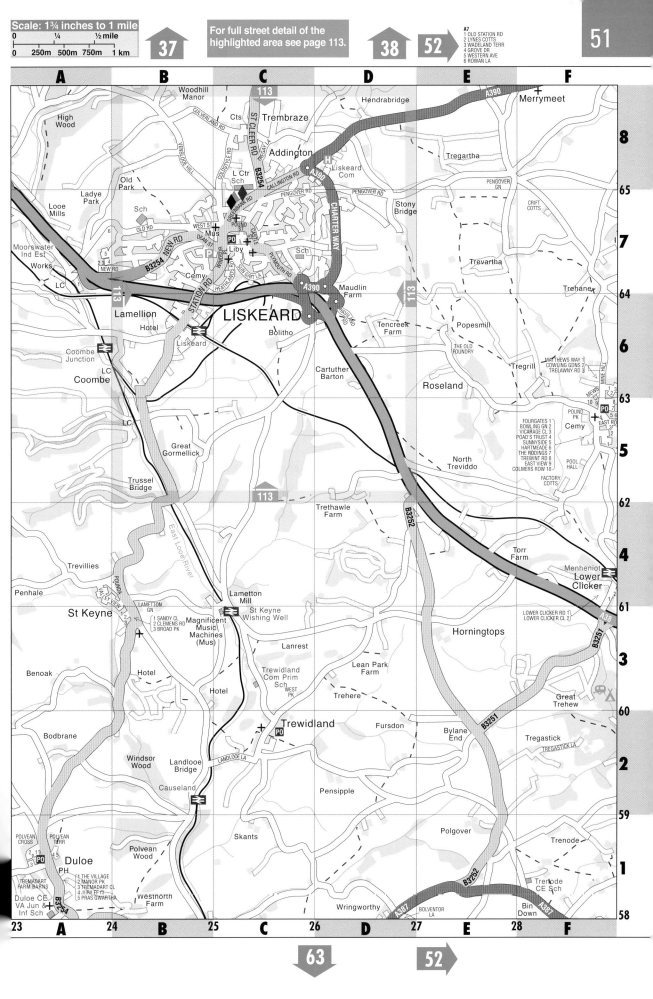

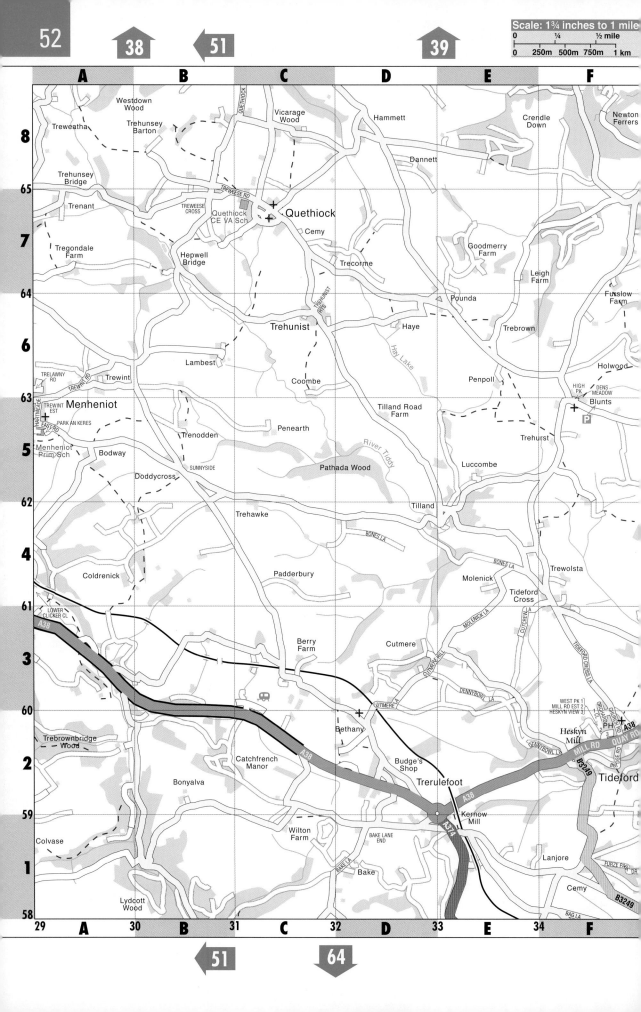

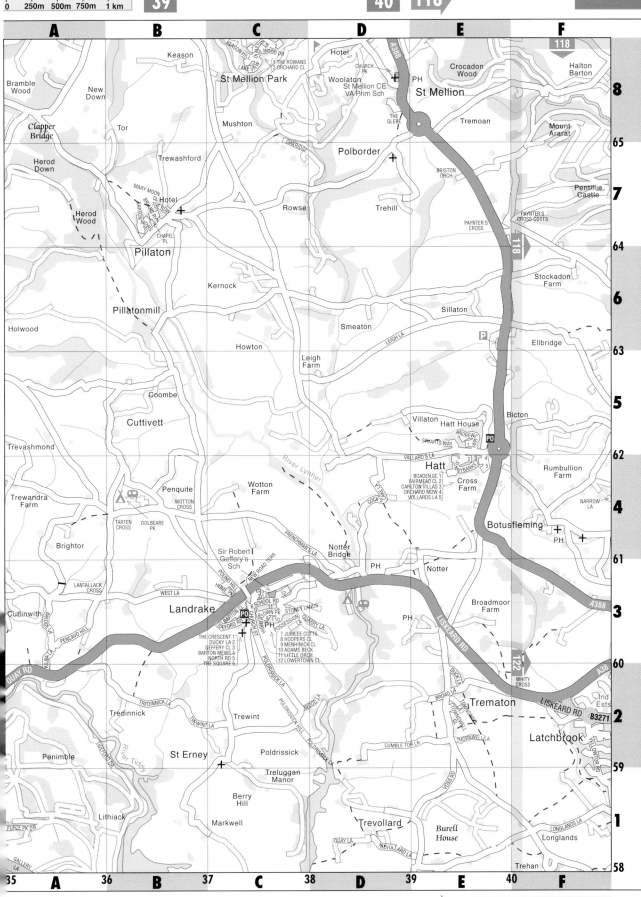

A   B   C   D   E   F

8
Bramble Wood
New Down
Keason
St Mellion Park
1 THE ROWANS
2 ORCHARD CL
Hotel
Woolaton
CHURCH PK
PH
St Mellion
Crocadon Wood
Halton Barton
St Mellion CE VA Prim Sch

65
Clapper Bridge
Tor
Mushton
THE GLEBE
Tremoan
Mount Ararat

7
Herod Down
Trewashford
MARY MOON
Hotel
Rowse
Trehill
Polborder
BRISTON ORCH
Pentillie Castle
PAYNTER'S CROSS COTTS

64
Herod Wood
THE ROW
BINNS PL
BARTON MDWS
CHAPEL PL
Pillaton
PAYNTER'S CROSS
118

6
Pillatonmill
Kernock
Smeaton
Sillaton
Stockadon Farm

63
Holwood
Howton
Leigh Farm
LEIGH LA
P
Ellbridge

5
Goombe
Cuttivett
Villaton
Hatt House
Bicton
ST ANDREW'S
STUARTS WAY
PO

62
Trevashmond
River Lynher
VALLARD'S LA
Hatt
IVYBANKS
Rumbullion Farm
BOADEN CL 1
FAIRMEAD CL 2
CARLTON VILLAS 3
ORCHARD MDW 4
MOLLARDS LA 5

4
Trewandra Farm
Wotton Cross
Wotton Farm
COCK'S
Cross Farm
Botusfleming
PH
NARROW LA

61
Brighton
TARTEN CROSS
DOLBEARE PK
FRENCHMAN'S LA
Sir Robert Geffery's Sch
Notter Bridge
PH
Notter

3
Lantallack Cross
WEST LA
POUND HILL
HOME PK
NEW ROAD TERR
SCHOOL RD
Landrake
STONEY LANDS
QUARRY LA
PH
Broadmoor Farm
A388
LISKEARD RD
Cutlinwith
PENCAVO HILL
BARTON CL
BEFORD HILL
CHAPEL ST
PO
PH
POSSESSION
7 JUBILEE COTTS
8 HOOPERS CL
9 MENHINICK CL
10 ADAMS BECK
11 LITTLE ORCH
12 LOWERTOWN CL
DUCK LA
122
WHITY CROSS

60
QUAY RD
THE CRESCENT 1
DUCKY LA 2
GEFFERY CL 3
BARTON MEWS 4
NORTH RD 5
THE SQUARE 6
POLDRISSICK LA
NIXON LA
BROAD LA
Trematon
LISKEARD RD
Ind Ests
B3271

2
Tredinnick
TREDINNICK LA
TREWINT LA
Trewint
POLDRISSICK HILL
POLDRISSICK LA
TOWNSEND
VOSS RD
Latchbrook
YELLOWTOR RD

59
Penimble
River Tiddy
St Erney
Poldrissick
Treluggan Manor
THORNWELL LA
CUMBLE TOR LA
FELLOWTOR RD

1
FURZE PK DR
Lithiack
Markwell
Berry Hill
Trevollard
Burell House
Longlands
LONGLANDS LA
QUAY LA
NEVOLLARD LA
VOSS RD
Trehan

58
GALLERY LA

A   B   C   D   E   F
35 36 37 38 39 40

65   122

For full street detail of the highlighted area see pages 118 and 122.

C1
1 BRECON CL
2 BEACONSFIELD PL
3 WHITE'S CL
4 ANGWIN AVE
5 CHURCHTOWN
6 CHEGWYN GDNS
7 KEMP'S CL
8 BOLSTER CL
9 FORDH TOBMEN

10 TREGELLAS CL
11 POLBREEN LA
12 POLBREEN AVE

D1
1 PENGARTH
2 CASTLE MDWS
3 COUNT HOUSE MEWS
4 PENWINNICK PARC
5 MIDDLEGATES
6 GRENVILLE DR
7 LAMBOURNE AVE
8 ATLANTIC MEWS
9 HIGHFIELD CT

10 THE OLD SCHOOL
11 STIPPY STAPPY
12 MINERS WAY
13 KERENSA GDNS
14 PARKLANDS

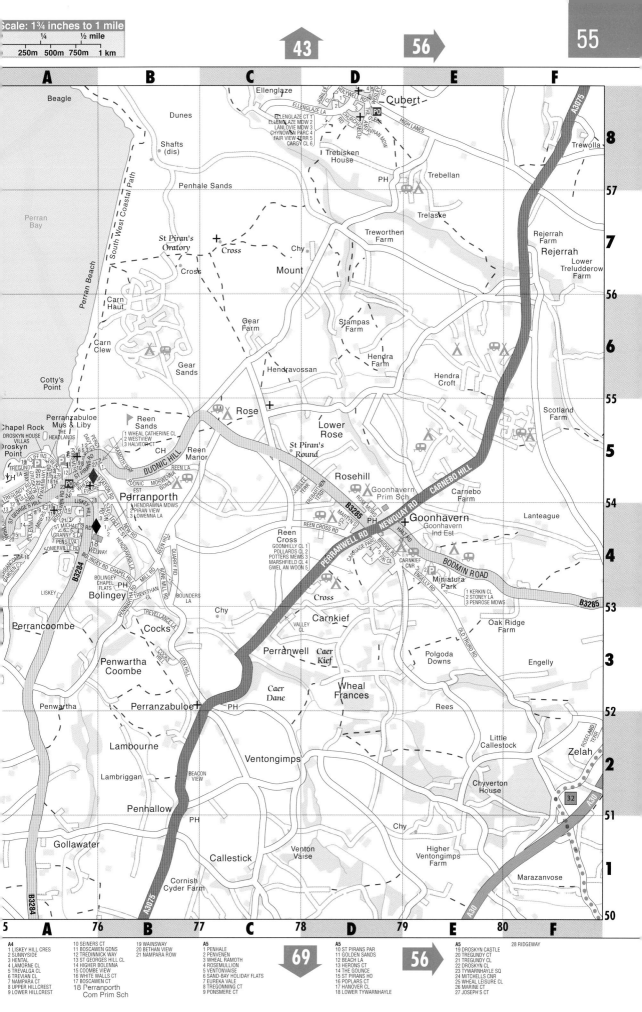

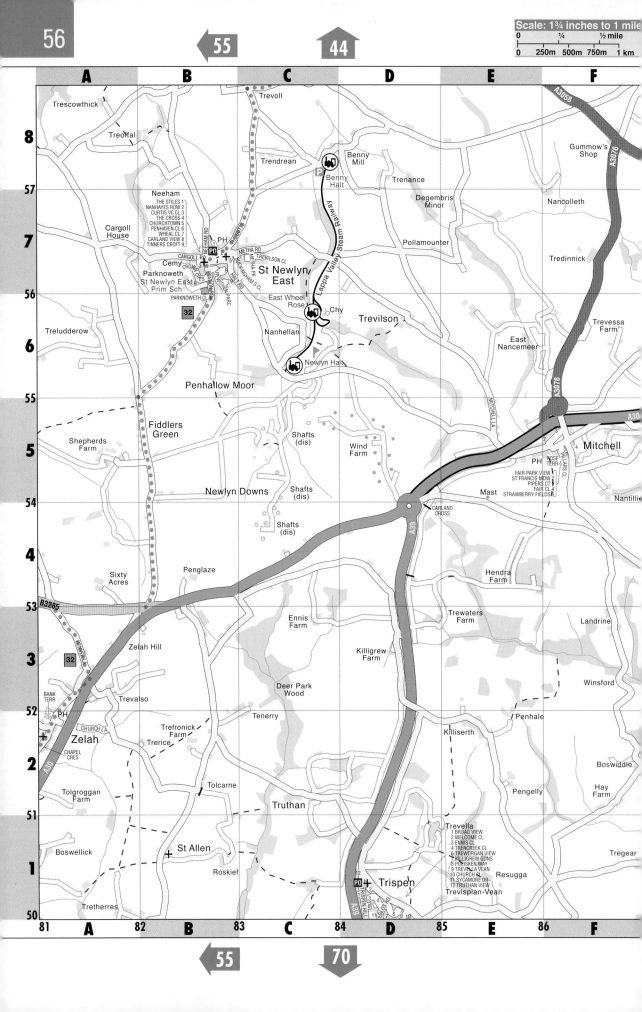

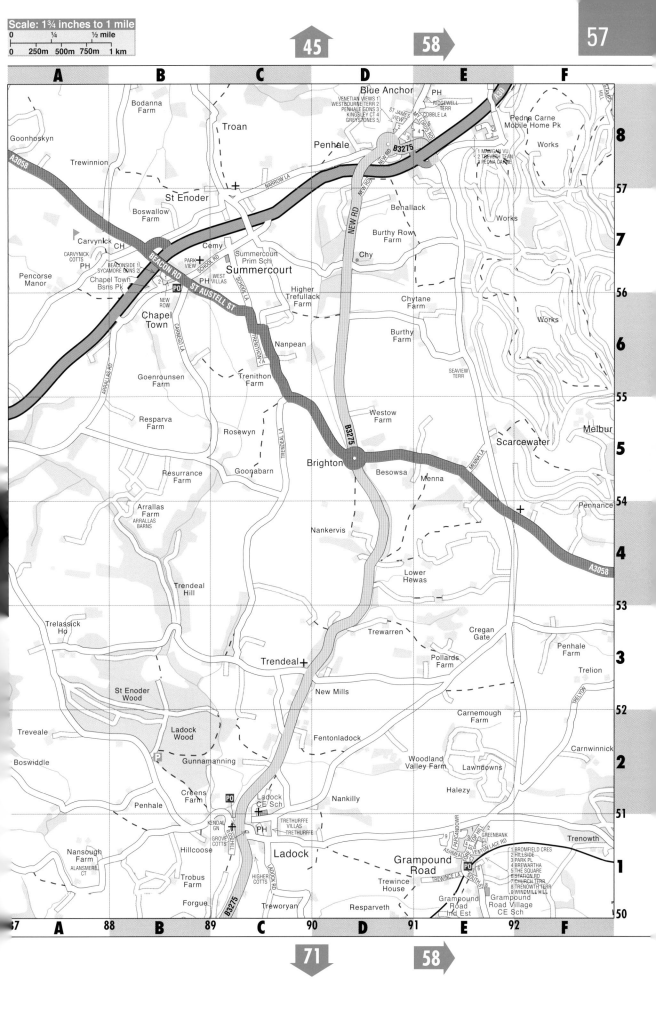

8

57

7

56

6

55

5

54

4

53

3

52

2

51

1

50

A   B   C   D   E   F

St Dennis

Whitemoor

Hendra

Trelavour Downs

Currian Vale

Carsella Farm

St Dennis Ind Est

Trerice Manor Farm

Bodella

Treviscoe Barton

Central Treviscoe

Treviscoe

Works

Rostowrack Downs

Chy

Chy

Nanpean

Nanpean Com Prim Sch

Old Pound

Goonamarth Farm

Fernleigh Terr

Works

Goverseth Terr

Foxhole Prim Sch

Foxhole

Trethosa

Stepaside

Goonabarn Cotts

Goonabarn

Carloggas

Carpalla Terr

Carpalla

St Stephen Church Town Prim Sch

Tregargus Farm

Tregargus View

High Street

Hornick

Hornick Hill

Tresweeta

Terras

Hallivick

St Stephen

The Square

The Brannel Sch

Gwindra

Gwindra Ind Est

Court Farm

High Street Ind Est

Hay Farm

Langerth Farm

Lanjeth

Works

Burngullow

Nanphysick Barton

Tregandanel

River Fal

Resugga

Tolgarrick

Resugga Lane-End

Coombe

Branell Farm

Hendra

Dowgas Farm

Trethullan Castle

Resugga Castle

Terhowth House

Chapel

Treway Farm

Downderry

Ventonwyn Farm

Ninnis Farm

Polclose

Trelower Farm

Little Trelower Park

Sticker

Trevan Wood

Garlenick Manor

A3058   TERRAS RD

GWINDRA RD

LONG LA

A3058

A390

B3279

HENDRA RD

QUARRY CL RD

CHAPEL RD

CARPALLA RD

COOMBE RD

93   94   95   96   97   98

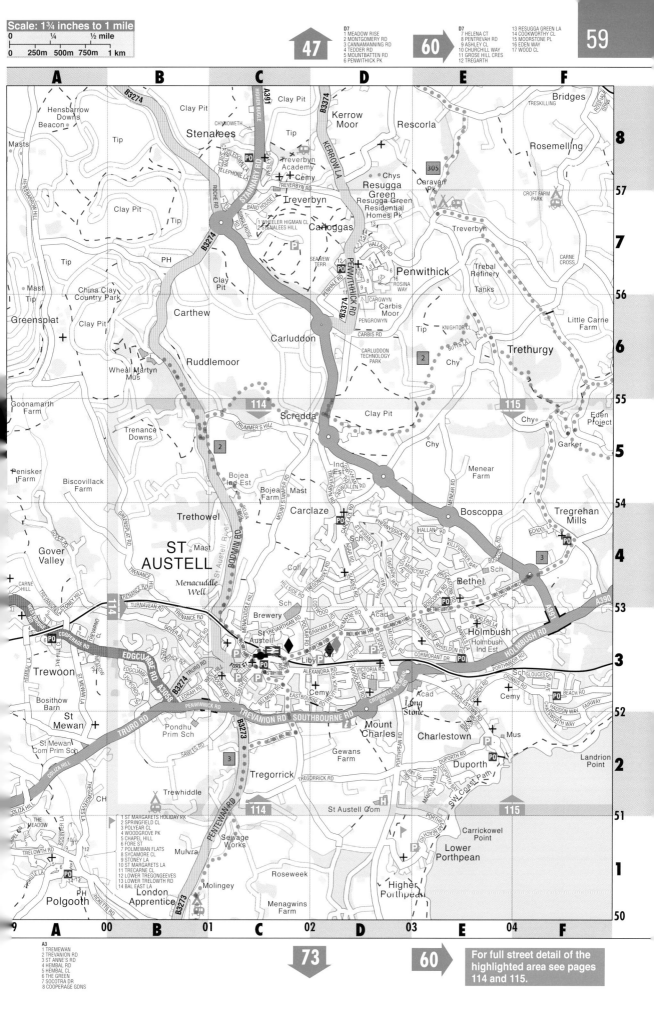

Scale: 1¾ inches to 1 mile

0   ¼   ½ mile
0   250m 500m 750m 1 km

47

D7
1 MEADOW RISE
2 MONTGOMERY RD
3 CANNAMANNING RD
4 TEDDER RD
5 MOUNTBATTEN RD
6 PENWITHICK PK

60

D7
7 HELENA CT
8 PENTREVAH RD
9 ASHLEY CL
10 CHURCHILL WAY
11 GROSE HILL CRES
12 TREGARTH

13 RESUGGA GREEN LA
14 COOKWORTHY CL
15 MOORSTONE PL
16 EDEN WAY
17 WOOD CL

59

73

60

For full street detail of the highlighted area see pages 114 and 115.

A3
1 TREMEWAN
2 TREVANION RD
3 ST ANNE'S RD
4 HEMBAL RD
5 HEMBAL CL
6 THE GREEN
7 SOCOTRA DR
8 COOPERAGE GDNS

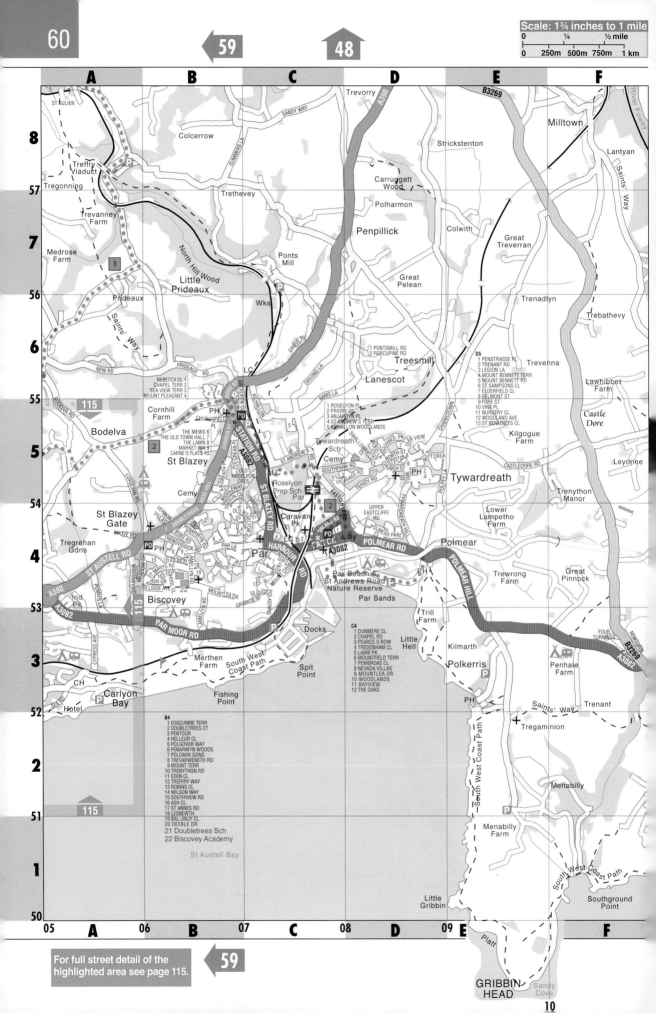

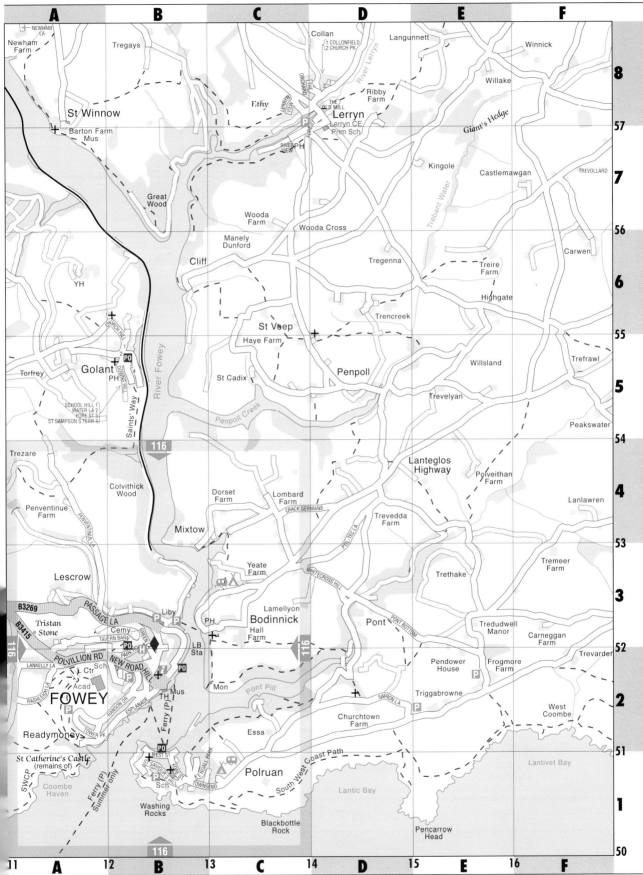

A   B   C   D   E   F

NEWHAM LA
Newham Farm

Tregays

8

St Winnow
Barton Farm
Mus

57

Collan
1 COLLONFIELD
2 CHURCH PK

Langunnett

Winnick

Ethy

THE ORCHARD
LERRYN VIEW

THE OLD MILL

Lerryn
Lerryn CE
Prim Sch

River Lerryn

Ribby Farm

Willake

RIVER VIEW   PH

Giant's Hedge

7

Great Wood

Kingole

Castlemawgan

TREVOLLARD

Wooda Farm

Wooda Cross

Trebant Water

56

Cliff

Manely Dunford

Tregenna

Treire Farm

Carwen

6

YH

St Veep

Trencreek

Highgate

55

Torfrey

Golant
PO
PH

Haye Farm

St Cadix

Penpoll

Trevelyan

Willsland

Trefrawl

5

SCHOOL HILL 1
WATER LA 2
FORE ST 3
ST SAMPSON S TERR 4

Saints' Way

River Fowey

Penpoll Creek

Peakswater

54

Trezare

116

Lanteglos Highway

Polveithan Farm

4

Penventinue Farm

Colvithick Wood

PENVENTINUE LA

Dorset Farm

Lombard Farm
CRACK GERMANS

Trevedda Farm

Lanlawren

Mixtow

PILL-TEG LA

53

Lescrow

Yeate Farm

WHITECROSS HILL

Trethake

Tremeer Farm

3

B3269
PASSAGE LA

Liby
P   P

PH

Lamellyon

Bodinnick
Hall Farm

Pont

PONT BOTTOM

Tredudwell Manor

Carneggan Farm

Tristan Stone

B3415

TAVERN BAR
GREEN ST

LB Sta

116

Trevarder

PARK LA
POLVILLION RD
H

PO

Pendower House
P

Frogmore Farm

52

LANKELLY LA
RASHLEIGH LA

Ctr
Sch
Acad

NEW ROAD HILL

PO
Mus

Mon

SAFRON LA

Triggabrowne
P

2

FOWEY

HANSON DR
Esplanade

TH

Pont Pill

Churchtown Farm

West Coombe

Readymoney

TOWER PK

Ferry (P)

Essa

51

St Catherine's Castle
(remains of)

PO
ST SAVIOUR'S HILL

KENDALL PARK

Polruan

South West Coast Path

Lantivet Bay

SWCP

Ferry (P)
Summer only

FORE ST
Sch
TOWNSEND

Lantic Bay

1

Coombe Haven

Washing Rocks

Blackbottle Rock

Pencarrow Head

Pencarrow Head

50

11   A   12   B   13   C   14   D   15   E   16   F

116

62

For full street detail of the highlighted area see page 116.

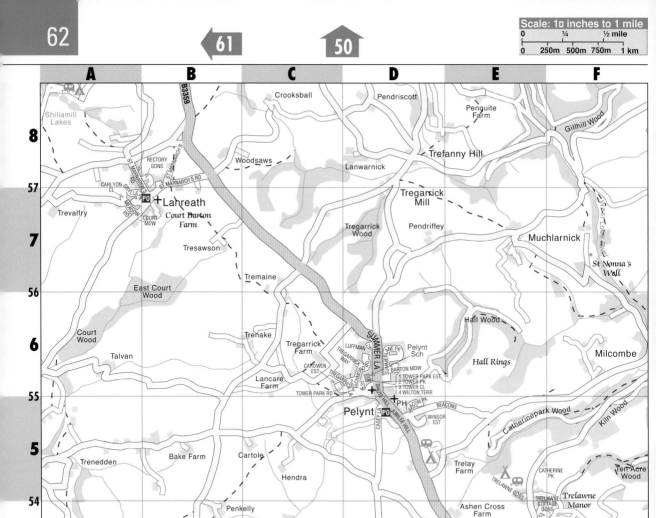

Shillamill Lakes

B3359

Crooksball

Pendriscott

Penguite Farm

Gillhill Wood

Woodsaws

Lanwarnick

Trefanny Hill

RECTORY GDNS

ST MARNARCH'S

ST MARNARCH'S RD

PO ⊕ Lanreath

CARLYON CL

Trevalfry

Court Barton Farm

COURT MDW

MEADOW RD

ST MARNARCH'S

Tregarrick Mill

Muchlarnick

Pendriffey

St Nonna's Well

Tresawson

Tregarrick Wood

East Court Wood

Tremaine

Trenake

Court Wood

Talvan

Tregarrick Farm

Hall Wood

Milcombe

SUMMER LA

LANE PK

Pelynt Sch

Hall Rings

CARDWEN EST

TREGARRICK LA

TREGARRICK WAY

Luffman

BARTON MDW

1 TOWER PARK EST
2 TOWER PK
3 TOWER CL
4 WILTON TERR

Lancare Farm

TOWER PARK RD

⊕ PH

CASEY LA

Pelynt PO

CHUTE HILL

JUBILEE HILL

BEACON PK

WINSOR EST

BEACONS

Catherinepark Wood

Kiln Wood

Ten Acre Wood

Trenedden

Bake Farm

Cartole

Hendra

Trelay Farm

TRELAWNE GDNS

CATHERINE PK

TRELAWNE COTTAGE GDNS

Trelawne Manor

Penkelly

Ashen Cross Farm

Hotel

TRELESKETH LA

Polean Farm

B3359

Trenewan

West Watergate

Barcelona

Cemy HENDERGULLING

SCLERDER LA

Sclerder Abbey

POLYNE COTTS

Tregamellyn

Treweers

West Kellow

Tarista

NEWTON FARM COTTS

Seaview Holiday Village

Tregavithick

Great Tratford

Cemy

Porthallow

Windsor

Tregue

Great Kellow Farm

LANGCOMBE LA

KELLOW HILL

CAREY PK

Hotel

BRIDALS LA

Lansallos

Landgreek

LANGREEK RD

LANGREEK BGLWS

Grenville WLK

HILLSVIEW

P

PLEYDON CL

CARELANE FELLS

P

Talland

Talland Bay

Lizzen

Landaviddy

Crumplehorn

Model Village

A387

PH

THE COOMBE

BRENTWARTHA

COASTGUARD COTTS

Polperro Com Prim Sch

Brent

East Coombe

Raphael

RAPHAEL RD

LANDAVIDDY LA

Hard Head

Mast

BIG GN

ROMAN BRIDGE 3

TALLAND ST 4

LITTLE GN 5

Polperro Her Mus of Smuggling & Fishing

Downend Point

Daymark

MILL HILL 1

THE LANEY

Chapel Cliff

Polperro

Shag Rock

South West Coast Path

The Bridges

Colors Cove

Larrick

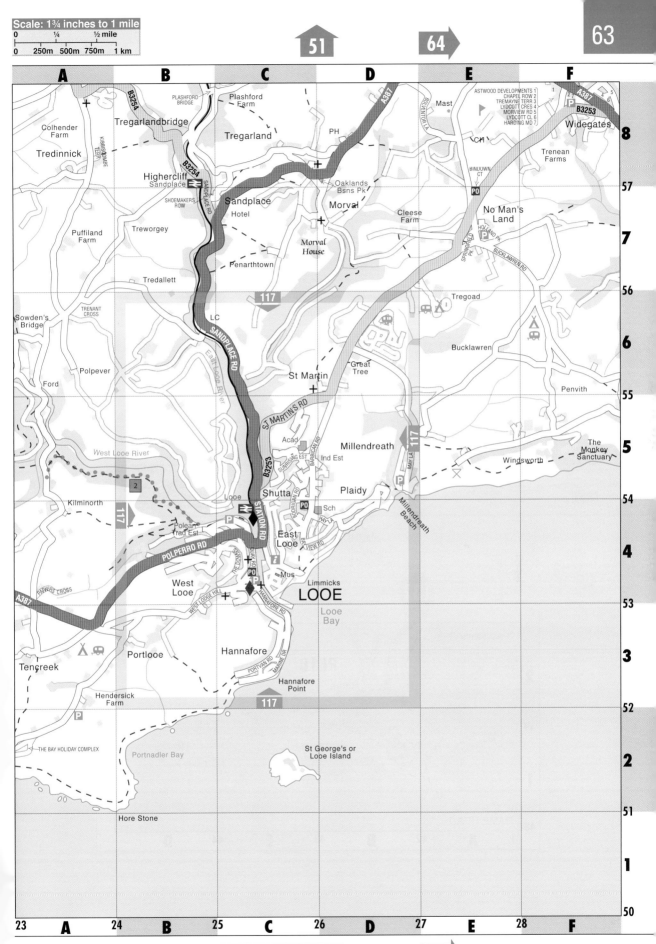

Scale: 1¾ inches to 1 mile

| 0 | ¼ | ½ mile |
| 0 | 250m | 500m | 750m | 1 km |

A   B   C   D   E   F

B3254
PLASHFORD BRIDGE
Plashford Farm
Tregarlandbridge
Plashford Farm
A387
Mast
BOLVENTOR LA

ASTWOOD DEVELOPMENTS 1
CHAPEL ROW 2
TREMAYNE TERR 3
LYDCOTT CRES 4
MORVIEW RD 5
LYDCOTT CL 6
HARDING MD 7

1
2
3
4
5
A387
B3253
Widegates

8

Colhender Farm
Tredinnick
B3254
Tregarland
PH
CH

57

Highercliff
Sandplace
SHOEMAKERS ROW
Sandplace
Hotel
Oaklands Bsns Pk
Morval
Cleese Farm
No Man's Land
PO

7

Puffiland Farm
Treworgey
Morval House
BINDOWN CT
SPRINGFIELD PK
HOLLAND PK

Tredallett
Penarthtown
117
BUCKLAWREN RD

56

Sowden's Bridge
TRENANT CROSS
LC
Tregoad

6

SANDPLACE RD
EAST LOOE RIVER
Bucklawren

Polpever
Ford
St Martin
Great Tree
Penvith

55

ST MARTIN'S RD
West Looe River
Acad
Millendreath
The Monkey Sanctuary

5

Kilminorth
117
B3253
Looe
SHUTTA
Ind Est
117
MAY LA
Windsworth

54

Polean Trad Est
Shutta
PO
Sch
HAY LA
P
Plaidy
Millendreath Beach

4

POLPERRO RD
STATION RD
RODRIGAN RD
BARBICAN RD
East Looe
BAY VIEW RD
i
Mus
Limmicks

West Looe
A387
PARKERS CROSS
WEST LODGE HILL
THE DOWNS
QUAY RD
PO
P
HANNAFORE RD
LOOE
Looe Bay

53

Tencreek
Portlooe
Hannafore
PORTVAN RD
MARINE DR

3

Hendersick Farm
P
Hannafore Point
117
St George's or Looe Island

52

THE BAY HOLIDAY COMPLEX
Portnadler Bay

2

Hore Stone

51

1

For full street detail of the highlighted area see page 117.

64

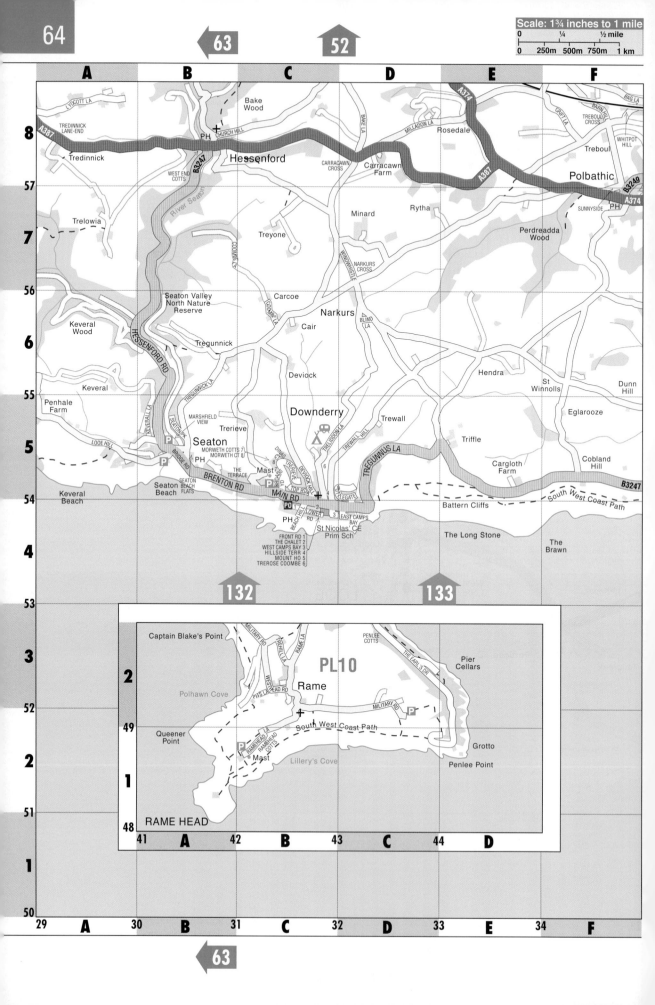

Scale: 1¾ inches to 1 mile

0   ¼   ½ mile
0 250m 500m 750m 1 km

A   B   C   D   E   F

8

Lyocott La

Tredinnick Lane-End

A387

Bake Wood

Tredinnick

PH CHURCH HILL

Hessenford

WEST END COTTS

B3247

Carracawn Cross

Carracawn Farm

Milladon La

A374

Rosedale

A387

Treboul

Whitpot Hill

Barn La

Treboul Cross

Bag La

Crift La

57

River Seaton

Trelowia

Treyone

Minard

Rytha

Polbathic

B3249

A374

PH

Sunnyside

57

7

Coombe Rd

Seaton Valley North Nature Reserve

Carcoe

Narkurs Cross

Ninnowhistle

Narkurs

Blind La

Perdreadda Wood

56

Keveral Wood

Coombe La

Tregunnick

Cair

Deviock

Hendra

St Winnolls

Dunn Hill

6

Keveral

HESSENFORD RD

Tregunnick La

Downderry

Treludom La

Trewall

Trewall Hill

Tregunnus La

Triffle

Eglarooze

Cobland Hill

55

Penhale Farm

Keleball La

Looe Hill

Seatom Rd

Marshfield View

Trerieve

Dinas Cross

Tregey

Carglath Farm

B3247

5

Seaton

P

P

PH

Morweth Cotts 7
Morweth Ct 8

Mast

The Terrace

BRENTON RD

P

Top Rd

Tor Rd

Treyard

Devlock Hill

Valegate

South West Coast Path

54

Keveral Beach

BRIDGE RD

Seaton Beach

Seaton Beach Flats

MAIN RD

PO

PH

BEACH HILL

Lower Rd

St Nicolas' CE Prim Sch

East Camps Bay

Battern Cliffs

The Long Stone

The Brawn

4

FRONT RD 1
THE CHALET 2
WEST CAMPS BAY 3
HILLSIDE TERR 4
MOUNT HO 5
TREROSE COOMBE 6

53

132   **133**

3

Captain Blake's Point

MILITARY RD

FERN LA

RAME LA

PENLEE COTTS

THE EARL'S DR

Pier Cellars

PL10

2

Polhawn Cove

PITTS LA

WESTHEAD RD

Rame

MILITARY RD

P

49

Queener Point

RAMEHEAD LA

RAMEHEAD COTTS

South West Coast Path

Grotto

2

Mast

Lillery's Cove

Penlee Point

1

51

48

RAME HEAD

41   **A**   42   **B**   43   **C**   44   **D**

1

50

29   **A**   30   **B**   31   **C**   32   **D**   33   **E**   34   **F**

A B C D E F

B3249
GALLERY LA
BAG LA
NEWPORT
TIDEFORD RD
CHURCH ST
St Germans
Port Eliot House
QUARRY ST 1
QUARRY LA 2
MILL LA 3
THE SIR WILLIAMS 4
MOYLES ALMSHOUSES 5
FAIRFIELD
LOWER FAIRFIELD
St Germans Prim Sch
OLD QUAY LA
LOVELY LA
St Germans
QUAY RD
THE QUAY RD
St Germans Quay

1 TIDDY CL
2 TREBOUL WAY
3 ELIOT DR
4 TREGALISTER GDNS
5 DUDDENBEAKE TERR
6 NUT TREE HILL

MARWELL LA

Grove

ELMGATE CROSSWAYS

Trehan

Elm Gate

Wivelscombe
Mon
Shillingham Manor

8

57

KELLOW PK

Erth Barton

Ince Castle

Black Rock

7

Trewin House

Sheviock Wood

Erth Hill

126
St Germans or Lynher River

56

Tredis

Haye
HAY LA

Sheviock

Berry Down

Bulland Quay

Clift Quay

West Clift

6

Dunn Hill

Tredrossel

B3247
HORSEPOOL LA
HORSEPOOL RD
GEORGES LA
CHURCH ROW

A374

55

Trewrickle Farm

The Beacon

CROSS PK
SHEVIOCK LA
KIMBERLEY FOSTER CL 1
WEST LA 2
DAWNEY TERR 3
THE TERRACE 4
TREDIS VW 5
CAMEN CL
B3247
PH
COOMBE LA
Crafthole

TRETHILL LA
Trethill

CROOKEDDR LA

Screasdon Fort

Antony
Antony CE VA Sch

HOLLONG PK
PH
ANY LOW HILL
ABBOTSCL

5

Cemy
Wolsdon House

54

OLD COASTGUARD COTTS
WHITSAND BAY VIEW
FINNYGOOK LA
BURNS VIEW
Cross
PO
Hotel
Hotel
Portwrinkle

Trethill Cliffs

Blerrick

B3247

Lower Tregantle

ST JOHNS LA

JACK'S LA
PH
St John

4

THE TERRACE
CH
P

DANGER AREA

DANGER AREA
Tregantle Fort

Mast Ranges

P
CLAMPIT LA

MENDENNICK HILL

B3247

53

Higher Tregantle Farm

Tregantle Cliff

P
Freathy

WITHNOE LA
BRAKE LA
Withnoe

52

Sharrow Point

132

WITHNOE TERR
Mon

CLIFF LA
Tregonhawke

MILITARY RD

2

51

Whitsand Bay

1

50

35 A 36 B 37 C 38 D 39 E 40 F

132

For full street detail of the highlighted area see pages 126 and 132.

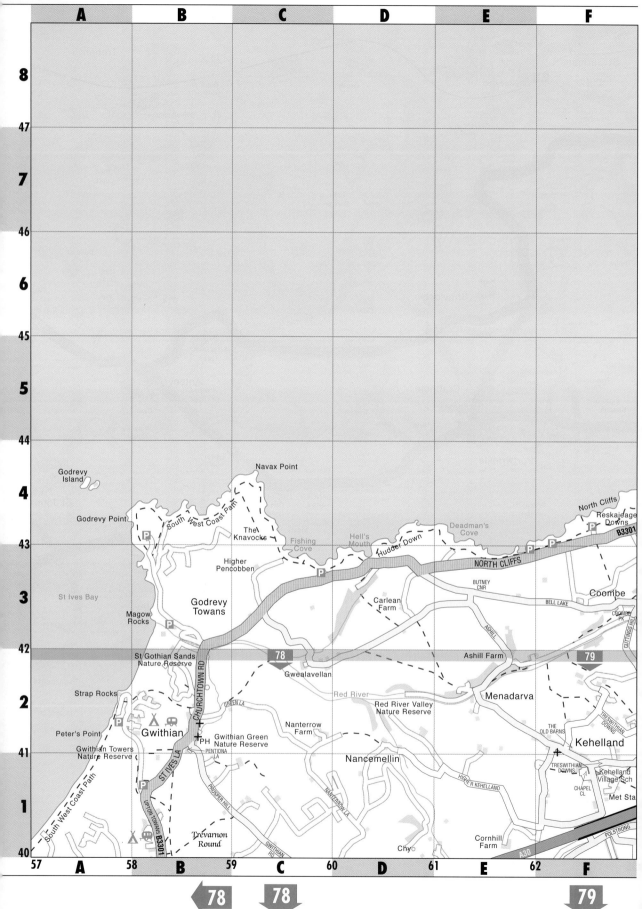

A   B   C   D   E   F

8
47
7
46
6
45
5
44
4
43
3
42
2
41
1
40

Godrevy
Island

Navax Point

Godrevy Point

South West Coast Path

The
Knavocks

Fishing
Cove

Hell's
Mouth

Hudder Down

Deadman's
Cove

North Cliffs

Reskajeage
Downs

NORTH CLIFFS

B3301

St Ives Bay

Godrevy
Towans

Higher
Pencobben

Carlean
Farm

BUTNEY
CNR

BELL LAKE

Coombe

COOMBE
PK

Magow
Rocks

St Gothian Sands
Nature Reserve

CHURCHTOWN RD

78

Gwealavellan

Ashill Farm

ASHILL

CUTTINGS HILL

79

Strap Rocks

GREEN LA

Red River

Red River Valley
Nature Reserve

Menadarva

TRESWITHIAN
DOWNS

Peter's Point

Gwithian

Nanterrow
Farm

THE
OLD BARNS

Kehelland

Gwithian Towers
Nature Reserve

ST IVES LA

PH

Gwithian Green
Nature Reserve

PENTIDNA
LA

Nancemellin

HIGHER KEHELLAND

TRESWITHIAN
DOWNS

Kehelland
Village Sch

PROSPER HILL

Trevarnon
Round

South West Coast Path

UPTON TOWANS B3301

GWITHIAN RD

NANTERROW LA

Chyo

Cornhill
Farm

A30

POLSTRONG

CHAPEL
CL

Met Sta

57   A   58   B   59   C   60   D   61   E   62   F

78   78   79

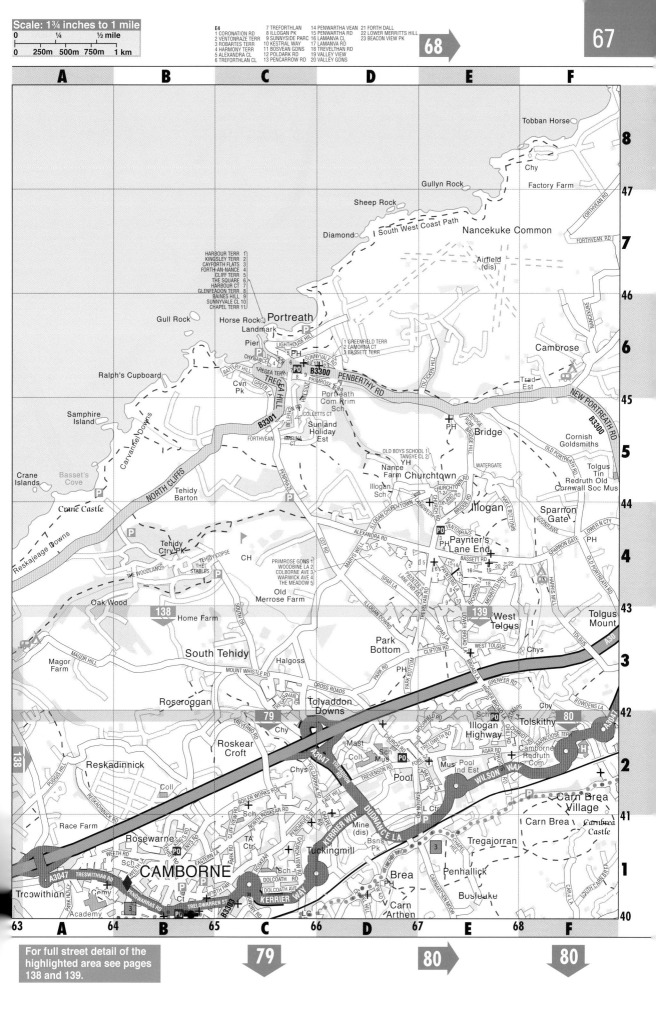

E4
1 CORONATION RD
2 VENTONRAZE TERR
3 ROBARTES TERR
4 ALEXANDRA CL
5 TREFORTHLAN
6 TREFORTHLAN CL
7 TREFORTHLAN
8 ILLOGAN PK
9 SUNNYSIDE PARC
10 KESTRAL WAY
11 BOSVEAN GDNS
12 POLDARK RD
13 PENCARROW RD
14 PENWARTHA VEAN
15 PENWARTHA
16 LAMANVA CL
17 LAMANVA RD
18 TREVELTHAN RD
19 VALLEY VIEW
20 VALLEY GDNS
21 FORTH DALL
22 LOWER MERRITTS HILL
23 BEACON VIEW PK

68

Tobban Horse

Chy

Factory Farm

Gullyn Rock

Sheep Rock

Diamond

South West Coast Path

Nancekuke Common

Airfield (dis)

Cambrose

Trad Est

HARBOUR TERR 1
KINGSLEY TERR 2
CAYFORTH FLATS 3
FORTH-AN-NANCE 4
CLIFF TERR 5
THE SQUARE 6
HARBOUR CT 7
GLENFEADON TERR 8
BAINES HILL 9
SUNNYVALE CL 10
CHAPEL TERR 11

Gull Rock

Horse Rock
Landmark

Portreath

Pier

PH

LIGHTHOUSE HILL

1 GREENFIELD TERR
2 LAMORNA CT
3 BASSETT TERR

Ralph's Cupboard

Cvn Pk

TREGEA HILL

SUNNYVALE RD

B3300

PENBERTHY RD

Cornish Goldsmiths

New Portreath Rd B3300

Samphire Island

CARVANNEL DOWNS

B3301

FORTHVEAN

Portreath Com Prim Sch

COLLETTS CT

Sunland Holiday Est

PH

Bridge

BRIDGE HILL

WATERGATE

Tolgus Tin
Redruth Old Cornwall Soc Mus

Crane Islands

NORTH CLIFFS

Tehidy Barton

OLD BOYS SCHOOL 1
TANGYE CL 2
YH

Nance Farm

Churchtown

Illogan Sch

CHURCHTOWN RD

Illogan

PO

Sparnon Gate

Crane Castle

RESKAJEAGE DOWNS

Tehidy Ctry Pk

THE STABLES

TEHIDY COPSE

CH

PRIMROSE GDNS 1
WOODBINE LA 2
COLBORNE AVE 3
WARWICK AVE 4
THE MEADOW 5

ALEXANDRA RD

MARYS WELL

Paynter's Lane End

PH

BASSETT RD

PAYNTERS LANE END

Oak Wood

Old Merrose Farm

COT RD

ILLOGAN DOWNS

SPAR LA

RICHARDS

MERRITTS HILL

HARRIS MILL

138

Home Farm

SOUTH DR

West Telgus

139

Tolgus Mount

Magor Farm

South Tehidy

Halgoss

Park Bottom

CLIFTON RD

WEST TOLGUS

Chys

Magor Hill

THE WOODLANDS

MOUNT WHISTLE RD

PARK RD

PH

BROAD LA

A30

Roscroggan

CROSS ROADS

Tolvaddon Downs

GRENFER RD

HIGHER BROAD LA

Sch

BOWDENS LA

79

TREVERNO RD

Chy

A3047

Mast Coll

Sch Mus

MOOR RD

Illogan Highway

CHURCH RD

Tolskithy

80

A3047

Roskear Croft

Reskadinnick

Coll

BOILER WORKS RD

Chys

Sch Mus

PO

Mus

Camborne Redruth Com

Pool Ind Est

WILSON WAY

Carn Brea Village

H

Race Farm

RESKADINNICK RD

Rosewarne

PO

Sch

NORTH ROSKEAR RD

Sch

TA Ctr

Tuckingmill

Mine (dis)

Bsns Pk

KERRIER WAY

DUDNANCE LA

STATION RD

L Ctr

3

Carn Brea

Cambrea Castle

Tregajorran

Treswithian

A3047

TRESWITHIAN RD

Cemy

Ct

PARK HOLLY

PUGIS HILL

WEETH RD

EDYS RD

CAMBORNE

PO

Sch

Ct

TRELOWARREN ST

NORTH PAR

DOLCOATH RD

DOLCOATH AVE

KERRIER WAY

Brea

PH

Carn Arthen

Penhallick

Busleake

Academy

3

PO

B3303

For full street detail of the highlighted area see pages 138 and 139.

79

80

80

Scale: 1¾ inches to 1 mile

0   ¼   ½ mile
0   250m   500m   750m   1 km

A B C D E F

8 7 49 48 6 47 5 46 4 45 3 44 2 43 1 42

Chapel Porth
Goonvrea
Shaft (dis)
Chy
Goonbell
Mithian Downs
Mingoose
Whitestreet
South West Coast Path
Towan Cross
1 EASTCLIFF AVE NO 1
2 EASTCLIFF AVENUE NO 2
3 EASTCLIFF AVE NO 3
4 LOWER EASTCLIFF
5 GOYNE'S FIELD
6 SEASPRAY LEISURE FLATS
7 KINGSLEY COVE
8 OCEAN CT
9 SANDY COVE TRAVEL LODGE
TOWAN RD
Hurlingbarrow Ind Est
Silverwell Farm
Silverwell
PH
Banns
Gover Farm
Porth Towan
THE SANDY COVE COVE
WEST BEACH RD
WEST CLIFF
PH
ATLANTIC WAY
Trevissick Farm
Mount Hawke
1 HENLEY CRES
2 HENLEY DR
3 HENLEY CL
4 SHORT CROSS MEWS
5 ALEXANDRA TERR
6 PENHALLOW CL
7 TRENITHICK MDW
8 GOVER CL
9 HIGH FIELD RD
10 MARSHALLEN RD
11 CHURCH RD
12 CHARLOTTE CL
13 ELLEN CL
Works
Porthtowan
Chy
Mount Hawke Academy
Chy
Penhallow Farm
Cemy
Wheal Bassett Farm
Goosewartha Farm
Two Burrows
THE OLD CHAPEL
Chiverton Cross
Manor Parsley
Menagissey
1 HIGHVIEW CRES
2 HIGHVIEW
3 SYMONDS CL
4 PASSMORE CL
Three Burrows
Blackwater
PO
Laity Moor
Mawla
Skinners Bottom
Blackwater Prim Sch
PH
CHAPEL HILL
Stencoose
Carnhot
Forge
1 GWEL GWARTHE
2 PARK LEDER
3 TREVEN NOWETH
4 PRAS COTH
Chy
Boscawen Farm
STATION RD
LAITY MOOR
OLD TRAM RD
Wheal Plenty
Wheal Busy
1 BUCKINGHAM NIP
2 SERGEANTS HILL
Sinns Barton
SINNS COMMON
GREEN LA
Chy
Chys
Chacewater
WHEAL BUSY LA
Parc Erissey
LITTLE SINNS
Wheal Rose
Hallenbeagle
1 SCORIA CL
2 RADNOR RD
THE TERRACE
HIGH ST
Parc Erissey Ind Est
WHITE CROSS
SAWMILLS LA
Salem
Motel
Scorrier
Chys
Cox Hill
B3300
NEW PORTREATH RD
North Downs
Radnor
RADNOR RD
SCORRIER RD   A3047
B3298
Scorrier House
Killifreth Farm
Creegbrawse
140
North Country
Treleigh
LC
SCORRIER HOUSE WORKSHOPS
Tregullow
1 TELEGRAPH HILL
2 NORTHFIELD CL
3 MILLS
4 SCORRIER ST
5 CHURCH ST
6 CAREW CL
7 BOSAWNA CL
8 MILLS GDNS
Todpool
BASSETT RD
A3047
Sch
Highway
Treskerby
WHEAL GORLAND RD
CHYROSE RD
FORTH-AN-PRAZE
BALCOATH
TRENANT
CHAPEL ST
BUCKINGHAM TERR
TELEGRAPH ST
MARKET SQ
FORE ST
WEST END
CAREW RD
FORTH-AN-EGLOS
BURNWITHIAN TERR
Tolgullow
POLDICE TERR
SANDY LA
Mount Ambrose
Mast
Goon Gumpas
REDRUTH
Trefula
TREFULA
Vogue
PH
VOGUE HILL
St Day
Crofthandy
LOWER GOONGUMPAS LA
HIGHER GOONGUMPAS LA
WHEAL JEWEL
MURDOCH CL
STRAWBERRY
PO
TRELEIGH AVE
NORTH ST
DRUMP RD
EAST END
A393
Cemy
Ninnis
St Day & Carharrack Com Sch
CHURCH HILL
Chys
Coll
TOLGUS HILL
Sch
P
P
Fords Row
Redruth
PO
B3300
W END

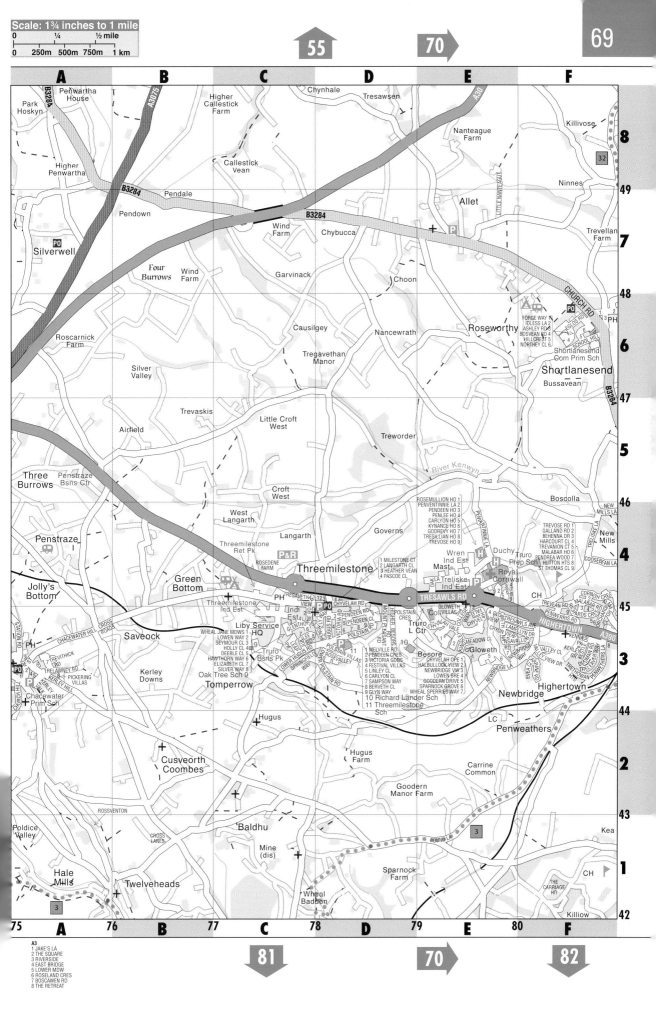

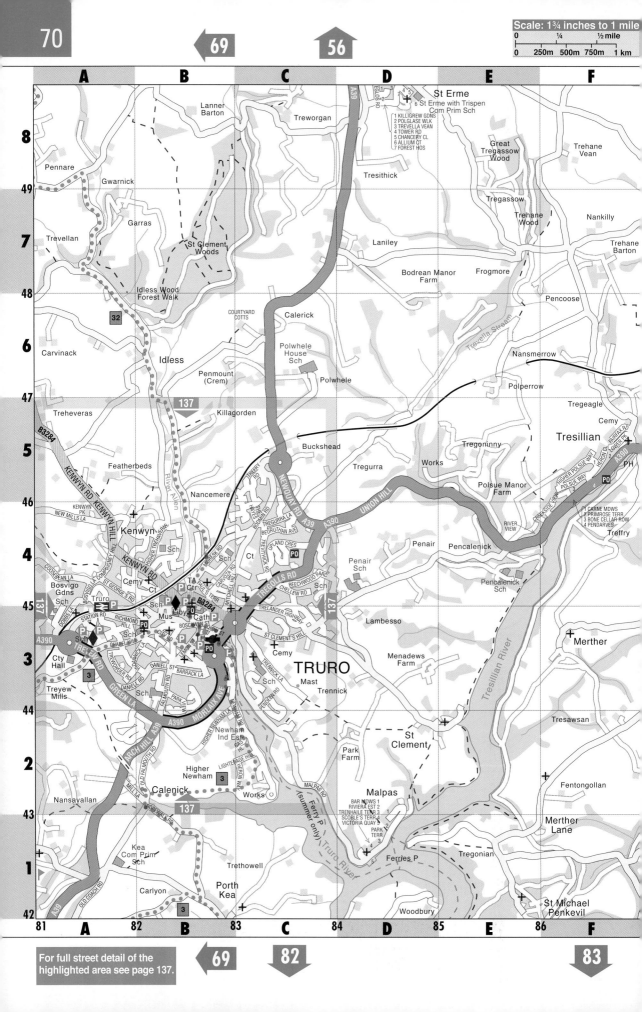

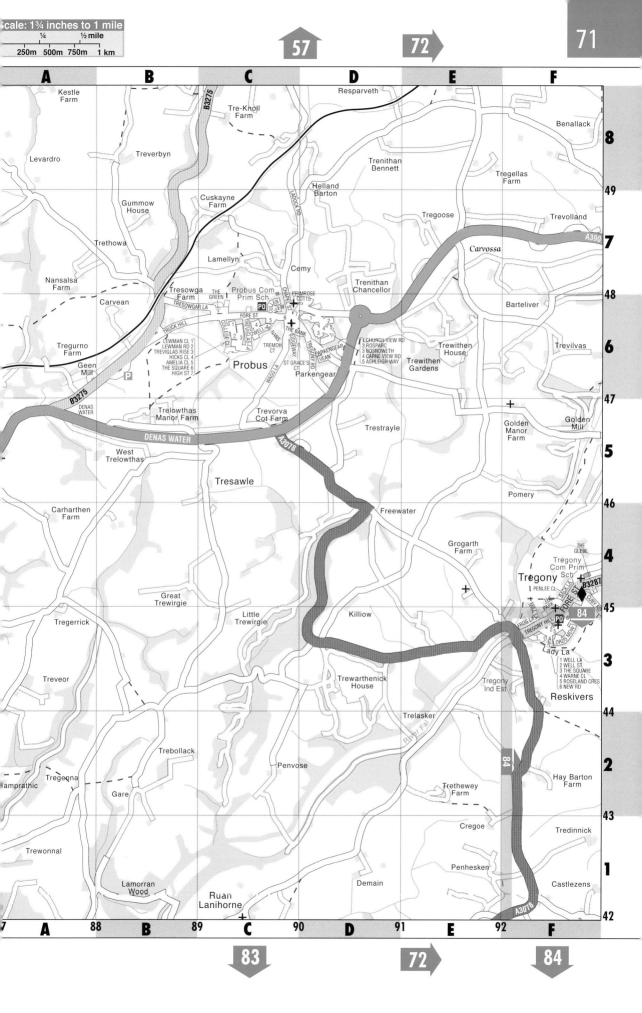

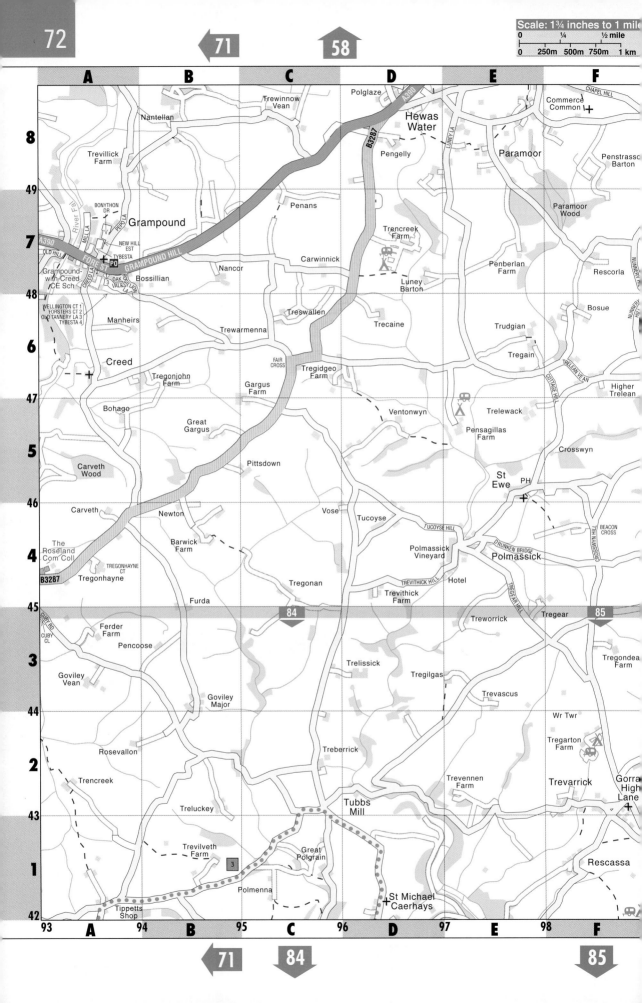

Scale: 1¾ inches to 1 mile

0   ¼   ½ mile

0   250m   500m   750m   1 km

A **B** **C** **D** **E** **F**

8

49

7

48

6

47

5

46

4

45

3

44

2

43

1

42

Trewinnow
Vean

Polglaze

Commerce
Common

Nantellan

Hewas
Water

Paramoor

Penstrassc
Barton

Trevillick
Farm

BONYTHON
DR

Penans

Pengelly

Paramoor
Wood

River Fal

Grampound

B3287

Trencreek
Farm

Penberlan
Farm

Rescorla

NEW HILL
EST
TYBESTA

Carwinnick

OLD HILL

A390

FORE ST

PO

GRAMPOUND HILL

Nancor

Luney
Barton

Grampound-
with-Creed
CE Sch

OAK
VALE

Bossillian

Treswallen

Bosue

WELLINGTON CT 1
FORSTERS CT 2
OLD TANNERY LA 3
TYBESTA 4

Manheirs

Trewarmenna

Trecaine

Trudgian

Creed

Tregonjohn
Farm

FAIR
CROSS

Tregidgeo
Farm

Tregain

TRELEAN VEAN

Higher
Trelean

Bohago

Gargus
Farm

Ventonwyn

Trelewack

COTTAGE HILL

Great
Gargus

Pensagillas
Farm

Crosswyn

Carveth
Wood

Pittsdown

St
Ewe

PH

Carveth

Newton

Vose

Tucoyse

TUCOYSE HILL

BEACON
CROSS

The
Roseland
Com Coll

Barwick
Farm

Polmassick
Vineyard

DRUNKEN BRIDGE

Polmassick

TRAMS CROSS

B3287

Tregonhayne
CT

Tregonhayne

Furda

Tregonan

Trevithick
Farm

TREVITHICK HILL

Hotel

TREGEAR HILL

Tregear

Tregondea
Farm

CUBY RD

CUBY
CL

Ferder
Farm

84

Treworrick

85

Pencoose

Trelissick

Tregilgas

Trevascus

Goviley
Vean

Goviley
Major

Wr Twr

Tregarton
Farm

Rosevallon

Treberrick

Trevennen
Farm

Trevarrick

Gorra
High
Lane

Trencreek

Treluckey

Tubbs
Mill

Trevilveth
Farm

3

Great
Polgrain

Rescassa

Polmenna

St Michael
Caerhays

Tippetts
Shop

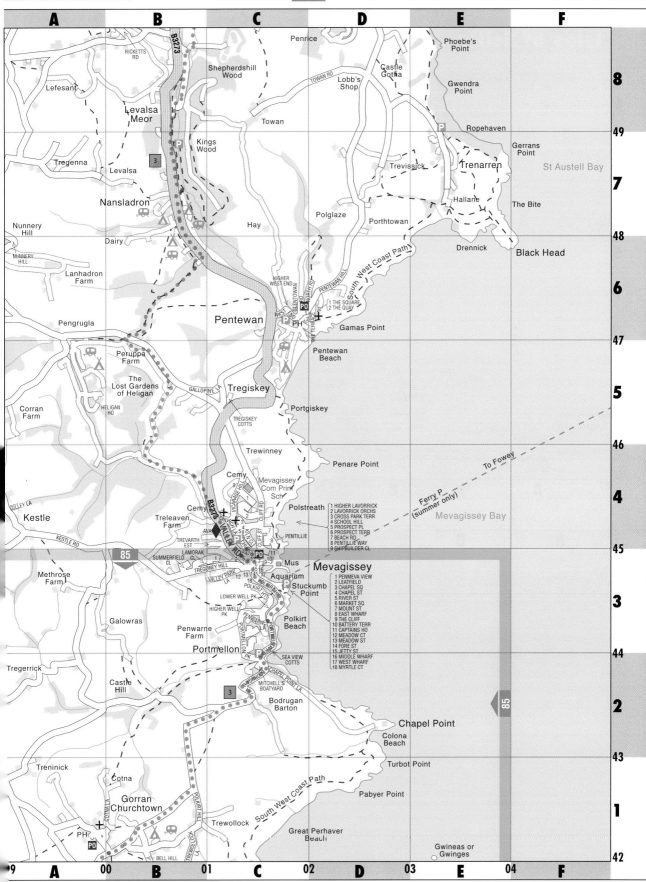

Scale: 1¾ inches to 1 mile

| 0 | ¼ | ½ mile |
| 0 | 250m | 500m | 750m | 1 km |

Penrice

Lobb's Shop

Phoebe's Point

Castle Gotha

Gwendra Point

Ropehaven

Shepherdshill Wood

TOWAN RD

RICKETTS RD

B3273

Lefesant

Levalsa Meor

Kings Wood

Towan

Trevissick

Gerrans Point

St Austell Bay

Tregenna

3

Levalsa

Trenarren

Hallane

The Bite

Nansladron

Hay

Polglaze

Porthtowan

Drennick

Black Head

Nunnery Hill

Dairy

NUNNERY HILL

Lanhadron Farm

HIGHER WEST END

GLENTOWAN RD

PENTEWAN HILL

NORTH RD

South West Coast Path

Pengrugla

Pentewan

WEST END

PO

THE TERRACE

PH

1 THE SQUARE
2 THE QUAY

Gamas Point

Peruppa Farm

Pentewan Beach

Corran Farm

The Lost Gardens of Heligan

GALLOPINE LA

Tregiskey

HELIGAN HO

Portgiskey

TREGISKEY COTTS

Trewinney

Portgiskey

Penare Point

To Fowey

Kestle

Cemy

KESTLE RD

GILLEY LA

Cemy

VICARAGE HILL

CLIFF RD

Mevagissey Com Prim Sch

Polstreath

Ferry P (summer only)

Mevagissey Bay

B3273

Treleaven Farm

CHURCH ST

VALLEY RD

CLIFF ST

PENTILLIE

1 HIGHER LAVORRICK
2 LAVORRICK ORCHS
3 CROSS PARK TERR
4 SCHOOL HILL
5 PROSPECT PL
6 PROSPECT TERB
7 BEACH RD
8 PENTILLIE WAY
9 SHIPBUILDER CL

TREVARTH EST

SUMMERFIELD CL

LAMORAK CL

TREGONEY HILL

85

Methrose Farm

VALLEY PARK LA

POLKIRT HTS

Mus

Aquarium

PO

Stuckumb Point

Mevagissey

1 PENMEVA VIEW
2 LEATFIELD
3 CHAPEL SQ
4 CHAPEL ST
5 RIVER ST
6 MARKET SQ
7 MOUNT ST
8 EAST WHARF
9 THE CLIFF
10 BATTERY TERR
11 CAPTAINS HO
12 MEADOW CT
13 MEADOW ST
14 FORE ST
15 JETTY ST
16 MIDDLE WHARF
17 WEST WHARF
18 MYRTLE CT

Galowras

Penwarne Farm

LOWER WELL PK

HIGHER WELL PK

PENWARNE RD

PORTMELLON PK

Polkirt Beach

Tregerrick

Portmellon

SEA VIEW COTTS

Castle Hill

3

MORRIS'S

CHAPEL POINT LA

Mitchell's Boatyard

Bodrugan Barton

Chapel Point

Colona Beach

85

Turbot Point

Treninick

Cotna

POLKIRT HILL

Gorran Churchtown

Trewollock

South West Coast Path

Pabyer Point

Great Perhaver Beach

Gwineas or Gwinges

PH

PO

TREWOLLOCK LA

BELL HILL

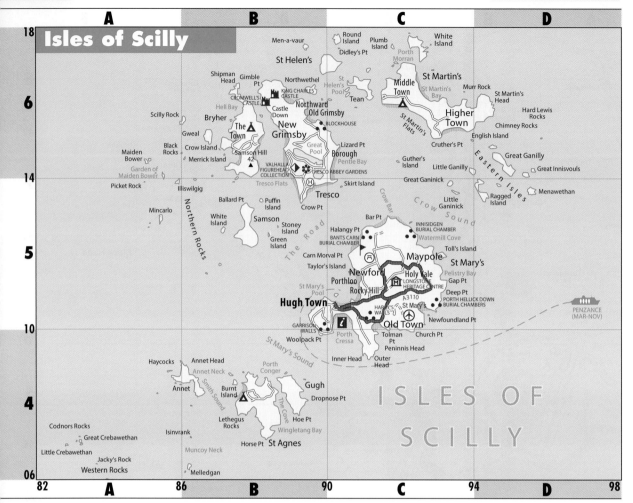

Isles of Scilly

Scale: 4 miles to 1 inch

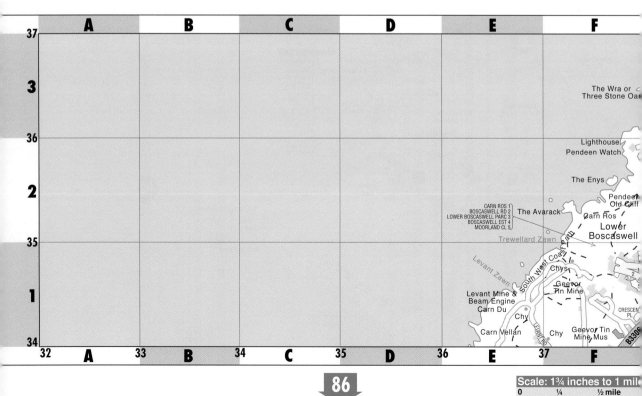

Scale: 1¾ inches to 1 mile

Scale: 1¾ inches to 1 mile

A1
1 PETERS ROW
2 PARK-AN-PYTH
3 TREASE
4 BOSCASWELL TERR
5 CALARTHA TERR
6 CRESCENT PL
7 THE SQUARE
8 ST JOHN'S TERR
9 GWEL-MOR
10 PORTHERRAS VILLAS
11 PORTHERRAS TERR

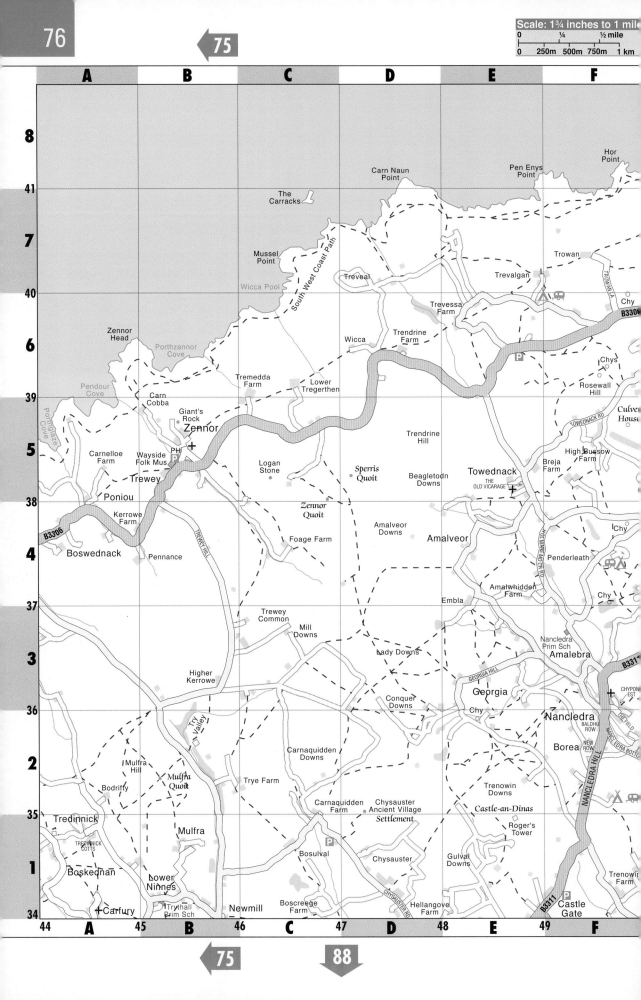

Scale: 1¾ inches to 1 mile

0   ¼   ½ mile

0 250m 500m 750m 1 km

A   B   C   D   E   F

8

41

7

Hor
Point

Pen Enys
Point

Carn Naun
Point

The Carracks

Trowan

Mussel
Point

Treveal

Trevalgan

Wicca Pool

South West Coast Path

Trevessa
Farm

40

Chy

B330

6

39

Zennor
Head

Porthzennor
Cove

Wicca

Trendrine
Farm

Rosewall
Hill

Chys

Pendour
Cove

Tremedda
Farm

Lower
Tregerthen

Culver
House

Carn
Cobba

TOWEDNACK RD

5

Portglaze
Cove

Giant's
Rock

Zennor

Trendrine
Hill

High Bussow
Farm

Carnelloe
Farm

Wayside
Folk Mus.

PH
P

Logan
Stone

Sperris
Quoit

Beagletodn
Downs

Towednack

THE
OLD VICARAGE

Breja
Farm

38

Trewey

Zennor
Quoit

Amalveor
Downs

Chy

Poniou

Kerrowe
Farm

Foage Farm

Amalveor

Penderleath

B3306

Boswednack

Pennance

HOLMANS MOOR RD

Amalwhidden
Farm

Chy

4

Embla

37

Trewey
Common

Mill
Downs

Nancledra
Prim Sch

B331

3

Higher
Kerrowe

Lady Downs

Amalebra

GEORGIA HILL

Georgia

CHYPONS
EST

36

Conquer
Downs

Chy

Nancledra

THE FIELD

BALDHU
ROW

Try
Valley

Borea

NEW
ROW

NANCLEDRA BOTTO

2

Mulfra
Hill

Mulfra
Quoit

Carnaquidden
Downs

NANCLEDRA HILL

Bodrifty

Trye Farm

Trenowin
Downs

35

Tredinnick

Carnaquidden
Farm

Chysauster
Ancient Village

Castle-an-Dinas

Roger's
Tower

TREDINNICK
COTTS

Mulfra

Settlement

Chysauster

Gulval
Downs

1

Boskednan

Lower
Ninnes

Bosulval

P

CHYSAUSTER RD

Hellangove
Farm

Trenowin
Farm

Boscreege
Farm

B3311

Castle
Gate

P

Carfury

Trythall
Prim Sch

Newmill

34

44   45   46   47   48   49

A   B   C   D   E   F

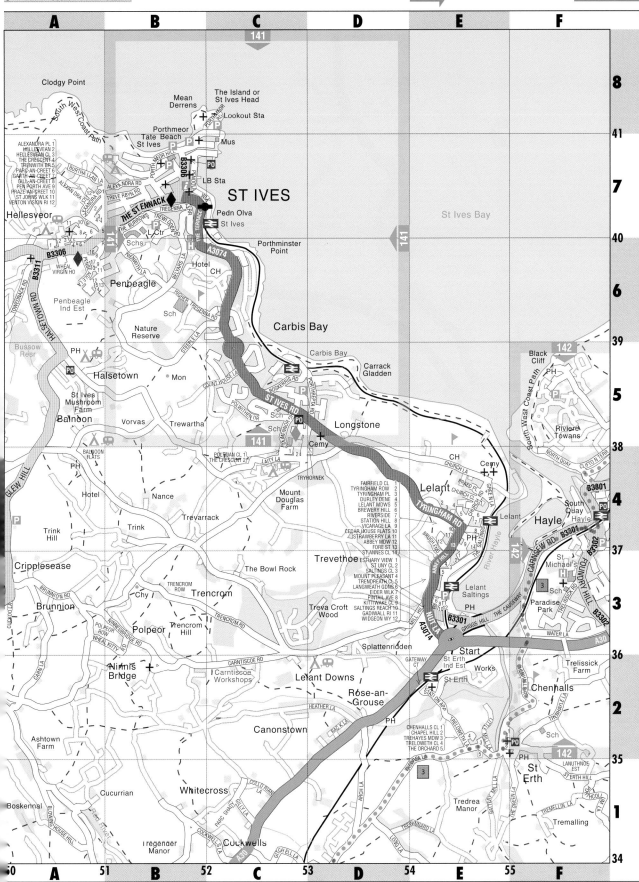

8
41
7
40
6
39
5
38
4
37
3
36
2
35
1
34

A   B   C   D   E   F

Clodgy Point

Mean Derrens

The Island or St Ives Head

Lookout Sta

Porthmeor Tate Beach St Ives

Mus

1 ALEXANDRA PL 1
2 HELLESVEAN 2
3 HELLESVEAN CL 3
4 THE CRESCENT 4
5 TRENWITH BR 5
6 PARC-AN-CREET 6
7 GARTH-AN-CREET 7
8 GILL-AN-CREET 8
9 PEN PORTH AVE 9
10 PRAZE-AN-CREET 10
11 ST JOHNS WLK 11
12 VENTON VISION RI 12

Helleveor

LB Sta

ST IVES

Pedn Olva St Ives

St Ives Bay

Porthminster Point

Penbeagle

Hotel

CH

Carbis Bay

Penbeagle Ind Est

Nature Reserve

Sch

Carbis Bay

Carrack Gladden

Bussow Resr

PH

PO

Halsetown

Mon

St Ives Mushroom Farm

Baldoon

Vorvas

Trewartha

141

Sch

Sch

Cemy

Longstone

Black Cliff

142

PH

Riviera Towans

NORTH QUAY

CLIFTON TERR

CH

CHURCH LA

Cemy

Lelant

B3301

South Quay Hayle

Hotel

Nance

Mount Douglas Farm

FAIRFIELD CL 1
TYRINGHAM ROW 2
TYRINGHAM PL 3
DURLEY DENE 4
LELANT MDWS 5
BREWERY HILL 6
RIVERSIDE 7
STATION HILL 8
VICARAGE LA 9
CEDAR HOUSE FLATS 10
STRAWBERRY LA 11
ABBEY MDW 12
FORE ST 13
ST ANNES CL 14

Lelant

Hayle

Trink Hill

Trevarrack

Trink

TYRINGHAM RD

PH

Lelant Saltings

St Michael's

Paradise Park

B3301

B3302

Cripplesease

The Bowl Rock

Trevethoe

ESTUARY VIEW 1
ST UNY CL 2
SALTINGS CL 3
MOUNT PLEASANT 4
TRENDREATH CL 5
LANGWEATH GDNS 6
EIDER WLK 7
PINTAIL AVE 8
KITTIWAKE CL 9
SALTINGS REACH 10
GADIWALL RI 11
WIDGEON WY 12

WATER LA

A30

Brunnion

Chy

TRENCROM ROW

Trencrom

Treva Croft Wood

Lelant Saltings

Trelissick Farm

Polpeor

Trencrom Hill

TRENCROM RD

MILL HILL

A3074

B3301

GRIGGS HILL

Chenhalls

Ninnis Bridge

CARNTISCOE RD

Carntiscoe Workshops

Lelant Downs

Splattenridden

GATEWAY CT

Start

St Erth Ind Est

Works

St Erth

Rose-an-Grouse

PH

CHENHALLS CL 1
CHAPEL HILL 2
TREHAYES MDW 3
TRELOWETH CL 4
THE ORCHARD 5

142

St Erth

LANUTHNOE EST

ST ERTH HILL

Ashtown Farm

Canonstown

BACK LA

PH

3

PO

PH

Cucurrian

Whitecross

Tredrea Manor

Tremalling

Boskennal

Tregender Manor

Cockwells

A30

A   B   C   D   E   F

89

78

For full street detail of the
highlighted area see pages
141 and 142.

A6
1 CHYANDOUR CL
2 HELLESVEAN
3 HELLESVEAN CL
4 PARC-AN-STAMPS
5 CROWS-AN-EGLOS
6 PARC-AN-FORTH
7 PENBEAGLE TERR
8 PENBEAGLE CRES
9 CORVA RD
10 PRIORS CL
11 CORVA CL
12 PORTHIA RD
13 CARNSTABBA RD
14 ALAN HARVEY CL
15 JUBILEE CT
16 TINNERS WAY
17 PENBEAGLE CL

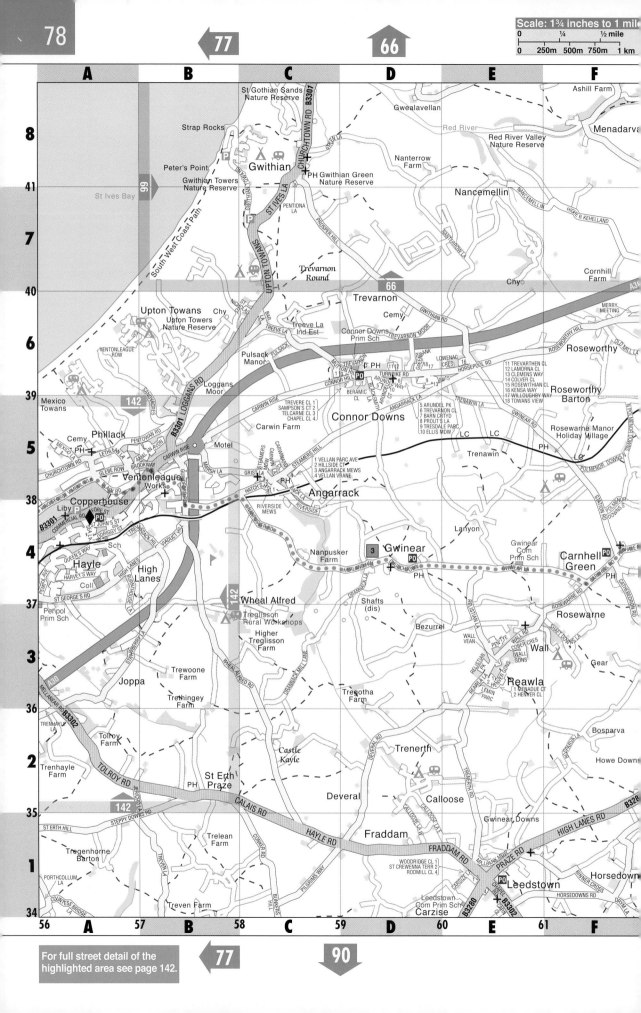

St Gothian Sands
Nature Reserve

Gwealavellan

Red River

Red River Valley
Nature Reserve

Menadarva

Strap Rocks

Ashill Farm

Peter's Point

Gwithian

PH Gwithian Green
Nature Reserve

Nanterrow
Farm

Nancemellin

St Ives Bay

Gwithian Towers
Nature Reserve

PENTIDNA
LA

NANCEMELLIN

HIGHER KEHELLAND

Cornhill
Farm

South West Coast Path

Trevarnon
Round

Chy

Trevarnon

66

Merry
Meeting

Upton Towans

Chy

Cemy

Roseworthy

Upton Towers
Nature Reserve

Treeve La

Connor Downs
Prim Sch

Roseworthy
Barton

VENTONLEAGUE
ROW

Pulsack
Manor

Treeve La
Ind Est

Loggans
Moor

142

Mexico
Towans

Carwin Rise

Carwin Farm

Connor Downs

11 TREVARTHEN CL
12 LAMORNA CL
13 CLEMENS WAY
14 COLVER CL
15 ROSEWITHIAN CL
16 KENSA WAY
17 WILLOUGHBY WAY
18 TOWANS VIEW

Rosewarne Manor
Holiday Village

Phillack

Cemy

PH

TREVERE CL 1
SAMPSON'S CT 2
TELCARNE CL 3
CHAPEL CL 4

5 ARUNDEL PK
6 TREVARNON CL
7 BARN CRTYD
8 PROUT'S LA
9 TRESDALE PARC
10 ELLIS MDW

Trenawin

Ventonleague

Works

STEAMERS HILL

1 VELLAN PARC AVE
2 HILLSIDE CT
3 ANGARRACK MEWS
4 VELLAN VRANE

Copperhouse

Liby

PH

Angarrack

RIVERSIDE
MEWS

Lanyon

Gwinear
Com Prim Sch

Carnhell
Green

Nanpusker
Farm

Gwinear

3

PO
PH

Hayle

High
Lanes

Coll

Wheal Alfred

Shafts
(dis)

Bezurrel

Rosewarne

Penpol
Prim Sch

142

Treglisson
Rural Workshops

Wall
Vean

Wall

Gear

Higher
Treglisson
Farm

Reawla

1 MENADUE CT
2 HENVER CL

Joppa

Trewoone
Farm

Tregotha
Farm

Bosparva

Trethingey
Farm

Trenerth

Howe Downs

TRENHAYLE
LA

Tolroy
Farm

Castle
Kayle

Deveral

Calloose

Trenhayle
Farm

142

St Erth
Praze

PH

Fraddam

Gwinear Downs

High Lanes Rd

St Erth Hill

Calais Rd

Hayle Rd

Fraddam Rd

Horsedown

Tregenhorne
Barton

Trelean
Farm

WOODRIDGE CL 1
ST CREWENNA TERR 2
RODMILL CL 4

Binner Cross

PORTHCOLLUM
LA

Leedstown

Treven Farm

Leedstown
Com Prim Sch

Carzise

COUNTESS BRIDGE
LA

Horsedowns Rd

For full street detail of the
highlighted area see page 142.

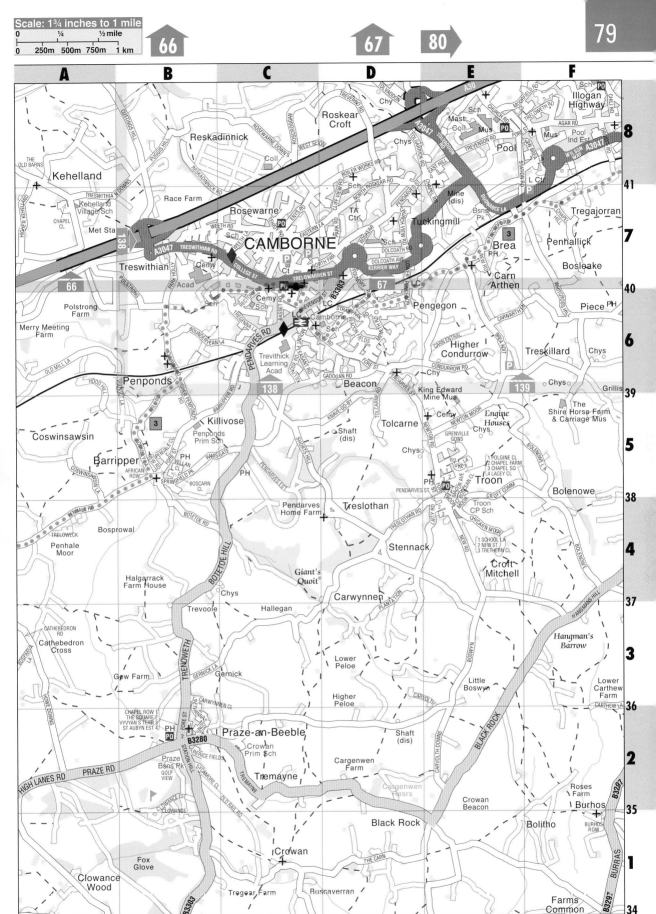

A   B   C   D   E   F

THE OLD BARNS

Kehelland

Higher Kehelland

Kehelland Village Sch

CHAPEL CL

Met Sta

Treswithian Downs

Race Farm

Reskadinnick

Rosewarne Downs

WEST SETON

Roskear Croft

Treverno Rd

TOLVADDON RD

Chy

Chys

Mast Coll

Sch

Mus

Illogan Highway

Sch

Pool Ind Est

Mus

Pool

8

A3047

Treswithian Rd

Cemy

College St

CAMBORNE

Trelowarren St

Trevenson St

Camborne

Sch

Kerrier Way

Dolcoath Ave

Tuckingmill

Brea

PH

Carn Arthen

Tregajorran

Penhallick

Bosleake

7

40

Polstrong Farm

Merry Meeting Farm

OLD MILL LA

Penponds

Pendarves Rd

Pengegon

Higher Condurrow

Piece PH

Treskillard

Chys

6

Coswinsawsin

Barripper

Killivose

Penponds Prim Sch

PH

Shaft (dis)

Tolcarne

Cemy

Engine Houses

King Edward Mine Mus

The Shire Horse Farm & Carriage Mus

Grillis

39

5

38

Bosprowal

Penhale Moor

Halgarrack Farm House

Pendarves Home Farm

Treslothan

Stennack

Troon

Troon CP Sch

Croft Mitchell

Bolenowe

4

37

Cathebedron Cross

Gew Farm

Gernick

Trevoole

Hallegan

Giant's Quoit

Carwynnen

Lower Peloe

Higher Peloe

Little Boswyn

Hangman's Barrow

Lower Carthew Farm

3

36

Praze-an-Beeble

Crowan Prim Sch

Tremayne

Shaft (dis)

Cargenwen Farm

Black Rock

Burhos

Roses Farm

2

35

High Lanes Rd

Praze Rd

Golf View

Black Rock

Crowan Beacon

Bolitho

Burhos Row

Fox Glove

Clowance Wood

Crowan

Tregear Farm

Buscaverran

THE CARN

Farms Common

1

34

62   63   64   65   66   67

A   B   C   D   E   F

For full street detail of the highlighted area see pages 138 and 139.

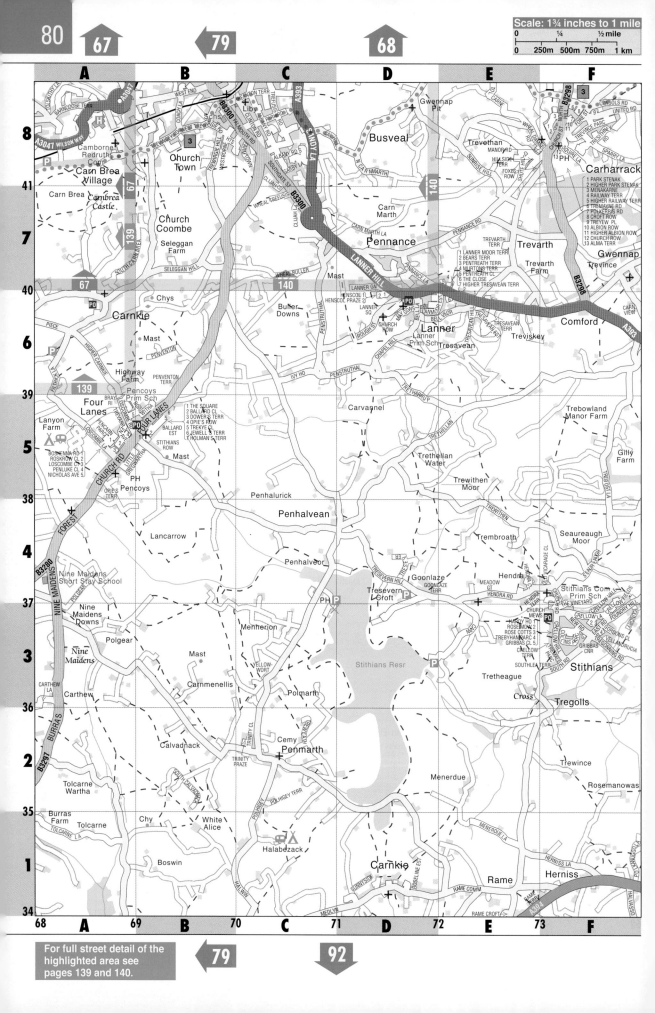

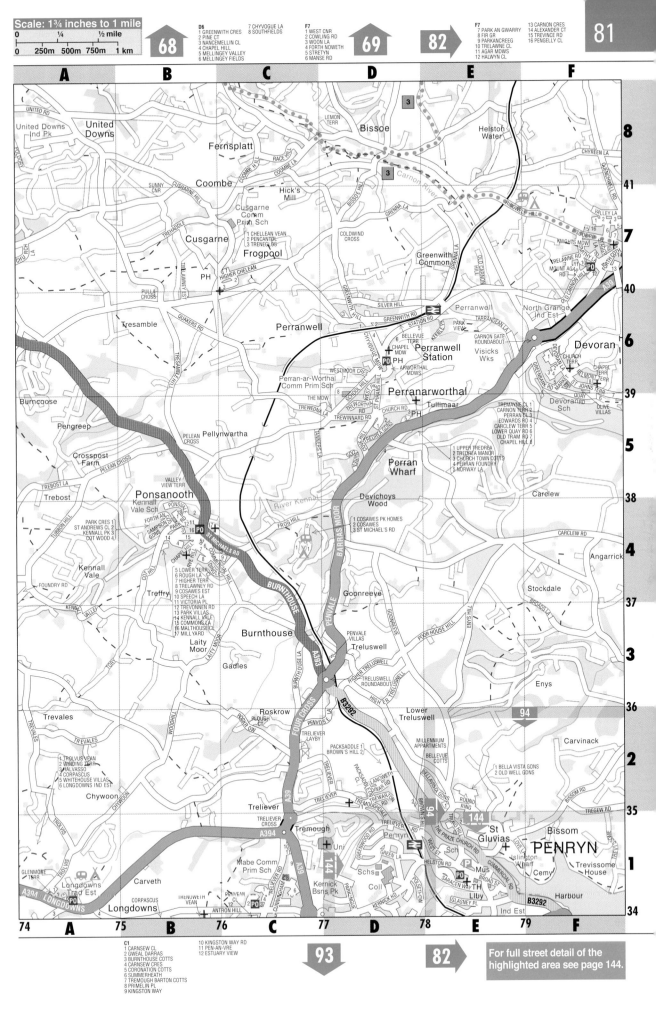

Scale: 1¾ inches to 1 mile
0   ¼   ½ mile
0   250m   500m   750m   1 km

For full street detail of the highlighted area see page 144.

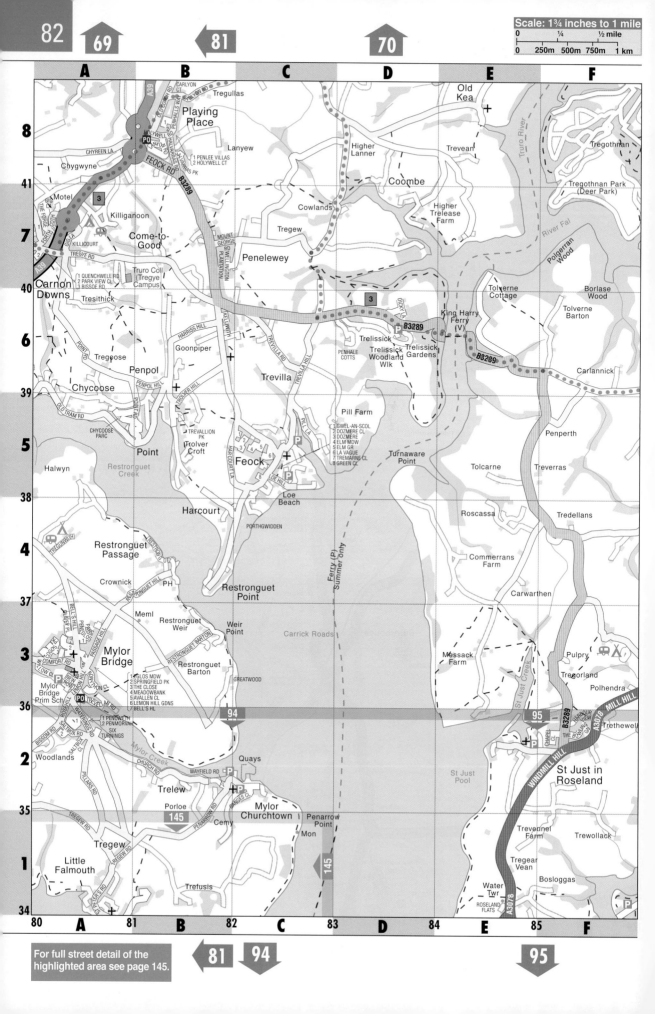

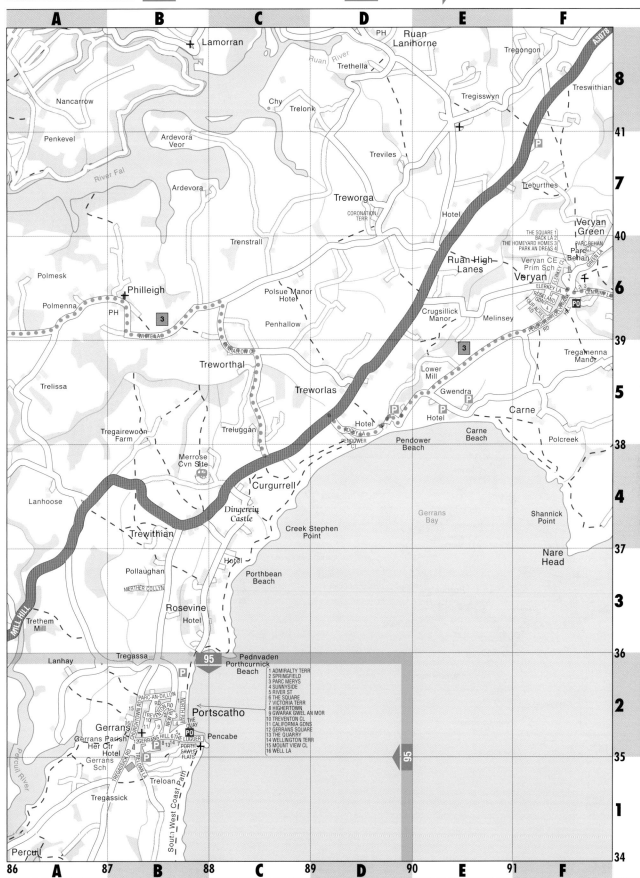

A   B   C   D   E   F

MILL LA
FROG LA
B3287
PO 7
LORDS MDW
Lady La
Tregony

1 TREGONY HILL
2 LADY LA
3 WELL ST
4 THE SQUARE
5 WARNE CL
6 ROSELAND CRES
7 NEW RD
8 ROSELAND PARC

Reskivers

CUBY RD
CUBY CL
Ferder Farm
Pencoose

Goviley Vean
Goviley Major

Treworrick
Tregear
Trelissick
Tregilgas
Trevascus

TREGEAR HILL

8

44

Rosevallon

Trencreek
Hay Barton farm

Treberrick

Trevennen Farm

7

43

Treluckey

Tubbs Mill

Tredinnick

Trevilveth Farm

Great Polgrain

6

Castlezens

3

A3078   71

Tippetts Shop

Polmenna

St Michael Caerhays

Study Ctr

Caerhays Castle

42

72

Trengrouse Farm

West Portholland

THE TERRACE

East Portholland

Porthluney Cove

5

Trelagossick

Tretheake Manor

PO

P

P

41

Calendra

Crohans
CROHANS CL

Perbargus Point

South West Coast Path

Tregenna

May's Rock

4

THE ROW

Treviskey
Trethennal Manor

TREVISKEY HILL

Caragloose Point
Shag Rock

40

Trewartha

Portloe

COASTGUARD TERR
Hartriza Point

3

CENTURY LA

Camels

The Jacka
BEACH HILL

Jacka Point

Veryan Bay

39

Manare Point

2

Caragloose

The Straythe

Parc Caragloose Rock

The Blouth

38

P

Kiberick Cove

1

Rosen Cliff

Lemoria Rock

37

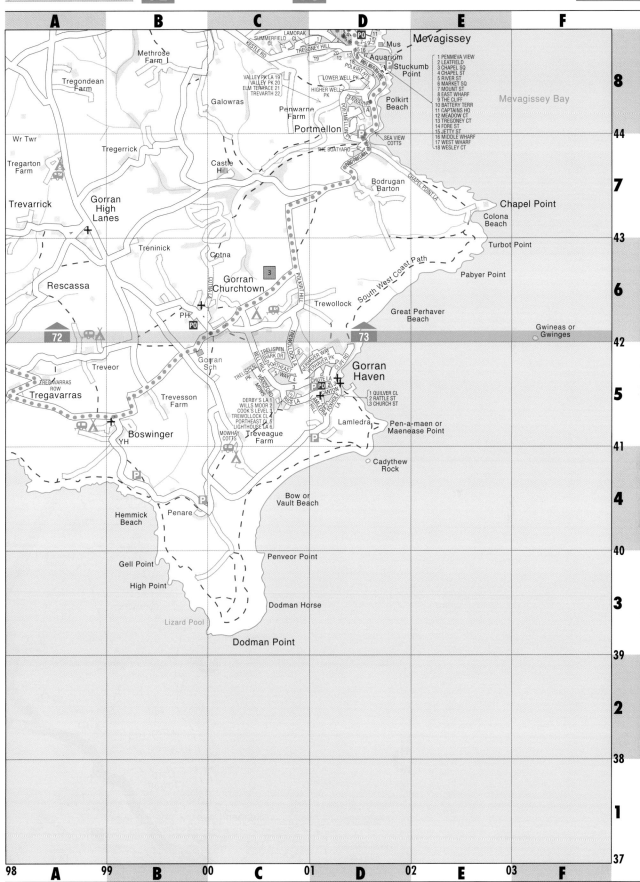

Mevagissey

1 PENMEVA VIEW
2 LEATFIELD
3 CHAPEL SQ
4 CHAPEL ST
5 RIVER ST
6 MARKET SQ
7 MOUNT ST
8 EAST WHARF
9 THE CLIFF
10 BATTERY TERR
11 CAPTAINS HO
12 MEADOW CT
13 TREGONEY CT
14 FORE ST
15 JETTY ST
16 MIDDLE WHARF
17 WEST WHARF
18 WESLEY CT

Mevagissey Bay

Methrose Farm

Tregondean Farm

Galowras

SUMMERFIELD CL

KESTLE RD

LAMORAK CL

TREGONEY HILL

VALLEY PK LA 19
VALLEY PK 20
ELM TERRACE 21
TREVARTH 22

LOWER WELL PK

HIGHER WELL PK

Penwarne Farm

Portmellon

Polkirt Beach

Stuckumb Point

Mus

Aquarium

SEA VIEW COTTS

THE BOATYARD

Wr Twr

Tregarton Farm

Trevarrick

Tregerrick

Castle Hill

Gorran High Lanes

Bodrugan Barton

Chapel Point

Colona Beach

Treninick

Cotna

Gorran Churchtown

Trewollock

Turbot Point

Pabyer Point

South West Coast Path

Rescassa

3

PH

PO

72

73

Great Perhaver Beach

Gwineas or Gwinges

Treveor

Gorran Sch

TRELISPEN PARK DR

BELL HILL

PORTHEAST WAY

MANOR RD

TRELISPEN PK

KERHAVER WAY

PERHAVER PK

Gorran Haven

Trevesson Farm

Tregavarras Row

Tregavarras

1 QUILVER CL
2 RATTLE ST
3 CHURCH ST

DERBY'S LA 1
WILLS MOOR 2
COOK'S LEVEL 3
TREWOLLOCK CL 4
PORTHEAST CL 5
LIGHTHOUSE LA 6

CHUTE LA

CANTON

RICE LA

LAMLEDRA HILL

FOXHOLE LA

CLIFF RD

Lamledra

Pen-a-maen or Maenease Point

Boswinger

YH

MOWHAY COTTS

Treveague Farm

Cadythew Rock

Hemmick Beach

Penare

Gell Point

High Point

Bow or Vault Beach

Penveor Point

Dodman Horse

Lizard Pool

Dodman Point

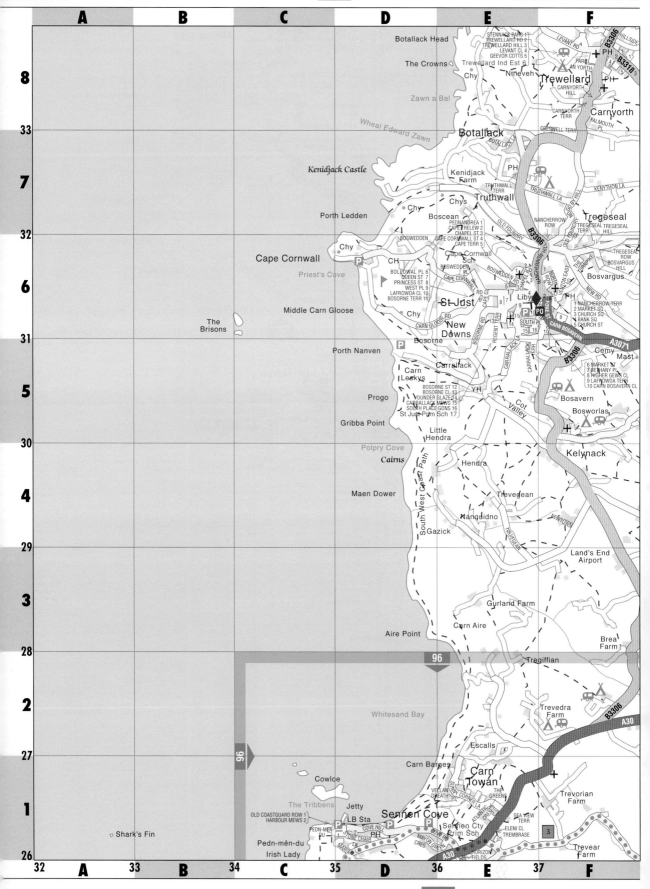

74

Scale: 1¾ inches to 1 mile

0   ¼   ½ mile

0   250m   500m   750m   1 km

A   **B**   **C**   **D**   **E**   **F**

Botallack Head

The Crowns

STENNACK PARK 1
TREWELLARD RD 2
TREWELLARD HILL 3
LEVANT CL 4
GEEVOR COTTS 5
Trewellard Ind Est 6

Nineveh

Chy

Trewellard

Carnyorth

CARNYORTH HILL

FALMOUTH PL

Carnyorth

Zawn a Bal

CARNYORTH TERR

33

Wheal Edward Zawn

Botallack

BOTALLACK

CRESWELL TERR

KENYTHON LA

Kenidjack Castle

7

Kenidjack Farm

TRUTHWALL TERR

TRUTHWALL LA

Truthwall

Tregeseal

NANCHERROW ROW

TREGESEAL TERR

TREGESEAL HILL

Porth Ledden

Chy

Chys

Boscean

32

BOSWEDDEN

PEDNANDREA 1
CAPE TRELEW 2
CAPE CORNWALL ST 4
CHAPEL ST 3
CAPE TERR 5

OLD FOUNDRY

B3306

TREGESEAL ROW
BOSVARGUS HILL

Chy

Cape Cornwall Sch

Bosvargus

Cape Cornwall

P

CH

BOSWEDDEN PL

BOLLOWAL PL 6
QUEEN ST 7
PRINCESS ST 8
WEST PL 9
LAFROWDA CL 10
BOSORNE TERR 11

CAPE CORNWALL RD

6

Priest's Cove

St Just

Libr

PO

1 NANCHERROW TERR
2 MARKET SQ
3 CHURCH SQ
4 BANK SQ
5 CHURCH ST

Middle Carn Gloose

Chy

CARN GLOOSE RD

New Downs

P

PH

31

The Brisons

Bosorne

Carrallack

Cemy

Mast

A3071

Porth Nanven

P

Carn Leskys

YH

B3306

6 MARKET ST
7 BETHANY PL
8 HIGHER GEWS CL
9 LAFROWDA TERR
10 CARN BOSAVERN CL

Bosavern

5

Progo

BOSORNE ST 12
BOSORNE CL 13
YOUNDER GLAZE 14
CARRALLACK MEWS 15
SOUTH PLACE GDNS 16
St Just Pri Sch 17

Cot Valley

Bosworlas

Gribba Point

Little Hendra

Kelynack

30

Polpry Cove

Cairns

Hendra

Maen Dower

4

Trevegean

Manquidno

NEWTOWN

Gazick

Land's End Airport

29

South West Coast Path

3

Gurland Farm

Carn Aire

Brea Farm

Aire Point

28

96

Tregiffian

Trevedra Farm

B3306

A30

2

Whitesand Bay

Escalls

96

27

Carn Barges

Carn Towan

Cowloe

VELLAN DREATH

THE GREENS

Trevorian Farm

1

The Tribbens

Jetty

Sennen Cove

OLD COASTGUARD ROW 1
HARBOUR MEWS 2

LB Sta

Sennen Cty Prim Sch

SEA VIEW TERR

ELENI CL
TREMBRASE

3

Shark's Fin

PEDN-MEN-DU

P

COVE HILL

PH

MAYON GREEN

ATLANTIC CREST

COVE RD

Trevear Farm

Pedn-mên-du
Irish Lady

ONE CHAIR

MARI

A30

HORIZON FIELDS

26

32   **A**   33   **B**   34   **C**   35   **D**   36   **E**   37   **F**

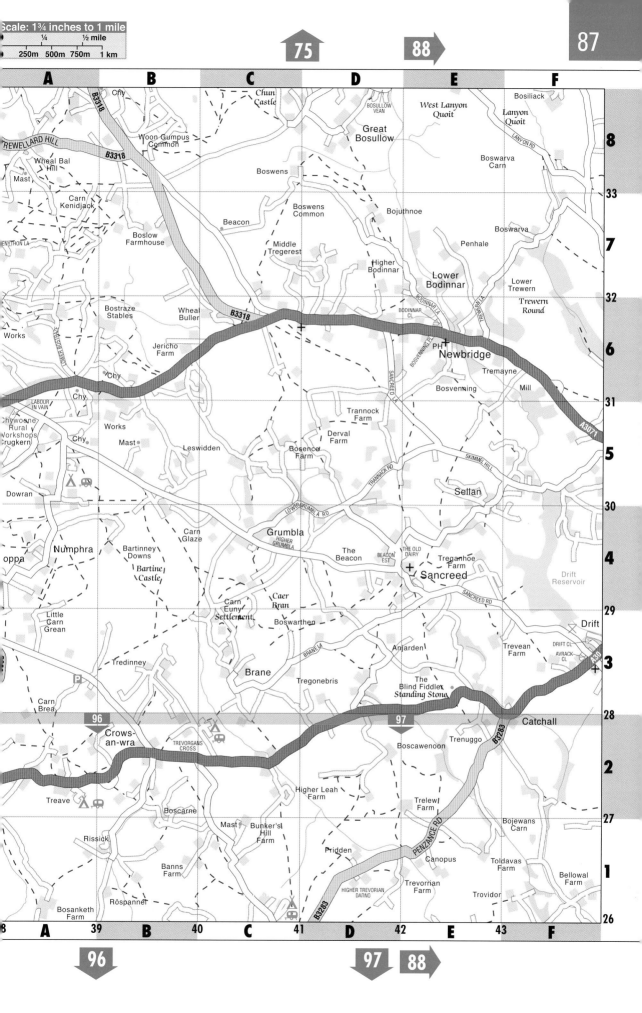

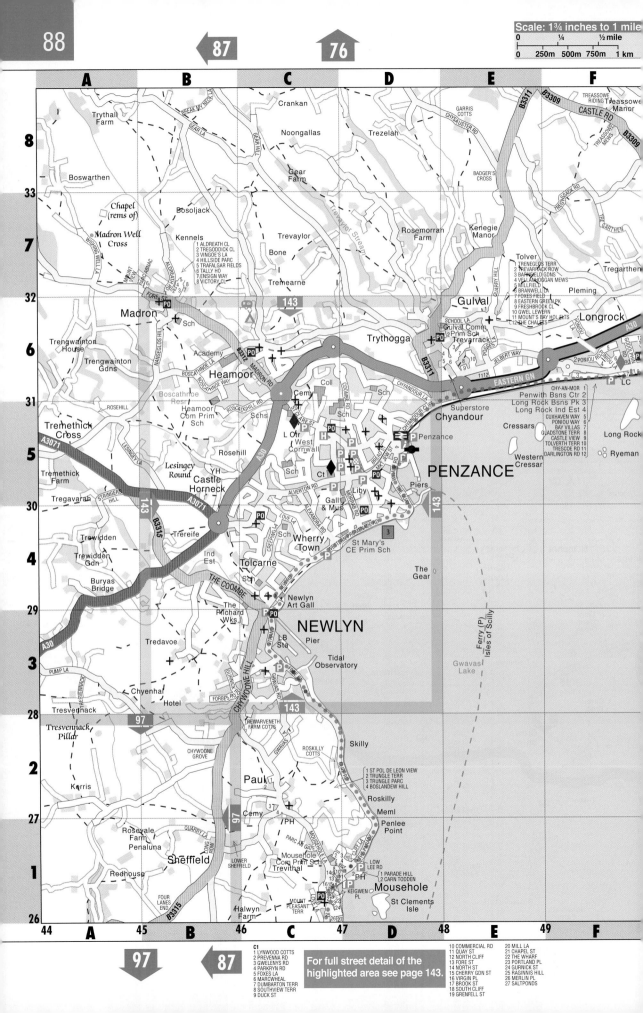

Scale: 1¾ inches to 1 mile

0   ¼   ½ mile
0   250m   500m   750m   1 km

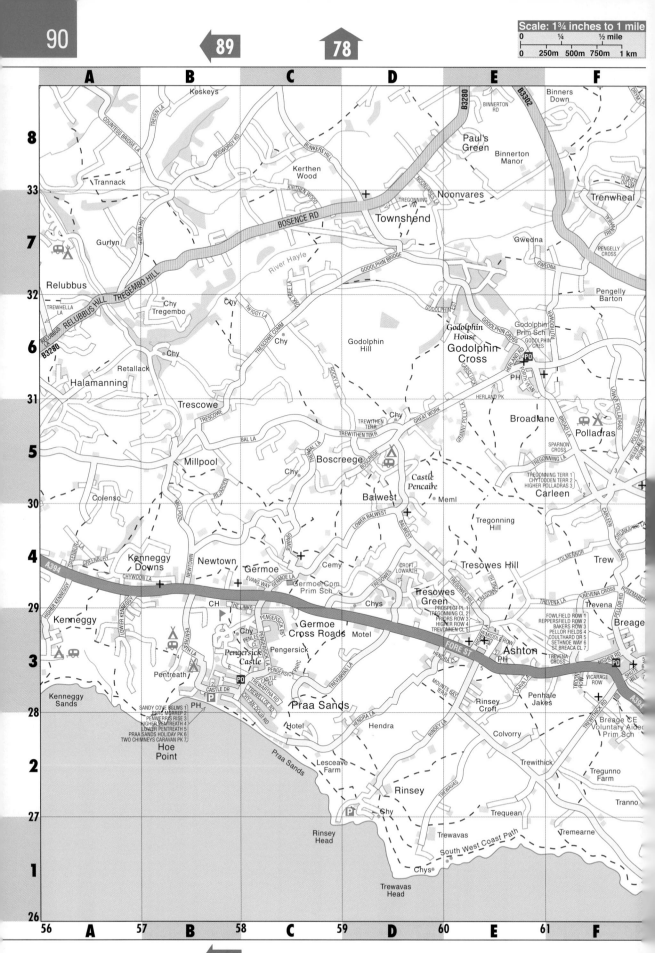

Scale: 1¾ inches to 1 mile

0   ¼   ½ mile

0   250m 500m 750m 1 km

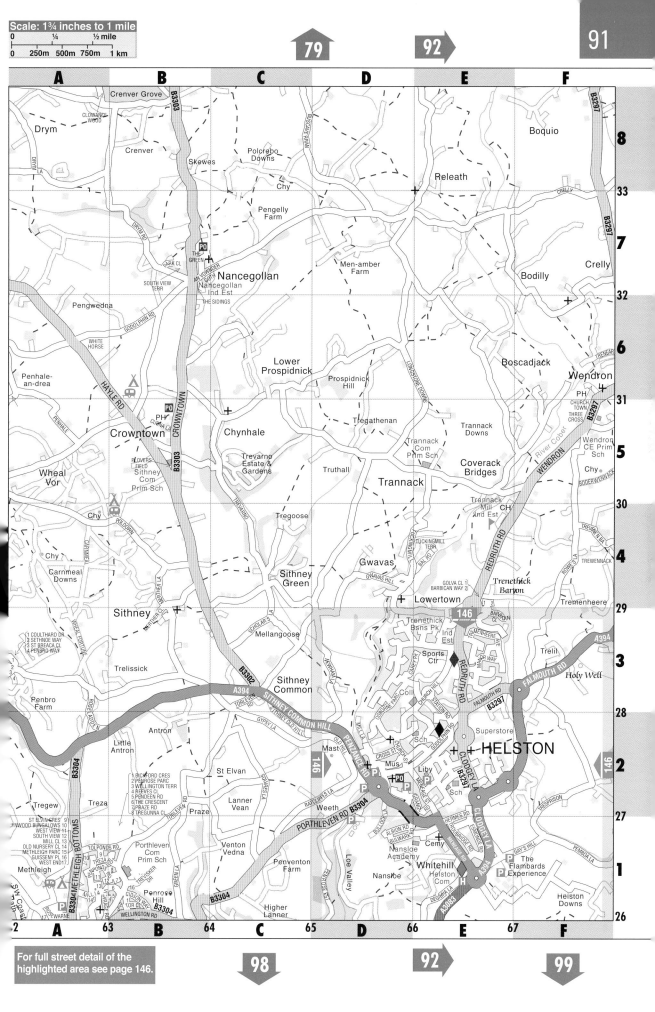

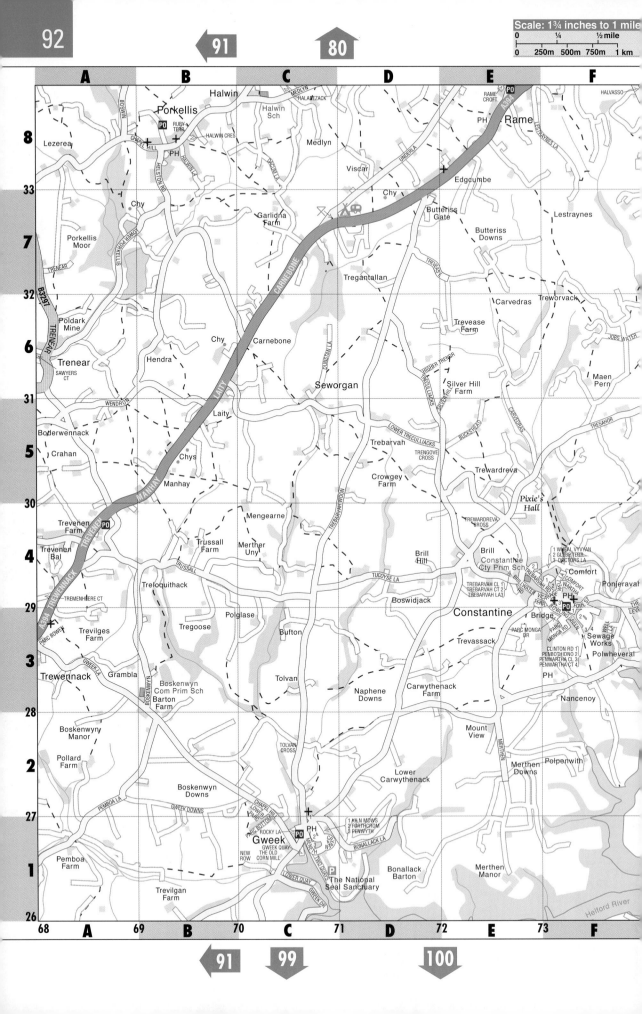

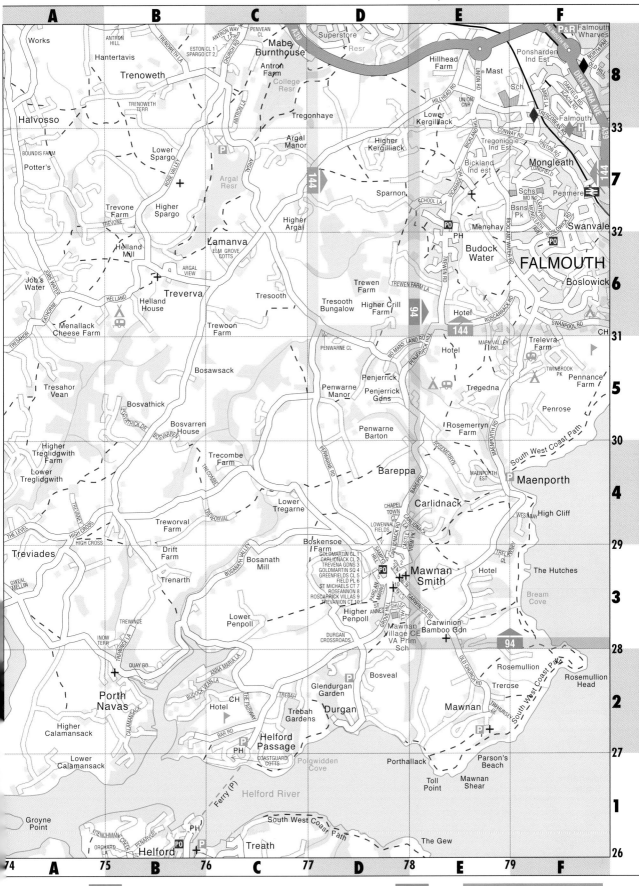

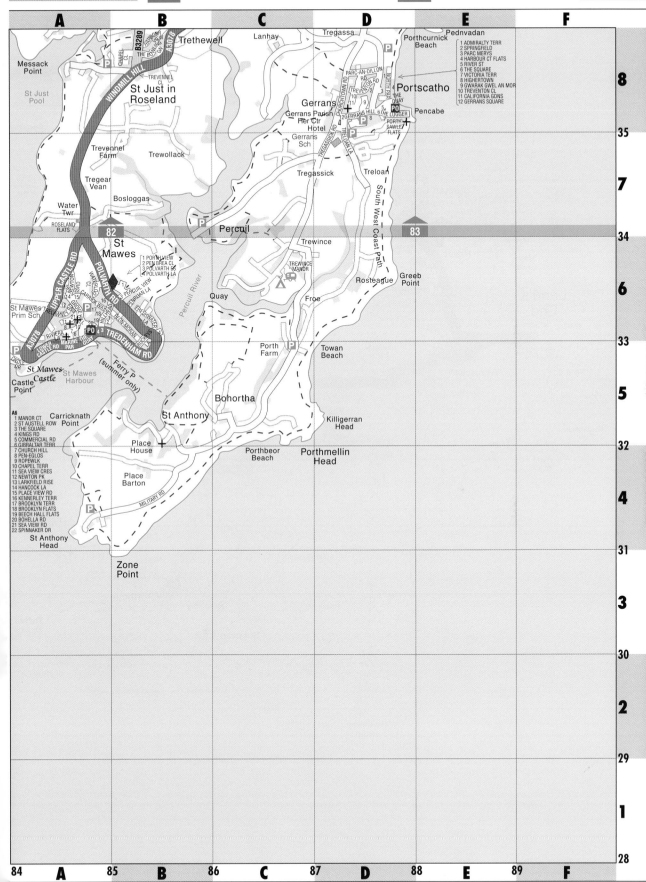

Scale: 1¾ inches to 1 mile

0   ¼   ½ mile
0   250m 500m 750m 1 km

82 ↑   **83** ↑

Messack Point

St Just Pool

B3289

Trethewell

WINDMILL HILL

CHIRGWIN RD
THE BOW LING GN
A3078
CHAPEL CL
TREVENNEL CL

St Just in Roseland

Lanhay

Tregassa

Porthcurnick Beach

Pednvadan

Portscatho

1 ADMIRALTY TERR
2 SPRINGFIELD
3 PARC MERYS
4 HARBOUR CT FLATS
5 RIVER ST
6 THE SQUARE
7 VICTORIA TERR
8 HIGHERTOWN
9 GWARAK GWEL AN MOR
10 TREVENTON CL
11 CALIFORNIA GDNS
12 GERRANS SQUARE

Trevennel Farm

Trewollack

Gerrans

Gerrans Parish Her Ctr Hotel

Gerrans Sch

PARC-AN-DILLON RD

CHURCHTOWN RD

LION CL

TREVES RD

NORTH PARR

THE QUAY

GERRANS HILL

PORTH SAWLES FLATS

Pencabe

Tregear Vean

Bosloggas

Tregassick

TRELOAN LA

Treloan

Water Twr

ROSELAND FLATS

82 ↑

Percuil

South West Coast Path

83 ↑

St Mawes

UPPER CASTLE RD

POLVARTH RD

1 PORTH VIEW
2 PEN BREA CL
3 POLVARTH RD
4 POLVARTH LA

Trewince

Greeb Point

A3078

WATERLOO

TREWITHAN GROVE

GREEN LA

PENDOWER RD

CARRICK WAY

PERCUIL VIEW

FRESHWATER LA

PENTEAN

FERRIS

TREDENHAM RD

RIVIERA

MARINE PAR

LOWER CASTLE RD

PO

TREWINCE MANOR

Quay

Froe

Rosteague

St Mawes Prim Sch

P

Percuil River

St Mawes Castle

Castle Point

CASTLE DR

St Mawes Harbour

Ferry P (summer only)

Carricknath Point

A6
1 MANOR CT
2 ST AUSTELL ROW
3 THE SQUARE
4 KINGS RD
5 COMMERCIAL RD
6 GIBRALTAR TERR
7 CHURCH HILL
8 PEN-EGLOS
9 ROPEWLK
10 CHAPEL TERR
11 SEA VIEW CRES
12 NEWTON PK
13 LARKFIELD RISE
14 HANCOCK LA
15 PLACE VIEW RD
16 KENNERLEY TERR
17 BROOKLYN TERR
18 BROOKLYN FLATS
19 BEECH HALL FLATS
20 BOHELLA RD
21 SEA VIEW RD
22 SPINNAKER DR

St Anthony

Bohortha

Porth Farm

P

Towan Beach

Killigerran Head

Place House

Porthbeor Beach

Porthmellin Head

Place Barton

MILITARY RD

P

St Anthony Head

Zone Point

84   A   85   B   86   C   87   D   88   E   89   F

8
35
7
34
6
33
5
32
4
31
3
30
2
29
1
28

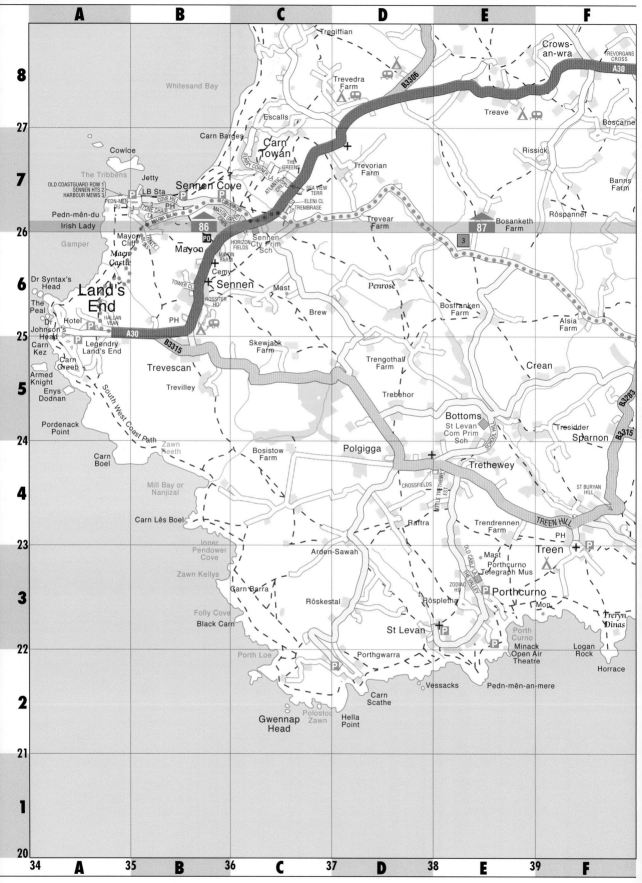

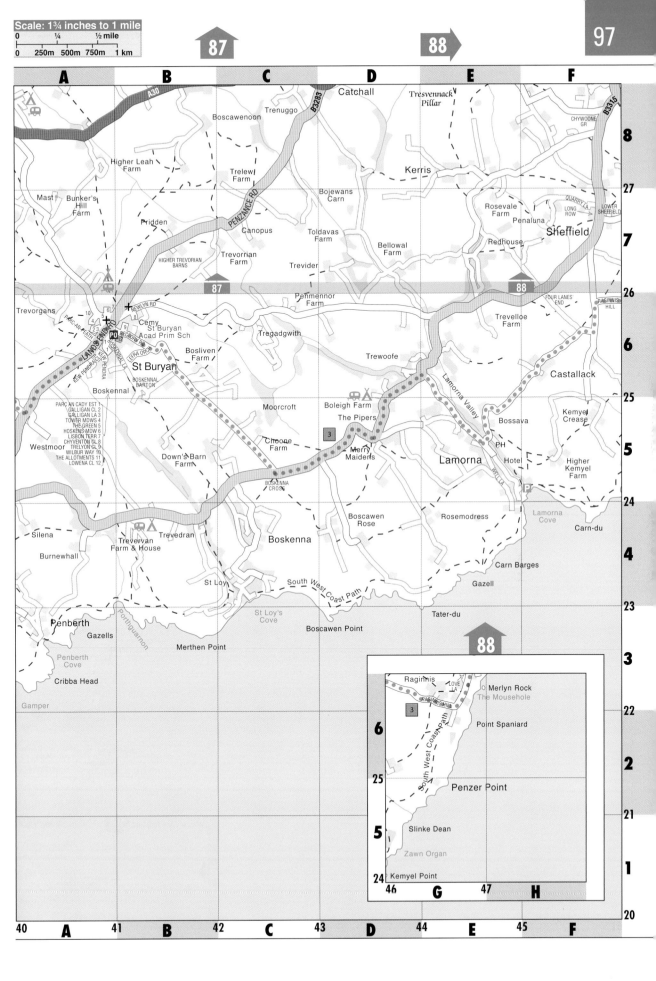

For full street detail of the
highlighted area see page 146.

Scale: 1¾ inches to 1 mile

0   ¼   ½ mile

0   250m 500m 750m 1 km

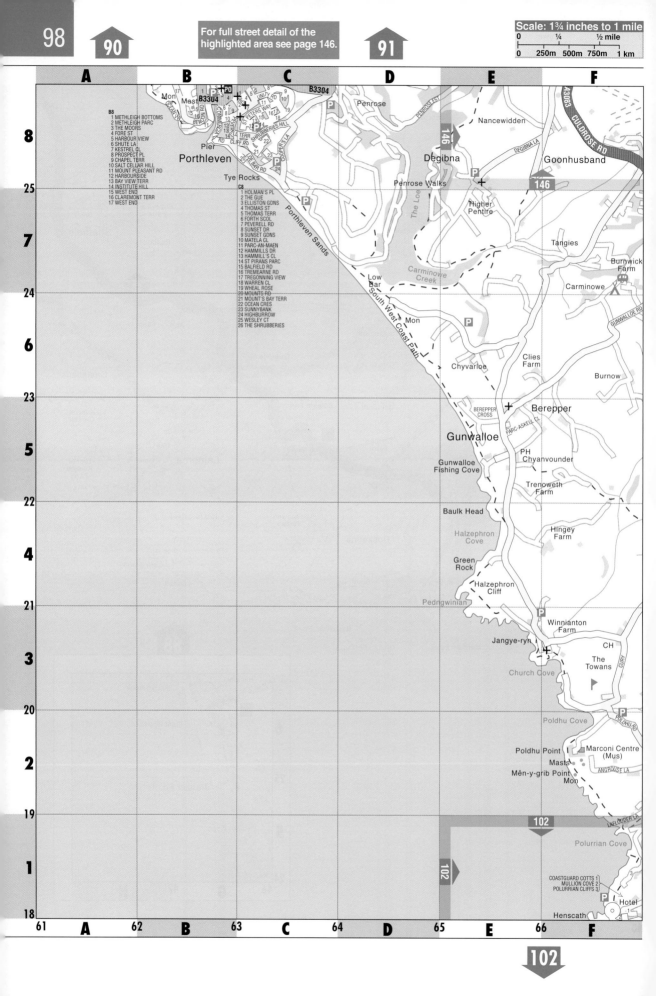

A   B   C   D   E   F

B8
1 METHLEIGH BOTTOMS
2 METHLEIGH PARC
3 THE MOORS
4 FORE ST
5 HARBOUR VIEW
6 SHUTE LA
7 KESTREL CL
8 PROSPECT PL
9 CHAPEL TERR
10 SALT CELLAR HILL
11 MOUNT PLEASANT RD
12 HARBOURSIDE
13 BAY VIEW TERR
14 INSTITUTE HILL
15 WEST END
16 CLAREMONT TERR
17 WEST END

C8
1 HOLMAN'S PL
2 THE GUE
3 ELLISTON GDNS
4 THOMAS ST
5 THOMAS TERR
6 FORTH SCOL
7 PEVERELL RD
8 SUNSET DR
9 SUNSET GDNS
10 MATELA CL
11 PARC-AN-MAEN
12 HAMMILLS DR
13 HAMMILL'S CL
14 ST PIRANS PARC
15 BALFIELD RD
16 TREMEARNE RD
17 TREGONNING VIEW
18 WARREN CL
19 WHEAL ROSE
20 MOUNTS RD
21 MOUNT'S BAY TERR
22 OCEAN CRES
23 SUNNYBANK
24 HIGHBURROW
25 WESLEY CT
26 THE SHRUBBERIES

Mon
Mast
B3304
B3304
B3304

Pier
Porthleven

Tye Rocks

Porthleven Sands

South West Coast Path

Low
Bar

Mon

Penrose

Penrose Walks

The Loe

Carminowe Creek

Degibna

146

Goonhusband

146

Nancewidden

Higher
Pentire

Tangies

Burnwick
Farm

Carminowe

Chyvarloe

Clies
Farm

Burnow

Berepper
Cross

Berepper

PARC-ASKELL CL

Gunwalloe

Gunwalloe
Fishing Cove

PH Chyanvounder

Trenoweth
Farm

Baulk Head

Halzephron
Cove

Hingey
Farm

Green
Rock

Halzephron
Cliff

Pedngwinian

Winnianton
Farm

Jangye-ryn

Church Cove

CH

The
Towans

CURY

Poldhu Cove

POLDHU RD

Poldhu Point

Marconi Centre
(Mus)

Masts

Mên-y-grib Point

ANGROUSE LA

Mon

102

LAFLOUDEN LA

Polurrian Cove

102

COASTGUARD COTTS 1
MULLION COVE 2
POLURRIAN CLIFFS 3

Hotel

Henscath

A   B   C   D   E   F

61   62   63   64   65   66

CULDROSE RD

A3083

GUNWALLOE RD

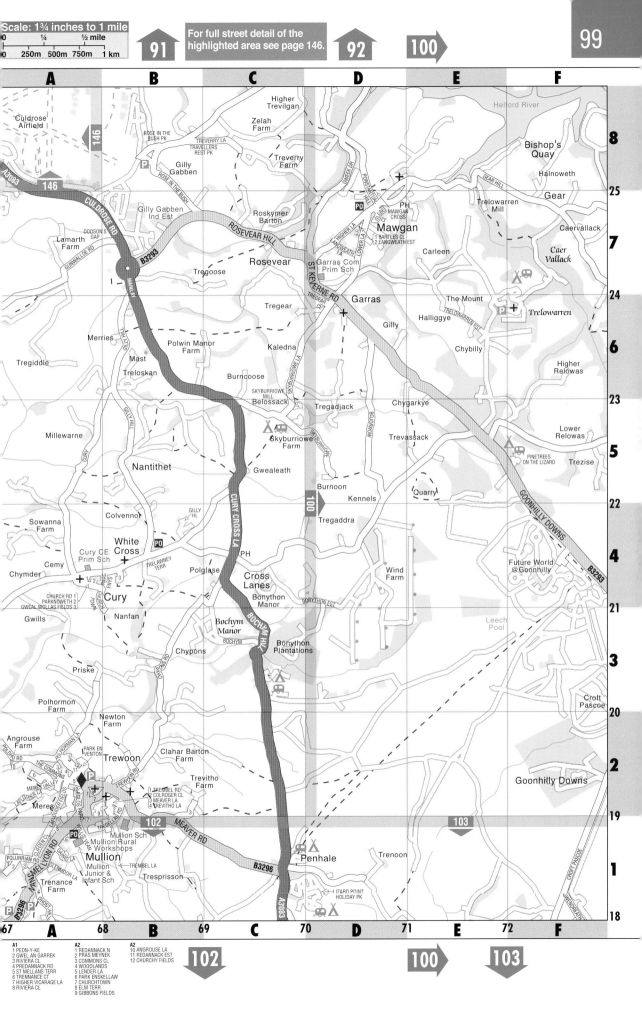

Scale: 1¾ inches to 1 mile

0   ¼   ½ mile
0   250m 500m 750m 1 km

91

For full street detail of the highlighted area see page 146.

92

100

99

A   B   C   D   E   F

Helford River

Culdrose
Airfield

146

A3083

146

CULDROSE RD

B3293

Higher
Trevilgan

Zelah
Farm

ROSE IN THE
BUSH PK

TREVERRY LA
TRAVELLERS
REST PK

Treverry
Farm

Gilly
Gabben

ROSE IN THE BUSH

Roskymer
Barton

Bishop's
Quay

Halnoweth

GEAR HILL

Gear

25

Trelowarren
Mill

Caervallack

Mawgan
MAWGAN
CROSS

Caer
Vallack

7

Lamarth
Farm

GUNWALLOE RD

DODSON'S
GAP

Gilly Gabben
Ind Est

ROSEVEAR HILL

Rosevear

ST KEVERNE RD

HIGHER LA
LANGWEATH LA
LOWER LA
GWEEK DR
POINSATIA HILL
GILBE

PH
PO

1 BARTLES CL
2 LANGWEATH EST

Garras Com
Prim Sch

GARRAS CT

Carleen

The Mount

Halliggye

Trelowarren

24

TRELOWARREN EST

PO

Merries

MARLIN

Tregoose

Tregear

TREGEAR

Garras

Gilly

Chybilly

Higher
Relowas

6

Tregiddle

TIM'S HO

Mast
Treloskan

Polwin Manor
Farm

Kaledna

Burncoose

SKYBURRIOWE LA

Tregadjack

Chygarkye

BALOROW

Trevassack

Lower
Relowas

23

SKYBURRIOWE
MILL

Belossack

Skyburriowe
Farm

SKYBURRIOWE

Pinetrees
on the Lizard

Trezise

5

GILLY HILL
CURY

Millewarne

Nantithet

Gwealeath

Burnoon

Kennels

Quarry

GOONHILLY DOWNS

22

Sowanna
Farm

Colvennor

GILLY
HL

PO

100

Tregaddra

Wind
Farm

Future World
@Goonhilly

B3293

4

CURY CROSS LA

White
Cross

TRELAWNEY
TERR

PH

Polglase

Cross
Lanes

Bonython
Manor

BONYTHON EST

Cemy

Chymder

CHURCH RD 1
PARKNOWETH 2
GWEAL WOLLAS FIELDS 3

Cury CE
Prim Sch

CHURCH TOWN

1 2

Cury

Nanfan

Bochym
Manor

BOCHYM

Bonython
Plantations

Leech
Pool

Croft
Pascoe

21

20

Gwills

Priske

CHYPONS RD

Chypons

BOCHYM HILL

3

Polhormon
Farm

Newton
Farm

Clahar Barton
Farm

Trevitho
Farm

Goonhilly Downs

2

Angrouse
Farm

POLDHU RD
POLHORMAN LA
THE COMMONS

PO

Trewoon

TREWOON RD

1 TREMBEL RD
2 COLROGER CL
3 MEAVER LA
4 TREVITHO LA

Meres
Valley

LAS LOWEN
MERES VALLEY
LANDLOWER FIELDS

Meres

EGLOS PARK
TREGELLESTA RD
CHURCH TOWN

19

102

MEAVER RD

103

POLURRIAN RD
NANSMELLYON RD
CLIFDEN CL
GLENMADOR LA
GHOST HILL

PO

Mullion Sch

Mullion Rural
Workshops

Mullion

Mullion
Junior &
Infant Sch

TREMBEL LA

Tresprisson

B3296

Penhale

Trenoon

1

P
P

B3296

Trenance
Farm

A3083

HARD POINT
HOLIDAY PK

18

A1
1 PEDN-Y-KE
2 GWEL AN GARREK
3 RIVIERA CL
4 PREDANNACK RD
5 ST MELLANS TERR
6 TRENNANCE CT
7 HIGHER VICARAGE LA
8 RIVIERA CL

A2
1 REDANNACK N
2 PRAS MEYNEK
3 COMMONS CL
4 WOODLANDS
5 LENDER LA
6 PARK ENSKELLAW
7 CHURCHTOWN
8 ELM TERR
9 GIBBONS FIELDS

A2
10 ANGROUSE LA
11 REDANNACK EST
12 CHURCHY FIELDS

Scale: 1¾ inches to 1 mile

0   ¼   ½ mile

0 250m 500m 750m 1 km

A **B** **C** **D** **E** **F**

Helford River

8

Bishop's
Quay

Tremayne   Trevedor   Kestle

ORCHARD
LA

25

Halnoweth

GEAR HILL

Gear

Mudgeon
Farm

Frenchman's
Pill

HIGH LA

Mudgeon
Vean

Withan

Tregithew

MAWGAN
CROSS

PO

Trelowarren
Mill

MUDGEON

Tregonwell

7

PH

Mawgan

1 BARTLES CL
2 LANGWEATH EST

Carleen

Caer
Vallack

Caervallack

FORDS HILL

Landrivick

Choon

Garras Com
Prim Sch

TRELOWARREN EST

24

ST KEVERNE RD

Garras

The Mount

Trelowarren

1 PORK ST
2 THE GREEN
3 BOSKERNOW
4 ST MARTINS GREEN

Tregevis
Farm

Trevaddra

Gilly

Halliggye

P

St Martin-
in-Meneage
Com Prim Sch

MOOR PARC

GREEN HILL

GREEN HILL

Higher
Trenower

6

Chybilly

St Martin

Higher
Relowas

PH

Newtown-
in-St Martin

TREWORGIE LA

23

Tregadjack

Chygarkye

Trethewey

NEWTOWN

Tregidden

TREGIDDEN HILL

BODRROW

Trevassack

Lower
Relowas

Tretharrup

Trewoon

POLKANUGGA

5

SKYBURRIOWE

PINETREES
ON THE LIZARD

Trezise

Trewince

Trelaminney

Tregeague

TREGIDDEN

Burnoon

Kennels

Quarry

Polkerth

Trelease
Mill

22

Tregaddra

Trenithon

GOONHILLY DOWNS

66

4

CURY CROSS LA

Wind
Farm

Future World
@Goonhilly

Traboe

BONYTHON EST

21

Leech
Pool

Rosuick

Grugwith

3

P

TRABOE
CROSS

Croft
Pascoe

Roscrowgey

Roskilly

B3293

Kernewas

20

Croft Pascoe
Pool

2

CROFT PASCOE

Goonhilly Downs

Trelanvean

The Lizard
Nature Reserve

19

102

103

Trelan

Trenoon

GWENDREATH

1

LIZARD POINT
HOLIDAY PK

The Lizard
Nature Reserve

PONSONGATH

18

70   71   72   73   74   75

A **B** **C** **D** **E** **F**

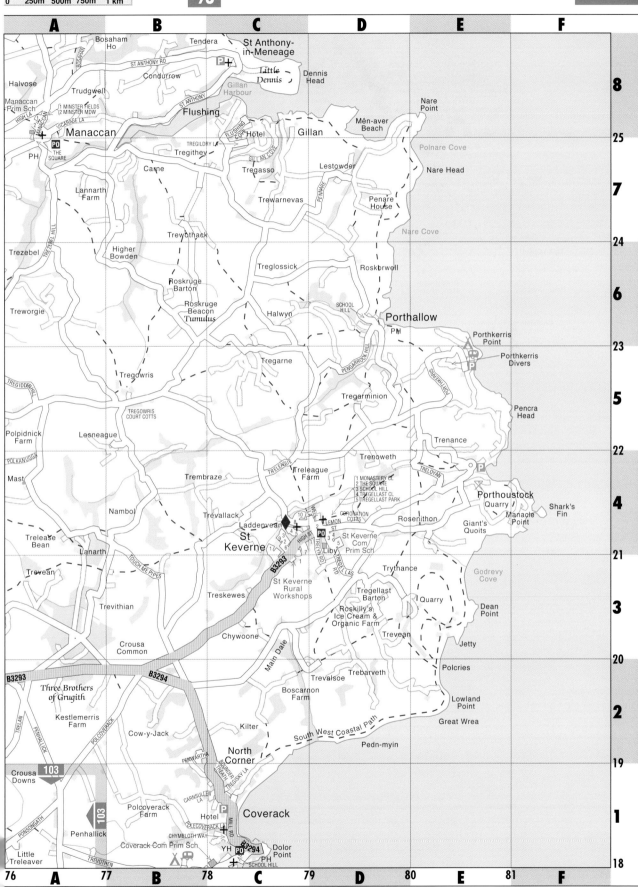

A   B   C   D   E   F

8

Bosaham Ho

Tendera

St Anthony-in-Meneage

Halvose

Condurrow

ST ANTHONY RD

Little Dennis

Dennis Head

Gillan Harbour

Trudgwell

Manaccan Prim Sch

1 MINSTER FIELDS
2 MINSTER MDW

ST ANTHONY

25

Flushing

Hotel

Gillan

Mên-aver Beach

Nare Point

Manaccan

VICARAGE LA

PO

THE SQUARE

Tregildry La

Tregithey

FLUSHING COVE

GILLAN COVE

Polnare Cove

PH

Came

Tregasso

Lestowder

Nare Head

7

Lannarth Farm

Trewarnevas

PENARE

Penare House

Trezebel

Trewothack

Higher Bowden

Treglossick

Roskorwell

Nare Cove

24

Roskruge Barton

SCHOOL HILL

Porthallow

Porthkerris Point

6

Treworgie

Roskruge Beacon Tumulus

Halwyn

PH

PENGARROCK HILL

23

Tregowris

Tregarne

Porthkerris Divers

5

Polpidnick Farm

Lesneague

Tregowris Court Cotts

Tregarminion

POLTHERRIS

Pencra Head

Mast

Trembraze

TRELEAGUE

Treleague Farm

Trenoweth

Trenance

22

POLKANUGGA

1 MONASTERY CL
2 THE SQUARE
3 SCHOOL HILL
4 TREGELLAST CL
5 TREGELLAST PARK

TRELOYAN

P

Porthoustock

Quarry

Shark's Fin

4

Nambol

Trevallack

CORONATION COTTS

Rosenithon

Manacle Point

Trelease Bean

Laddenvean

St Keverne

HIGH ST

PO

Liby

St Keverne Com Prim Sch

Giant's Quoits

21

Lanarth

TOUCH ME PIPES

B3293

TREGEL LAS

Trythance

Godrevy Cove

Trevean

St Keverne Rural Workshops

Tregellast Barton

I Quarry

Dean Point

3

Trevithian

Treskewes

Roskilly's Ice Cream & Organic Farm

Trevean

Chywoone

MAIN DALE

Jetty

Crousa Common

20

B3293

B3294

Trevalsoe

Trebarveth

Polcries

2

Three Brothers of Grugith

Boscarnon Farm

Lowland Point

Kestlemerris Farm

Cow-y-Jack

Kilter

Great Wrea

TRELAN

PENHALLICK

POLCOVERACK

PENWARTHA

North Corner

Pedn-myin

South West Coastal Path

19

103

Crousa Downs

BLUNDER TREATH

TREGISKY LA

CARNSULLEN LA

Polcoverack Farm

Hotel

P

Coverack

1

103

Penhallick

CHYMBLOTH WAY

MILL RD

PLECOVERACK LA

Little Treleaver

TREVOTHEN

Coverack Com Prim Sch

YH

PO

B3294

Dolor Point

PH

SCHOOL HILL

18

76   A   77   B   78   C   79   D   80   E   81   F

C4
1 TRESKEWES EST
2 TREVALLACK VIEW
3 TREVALLACK PARC
4 LANHEVERNE PARC
5 DOCTORS HILL
6 POLVENTON PARC
7 PENMENNER EST
8 COMMERCIAL RD
9 TREVALLACK CL

C4
10 TREGONNING PARC

C3
1 Treskewes Ind Est

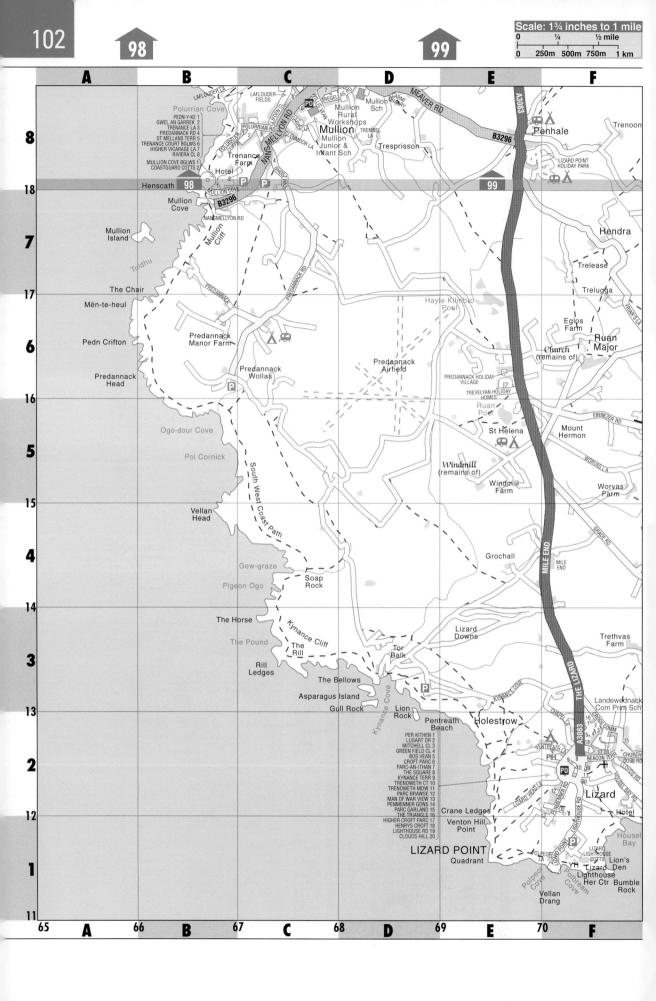

Scale: 1¾ inches to 1 mile

0   ¼   ½ mile

0   250m   500m   750m   1 km

A   B   C   D   E   F

8

LAFLOUDER LA
LAFLOUDER
FIELDS
Polurrian Cove
TREGELLAS RD
Mullion Sch
MEAVER RD
Trenoon
PO
PEDN-Y-KE 1
GWEL AN GARREK 2
TRENANCE LA 3
PREDANNACK RD 4
ST MELLANS TERR 5
TRENANCE COURT BGLWS 6
HIGHER VICARAGE LA 7
RIVIERA CL 8
Mullion
Rural
Workshops
CARNE QUARRY
B3296
Penhale
Mullion
MULLION COVE BGLWS 1
COASTGUARD COTTS 2
Trenance
Farm
Mullion
Junior &
Infant Sch
TREMBEL LA
Trespisson
LIZARD POINT
HOLIDAY PARK

18   Henscath **98**   Hotel   P   P

B3296

Mullion
Cove

NANSMELLYON RD

99

Hendra

7   Mullion
Island

Mullion
Cliff

17   The Chair   PREDANNACK

Trelease

Mên-te-heul

Hayle Kilmbro
Pool

Trelugga

6   Pedn Crifton   Predannack
Manor Farm

Eglos
Farm

Ruan
Major

PREDANNACK RD

Predannack
Wollas

Predannack
Airfield

Church
(remains of)

Predannack
Head

PREDANNACK HOLIDAY
VILLAGE

16   P

TREVELYAN HOLIDAY
HOMES

Ruan
Pool

EBENEZER RD

Ogo-dour Cove

St Helena

Mount
Hermon

5   Pol Cornick

Windmill
(remains of)

WORVAS LA

15   Vellan
Head

South West Coast Path

Windmill
Farm

Worvas
Farm

GRADE RD

4   Gew-graze

Soap
Rock

Grochall

MILE END

MILE
END

Pigeon Ogo

14

The Horse

Kynance Cliff

Lizard
Downs

Trethvas
Farm

3   The Pound

The
Rill

Tor
Balk

THE LIZARD

Rill
Ledges

The Bellows

P

Landewednack
Com Prim Sch

13

Asparagus Island

Gull Rock

Lion
Rock

Kynance Cove

Pentreath
Beach

Holestrow

KYNANCE COVE

CHAPEL LA

A3083

CROSS COMM

CHURCH
COVE RD

PER KITHEN 1
LUSART DR 2
MITCHELL CL 3
GREEN FIELD CL 4
BOS VEAN 5
CROFT PARC 6
PARC-AN-ITHAN 7
THE SQUARE 8
KYNANCE TERR 9
TRENOWETH CT 10
TRENOWETH MDW 11
PARC BRAWSE 12
MAN OF WAR VIEW 13
PENMENNER GDNS 14
PARC GARLAND 15
THE TRIANGLE 16
HIGHER CROFT PARC 17
HENRYS CROFT 18
LIGHTHOUSE RD 19
CLOUDS HILL 20

PENTREATH LA
PH
BEACON TERR

2   PO

Lizard

Hotel

LIZARD HEAD LA

Crane Ledges

Venton Hill
Point

PENMENNER RD

Housel
Bay

12

P

LIZARD
COTTS

Lion's
Tizard
Den

1   LIZARD POINT
Quadrant

POLPEOR LA

Polpeor
Cove

Polbream
Cove

YH   Lighthouse
Her Ctr   Bumble
Rock

LIGHTHOUSE RD

Vellan
Drang

11

65   **A**   66   **B**   67   **C**   68   **D**   69   **E**   70   **F**

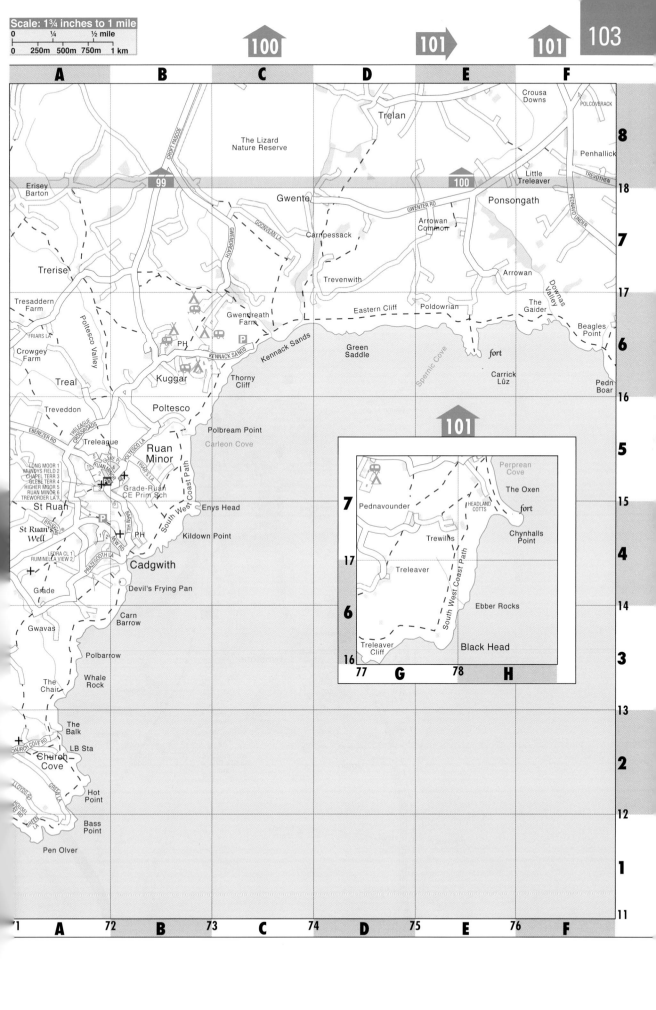

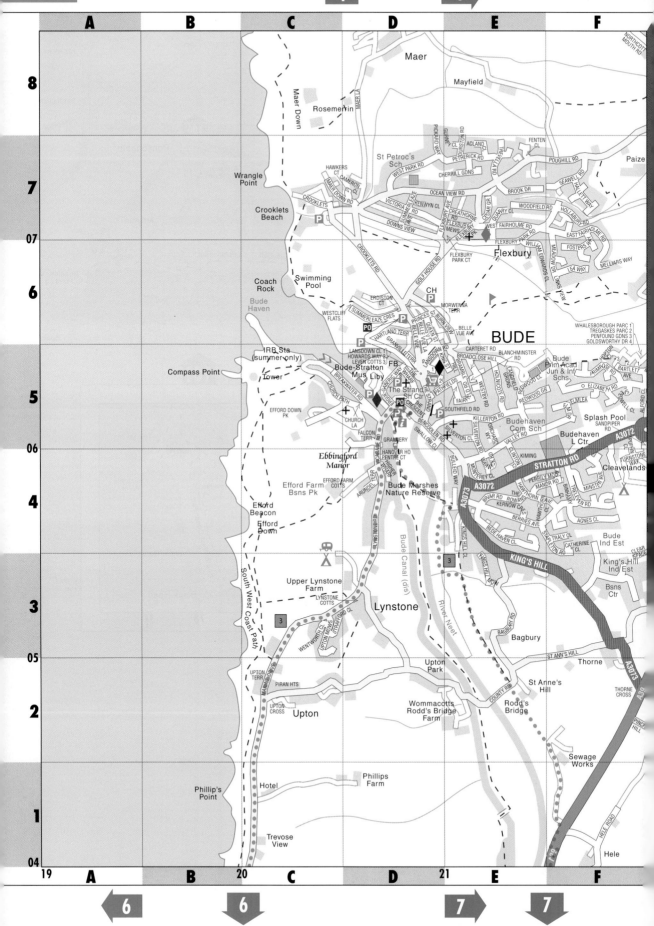

Maer

Mayfield

Rosemerrin

Maer Down

Wrangle Point

Crooklets Beach

Coach Rock

Bude Haven

St Petroc's Sch

HAWKERS CT

WEST PARK RD

CHERILL GDNS

PICKFORD WAY

GURNEY

ACLAND

PETHERICK RD

TREVELLA RD

FENTEN CL

POUGHILL RD

SEAWEL WAY

HALLETT WAY

PAIZE

OCEAN VIEW RD

BROOK DR

WOODFIELD RD

HOLLABURY RD

EAST FAIRHOLME RD

MELLIARS WAY

Flexbury

FLEXBURY PARK RD

FLEXBURY PARK CT

CH

MORWENNA TERR

BELLE VUE AVE

BUDE

WHALESBOROUGH PARC 1
TREGASKES PARC 2
PENFOUND GDNS 3
GOLDSWORTHY DR 4

CARTERET RD

BLANCHMINSTER RD

Bude Prim Acad Jun & Inf Schs

IRB Sta (summer only)

Tower

Compass Point

Bude-Stratton Mus

Liby

The Strand Sh Ctr

Budehaven Com Sch

Budehaven L Ctr

Splash Pool

SANDPIPER

Cleavelands

STRATTON RD

A3072

Ebbingford Manor

Efford Farm Bsns Pk

EFFORD DOWN PK

CHURCH LA

FALCON TERR

GRANARY

HANOVER HO

PENTRE CT

Bude Marshes Nature Reserve

Efford Beacon

Efford Down

Bude Canal (dis)

River Neet

Bude Ind Est

King's Hill Ind Est

KING'S HILL

Bsns Ctr

CLEAR SPACE

South West Coast Path

Upper Lynstone Farm

LYNSTONE COTTS

Lynstone

Bagbury

Thorne

ST ANN'S HILL

St Anne's Hill

THORNE CROSS

Upton Park

Wommacotts Rodd's Bridge Farm

Rodd's Bridge

Sewage Works

Upton

UPTON TERR

PIRAN HTS

UPTON CROSS

Phillip's Point

Hotel

Phillips Farm

Trevose View

Hele

HELE ROAD

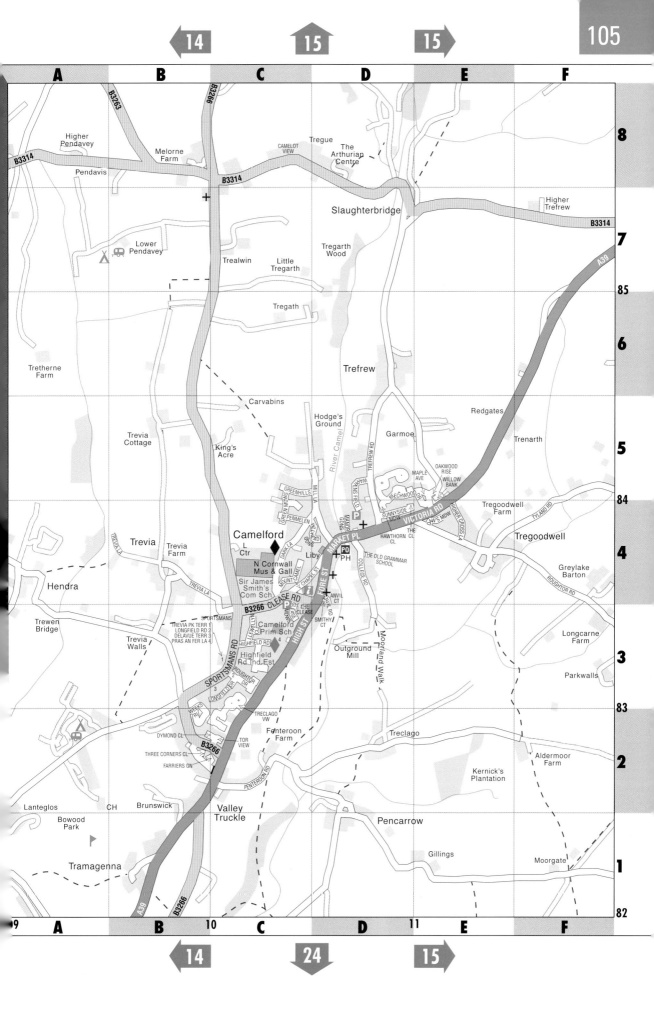

A B C D E F

8
7
85
6
5
84
4
3
83
2
1
82

Higher Pendavey
Melorne Farm
Pendavis
Tregue
Camelot View
The Arthurian Centre
Higher Trefrew
B3314
B3314
B3263
B3266
Slaughterbridge
A39

Trealwin
Little Tregarth
Tregarth Wood
Lower Pendavey
Tregath

Tretherne Farm
Trefrew
Redgates
Trenarth

Carvabins
Trevia Cottage
King's Acre
Hodge's Ground
Garmoe
Oakwood Rise
Willow Bank
Maple Ave
Beechwood
Tregoodwell Farm
Tyland Rd
River Camel

Trevia
Trevia Farm
Camelford
L Ctr
N Cornwall Mus & Gall
Sir James Smith's Com Sch
Greenhills
Penmelen
Green Mdws
Mill La
Village Rd
Manor Gdns
Trefrew Rd
Wadfield Rd
Sunnyside
MDW
The CL
Victoria Rd
Hawthorn CL
Higher Cross La
Oakwood Rise
Mdw's Mdw
Tregoodwell
Greylake Barton
Roughtor Rd

Hendra
Trevia La
Liby
Market Pl
PO
PH
The Old Grammar School
College Rd

Trewen Bridge
Trevia Walls
Sportsmans
Trevia Pk Terr 1
Longfield Rd 2
Delavue Terr 3
Pras An Fer La 4
Camelford Prim Sch
Highfield Rd
Highfield Rd Ind Est
Longfielder Dr
Roughtor Dr
Sportsmans Rd
B3266 Cleasé Rd
Fore St
High St
Anvil Ct
Smithy Ct
The Cleasé
Outground Mill
Moorland Walk
Longcarne Farm
Parkwalls

Weeks Rí
Dymond Cl
Three Corners Cl
Farriers Gn
Tor View
Treclago VW
Fenteroon Farm
Treclago
Kernick's Plantation
Aldermoor Farm

Lanteglos
CH
Brunswick
Valley Truckle
Pencarrow
Gillings
Moorgate

Bowood Park
Tramagenna
B3266
A39
Penteroon Rd

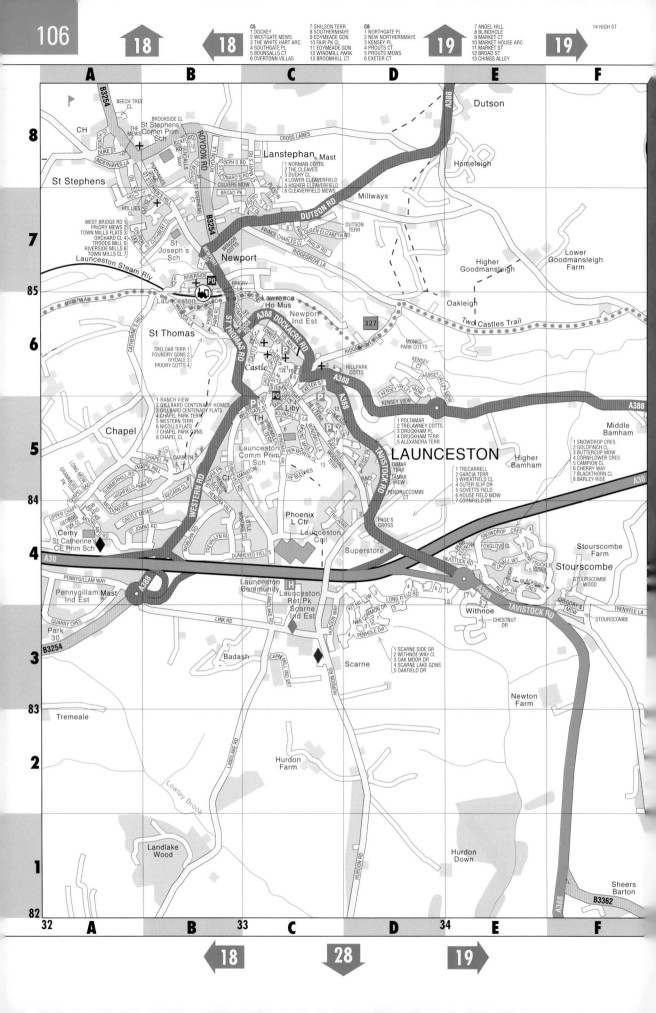

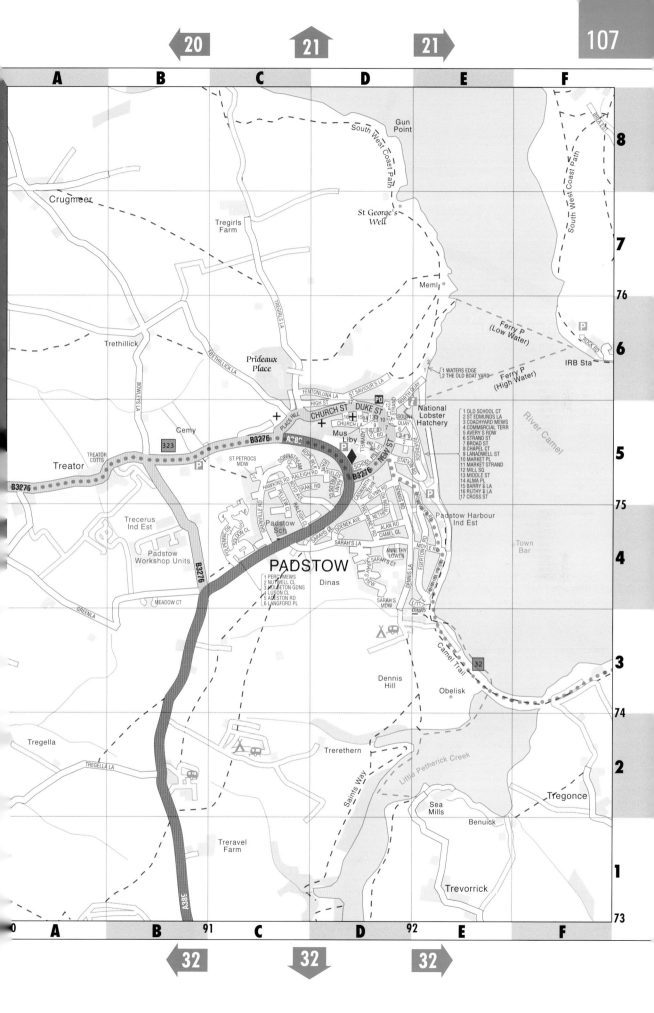

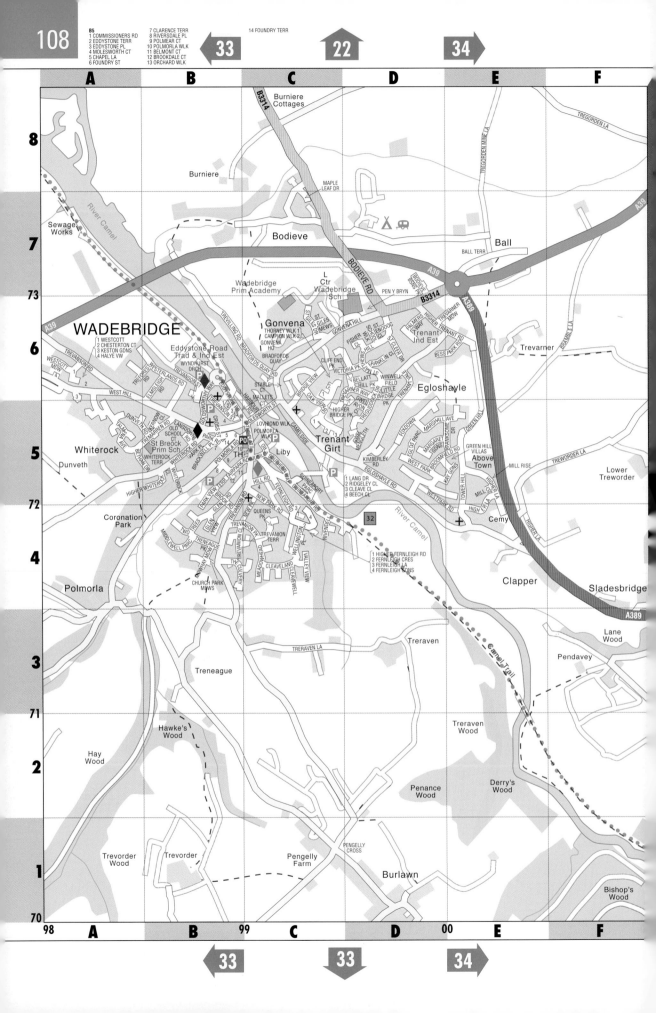

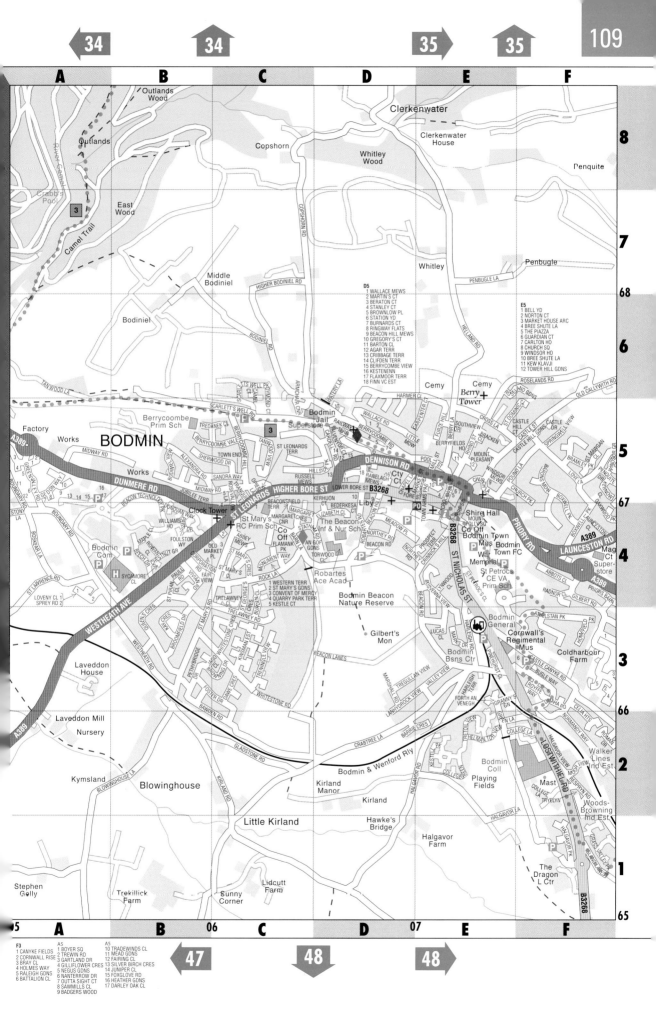

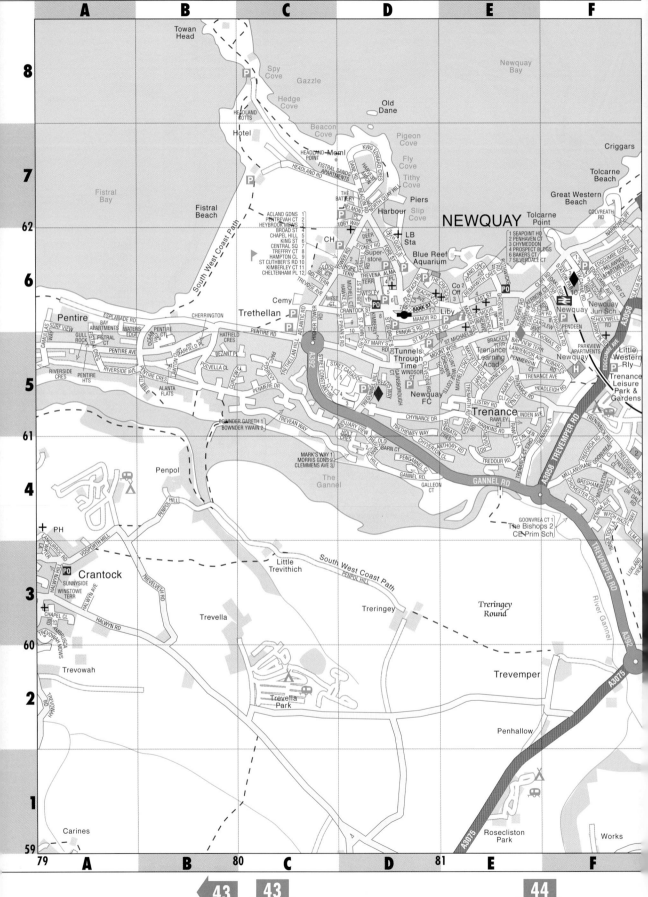

43
43
44

D5
1 CAERNARVON LODGE
2 ST MARY'S CT
3 BOWNDER SARRAS
4 BOWNDER MARHAUS
5 BOWNDER CORBENIC

F6
1 TREVANION CT
2 WESTCOVE HO
3 STATION APP
4 ALBANY CT
5 ALBANY RD
6 IVANHOE

7 TOLCARNE MEWS
8 MORRAB CT
9 PERGOLLA CT
10 Newquay
Adult Ed Ctr

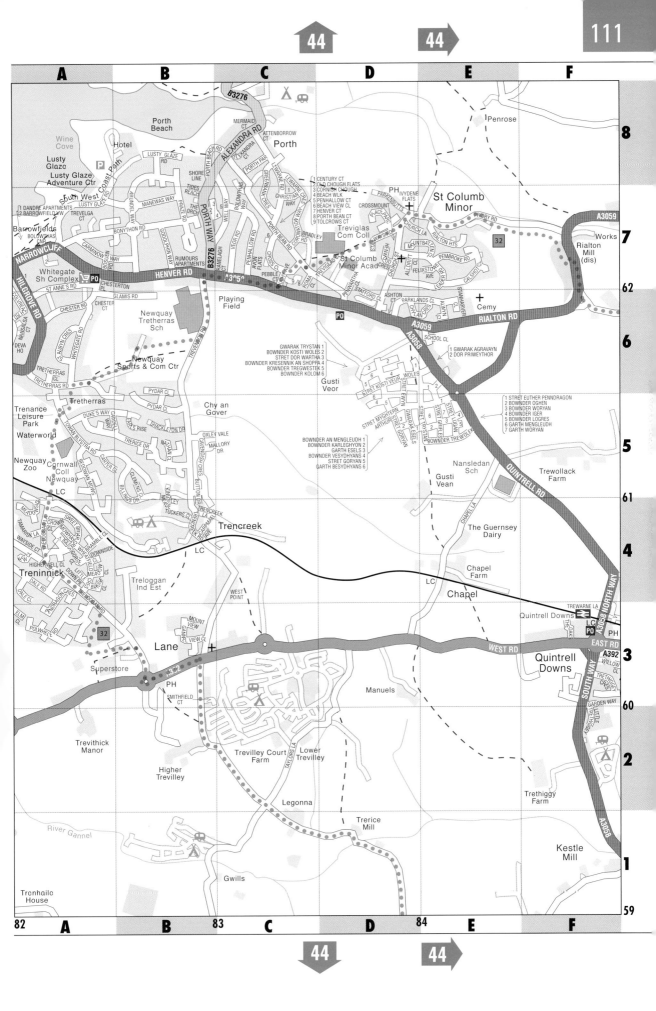

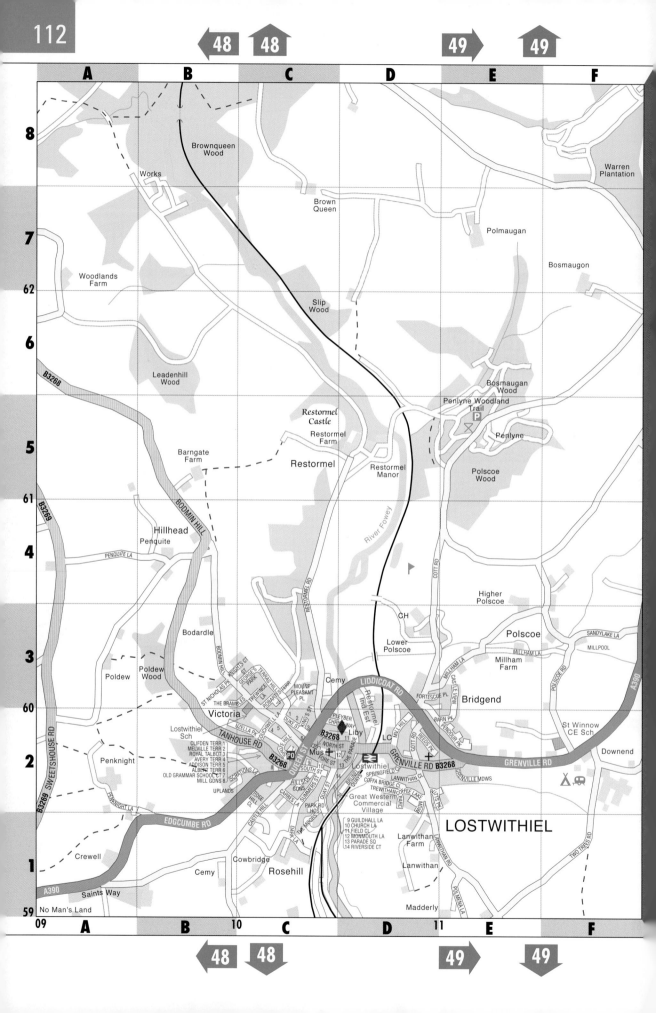

A   B   C   D   E   F

8

7

62

6

5

61

4

3

60

2

1

59

09   A   10   B   C   11   D   E   F

Brownqueen Wood

Works

Brown Queen

Warren Plantation

Polmaugan

Bosmaugon

Woodlands Farm

Slip Wood

Leadenhill Wood

Bosmaugan Wood

Penlyne Woodland Trail

B3268

Restormel Castle

Restormel Farm

Penlyne

Restormel

Restormel Manor

Polscoe Wood

Barngate Farm

BODMIN HILL

River Fowey

B3269

Hillhead
Penquite

PENQUITE LA

Higher Polscoe

COTT RD

Bodardle

CH

Lower Polscoe

Polscoe

SANDYLAKE LA

MILLHAM LA

MILLPOOL

Poldew

Poldew Wood

RESTORMEL RD

Cemy

LIDDICOAT RD

Bridgend

Millham Farm

POLSCOE RD

A390

KNIGHTS CT
ST GEORGE'S PK

ST NICHOLAS PK

TREVINCE LA

MOUNT PLEASANT PL

CASTLE VIEW

FORTESCUE PL

St Winnow CE Sch

THE BRAMBLES

Victoria

Lostwithiel Sch

TANHOUSE RD

UZELLA PK

SCRATIONS LA

MILL HILL

COUCHWELL LA

DUKE ST

KING'S ST

PLEYBER CHRISTWAY

B3268
NORTH ST

Restormel Ind Est

BARN PK

REEDS CT

Downend

Penknight

CLIFDEN TERR 1
MELVILLE TERR 2
ROYAL TALBOT 3
AVERY TERR 4
ADDISON TERR 5
ALBERT TERR 6
OLD GRAMMAR SCHOOL CT 7
MILL GDNS 8

PO
B3268

Mus
FORE ST
SOUTH ST

Liby

LC

MILL HILL

COTT RD

Lostwithiel

GRENVILLE RD

B3268

GRENVILLE RD

UPLANDS

HILLSIDE GDNS

SUMMER'S ST

CLAY ST

PARK RD
LHOS

LANWITHAN CL

GRENVILLE MDWS

PENKNIGHT LA

EDGCUMBE RD

CASTLE HILL

ROSE HILL

CARBES LA

DARK LA

THE MINORS

Great Western Commercial Village

COFFA BRIDGE CL

TREWITHAN PARC

COFFEE LAKE

BUTTS PK

Lanwithan Farm

LANWITHAN RD

TWO TREES RD

Crewell

Cowbridge

Cemy

Rosehill

9 GUILDHALL LA
10 CHURCH LA
11 FIELD CL
12 MONMOUTH LA
13 PARADE SQ
14 RIVERSIDE CT

LOSTWITHIEL

A390

Saints Way

No Man's Land

Lanwithan

POLMENA LA

Madderly

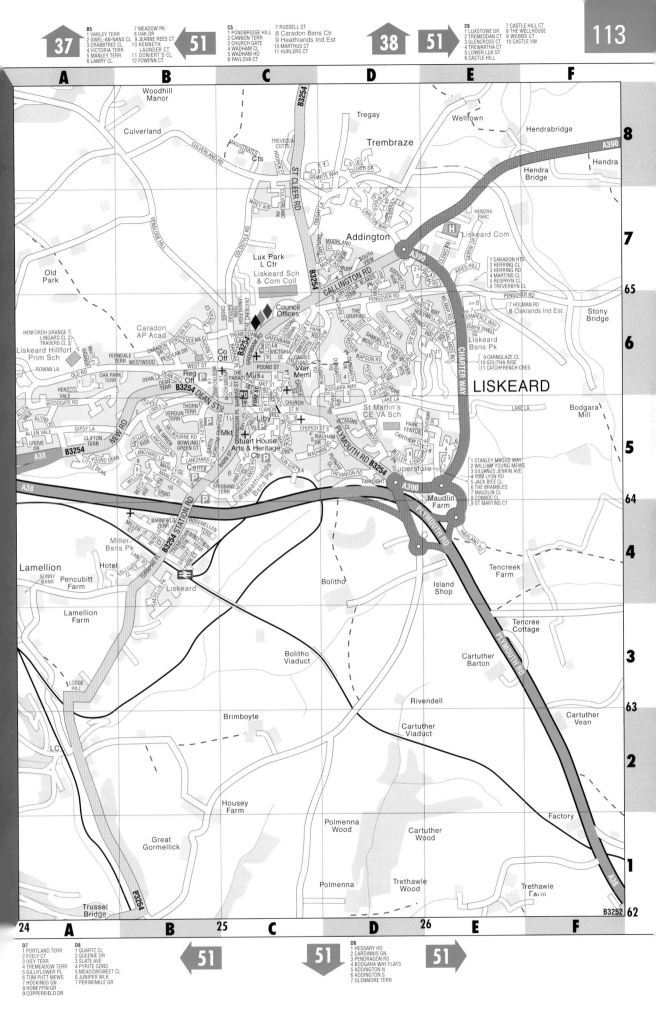

37

B5
1 VARLEY TERR
2 GWEL-AN-NANS CL
3 CRABBTREE CL
4 VICTORIA TERR
5 MANLEY TERR
6 LAWRY CL
7 MEADOW PK
8 OAK DR
9 JEANNE REES CT
10 KENNETH LAUNDER CT
11 DONIERT CL
12 FOWENN CT

51

C5
1 PONDBRIDGE HILL
2 CANNON TERR
3 CHURCH GATE
4 WADHAM CL
5 WADHAM HO
6 PAVLOVA CT
7 RUSSELL ST
8 CARADON BSNS CTR
9 HEATHLANDS IND EST
10 MARTHUS CT
11 HURLERS CT

38

51

C6
1 LUXSTOWE DR
2 TREMEDDAN CT
3 GLENCROSS CT
4 TREWARTHA CT
5 LOWER LUX ST
6 CASTLE HILL
7 CASTLE HILL CT
8 THE WELLHOUSE
9 WEBBS CT
10 CASTLE VW

51

D7
1 PORTLAND TERR
2 EVELY CT
3 IVEY TERR
4 TREMEADOW TERR
5 GILLIFLOWER PL
6 TOM PUTT MEWS
7 HOCKINGS GN
8 HONEYPIN GR
9 COPPERFIELD DR

D8
1 QUARTZ CL
2 QUEENIE DR
3 SLATE AVE
4 PYRITE GDNS
5 MEADOWSWEET CL
6 JUNIPER WLK
7 PERIWINKLE CL

51

D6
1 HESSARY HO
2 CARDINNIS GN
3 PENDRAGON RD
4 BODGARA WAY FLATS
5 ADDINGTON N
6 ADDINGTON S
7 GLENMORE TERR

51

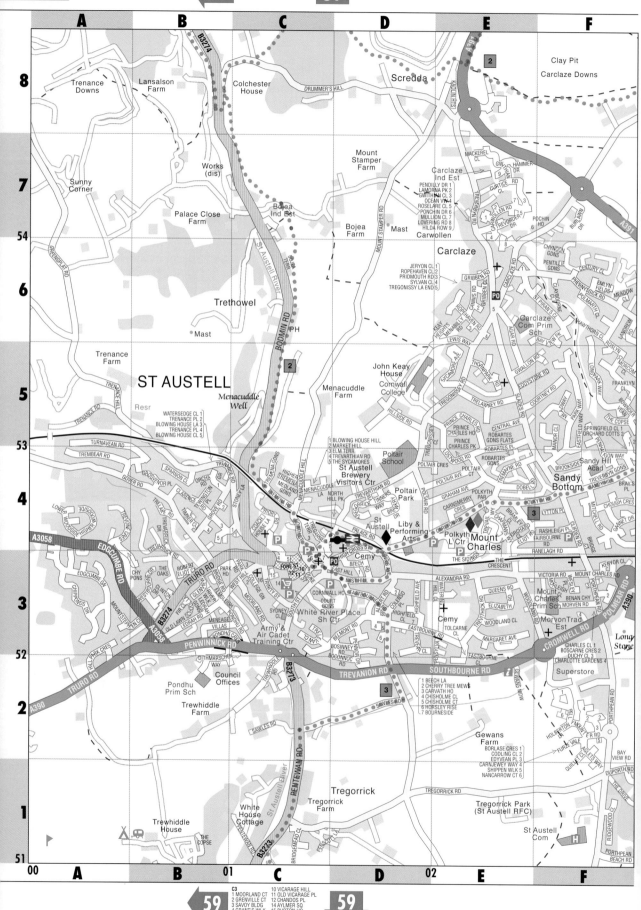

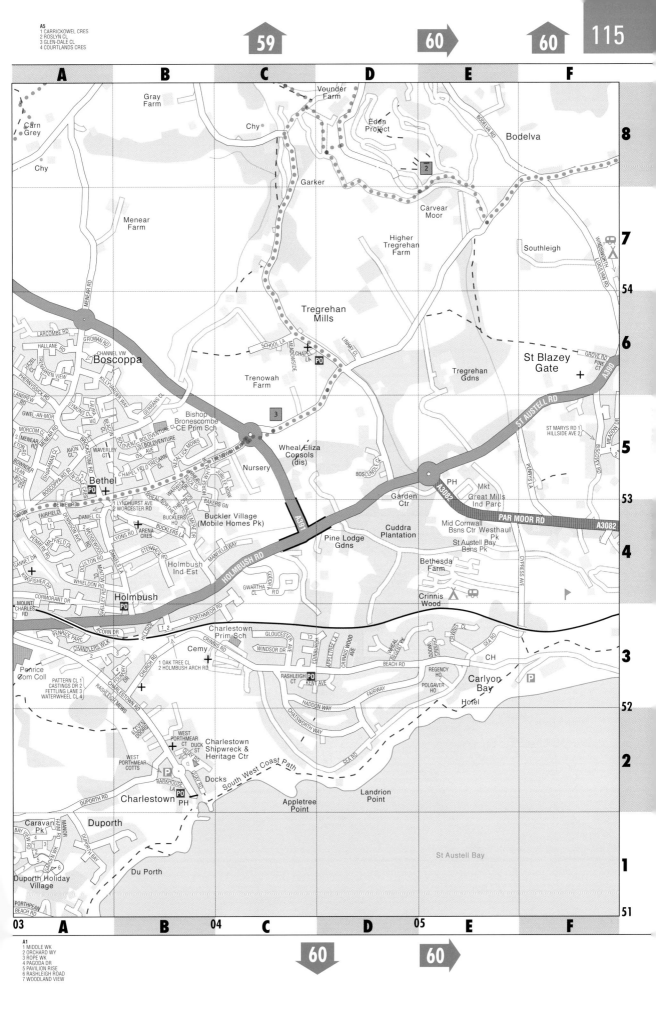

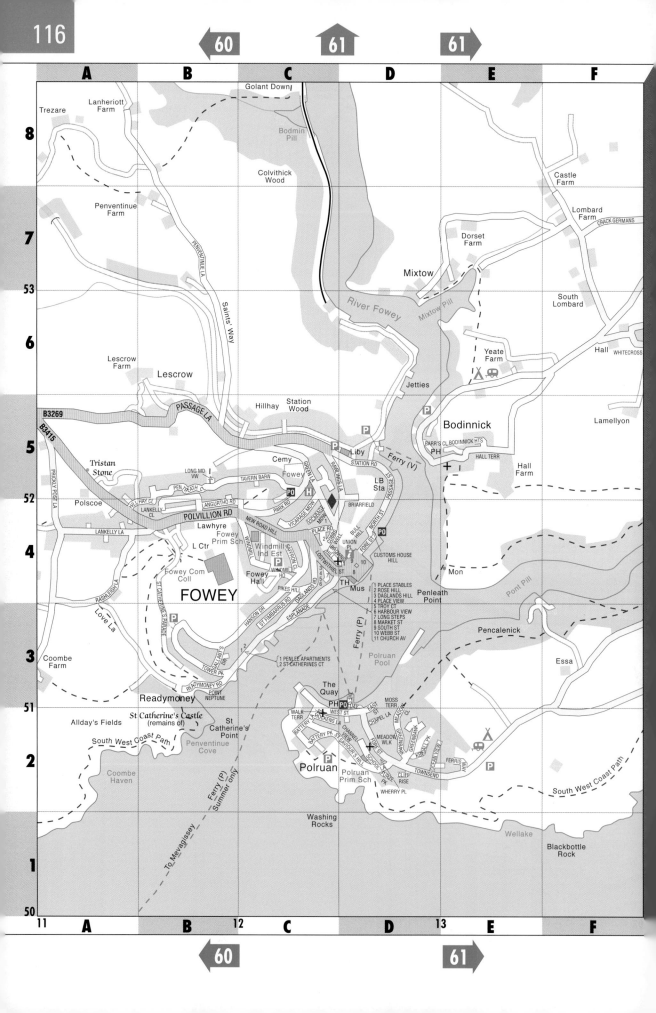

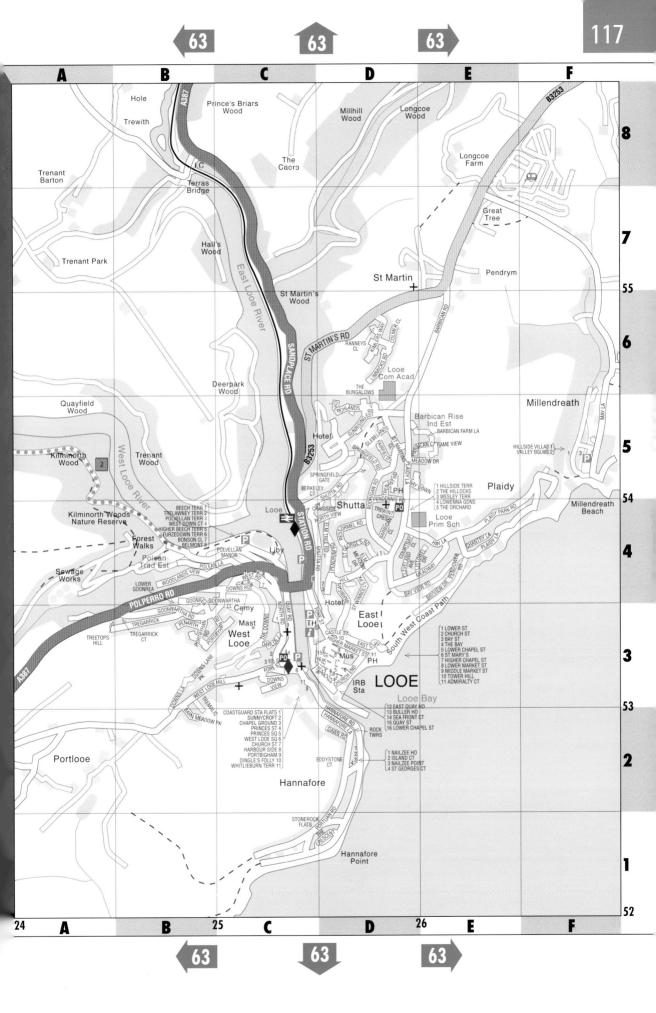

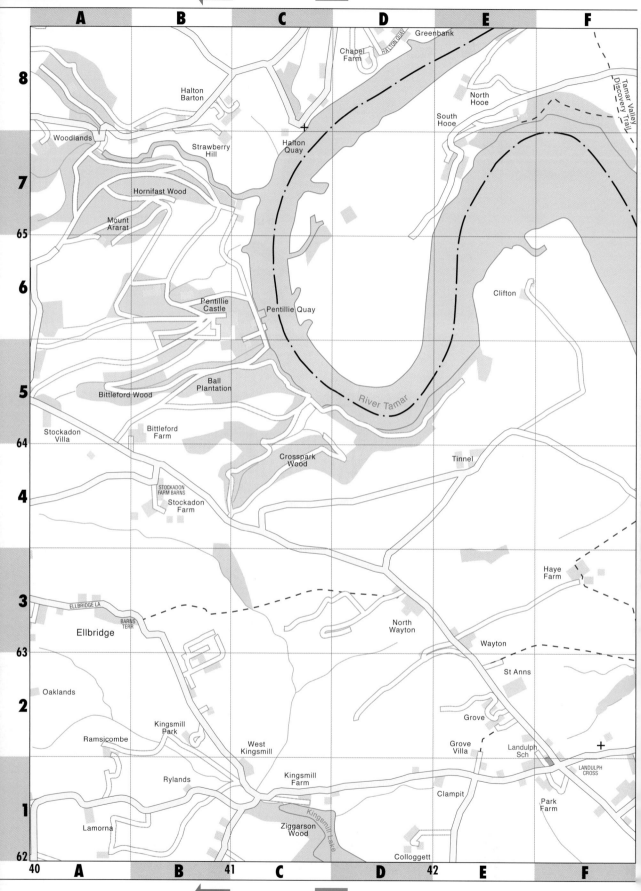

A B C D E F

8

Woodlands

Halton
Barton

Strawberry
Hill

Chapel
Farm

Greenbank

HALTON QUAY

North
Hooe

Tamar Valley
Discovery Trail

7

Hornifast Wood

Halton
Quay

South
Hooe

65

Mount
Ararat

6

Pentillie
Castle

Pentillie Quay

Clifton

5

Bittleford Wood

Ball
Plantation

River Tamar

64

Stockadon
Villa

Bittleford
Farm

Crosspark
Wood

Tinnel

4

STOCKADON
FARM BARNS

Stockadon
Farm

3

ELLBRIDGE LA

BARNS
TERR

North
Wayton

Haye
Farm

Ellbridge

63

Wayton

St Anns

2

Oaklands

Grove

Ramsicombe

Kingsmill
Park

West
Kingsmill

Grove
Villa

Landulph
Sch

LANDULPH
CROSS

Rylands

Kingsmill
Farm

Clampit

Park
Farm

1

Lamorna

Ziggarson
Wood

Kingsmill Lake

Colloggett

62

40 A B 41 C D 42 E F

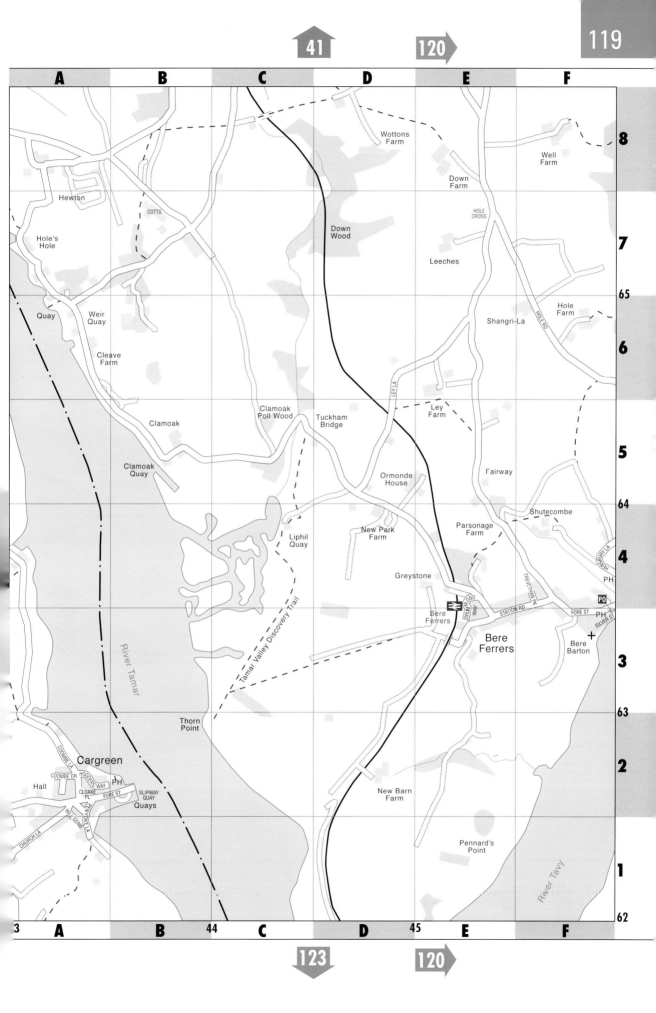

41
120

A B C D E F

8

Wottons
Farm

Well
Farm

Hewton

COTTS

Down
Farm

HOLE
CROSS

7

Hole's
Hole

Down
Wood

Leeches

65

Quay

Weir Quay

Shangri-La

Hole
Farm

HOLE RD

6

Cleave
Farm

Clamoak

Clamoak
Poll Wood

Tuckham
Bridge

Ley
Farm

LEY LA

Ley
Farm

5

Clamoak
Quay

Fairway

64

Liphil
Quay

New Park
Farm

Ormonde
House

Parsonage
Farm

Shutecombe

HEASBURY LA

4

Tamar Valley Discovery Trail

Greystone

Bere
Ferrers

DREAM OLD WAY

TREVETHAN PK

STATION RD

Bere
Ferrers

FORE ST

PH

PO

PH

SILVER ST

Bere
Barton

River Tamar

Thorn
Point

63

Cargreen

COOMBE LA

COOMBE DR

HOLDERS WAY

PH

SLIPWAY
QUAY

New Barn
Farm

2

Hall

CLOAKE
PL

FORE ST

Quays

CHURCH LA

HILL GDNS

PENYOKE LA

Pennard's
Point

River Tavy

1

62

3 A 44 B C 45 D E F

123
120

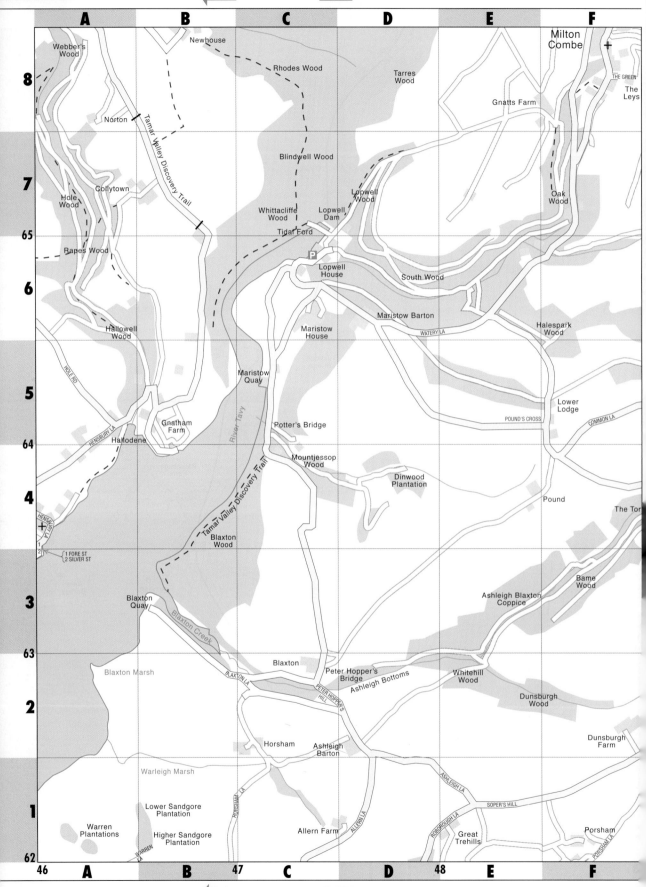

A   B   C   D   E   F

8   Webber's Wood   Newhouse
    Rhodes Wood   Tarres Wood   Milton Combe   THE GREEN   The Leys
    Norton   Gnatts Farm
7   Hole Wood   Collytown   Blindwell Wood   Lopwell Wood   Oak Wood
65 Rapes Wood   Whittacliffe Wood   Lopwell Wood
    Tidal Ford   Lopwell Dam
    P
6   Hallowell Wood   Lopwell House   South Wood   Halespark Wood
    Maristow Barton
    Maristow House   WATERY LA
5   HOLE RD   Gnatham Farm   Maristow Quay   River Tavy   Lower Lodge
    POUND'S CROSS   COMMON LA
64 HENSBURY LA   Hallodene   Potter's Bridge
    Mountjessop Wood   Dinwood Plantation
4   HENSBURY LA   Pound   The Tor
    1 FORE ST   Blaxton Wood   Ashleigh Blaxton Coppice   Bame Wood
    2 SILVER ST
3   Blaxton Quay   Blaxton Creek   Whitehill Wood
    Blaxton   Peter Hopper's Bridge   Ashleigh Bottoms   Dunsburgh Wood
63 Blaxton Marsh   BLAXTON LA   ASHLEIGH LA
2   PETER HOPPER'S HILL   Dunsburgh Farm
    Warleigh Marsh   Horsham   Ashleigh Barton   SOPER'S HILL
1   HORSHAM LA   ALLERN LA   ROBOROUGH LA   PORSHAM LA
    Lower Sandgore Plantation   Porsham
    Warren Plantations   Higher Sandgore Plantation   Allern Farm   Great Trehills
62
46   A   B   47   C   D   48   E   F

Tamar Valley Discovery Trail

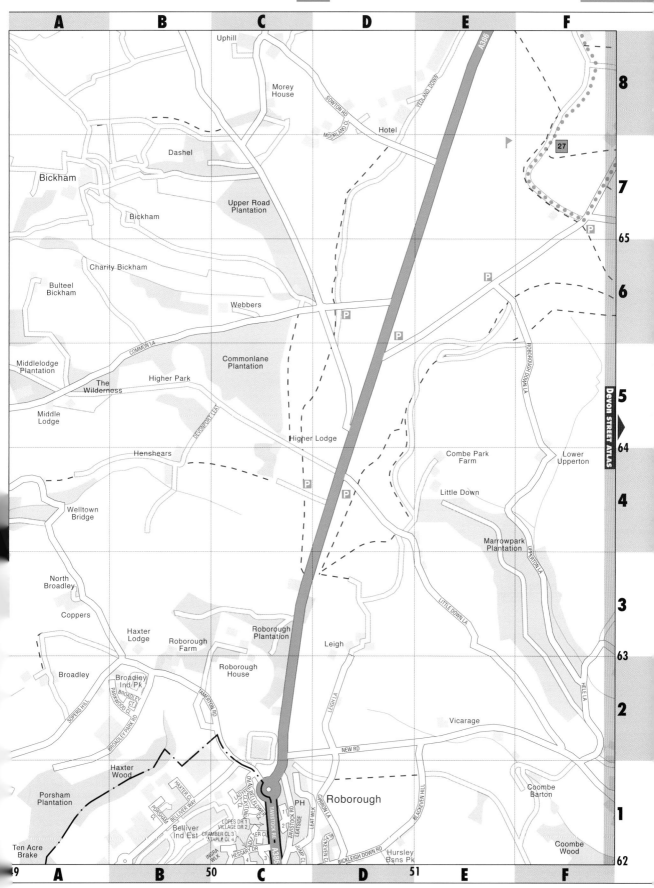

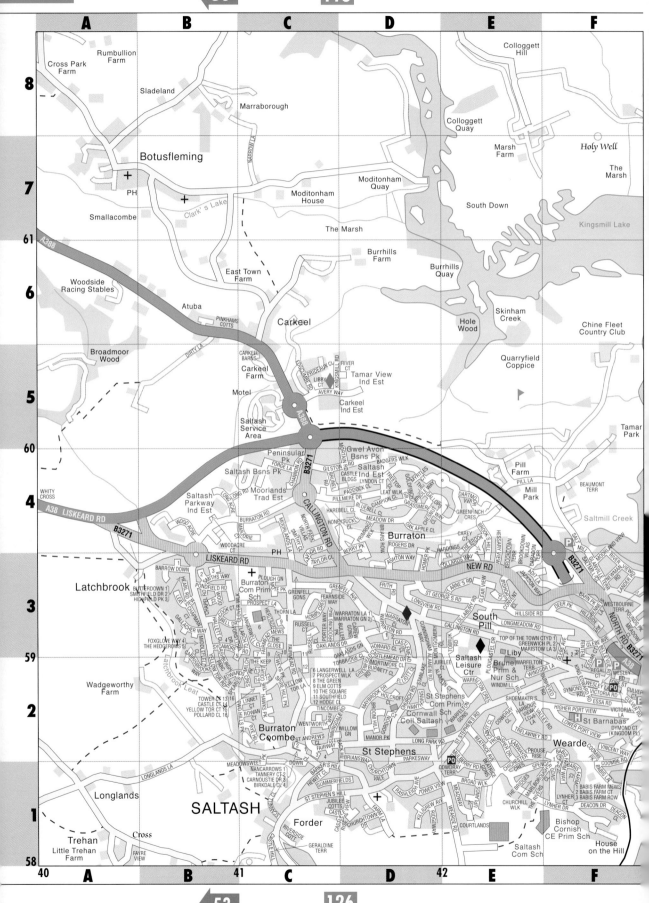

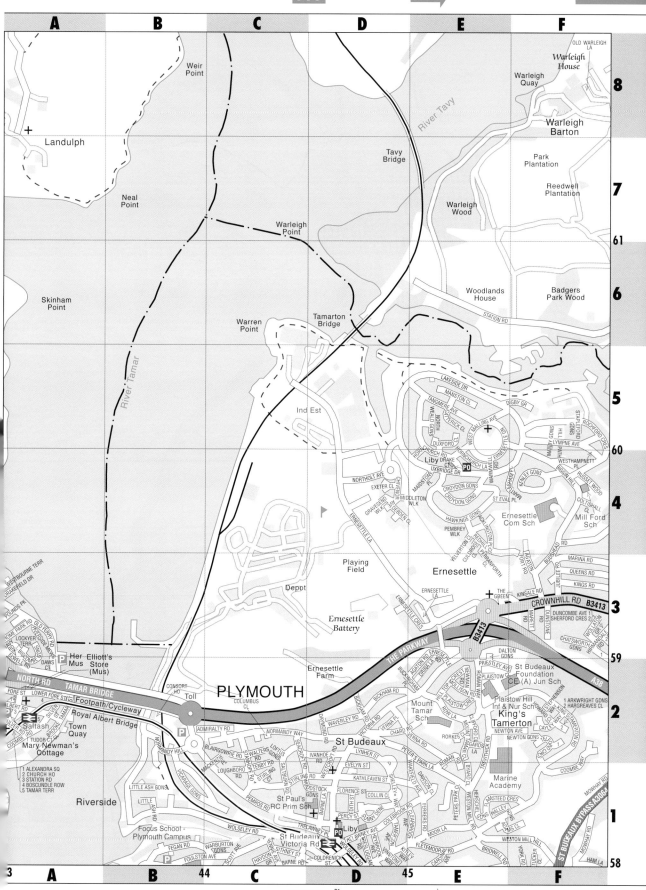

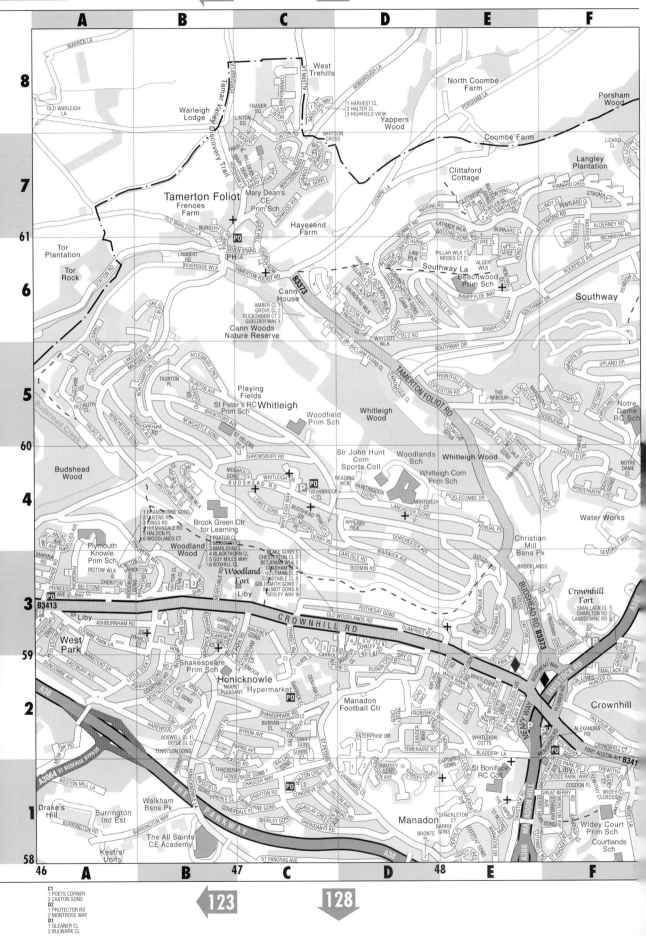

C1
1 POETS CORNER
2 CAXTON GDNS
D2
1 PROTECTOR RD
2 MONTROSE WAY
D1
1 GLEANER CL
2 BULWARK CL

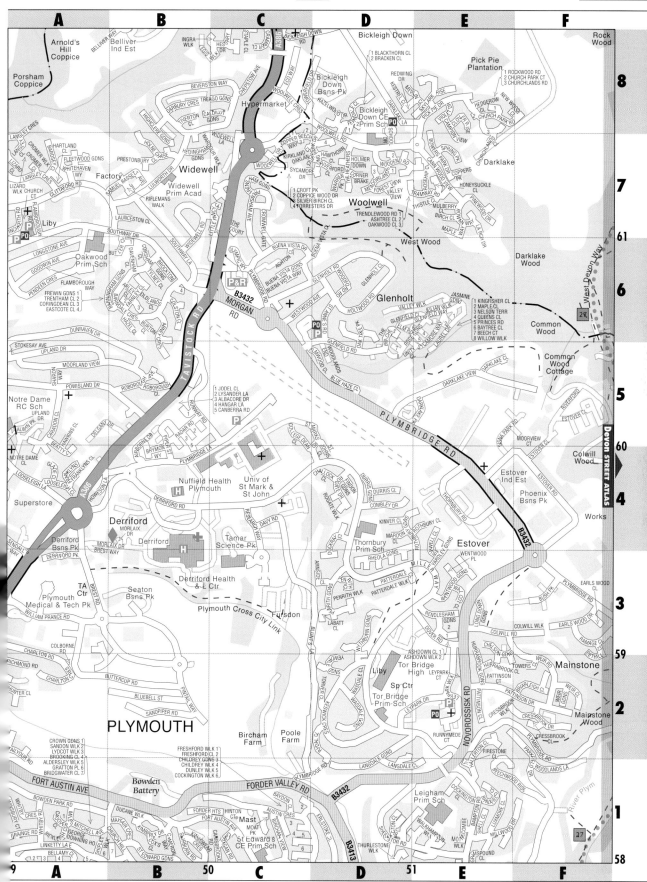

F5
1 NEPEAN ST
2 ADELAIDE ST
3 BRUNEL TERR
4 EPWORTH TERR
5 SUSSEX TERR
6 RAILWAY COTTS
7 YORK TERR
8 ST MAWES TERR

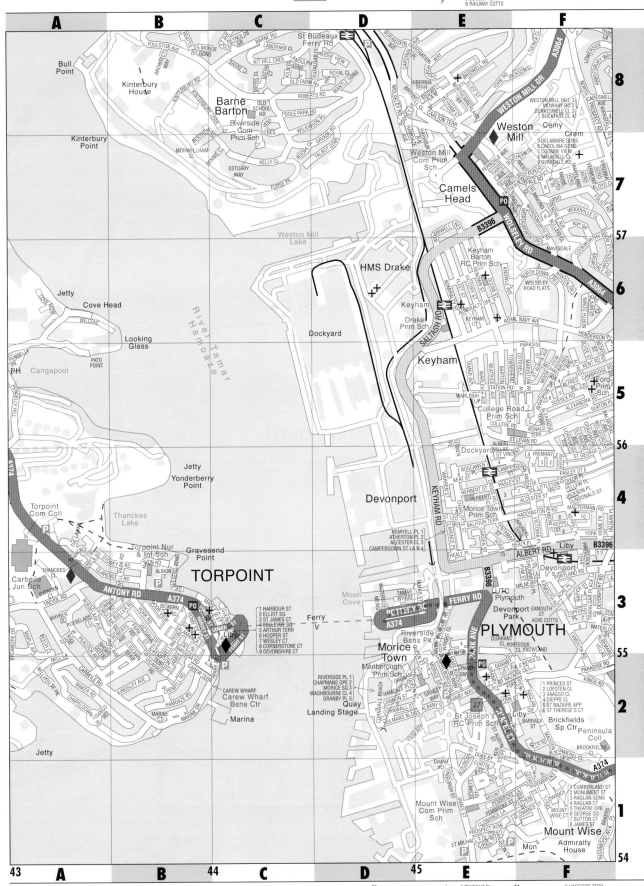

F3
1 CLARENDON HO
2 GARFIELD TERR
3 TRAFALGAR PL
4 THE MEWS
5 NELSON GDNS
6 BEYROUT PL
7 ST MICHAEL'S CT
8 ST MICHAEL'S TERR
9 PORTLAND CT
10 MOLYNEAUX PL
11 CLARENDON LA
F4
1 ST GEORGES CT
2 HORNBY ST
3 PHILLIMORE ST
4 FREMANTLE GDNS
5 FAIRFAX TERR
6 HARGOOD TERR
7 HARRISON ST
8 KEPPEL TERR
9 HEALY CT
10 BRUNSWICK PL

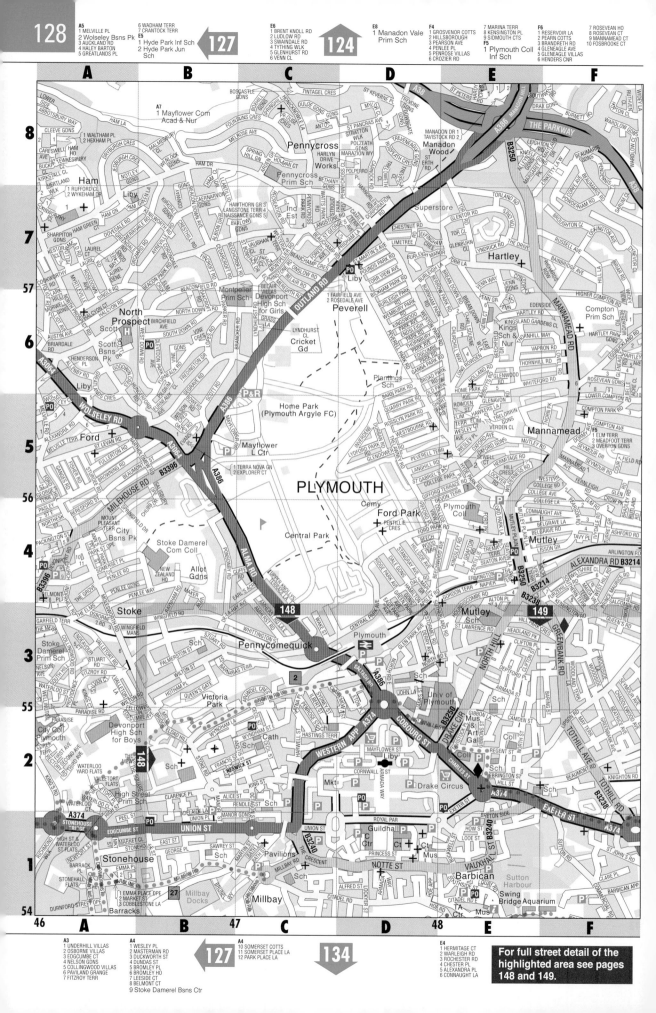

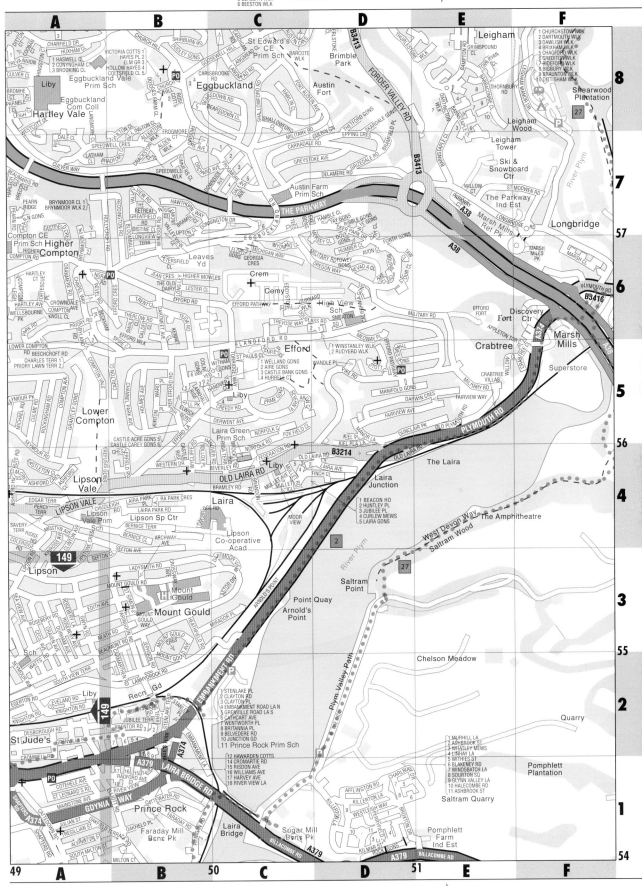

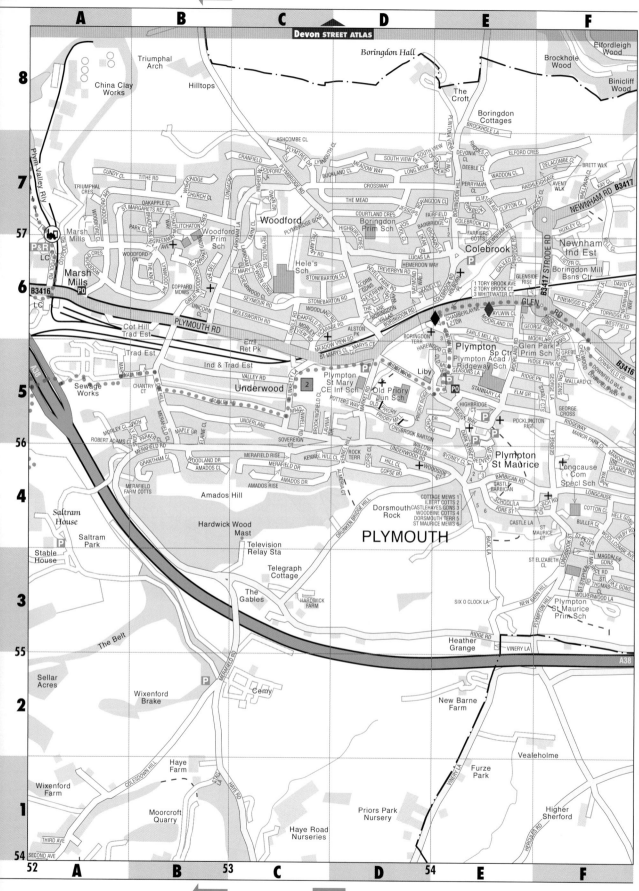

B5
1 CALEDONIA CL
2 ELDER CL
3 MAGNOLIA CL
4 TURBILL GDNS
5 PAYNTER WLK
6 Glen Park Prim Sch

C5
1 EIGHT ACRE CL
2 LAWN CL
3 ORCHARD CL
4 GREAT PARK CL
5 LONG TERRACE CL
6 CYPRESS CL

7 CAMPION CL
8 RODDICK WAY
9 BRANSON CT

Devon STREET ATLAS

A **B** **C** **D** **E** **F**

Sparkwell Farm

Newnham Park

Furzeacre Wood

B3417

Windwhistle

Sparkwell

8

Furzeacre Bridge

Holly Wood

Lowdamoor

HEMERDON LA

BEECHWOOD CROSS

LEGGATE LA

Beechwood

Old Newnham Farm

Hemerdon

Hemerdon House

Hemerdon Cross

Old Newnham

Hemerdon Farm

PH

Lodge

Sherwell

7

NEWNHAM RD

WEST PARK HILL

RIDINGS

Lodge

Sparkwell Bridge

57

Newnham Ind Est

CORNFIELD GDNS

UPPER RIDINGS

LOWER RIDINGS

Moor Bridge

6

STOGGY LA

GREENWOOD PARK CL

WESTMOOR CL

LANGAGE CROSS

Chaddlewood

GREENWOOD PARK RD

ROSECLAVE CL

Langage Science Pk

Combe Farm

5

Chaddlewood Prim Sch

GLEN RD

PO

WALNUT

BEECHWOOD WAY

HOLLAND RD

Higher Langage

Lower Langage

56

2

Langage Pk

Langage Ind Est

Ley Farm

Voss

PH

A38

A38 Exeter, M5

3

Yealmpstone Farm Prim Sch

DEEP LA

B3416

WOLVERWOOD CL

Battisford Pk

55

SPRINGWOOD CL

RIDGE RD

WOLVERWOOD LA

DEEP LA

Wiverton House

Battisford

2

Butlas Farm

Wiverton Acre

Tuxton Farm

Tuxton Wood

1

East Sherford

Blackpool

54

55 **A** **B** **56** **C** **D** **57** **E** **F**

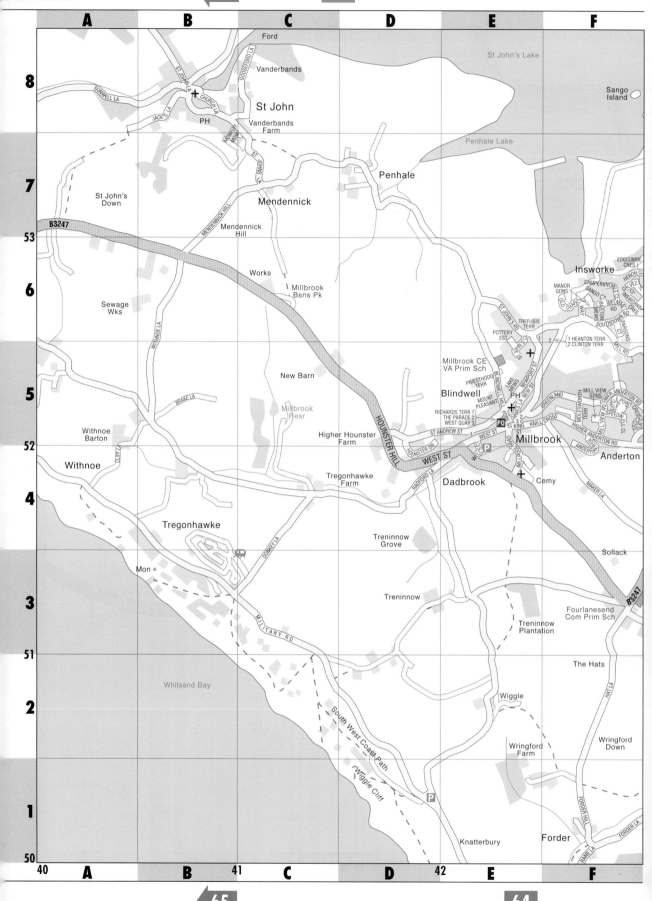

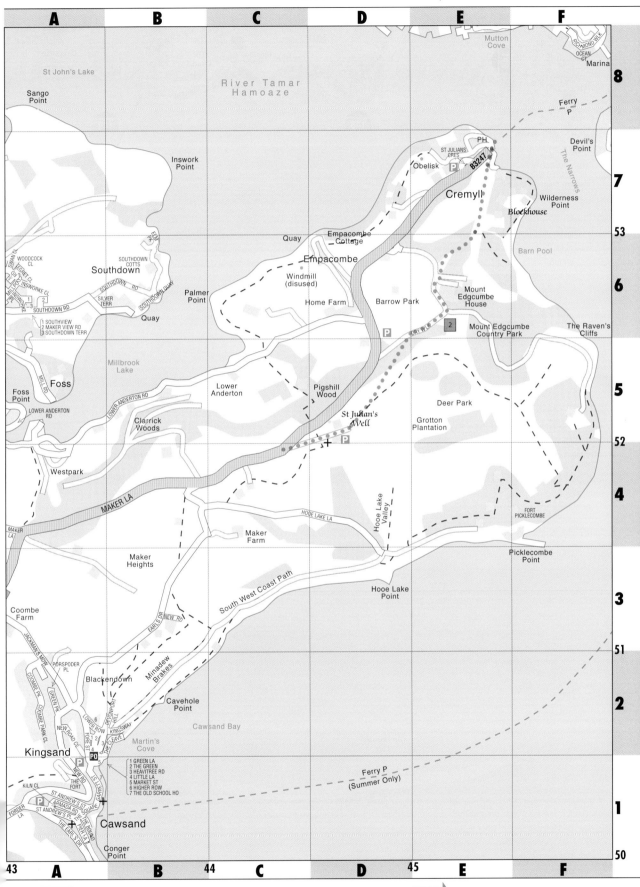

Mutton Cove

OCEAN
RICHMOND WALK
Marina

St John's Lake

River Tamar
Hamoaze

Sango Point

Ferry P

8

Devil's Point

Inswork Point

PH

St JULIANS CRES
Obelisk
P
B3247
Cremyll

The Narrows

Wilderness Point

Blockhouse

7

53

Empacombe Cottage
Quay

Barn Pool

Southdown

WOODCOCK CL
SWAN CL
EGRET CL
INSWORKE CL
MILLBROOKE

SOUTHDOWN COTTS

ELM
SOUTHDOWN RD
SILVER TERR
SOUTHDOWN QUAY

1 SOUTHVIEW
2 MAKER VIEW RD
3 SOUTHDOWN TERR

Quay

Palmer Point

Empacombe

Windmill (disused)

Home Farm

Barrow Park

Mount Edgcumbe House

2

Mount Edgcumbe Country Park

The Raven's Cliffs

6

53

Foss
Foss Point

MILL RD

LOWER ANDERTON RD

Millbrook Lake

Lower Anderton

Pigshill Wood

DRY WLK
P

P

5

LOWER ANDERTON RD

Clarrick Woods

St Julian's Well

Deer Park

Grotton Plantation

52

Westpark

MAKER LA

MAKER LA

Maker Farm

HOOE LAKE LA

Hooe Lake Valley

Hooe Lake Point

FORT PICKLECOMBE

4

Picklecombe Point

51

Coombe Farm

Maker Heights

South West Coast Path

EARLS DR
NEW RD

Minadew Brakes

Blackendown

PORSPODER PL

GREEN PK
COOMBE PK
COOMBE PARK CL

LOWER ROW

NEW ROAD CL

KINGSWAY

DEVONPORT HILL

THE CLEAVE

FORE ST

Cavehole Point

Cawsand Bay

3

51

2

Kingsand

P
PO

Martin's Cove

1 GREEN LA
2 THE GREEN
3 HEAVITREE RD
4 LITTLE LA
5 MARKET ST
6 HIGHER ROW
7 THE OLD SCHOOL HO

Ferry P
(Summer Only)

THE FORT

KILN CL

FORDER LA

ST ANDREWS ST
ARMADA RD
ST ANDREW'S PL

NEW RD

THE EARL'S DR
THE PIER LA
THE BOUND

JACKMAN'S MDW

Cawsand

Conger Point

1

50

133

128

For full street detail of the highlighted area see pages 148 and 149.

A B C D E F

ADMIRAL'S HARD
THE QUARTERDECK
ST STRAND ST
POUND ST
ADMIRAL ST
Ferryport
TA Ctr
WALKER TERR
Coxside

TELEGRAPH WHARF
ST PAUL'S ST
Millbay Docks
SOAP ST
WINSTON AVE
CLIFF RD
PIER ST
The Hoe
Smeaton's Tower
27
The Citadel

FREEMANS WHARF
THE MANSION HO
27
West Hoe
West Hoe Pier
MADEIRA RD

8

ROYAL WILLIAM YARD
MOUNT STONE RD
ROYAL WILLIAM RD
St George's CE Prim Sch

ADMIRALTY COTTS
ADMIRALTY RD
Tower
Eastern King Point

148

149

Mount Batten Breakwater
SPINNAKER QUAY
P
Clovelly Bay

Firestone Bay

7 Western King Point
Mount Batten Point
Mount Batten Tower
SHAW WAY
LAWRENCE RD

53
Mount Batten Ctr
LORD LOUIS CRES

6 Drake's or St Nicholas's Island
Mast
The Bridge
Batten Bay
Dunstone Point
Rum Bay

Ferry P (Summer Only)

5

52
Jennycliff Bay

4 The Sound

Ramscliff Point
Rams Cliff
South West Coast Path
Wall

3

51 Leekbed Bay

2 Bovisand Pier
Staddon Point
Bovisand Fort
BOVISAND CT
COASTGUARD COTTS

Breakwater Fort

1 Plymouth Breakwater

50

46 A B 47 C D 48 E F

For full street detail of the highlighted area see page 149.

129

136

135

F5
1 CHALLGOOD CL
2 ORCHARDTON TERR

F7
1 THE DUKES RYDE
2 MAPLE CT
3 MAGNOLIA CT
4 HORN LANE FLATS
5 SELKIRK HO

E8
1 CAPELLA DR
2 LYNX LA
3 INDUS PL
4 CYGNUS MEWS
5 LIBRA AVE
6 OCTANS WAY

E8
7 CANIS MEWS
8 AQUARIUS DR
9 CARINA PL
10 PAVO ST
11 SCULPTOR WAY
12 LEO AVE

E8
13 CENTAUR MEWS
14 CAPRICORN WAY
15 CORVUS MEWS
16 AQUILA DR
17 PERSEUS CRES
18 VOLANS LA

E8
19 TITAN AVE
20 ELECTRA WAY
21 URSA GDNS
22 ARIEL MEWS

135 ◄

130 ⌂

	A	B	C	D	E	F

PLYMOUTH

Moorcroft Quarry

A379

ELBURTON RD

Dunstone Prim Sch

Dunstone Woods

Elburton Prim Sch

Widegate Nursery

Thornville Nurseries

Elburton Vineries

West Sherford

1 SERPENS VALE
2 POLARIS MEWS
3 ANDROMEDA GR

Elburton

ELBURTON RD

Chittleburn Wood

28

Sterts Farm

Halwell

Halwell Wood

Wopplewell

CHITTLEBURN HILL

Chittleburn Cross

Dodovens Farm

Hilltop Cotts

Combe

Fordbrook Farm

Popplestone Pk

Brixton Lodge Gdns

Vicarage

Chittleburn Bsns Pk

Court View

A379 Modbury

Brixton

A379

Coombe Dean Sch

Jew's Wood

Coombe Wood

Coombe Farm

Torr Hill Farm

Spriddlestone

Higher Spriddlestone

Spriddlestone Barton

Coflete

Leyford Parks

Cemy

Ridge Cross

Higher Leyford

Knapps Wood

Spriddlestone House

Andron Wood

Hollacombe Hill

Hollacombe Wood

Train Brake

Train Wood

Coflete Creek

Western Park Wood

South Barton

Steer Point Cotts

Brick Works

River Yealm

Spirewell

Wembury

Trescan

Wembury Wood

Devon **STREET ATLAS**

69

C5
1 SANDHURST TERR
2 CORNWALL TERR
3 TREHAVERNE TERR
4 ST MARY'S TERR
5 HENDRA CL

70

D5
1 BENSON HO
2 BENSON GDNS
3 ST CLEMENT'S TERR
4 MITCHELL HILL TERR
5 PROSPECT PL
6 SOLAR ROW

70

D5
7 PARKINS TERR
8 MIDDLE ROSEWIN ROW
9 LOWER ROSEWIN ROW
10 EAST ROSEWIN ROW
11 MITCHELL CT
12 CHURCH WLK

13 BELMONT VILLAS

137

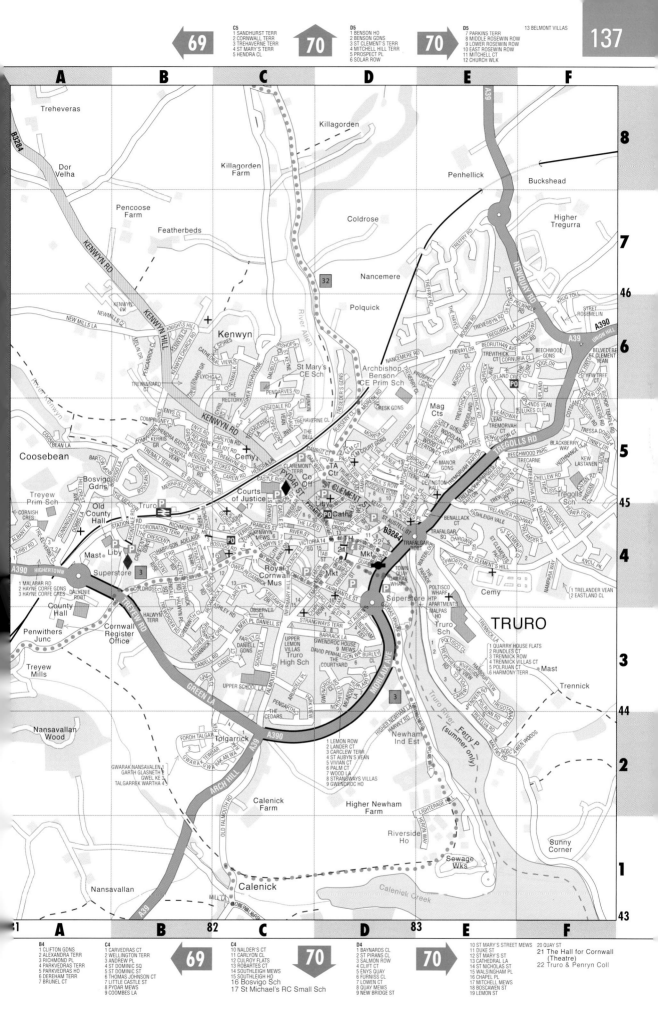

B4
1 CLIFTON GDNS
2 ALEXANDRA TERR
3 RICHMOND PL
4 PARKVEDRAS TERR
5 PARKVEDRAS HO
6 DEREHAM TERR
7 BRUNEL CT

C4
1 CARVEDRAS CT
2 WELLINGTON TERR
3 ANDREW PL
4 ST DOMINIC SQ
5 ST DOMINIC CT
6 THOMAS JOHNSON CT
7 LITTLE CASTLE ST
8 PYDAR MEWS
9 COOMBES LA

69

C4
10 NALDER'S CT
11 CARLYON CL
12 CULROY FLATS
13 ROBARTES CT
14 SOUTHLEIGH MEWS
15 SOUTHLEIGH HO
16 Bosvigo Sch
17 St Michael's RC Small Sch

70

D4
1 BAYNARDS CL
2 ST PIRANS CL
3 SALMON ROW
4 CLIFT CT
5 ENYS QUAY
6 FURNISS CL
7 LOWEN CT
8 QUAY MEWS
9 NEW BRIDGE ST

70

10 ST MARY'S STREET MEWS
11 DUKE ST
12 ST MARY'S ST
13 CATHEDRAL LA
14 ST NICHOLAS ST
15 WALSINGHAM PL
16 CHAPEL PL
17 MITCHELL MEWS
18 BOSCAWEN ST
19 LEMON ST

20 QUAY ST
21 The Hall for Cornwall (Theatre)
22 Truro & Penryn Coll

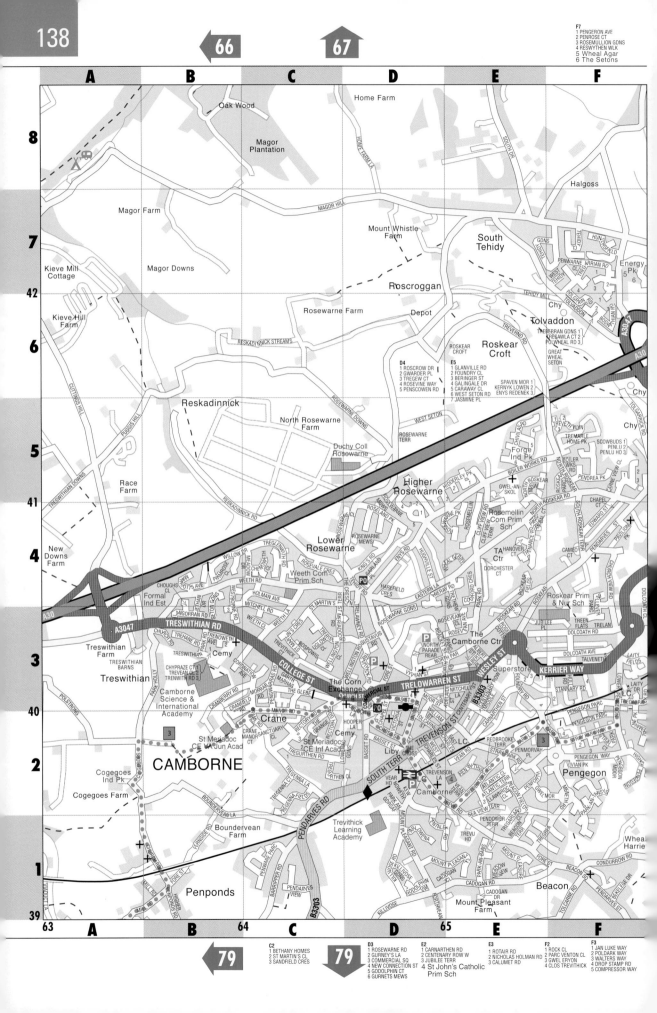

66 67

F7
1 PENGERON AVE
2 PENROSE CT
3 ROSEMULLION GDNS
4 RESWYTHEN WLK
5 Wheal Agar
6 The Setons

D4
1 ROSCROW DR
2 GWARDER PL
3 TREGEW CT
4 ROSEVINE WAY
5 PENSCOWEN RD

E5
1 GLANVILLE RD
2 FOUNDRY CL
3 BERINGER ST
4 GALINGALE DR
5 CARAWAY CL
6 WEST SETON RD
7 JASMINE PL

SPAVEN MOR 1
KERNYK LOWEN 2
ENYS REDENEK 3

THEBERRAN GDNS 1
TRESAWLA CT 2
POLWHEAL RD 3

C2
1 BETHANY HOMES
2 ST MARTIN'S CL
3 SANDFIELD CRES

D3
1 ROSEWARNE RD
2 GURNEY'S LA
3 COMMERCIAL SQ
4 NEW CONNECTION ST
5 GODOLPHIN CT
6 GURNETS MEWS

E2
1 CARNARTHEN RD
2 CENTENARY ROW W
3 JUBILEE TERR
4 St John's Catholic Prim Sch

E3
1 ROTAIR RD
2 NICHOLAS HOLMAN RD
3 CALUMET RD

F2
1 ROCK CL
2 PARC VENTON CL
3 GWEL ERYON
4 CLOS TREVITHICK

F3
1 JAN LUKE WAY
2 POLDARK WAY
3 WALTERS WAY
4 DROP STAMP RD
5 COMPRESSOR WAY

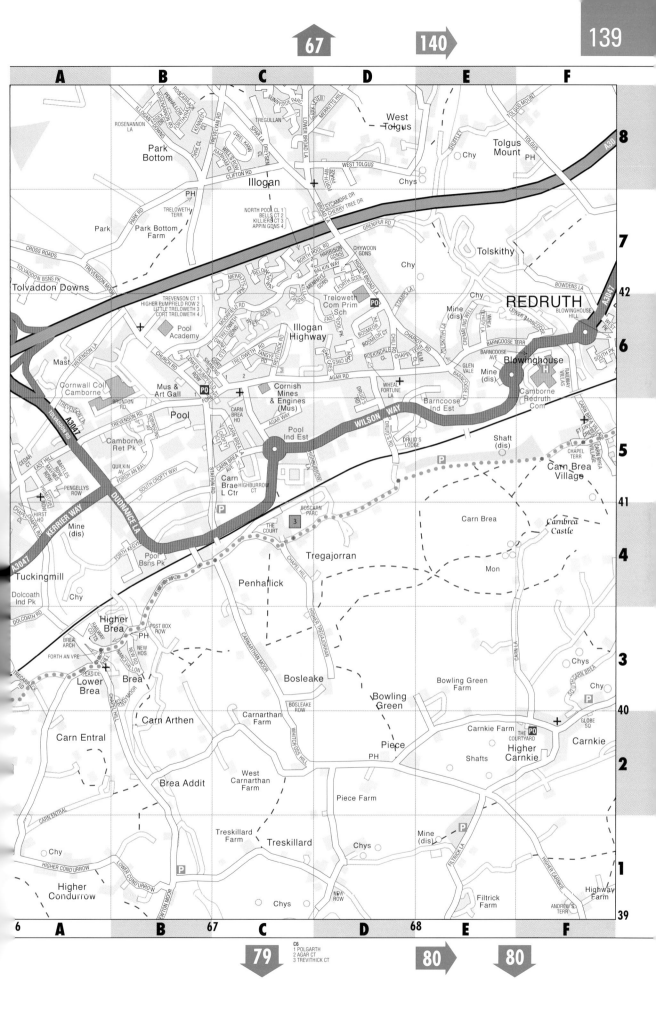

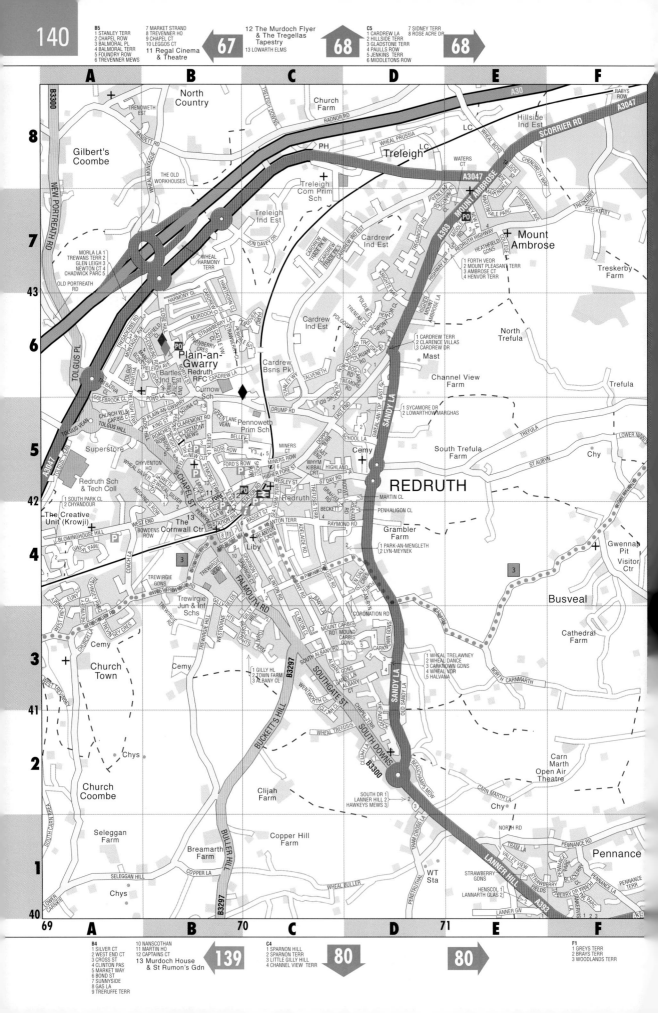

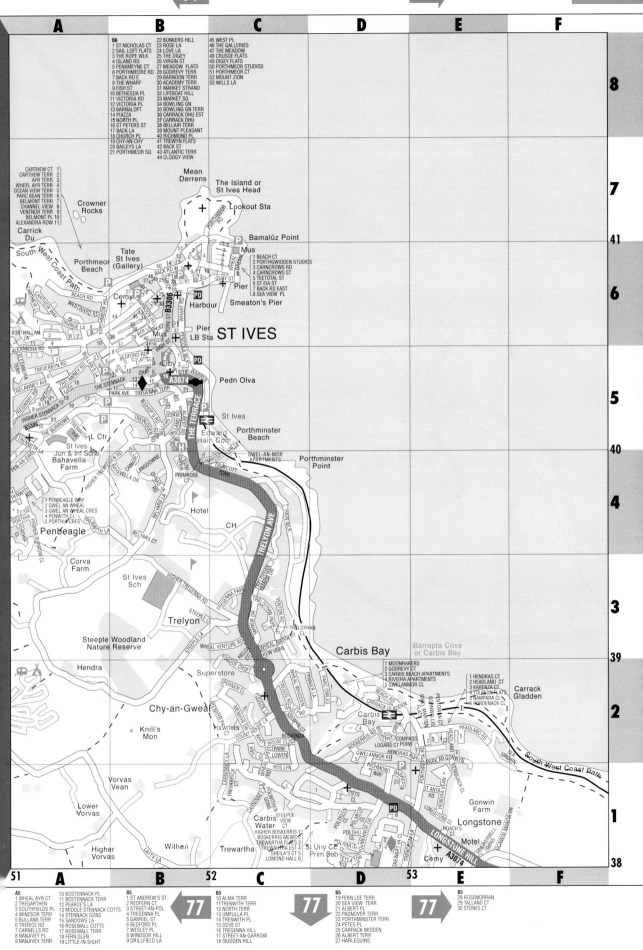

B6
1 ST NICHOLAS CT
2 SAIL LOFT FLATS
3 THE ROPE WLK
4 ISLAND RD
5 PENAMEYNE CT
6 PORTHMEORE RD
7 BACK RD E
8 THE WHARF
9 FISH ST
10 BETHESDA PL
11 VICTORIA RD
12 VICTORIA PL
13 BARNALOFT
14 PIAZZA
15 NORTH PL
16 ST PETERS ST
17 BACK LA
18 CHURCH PL
19 CHY-AN-CHY
20 BAILEYS LA
21 PORTHMEOR SQ

22 BUNKERS HILL
23 ROSE LA
24 LOVE LA
25 THE DIGEY
26 VIRGIN ST
27 MEADOW FLATS
28 GODREVY TERR
29 BARNOON TERR
30 ACADEMY TERR
31 MARKET STRAND
32 LIFEBOAT HILL
33 MARKET SQ
34 BOWLING GN
35 BOWLING GN TERR
36 CARRACK DHU EST
37 CARRACK DHU
38 BELLAIR TERR
39 MOUNT PLEASANT
40 RICHMOND PL
41 TREWYN FLATS
42 BACK ST
43 ATLANTIC TERR
44 CLODGY VIEW

45 WEST PL
46 THE GALLERIES
47 THE MEADOW
48 CRUSOE FLATS
49 DIGEY FLATS
50 PORTHMEOR STUDIOS
51 PORTHMEOR CT
52 MOUNT ZION
53 WILLS LA

CARTHEW CT 1
CARTHEW TERR 2
AYR TERR 3
WHEEL AYR TERR 4
OCEAN VIEW 5
PARC BEAN TERR 6
BELMONT TERR 7
CHANNEL VIEW 8
VENTNOR TERR 9
BELMONT PL 10
ALEXANDRA ROW 11

1 BEACH CT
2 PORTHGWIDDEN STUDIOS
3 CARNCROWS RD
4 CARNCROWS ST
5 TEETOTAL ST
6 ST EIA ST
7 BACK RD EAST
8 SEA VIEW PL

1 PENBEAGLE WAY
2 GWEL AN WHEAL
3 GWEL AN WHEAL CRES
4 PENWITH CL
5 PORTHIA CRES

1 MOONRAKERS
2 GODREVY CT
3 CARBIS BEACH APARTMENTS
4 RIVIERA APARTMENTS
5 GWELANMOR CL

1 HENDRAS CT
2 HEADLAND CT
3 KARENZA CT
4 TOLEDNH FLATS
5 RAMPARA CT
6 BORDENACK CL

A5
1 WHEAL AYR CT
2 TREGARTHEN
3 SOUTHFIELDS PL
4 WINDSOR TERR
5 BULLANS TERR
6 TRERICE RD
7 CARNELLS RD
8 NANJIVEY PL
9 NANJIVEY TERR
10 BOSTENNACK PL
11 BOSTENNACK TERR
12 PEARCE'S LA
13 MIDDLE STENNACK COTTS
14 STENNACK GDNS
15 SANDOWS LA
16 ROSEWALL COTTS
17 ROSEWALL TERR
18 FERN GLEN
19 LITTLE-IN-SIGHT

B5
1 ST ANDREW'S ST
2 REDFERN ST
3 STREET-AN-POL
4 TREGENNA PL
5 GABRIEL ST
6 BEDFORD RD
7 WESLEY PL
8 WINDSOR HILL
9 DRILLFIELD LA
10 ALMA TERR
11 TRENWITH TERR
12 NORTH TERR
13 UMFULLA PL
14 TRENWITH PL
15 DOVE ST
16 TREGENNA HILL
17 STREET-AN-GARROW
18 SKIDDEN HILL

B5
19 FERN LEE TERR
20 SEA VIEW TERR
21 ALBERT PL
22 PADNOVER TERR
23 PORTHMINSTER TERR
24 PETES PL
25 CARRACK WIDDEN
26 ALBERT TERR
27 HARLEQUINS

B5
28 ROSEMORRAN
29 TALLAND CT
30 STONES CT

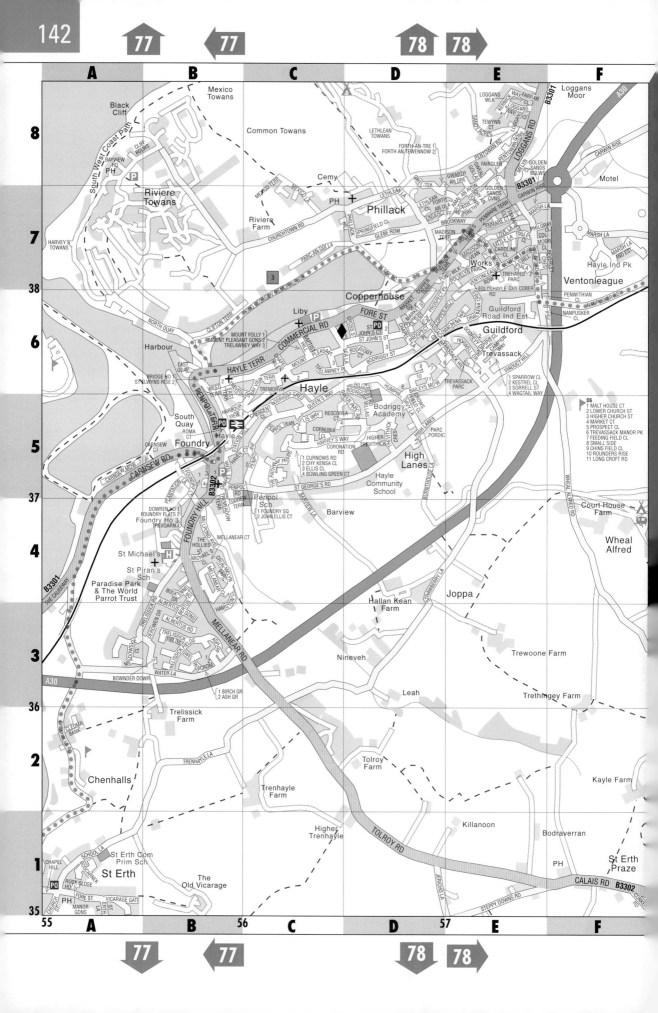

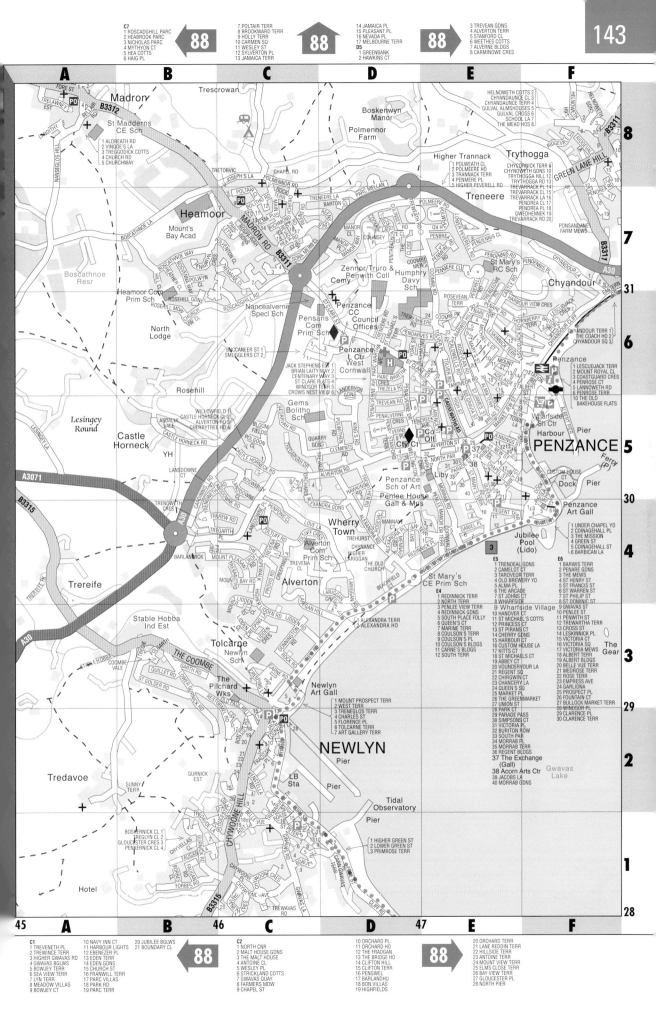

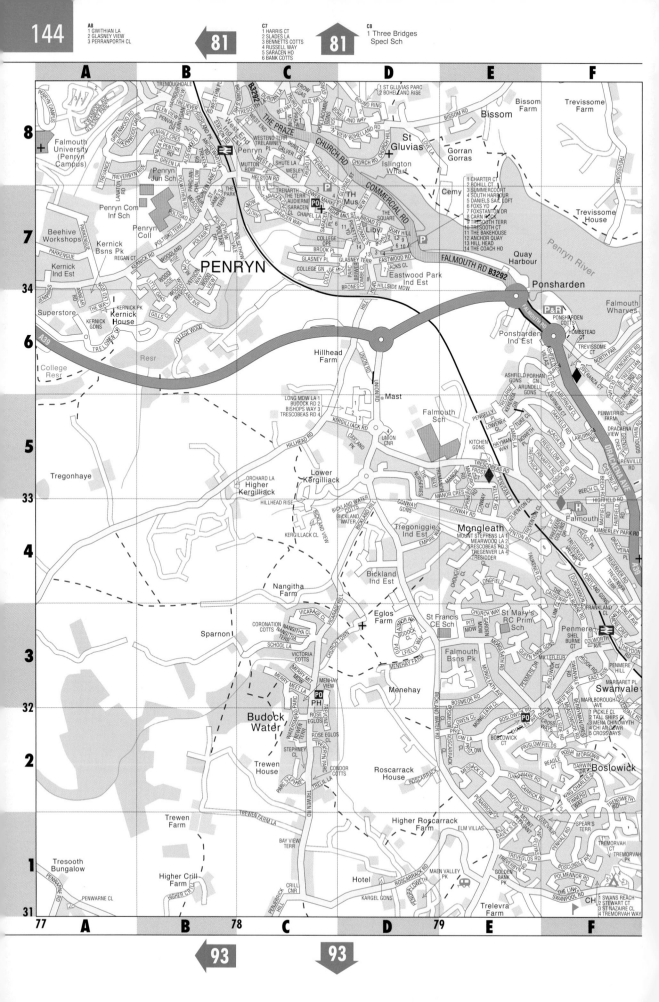

A8
1 GWITHIAN LA
2 GLASNEY VIEW
3 PERRANPORTH CL

C7
1 HARRIS CT
2 SLADES LA
3 BENNETTS COTTS
4 RUSSELL WAY
5 SARACEN HO
6 BANK COTTS

C8
1 Three Bridges
Specl Sch

81

81

A B C D E F

8 7 34 6 5 33 4 3 32 2 1 31

77 A 78 C 78 D 79 E F

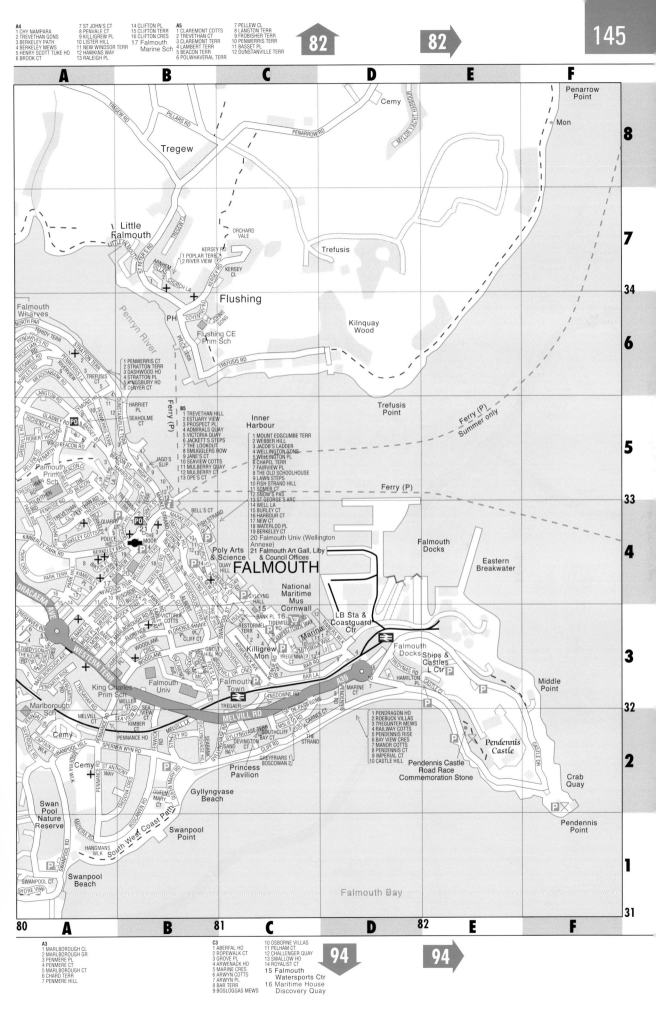

A4
1 CHY NAMPARA
2 TREVETHAN GDNS
3 BERKELEY PATH
4 BERKELEY MEWS
5 HENRY SCOTT TUKE HO
6 BROOK CT
7 ST JOHN'S CT
8 PENVALE CT
9 KILLIGREW PL
10 LISTER HILL
11 NEW WINDSOR TERR
12 HAWKINS WAY
13 RALEIGH PL
14 CLIFTON PL
15 CLIFTON TERR
16 CLIFTON CRES
17 Falmouth Marine Sch

A5
1 CLAREMONT COTTS
2 TREVETHAN CT
3 CLAREMONT TERR
4 LAMBERT TERR
5 BEACON TERR
6 POLWHAVERAL TERR
7 PELLEW CL
8 LANGTON TERR
9 FROBISHER TERR
10 PENWERRIS TERR
11 BASSET PL
12 DUNSTANVILLE TERR

Penarrow Point

Mon

Tregew

Little Falmouth

Cemy

Orchard Vale

Trefusis

Kersey Rd
1 POPLAR TERR
2 RIVER VIEW

Kersey Cl

Flushing

Kilnquay Wood

Falmouth Wharves

Flushing CE Prim Sch

PH

COVENT

JOHNS GDNS

Penryn River

Ferry (P)

Trefusis Rd

Trefusis Point

Ferry (P) Summer only

B5
1 TREVETHAN HILL
2 ESTUARY VIEW
3 PROSPECT PL
4 ADMIRALS QUAY
5 VICTORIA QUAY
6 JACKETT'S STEPS
7 THE LOOKOUT
8 SMUGGLERS ROW
9 JANE'S CT
10 SEAVIEW COTTS
11 MULBERRY QUAY
12 MULBERRY CT
13 OPE'S CT

Inner Harbour

1 MOUNT EDGCUMBE TERR
2 WEBBER HILL
3 JACOB'S LADDER
4 WELLINGTON GDNS
5 WELLINGTON PL
6 CHAPEL TERR
7 FAIRVIEW PL
8 THE OLD SCHOOLHOUSE
9 LAWN STEPS
10 FISH STRAND HILL
11 SOMER CT
12 SNOW'S PAS
13 ST GEORGE'S ARC
14 WELL LA
15 BURLEY CT
16 HARBOUR CT
17 NEW CT
18 WATERLOO PL
19 BERKELEY CT
20 Falmouth Univ (Wellington Annexe)
21 Falmouth Art Gall, Liby & Council Offices

Ferry (P)

Falmouth Docks

Eastern Breakwater

Falmouth Prim Sch

Poly Arts & Science

FALMOUTH

National Maritime Mus Cornwall

LB Sta & Coastguard Ctr

Falmouth Docks

Ships & Castles L Ctr

Marina

Killigrew Mon

Falmouth Univ

King Charles Prim Sch

Falmouth Town

Middle Point

DRACAENA AVE

WESTERN TERR

Marlborough Sch

MELVILL RD

Princess Pavilion

1 PENDRAGON HO
2 ROEBUCK VILLAS
3 TREGUNTER MEWS
4 RAILWAY COTTS
5 PENDENNIS RISE
6 BAY VIEW CRES
7 MANOR COTTS
8 PENDENNIS CT
9 IMPERIAL CT
10 CASTLE HILL

Pendennis Castle

Crab Quay

Cemy

Cemy

Swan Pool Nature Reserve

Gyllyngvase Beach

South West Coast Path

Swanpool Point

Pendennis Castle Road Race Commemoration Stone

Pendennis Point

Swanpool Beach

Falmouth Bay

A3
1 MARLBOROUGH CL
2 MARLBOROUGH GR
3 PENMERE PL
4 PENMERE CT
5 MARLBOROUGH CT
6 CHARD TERR
7 PENMERE HILL

C3
1 ABERFAL HO
2 ROPEWALK CT
3 GROVE PL
4 ARWENACK HO
5 MARINE CRES
6 ARWYN COTTS
7 ARWYN PL
8 BAR TERR
9 BOSLOGGAS MEWS
10 OSBORNE VILLAS
11 PELHAM CT
12 CHALLENGER QUAY
13 SWALLOW HO
14 ROYALIST CT
15 Falmouth Watersports Ctr
16 Maritime House Discovery Quay

82
94

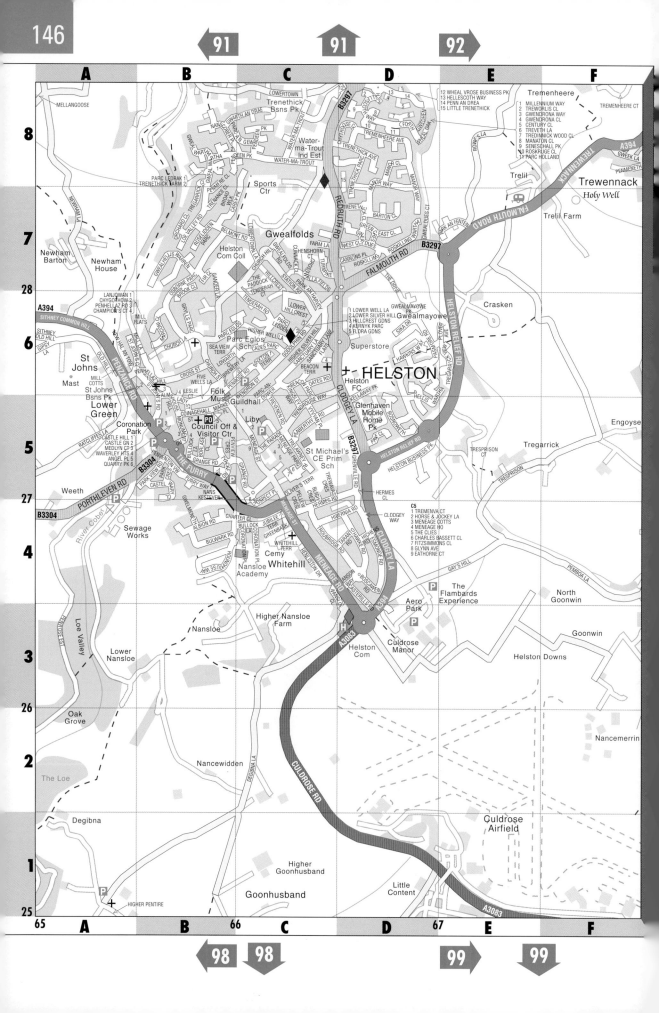

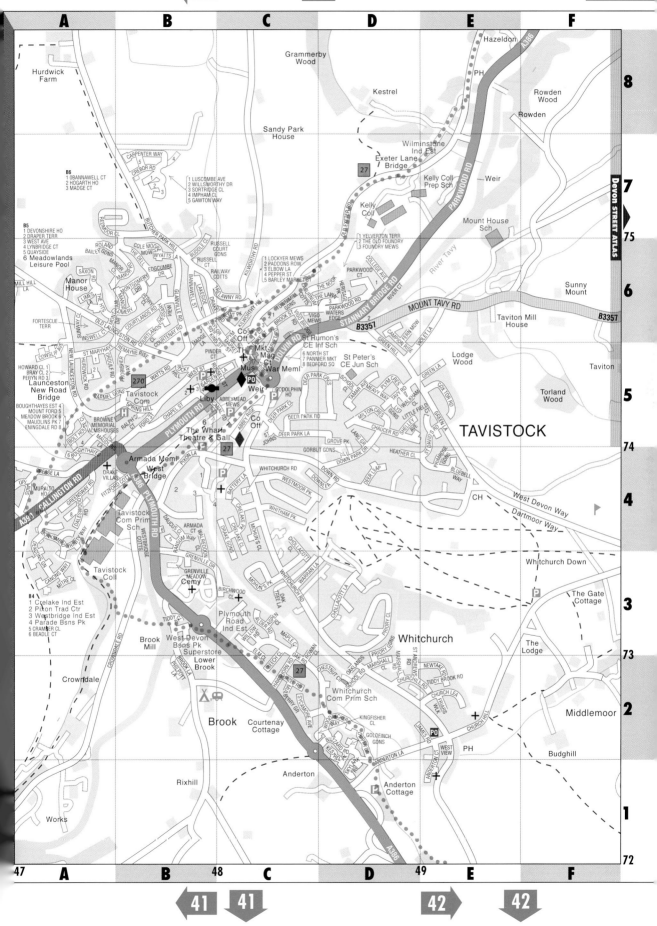

One-way Streets

House numbers
1 | 59
HIGH ST

A   B   C

4

550

3

2

545

540

1

535

465   A   470   B   475   C

Pennycomequick

Plymouth

Victoria Park

Stuart Road Prim Sch

1 VALLETORT TERR
2 FELLOWES PL
3 SEYMOUR PL
4 FELLOWES LA

WYNDHAM MEWS 1
HOLLYWOOD TERR 2

Plymouth Cath

Cathedral Sch of St Mary

Notre Dame Ho

Plymouth Coll Prep Sch

Adelaide St

St Peters CE VA Prim Sch & Nur

Plymouth Sch of Creative Arts

Plymouth Pavilions

Miller Court Workshop Units

1 ATHLONE HO
2 DAVID SOUTHGATE CT
3 BATTERY STREET FLATS

Millbay

CHICHESTER HO 1
LEIGHAM CT 2
LEIGHAM TERR LA 3
ST JAMES CT 4
ST JAMES MEWS 5

TA Ctr

St Andrew's CE VA Prim Sch

Continental Ferryport

Millbay Docks

St George's CE Prim Sch

West Hoe

West Hoe Pier

LB Sta

The Bridge

Armada Ctr

Pilgrim Prim Sch

Univ of Plymouth

Univ Bsns Sch

Plymouth Sta

City Mkt

City Coll Plymouth

Theatre Royal

Plymouth Athenaeum & Theatre

Guildhall Crown & Cty Cts

Merchant's House (Mus)

Guildhall Sq

War Memorial

1 RUSSELL CT
2 HOEGATE CT
3 HOEGATE PL
4 HOE GDNS
5 CITADEL RD E

Plymouth Hoe

PLYMOUTH

The Hoe

Smeaton's Tower

Royal Citadel

Tinside Lido

Grand Hotel

B3
1 ANSON HO
2 MELBOURNE GN
3 ETON TERR
4 OXFORD TERR
5 CAMBRIDGE LA W
6 FREDERICK ST W
7 ALICE LA
8 HARWELL CT
9 FRANKFORT GATE
10 COLIN CAMPBELL CT

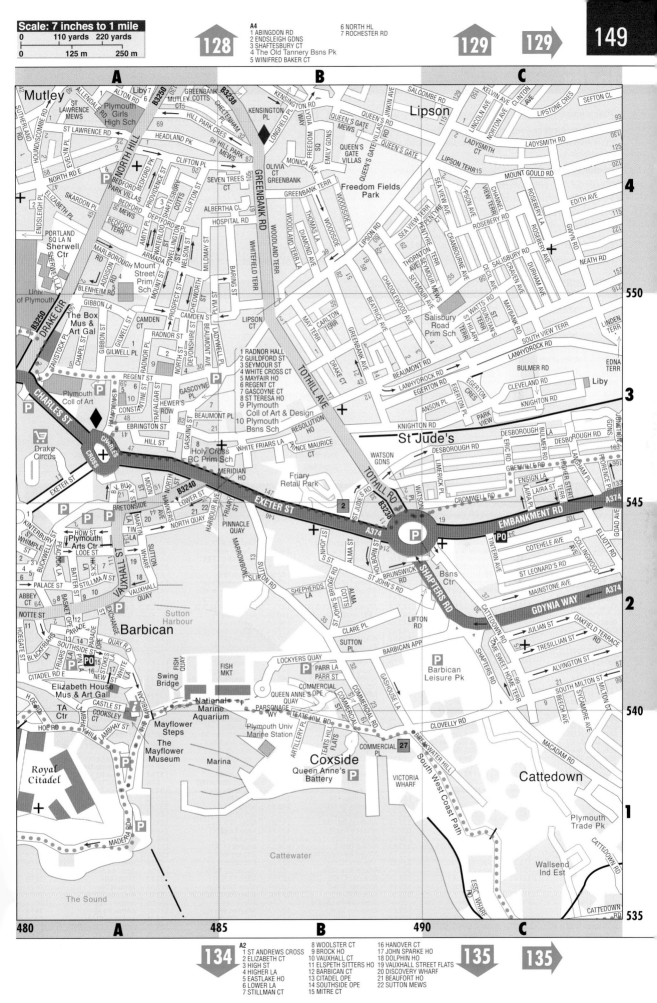

A4
1. ABINGDON RD
2. ENDSLEIGH GDNS
3. SHAFTESBURY CT
4. The Old Tannery Bsns Pk
5. WINIFRED BAKER CT
6 NORTH HL
7 ROCHESTER RD

A   B   C

Mutley

Lipson

Freedom Fields Park

St Jude's

The Box Mus & Art Gal

Plymouth Coll of Art

Drake Circus

Friary Retail Park

Salisbury Road Prim Sch

Exeter St   Embankment Rd

Plymouth Arts Ctr

Barbican

Sutton Harbour

Elizabeth House Mus & Art Gall

Swing Bridge

National Marine Aquarium

Mayflower Steps

The Mayflower Museum

Marina

Coxside

Queen Anne's Battery

Barbican Leisure Pk

South West Coast Path

Cattedown

Royal Citadel

The Sound

Cattewater

Plymouth Trade Pk

Wallsend Ind Est

480   485   490   535

A   B   C

A2
1 ST ANDREWS CROSS
2 ELIZABETH CT
3 HIGH ST
4 HIGHER LA
5 EASTLAKE HO
6 LOWER LA
7 STILLMAN CT
8 WOOLSTER CT
9 BROCK HO
10 VAUXHALL CT
11 ELSPETH SITTERS HO
12 BARBICAN CT
13 CITADEL OPE
14 SOUTHSIDE OPE
15 MITRE CT
16 HANOVER CT
17 JOHN SPARKE HO
18 DOLPHIN HO
19 VAUXHALL STREET FLATS
20 DISCOVERY WHARF
21 BEAUFORT HO
22 SUTTON MEWS

Index

Place name May be abbreviated on the map

Church Rd 6 Beckenham BR2..........**53** C6

Location number Present when a number indicates the place's position in a crowded area of mapping

Locality, town or village Shown when more than one place has the same name

Postcode district District for the indexed place

Page and grid square Page number and grid reference for the standard mapping

Cities, towns and villages are listed in CAPITAL LETTERS

Public and commercial buildings are highlighted in **magenta**   **Places of interest** are highlighted in blue with a star★

Abbreviations used in the index

Acad	Academy	Comm	Common	Gd	Ground	L	Leisure	Prom	Promenade
App	Approach	Cott	Cottage	Gdn	Garden	La	Lane	Rd	Road
Arc	Arcade	Cres	Crescent	Gn	Green	Liby	Library	Recn	Recreation
Ave	Avenue	Cswy	Causeway	Gr	Grove	Mdw	Meadow	Ret	Retail
Bglw	Bungalow	Ct	Court	H	Hall	Meml	Memorial	Sh	Shopping
Bldg	Building	Ctr	Centre	Ho	House	Mkt	Market	Sq	Square
Bsns, Bus	Business	Ctry	Country	Hospl	Hospital	Mus	Museum	St	Street
Bvd	Boulevard	Cty	County	HQ	Headquarters	Orch	Orchard	Sta	Station
Cath	Cathedral	Dr	Drive	Hts	Heights	Pal	Palace	Terr	Terrace
Cir	Circus	Dro	Drove	Ind	Industrial	Par	Parade	TH	Town Hall
Cl	Close	Ed	Education	Inst	Institute	Pas	Passage	Univ	University
Cnr	Corner	Emb	Embankment	Int	International	Pk	Park	Wk, Wlk	Walk
Coll	College	Est	Estate	Intc	Interchange	Pl	Place	Wr	Water
Com	Community	Ex	Exhibition	Junc	Junction	Prec	Precinct	Yd	Yard

Index of towns, villages, streets, hospitals, industrial estates, railway stations, schools, shopping centres, universities and places of interest

Abb–Amh

A

Abbey Cl PL20 . . . . **42** B2
Abbey Ct 19 Penzance TR18 **143** E5
Plymouth PL1. . . . . **149** A2
Abbey Hill TR26 . . . . **77** E3
Abbey Mdw
 5 Crapstone PL20 . . . . **42** A2
 Lelant TR26 . . . . **77** E4
Abbeymead Mews PL19 . .**147** C5
Abbey Mews PL31 . . . .**109** C4
Abbey Pl Plymouth PL1 . . . .**148** C2
 Tavistock PL19. . . . .**147** C5
Abbey Rise PL19 . . . .**147** C5
Abbey St TR18 . . . .**143** E5
Abbotsbury Way PL2 . . . . .**127** F8
Abbots Cl PL31 . . . .**109** F4
Abbotscourt La PL11. . . . . .**126** A2
Abbotsfield Cl PL19. . . . .**41** D8
Abbotsfield Cres PL19 . . . . . .**41** A8
Abbotts Rd PL3. . . . .**128** E6
Aberdeen Ave PL5 . . . .**124** D1
Aberdeen CI PL24 . . . . **60** B6
Aberfal Ho 1 TR11 . . . .**145** C3
Abingdon Rd 1 PL4 . . . . . .**149** A4
Abney Cres PL6. . . . .**125** B6
Above La PL15. . . . . **16** F3
Above Town Cl PL27 . . . . **21** F3
Abscott La PL9 . . . .**135** C5
Acacia Rd TR11. . . . .**144** F5
Academy Terr 30 TR26 . . .**141** B6
Acklington Pl PL5 . . . .**123** E4
Acland Cl EX23 . . . .**104** E7
Acland Gdns TR7 . . . .**110** D6
Acorn Arts Ctr★ 38 TR18 .**143** E5
Acorn Dr PL25 . . . .**115** A3
Acorn Gdns PL7 . . . .**130** D6
Acre Cotts PL1 . . . .**127** F3
Acre Pl PL1. . . . .**127** F3
Adams Cl Plymouth PL5 . . .**123** F1
 Torpoint PL11 . . . .**126** F3
Adams Cres PL11 . . . .**126** E3
ADDINGTON. **113** D7
Addington N 5 PL14. . . . . .**113** D6
Addington S 6 PL14. . . . . . .**113** D6
Addison Rd PL4 . . . .**149** A4
Addison Terr PL22. . . . .**112** C2
Adelaide La PL1 . . . .**148** A2
Adelaide Pl PL1. . . . .**148** A3

Adelaide Rd TR15. . . . .**140** C4
Adelaide St Camborne TR14 **138** E3
 Penzance TR18 . . . .**143** E6
 Plymouth PL1. . . . .**148** A3
  2 Plymouth, Ford PL2 . . .**127** F5
Adelaide Street Ope PL1. .**148** A3
Adelaide Terr TR1 . . . .**137** B4
Adela Rd PL11. . . . .**127** A3
Adeston Rd 5 PL28. . . . . . .**107** C4
Adit La Newlyn TR18 . . . . . .**143** C1
 Saltash PL12 . . . .**122** E3
Adits The PL18 . . . .**41** A3
Admiral's Hard PL1 . . . .**134** A8
Admirals Quay 4 PL1 . . . . .**145** B5
Admiralty Cotts PL1 . . . . . .**134** A7
Admiralty Ct PL13 . . . .**117** D3
Admiralty Ope S PL2. . . . . .**127** F6
Admiralty Rd
 Plymouth, Millbay PL1. . . . .**134** A8
 Plymouth, St Budeaux PL5. .**123** C2
Admiralty St
 Plymouth, Keyham PL2 . . . .**127** E6
 Plymouth, Millbay PL1. . . . .**134** A8
Admiralty Terr TR2 . . . . **83** B2
Aerohub Business Park TR8 **44** F6
Affaland Moor Rd EX22 . . . . . **8** E3
Afflington Rd PL9 . . . .**129** D1
African Row TR14 . . . . **79** B5
Agar Cres TR15. . . . .**139** D6
Agar Ct 2 Camborne TR15. .**139** C6
 Truro TR1. . . . .**137** D5
Agar Mdws 11 TR3. . . . . **81** F7
Agar Rd Camborne TR15 . . .**139** D6
 Newquay TR7. . . . .**110** E5
 St Austell PL25. . . . .**114** E6
 Truro TR1. . . . .**137** C5
Agar Terr 12 PL31. . . . .**109** D5
Agar Way TR15 . . . .**139** C5
Agaton Fort Rd PL5. . . . . . .**123** F3
Agaton Rd PL5 . . . .**123** E3
Aglets Way PL26. . . . .**114** F2
Agnes Cl EX23 . . . .**104** F4
Ainslie Terr PL2 . . . .**127** E7
Airborne Dr PL6 . . . .**125** B4
Aire Gdns PL3 . . . .**129** B5
Airfield Rd PL30. . . . . **35** E4
Alamein Ct PL12. . . . .**122** E2
Alamein Rd PL12 . . . .**122** D2
Alan Harvey Ct 14 TR26 . .**141** B4
Alan Rd PL28 . . . .**107** D4
Alansmere Ct TR2 . . . . **57** A1
Alanta Flats TR7. . . . .**110** B5
Albacore Dr 3 PL6. . . . .**125** B5
Albany Cl Redruth TR15 . . . .**140** C3

Albany Cl continued
 Redruth TR15. . . . .**140** C3
 St Agnes TR5 . . . . **68** D8
Albany Ct 4 Newquay TR7 .**110** F6
 Redruth TR15. . . . .**140** D3
Albany Gdns TR15 . . . .**140** D3
Albany La TR15 . . . .**140** C4
Albany Pl TR11 . . . .**145** A3
Albany Rd Falmouth TR11. . .**145** A3
  5 Newquay TR7. . . . .**110** F6
 Redruth TR15. . . . .**140** C4
 Truro TR1. . . . .**137** A4
Albany St PL1 . . . .**127** E2
Albany Terr TR26 . . . .**141** B4
ALBASTON. **40** E5
Albemarle Villas PL1 . . . . . .**127** F3
Albert Bldgs 19 TR18. . . . . .**143** E6
Albert Cotts TR11. . . . .**145** B4
Albertha Cl PL4. . . . .**149** B4
Albert Pier TR18 . . . .**143** F5
Albert Pl Camborne TR14 . .**138** E3
  21 St Ives TR26 . . . .**141** B5
 Truro TR1. . . . .**137** C3
Albert Rd Plymouth PL2 . . . .**127** F3
 St Austell PL25. . . . .**114** D3
 St Ives TR26. . . . . **77** A7
Albert St Camborne TR14 . .**138** E3
 Penzance TR18 . . . .**143** F6
Albert Terr Gunnislake PL18 . **40** F5
 Lostwithiel PL22 . . . .**112** C2
  18 Penzance TR18. . . . . . .**143** E6
  26 St Ives TR26. . . . .**141** B5
Albertus Dr TR27 . . . .**142** B3
Albertus Gdns TR27. . . . . . .**142** B3
Albertus Rd TR27 . . . .**142** B3
Albert Villas PL2. . . . .**127** E4
Albion Ct PL11. . . . .**127** B3
Albion Dr PL2 . . . .**128** B7
Albion Rd Helston TR13 . . . .**146** B4
 Torpoint PL11 . . . .**127** B3
Albion Row TR16 . . . . **80** F8
Alcester Cl PL2. . . . .**127** E4
Alcester St PL2. . . . .**127** F4
Alden Wlk PL6. . . . .**129** B7
Aldercombe La EX23. . . . . **5** A6
Alderney Rd PL6. . . . .**124** F7
Alder Rd PL19 . . . .**147** C3
Aldersley Wlk PL6 . . . .**125** A1
Alderwood Parc TR10. . . . . .**144** B8
Aldreath Cl TR20 . . . . **88** B7
Aldreath Rd TR20. . . . . **88** B7
Alexander Ct
  14 Carnon Downs TR3. . . . . **81** F7
Albany Cl Redruth TR15 . . . .**140** C3

Alexander Ct continued
 Gorran Haven PL26 . . . . **85** D5
Alexandra Cl 5 Illogan TR16 **67** E4
 Plymouth PL9. . . . .**136** B8
 St Ives TR26. . . . . **77** A7
Alexandra Ct TR7. . . . .**111** C8
Alexandra Dr PL20. . . . . **41** C1
Alexandra Gdns TR18 . . . . .**143** D4
Alexandra Ho TR18 . . . .**143** D3
Alexandra Pl
 Penzance TR18 . . . .**143** D4
  5 Plymouth PL4. . . . .**128** E4
 St Ives TR26. . . . . **77** A7
Alexandra Rd Bodmin PL31 .**109** B5
 Illogan TR16 . . . . **67** D4
 Newquay TR7. . . . .**111** C8
 Penzance TR18 . . . .**143** D4
 Plymouth, Crownhill PL6 . . .**124** F2
 Plymouth, Ford PL2 . . . .**127** F5
 Plymouth, Mutley PL4 . . . . .**128** F4
 St Austell PL25. . . . .**114** E3
 St Ives TR26. . . . . **77** A7
Alexandra Sq PL12. . . . .**123** A2
Alexandra Terr
 Mount Hawke TR4. . . . . **68** C6
 Penzance TR18 . . . .**143** D3
 Plymouth PL2. . . . .**127** F5
 St Ives TR26. . . . .**141** A5
 Tremar PL14 . . . . **38** A4
  2 Truro TR1 . . . .**137** B4
ALFARDISWORTHY **5** E6
Alford Cl EX23. . . . .**104** F5
Alfred Pl PL2 . . . .**127** F5
Alfred Rd PL2 . . . .**127** F5
Alfred St PL1. . . . .**148** C2
Alger Wlk PL6 . . . .**124** E6
Alice La 7 PL1 . . . .**148** B3
Alice St PL1 . . . .**148** A3
Alldritt Cl TR7. . . . .**111** D7
Allenby Rd PL2 . . . .**128** A6
Allendale PL26 . . . . **58** E8
Allendale Rd PL4 . . . .**149** A4
Allen Pk PL30 . . . . **23** B2
Allen Vale PL14. . . . .**113** A5
Allen Valley Rd PL30. . . . . . . **23** E6
Allern La PL5. . . . .**120** D1
Allerton Wlk PL6 . . . .**129** B7
Alley Hill PL20. . . . . **42** A1
Alleyn Gdns PL3 . . . .**128** E8
Allium Ct TR4 . . . . **70** D8
All Saints Pk PL18 . . . . **40** E5
Alma Cl TR5 . . . . **68** D8
Alma Cotts PL4 . . . .**149** B2
Alma Pl Heamoor TR18 . . . .**143** C7

Alma Pl continued
 Newquay TR7. . . . .**110** D6
 Padstow PL28 . . . .**107** D5
  5 Penzance TR18. . . . .**143** E5
 Redruth TR15. . . . .**140** B5
Alma Rd Plymouth PL3 . . . . .**128** C4
 Truro TR1. . . . . **69** F3
Alma St PL4 . . . .**149** B2
Alma Terr Carharrack TR16 . . **80** F8
 Gunnislake PL18. . . . . **41** A6
 Penzance TR18 . . . .**143** E5
  10 St Ives TR26 . . . .**141** B5
Almeria Ct PL7 . . . .**130** C4
Almond Dr PL7 . . . .**131** B6
Almshouse Hill TR13. . . . . .**146** B5
Alouts PL32 . . . . **15** D7
Alston Pk PL7 . . . .**130** D6
ALTARNUN **26** C8
Altarnun Com Prim Sch
 PL15 . . . . **26** C7
Altarnun Rd PL15. . . . . **16** E2
Alton Pl PL4. . . . .**128** E4
Alton Rd PL4 . . . .**149** A4
Alverne Bldgs 7 TR18 . . . .**143** D5
ALVERTON **143** C4
Alverton Com Prim Sch
 TR18. . . . .**143** C4
Alverton Ct TR1 . . . .**137** E5
Alverton Ho TR18. . . . .**143** C5
Alverton Rd TR18 . . . .**143** D5
Alverton St TR18 . . . .**143** D5
Alverton Terr
  4 Penzance TR18. . . . .**143** D5
 Truro TR1. . . . .**137** D5
Alvington St PL4. . . . .**149** C2
Alwin Pk PL6. . . . .**125** A5
Alwyn Cl TR7 . . . .**111** E6
Amacre Dr PL9 . . . .**135** B6
Amados Cl PL7 . . . .**130** B4
Amados Dr PL7 . . . .**130** C4
Amados Rise PL7. . . . .**130** B4
Amal An Avon TR27. . . . . . .**142** E7
AMALEBRA. **76** F3
AMALVEOR. **76** E4
Amanda Way PL14. . . . . **38** E4
Amber Cl 1 PL6. . . . .**124** C6
Amble Rd 28 PL17 . . . . **39** F4
Ambrose Ct TR15 . . . .**140** E5
Ambrose Lake Hill PL14. . . . **37** A2
Amelia Ct PL7. . . . .**130** B4
Amherst Rd PL3 . . . .**148** B4
Amherst Rd La E PL3. . . . . .**128** C4
Amherst Road Lane East
 PL3 . . . .**148** B4

Amity Pl PL4 . . . . .149 A4
Anchor Quay **12** TR10 . .144 D7
ANDERTON. 132 F4
Anderton Ct PL19. . . . . . .147 E2
Anderton La PL19. . . . . . .147 D2
Anderton Rise PL10. . . . . .132 F4
Andrewartha Rd TR10 . . .144 B8
Andrew Pl **3** TR1. . . . . . .137 C4
Andrew's Terr TR16 . . . . .139 F1
Andrews Way PL12 . . . . . .53 E5
Andromeda Gr **3** PL9 . . .136 E7
Andurn Cl PL9. . . . . .136 B6
Aneray Rd TR14 . . . . .138 D4
ANGARRACK 78 C5
Angarrack Ct PL26. . . . . . .46 F2
Angarrack La TR27. . . . . . .78 C5
Angarrack Mews TR27. . . .78 C5
Angavran Mdw TR8. . . . . .55 D8
Angel Hill **7** PL15 . . . . .106 C6
Angel Pl **5** TR13. . . . . . .146 B5
An Gof Gdns PL31. . . . . . .109 C4
Angrouse La
    Poldhu Cove TR12 . . . . . .98 F2
    10 Trewoon TR12. . . . . .99 A2
Angwin Ave **4** TR5 . . . . .54 C1
Anjardyn Pl PL24 . . . . . . .60 C5
Ankervis La TR16 . . . . . . .140 F1
Anna Maria La TR11 . . . . .93 C2
Annear Rd TR10 . . . . .144 A6
Ann's Pl PL3. . . . . .128 A4
Anson Ho **1** PL1 . . . . . . .148 B3
Anson Pl
    Plymouth, Devonport PL2 . . . .127 F4
    Plymouth, St Jude's PL4 . . .149 C3
Anson Rd PL27. . . . . .31 F3
Anson Way TR13. . . . . . . .146 D4
Anstis St PL1 . . . . .148 A3
Anthony Cl EX23. . . . . .4 C3
Anthony Lowen PL28 . . . .107 D4
Anthony Rd TR7. . . . . . . .110 E4
Antoine Cl **4** TR18 . . . . .143 C2
Antoine Terr **23** TR18 . . .143 C2
ANTONY 65 E5
Antony CE VA Sch PL11. . . .65 E5
Antony Gdns PL2 . . . . . . .128 C8
Antony Hill PL11. . . . . .65 E5
Antony House★ PL11 . . . .126 D5
Antony Rd PL11. . . . . .127 B3
Antony Woodland Gdn★
    PL11. . . . . .126 D6
Antron Hill TR10. . . . . .81 B1
Antron La
    Mabe Burnthouse TR10 . . . .93 C8
    Trenowth TR10. . . . . .93 C8
Antron Way TR10 . . . . .93 C8
Anvil Ct Camelford PL32 . . .105 D3
    Venterdon PL17. . . . . .28 D1
Anvil Rd PL32. . . . . .105 D3
An Vownder Goth TR13 . . .91 B7
Anwyl Cl PL1. . . . . .148 B3
Anzac Ave PL5. . . . . .124 A4
Appin Gdns TR15 . . . . . . .139 C7
Appleby Wlk PL5 . . . . . . .124 D4
Appledore La PL14 . . . . . . .39 B3
Appleton Tor Cl PL3 . . . . .129 F5
Appletree La PL25 . . . . . .115 D3
Apsley Rd PL4 . . . . .136 E8
Aquarius Dr **8** PL9 . . . . .136 E8
Aquila Dr **16** PL9 . . . . . .136 E8
Arbour The PL6 . . . . .124 E5
Arcade The **6** TR18. . . . .143 E5
Arcadia PL9 . . . . .136 D6
Arcadia Rd TR10 . . . . .93 C6
Archbishop Benson CE Prim
    Sch TR1. . . . . .137 D6
Archer Pl PL1 . . . . .148 B4
Archer Terr PL1 . . . . .148 B3
Arch Hill TR1 . . . . .137 C2
Architects Way PL5 . . . . . .127 B8
Arch La TR27 . . . . .77 D1
Archway Ave PL4 . . . . . . .129 B3
Arden Gr PL2. . . . . .128 C8
Ardhow TR10. . . . . .94 A8
Arena Cres PL25. . . . . . . .115 B4
Argal TR11 . . . . .93 C7
Argal View TR10. . . . . .93 B6
Ariel Mews **22** PL9 . . . . .136 E8
Aries Hill PL14. . . . . .113 E7
Aries La PL9. . . . . .136 D8
Ark Royal Cl PL5. . . . . . . .127 D8
Arkwright Gdns PL5 . . . . .123 F2
Arley Cl PL6 . . . . .125 B6
Arlington Rd PL4 . . . . .128 F4
Armada Ct PL19 . . . . .147 B4
Armada Ctr PL1 . . . . .148 C3
Armada Rd PL10. . . . . . . .133 A1
Armada St PL4 . . . . .149 A4
Armada Way PL1 . . . . . . .148 C2
Armchair Cnr PL31 . . . . . .109 C5
Arnheim Terr TR11 . . . . . .145 B7
Arnhem Villas TR11. . . . . .145 B7
Arnison Cl PL9 . . . . .135 F5
Arnold's Point PL4. . . . . . .129 C5
Arnside Cl PL6. . . . . .125 D3
Arrallas Barns TR2. . . . . . .57 B4
Arrallas Rd TR8. . . . . .57 A6
Arscott Gdns PL9. . . . . . . .135 C5
Arscott La PL9. . . . . .135 D5
Art Gallery Terr TR18 . . . .143 C3
Arthurian Ctr The★ PL32 . .105 D8
Arthur Terr PL11 . . . . .127 B2
Artillery Pl PL4 . . . . .149 B1
Arun Cl PL3 . . . . .129 C5
Arundel Cl PL16. . . . . .19 F4
Arundel Ct TR27 . . . . .78 D6
Arundell Gdns
    Falmouth TR11. . . . . .144 E6
    Lifton PL16. . . . . .19 F4

Arundell Pl TR1 . . . . .137 C3
Arundel Pk TR27. . . . . .78 D6
Arundel Terr Bude EX23 . . .104 D4
    Plymouth PL2. . . . . .127 F4
Arundel Way
    Connor Downs TR27 . . . . . .78 D6
    Newquay TR7. . . . . .111 B7
Arwenack Ave TR11 . . . . .145 C3
Arwenack Ho **4** TR11. . . .145 C3
Arwenack St TR11 . . . . . .145 C3
Arworthal Mdws TR3 . . . . .81 D6
Arwyn Cotts **6** TR11. . . .145 C3
Asdally Vale TR18 . . . . . . .143 B5
Ashbrook St
    11 Prince Rock PL9. . . . .129 D1
    2 Prince Rock PL9. . . . . .129 D1
Ashburgh Parc PL12. . . . . .122 B3
Ashburnham Rd PL5. . . . .124 A3
Ashbury Gr EX22. . . . . .11 E8
Ash Cl **16** Par PL24. . . . . .60 B4
    7 Yelverton PL20. . . . . . .42 C3
Ashcombe Cl PL7. . . . . . . .130 C7
Ashdown Cl Plymouth PL6 . .125 E3
    Sticker PL26. . . . . .58 E1
Ashdown Wlk PL6 . . . . . . .125 E3
Ash Dr TR27. . . . . .142 B3
Ashery Dr PL9 . . . . .135 C6
Ashfield Gdns TR11. . . . . .144 E6
Ashfield Rd TR11 . . . . .144 F6
Ashfield Villas TR11 . . . . .144 F6
Ashford Cl PL3 . . . . .129 A4
Ashford Cres PL3. . . . . . . .129 A4
Ashford Hill PL4. . . . . .129 A4
Ashford Rd PL4. . . . . .128 F4
Ash Gr Hayle TR27 . . . . . .142 B3
    Par PL24. . . . . .60 B4
    Plymouth PL2. . . . . .127 F7
Ashill TR14 . . . . .66 E3
Ashleigh Cl PL5 . . . . .124 C7
Ashleigh La PL5 . . . . .120 D1
Ashleigh Way Plymouth PL7 .131 C4
    Probus TR2. . . . . .71 D6
Ashley Cl **9** PL26 . . . . . . .59 D7
Ashley Pl PL1. . . . . .148 B2
Ashley Rd Shortlanesend TR4. .69 F6
    Truro TR1. . . . . .137 C4
Ashmead TR2 . . . . .57 E1
Ash Park Cl PL14 . . . . .38 A4
Ashridge Gdns PL5 . . . . . .124 B2
ASHTON 90 E3
Ashton Cl PL6 . . . . .125 C6
Ashton Ct TR7 . . . . .111 D6
Ashton Way PL12 . . . . . . .122 D3
Ashton Wlk EX23 . . . . .6 F5
Ashtree Cl PL6 . . . . .125 D7
Ashtree Gr PL9 . . . . .136 C8
Ash Vale PL16 . . . . .19 F4
Ashwood Cl PL7 . . . . .131 B6
Ashwood Park Rd PL7 . . . .131 C6
Aspen Cl PL19 . . . . .147 C3
Aspen Gdns PL7. . . . . .131 B5
Astor Dr PL4 . . . . .129 C1
Astwood Developments
    PL13 . . . . .63 F8
Athelstan Pk PL31 . . . . . . .109 F3
Athenaeum La PL1 . . . . . .148 B2
Athenaeum Pl PL1. . . . . . .148 C2
Athenaeum St PL1. . . . . . .148 B2
Atherton Pl PL2 . . . . .127 E4
Athlone Ho PL1. . . . . .148 A2
Atlanta PL28 . . . . .20 E2
Atlantic Bays Holiday Pk
    PL28 . . . . .31 F6
Atlantic Cl Camborne TR14 . .138 E2
    Treknow PL33. . . . . .14 C5
    Widemouth Bay EX23 . . . . . .6 F5
Atlantic Cres TR19. . . . . . . .96 C5
Atlantic Highway PL32. . . .10 D2
Atlantic Mews
    New Polzeath PL27 . . . . . . .21 D6
    8 St Agnes TR5. . . . . . . .54 C1
Atlantic Rd Delabole PL33 . .14 D2
    Newquay TR7. . . . . .110 C6
    Tintagel PL34. . . . . .14 C7
Atlantic Reach TR8 . . . . . . .45 D3
Atlantic Terr
    Camborne TR14. . . . . .138 E2
    New Polzeath PL27 . . . . . . .21 D6
    43 St Ives TR26. . . . . . . .141 B6
    Trevone PL28. . . . . .20 E2
Atlantic View Rd EX23 . . . . .5 A6
Atlantic Way Porthtowan TR4 .68 A6
    4 Tintagel PL34. . . . . . . .14 C7
Attenborrow Ct TR7 . . . . .111 C8
Attery View PL15 . . . . .18 E6
Attwood La PL14. . . . . .38 D3
Auckland Rd **3** PL2 . . . . .128 A5
Audierne Rd PL10 . . . . . . .144 C7
Austin Ave PL2 . . . . .128 A6
Austin Cres PL6 . . . . .125 C1
Austin Farm Prim Sch PL6 .129 C7
Ava PL26 . . . . .73 C4
Avallen Cl TR11. . . . . .82 A3
Avent Wlk PL7. . . . . .130 F7
Avenue Rd TR11 . . . . .145 C4
Avenue The St Hilary TR20. . .89 F6
    Truro TR1. . . . . .137 D5
Averys Gn PL30 . . . . .35 F3
Avery's Row PL28. . . . . . . .107 D5
Avery Terr PL22 . . . . .112 C2
Avon Cl Plymouth PL3 . . . . .129 D6
    St Austell PL25. . . . . .115 A5
Avondale Rd TR1. . . . . . . .137 B4
Avon Flats TR7 . . . . .111 C7
Avrack Cl TR19 . . . . .87 F3

Axe Cl PL3. . . . . .129 D6
Axford Hill PL17 . . . . .39 F2
Axtown La PL20 . . . . .42 C2
Aycliffe Gdns PL7. . . . . . . .131 A3
Aylesbury Cres PL5 . . . . . .124 B5
Aylmer Sq **14** PL25 . . . . .114 C3
Aylwin Cl PL7. . . . . .130 E6
Ayreville Rd PL2. . . . . .128 B7
Ayr La TR26 . . . . .141 B6
Ayr Terr TR26 . . . . .141 A6
Aysshton Gdns **15** PL17 . .39 F4
Azenor Ave TR11. . . . . . . .144 D3

B

Babbacombe Cl PL6 . . . . .129 E8
Baber Cl PL12. . . . . .40 C2
Baber Ct PL12. . . . . .40 D2
Babis Farm Cl PL12. . . . . .122 F1
Babis Farm Ct PL12. . . . . .122 F1
Babis Farm Mews PL12. . . .122 F2
Babis Farm Row PL12. . . .122 F1
Babis Farm Way PL12. . . .122 F2
Babis La PL12 . . . . .122 F1
Baby Beach La PL27 . . . . . .21 D6
Backen La PL32. . . . . .10 D2
Back Hill Port Isaac PL29 . . .22 D7
    Saltash PL12. . . . . .122 D2
Back La Angarrack TR27. . . .78 C5
    Callington PL17. . . . . .39 F4
    Crowlas TR20. . . . . .89 B8
    Marazion TR17. . . . . .89 B5
    Plymouth PL7. . . . . .130 E4
    17 St Erth TR27. . . . . . . .77 D2
    17 St Ives TR26 . . . . . . .141 B6
    St Neot PL14 . . . . .36 F2
    Tintagel PL34. . . . . .14 D7
    Tregony TR2. . . . . .71 F4
    Veryan TR2. . . . . .83 F6
Back Lane W TR15. . . . . . .140 B4
Back Quay TR1 . . . . .137 D4
Back Rd PL18. . . . . .41 A3
Back Road E **7** TR26. . . . .141 B6
Back Road W TR26. . . . . . .141 B6
Back St **42** TR26. . . . . . .141 B6
BADGALL 17 C5
Badgall Rd PL15 . . . . .17 C5
Badger's Cross TR20. . . . . .88 E8
Badgers Wlk PL12 . . . . . . .122 D4
Badgers Wood **9** PL31 . .109 A5
Badger View PL9 . . . . .135 E5
BADHARLICK 17 E5
Bagbury Rd EX23 . . . . .104 E3
Bag La Lanjore PL12. . . . . . .52 F1
    Polbathic PL12. . . . . .64 F8
    St Germans PL12. . . . . .65 A8
Bahavella Dr TR26 . . . . . . .141 B4
Bailey Gdns EX22. . . . . .8 A5
Baileys Field **7** EX23 . . . . .5 A6
Baileys La **20** TR26. . . . . .141 B6
Bailey Terr EX22. . . . . .8 A5
Bainbridge Ave PL3. . . . . .128 F7
Bainbridge Ct PL7 . . . . . . .130 E7
Baines Hill TR16 . . . . .67 C6
Bakehouse La **12** PL17. . . .39 E4
Bakehouse The TR10 . . . . .144 D7
Bake La Bake PL12. . . . . . . .52 D1
    Rosedale PL12. . . . . .64 D8
Bake Lane End PL12. . . . . .52 D1
Bakers Cl PL7 . . . . .131 C5
Bakers Ct TR7 . . . . .110 E6
Bakers Gn PL25. . . . . .115 B4
Bakers La Gunnislake PL18. . .40 F5
    Oakenhayes PL18 . . . . .41 A5
Bakers Pl PL1 . . . . .127 F1
Bakers Row TR13. . . . . .90 F3
BAKESDOWN. 7 D3
Balcoath TR16. . . . . .68 D1
BALDHU 69 C1
Baldhu Row TR20. . . . . . . .76 F2
Bal East La PL26 . . . . .59 A1
Balfield St **5** TR13. . . . . . .98 C8
Balfour Terr PL2. . . . . .127 E4
Bal–Jinjy Cl **19** PL24 . . . . .60 B4
Balkin Way TR15. . . . . . . .139 D7
BALL 108 E7
Bal La TR27. . . . . .90 C5
Ballad Gdns PL5. . . . . .124 C1
Ballaminers La PL27 . . . . . .32 C6
Ballard Cl TR16. . . . . .80 B5
Ballard Est TR16. . . . . .80 B5
Ball La TR8. . . . . .45 A8
Ball Terr PL27 . . . . .108 E7
Balmoral Ave PL2 . . . . . . .127 F5
Balmoral Pl **3** TR15 . . . .140 B5
Balmoral Terr **4** TR15 . . .140 B5
BALNOON. 77 A5
Balnoon Flats TR26. . . . . . .77 A4
Bal Rd TR13 . . . . .91 E4
BALWEST 90 D5
Bambry Cl TR20 . . . . .89 C5
Bampfylde Way
    Goldsithney TR20. . . . . .89 F5
    Plymouth PL6. . . . . .124 D4
Bampton Rd PL6. . . . . .125 E1
Band House La PL26 . . . . . .59 C7
BANGORS. 6 F2
Bangors Est EX23. . . . . .6 F2
Bangors Rd PL15 . . . . .18 E2
Banjo La PL27 . . . . .32 D6
Bank Cotts **6** TR10. . . . . .144 C7
Bank Pl TR11. . . . . .145 C3
Bank Sq TR19 . . . . .86 F6
Bank St Newquay TR7. . . . .110 D6
    St Columb Major TR9 . . . . .45 E6
Bank Terr TR4. . . . . .56 A2
Bannawell Ct **1** PL19. . . .147 B6

Bannawell St PL19 . . . . . . .147 B6
Banns Rd TR4 . . . . .68 C3
Baptist Hill TR27 . . . . .142 C6
Baptist St PL17 . . . . .41 A3
Bara Pl PL17. . . . . .39 F6
Barbara Hepworth Mus &
    Sculpture Gdn★ TR26 . . .141 B6
BARBICAN 149 A2
Barbican App PL4. . . . . . . .149 B2
Barbican Cl PL13 . . . . .117 D4
Barbican Ct Looe PL13. . . . .117 D5
    12 Plymouth PL4 . . . . . .149 A2
Barbican Farm La PL13 . . .117 E5
Barbican Hill PL13. . . . . . .117 D4
Barbican La TR18. . . . . . . .143 F4
Barbican Leisure Pk PL4 . .149 C2
Barbican Rd Looe PL13 . . .117 E6
    Plymouth PL7. . . . . .130 E4
Barbican Rise Ind Est
    PL13 . . . . .117 E5
Barbican The PL1 . . . . .149 A1
Barbican Theatre PL1. . . . .149 A1
Barbican Way TR13. . . . . . .91 E4
Barbury Cres PL6. . . . . . . .125 B8
BARCELONA. 62 E4
Barcote Wlk PL6. . . . . .129 C8
Bardsey Cl PL6 . . . . .125 A7
BAREPPA 93 B4
Bareppa Bareppa TR11. . . . .93 E4
    Carlidnack TR16. . . . . .94 A2
Baring St PL4. . . . . .149 B4
Barker's Hill PL12 . . . . . . .122 C1
Barkhouse La PL25 . . . . . .115 B2
BARKLA SHOP 54 E1
Bar La Connor Downs TR27 . .78 C6
    Falmouth TR11. . . . . .145 C3
Barlandhu **17** TR18 . . . . .143 C2
Barlanwick TR18 . . . . .143 B2
Barley Market St PL19 . . . .147 C6
Barlowena TR14 . . . . .138 D1
Barlow Gdns PL2 . . . . .128 B7
Bar Mdws TR1. . . . . .70 D2
Barnaloft **13** TR26. . . . . . .141 B6
Barn Cl Plymouth PL7. . . . .131 D4
    Wainhouse Corner EX23 . . . .10 F6
Barncoose Ind Est TR15 . . .139 F6
Barncoose La TR15 . . . . . . .139 E6
Barncoose Terr TR15 . . . . .139 F6
Barn Courtyard TR27 . . . . .78 D6
Barndale Cres PL6. . . . . . .125 B6
BARNE BARTON 127 C8
Barne Cl PL5 . . . . .127 C8
Barnecutt Cl **6** PL14. . . . .38 A3
Barne La PL5 . . . . .123 D1
Barne Rd PL5. . . . . .127 C8
Barnfield Dr PL7 . . . . .131 C5
Barnfield Gdns TR18. . . . . .88 E6
Barnfield Pk EX23 . . . . .4 E1
Barnfield Terr
    3 Indian Queens TR9 . . . . .45 E1
    Liskeard PL14 . . . . .113 B4
Barn Hill Cadgwith TR12 . .103 B3
    Polbathic PL12. . . . . .64 F8
    Tideford PL12. . . . . .52 F1
Barningham Gdns PL6. . . .125 B6
Barn La Bodmin PL31. . . . .109 C4
    Bokelly PL30 . . . . .23 C3
    18 St Columb Major TR9 . . .45 E6
Barn Meadow Pk PL13 . . .117 B2
Barnoon Hill TR26. . . . . . .141 B6
Barnoon Terr **29** TR26 . . .141 B6
Barn Park La PL31. . . . . . . .35 B2
Barnpark Rd PL35. . . . . .9 C1
Barn Park Rd PL3. . . . . . . .128 D6
Barn Pk South Petherwin PL22 .112 C2
    Saltash PL12. . . . . .122 F3
Barn St PL14 . . . . .113 C5
Barnstaple Cl PL6. . . . . . . .129 E7
Barns Terr PL12 . . . . .118 A3
Barnwood Cl PL9. . . . . . . .135 E5
Baron Ct PL15 . . . . .17 D5
Barons Mdw PL31 . . . . . . .109 F5
Barons Rd PL20. . . . . .42 E3
Barossa Rd PL11. . . . . .127 B3
Barracadoes PL15 . . . . .18 E5
Barrack La TR1 . . . . .137 D3
Barrack Pl PL1 . . . . .128 A1
Barrack's La TR16 . . . . .68 E1
Barrack St PL1 . . . . .127 E2
Barras Cross PL14 . . . . . . .113 C6
Barras Moor TR10 . . . . .81 D4
Barras Pl PL14. . . . . .113 C6
Barras St PL14 . . . . .113 C6
Bar Rd Falmouth TR11 . . . .145 C3
    Mawnan Smith TR11. . . . . . .93 C2
Barrepta Cl TR26 . . . . .141 D1
Barrie Cres PL31 . . . . .109 E2
BARRIPPER 79 B5
Barripper Rd
    Camborne TR14. . . . . .138 C1
    Penponds TR14 . . . . .79 C5
Barrow Down PL12 . . . . . .122 B3
Barrowfield View TR7 . . . .111 A7
Barr's Cl PL23. . . . . .116 D5
Barry's La PL28. . . . . .107 D5
Bar Terr **8** TR11. . . . . . . .145 C3
Bartholomew Rd PL2 . . . . .128 B5
Bartles Cl PL16 . . . . .19 D7
Bartles Ind Est TR15. . . . . . .90 D7
Bartlett Ave EX23 . . . . . . .104 F5
Barton Cl **11** Bodmin PL31. .109 D5
    Heamoor TR18. . . . . .143 D7
    Helston TR13. . . . . .146 D7
    Landrake PL12. . . . . .53 C3
    Plymouth PL7. . . . . .131 C5

Barton Ct PL26 . . . . .58 A7
Barton La TR9 . . . . .45 D1
Barton Mdw Pelynt PL13 . . .62 D6
    Truro TR1. . . . . .137 A5
Barton Mdws PL12. . . . . . . .53 B7
Barton Mews Landrake PL12. .53 C3
    Millbrook PL10. . . . . .132 F6
Barton Rd Helland PL30 . . . .35 A5
    St Dennis PL26. . . . . .58 A7
Barton Row PL30 . . . . .23 A3
Barton The PL29 . . . . .22 D6
Barview La TR27 . . . . .142 C4
Barwis Hill TR18 . . . . .143 E6
Barwis Terr **1** TR18 . . . . .143 E6
Basil Rd PL15. . . . . .16 F3
Basinghall Cl PL9. . . . . . . .135 E5
Basket Ope PL4 . . . . .149 A2
Basset Rd TR14. . . . . .138 D2
Basset St Camborne TR14. . .138 D2
    Falmouth TR11. . . . . .145 A5
    Redruth TR15. . . . . .140 C4
Bassett Cl PL26 . . . . .47 A1
Bassett Pl **11** TR11 . . . . .145 A5
Bassett Rd Illogan TR16. . . .67 E4
    Redruth TR15. . . . . .140 B8
Bassett Terr TR16 . . . . .67 D6
Bastville EX22 . . . . .11 E8
Bath La PL1 . . . . .148 B2
Bath Pl PL1. . . . . .148 B2
Bath Place W PL1 . . . . . . .148 B2
BATHPOOL 27 C1
Bath St PL1. . . . . .148 B2
Battalion Cl **6** PL31 . . . . .109 F3
Battershall Cl PL9 . . . . . . .135 F5
Batter St PL4. . . . . .149 A2
Battery Hill TR16 . . . . .67 C6
Battery La Polruan PL23 . . .116 C2
    Tavistock PL19. . . . . .147 C4
Battery Mill La TR27 . . . . . .77 C1
Battery Pk PL3. . . . . .116 C2
Battery Rd TR18. . . . . .143 F4
Battery St PL1. . . . . .148 A2
Battery Terr PL26. . . . . .73 C3
Battery The TR7. . . . . .110 D7
Battisford Pk PL7. . . . . . . .131 E3
Bawden Rd PL31. . . . . .109 B3
Bay Apartments PL7 . . . . .110 A6
Bay Ct TR11. . . . . .145 C2
Baydon Cl PL6. . . . . .125 C1
Bay Down PL13 . . . . .117 D5
Bayly's Rd PL9. . . . . .135 B7
Baynards Cl **1** TR1 . . . . .137 D4
Baynes Cl **3** PL4 . . . . .38 A3
Bay Rd PL28 . . . . .20 F2
Bay Retreat Padstow PL28. . .31 F7
    19 Tregolds PL28. . . . . . .31 F7
Bay St PL13. . . . . .117 D3
Bayswater Rd PL1. . . . . . . .148 B4
Bay The PL13. . . . . .117 D3
Baytree Cl PL6 . . . . .125 D6
Bay Tree Cotts **3** EX23 . . . .4 D1
Baytree Gdns PL2 . . . . . . .128 A7
Baytree Hill PL14 . . . . .113 C5
Bay Tree Orch EX23. . . . . . .4 D2
Bayview **11** PL24. . . . . . . .60 C4
Bay View Cres TR11. . . . . .145 D3
Bayview Dr PL13. . . . . .117 E4
Bayview Ho TR27 . . . . .142 A8
Bay View Pk PL25. . . . . . . .114 F6
Bay View Rd Looe PL13. . . .117 D4
    St Austell PL26. . . . . .115 A1
Bay View Terr
    Budock Water TR11. . . . . . .144 C1
    Hayle TR27. . . . . .142 C6
    26 Newlyn TR18. . . . . . . .143 C2
    Newquay TR7. . . . . .110 C5
    Penzance TR18 . . . . .143 D4
    13 Porthleven TR13. . . . . .98 B8
Bay Villas TR20 . . . . .88 F6
Beach Ct TR26. . . . . .141 C6
Beachfield Ave TR7. . . . . . .110 D6
Beachfield Ct TR18 . . . . . .143 D4
Beach Hill Downderry PL11. . .64 C4
    Portloe TR2. . . . . .84 B3
Beach La **12** TR26. . . . . . .55 A5
Beach Rd Carbis Bay TR26 . .141 D2
    Crantock TR8. . . . . .43 D3
    Marazion TR17. . . . . .89 B6
    Mevagissey PL26. . . . . .73 C4
    Newquay TR7. . . . . .110 D6
    Perranporth TR6. . . . . .55 A5
    Porthtowan TR4. . . . . .68 A6
    St Austell PL25. . . . . .115 D3
    St Ives TR26. . . . . .141 A6
    Trevone PL28. . . . . .20 F2
Beachside Ct TR4. . . . . .68 A6
Beach View Cl TR7. . . . . . .111 C7
Beachview Flats TR4 . . . . . .68 A6
Beach Way PL15 . . . . .27 C1
Beach Wlk TR7. . . . . .111 C7
BEACON 138 F1
Beacon Cl Falmouth TR11. . .145 A5
    St Austell PL25. . . . . .115 A5
Beacon Cross 72 F4
Beacon Down Ave PL2. . . .128 B7
Beacon Dr TR5 . . . . .54 B1
Beacon Est TR20. . . . . .87 D4
Beacon Farm TR5 . . . . .54 C1
Beaconfield Rd PL2. . . . . . .128 B7
Beacon Fields TR14. . . . . . .138 E2
Beacon Hill Bodmin PL31. . .109 C4
    Withielgoose Mills PL30 . . . .47 B8
Beacon Hill Mews **9** PL31 .109 D5

Beacon Ho PL3 . . . .**129** D4
Beacon Inf & Nur Sch The
PL31 . . . .**109** D4
Beacon La Henon PL30 . . . . . . 24 A6
Treveighan PL30 . . . . 23 F6
Beacon Lanes PL31 . . . .**109** D3
Beacon Parc TR13 . . . .**146** C6
Beacon Park Rd PL2 . . . .**128** B7
Pelynt PL13 . . . . 62 D5
Beacon Pk Boyton PL15 . . . . . 13 A2
Beacon Rd Belowda PL26 . . . . 46 E4
Bodmin PL31 . . . .**109** D4
Bodmin PL31 . . . .**109** E3
Falmouth TR11 . . . .**145** A5
Foxhole PL26 . . . . 58 D5
Marazion TR17 . . . . 89 B5
Newquay TR7 . . . .**110** D7
Porthleven TR13 . . . . 98 B8
St Agnes TR5 . . . . 54 C1
Summercourt TR8 . . . . 57 B7
Beacons PL13 . . . . 62 E5
Beaconsfield Pl **2** TR5 . . . . 54 C1
Beaconsfield Terr PL31 . . . . .**109** C4
Beaconside Foxhole PL26 . . . . 58 D5
Summercourt TR8 . . . . 57 B7
Beacon Sq TR14 . . . .**138** F1
Beacon St TR11 . . . .**145** B5
Beacon Technology Pk
PL31 . . . .**109** B4
Beacon Terr
Camborne TR14 . . . .**138** E1
5 Falmouth TR11 . . . .**145** A5
Foxhole PL26 . . . . 58 D5
Helston TR13 . . . .**146** C6
Lizard TR12 . . . .**102** F2
BEACON THE 10 F6
Beacon The TR11 . . . .**145** A5
Beacon View TR4 . . . . 55 B2
Beacon View Pk **23** TR16 . . . 67 E4
Beacon Vw PL15 . . . . 27 B7
Beadle Ct **6** PL19 . . . .**147** B4
Beagle Ct TR11 . . . .**144** F2
BEALSMILL 28 E3
Bealswood Cl PL18 . . . . 41 A6
Bealswood Rd PL18 . . . . 41 A6
Beam Rd PL26 . . . . 47 C1
Beam Terr PL26 . . . . 47 B1
Beam Villas PL30 . . . . 47 D5
Beare Cl PL9 . . . .**135** B5
Bearsdown Cl PL6 . . . .**129** C8
Bearsdown Rd PL6 . . . .**129** C8
Bears Terr TR16 . . . . 80 E7
Beatrice Ave
Plymouth, Keyham PL2 . . . . .**127** E5
Plymouth, St Jude's PL4 . . . .**149** B3
Saltash PL12 . . . .**122** E1
Beatrice Gdns PL12 . . . .**122** E1
Beatrice Rd PL31 . . . . 48 D8
Beatrice Terr TR27 . . . .**142** D7
Beattie Rd PL5 . . . .**127** B8
Beatty Cl PL6 . . . .**125** A4
Beauchamp Cres PL2 . . . . . .**128** C7
Beauchamp Rd PL2 . . . .**128** C7
Beauchamps Mdw TR15 . . . .**140** D2
Beaudyn Wlk **5** PL6 . . . . . .**129** C7
Beaufighter Ave PL27 . . . . . . 31 F3
Beaufort Ave **8** PL27 . . . . . 31 F3
Beaufort Ho **21** PL4 . . . . . .**149** A2
Beauly Cl PL7 . . . .**131** A5
Beaumaris Gdns PL3 . . . . . .**128** F8
Beaumaris Rd PL3 . . . .**128** F7
Beaumont Ave PL4 . . . .**149** A3
Beaumont Pl PL4 . . . .**149** A3
Beaumont Rd PL4 . . . .**149** B3
Beaumont St PL2 . . . .**128** A5
Beaumont Terr PL12 . . . .**122** F4
Beck Adams PL12 . . . . 53 C3
Beckett Cl TR15 . . . .**140** C4
Beckford Cl PL7 . . . .**131** A5
Beckham Pl PL3 . . . .**129** A6
Beckly Ct PL1 . . . .**148** C3
Beckys La PL27 . . . . 31 E6
Bede Gdns PL5 . . . .**124** C1
Bede Haven Cl EX23 . . . . . .**104** E4
Bederkesa Ct PL31 . . . .**109** D4
Bedford Cl PL18 . . . . 40 F6
Bedford Mews PL4 . . . .**149** A4
Bedford Park Villas PL4 . .**149** A4
Bedford Pk
10 Bere Alston PL20 . . . . . 41 B1
Plymouth PL4 . . . .**149** A4
Bedford Pl
6 Bere Alston PL20 . . . . . 41 B1
5 St Ives TR26 . . . .**141** B5
Bedford Rd Horrabridge PL20 42 C4
Plymouth PL9 . . . .**135** E8
St Ives TR26 . . . .**141** B5
Bedford Sq PL19 . . . .**147** C5
Bedford St Bere Alston PL20 . 41 B1
Plymouth PL2 . . . .**127** F5
Bedford Terr PL4 . . . .**149** A4
Bedford Units PL18 . . . . 40 F5
Bedford Villas **7** PL20 . . . . 41 B1
Bedford Way PL3 . . . .**148** C3
Bedowan Mdws TR7 . . . . . .**111** A4
Bedruthan Ave TR1 . . . .**137** E6
Bedruthan Steps* PL27 . . . 31 B4
Beech Ave Liskeard PL14 . . . .**113** B5
Plymouth PL4 . . . .**149** C2
Beech Cl Down Thomas PL9 . .**135** B1
Falmouth TR11 . . . .**144** F5
Tavistock PL19 . . . .**147** C2
Torpoint PL11 . . . .**127** A3
4 Whiterock PL27 . . . . . .**108** C5
Beechcombers TR8 . . . . 44 D7

Beechcroft Rd
Plymouth, Lower Compton
PL3 . . . .**129** A6
Plymouth, North Prospect
PL2 . . . .**128** B7
Beech Ct PL6 . . . .**125** D5
Beech Dr Bodmin PL31 . . . . .**109** B4
4 St Columb Major TR9 . . . 45 D6
Beeches The
Launceston PL15 . . . .**106** C5
5 Pensilva PL14 . . . . 38 E4
Beechfield Ave PL20 . . . . 42 D3
Beechfield Gr PL3 . . . .**128** B7
Beech Hall Flats **19** TR2 . . . 95 A6
Beeching Pk PL17 . . . . 39 F6
Beech La PL25 . . . .**114** D3
Beech Terr PL13 . . . .**117** C4
Beech Tree Cl PL15 . . . .**106** A8
Beechwood Ave PL4 . . . .**128** D4
Beechwood Cross PL7 . . . . .**131** F7
Beechwood Dr PL32 . . . .**105** D5
Beechwood Gdns PL1 . . . . . .**137** E6
Beechwood Parc TR1 . . . . . .**137** F5
Beechwood Prim Sch PL6 . .**124** E6
Beechwood Rise PL6 . . . . . .**125** E1
Beechwood Terr PL4 . . . . . .**128** D4
Beechwood Way PL7 . . . . . .**131** D5
Beehive Workshops TR10 . . .**144** A7
BEENY 9 E3
Beeston Wlk **6** PL6 . . . . . .**129** C7
Behenna Dr TR1 . . . . 69 F3
Bekelege Dr TR14 . . . .**138** F1
Belah Mdws PL15 . . . . 16 A8
Belair Rd PL2 . . . .**128** C7
Belair Villas PL2 . . . .**128** C7
Belerion Rd TR16 . . . . 67 C5
Belgrave La PL4 . . . .**128** F4
Belgrave Rd PL4 . . . .**128** F4
Belgrave Terr PL14 . . . .**113** D6
Belgravia St TR18 . . . .**143** E5
Belhay TR10 . . . .**144** C8
Bellair Rd TR20 . . . .**143** A8
Bellair Terr **38** TR26 . . . . .**141** B6
Bellamy Cl PL6 . . . .**125** A1
Bellatt PL27 . . . .**108** D6
Bella Vista Gdns TR10 . . . . . 81 E2
Bell Cl PL7 . . . .**130** F6
Belle Acre Cl PL3 . . . .**128** F6
Bellever Parc TR14 . . . .**138** F4
Belle Vue TR15 . . . .**140** C5
Newlyn TR18 . . . .**143** C1
Belle Vue Ave Bude EX23 . . .**104** D6
Plymouth PL9 . . . .**135** B5
Bellevue Cotts TR10 . . . . 81 E2
Belle Vue Dr PL9 . . . .**135** B5
Belle Vue La EX23 . . . .**104** D6
Belle Vue Rd Plymouth PL9 . .**135** C5
Saltash PL12 . . . .**122** F2
Belle Vue Rise PL9 . . . .**135** B5
Bellevue Sq PL11 . . . .**127** B2
Bellevue Terr TR3 . . . . 81 D6
Belle Vue Terr **20** PL18 . . . .**143** E6
Bellflower Cl PL6 . . . .**121** C1
Belliers La TR26 . . . .**141** B5
Bellingham Cres PL7 . . . . . .**131** C4
Belliver Ind Est PL6 . . . .**121** B1
Belliver Way PL6 . . . .**121** B1
Bell La TR16 . . . . 80 D6
Bell Lake TR14 . . . . 66 F3
Bells Ct TR15 . . . .**139** C7
Bell's Ct TR11 . . . .**145** B4
Mylor Bridge TR11 . . . . 82 A3
Bell Veor TR16 . . . . 80 E6
Bell Yd **1** PL31 . . . .**109** E5
Belmont Cl PL33 . . . . 14 D2
Belmont Ct
8 Plymouth PL3 . . . .**128** A4
11 Wadebridge PL27 . . . . .**108** B5
Belmont Mews PL14 . . . . 38 D4
Belmont Pk PL14 . . . . 38 D4
Belmont Pl Newquay TR7 . . .**110** D7
Plymouth PL3 . . . .**128** A4
St Ives TR26 . . . .**141** A6
Belmont Rd Falmouth TR11 .**145** A3
Helston TR13 . . . .**146** B7
St Austell PL25 . . . .**114** D3
Belmont St Plymouth PL1 . . .**148** B3
3 Tywardreath PL24 . . . . . 60 D5
Belmont Terr Devoran TR3 . . . 81 F6
13 St Ives TR26 . . . .**141** A6
Belmont Villas **13** TR1 . . . .**137** D6
BELOWDA 46 D4
Belstone Cl PL5 . . . .**124** A3
Belvedere TR1 . . . .**137** F6
Belvedere La TR26 . . . . 89 F5
Belvedere Rd PL4 . . . .**129** B2
Belyars Ct TR26 . . . .**141** B4
Belyars La TR26 . . . .**141** B4
Benallack Ct TR1 . . . .**137** E4
Benan Chy TR2 . . . .**114** F3
Benbow St PL2 . . . .**127** F4
Bencoolen Rd EX23 . . . .**104** D5
Beneathway PL14 . . . . 50 E7
BENNACOTT 12 E2
Bennets La PL12 . . . .**122** F3
Bennetts Cotts **3** TR10 . . .**144** C7
Bennett St PL1 . . . .**127** E1
Benny Halt Sta* TR8 . . . . . 56 C8
Benson Dens **2** TR1 . . . . . .**137** D5
Benson Ho **1** TR1 . . . .**137** D5
Benson Rd TR1 . . . .**137** B5

Bentley Dr **5** EX23 . . . . 4 D1
Beramic Cl TR27 . . . . 78 D6
Beraton Ct **3** PL31 . . . .**109** D5
BERE ALSTON 41 B1
Bere Alston Prim Sch PL20 . 41 B1
Bere Alston Sta PL20 . . . . . . 41 B2
BERE FERRERS **119** E3
Bere Ferrers Sta PL20 . . . . .**119** E3
BEREPPER 98 F5
Berepper Cross TR12 . . . . . . 98 E5
Beresford St PL2 . . . .**128** A4
Beringer St **3** TR14 . . . . . .**138** E5
Berkeley Cl EX23 . . . . 4 D1
Berkeley Cotts TR11 . . . .**145** A4
Berkeley Ct Falmouth TR11 . .**145** B4
Looe PL13 . . . .**117** C5
Berkeley Hill TR11 . . . .**145** A4
Berkeley Mews **3** TR11 . . .**145** A4
Berkeley Path **3** TR11 . . . .**145** A4
Berkeley Vale TR11 . . . .**145** A4
Berkshire Dr PL2 . . . .**127** F5
Bernice Cl PL4 . . . .**129** B4
Bernice Terr PL4 . . . .**129** B4
Berries Ave EX23 . . . .**104** E4
Berries Mount EX23 . . . .**104** F4
BERRIOWBRIDGE 27 B2
Berrow Park Rd PL3 . . . .**128** E6
Berrycombe View **18** PL31 **109** D5
Berrycoombe Hill PL31 . . . .**109** C5
Berrycoombe Prim Sch
PL31 . . . .**109** B5
Berrycoombe Rd PL31 . . . . .**109** D5
Berrycoombe Vale PL31 . . . .**109** C5
Berryfields Ho PL31 . . . .**109** E5
Berry Head Gdns PL6 . . . . .**124** E1
Berryhill PL30 . . . . 47 C6
Berry La PL31 . . . .**109** E5
Berryman Cres TR11 . . . . . .**144** F3
Berry Park Cl PL9 . . . .**135** E6
Berry Park Rd PL9 . . . .**135** E7
Berry Pk PL12 . . . .**122** D4
Berry Rd TR7 . . . .**110** E6
Berthon Rd PL5 . . . .**127** C8
Berveth Cl TR3 . . . . 69 D3
Berwick Ave PL5 . . . .**124** E3
BESOUGHAN 45 A3
Bess Park Rd PL27 . . . .**108** E6
Beswetherick Field PL30 . . . 47 F1
Bethan Dr PL7 . . . .**131** B5
Bethan View **20** TR6 . . . . . . 55 A4
Bethany Homes **1** TR14 . . .**138** C2
Bethany Pl TR19 . . . . 86 F6
BETHEL **115** A5
Bethel Rd PL25 . . . .**115** A4
Bethesda Pl **10** TR26 . . . . .**141** B6
Betjeman Wlk PL5 . . . .**124** C3
Beverley Cres TR27 . . . .**142** E7
Beverley Rd PL3 . . . .**129** C4
Beverston Way PL6 . . . .**125** B8
Beweys Pk PL12 . . . .**122** C2
Beyrout Pl **6** PL1 . . . .**127** F3
Bezant Pl TR7 . . . .**110** B5
Bickern Rd PL11 . . . .**127** B3
Bickford Cres TR13 . . . . 91 B1
Bickford Rd PL15 . . . .**106** B8
BICKHAM **121** A7
Bickham Park Rd PL3 . . . . . .**128** D7
Bickham Rd PL5 . . . .**123** D2
Bickland Hill TR11 . . . .**144** D4
Bickland Ind Est TR11 . . . . .**144** D4
Bickland Wlk TR11 . . . .**144** C4
Bickland Water Cotts
TR11 . . . .**144** D4
Bickland Water Rd TR11 . . .**144** D2
Bickland Wlk TR11 . . . .**144** D4
Bickleigh Cl PL6 . . . .**125** A1
Bickleigh Down Bsns Pk
PL6 . . . .**125** D7
Bickleigh Down CE Prim Sch
PL6 . . . .**125** D7
Bickleigh Down Rd PL6 . . . .**125** D1
Bicton Cl PL6 . . . .**125** D1
Bicton Rd Gang PL14 . . . . . . 38 F3
Penwarden PL14 . . . . 39 A4
Biddick Dr PL2 . . . .**127** F6
Biddick's Ct **5** PL25 . . . . . .**114** C3
Bideford Mews **13** EX23 . . . . 4 E1
Bideford Wlk PL6 . . . .**129** E8
Bigbury Wlk PL6 . . . .**129** E8
Biggin Hill PL5 . . . .**123** F4
Big Gn PL13 . . . . 62 D1
Big Treslea Hill PL30 . . . . . . 36 A3
Bilbury St PL4 . . . .**149** A3
BILLACOMBE **135** F8
Billacombe Rd PL9 . . . .**129** E1
Billacombe Villas PL9 . . . . .**135** F8
BILLACOTT 12 B1
Billacott Rd PL15 . . . . 12 A1
Billings Cl PL6 . . . .**124** D6
Billings Dr PL7 . . . .**111** B5
Billington Ct PL13 . . . .**129** B7
Bindown Ct PL13 . . . . 63 E8
Binhamy Cl EX23 . . . .**104** F4
Binhamy Rd EX23 . . . . 7 B8
Binkham Hill PL20 . . . . 42 D3
Binner Cross TR27 . . . . 78 F1
Binnerton Rd TR27 . . . . 90 E8
Bircham View PL6 . . . .**125** C1
Birch Cl PL6 . . . .**125** E7
Birches The PL6 . . . .**125** D6
Birchfield Ave PL2 . . . .**128** B6
Birch Gr PL27 . . . .**142** B3
Birchill PL30 . . . . 47 C6
Birch Pond Rd PL9 . . . .**135** D7
Birchwood Cl PL19 . . . .**147** C3
Birchwood Gdns PL7 . . . . . .**131** A7

Birlea Business Pk EX23 . . . . 7 C8
Biscombe Gdns PL12 . . . . . .**123** A2
Biscombes La **8** PL17 . . . . . 39 E4
BISCOVEY 60 B4
Biscovey Academy **22** PL24 . 60 B4
Biscovey Rd PL24 . . . .**115** F5
Bishop Bronescombe CE Prim
Sch PL25 . . . .**122** F1
Bishop Cornish CE Prim Sch
PL12 . . . .**122** F1
Bishops Cl Saltash PL12 . . . .**122** E3
Truro TR1 . . . .**137** C6
Bishops Ct TR9 . . . . 45 E6
Bishop's Hill Rd PL27 . . . . . . 21 D6
Bishop's Pl PL1 . . . .**148** B1
Bishop's Rd TR26 . . . .**141** B5
Bishops Way TR1 . . . .**144** D5
Bishop Temple Rd TR1 . . . . .**137** F6
BISSOE 81 D8
Bissoe Hill TR4 . . . . 81 D7
Bissoe Rd TR3 . . . . 81 F7
BISSOM **144** E8
Bissom Rd Carvinack TR11 . . 81 F2
Penryn TR10 . . . . 81 F2
Bittern Cl **3** EX23 . . . . 7 B8
Bitthams La PL18 . . . . 40 E7
Blable La PL27 . . . . 32 E5
Blackberry Cl PL9 . . . .**135** E8
Blackberry La PL9 . . . .**135** E8
Blackberry Way TR1 . . . .**137** F5
Blackbird Cres PL15 . . . .**106** E4
Blackbrook Cl PL20 . . . . 42 E4
BLACK CROSS 45 E3
Blackerry Cl TR16 . . . .**140** F1
Blackeven Cl PL6 . . . .**121** D1
Blackeven Hill PL6 . . . .**121** C1
Blackfriars La PL1 . . . .**149** A2
Blackhall Gdns PL6 . . . .**124** D6
Black La PL15 . . . . 18 A8
Blackmore Cres PL6 . . . .**124** D6
Black Rd TR27 . . . .**142** D7
BLACK ROCK 79 D1
Blacksmith La TR27 . . . . 78 D6
Blacksmiths Mdw **5** PL15 . 27 D3
Blackstone Cl PL9 . . . .**136** B6
Blackthorn Cl
Plymouth, Honicknowle
PL5 . . . .**124** B3
Plymouth, Woolwell PL6 . . . .**125** D8
Withnoe PL15 . . . .**106** E4
BLACKWATER 68 D5
Blackwater Prim Sch TR4 . . . 68 E5
Bladder La PL5 . . . .**124** E2
Blagdon Cross EX21 . . . .**13** F7
Blagdon Lodge Cross EX21 . 13 F8
Blairgowrie Rd PL5 . . . .**123** C2
Blake Gdns PL5 . . . .**124** C3
Blakeney Rd **6** PL9 . . . . . .**129** D1
Blakes Pk PL14 . . . .**113** D7
Blanchard Pl **2** PL7 . . . . . .**130** E7
Blanchdown Dr
Gunnislake PL18 . . . . 40 F7
Horsebridge PL19 . . . . 29 D1
Saw Mill PL19 . . . . 41 A7
Blanchminster Rd EX23 . . . .**104** E5
Blandford Rd PL3 . . . .**129** C6
Blatchborough Cross EX22 . . 3 E1
Blaxton La PL5 . . . .**120** C2
Blenheim Rd PL4 . . . .**149** A4
Bligh Cres TR13 . . . .**146** C5
Blight's Row TR15 . . . .**140** B5
Blindhole **8** PL15 . . . .**106** C6
Blind La PL11 . . . . 64 D6
BLINDWELL **132** E5
Blindwell Hill PL10 . . . .**132** E5
BLISLAND 35 D8
Blisland Com Prim Sch
PL30 . . . . 35 D7
Bloomball Cl PL3 . . . .**129** B6
Bloom Fields PL18 . . . .**143** E5
BLOWINGHOUSE Bodmin . .**109** B2
Redruth **139** F6
Blowinghouse Cl PL25 . . . . .**114** B4
Blowinghouse Hill TR15 . . . .**140** A4
Blowing House Hill
Crowlas TR20 . . . . 89 B8
Hayle TR20 . . . . 77 A1
St Austell PL25 . . . .**114** C4
Blowinghouse La PL30 . . . . .**109** B2
Blowing House La PL25 . . . .**114** B4
BLUE ANCHOR 57 D8
Bluebell Cl PL12 . . . .**122** D4
Bluebell La PL14 . . . . 38 F6
Bluebell St PL6 . . . .**125** B2
Bluebell Way
Launceston PL15 . . . .**106** E4
Tavistock PL19 . . . .**147** E4
Blue Haze Cl PL25 . . . .**125** D5
Blue Reef Aquarium*
TR7 . . . .**110** D6
Blunt's La PL6 . . . .**125** C3
Boaden Cl PL12 . . . . 53 E5
Boase St TR18 . . . .**143** C1
Boatyard, The PL26 . . . . 85 D7
Bobs Rd PL24 . . . . 60 B4
Bochym TR12 . . . . 99 C3
Bochym Hill TR12 . . . . 99 C3
Boconnic La PL20 . . . . 42 D3
Boconnoc Ave PL17 . . . . 39 F3
Boconnoc Rd PL25 . . . .**114** D2
BODELVA **115** F8
Bodelva Rd PL24 . . . .**115** E8
Boderwennack TR13 . . . . 91 F5
Bodgara Way PL14 . . . .**113** D6
Bodgara Way Flats **4**
PL14 . . . .**113** D6
Bodgate Rd PL15 . . . . 12 C1

BODIEVE **108** C7
Bodieve Bsns Pk PL27 . . . . .**108** D7
Bodieve Rd PL27 . . . .**108** D7
BODILLY 91 F7
Bodinar Rd TR10 . . . . 81 D7
Bodinnel Rd PL31 . . . .**109** C6
Bodiniel View PL31 . . . .**109** B5
Bodinnar Cl TR20 . . . . 87 E6
Bodinnar La TR20 . . . . 87 E6
BODINNICK **116** E5
Bodinnick Hts PL23 . . . .**116** E5
Bodinnick Parc PL30 . . . . . . 23 E3
Bodinnick Rd PL30 . . . . 23 E3
BODMIN **109** B5
Bodmin Beacon Nature
Reserve* PL31 . . . .**109** D4
Bodmin Bsns Ctr PL31 . . . . .**109** E3
Bodmin Bsns Pk PL31 . . . . . 35 B2
Bodmin Coll PL31 . . . .**109** F2
Bodmin Community Hospital
PL31 . . . .**109** D4
Bodmin General Sta* **109** E3
Bodmin Hill PL22 . . . .**112** B4
Bodmin Jail* PL31 . . . . . .**109** E4
Bodmin Parkway PL22 . . . . . 48 F6
Bodmin Parkway Sta PL30 . 49 A7
Bodmin Rd Plymouth PL5 . . .**124** D3
St Austell PL25 . . . .**114** C6
Trebyan PL30 . . . . 48 D5
Trenhorne PL15 . . . . 27 C5
Truro TR1 . . . .**137** E6
Bodmin Ret Pk PL31 . . . . . . 35 B1
Bodmin Road TR4 . . . . 55 B4
Bodmin Town Mus* PL31 .**109** E4
Bodmin & Wenford Rly*
PL30 . . . .**109** D2
Bodrigan Rd PL13 . . . .**117** D5
Bodriggy Academy TR27 . . .**145** D5
Bodriggy Cres TR27 . . . .**142** D6
Bodriggy St TR27 . . . .**142** D6
Bodriggy Villas TR27 . . . . . .**142** D6
Bodrugan Hill
Portmellon PL26 . . . . 73 C2
Portmellon PL26 . . . . 85 D8
Tregony PL26 . . . . 85 D7
BODWEN 47 E3
Bodwen La PL30 . . . . 35 A6
Body's Ct PL18 . . . . 40 F6
Bohelland Rd TR10 . . . .**144** D8
Bohelland Rise TR10 . . . . . .**144** D8
Bohelland Way TR10 . . . . . .**144** D8
Bohella Rd **20** TR2 . . . . 95 A6
BOHETHERICK 40 F2
Bohill TR10 . . . .**144** D7
Bohill Ct TR10 . . . .**144** D7
BOHORTHA 95 C5
Boiler Works Rd TR14 . . . . .**138** E5
Bojea Ind Est PL25 . . . .**114** C7
Bojea Terr PL25 . . . .**114** C6
Bojewyan Stennack TR19 . . 75 B1
Bojorrow Trevassack TR12 . . . 99 D5
Trevassack TR12 . . . .**100** A5
Bokelly La PL30 . . . . 23 B3
Bokenna Cl **12** PL14 . . . . . 50 E7
Bokenna Cross TR15 . . . . 37 C1
Boldventure Ave PL25 . . . . .**115** B5
Boldventure Cl PL25 . . . . . .**115** B5
Boldventure Rd PL25 . . . . . .**115** B5
Bolenna La TR6 . . . . 55 A4
BOLENOWE 79 F5
Bolenowe TR14 . . . . 79 F4
Bolenowe La TR14 . . . . 79 F5
BOLINGEY 55 B4
Bolingey Chapel Flats TR6 . . 55 B4
Bolingey Rd TR6 . . . . 55 A4
BOLITHO 79 F1
Bolitho Rd TR18 . . . .**143** C7
Bollowal Pl TR19 . . . . 86 E6
Bolowthas Cnr TR7 . . . .**111** A7
Bolowthas Way TR7 . . . .**111** C7
Bolster Ct **8** TR5 . . . . 54 C1
Boltern Rd TR17 . . . . 89 C5
Bolt House Cl PL19 . . . .**147** A5
BOLVENTOR 25 E3
Bolventor La PL13 . . . . 63 E8
Bonallack La TR12 . . . . 92 D1
Bon Cot Rd TR18 . . . .**143** C2
Bond St Plymouth PL6 . . . . .**124** E6
6 Redruth TR15 . . . .**140** B4
Bone Cellar Row TR2 . . . . . . 70 F5
Bone Mill Rd TR6 . . . . 55 B4
Bones La Padderbury PL14 . . 52 D4
Tideford PL12 . . . . 52 E4
Bonson Cl PL13 . . . .**117** C4
Bon Villas **18** TR18 . . . . . .**143** C2
Bonville Rd PL6 . . . .**124** E6
Bonython Cl TR11 . . . . 82 A3
Bonython Dr TR12 . . . . 72 A7
Bonython Est
Tregadara TR12 . . . . 99 D4
Tregadara TR12 . . . .**100** A4
Bonython Rd TR7 . . . .**111** B7
Bonython Terr PL14 . . . .**113** B4
Boon's Pl PL1 . . . .**148** C4
BOQUIO 91 F8
BOREA 76 F2
Borgwitha TR16 . . . . 80 B5
Boringdon Ave PL5 . . . .**127** D8
Boringdon Cl PL7 . . . .**130** D7
Boringdon Hill PL7 . . . .**130** E7
Boringdon Mill Bsns Ctr
PL7 . . . .**130** F6
Boringdon Prim Sch PL7 . .**130** D7
Boringdon Rd
Plymouth, Plympton PL7 . . .**130** D6
Plymouth, Turnchapel PL9 . .**135** A4

Boringdon Terr
Plymouth, Plympton PL7 ... 130 D6
Plymouth, Turnchapel PL9 ... 135 A7
Boringdon Villas PL7 ... 130 D6
Borlase Cl TR13 ... 146 B5
Borlase Cres ❶ PL25 ... 114 F2
Borough Cross EX22 ... 7 F5
Borough Ct PL11 ... 126 E4
Borough Pk PL11 ... 126 E4
Borrowdale Cl PL6 ... 124 D5
Bosahan TR12 ... 101 A8
Bosanath Valley TR11 ... 93 C3
Bosawna Cl TR16 ... 68 E1
BOSCADJACK ... 91 F6
Boscarn Cl TR14 ... 79 B5
BOSCARNE ... 34 C2
Boscarne Cres PL25 ... 114 F3
Boscarne Junction Sta★
PL30 ... 34 D2
Boscarnek TR27 ... 142 A1
Boscarne View PL30 ... 34 D2
Boscarn Parc TR15 ... 139 C4
Boscarn Rd TR15 ... 140 D6
BOSCASTLE ... 9 C1
Boscastle Com Prim Sch
PL35 ... 9 C1
Boscastle Gdns PL2 ... 128 A8
Boscastle Visitor Ctr★ PL35 . 9 D2
Boscaswell Downs TR19 ... 75 A1
Boscaswell Est TR19 ... 74 F1
Boscaswell Rd TR19 ... 75 A1
Boscaswell Terr ❹ TR19 ... 75 A1
Boscathnoe La TR18 ... 143 B7
Boscathnoe Way TR18 ... 143 B7
Boscawen Ct ⓱ TR6 ... 55 A4
Boscawen Gdns ⓫ TR6 ... 55 A4
Boscawen Pk PL26 ... 58 B8
Boscawen Pl PL2 ... 127 E4
Boscawen Rd
❼ Chacewater TR4 ... 69 A3
Falmouth TR11 ... 145 B2
Helston TR13 ... 146 D4
Perranporth TR6 ... 55 A4
St Dennis PL26 ... 58 C8
Boscawen St ⓲ TR1 ... 137 D4
Boscawen Woods TR1 ... 137 F2
Boscean Cl TR14 ... 79 E4
BOSCOPPA ... 115 A6
Boscoppa Cl TR15 ... 140 D7
Boscoppa Rd
St Austell, Bethel PL25 ... 115 A5
St Austell, Boscoppa PL25 ... 115 B5
Boscowan TR11 ... 145 C2
BOSCREEGE ... 90 C5
Boscrege TR13 ... 90 D5
Boscundle Ave TR11 ... 144 F1
Boscundle Cl PL25 ... 115 D5
Boscundle Row PL12 ... 123 A2
Bosence Rd TR27 ... 90 C7
Bosillion La TR2 ... 72 A7
Bosil Rd PL15 ... 16 E3
Bosinney Rd PL25 ... 114 D3
Bosinver La PL26 ... 59 A1
Boskear La PL31 ... 109 A4
BOSKEDNAN ... 76 A1
BOSKENNA ... 97 C4
Boskenna Cross TR19 ... 97 C5
Boskennal Barton TR19 ... 97 B6
Boskennal La TR19 ... 97 B6
Boskenna Rd TR16 ... 80 A5
Boskennel Dr TR27 ... 142 B4
Boskenwyn TR13 ... 92 B3
Boskenwyn Com Prim Sch
TR13 ... 92 B3
Boskenza Ct TR26 ... 141 C2
Boskernick Cl TR18 ... 143 B1
Boskernow TR12 ... 100 D6
Boskerris Cres TR26 ... 141 D2
Boskerris Mews TR26 ... 141 D1
Boskerris Rd TR26 ... 141 D2
Boslandew Hill ❹ TR19 ... 88 C2
BOSLEAKE ... 139 C3
Bosleake Row TR15 ... 139 C3
Bosloggas Mews ❾ TR11 . 145 C3
BOSLOWICK ... 144 F2
Boslowick Cl TR11 ... 144 F3
Boslowick Ct TR11 ... 144 E2
Boslowick Rd TR11 ... 144 E2
Boslymon Hill PL30 ... 48 D4
Bosmeor Cl TR11 ... 144 E2
Bosmeor Ct TR15 ... 139 D6
Bosmeor Pk TR15 ... 139 D6
Bosmeor Rd TR11 ... 144 E3
Bosneives Hill PL30 ... 33 D2
Bosneives Rd PL30 ... 33 E1
Bosnoweth Helston TR13 ... 146 D5
Probus TR2 ... 71 D6
Bosorne Cl TR19 ... 86 E6
Bosorne Rd TR19 ... 86 E6
Bosorne St TR19 ... 86 E6
Bosorne Terr TR19 ... 86 E6
Bosparva La
Leedstown TR27 ... 78 F2
Praze-an-Beeble TR14 ... 79 A3
Bospolvans Rd ❷ TR9 ... 45 D6
BOSPORTHENNIS ... 75 F3
Bospowis TR14 ... 138 C3
BOSSINEY ... 14 D8
Bossiney Rd PL34 ... 14 D7
Bostennack Pl ❿ TR26 ... 141 A5
Bostennack Terr ⓫ TR26 . 141 A5
Boston Cl PL9 ... 135 B7
Bosuen Rd TR7 ... 111 A7
Bosullow Vean TR20 ... 87 D8
Bosvargus Hill ❻ TR19 ... 86 F6
Bosvarren TR11 ... 93 B5
Bosvathick Dr TR11 ... 93 B6
Bos Vean TR12 ... 102 F2
Bosvean Gdns
⓫ Illogan TR16 ... 67 E4
Truro TR1 ... 137 B5
Bosvean Rd TR4 ... 69 F6
Bosvenna View PL31 ... 109 E4
Bosvenna Way TR18 ... 143 B7
Bosvenning Pl TR20 ... 87 E6
Bosvigo Gdns★ TR1 ... 137 A5
Bosvigo La TR1 ... 137 B5
Bosvigo Rd TR1 ... 137 C4
Bosvigo Sch ⓰ TR1 ... 137 C4
Boswedden TR19 ... 86 D6
Boswedden Pl TR19 ... 86 E6
Boswedden Rd TR19 ... 86 E6
BOSWEDNACK ... 76 A4
Boswell Cl PL5 ... 124 B2
Boswergy TR18 ... 143 C5
Boswin TR13 ... 92 A8
BOSWINGER ... 85 B5
Boswithian Rd TR14 ... 138 F6
Bosworgey Cl ❸ TR9 ... 45 D6
Bosworgy Rd TR20, TR27 ... 90 B8
Boswyn TR14 ... 79 E3
BOTALLACK ... 86 E7
Botallack La TR19 ... 86 E7
Botetoe Hill TR14 ... 79 C4
Botetoe Rd TR14 ... 79 B4
Botha Rd ❶ PL27 ... 31 F3
Bothwicks Rd TR7 ... 110 E6
BOTTOMS ... 96 E5
BOTUSFLEMING ... 122 B7
Boughthayes Est PL19 ... 147 A5
Boulden Cl PL7 ... 131 C5
Boulter Cl PL6 ... 121 C1
Boundary Cl ㉑ TR18 ... 143 C1
Boundary Dr EX23 ... 7 B6
Boundary Rd Bodmin PL31 . 109 A4
Bodmin PL31 ... 109 A5
Dousland PL20 ... 42 E3
Bounders La TR6 ... 55 B4
Bounder Treath TR12 ... 101 C1
Boundervean La TR14 ... 138 B2
Boundis Farm TR10 ... 93 A7
Bounds Cross EX22 ... 8 B4
Bounds Pl PL1 ... 148 B2
Bound The PL10 ... 133 A1
Bounsalls Ct ❺ PL15 ... 106 C5
Bounsall's La PL15 ... 106 C5
Bourne Cl PL3 ... 129 D6
Bourneside PL25 ... 114 D3
Boveway Dr PL14 ... 113 E5
Boville La PL9 ... 136 C7
Bovisand Ct PL9 ... 134 F2
Bovisand La
Down Thomas PL9 ... 135 B2
Staddiscombe PL9 ... 135 D3
Bovisand Pk PL9 ... 135 A1
Bovisand Rd PL9 ... 135 E3
Bowden ⓮ EX23 ... 4 D1
Bowden Park Rd PL6 ... 125 A1
Bowdens La Redruth TR15 .. 139 F7
Tolskithy TR15 ... 67 F2
Bowdens Row TR15 ... 140 A4
Bowers Park Dr PL6 ... 125 E7
Bowers Rd PL2 ... 128 B5
Bowglas Cl TR20 ... 89 A8
Bowhays Wlk ❷ PL6 ... 129 C7
Bowithick Rd PL15 ... 16 C2
Bowjey Ct ❾ TR18 ... 143 C1
Bowjey Hill TR18 ... 143 C1
Bowjey Terr ❺ TR18 ... 143 C1
Bow La EX23 ... 4 D2
Bowles Rd TR11 ... 145 A6
Bowleys La Trethellick PL28 .. 21 A2
Trethillick PL28 ... 107 B6
Bowling Gn Menheniot PL14 . 51 F5
㉞ St Ives TR26 ... 141 B6
Bowling Gn The TR2 ... 82 F2
BOWLING GREEN Bugle ... 47 E1
Redruth ... 139 D3
Bowling Green TR11 ... 92 F3
Bowling Green Ct
Hayle TR27 ... 142 D5
Liskeard PL14 ... 113 B5
Bowling Green Rd TR11 ... 92 F3
Bowling Green Terr ㉟
TR26 ... 141 B6
Bownder An Mengleudh ❶
TR8 ... 111 D5
Bownder An Sycamor TR16 68 F2
Bownder Corbenic ❺ TR7 110 D5
Bownder Dowr TR27 ... 142 B3
Bownder Gareth TR7 ... 110 C5
Bownder Iger ❹ TR7 ... 111 E5
Bownder Karleghyon ❷
TR8 ... 111 D5
Bownder Kolom ❻ TR7 ... 111 D6
Bownder Kosti Woles ❷
TR7 ... 111 D6
Bownder Kresennik An Shoppa
❹ TR7 ... 111 D6
Bownder Logres ❺ TR7 ... 111 E5
Bownder Marhaus ❹ TR7 110 D5
Bownder Oghen ❷ TR7 ... 111 E5
Bownder Sarras ❸ TR7 ... 110 D5
Bownder Tregwestek ❺
TR7 ... 111 D6
Bownder Trewolek TR8 ... 111 E5
Bownder Vean PL25 ... 115 A5
Bownder Vesydhyans ❹
TR8 ... 111 D5
Bownder Woryan ❸ TR7 ... 111 E5
Bownder Ywain TR7 ... 110 C5
Bowood Pk Delabole PL33 ... 14 F1
Helstone PL32 ... 24 B8
Box Heater PL28 ... 31 F7
Boxhill Cl PL5 ... 124 B3
Boxhill Gdns PL2 ... 128 C8
Box's Shop EX23 ... 7 A4
Boxwell Pk PL31 ... 109 F4
Boyd Ave PL28 ... 107 C5
Boyer Sq ❶ PL31 ... 109 A5
BOYTON ... 13 B2
Boyton Com Prim Sch PL15 13 A3
Bracken Cl Bodmin PL31 ... 109 E5
Plymouth PL6 ... 125 D8
Brackenside PL13 ... 62 D1
Bracken Terr TR7 ... 110 E5
Brackwell Pl PL27 ... 108 B5
BRADDOCK ... 49 F5
Braddock CE Prim Sch
PL14 ... 50 B6
Braddock Cl PL26 ... 58 D6
Braddons Hill PL7 ... 130 B7
Bradfield Cl PL6 ... 125 E1
BRADFORD ... 24 D2
Bradford Cl PL6 ... 129 B7
Bradfords Quay PL27 ... 108 C6
Bradfords Quay Rd PL27 . 108 C6
Bradley Rd Newquay TR7 .. 111 C7
Plymouth PL4 ... 128 F4
Bradridge Ct PL15 ... 13 A4
Braemar Cl PL7 ... 131 C4
Braeside Pk PL14 ... 50 E8
Braggs Hill PL15 ... 13 B3
Brake La PL10 ... 132 B5
Brake Rd PL5 ... 124 E2
Brake The PL14 ... 37 F4
Bramble Cl Newquay TR7 .. 111 A4
Plymouth PL3 ... 129 B7
Widemouth Bay EX23 ... 6 F5
Bramble Hill EX23 ... 104 E5
Bramble La Egloshayle PL27 . 33 F7
Trevarner PL27 ... 108 F6
Brambleside ❶ PL30 ... 23 E7
Brambles The
Liskeard PL14 ... 113 E5
Lostwithiel PL22 ... 112 C3
Bramble Wlk ❶ PL6 ... 129 C7
Bramfield Pl PL6 ... 129 D7
Bramley Cl PL25 ... 114 E4
Bramley Pk PL31 ... 109 F5
Bramley Rd PL3 ... 129 C4
Brancker Rd PL2 ... 128 C6
Brandon Rd PL3 ... 129 C4
Brandon Wlk EX23 ... 6 F5
Brandreth Rd ❸ PL3 ... 128 F6
Brandy La TR20 ... 89 F4
BRANE ... 87 C3
Brane La TR20 ... 87 D3
Branksome Dr PL27 ... 108 E5
Brannel Rd PL26 ... 58 C2
Brannel Sch The PL26 ... 58 B3
Branscombe Gdns PL5 ... 124 A3
Branson Ct ❾ PL7 ... 131 C5
Branson Pk PL19 ... 42 A6
Branwell La TR18 ... 88 E6
Braunton Wlk PL6 ... 129 E8
Bray Cl ❸ Kirkland PL31 ... 109 F3
Tavistock PL19 ... 147 A5
Brayford Cl PL5 ... 124 B3
Bray Rise TR16 ... 80 A5
BRAY SHOP ... 28 B1
Bray's Pl PL25 ... 114 F4
Brays Terr ❷ TR16 ... 140 F1
BRAZACOTT ... 12 B2
Brazacott Cross PL15 ... 12 B2
BREA ... 139 B3
BREA ADDIT ... 139 B2
Brea Arch TR14 ... 139 A3
Bread St TR18 ... 143 E5
Brea Est Crugmeer PL27 ... 107 F8
Rock PL27 ... 21 D3
BREAGE ... 90 F3
Breage CE Voluntary Aided
Prim Sch TR13 ... 90 F3
Break My Neck La TR20 ... 88 B8
Breakwater Hill PL4 ... 149 C1
Breakwater Ind Est PL9 ... 135 C8
Breakwater Rd Bude EX23 . 104 D5
Plymouth PL9 ... 135 C8
Brean Down Cl PL3 ... 128 E6
Brean Down Rd PL3 ... 128 E7
Brea Rd Rock PL27 ... 21 D2
Rock PL27 ... 21 D3
Breaside TR14 ... 139 A3
Brecon Cl Plymouth PL3 ... 129 A7
❶ St Agnes TR5 ... 54 C1
Bredon Ct TR7 ... 110 C6
Bree Shute La ❿ PL31 ... 109 E5
❹ Bodmin PL31 ... 109 E5
BRENT ... 62 E2
Brentford Ave PL5 ... 124 B5
Brent Knoll Rd ❶ PL3 ... 128 E6
Brenton Rd PL11 ... 64 B5
Brentons Pk PL29 ... 22 D6
Brentor Rd Mary Tavy PL19 .. 30 F6
Plymouth PL4 ... 129 B2
Brent Tor★ PL19 ... 30 D7
Brentwartha PL13 ... 62 E2
Brest Rd PL6 ... 125 A3
Brest Way PL6 ... 125 A3
Bretonside PL4 ... 149 A2
Brett Wlk PL7 ... 130 F7
Brewartha TR2 ... 57 E1
Brewers Cl PL30 ... 47 F6
Brewers Hill PL26 ... 58 C8
Brewers Rd TR1 ... 137 F5
Brewery Hill TR26 ... 77 E4
Brewery La TR13 ... 146 B6
Brian Laity Way ❷ TR18 .. 143 D6
Briansway PL12 ... 122 D2
Briardale Rd PL2 ... 127 F6
Briarfield PL23 ... 116 D4
Briarleigh Cl PL6 ... 125 F2
Briar Rd Bude EX23 ... 104 E4
Briar Rd *continued*
Plymouth PL3 ... 128 F7
Briars Row PL12 ... 122 D4
Briars Ryn PL12 ... 53 B7
Briar Tor PL20 ... 42 D3
Briarwood PL14 ... 113 D5
Brickfields Sp Ctr PL1 ... 127 F2
Brickworks Hill TR16 ... 68 D1
Bridals La PL13 ... 62 E2
BRIDGE ... 67 E5
Bridge TR9 ... 45 E7
Bridge Cl TR7 ... 111 A4
Bridge Ct PL25 ... 114 F4
Bridge Hill Illogan TR16 ... 67 E5
St Columb Major TR9 ... 45 E6
Trebyan PL30 ... 48 C5
Bridge Ho Delabole PL33 ... 14 E2
Hayle TR27 ... 142 B6
Bridge Ho The ⓭ TR18 ... 143 C2
Bridge La PL12 ... 53 A3
Bridgemead Cl PL26 ... 114 C1
Bridgemoor Cross EX22 ... 8 C6
BRIDGEND ... 112 E3
Bridge Pk EX22 ... 8 A5
Bridge Rd Goonhavern TR4 .. 55 D4
Illogan TR16 ... 67 E4
St Austell PL25 ... 114 B3
Seaton PL11 ... 64 B5
Tideford PL12 ... 52 F2
Bridge Row TR16 ... 67 E5
BRIDGERULE ... 8 A6
Bridgerule CE Prim Sch
EX22 ... 8 A5
Bridgerule Ind Est EX22 ... 7 F4
BRIDGES ... 59 F8
Bridge St Par PL24 ... 60 B6
❼ Stratton EX23 ... 4 D1
Bridges The PL12 ... 122 E1
Bridge The PL1 ... 148 B1
BRIDGETOWN ... 19 B8
Bridge View PL5 ... 127 D8
Wadebridge PL27 ... 108 C6
Bridge Wlk ❷ PL35 ... 9 C2
Bridgwater Cl PL6 ... 125 B1
Bridle Cl PL7 ... 131 B7
Bridle Way
Quintrell Downs TR8 ... 44 E3
Saltash PL12 ... 122 D4
Bridwell Cl PL5 ... 127 E8
Bridwell Lane N PL5 ... 127 E8
Bridwell Rd PL5 ... 127 E8
Brighter La PL30 ... 23 C3
BRIGHTON ... 57 D5
Brighton Water Hill
Cardinham PL30 ... 35 F3
Welltown PL30 ... 36 A3
Brighton Water La PL30 ... 36 A3
Brillwater Rd TR11 ... 92 E4
Brimford Cross EX22 ... 3 D4
Brimhill Cl PL7 ... 131 B3
Brimstone Hill PL30 ... 35 E3
Brinky Well Rd PL30 ... 34 E6
Brisbane Terr PL14 ... 113 C5
Brismar Wlk ❸ PL6 ... 129 C7
Briston Orch PL12 ... 53 E7
Britannia Pl PL4 ... 129 B2
Briticheston Cl PL9 ... 136 A5
British Rd TR5 ... 54 D1
Briton's Hill TR18 ... 143 F6
Brixham Wlk PL6 ... 129 E8
BRIXTON ... 136 F4
Brixton Lodge Gdns PL8 .. 136 F5
Brixton Terr TR13 ... 146 C6
Broad Cl EX22 ... 11 E7
Broadclose Hill EX23 ... 104 E5
Broad La Broadlane TR13 ... 90 F5
Illogan TR15 ... 139 D7
Trematon PL12 ... 53 E2
Welltown PL30 ... 36 A2
Broadland Gdns PL9 ... 136 A8
Broadland La PL9 ... 135 F8
Broadlands Cl PL7 ... 131 A3
BROADLANE ... 90 E5
Broadley Ct PL6 ... 121 B2
Broadley Ind Pk PL6 ... 121 B2
Broadley Park Rd PL6 ... 121 B2
Broad Mead PL17 ... 39 E5
Broad Park Rd
Bere Alston PL20 ... 41 B2
Plymouth PL3 ... 128 D6
Broad Pk Launceston PL15 . 106 C7
Plymouth PL9 ... 135 C7
St Keyne PL14 ... 51 B3
Broadshell Cross EX22 ... 8 E5
Broads La TR11 ... 81 F3
Broad St
⓬ Launceston PL15 ... 106 C6
Lifton PL16 ... 19 F4
Newquay TR7 ... 110 D6
Padstow PL28 ... 107 D5
Penryn TR10 ... 144 D7
❼ St Columb Major TR9 ... 45 E6
Truro TR1 ... 137 E5
Broads Yd PL11 ... 64 C5
Broadview PL19 ... 30 A6
Broad View TR4 ... 56 D1
Broadway The PL9 ... 135 E7
Broad Wlk Helston TR13 ... 146 B7
Saltash PL12 ... 122 E1
Brock Ho ❾ PL4 ... 149 A2
Brockhole La PL7 ... 130 E8
Brockley Rd PL3 ... 129 C4
Brocks La PL10 ... 132 F5
Brockstone Rd PL25 ... 115 A5
Brockton Gdns PL6 ... 125 B6
BROCTON ... 34 A3
Bromfield Cres TR2 ... 57 E1
Bromhead Ct PL6 ... 129 A8
Bromley Ho ❻ PL2 ... 128 A4
Bromley Pl ❺ PL2 ... 128 A4
Bronescombe Cl TR10 ... 144 D7
Bronte Pl PL5 ... 124 D1
BROOK ... 147 B2
Brook Cl Helston TR13 ... 146 B7
Plymouth PL7 ... 131 A3
Brook Ct ❻ TR11 ... 145 A4
Brookdale Ct ⓬ PL27 ... 108 B5
Brookdown Terr PL12 ... 122 E3
Brookdown Villas PL12 ... 122 E3
Brook Dr EX23 ... 104 E7
Brooke Cl PL12 ... 123 A2
Brookfield Cl Lanjeth PL26 .. 58 E3
Plymouth PL7 ... 131 B5
Brookfields Cl PL1 ... 127 F1
Brook Green Ctr for Learning
PL5 ... 124 B4
Brooking Cl PL6 ... 129 A8
Brookingfield Cl PL7 ... 130 C5
Brooking Way PL12 ... 122 C3
Brook La PL19 ... 147 B2
Brooklands Ct PL6 ... 124 E3
Brooklands View PL29 ... 22 E7
Brooklyn Flats ⓲ TR2 ... 95 A6
Brooklyn Terr ⓱ TR2 ... 95 A6
Brook Pl Falmouth TR11 ... 145 A4
Penryn TR10 ... 144 C7
Brook Rd Falmouth TR11 ... 144 F3
Wadebridge PL27 ... 108 B5
Brooks PL22 ... 49 E3
Brookside PL25 ... 114 F4
Brookside Cl PL15 ... 106 B8
Brook St Falmouth TR11 ... 145 A4
⓱ Mousehole TR19 ... 88 C1
Tavistock PL19 ... 147 C6
Brook The PL12 ... 122 E4
Brookward Terr ❽ TR18 .. 143 C7
Brookway TR27 ... 142 E7
Brookwood Rd PL9 ... 136 D7
Broomfield Dr Bodmin PL31 109 B3
Plymouth PL9 ... 135 C5
Broomfield Rd PL27 ... 108 D5
Broom Hill PL12 ... 122 D2
Broomhill Cross EX22 ... 5 E3
Broomhill La EX23 ... 4 D2
Broom Pk PL9 ... 135 D5
Broughton Cl PL3 ... 128 F7
Browne Memorial Almshouses
PL19 ... 147 A5
Browning Cl ⓮ TR9 ... 45 D6
Browning Dr PL31 ... 109 C3
Browning Rd PL2 ... 128 A5
Brownlow Pl ❺ PL31 ... 109 D5
Brownlow St PL1 ... 148 A2
Browns Hill PL23 ... 116 C4
Brown's Hill Penryn TR10 .. 144 C8
❷ Treliever TR10 ... 81 D2
Broxton Dr PL9 ... 129 E1
Bruallen Cl PL30 ... 23 E7
Bruggan TR12 ... 103 A4
Brunel Ave PL2 ... 127 F5
Brunel Ct ❼ TR1 ... 137 B4
Brunel Prim & Nur Sch
PL12 ... 122 E2
Brunel Quays PL22 ... 112 D2
Brunel Rd PL12 ... 122 C4
Brunel Terr ❸ PL2 ... 127 F5
Brunel Way PL1 ... 148 A2
BRUNNION ... 77 A3
Brunnion Rd TR27 ... 77 A3
Brunswick Pl ❿ PL2 ... 127 F4
Brunswick Rd PL4 ... 149 B2
Brunton Rd TR15 ... 23 B5
Brush End TR26 ... 77 E4
Bryher Cl PL17 ... 39 E6
Brymon Way PL6 ... 125 B4
Brynmoor Cl PL3 ... 129 A7
Brynmoor Pk PL3 ... 129 A6
Brynmoor Wlk PL3 ... 129 A6
Bryny Cl PL30 ... 23 E7
Buccaneer St ❶ TR18 ... 143 D6
Buckett's Hill TR15 ... 140 C2
Buckeys La TR2 ... 95 B6
Buckfast Cl PL2 ... 128 A8
Buckingham Nip TR4 ... 68 F3
Buckingham Pl PL5 ... 123 E2
Buckingham's Cl TR8 ... 56 B7
Buckingham Terr TR16 ... 68 D1
Buckland Abbey★ PL20 ... 41 F1
Buckland Cl PL7 ... 130 D7
BUCKLAND
MONACHORUM ... 42 A3
Buckland St PL1 ... 148 B2
Buckland Terr PL20 ... 42 C2
Bucklawren Rd PL13 ... 63 E7
Bucklers Ho PL25 ... 115 B4
Bucklers La PL25 ... 115 B4
Buckler Village (Mobile Homes
Pk) PL25 ... 115 B4
Buckles Hill PL15 ... 10 E1
Buckthorn Ct ❸ PL6 ... 124 C6
Buckwell St PL1, PL4 ... 149 A2
Buctor Pk PL19 ... 41 D8
Buddle Cl Plymouth PL9 ... 136 A5
Tavistock PL19 ... 147 B6
BUDE ... 104 E6
Budehaven Com Sch EX23 104 F5
Budehaven L Ctr EX23 ... 104 F5
Bude Ind Est EX23 ... 104 F4
Bude Marshes Nature
Reserve★ EX23 ... 104 D4
Bude Primary Academy Junior
& Infants School EX23 ... 104 E5
Bude-Stratton Bsns Pk EX23 7 B8

Bude-Stratton Mus ★
  EX23 . . . . **104** D5
Budge Mdws PL15 . . . . **28** C4
Budleigh Cl PL9 . . . . **135** F5
Budnic Est TR6 . . . . **55** B5
Budnic Hill TR6 . . . . **55** B5
Budock Cl TR11 . . . . **144** D3
Budock Pl TR11 . . . . **145** B4
Budock Terr TR11 . . . . **145** B3
Budock Vean La TR11 . . . . . **93** B2
BUDOCK WATER **144** C2
Budshead Gn PL5 . . . . **124** C4
Budshead Rd PL5 . . . . **124** C4
Budshead Way PL5 . . . . . . **124** E2
Buena Vista Cl PL6 . . . . . . **125** D6
Buena Vista Dr PL6 . . . . . . **125** C6
Buena Vista Gdns PL6 . . . . **125** C6
Buena Vista Way PL6 . . . . **125** C6
BUGLE **47** D1
Bugle Rural Workshops
  PL26 . . . . **47** C1
Bugle Sch PL26 . . . . **47** C1
Bugle Sta PL26 . . . . **47** C2
Bugle Way PL31 . . . . **109** F3
Buildings The TR20 . . . . **89** A6
Bullan's La TR26 . . . . **141** A5
Bullans Terr 5 TR26 . . . . . **141** A5
Bulleid Cl PL2 . . . . **127** F7
Bulleid Way EX23 . . . . **104** E4
Buller Cl Plymouth PL7 . . . **130** F4
  Torpoint PL11 . . . . **127** A3
Buller Hill TR16 . . . . **80** B6
Buller Ho PL13 . . . . **117** D3
Buller Pk Liskeard PL14 . . **113** D5
  Saltash PL12 . . . . **122** D3
Buller Rd PL11 . . . . **127** D3
Buller St PL13 . . . . **117** C3
Bull Hill PL23 . . . . **116** D4
Bullock La
  Helston, Lower Green
   TR13 . . . . **146** B5
  Helston, Whitehill TR13 . **146** C4
  Whitehill TR13 . . . . **146** B4
Bullock Market Terr 27
  TR18 . . . . **143** E6
Bulmer Rd PL4 . . . . **149** C3
Bulsworthy La PL15 . . . . **19** C2
Bulteel Gdns PL6 . . . . **124** E7
Bulwark Cl 2 PL5 . . . . **124** D1
Bulwark Rd TR13 . . . . **146** B4
Bungalows The Looe PL13 **117** D6
  Tintagel PL34 . . . . **14** D7
Bunkers Hill
  22 St Ives TR26 . . . . **141** B6
  Townshend TR27 . . . . **90** C8
Bunneys Side PL14 . . . . **36** E1
Bunnys Hill PL30 . . . . **35** E2
Bunyan Cl PL5 . . . . **124** C2
Burden Cl PL31 . . . . **109** C4
Burgess Cl EX23 . . . . **4** D2
Burgois Rd PL27 . . . . **32** D7
BURHOS **79** F2
Burhos Row TR13 . . . . **79** F1
Buriton Row 32 TR18 . . . . **143** E5
BURLAWN **108** D1
Burlawn Dr PL25 . . . . **114** F7
Burleigh La PL3 . . . . **128** D7
Burleigh Manor PL3 . . . . . **128** D7
Burleigh Park Rd PL3 . . . . **128** D6
Burley Cl PL3 . . . . **137** D3
Burley Ct TR11 . . . . **145** B4
Burnard Cl PL6 . . . . **124** E7
Burnards Ct 7 PL31 . . . . . **109** D5
Burnett Cl PL12 . . . . **122** D2
Burnett Rd PL6 . . . . **128** E8
Burngullow Rd PL26 . . . . . . **58** F3
Burnham Park Rd PL3 . . . . **128** C8
Burniston Cl PL7 . . . . **131** A3
Burnistone Cl PL7 . . . . **131** A3
Burn La PL19 . . . . **30** E8
Burns Ave PL5 . . . . **124** C2
Burns View PL11 . . . . **65** B5
Burnthouse Burnthouse TR10 **81** C4
  Dobwalls PL14 . . . . **37** C1
Burnthouse Cotts TR10 . . . **81** C1
Burnthouse La Hayle TR27 **142** D5
  Roskrow TR10 . . . . **81** C3
Burn View EX23 . . . . **104** D6
Burnwithian Terr TR16 . . . . **68** D1
Burras Bolitho TR14 . . . . . . **79** F1
  Tolcarne TR13 . . . . **80** A2
BURRATON **122** D4
Burraton Com Prim Sch
  PL12 . . . . **122** C3
BURRATON COOMBE **122** C2
Burraton Rd PL12 . . . . **122** C4
Burrator Rd PL20 . . . . **42** E3
Burrington Ind Est PL5 . . . **124** A1
Burrington Rd PL5 . . . . . . **124** A1
Burrington Way PL5 . . . . . **124** B1
Burrow Hill PL9 . . . . **135** E6
Burrows The TR26 . . . . **141** A5
BURSDON **3** B6
Bursdon Moor Cross EX39 . . **3** B7
Burthallan La TR26 . . . . **77** A7
Burton Cl PL6 . . . . **125** B6
Burton Ho 15 PL25 . . . . . . **114** C3
Burwell Cl PL6 . . . . **125** C4
Bury Cl PL15 . . . . **11** B1
Buscaverran PL14 . . . . **91** C8
Bush Hill PL14 . . . . **36** F2
Bush Pk Launceston PL15 . **106** D5
  Plymouth PL6 . . . . **125** F3
BUSVEAL **140** F4

Butcher Park Hill PL19 . . . **147** B7
Bute Rd PL4 . . . . **129** A4
Butler Cl PL6 . . . . **125** B6
Butney Cnr TR14 . . . . **66** E3
Butson Pk TR5 . . . . **68** D8
Buttercup Field EX23 . . . . . . **6** F2
Buttercup Mdw PL15 . . . . **106** E4
Buttercup Rd PL6 . . . . **125** B2
Butterdown PL12 . . . . **122** B3
Buttlegate PL11 . . . . **64** D5
Button Dr TR8 . . . . **111** B5
Butt Park Rd PL5 . . . . **124** B3
BUTTSBEAR CROSS **7** F7
Butts La PL31 . . . . **9** D1
Butts Pk PL22 . . . . **112** D2
Butts The St Newlyn East TR8 **56** B7
  Tintagel PL34 . . . . **14** D7
Buzzard Rd PL19 . . . . **147** D2
Buzzard Rise 8 PL18 . . . . . **40** F5
Byard Cl PL5 . . . . **123** E1
Byland Rd PL3 . . . . **129** A6
Byron Ave PL5 . . . . **124** C2

C

Cabot Cl PL12 . . . . **122** E2
Cades Parc TR13 . . . . **146** C6
CADGWITH **103** B4
Cadoc Cl PL28 . . . . **20** E1
Cadogan Cl TR14 . . . . **138** E1
Cadogan Dr TR14 . . . . **138** E1
Cadogan Rd TR14 . . . . **138** E1
Cadover Cl PL6 . . . . **125** A1
Caernarvon Gdns PL2 . . . . **128** B7
Caernarvon Lodge 1 TR7 **110** D5
Calais Rd TR27 . . . . **78** C2
Calamansack TR11 . . . . **93** B2
Calartha Rd TR19 . . . . **75** A1
Calartha Terr 5 TR19 . . . . . **75** A1
Calder Cl PL3 . . . . **129** B6
Caldicot Gdns PL6 . . . . . . **125** C8
Caldwells Rd TR18 . . . . . . **143** E6
Caledonia Cl 1 PL7 . . . . . **131** B5
CALENICK **137** C1
Calenick St TR1 . . . . **137** C4
Cal Hill TR16 . . . . **140** D3
California Gdns
  Plymouth PL3 . . . . **129** D6
  Portscatho TR2 . . . . **83** B2
CALLESTICK **55** C1
CALLINGTON **39** F5
Callington Com Coll PL17 . **39** F5
Callington Her Ctr ★ PL17 . **39** E4
Callington Prim Sch 20
  PL17 . . . . **39** E4
Callington Rd
  Harrowbarrow PL17 . . . . . **40** C4
  Lewannick PL15 . . . . **27** B7
  Liskeard PL14 . . . . **113** D7
  Saltash PL12 . . . . **122** E3
  Tavistock PL19 . . . . **147** A4
CALLOOSE **78** D2
Calloose Lane E TR27 . . . . **78** D1
Calloose Lane W TR27 . . . . **78** D1
Callybarrett Rd
  Callywith PL31 . . . . **35** B2
  Milltown PL30 . . . . **35** D2
Callywith Gate Ind Est PL31 **35** B3
Calshot Cl TR7 . . . . **111** E7
CALSTOCK **41** A3
Calstock Com Prim Sch
  PL18 . . . . **41** A3
Calstock Rd PL18 . . . . **41** A6
Calstock Sta PL17 . . . . **41** A3
Calumet Rd 3 TR14 . . . . . **138** E3
Calver Cl TR10 . . . . **144** C8
Calvez Cl PL10 . . . . **132** F6
Camaret Dr TR26 . . . . **141** B4
Cambeak PL35 . . . . **9** C1
Cambeak Cl EX23 . . . . **10** C6
Camber Rd PL1 . . . . **148** A1
CAMBORNE **138** B2
Camborne Cl PL5 . . . . **124** A5
Camborne Ctr The ★ TR14 **138** E3
Camborne Geological Mus &
  Art Gal ★ TR15 . . . . **139** B2
Camborne Redruth Com Hospl
  TR15 . . . . **139** F6
Camborne Ret Pk TR15 . . . **139** B5
Camborne Science &
  International Academy
  TR14 . . . . **138** B3
Camborne Sta TR14 . . . . . **138** D3
Cambridge La W 5 PL1 . . **148** B3
Cambridge Pl TR11 . . . . . . **145** A3
Cambridge Rd PL2 . . . . . . **127** F5
CAMBROSE **67** F6
Camden Ct PL4 . . . . **149** A3
Camden St PL4 . . . . **149** A3
Camel Cl PL28 . . . . **20** E1
Camel Ct PL30 . . . . **109** C6
Camelford **105** C4
Camelford L Ctr PL32 . . . . **105** C4
Camelford Prim Sch PL32 **105** C3
Camelot Cl 2 TR18 . . . . . . **143** E5
Camelot View PL32 . . . . . . **105** C8
Camel Rd Carlyon PL27 . . . **21** F2
  Dinham PL27 . . . . **22** A1
CAMELS HEAD **127** E7
Camelside PL27 . . . . **108** C5
Camel Valley Vineyard ★
  PL30 . . . . **34** B2
Cameo Ct TR14 . . . . **138** F4
Cameron Cl EX23 . . . . **104** D7
Cameron Way PL6 . . . . . . **125** B1
Camilla Terr PL2 . . . . **128** D7
Campbell Rd PL9 . . . . **135** F7

Campbeltown Way TR11 . . **145** C3
Camp Cross PL15 . . . . **19** F7
Camperdown St La N 4
  PL2 . . . . **127** F4
Camperdown St PL2 . . . . . **127** F4
Camperknowle Cl PL10 . . **132** F6
Campfield Hill TR1 . . . . . . **137** D5
Camp Hall Rd TR8 . . . . **43** B1
Campion Cl PL15 . . . . **106** E4
  7 Plymouth PL7 . . . . **131** C5
  Saltash PL12 . . . . **122** D4
Campion Rise PL19 . . . . . . **147** D6
Campion View PL6 . . . . . . **125** E8
Campion Way TR27 . . . . . . **142** E6
Campion Wlk 2 PL27 . . . . **108** C6
Camp Rd TR8 . . . . **43** B1
Camullas Way TR7 . . . . . . **110** A5
Canal Rd PL19 . . . . **147** B5
Canberra Rd 5 PL6 . . . . . **125** D6
Candish Dr PL9 . . . . **136** D7
Canefields Ave PL7 . . . . . . **131** B3
Canhaye Cl PL7 . . . . **131** A3
Canis Mews 7 PL9 . . . . . . **136** A5
CANNALIDGEY **32** E4
Cannalidgey Rd PL27 . . . . . **32** E4
Cann Gdns PL6 . . . . **124** D6
Cannis Rd PL25 . . . . **114** E6
Cannon Hill PL14 . . . . **113** C5
Cannons Pl TR13 . . . . **146** D7
Cannon St PL1 . . . . **127** D2
Cannon Terr 2 PL14 . . . . . **113** C5
Cann Woods Nature Reserve ★
  PL5 . . . . **124** C6
Cann Wood View PL6 . . . . **125** E7
CANONSTOWN **77** C2
Canons Way PL19 . . . . **147** A3
Cansford Dip EX23 . . . . **10** E5
Canterbury Dr PL5 . . . . . . **124** B4
Cantillion Cl PL27 . . . . **21** E3
Canton PL26 . . . . **85** D5
CANWORTHY WATER **11** D2
Canyke Fields 1 PL31 . . . **109** F3
Canyke Rd PL31 . . . . **48** D8
Cape Cl TR19 . . . . **86** E6
Cape Terr TR19 . . . . **86** E6
Cape Cornwall Rd TR19 . . . **86** E6
Cape Cornwall Sch TR19 . . **86** E6
Cape Cornwall St TR19 . . . **86** E6
Capella Dr 1 PL9 . . . . **136** E8
Cape Terr TR19 . . . . **86** E6
Cape Trelew TR19 . . . . **86** E6
Caprera Terr La PL4 . . . . . **148** C4
Capricorn Way 14 PL9 . . . **136** E8
Captains Gdns PL25 . . . . . **124** E1
Captains Ho PL26 . . . . **73** C3
Captain's Wlk TR11 . . . . . . **145** A2
Caradon Bsns Ctr 8 PL14 **113** C5
Caradon Cl
  9 Callington PL17 . . . . . . **39** E4
  1 Pensilva PL14 . . . . **38** E4
  Plymouth PL6 . . . . **125** A5
Caradon Ct 2 PL20 . . . . . . **42** C4
Caradon Dr PL14 . . . . **113** B6
Caradon Hts Liskeard PL14 **113** D7
  Tremar PL14 . . . . **38** B4
Caradon Terr PL12 . . . . . . **122** E3
CARADON TOWN **38** E6
Caradon View PL14 . . . . . . **37** F3
Caravan Pk TR20 . . . . **89** C6
Caraway Cl 5 TR14 . . . . . **138** E5
Carbeile Jun Sch PL11 . . . **127** A3
Carbeile Rd PL11 . . . . **127** A2
Carbes La PL22 . . . . **112** C2
CARBIS **47** A2
CARBIS BAY **141** D3
Carbis Bay Sta TR26 . . . . . **141** D2
Carbis Cl TR15 . . . . **140** A5
Carbis Rd PL26 . . . . **59** D6
Carboth La PL15 . . . . **106** B5
CARCLAZE **114** E6
Carclaze Com Prim Sch
  PL25 . . . . **114** E6
Carclaze Ind Est PL25 . . . . **114** E7
Carclaze La PL27 . . . . **22** E2
Carclaze Rd PL25 . . . . **114** E6
Carclew Ave TR7 . . . . **110** E6
Carclew Rd TR11 . . . . **81** F4
Carclew St TR1 . . . . **137** D3
Carclew Terr Devoran TR3 . **81** F6
  Truro TR1 . . . . **137** D3
Cardeast La PL30 . . . . **35** E4
Cardell Rd PL31 . . . . **109** D5
Cardell Way TR7 . . . . **111** A5
Cardiff Cl PL7 . . . . **131** B4
Cardigan Rd PL6 . . . . **125** C1
Cardinal Ave PL5 . . . . **127** D8
CARDINHAM **35** E3
Cardinham Prim Sch PL30 . **35** F3
Cardinham Woods Forest
  Walks ★ PL30 . . . . **35** C1
Cardinnis Gn 2 PL14 . . . . **113** D6
Cardinnis Rd TR18 . . . . . . **143** B5
Cardrew Bsns Pk TR15 . . . **140** C6
Cardrew Cl TR15 . . . . **140** B6
Cardrew Dr TR15 . . . . **140** D6
Cardrew Ind Est
  Redruth TR15 . . . . **140** D7
  Redruth TR16 . . . . **68** B2
  Treleigh TR15 . . . . **140** C7
Cardrew La 1 TR15 . . . . . **140** C5
Cardrew Terr TR15 . . . . . . **140** D6
Cardrew Trade Park N
  TR15 . . . . **140** C7
Cardrew Trade Park S
  TR15 . . . . **140** C7
Cardwen Est PL13 . . . . **62** C6

Careswell Ave PL2 . . . . . . **127** F8
Carew Ave PL5 . . . . **124** B3
Carew Cl Crafthole PL11 . . **65** B5
  St Day TR16 . . . . **68** E1
Carew Gdns Plymouth PL5 **124** B3
  Saltash PL12 . . . . **122** D3
Carew Gr PL5 . . . . **124** B3
Carew-Pole Cl TR11 . . . . . **137** E3
Carew Rd St Day TR16 . . . . **68** E1
  Truro TR1 . . . . **137** C5
Carew Terr PL11 . . . . **127** B2
Carew Wharf PL11 . . . . . . **127** C2
Carew Wharf Bsns Ctr
  PL11 . . . . **127** C2
Carey Ct PL12 . . . . **122** E3
Carey Pk Helston TR13 . . . **146** B7
  Polperro PL13 . . . . **62** E2
  Truro TR1 . . . . **137** C4
CARFURY **76** A1
Cargoll Rd TR8 . . . . **56** B7
CARGREEN **119** A2
Cargwyn PL26 . . . . **59** D6
Cargy Cl TR8 . . . . **55** D8
CARHARRACK **80** F8
Carina Pl 9 PL9 . . . . **136** E8
Carisbrooke Rd PL6 . . . . . **125** C1
Carkeek's Cl PL26 . . . . **58** B3
CARKEEL **122** C6
Carkeel Barns PL12 . . . . . **122** C5
Carkeel Ind Est PL12 . . . . **122** D5
Carknown Gdns TR15 . . . . **140** D3
Carland Cross TR8 . . . . **56** D4
Carland View TR8 . . . . **56** B7
CARLEEN **90** F5
Carleen TR13 . . . . **90** F4
CARLIDNACK **93** E4
Carlidnack Cl TR11 . . . . **93** D3
Carlidnack La TR11 . . . . **93** D4
Carlidnack Rd TR11 . . . . . . **93** E4
Carlisle Rd PL5 . . . . **124** D3
CARLOGGAS Foxhole **58** C5
  Penwithick **59** D7
  St Mawgan **45** A8
Carloggas Cl TR8 . . . . **45** A8
Carloggas Farm TR8 . . . . . **45** A8
Carloggas Gr 6 TR9 . . . . . **45** D6
Carloggas La PL26 . . . . **58** C4
Carloggas Way 10 TR9 . . . **45** D6
Carlton Cl PL3 . . . . **129** B5
Carlton Ho 6 PL31 . . . . . . **109** E5
Carlton Terr
  Plymouth, Lipson PL4 . . . **149** B3
  Plymouth, Weston Mill PL5 **127** E8
Carlton Vills PL12 . . . . **53** E4
Carlton Way PL14 . . . . **113** D7
CARLUDDON **59** D6
Carluddon Technology Park
  PL26 . . . . **59** D6
CARLYON BAY **115** E3
Carlyon Cl Looe PL13 . . . . . **62** A7
  Threemilestone TR3 . . . . . **69** D3
  Torpoint PL11 . . . . **126** F4
  11 Truro TR1 . . . . **137** C4
Carlyon Ct TR3 . . . . **82** B8
Carlyon Ho TR1 . . . . **69** E4
Carlyon Rd Playing Field TR3 **82** B8
  St Austell PL25 . . . . **114** E4
  Truro TR1 . . . . **137** C5
Carmarthen Rd PL4 . . . . . **129** B2
Carmel Gdns PL19 . . . . . . **147** A5
Carmen Sq 10 TR18 . . . . . **143** C7
Carminow Cross PL30 . . . . **48** D8
Carminowe Cres 8 TR18 . **143** D5
Carminow Rd PL31 . . . . **48** D8
Carminow Road Ind Est 4
  PL31 . . . . **48** D8
Carminow Way TR7 . . . . . **111** A7
Carn TR3 . . . . **80** E3
Carnanton Rd TR8 . . . . **45** C6
Carnarthen Moor TR15 . . . **139** C3
Carnarthen La TR15 . . . . . . **79** E6
CARN ARTHEN **139** B2
Carnarthen Moor TR15 . . . . **67** E1
Carnarthen Rd 1 TR14 . . . **138** C2
Carnarthen St TR14 . . . . . **138** E2
Carn Ave TR14 . . . . **138** F2
Carn Bargus PL26 . . . . **58** E8
Carn Bosavern TR19 . . . . . . **86** F6
Carn Bosavern Cl TR19 . . . . **86** F6
Carn Brae L Ctr TR15 . . . . **139** C5
Carn Brea Ave TR15 . . . . . **139** C5
Carn Brea Ho TR15 . . . . . . **139** C5
Carn Brea La TR15 . . . . . . **139** C5
CARN BREA VILLAGE **139** F5
Carn Brea Village TR15 . . . **139** F5
Carn Cl TR27 . . . . **78** E1
Carncrows Rd TR26 . . . . . **141** C6
Carncrows St TR26 . . . . . . **141** C6
CARNE St Dennis **46** C1
  Veryan **83** F5
Carnebo Hill TR4 . . . . **55** E5
Carnebone TR13 . . . . **92** C7
Carne Cross PL24 . . . . **59** F7
Carne Ct PL26 . . . . **58** C8
Carnedon PL14 . . . . **38** C7
Carnego La TR8 . . . . **57** B6
Carne Hill St Dennis PL26 . . **46** C1
  Trewoon PL25 . . . . **58** F4
Carnellis Rd 7 TR26 . . . . . **141** B5
Carne Mdws TR2 . . . . **70** F5
CARN ENTRAL **139** A2
Carn Entral Brea Addit TR14 **139** A1
  Pengegon TR14 . . . . **79** B2
Carne Quarry TR12 . . . . . **102** D8
Carne Rd TR18 . . . . **143** C3
Carne's Bldgs 11 TR18 . . . **143** E4
Carnes Ct TR11 . . . . **145** C2
Carne's Flats PL24 . . . . **60** B5

Carneton Cl TR8 . . . . **43** D3
Carn Euny Settlement ★
  TR20 . . . . **87** C3
Carne View Cl TR14 . . . . . **138** F5
Carne View Rd TR2 . . . . **71** D6
Carnglaze Caverns ★ PL14 . **36** F1
Carnglaze Cl PL14 . . . . . . **113** C6
Carn Gloose Rd TR19 . . . . . **86** E6
Carn Gwavas Terr TR18 . . **143** D1
CARNHELL GREEN **78** F4
Carnhell Rd TR14, TR27 . . . **78** F4
CARNHOT **68** F4
Carninney La TR26 . . . . . . **141** C1
Carnjewey Way 4 PL25 . . **114** F2
CARNKIE **139** F2
Carnkie Cnr TR4 . . . . **55** D4
Carnkief Cnr TR4 . . . . **55** D4
Carn La Bosleake TR16 . . . . **67** F1
  Brunnion TR20 . . . . **77** A2
  Carnkie TR16 . . . . **139** F3
Carn Marth La TR16 . . . . . **140** E2
Carnmeal TR13 . . . . **91** A4
Carnock Rd PL2 . . . . **128** D8
Carnon Cres 13 TR3 . . . . . **81** F7
CARNON DOWNS **82** A7
Carnon Gate Roundabout
  TR3 . . . . **81** E6
Carnon Terr TR3 . . . . **81** F6
Carnoustie Dr PL12 . . . . . **122** C2
Carn Rock TR10 . . . . **144** D7
Carn Ros TR19 . . . . **74** F1
Carnsew Cl TR10 . . . . **81** C1
Carnsew Cres TR10 . . . . . . **81** C1
Carnsew Ct TR27 . . . . **142** B5
Carnsew Mdw TR27 . . . . . **142** A5
Carnsew Rd TR27 . . . . **142** A5
Carnsmerry PL26 . . . . **47** C1
Carnsmerry Cres PL25 . . . **114** E4
Carnstabba Rd 13 TR26 . . . **77** A6
Carnsullen La TR12 . . . . . . **101** B1
Carntiscoe Rd TR27 . . . . . . **77** C2
Carntiscoe Workshops
  TR27 . . . . **77** C2
Carn Todden TR19 . . . . **88** D1
CARN TOWAN **96** C7
Carn View TR16 . . . . **80** F6
Carn View Terr TR19 . . . . . . **75** A1
CARNYORTH **86** F8
Carnyorth Hill TR19 . . . . . . **86** F8
Carnyorth Terr
  Carnyorth TR19 . . . . **86** F8
  Trewellard TR19 . . . . **86** F8
Caroe Rd PL32 . . . . **10** D2
Carolina Gdns PL2 . . . . . . **127** F7
Caroline Cl TR27 . . . . **142** E7
Caroline Row TR27 . . . . . . **142** E7
CARPALLA **58** D4
Carpalla Terr PL26 . . . . **58** D5
Carpenter Ct PL31 . . . . . . **109** E5
Carpenter Rd PL9 . . . . **135** F8
Carpenter Way PL19 . . . . . **147** B7
Carpmael Ave TR8 . . . . . . **111** B4
Carracawn Cross PL12 . . . . **64** D8
Carrack Dhu 37 TR26 . . . . **141** B6
Carrack Dhu Est 36 TR26 . **141** B6
Carrack Gladden TR26 . . . **141** D2
Carrack Widden 25 TR26 . **141** B5
Carradale Rd PL6 . . . . **129** C2
Carrallack La TR19 . . . . **86** E5
Carrallack Mews TR19 . . . . **86** E5
Carrallack Terr TR19 . . . . . . **86** E5
Carriage Ho The TR3 . . . . . **69** F1
Carriage Parc TR3 . . . . **55** D4
Carrickowel Cres 1 PL25 . **115** A5
Carrick Rd TR11 . . . . **144** E2
Carrick Way TR2 . . . . **95** A6
Carrine Rd TR1 . . . . **69** F3
Carrisbrooke Way PL12 . . **122** B2
Carrnown Gdns TR15 . . . . **140** D3
Carroll Rd PL5 . . . . **124** C2
Carrolls Way PL9 . . . . **136** A5
Carron La PL6 . . . . **121** D1
Carsize La TR27 . . . . **78** E1
Carter Cl TR7 . . . . **111** A5
Carteret Rd EX23 . . . . **104** E5
CARTHEW **59** B6
Carthew Cl Liskeard PL14 . **113** D5
  St Ives TR26 . . . . **141** A6
Carthew Ct TR26 . . . . **141** A6
Carthew La Four Lanes TR13 . **80** A3
  Praze-an-Beeble TR13 . . . **79** F2
Carthew Terr TR26 . . . . . . **141** A6
Carthew Way TR26 . . . . . . **141** A6
Carvath Ho PL25 . . . . **114** D3
Carvedras TR11 . . . . **92** E5
Carvedras Ct 1 TR1 . . . . . **137** C4
Carvolth TR14 . . . . **79** D3
Carvolth Downs TR14 . . . . . **79** E2
Carvossa Est TR20 . . . . **89** B8
Carvoza Rd TR1 . . . . **137** D5
Carvynick Cotts TR8 . . . . . . **57** A7
Carwen Rd PL30 . . . . **35** D8
Carwinard TR7 . . . . **78** C5
Carwinion Bamboo Gdn ★
  TR11 . . . . **93** E3
Carwinion Rd TR11 . . . . **93** E3
Carwin La TR27 . . . . **78** C5
Carwin Rise Angarrack TR27 . **78** C5
  Hayle TR27 . . . . **142** E7
Carwollen Rd PL25 . . . . . . **114** E7
Carworgie Ct 10 TR9 . . . . . **45** E2
Carworgie Manor TR9 . . . . **45** E2
Carworgie Way 7 TR9 . . . . **45** E2
CARWYNNEN **79** D4
Carwynnen Cl TR14 . . . . . . **79** B3
CARZISE **78** D1
Casey La PL13 . . . . **62** D5

Cassacawn Hill PL30 . . . . . . 35 D8
CASTALLACK 97 F6
Castel Wary Cl TR13 . . . . 146 B5
Casterills Rd TR13 . . . . 146 D4
Castings Dr 2 PL25. . . . . . . 115 A3
Castle Acre Gdns PL3 . . . . 129 B5
Castle Bank Gdns PL3 . . . . 129 B5
Castle Barbican PL7 . . . . . . 130 E4
Castle Bldgs PL12 . . . . 122 D4
Castle Canyke Rd
  Bodmin PL31 . . . . 109 F3
  Bodmin PL31 . . . . 109 F3
Castle Carey Gdns PL3 . . . . 129 B5
Castle Cl TR11. . . . . 145 B3
Castle Ct Praa Sands TR20 . . 90 C3
  Saltash PL12. . . . . 122 C2
Castledore Rd PL24. . . . . . . 60 E5
Castle Dr Bodmin PL31 . . . . 109 F5
  Falmouth TR11. . . . . 145 E4
  Praa Sands TR20 . . . . 90 B3
  St Mawes TR2 . . . . 94 F5
Castle Dyke PL15 . . . . 106 C6
CASTLE GATE 76 F1
Castle Gdns PL14 . . . . 113 C6
Castle Gn 2 PL14 . . . . 146 B5
Castlehayes Gdns PL7 . . . . 130 E4
Castle Hill Falmouth TR11 . . 145 D3
  1 Helston TR13 . . . . 146 B5
  5 Liskeard PL14 . . . . 113 C6
  Lostwithiel PL22 . . . . 112 C2
  Saltash PL12 . . . . 122 C1
Castle Hill Ct Bodmin PL31 . 109 E5
  7 Liskeard PL14 . . . . 113 C6
Castle Hill Gdns PL31 . . . . . 109 F5
Castle Hts 3 PL34. . . . . 14 C7
Castlek La PL15. . . . . 27 A4
Castle La Liskeard PL14 . . . 113 C6
  Plymouth PL7. . . . . 130 E4
Castle Mdws
  Launceston PL15. . . . . 106 A4
  2 St Agnes TR5. . . . . 54 D1
Castlemead Cl PL12 . . . . . . 122 D3
Castlemead Dr PL12 . . . . . . 122 D3
Castle Rd Castle Down TR9 . . 46 B4
  Longrock TR20. . . . . 88 F8
  Ludgvan TR20 . . . . 89 A8
  Penzance TR18 . . . . 143 E7
  Tintagel PL34. . . . . 14 C7
Castle Rise Plymouth PL3. . 129 B4
  Saltash PL12. . . . . 122 C1
  Truro TR1. . . . . 137 C5
Castle Rock PL29 . . . . 22 D8
Castle St Bodmin PL31 . . . . 109 F5
  Launceston PL15. . . . . 106 C6
  Liskeard PL14 . . . . 113 C6
  Looe PL13 . . . . 117 D3
  Plymouth PL1. . . . . 149 A2
  Truro TR1. . . . . 137 C4
Castleton Cl PL3. . . . . 129 A4
Castle View
  10 Liskeard PL14. . . . . 113 C6
  Longrock TR20. . . . . 88 F6
  Lostwithiel PL22 . . . . 112 E3
  Saltash PL12. . . . . 122 D1
  Tintagel PL34. . . . . 14 C7
Castle View Cl TR15 . . . . . . 140 B6
Castle View Pk TR11 . . . . . . 93 D3
Caswarth Terr PL28. . . . . . . 107 D5
Catalina Row PL27. . . . . 31 F3
Catalina Villas PL9 . . . . 135 A6
CATCHALL 97 D8
Catchfrench Cres PL14 . . . . 113 E6
Cathcart Ave PL4. . . . . 129 B2
Cathebedron Rd
  Carnhell Green TR14 . . . . . . 78 F4
  Praze-an-Beeble TR14. . . . . 79 A3
Cathedral Church of the
  Blessed Virgin Mary *
  TR1. . . . . 137 D4
Cathedral La 13 TR1 . . . . . 137 D4
Cathedral of St Mary & St
  Boniface PL1. . . . . 148 B3
Cathedral School of St Mary
  PL1 . . . . 148 B3
Cathedral St PL1 . . . . 148 B3
Cathedral View TR1 . . . . . . 137 C6
Catherine Cl EX23 . . . . 104 F4
Catherine Pk PL13. . . . . 62 E5
Catherine's Hill PL15 . . . . . 106 A6
Catherine St PL1 . . . . 148 C2
CATTEDOWN 149 C1
Catterick Cl PL5. . . . . 123 E5
Cattewater Rd PL4. . . . . . . 129 B1
Caudledown La PL26 . . . . . . 59 C8
Caunter Rd PL14. . . . . 113 D6
Causeland Sta PL14. . . . . . . 51 B2
Causewayhead PL18. . . . . . 143 E5
Causeway The
  Falmouth TR11. . . . . 144 F4
  Hayle TR27. . . . . 142 A4
Causley Cl PL15 . . . . 106 C7
Cavendish Cres TR7 . . . . . . 111 B5
CAWSAND 133 B1
Caxton Gdns
  2 Manadon PL5. . . . . 124 C1
  Plymouth PL5. . . . . 124 C1
Cayforth Flats TR16. . . . . . . 67 C6
Cayley Way PL5 . . . . 123 F2
Cecil Ave PL4. . . . . 149 C4
Cecil Cotts PL1. . . . . 148 A3
Cecil St PL1 . . . . 148 B3
Cedar Ave PL9. . . . . 135 C5
Cedar Cl 21 Callington PL17 . 39 F4
  Torpoint PL11. . . . . 126 F2
Cedarcroft Rd PL2. . . . . 128 B7

Cedar Ct Camborne TR14 . . 139 A5
  Saltash PL12 . . . . 122 F2
Cedar Dr PL11 . . . . 126 F2
Cedar Gr EX23 . . . . 104 E7
Cedar House Flats TR26 . . . 77 E4
Cedar Pk PL9. . . . . 135 A1
Cedars The TR1 . . . . 137 C2
Celandine Gdns PL7. . . . . . 131 C5
Celia Hts PL31. . . . . 109 F2
Celtic Rd PL17 . . . . 39 F4
Cemetery Rd PL18. . . . . 40 F5
Centaur Mews 18 PL9. . . . 136 E8
Centenary Row Middle
  TR14 . . . . 138 E3
Centenary Row W 2 TR14 138 E2
Centenary St TR14. . . . . . . 138 E3
Centenary Way 3 PL18. . . . 143 D6
Central Ave PL25 . . . . 114 E5
Central Cl PL26. . . . . 58 B4
Central Park Ave PL4 . . . . . 148 C4
Central Sq TR7 . . . . 110 D6
Central Treviscoe
  St Dennis PL26. . . . . 58 A7
  Treviscoe PL26 . . . . 58 B7
Century Cl Helston TR13 . . . 146 D2
  St Austell PL25. . . . . 114 F6
Century Ct TR7 . . . . 111 C7
Century La TR2 . . . . 83 F6
Century Sq 6 PL14 . . . . 38 E4
CHACEWATER 68 F3
Chacewater Hill TR4. . . . . . . 69 A3
Chacewater Prim Sch TR4 . . 69 A3
CHADDLEWOOD 131 B6
Chaddlewood Ave PL4. . . . . 148 C4
Chaddlewood Cl PL7 . . . . . 131 A4
Chaddlewood Ho PL7. . . . . 131 B5
Chaddlewood Prim Sch
  PL7 . . . . 131 A5
Chadwick Parc TR15. . . . . . 140 B6
Chagford Wlk PL6 . . . . 129 E8
Chainwalk Dr TR1 . . . . 137 C6
Chalets The TR18. . . . . 88 E6
Chalet The PL11 . . . . 64 C4
Challacombe Gdns TR10 . . 144 C8
Challenger Quay 12 TR11 . 145 C3
Challgood Cl 1 PL9 . . . . . . 135 F5
Challgood Rise PL9. . . . . . . 135 F5
Challis Ave TR8. . . . . 45 A8
Challock Cl PL6 . . . . 125 D4
Chamberlayne Dr PL7 . . . . 130 E6
Champion's Ct TR13 . . . . . . 146 B6
Chancery Cl TR4. . . . . 70 D8
Chancery La 23 TR18 . . . . . 143 E5
Chandler Pk 4 TR10. . . . . . . 94 A8
Chandlers Wlk PL25 . . . . . . 115 A3
Chandos Pl 12 PL25. . . . . . 114 C3
Channel Park Ave PL3 . . . . 129 B5
Channel View Polruan PL23 116 D2
  St Austell PL25. . . . . 115 A6
  St Ives TR26 . . . . 141 A6
Channel View Terr
  Plymouth PL4. . . . . 149 C4
  4 Redruth TR15 . . . . 140 C4
Channon Rd PL12. . . . . 122 C4
Chantry Ct PL7 . . . . 130 B5
Chantry La PL13. . . . . 117 E4
CHAPEL Launceston 106 A5
  Quintrell Downs. 111 E4
Chapel Amble Rd PL27. . . . . 22 E2
Chapel Cl
  Camborne, Kehelland TR14 . 66 F1
  Camborne, Tuckingmill TR14 139 A4
  8 Chapel PL15 . . . . 106 B5
  Connor Downs TR27 . . . . . . 78 D6
  Crantock TR8. . . . . 110 A3
  Gunnislake PL18 . . . . 40 E5
  4 Horrabridge PL20. . . . . . 42 C4
  Lanivet PL30 . . . . 47 E6
  St Just in Roseland TR2 . . . . 82 F7
Chapel Cnr EX22. . . . . 8 A5
Chapel Cotts EX23 . . . . 4 C8
Chapel Cres TR4. . . . . 56 A4
Chapel Ct Camborne TR14 . 138 F3
  Padstow PL28 . . . . 107 D5
  9 Redruth TR15 . . . . 140 B5
Chapeldown PL24 . . . . 60 D5
Chapeldown Rd PL11 . . . . . 127 A2
Chapel Farm TR14 . . . . 79 E5
Chapel Field PL25 . . . . 115 B5
Chapel Gate PL15. . . . . 106 A5
Chapel Gn PL26 . . . . 59 A1
Chapel Ground PL13. . . . . . 117 C3
Chapel Hill
  Camborne, Brea TR14 . . . . 139 A3
  Camborne, Tregajorran
  TR15. . . . . 139 C4
  Carwen PL30 . . . . 35 E8
  Devoran TR3 . . . . 81 F6
  Gweek TR12. . . . . 92 C2
  Hayle TR27. . . . . 142 C6
  Kerrow PL30 . . . . 24 D1
  Lanner TR16. . . . . 80 D6
  Launceston PL15. . . . . 106 B5
  Newquay TR7. . . . . 110 D6
  Perranporth TR6 . . . . 55 B4
  4 Perranwell TR3. . . . . 81 D6
  Polgooth PL26 . . . . 59 A1
  Ponsanooth TR3. . . . . 81 B4
  Porkellis TR13 . . . . 92 B8
  Porthtowan TR4. . . . . 68 A5
  Redruth TR16. . . . . 68 A4
  St Erth TR27. . . . . 142 A1
  Sticker PL26 . . . . 58 F1
  Truro TR1. . . . . 137 B4
Chapel La
  Berriowbridge PL15 . . . . . . 27 B3

Chapel La continued
  Bodmin PL31. . . . . 109 D5
  Goldsithney TR20. . . . . 89 F5
  Hayle TR27. . . . . 142 D6
  Horrabridge PL20. . . . . 42 C4
  Lizard TR12. . . . . 102 F2
  Penryn TR10 . . . . 144 C7
  Polmenna PL14 . . . . 36 E1
  Polruan PL23. . . . . 116 D2
  St Austell PL25. . . . . 115 C6
  St Mabyn PL30. . . . . 34 D8
  St Teath PL30. . . . . 23 F6
  Treswithick PL30. . . . . 35 E5
  Trevenna PL34 . . . . 36 E2
  5 Wadebridge PL27 . . . . . 108 B5
Chapel Mdw
  Buckland Monachorum PL20 . 41 F3
  21 Callington PL17/ 39 E4
  Perranarworthal TR3. . . . . . 81 D6
Chapel Park Gdns PL15 . . . 106 B5
Chapel Park Terr PL15 . . . . 106 B5
Chapel Pk PL15 . . . . 106 B5
Chapel Pl Pillaton PL12 . . . . 53 B7
  16 Truro TR1 . . . . 137 D4
Chapel Point La PL26 . . . . . 73 C2
Chapel Rd Camborne TR14 . 139 A4
  Foxhole PL26. . . . . 58 D5
  Heamoor TR18. . . . . 143 C8
  Indian Queens TR9 . . . . 45 E1
  Langore PL15 . . . . 18 D5
  Leedstown TR27 . . . . 78 E1
  Nanstallon PL30 . . . . 34 C1
  2 Par PL24. . . . . 60 C4
  Roche PL26 . . . . 46 F3
  St Just TR19. . . . . 86 E6
  St Tudy PL30. . . . . 23 E3
  Saltash PL12 . . . . 122 B3
Chapel Row
  Praze-an-Beeble TR14. . . . . 79 B2
  2 Redruth TR15 . . . . 140 B5
  Tremar PL14. . . . . 38 A3
  Truro TR1. . . . . 137 D4
  Widegates PL13 . . . . 63 F8
Chapel Sq Crowlas TR20 . . . 89 B8
  Mevagissey PL26 . . . . 73 C3
  Troon TR14. . . . . 79 E5
Chapel St
  4 Bere Alston PL20 . . . . . . 41 B1
  4 Callington PL17 . . . . 39 F4
  Camborne TR14 . . . . 138 D2
  Camelford PL32 . . . . 105 C4
  Grimscott EX23 . . . . 5 B2
  Gunnislake PL18 . . . . 40 F6
  Lifton PL16. . . . . 19 F4
  Marazion TR17. . . . . 89 B5
  21 Mousehole TR19. . . . . . 88 C1
  9 Newlyn TR18. . . . . 143 C1
  Penzance TR18 . . . . 143 E5
  Plymouth PL4. . . . . 149 A3
  Plymouth, Mount Wise PL1 . 127 E2
  Probus TR2 . . . . 71 C6
  Redruth TR15. . . . . 140 B5
  St Day TR16 . . . . 68 D1
  St Ives TR26. . . . . 141 B5
  St Just TR19. . . . . 86 E6
  Tavistock PL19. . . . . 147 B5
Chapel Terr
  Camborne TR15 . . . . 139 C6
  Devoran TR3 . . . . 81 F6
  Falmouth TR11. . . . . 145 B4
  Hayle TR27. . . . . 142 B5
  Par PL24 . . . . 60 B6
  9 Porthleven TR13. . . . . . . 98 B8
  Portreath TR16 . . . . 67 C6
  Redruth TR15. . . . . 140 D2
Chapel Town Bsns Pk TR8 . 57 B7
Chapel Town Ct TR11 . . . . . 93 D4
Chapel Way PL3 . . . . 129 A6
CHAPLE AMBLE. 22 D7
Chapman Ct PL12. . . . . 122 B3
Chapmans Ope PL1. . . . . . . 127 E2
CHAPMAN'S WELL 13 E4
Chapmans Wy PL25. . . . . . 114 E4
Charaton Cross PL14 . . . . . 38 F4
Charaton Rd PL14 . . . . 38 F4
Chard Barton PL5 . . . . 124 B3
Chard Rd PL5. . . . . 123 D2
Chard Terr 6 TR11 . . . . . . 145 A3
Charfield Dr PL6. . . . . 129 A8
Chariot Rd TR15 . . . . 139 E6
Chark La PL30. . . . . 48 D4
Charlbury Dr PL9 . . . . 129 D1
Charles Ave TR11 . . . . 144 E2
Charles Bassett Cl 6
  TR13 . . . . 146 C5
Charles Cl PL25. . . . . 114 F3
Charles Cross PL4 . . . . 149 A3
Charles St Bugle PL26 . . . . . 47 C1
  Newlyn TR18 . . . . 143 C1
  Plymouth PL4. . . . . 149 A3
  Truro TR1. . . . . 137 C4
Charles Terr PL3 . . . . 129 A6
CHARLESTOWN. 115 B2
Charlestown Prim Sch
  PL25. . . . . 115 C3
Charlestown Rd PL25 . . . . . 115 B3
Charlestown Shipwreck &
  Heritage Ctr * PL25. . . . . 115 B2
Charlotte Cl TR4. . . . . 68 C6
Charlotte Gardens PL25 . . 114 F3

Charlotte St PL2. . . . . 127 E4
Charlton Cres PL6 . . . . 125 A4
Charlton Rd PL6 . . . . 125 A3
Charnhill Cl PL9 . . . . 136 A6
Charnhill Way PL9. . . . . 136 A6
Charter Cl TR13 . . . . 146 C4
Charter Ct TR10 . . . . 144 B7
Charter Way PL14 . . . . 113 E6
Chateau Cl PL26 . . . . 46 D1
Chatry Pk 23 PL17 . . . . 39 E4
Chatsworth Gdns PL5. . . . . 123 F3
Chatsworth Way PL25 . . . . 115 C2
Chaucer Rd PL19 . . . . 147 D5
Chaucer Way PL5. . . . . 124 C1
Chawleigh Cl PL18. . . . . 40 F5
Chedworth St PL4 . . . . 149 A3
Chegwin Gdns TR7 . . . . . . 110 E5
Chegwyn Gdns 6 TR5 . . . . . 54 C1
Chegwyns PL26. . . . . 58 D5
Chegwyns Hill PL26. . . . . . . 58 D5
Chelfham Senior Sch PL20 . 40 F3
Chellean Vean TR4 . . . . 81 C7
Chellew Rd TR1 . . . . 137 E5
Chelmer Cl PL7. . . . . 131 A5
Chelmsford Pl PL5. . . . . . . 124 C4
Chelson Gdns PL6. . . . . 125 E3
Cheltenham Pl
  Newquay TR7. . . . . 110 D6
  Plymouth PL4. . . . . 149 B4
Chelwood Gr PL7 . . . . 130 F5
CHENHALLS 142 A2
Chenhalls Cl TR27 . . . . 77 E2
Chenhalls Rd TR27 . . . . . . 142 A2
Chenoweth Cl TR14. . . . . . 138 C4
Chenoweth Way TR16 . . . . 140 E8
Chepstow Ave PL6. . . . . . . 125 C8
Chequer Tree Ct PL18 . . . . . 40 F5
Chequetts Cl 10 PL17 . . . . . 39 E4
Cheriton Cl PL5 . . . . 124 A3
Cherrill Gdns EX23 . . . . . . 104 E7
Cherrington TR7 . . . . 110 B5
Cherry Cross EX22. . . . . 12 B7
Cherry Ct 1 PL19. . . . . 30 A3
Cherry Gdns 14 PL18. . . . . 143 E5
Cherry Gdn St 15 TR19 . . . . 88 C1
Cherry Hill TR9. . . . . 44 C8
Cherry Pk PL7. . . . . 131 A3
Cherry Tree Dr TR15 . . . . . 139 D7
Cherrytree Ho TR18 . . . . . . 143 C5
Cherry Tree La PL7 . . . . . . 131 A4
Cherry Tree Mews PL25. . . 114 D3
Cherry Way PL15 . . . . 106 E4
Cheshire Dr PL6 . . . . 124 D6
Chesnut Cl PL12 . . . . 122 D4
Chester Ct TR7 . . . . 111 A6
Chesterfield Rd PL3 . . . . . . 129 B4
Chester Pl 4 PL4. . . . . 128 E4
Chester Rd TR7. . . . . 111 A6
Chesterton Cl PL5 . . . . 124 C3
Chesterton Ct PL27 . . . . . . 108 A6
Chesterton Pl TR7 . . . . 111 A7
Chestnut Ave PL9. . . . . 135 C5
Chestnut Cl Callington PL17. . 40 A4
  Falmouth TR11. . . . . 144 F5
  Lamerton PL19 . . . . 30 A4
  St Tudy PL30. . . . . 23 E3
  Tavistock PL19. . . . . 147 D2
  Torpoint PL11. . . . . 126 F3
  24 Yelverton PL20 . . . . 41 B1
Chestnut Dr 1 PL14. . . . . . . 50 D7
Chestnut Gr PL31 . . . . 109 B4
Chestnut Rd PL3. . . . . 128 D7
Chestnut Terr PL19 . . . . 30 A4
Cheviot Rd TR7 . . . . 110 E4
Chi An Dowr 4 TR11. . . . . . 144 F2
Chichester Cl PL26 . . . . 58 E5
Chichester Cres
  Newquay TR7. . . . . 110 F4
  Saltash PL12 . . . . 122 A4
Chichester Ct PL20 . . . . 42 C4
Chichester Ho PL1. . . . . . . 148 B2
Childrey Gdns PL6 . . . . 125 C1
Childrey Wlk PL6 . . . . 125 C1
Chili Rd TR15 . . . . 139 D6
Chilton Cl PL6 . . . . 129 B7
CHILLATON 29 F8
Chilton Cl PL6 . . . . 129 B7
Chimney Tops PL26. . . . . . . 47 C8
China Clay Ctry Pk * PL26 . 59 A7
China Downs Rd PL30. . . . . 23 C8
Chings Alley 13 PL15. . . . . 106 C6
Chins Field Cl 9 TR27 . . . . 142 D6
Chippdon Dr PL25 . . . . 114 A3
Chirgwin Ct 22 TR18. . . . . 143 E5
Chirgwin Rd TR1 . . . . 137 E4
Chisholme Cl PL25. . . . . . . 114 D3
Chisholme Ct PL25. . . . . . . 114 D3
Chittleburn Bsns Pk PL8. . 136 F6
Chittleburn Cross PL8 . . . . 136 E5
Chittleburn Hill PL8. . . . . . 136 E5
Chivenor Ave PL5. . . . . 123 D4
Chiverton Cl TR27 . . . . 89 F4
Chiverton Cross
  Blackwater TR4 . . . . 68 F5
  Rosudgeon PL20 . . . . 89 F4
Chiverton Greenacres TR5 . 68 D8
Chiverton Way TR20 . . . . . . 89 F4
Chivilas Rd TR14. . . . . 138 E5
Chollacott Cl PL19. . . . . . . 147 C4
Chollacott La PL19. . . . . . . 147 D3
Chough Cl 12 Binhamy EX23 . . 7 B8
  Falmouth TR11. . . . . 144 E4
  Launceston PL15. . . . . 106 E4
Chough Cres PL25 . . . . 114 F4
Choughs Ct TR14 . . . . 138 B3
Christa Cl PL14. . . . . 38 D7
Christian Mill Bsns Pk PL6 124 E4
Christian Way TR7 . . . . 111 C7

Cas–Chu **155**

Chubb Dr PL3 . . . . 128 B4
Chudleigh Rd PL4 . . . . 129 A4
Chun Castle * TR20 . . . . . . 87 C8
Church Av PL23. . . . . 116 C4
Church Ave PL19 . . . . 30 B3
CHURCHBRIDGE 50 F1
Church Cl Blisland PL30 . . . . 35 D8
  Lelant TR26 . . . . 77 E4
  Plymouth PL7. . . . . 130 B7
  Trispen TR4 . . . . 56 D1
CHURCH COMBE 140 A2
CHURCH COVE. 103 A2
Church Cove Rd TR12. . . . . 103 A2
Church Ct PL6 . . . . 125 A7
Church End PL13. . . . . 117 D3
Churchfield Cl TR20 . . . . 89 A8
Churchfield Pl PL24 . . . . 60 B5
Churchfields PL18. . . . . 55 D8
Church Gate 3 PL14. . . . . . 113 C5
Church Hill Calstock PL18 . . 41 A3
  Chacewater TR4 . . . . 68 F2
  Golant PL23. . . . . 61 B6
  Helston TR13. . . . . 146 C7
  Herodsfoot PL14 . . . . 50 E3
  Hessenford PL11, PL12. . . . 64 B8
  Ludgvan TR20 . . . . 89 A8
  Milton Combe PL20 . . . . . . 41 F1
  Navarino PL15 . . . . 18 A8
  Penryn TR10 . . . . 144 D8
  4 Pensilva PL14. . . . . 38 E4
  Plymouth PL6. . . . . 125 B1
  Port Isaac PL29. . . . . 22 D7
  St Day TR16 . . . . 68 E1
  7 St Mawes TR2. . . . . 95 A6
  Sticker PL26 . . . . 58 F1
  Tavistock PL19. . . . . 147 E2
  Tintagel PL34. . . . . 14 C7
  Trefranck PL15 . . . . 16 F3
Church Hill Rd PL9 . . . . . . 135 A6
Church Ho PL12. . . . . 123 A2
Churchill Rd PL19 . . . . 147 D2
Churchill Way
  10 Penwithick PL26. . . . . . 59 D7
  Plymouth PL6. . . . . 128 E6
Churchill Wlk PL12 . . . . . . 122 E1
Church La Bodmin PL31 . . . 109 E5
  Bude PL35 . . . . 104 D5
  Calstock PL18 . . . . 41 A3
  Camborne TR14 . . . . 138 D3
  Cargreen PL12. . . . . 119 A1
  Flushing TR11 . . . . 145 B7
  Helston TR13. . . . . 146 B6
  Lelant TR26 . . . . 77 E4
  Lostwithiel PL22 . . . . 112 C2
  Mevagissey PL26. . . . . 73 C4
  Padstow PL28 . . . . 107 D5
  St Columb Minor TR7. . . . . 111 E7
  St John PL11 . . . . 132 B8
  Tamerton Town EX22. . . . . 13 A8
  Tresamble TR16. . . . . 81 A7
  Zelah TR4 . . . . 56 A2
Churchlands PL13. . . . . 117 D5
Churchlands Cl PL6. . . . . . . 125 E7
Churchlands Rd PL6 . . . . . . 125 E8
Church Lea
  Launceston PL15. . . . . 106 A7
  Tavistock PL19. . . . . 147 E2
Church Mews Stithians TR3 . 80 F8
  Week St Mary EX22. . . . . . . 11 E8
Church Park Ct PL6. . . . . . . 125 E8
Church Park Mews PL27. . . 108 B4
Church Park Rd
  Crackington Haven EX23. . . 10 C6
  Plymouth PL6. . . . . 125 E8
Church Path EX23 . . . . 104 C5
Church Pk Bodmin PL31. . . 109 F5
  Horrabridge PL20. . . . . 42 C4
  Lerryn PL22 . . . . 61 D8
  St Mellion PL12 . . . . 53 D8
Church Pl Liskeard PL14. . . 113 C5
  18 St Ives TR26 . . . . 141 B6
Church Rd Camborne TR15 . 139 B6
  Cardinham PL30 . . . . 35 F3
  Cury TR12 . . . . 99 A5
  Four Lanes TR16 . . . . 80 A5
  Heamoor TR18. . . . . 143 C7
  Illogan TR16 . . . . 67 E4
  Lanivet PL30 . . . . 47 E7
  Launceston PL15. . . . . 18 F6
  Lelant TR26 . . . . 77 E4
  Mabe Burnthouse TR10 . . . 93 C8
  Madron TR20. . . . . 143 A8
  Merrymeet PL14 . . . . 38 C1
  Mount Hawke TR4 . . . . 68 C6
  Mylor Bridge TR11. . . . . . . 82 B2
  Pendeen TR19 . . . . 75 A1
  Penponds TR14 . . . . 138 B1
  Penryn TR10 . . . . 144 C8
  Perranarworthal TR3. . . . . . 81 D5
  Plymouth, Plympton PL7. . 130 F4
  Plymouth, Plymstock PL9 . . 135 F7
  St Austell PL25. . . . . 115 B3
  St Dennis PL26. . . . . 46 C1
  St Tudy PL30. . . . . 23 E3
  Saltash PL12 . . . . 122 D2
  Shortlanesend TR4 . . . . 69 F6
  Stithians TR3. . . . . 80 F4
  Tideford PL12 . . . . 52 F2
Church Road EX23 . . . . 10 C7
Church Row Carharrack TR16 80 F8
  Lanner TR16. . . . . 80 D6
  Shevick PL15 . . . . 18 B3
Church Row La PL5. . . . . . . 124 C6
Church Sq 8 Bodmin PL31 . 109 E5
  St Just TR19. . . . . 86 F6

Church Sq *continued*
4 Stratton EX23 . . . . 4 E1
Church St Callington PL17 . . 39 E4
Calstock PL18 . . . . 41 A3
Camborne TR14. . . . . 138 D3
Carharrack TR16 . . . . 80 F8
Falmouth TR11 . . . . 145 B4
Gorran Haven PL26 . . . . 85 D5
Helston TR13 . . . . 146 B6
Landrake PL12 . . . . 53 C3
Launceston PL15 . . . . 106 C6
Liskeard PL14 . . . . 113 C5
Looe, East Looe PL13 . . . . . 117 D3
Looe, West Looe PL13 . . . . 117 C3
Mevagissey PL26 . . . . 73 C3
15 Newlyn TR18 . . . . 143 C1
Padstow PL28 . . . . 107 D5
Par PL24 . . . . 60 B5
Plymouth PL3 . . . . 128 A4
Poughill EX23 . . . . 4 D2
8 St Austell PL25 . . . . 114 C3
St Columb Minor TR7 . . . . . 111 D7
St Day TR16 . . . . 68 E1
St Erth TR27 . . . . 142 A1
St Germans PL12 . . . . 65 A8
St Just TR19 . . . . 86 F6
5 Stratton EX23 . . . . 4 E1
Tywardreath PL24 . . . . 60 D5
Churchstow Wlk PL6 . . . 129 E8
Church Street N PL14 . . . 113 C5
Church Street S PL14 . . . 113 C5
Church Terr Devoran TR3 . 81 F6
Grampound Road TR2 . . . . . 57 E1
St Kew PL30 . . . . 23 A3
CHURCHTOWN Bridgerule . . 8 B6
Camborne 67 E5
Lanivet 47 E7
St Breward 24 B4
Churchtown Cardinham PL30 35 F3
Colvennor TR12 . . . . 99 A4
Gwinear TR27 . . . . 78 D4
Mellingey PL27 . . . . 32 D6
7 Mullion TR12 . . . . 99 A2
5 St Agnes TR5 . . . . 54 C1
St Kew PL30 . . . . 23 A3
St Minver PL27 . . . . 22 A4
St Newlyn East TR8 . . . . 56 B7
CHURCH TOWN 140 A3
Church Town
Falmouth TR11 . . . . 144 D3
Wendron TR13 . . . . 91 F6
Church Town Cl PL26 . . . . 46 F2
Church Town Cotts TR3 . . 81 D5
Churchtown Dr PL12 . . . . 122 D1
Churchtown Mdws PL26 . . 58 B4
Churchtown Mews PL30 . . 35 C8
Churchtown Rd
Gwithian TR27 . . . . 66 B2
Illogan TR16 . . . . 67 E5
Phillack TR27 . . . . 142 C7
Portscatho TR2 . . . . 83 B2
St Stephen PL26 . . . . 58 B4
Church Town Rd PL32 . . . . 10 D2
Churchtown Terr PL27 . . . 32 D6
Churchtown Vale PL12 . . 122 D1
Church View Navarino PL15 18 A8
St Cleer PL14 . . . . 37 F3
St Dominick PL12 . . . . 40 D2
St Neot PL14 . . . . 36 F2
Treburley PL15 . . . . 28 B5
Walkhampton PL20 . . . . 42 E4
Church View Cl TR18 . . . . 143 B6
Church View Rd
Camborne TR14 . . . . 138 F4
Probus TR2 . . . . 71 D6
Churchway Madron TR20 . 143 A8
11 Marazion TR17 . . . . 89 C5
Church Way Falmouth TR11 144 E3
Plymouth PL5 . . . . 127 E8
St Clether PL15 . . . . 17 B2
Church Wlk Redruth TR15 140 A5
South Petherwin PL15 . . . . 27 E8
12 Truro TR1 . . . . 137 D5
Churchy Fields 12 TR12 . . 99 A2
Chute La PL26 . . . . 85 D5
Chy-an-Chy 19 TR26 . . . . 141 B6
Chyandaunce Cl TR18 . . . 143 F8
Chyandaunce Terr TR18 . 143 F8
Chyandor Cl PL24 . . . . 60 C4
CHYANDOUR 143 F7
Chyandour TR15 . . . . 140 A4
Chyandour Cl 1 TR18 . . . . 77 A6
Chyandour Cliff TR18 . . . 143 F6
Chyandour La TR18 . . . . . 143 F7
Chy-an-Dour Rd TR20 . . . 90 C3
Chyandour Sq TR18 . . . . . 143 F7
Chyandour Terr TR18 . . . 143 F7
Chy an Dowr TR27 . . . . . . 142 E7
CHY-AN-GWEAL 141 B2
Chy-an-Gweal Est TR20 . . 89 A7
Chy-an-Mor TR20 . . . . 88 F6
Chycarn Moor TR14 . . . . . 79 E4
Chy Cober TR27 . . . . 142 E7
CHYCOOSE 82 A6
Chycoose Parc TR3 . . . . . . 82 A5
Chycornick Terr TR18 . . . 143 F8
Chygothow TR13 . . . . 146 B6
Chy Hwel TR1 . . . . 137 F6
Chy Kensa Cl TR27 . . . . . . 142 C5
Chylan Cres TR7 . . . . 111 E6
Chymbloth Way TR12 . . . 101 C1
Chymeddon TR7 . . . . 110 E6
Chy Nampara 1 TR11 . . . . 145 A4
Chynance Penzance TR18 143 D4
Portreath TR16 . . . . 67 C6

Chynance Dr TR7 . . . . 43 F4
Newquay TR7 . . . . 110 D5
CHYNHALE 91 C5
Chynoon Gdns PL25 . . . . 114 F6
Chynowen La TR8 . . . . 43 D1
Chynowen Parc TR8 . . . . . 43 D1
Chynoweth PL26 . . . . 59 C8
Chynoweth Gdns TR18 . . 143 F8
Chynoweth La TR20 . . . . . 89 F6
Chy Pons PL25 . . . . 114 A4
Chypons Est TR20 . . . . . . 76 F3
Chypons Rd TR12 . . . . 99 B3
Chypraze Ct TR14 . . . . . . 138 B3
Chyreen La
Carnon Downs TR3 . . . . 81 F8
Playing Place TR3 . . . . 82 A8
Chyrn Dr PL30 . . . . 24 B3
Chyrose Rd TR16 . . . . 68 D1
Chysauster Ancient Village ★
TR20 . . . . 76 D2
Chysauster Rd
Chysauster TR20 . . . . 76 D1
Trezelah TR20 . . . . 88 E8
Chytodden Terr TR13 . . . . 90 F5
Chytroose Cl TR13 . . . . . . 146 D8
Chyvelah Ope TR1 . . . . 69 E3
Chyvelah Rd TR3 . . . . 69 D4
Chyvelah Vale TR1 . . . . . . 69 E3
Chyvellas LaTR18 . . . . 143 B1
Chyventon Cl TR19 . . . . . . 97 B6
Chyventon Ho TR15 . . . . . 140 B5
Chyverton Cl TR7 . . . . 110 D4
Chyvogue Mdw TR3 . . . . . 81 D6
Chywoone TR10 . . . . 81 A2
Chywoone Ave TR18 . . . . 143 C1
Chywoone Cres TR18 . . . . 143 C1
Chywoone Gr TR19 . . . . . . 97 F8
Chywoone Hill TR18 . . . . 143 C1
Chywoone Pl TR18 . . . . . . 143 C1
Chywoone Rural Workshops
TR19 . . . . 87 A5
Chywoon Gdns TR15 . . . . 139 D7
Chywoon La TR20 . . . . 90 A4
Citadel Ope 13 PL1 . . . . . . 149 A4
Citadel Road E PL1 . . . . . . 149 A2
Citadel Road W PL1 . . . . . 148 C2
Citadel The ★ PL1 . . . . 149 A1
City Bsns Pk PL3 . . . . 128 A4
City Coll Plymouth (Kings
Road Ctr) PL1 . . . . 128 A2
City Coll Plymouth (Learning
Warehouse) PL1 . . . . . . 148 B2
City Rd TR1 . . . . 137 C4
Clairemont Pl 1 PL14 . . . . 38 A3
Clampet La PL11 . . . . 65 E4
Clann Hl PL30 . . . . 47 E7
Clann La PL30 . . . . 47 E7
Clann Mdws PL30 . . . . 47 E7
CLAPPER 108 E4
Claremont Cotts TR11 . . . 145 A5
Claremont Falls PL13 . . . . . 62 E2
Claremont Mews TR15 . . . 140 B5
Claremont Rd TR15 . . . . . . 140 B5
Claremont St PL1 . . . . 148 C4
Claremont Terr
3 Falmouth TR11 . . . . 145 A5
16 Porthleven TR13 . . . . 98 B8
Truro TR1 . . . . 137 C5
Clarence Ct PL1 . . . . 148 A3
Clarence Pl
29 Penzance TR18 . . . . 143 E6
Plymouth, Morice Town PL2 . 127 E4
Plymouth, Stonehouse PL1 . 148 A3
Clarence Rd St Austell PL25 114 B4
Torpoint PL11 . . . . 127 B3
Clarence St TR18 . . . . 143 E5
Clarence Terr
30 Penzance TR18 . . . . 143 E6
7 Wadebridge PL27 . . . . . . 108 B5
Clarence Villas TR15 . . . . 140 D6
Clarendon Ho 4 PL1 . . . . . 127 F3
Clarendon La 11 PL3 . . . . . 127 F3
Clare Pl PL4 . . . . 149 B2
Clare Terr TR11 . . . . 145 B4
Claybourne Cl PL25 . . . . . 114 F6
Claylands PL30 . . . . 24 A1
Claypit La PL15 . . . . 12 B2
Clay Rd PL30 . . . . 36 B4
Clays Walk PL26 . . . . 59 C8
Claytonia Cl PL6 . . . . 121 C1
Clayton Pl PL4 . . . . 129 B2
Clayton Rd PL4 . . . . 129 B2
Clearbrook Ave PL5 . . . . . 123 E1
Clear Space EX23 . . . . 104 F3
Clear View TR12 . . . . 122 E3
Clease Mdws PL32 . . . . . . 105 C3
Clease Rd PL32 . . . . 105 C4
Clease The PL32 . . . . 105 C3
Cleave Cl 3 PL27 . . . . 108 C5
Cleave Cres EX23 . . . . 4 B8
Cleaveland PL27 . . . . 108 C4
Cleaverfield Mews PL15 . 106 C7
Cleaves The PL15 . . . . 106 C7
Cleave The PL10 . . . . 133 B2
Cleavewell PL27 . . . . 108 C4
Cledma Bank TR27 . . . . . . 142 A2
CLEERS 46 E1
Cleers Hill St Dennis PL26 . 46 E1
Whitemoor PL26 . . . . 58 E8
Whitemoor PL26 . . . . 58 E8
Clegg Ave PL11 . . . . 126 E3
Clemens Cl TR7 . . . . 111 B5
Clemens Rd PL14 . . . . 51 B3
Clemens Way TR27 . . . . . . 78 D6
Clement Rd PL7 . . . . 131 B5
Clements Rd TR18 . . . . . . 143 D5
Clemmens Ave TR7 . . . . . 110 D4

Clemo Rd PL14 . . . . 113 E7
CLERKENWATER 109 D8
Clevedon Park Ave PL2 . . 128 B6
Clevedon Rd TR7 . . . . 110 D5
Cleveland Ave PL13 . . . . . 117 D4
Cleveland Rd PL4 . . . . 149 C3
Clies The 5 TR13 . . . . 146 C5
Clifden Cl Mullion TR12 . . . 99 A1
Newquay TR7 . . . . 110 E5
Clifden Dr PL27 . . . . 21 D6
Clifden Rd PL27 . . . . 21 D6
Clifden Terr
14 Bodmin PL31 . . . . 109 D5
Lostwithiel PL22 . . . . 112 C2
CLIFF 61 B6
Cliff Bglws TR27 . . . . 142 A8
Cliff Ct Falmouth TR11 . . . 145 B3
Plymouth PL1 . . . . 148 B1
Cliff End Pk PL27 . . . . 108 D6
Cliff La Millbrook PL10 . . . 132 A4
Mousehole TR19 . . . . 88 D1
New Polzeath PL27 . . . . 21 D6
CLIFFORD 3 F8
Clifford Cl PL5 . . . . 123 E2
Cliff Rd Falmouth TR11 . . . 145 C2
Gorran Haven PL26 . . . . 85 D5
Mevagissey PL26 . . . . 73 C4
Mousehole TR19 . . . . 88 D2
Newlyn TR18 . . . . 143 D1
Newquay TR7 . . . . 110 F6
Perranporth TR6 . . . . 55 A5
Plymouth PL1 . . . . 148 B1
Porthleven TR13 . . . . 98 B8
Cliff Rise PL23 . . . . 116 D2
Cliff St PL26 . . . . 73 C4
Cliff Terr TR16 . . . . 67 C6
Cliff The PL26 . . . . 73 C3
Cliff View Rd TR14 . . . . . . 138 E4
Cliff View Terr TR14 . . . . . 138 E4
Clift Ct 4 TR1 . . . . 137 D4
Clifton Ave PL7 . . . . 130 E7
Clifton Cl PL7 . . . . 130 E7
Clifton Cres 16 TR11 . . . . 145 A4
Clifton Gdns 1 TR1 . . . . . . 137 B4
Clifton Hill 14 TR18 . . . . . 143 C2
Clifton Pl 14 Falmouth TR11 145 A4
Plymouth PL4 . . . . 149 A4
Clifton Rd TR15 . . . . 139 C8
Clifton St PL4 . . . . 149 A4
Clifton Terr
15 Falmouth TR11 . . . . 145 A4
Hayle TR27 . . . . 142 B6
Liskeard PL14 . . . . 113 A5
15 Newlyn TR18 . . . . 143 C2
Cligga Head Ind Est 3 TR6 . 54 F4
Cligga Workshops TR6 . . . . 54 F4
Clijah Cl TR15 . . . . 140 C2
Clijah La TR15 . . . . 140 D2
Clinton Ave PL4 . . . . 129 A4
Clinton Cl Bude EX23 . . . . . 104 E4
Redruth TR15 . . . . 140 C3
Clinton Dr PL25 . . . . 114 B3
Clinton Pas 4 TR15 . . . . . 140 B4
Clinton Rd Constantine TR11 . 92 F3
Redruth TR15 . . . . 140 C4
Clinton Terr PL10 . . . . 132 F6
Clittaford Rd PL6 . . . . 124 F7
Clittaford View PL6 . . . . . 124 E7
Cloake Pl PL12 . . . . 119 A2
Clodan Mews 11 TR9 . . . . . 45 E2
Clodgey La Helston TR13 . 146 D5
Whitehill TR13 . . . . 91 E1
Clodgey Way TR13 . . . . . . 146 D4
Clodgy View 44 TR26 . . . . 141 B6
Clonway 1 PL20 . . . . 42 C3
Close Hill TR15 . . . . 140 B6
Close The
17 Bere Alston PL20 . . . . . . 41 B1
Lanner TR16 . . . . 80 E6
Mylor Bridge TR11 . . . . 82 A3
Penzance TR18 . . . . 143 D7
Saltash PL12 . . . . 122 C3
Trevone PL28 . . . . 20 F2
Truro TR1 . . . . 137 F6
Clos Trevithick 4 TR14 . . 138 F2
Clouds Hill 20 PL12 . . . . . 102 F2
Clovelly Rd PL4 . . . . 149 C1
Clovelly View PL9 . . . . 135 A7
Clover Dr PL14 . . . . 113 D8
Clover Lane Cl 6 PL35 . . . . 9 C1
Clover Rise PL6 . . . . 125 E8
Clover Wlk PL12 . . . . 122 C3
Clowance TR14 . . . . 79 B2
Clowance Cl PL1 . . . . 127 F1
Clowance Est TR14 . . . . . . 79 B2
Clowance La PL1 . . . . 127 E1
Clowance St PL1 . . . . 127 F1
CLOWANCE WOOD 79 A1
Clowance Wood TR14 . . . . 91 A8
CLUBWORTHY 12 C3
Clyde St PL2 . . . . 127 F5
Coach Ho The Penryn TR10 144 D7
Penzance TR18 . . . . 143 F7
Coach House La PL25 . . . . 114 F7
Coach House Mews PL9 . . 136 B6
Coach La TR15 . . . . 140 A4
Coachyard Mews PL28 . . . 107 D5
COAD'S GREEN 27 D4
Coad's Green Prim Sch
PL15 . . . . 27 D3
Coastguard Cotts
Down Thomas PL9 . . . . 134 F2
Mawnan Smith TR11 . . . . . . 93 C1
Mullion TR12 . . . . 98 F1
Polperro PL13 . . . . 62 E2
Rosudgeon TR20 . . . . 89 F3
Coastguard Cres TR18 . . . 143 F6
Coastguard Hill PL29 . . . . 22 D8

Coastguard Hos PL28 . . . . 21 B4
Coastguard Sta Flats PL13 117 C3
Coastguard Terr TR2 . . . . . 84 B3
Coastline Ct TR8 . . . . 44 C6
Coast Rd Millook Common EX23 6 C2
Newton farm PL35 . . . . 10 A4
Porthtowan TR4 . . . . 68 A7
Cobbett Rd PL5 . . . . 124 B2
Cobb La PL9 . . . . 135 F6
Cobble La TR9 . . . . 57 E8
Cobblestone La PL1 . . . . . 128 A1
Cobber Cres TR27 . . . . 78 E3
Cobourg St PL1 . . . . 148 C3
Cockington Cl PL6 . . . . . . 125 E1
Cockington Wlk PL6 . . . . . 125 C1
Cocklawelva PL27 . . . . 21 D2
COCKS 55 B3
Cocks Hill TR6 . . . . 55 B3
Cock's Lake La PL12 . . . . . 53 D4
Cocksport Rd PL32 . . . . . . 10 D3
COCKWELLS 77 C1
Cockwells La TR26 . . . . . . 77 C1
Coddles La PL30 . . . . 47 A8
Codiford Cres TR14 . . . . . 138 E4
Codling Cl 2 PL25 . . . . 114 F2
Coffa Bridge Cl PL22 . . . . 112 D2
Coffee Lake Mdw PL22 . . . 112 D2
Cogegoes TR14 . . . . 138 B2
Cogegoes Ind Pk TR14 . . . 138 A2
Cogos Pk TR11 . . . . 82 A3
Co Hill PL15 . . . . 27 B3
Coinagehall Pl TR18 . . . . . 143 F4
Coinagehall St
Helston TR13 . . . . 146 B5
Penzance TR18 . . . . 143 F4
COLAN 44 F4
Colborne Ave TR16 . . . . . . 67 D4
Colborne Rd PL6 . . . . 125 C4
COLD NORTHCOT 16 F5
Coldrenick St PL5 . . . . . . 123 D1
Coldrose Ct TR1 . . . . 137 B4
Coldstyle Rd PL14 . . . . . . 113 C7
COLDVREATH 46 F1
Coldvreath Rd PL26 . . . . . . 46 F1
Coldwind Cross TR3 . . . . . 81 D7
COLEBROOK 130 E6
Colebrook Cl PL5 . . . . 140 A5
Colebrook La PL7 . . . . 130 E7
Colebrook Rd
Plymouth, Plympton PL7 . . 130 E6
Plymouth, St Budeaux PL5 . 123 D1
Coleman Dr PL4 . . . . 135 F4
Colemans Cross PL15 . . . . 19 C5
Cole Moore Mdw PL19 . . . 147 B6
Colenso Cross TR20 . . . . . 89 F5
Colenso Pl PL25 . . . . 114 D3
Coleridge Ave PL6 . . . . . . 124 F2
Coleridge Rd PL4 . . . . 129 A4
Coles Cotts PL9 . . . . 135 C1
Colesdown Hill PL9 . . . . . 130 B1
Colesloggett Halt Sta ★
PL30 . . . . 48 F8
Colin Campbell Ct 10 PL1 . 148 B3
Colinsey Pl TR18 . . . . 143 D7
Colinsey Rd TR18 . . . . 143 D7
Coliza Hill PL26 . . . . 59 A2
Collacombe Cross PL19 . . . 29 F4
Collaford Cl PL7 . . . . 131 A4
Collan's Cross PL32 . . . . . . 15 C4
College Plymouth PL3 . . . . 128 E5
Tavistock PL19 . . . . 147 D6
College Cl TR1 . . . . 71 C6
College Dean Cl PL6 . . . . . 125 C5
College Gn Bodmin PL31 . . 109 E2
Penryn TR10 . . . . 144 C2
St Austell PL25 . . . . 114 C3
College Green PL31 . . . . . 109 E2
College Hill PL10 . . . . 144 C7
College La Bodmin PL31 . . 109 F2
Plymouth PL4 . . . . 128 F4
Redruth TR15 . . . . 140 E7
College Ope TR10 . . . . 144 D7
College Park Pl PL3 . . . . . 128 E5
College Rd Camelford PL32 105 D4
Plymouth PL2 . . . . 127 E5
College Road Prim Sch
PL2 . . . . 127 E5
College St TR14 . . . . 138 C3
College View PL3 . . . . 128 E4
College Way TR1 . . . . 69 E3
College Wood TR10 . . . . . 144 B6
Colletts Ct TR16 . . . . 67 C5
Colliford Lake Pk ★ PL14 . . 36 E8
Collin Cl PL7 . . . . 123 D1
Collingwood Ave PL4 . . . . 149 C2
Collingwood Rd PL4 . . . . . 149 B2
Collingwood Villas 5 PL1 128 A3
Collins Parc TR3 . . . . 80 F3
Collon Field PL22 . . . . 61 D8
Collorian La TR26 . . . . 77 C1
Collygree Parc TR20 . . . . . 89 C5
Colmer Cl PL13 . . . . 117 D6
Colmers La PL14 . . . . 39 E4
Colmers Row PL14 . . . . 51 F5
Col-Moor Cl TR27 . . . . 142 E7
Colne Gdns PL3 . . . . 129 B5
Cologer Cl TR12 . . . . 99 B2
Colston Cl PL6 . . . . 125 B6
Coltishall Cl PL5 . . . . 123 C4
Coltness Rd PL9 . . . . 136 B5
Coltsfield Cl PL6 . . . . 129 B8
Columbus Cl PL5 . . . . 123 C2
Colver Cl TR27 . . . . 78 E3
Colvreath Rd TR7 . . . . 110 F6
Colwill Rd PL6 . . . . 125 D4
Colwill Wlk PL6 . . . . 125 D5
Colworth Ave TR11 . . . . . 144 F3

Colwyn Rd PL11 . . . . 127 A3
COMBE 136 E5
Combe La EX23 . . . . 6 F4
Combley Dr PL6 . . . . 125 D4
COME-TO-GOOD 82 B7
COMFORD 80 F6
Comfort Rd TR11 . . . . 82 A3
Comfort Wartha TR11 . . . . 92 F4
Commercial Hill TR3 . . . . . 81 B4
Commercial Ope PL4 . . . . 149 B2
Commercial Pl PL4 . . . . . . 149 B1
Commercial Rd
Calstock PL18 . . . . 41 A3
Hayle TR27 . . . . 142 C6
Horrabridge PL20 . . . . 42 C4
10 Mousehole TR19 . . . . 88 C1
Penryn TR10 . . . . 144 D7
Plymouth PL4 . . . . 149 B2
Porthleven TR13 . . . . 98 B8
8 St Keverne TR12 . . . . 101 C4
5 St Mawes TR2 . . . . 95 A6
Commercial Sq 3 TR14 . . 138 D3
Commercial St
Camborne TR14 . . . . 138 D3
Gunnislake PL18 . . . . 41 A6
Plymouth PL4 . . . . 149 B2
Commercial Terr PL28 . . . 107 D5
Commissioners Rd 1
PL27 . . . . 108 B5
Common La PL6 . . . . 121 B5
COMMON MOOR 37 F4
Commons Cl 3 TR12 . . . . . 99 A2
Commons Gate EX22 . . . . . 13 B8
Commons La 15 TR3 . . . . . 81 B4
Commons Rd TR18 . . . . . . 43 D1
Commons The TR12 . . . . . . 99 A2
Compass Dr PL7 . . . . 131 A7
Compass Point TR26 . . . . 141 D2
Compass W PL15 . . . . 18 C2
Compressor Way 5 TR14 138 F3
Comprigney Cl TR1 . . . . . . 137 B5
Comprigney Hill TR1 . . . . 137 B5
Compton Ave PL3 . . . . 129 A5
Compton CE Prim Sch
PL3 . . . . 129 A6
Compton Knoll Cl PL3 . . . 129 A6
Compton Leigh PL3 . . . . . 129 A6
Compton Park Rd PL3 . . . 128 F5
Compton Rd 2 PL17 . . . . . 39 E4
Compton Vale PL3 . . . . . . 129 A5
CONDON'S SHOP 27 B5
Condor Cotts TR11 . . . . . . 144 C2
Congreve Gdns PL5 . . . . . 124 C1
Coniston Gdns PL6 . . . . . . 124 F4
Conker Rd TR27 . . . . 78 C1
Connaught Ave PL4 . . . . . 128 E4
Connaught La 6 PL4 . . . . . 128 E4
Connoc Cl PL14 . . . . 113 D5
CONNOR DOWNS 78 D5
Connor Downs Prim Sch
TR27 . . . . 78 D6
Connor Hill TR27 . . . . 78 D6
Conqueror Dr PL5 . . . . 124 E1
Conrad Rd PL5 . . . . 124 D1
Consols Rd TR16 . . . . 80 F8
Consort Cl PL3 . . . . 128 E7
Consort Ho PL5 . . . . 123 B2
Constable Cl PL5 . . . . 124 D3
Constance Pl PL1 . . . . 148 A3
CONSTANTINE 92 E3
CONSTANTINE BAY 20 D1
Constantine Cty Prim Sch
TR11 . . . . 92 E4
Constantine St PL4 . . . . . 149 A3
Convent Cl PL12 . . . . 122 E3
Convent of Mercy PL31 . . 109 C4
Conway Cl TR11 . . . . 144 E4
Conway Gdns
Falmouth TR11 . . . . 144 D4
Plymouth PL2 . . . . 128 B7
Conway Rd TR11 . . . . 144 D4
Conyngham Ct PL6 . . . . . . 129 A8
Cooban Ct PL6 . . . . 129 A8
Cook Ct PL12 . . . . 122 B3
COOKSLAND 35 B2
Cooksland Ind Est PL31 . . 35 B2
Cooksland La PL31 . . . . 35 B2
Cooksland Rd PL31 . . . . . . 35 B1
Cook's Level PL26 . . . . 85 C5
Cooksley Ct PL1 . . . . 149 A1
Cookworthy Cl 14 PL26 . . 59 D7
Cookworthy Rd PL2 . . . . . 127 F6
COOMBE Camborne 66 F3
Perranarworthal 81 B8
Playing Place 82 D8
St Stephen 58 B2
Coombe Dean Sch PL9 . . 136 A6
Coombe Dean Sp Ctr PL9 136 A6
Coombe Dr PL12 . . . . 119 A2
Coombe Hill Coombe PL26 . 58 C2
Saltash 81 C8
Coombe Junction Halt
PL14 . . . . 51 A6
Coombe La Cargreen PL12 . 119 A2
Combe PL8 . . . . 136 E5
Crafthole PL11 . . . . 65 B5
Penzance TR18 . . . . 143 D7
Plymouth PL5 . . . . 124 D7
Seaton PL11 . . . . 64 B7
Trebyan PL30 . . . . 48 D5
Trelill PL30 . . . . 23 D5
Truro TR4 . . . . 81 C8
Coombe Ln PL15 . . . . 17 C8
Coombe Mews TR18 . . . . . 143 E7
Coombe Park Cl PL10 . . . . 133 A2
Coombe Park La PL5 . . . . 124 A3
Coombe Pk Camborne TR14 . 66 F3
Kingsand PL10 . . . . 133 A2

Coombe Pk *continued*
Penzance TR18 . . . .**143** E6
Saltash PL12 . . . .**122** F2
Coombe Rd Callington PL17. . **39** F4
Lanjeth PL26 . . . .**58** D3
Lanjeth PL26 . . . .**58** E3
Penzance TR18 . . . .**143** E7
St Breward PL30 . . . .**24** A3
Saltash PL12 . . . .**123** A4
Coombes La 9 TR1. . . . . . .**137** C4
Coombe The
Crumplehorn PL13. . . . .**62** D2
Newlyn TR18 . . . .**143** B3
Coombe Vale TR18 . . . .**143** B3
Coombe View
15 Perranporth TR6. . . . . . .**55** A4
Plymouth PL2. . . . .**127** F7
Coombe Way PL5. . . . .**123** F1
Cooperage Gdns 8 PL25 . .**59** A3
Cooperage Rd PL25. . . . . . .**59** A3
Cooper's La TR13. . . . .**98** C8
COOSEBEAN **137** A5
Coosebean La TR4. . . . .**137** A5
Copes Gdns TR1 . . . .**137** C5
Copleston Rd PL6 . . . .**124** E5
COPPATHORNE **7** A3
Copper Beech Way PL6. . . .**125** C7
Copperfield Dr 9 PL14 . . .**113** D7
Copperfields PL20. . . . .**42** B5
Copper Hill TR27 . . . .**142** D6
COPPERHOUSE **142** D6
Copper La TR16 . . . .**140** A1
Copper Pl PL1. . . . .**148** A3
Coppers Pk PL6 . . . .**125** E4
Copper Terr TR27 . . . .**142** D7
Coppice Gdns PL5 . . . .**124** E2
Coppice Wood Dr PL6 . . . . .**125** C7
Copse Cl PL7 . . . .**130** D4
Copse Rd PL7 . . . .**130** D4
Copse The
St Austell, Sandy Bottom
PL25. . . . .**114** F5
St Austell, Tregorrick PL26. .**114** B1
Copshorn Rd PL31. . . . .**109** C7
COPTHORNE **12** B3
Copthorne Cross PL15. . . . . .**12** B2
Copthorne Gdns PL9. . . . . .**135** F5
Copthorne Rd PL15. . . . .**12** B3
Corea Terr PL1. . . . .**128** A2
Corfe Ave PL3 . . . .**128** F8
Coringdean Ct TR17. . . . .**89** C5
Cormorant Cl 2 EX23 . . . .**7** B8
Cormorant Dr PL25. . . . . . .**115** A4
Corner Brake PL6 . . . .**125** D7
Corner Gdns EX23 . . . .**4** D1
Corner Pk PL15. . . . .**26** C7
Cornerstone Ct PL11. . . . . .**127** B3
Cornfield Dr 7 PL15. . . . . .**106** D4
Cornfield Gdns PL7 . . . .**131** B7
Cornflower Cres PL15 . . . . .**106** E4
Cornhill Rd PL24. . . . .**60** B5
Cornish Birds of Prey Ctr
The ★ TR9 . . . .**32** D1
Cornish Chough PL7 . . . . . .**111** B7
Cornish Cider Farm ★ TR4 . .**55** B1
Cornish Cres TR1. . . . .**137** C5
Cornish Goldsmiths ★ TR16. **67** F5
Cornish Mines & Engines
(Mus) ★ TR15. . . . .**139** C6
Cornubia Cl Hayle TR27. . . .**142** C5
Truro TR1. . . . .**137** F6
Cornwall Beach PL1. . . . . . .**127** D2
Cornwall Coll Camborne
TR15. . . . .**139** B6
Cornwall Coll Newquay
TR7. . . . .**111** A5
Cornwall Coll St Austell
PL25. . . . .**114** D5
Cornwall Coll Saltash
PL12. . . . .**122** D2
Cornwall Ctr ★ TR15. . . . . . .**140** B4
Cornwall Ho PL25 . . . .**114** C3
Cornwallis TR26. . . . .**141** E2
Cornwall Rise 2 PL31 . . . . .**109** F3
Cornwall's Regimental Mus
(Duke of Cornwall's Light
Infantry Mus) ★ PL31. . . . .**109** F3
Cornwall St Bere Alston PL20 .**41** B1
Plymouth PL1. . . . .**148** C3
Plymouth, Morice Town PL1. .**127** D2
Cornwall Terr
Penzance TR18 . . . .**143** E4
2 Truro TR1. . . . .**137** C3
Cornwood Rd PL7 . . . .**131** B4
Cornworthy Cl PL2 . . . .**128** A4
Coronation Ave TR14. . . . . .**138** C3
Coronation Cl 2 PL17 . . . . . .**39** F4
Coronation Cotts
Budock Water TR11. . . . . . .**144** C3
Mabe Burnthouse TR10. . . . . .**81** C1
St Keverne TR12 . . . .**101** D4
Coronation Pl Helston TR13 . **146** C4
Plymouth PL5. . . . .**127** E8
Coronation Rd
10 Callington PL17 . . . .**39** F4
Hayle TR27. . . . .**142** D5
1 Illogan TR16. . . . .**67** E1
Redruth TR15. . . . .**140** D4
Coronation Terr Truro TR1 . .**137** B4
Veryan TR2. . . . .**83** D7
Coronation Way TR7. . . . . .**111** C4
Corondale Rd PL2 . . . .**128** B7
Corpascus Carveth TR10 . . . .**81** B1
4 Longdowns TR10 . . . .**81** A1
Corporation Rd
Bodmin PL31. . . . .**109** B4

Corporation Rd *continued*
Plymouth PL2. . . . .**128** D7
Cort Simmons TR15 . . . . . .**139** C6
Cort Treloweth TR15. . . . . .**139** B6
Corva Cl 11 TR26. . . . .**77** A6
Corva Rd 9 TR26 . . . .**77** A6
Corvus Mews 15 PL9 . . . . . .**136** E8
Cory Cl EX23 . . . .**10** F6
Cosawes 2 TR3 . . . .**81** C4
Cosawes Est TR3 . . . .**81** B4
Cosawes Pk Homes 1 TR3. .**81** C4
Cosdon PL6. . . . .**124** F1
COSWINSAWSIN **79** A5
Coswinsawsin La TR14. . . . . .**79** A5
Cotehele Ave
Plymouth, Keyham PL5. . . . .**127** F5
Plymouth, Prince Rock PL4 . .**149** C2
Cotehele Ho ★ PL12. . . . .**40** F7
Cotehele Quay Discovery Ctr ★
PL12 . . . .**40** F7
Cotehele View PL18 . . . .**41** A3
Cothele Cl PL17 . . . .**39** E3
Cot Hill Plymouth PL7 . . . . .**130** B5
Ponsanooth TR3. . . . .**81** B4
2 Stratton EX23 . . . .**4** E1
Cot Hill Trad Est PL7 . . . . . .**130** B6
Cotna La Cotna PL26. . . . .**73** A1
Cotna PL26. . . . .**85** C6
Cot Rd TR15, TR16. . . . .**67** D4
Cotsland Rd TR1. . . . .**137** F5
Cotswold Ave PL26 . . . .**58** E1
Cotswold Cl PL26 . . . .**58** E1
Cottage Gdns PL15 . . . .**27** B7
Cottage Hill PL26 . . . .**72** F6
Cottage Mews PL7. . . . .**130** E4
Cotton Cl PL7 . . . .**130** F4
Cott Rd Lostwithiel PL22 . . . .**112** D2
Lostwithiel, Polscoe PL22 . . .**112** D4
Cotts PL20. . . . .**119** B7
Cot Wood TR3 . . . .**81** B4
Couchwell La PL22. . . . .**112** C2
Coulson's Bldgs 10 TR18. . .**143** E4
Coulson's Pl 9 TR18 . . . .**143** E4
Coulson's Terr 8 TR18 . . . . .**143** E4
Coulthard Dr TR13. . . . .**91** A3
Countess Bridge La TR27 . . .**90** A8
Count House La TR26 . . . . . .**141** C2
Count House Mews 3 TR5 . .**54** D1
County Cl PL7 . . . .**131** A5
County Rd EX23 . . . .**104** E2
Court Barton Cotts PL9 . . . .**135** C1
Court Barton Mews PL19. . . .**30** B4
Courtenay Rd PL19 . . . .**147** B6
Courtenay St PL1 . . . .**148** C3
Courtfield Rd PL3 . . . .**128** F5
Court Gdns PL25. . . . .**114** C3
Courtland Cres PL7. . . . .**130** D7
Courtlands PL12. . . . .**122** E1
Courtlands Cl PL19 . . . .**147** B6
Courtlands Cres 4 PL25 . . . .**115** A5
Courtlands Rd PL19. . . . .**147** B6
Courtlands Sch PL6. . . . .**124** F1
Court Mdw PL13. . . . .**62** B7
Courtnay Cl PL13 . . . .**117** D4
Courtney Ho PL5 . . . .**124** B2
Courtney Rd Liskeard PL14. .**113** D6
St Austell PL25. . . . .**114** F5
Truro TR1. . . . .**137** B5
Court The Camborne TR15 . .**139** C4
Plymouth PL6. . . . .**125** C7
Saltash PL12. . . . .**122** C2
Court View PL6. . . . .**136** F4
Courtyard Cotts TR4. . . . .**70** C6
Courtyard The
Redruth TR16. . . . .**139** F2
Truro TR1. . . . .**137** D3
Cove Hill
Perranworthal TR3. . . . .**81** D5
Sennen Cove TR19 . . . .**96** B7
Cove Mdw PL11 . . . .**127** A6
Cove Rd TR19 . . . .**96** C7
Coverdale Pl PL5 . . . .**124** C1
Cove The TR4 . . . .**68** A7
Cowdray Cl PL12 . . . .**122** E2
Cowdray Terr PL12. . . . .**122** E1
Cow Lard Cl PL15. . . . .**106** A4
Cowley Rd PL5 . . . .**124** D3
Cowling Gdns PL14 . . . .**51** F6
Cowling Rd 2 TR3. . . . .**81** F7
Cowslip Ave PL19. . . . .**147** A5
COXFORD **10** D7
Cox Hill TR6 . . . .**55** B3
COXPARK **40** D7
Cox Park Terr PL18 . . . .**40** C6
Cox's Cl PL6 . . . .**125** B1
COXSIDE **149** B1
Coxs Mdw EX22. . . . .**13** C7
Cox Tor Cl 6 PL20 . . . .**42** C3
Cox Tor Rd PL19. . . . .**147** E5
Coypool Rd PL7 . . . .**130** A6
Crabbs Cl PL15 . . . .**18** D4
Crabbtree Cl 3 PL14 . . . . . .**113** D5
CRABTREE **129** E5
Crabtree Cl PL3 . . . .**129** E5
Crabtree La PL30, PL31 . . . .**109** D2
Crabtree Villas PL3 . . . .**129** E5
Crack Germans Mixtow PL23 **61** C4
Mixtow PL23 . . . .**2** D4
CRACKINGTON HAVEN **10** B7
Crackston Cl PL6 . . . .**129** B7
CRAFTHOLE **65** B5

Craigie Dr PL1. . . . .**148** A3
Craigmore Ave PL2. . . . . . .**127** F5
Craigside PL13 . . . .**117** D4
Cramber Cl Roborough PL6 . .**125** C8
5 Tavistock PL19 . . . .**147** B4
Cranberry Rd TR14 . . . .**138** B3
Cranbourne Ave PL4. . . . . . .**149** C4
CRANE **138** C2
Crane Manor Ct TR14 . . . . .**138** C2
Crane Rd TR14 . . . .**138** C2
Cranfield PL7 . . . .**130** C7
Cranfield Rd TR14 . . . .**138** B3
Cranmere Rd PL3. . . . .**129** A6
CRANTOCK **43** D3
Crantock St TR7 . . . .**110** D6
Crantock Terr 7 PL2 . . . . . .**128** A5
CRAPSTONE **42** B2
Crapstone Rd PL20. . . . .**42** C2
Crapstone Terr PL20. . . . .**42** B2
Crashaw Cl PL5. . . . .**124** D3
Crava La TR20 . . . .**90** E3
Craven Ave PL4. . . . .**149** C4
Crawford Rd PL1 . . . .**148** A4
Creakavose PL26 . . . .**58** B4
Creakavose Pk PL26 . . . .**58** A4
Crealy Adventure Park
(Cornwall) ★ PL27 . . . .**32** D4
CREAN **96** F5
Crease La Millhill PL19 . . . . . .**30** B1
Tavistock PL19. . . . .**147** A4
Creathorne Rd EX23 . . . . . .**104** E7
Creative Unit (Krowji) ★
TR15. . . . .**140** A4
Creaz-an-Bre PL26. . . . .**58** D5
Crebor Rd PL19 . . . .**147** B7
Crediton Wlk PL6. . . . .**129** E8
CREED **72** A6
Creed La TR7 . . . .**72** A7
Creedy Rd PL3. . . . .**129** C5
CREEGBRAWSE **68** F2
Creekside View TR2 . . . .**70** F4
Creeping La Newlyn TR18 . . .**143** C3
Penzance TR18 . . . .**143** C4
Crelake Cl PL19 . . . .**147** C4
Crelake Ind Est 1 PL19 . . . .**147** B4
Crelake Pk PL19. . . . .**147** C4
Crellow Fields TR3 . . . .**80** F3
Crellow Hill TR3. . . . .**80** F3
Crellow La TR3 . . . .**80** F3
Crellow Terr TR3 . . . .**80** F3
Crellow Vale TR3. . . . .**80** F3
CRELLY **91** F7
Crelly TR13. . . . .**91** F7
Crembling Well TR15 . . . . . .**139** E6
CREMYLL **133** E7
Cremyll Rd PL11 . . . .**127** B2
Cremyll St PL1. . . . .**134** A8
Crescent Ave PL1. . . . .**148** B2
Crescent Avenue Mews
PL1 . . . .**148** B2
Crescent Cl Hayle TR27 . . . .**142** C5
Widemouth Bay EX23 . . . .**6** F5
Crescent Gdns TR1 . . . .**137** B4
Crescent Pl 6 TR1 . . . .**74** F1
Crescent Rd Bugle PL26. . . . .**47** C1
Truro TR1. . . . .**137** B4
Crescent Rise
Constantine Bay PL28 . . . . . .**20** C1
Truro TR1. . . . .**137** B4
Crescent The Bude EX23 . . .**104** D5
Camborne TR14 . . . .**138** D4
Carbis Bay TR26 . . . .**77** C4
Common Moor PL14 . . . .**37** F4
Crapstone PL20. . . . .**42** B3
Gunnislake PL18 . . . .**41** A6
Landrake PL12. . . . .**53** C3
Lifton PL16. . . . .**19** F4
Liskeard PL14. . . . .**113** C6
Looe PL13 . . . .**117** D1
Newquay PL7. . . . .**110** E6
Plymouth PL1. . . . .**148** B2
Porthleven PL13 . . . .**91** B1
St Austell PL25. . . . .**115** B5
St Ives TR26. . . . .**77** A7
St Mabyn PL30. . . . .**34** D8
Truro TR1. . . . .**137** B4
Widemouth Bay EX23 . . . .**6** F5
Cressbrook Cl PL6. . . . .**125** F2
Cressbrook Dr PL6 . . . .**125** F2
Cressbrook Wlk PL6. . . . . . .**125** E2
Cresthill Rd PL2 . . . .**128** B7
Creswell Terr TR19 . . . .**86** F7
Creykes Ct PL1. . . . .**148** A3
Cribbage Terr 13 PL31 . . . .**109** D5
Cricketers Cl 3 PL27 . . . .**21** E3
Cricketers Hollow PL27. . . . .**21** E3
Cricket Pk EX23 . . . .**7** B6
Cricks PL30. . . . .**23** A3
Crift Cotts PL14. . . . .**51** F7
Crift La PL12 . . . .**64** F8
Criftoe Rd TR9 . . . .**46** B6
Crill Cnr TR11 . . . .**144** C1
CRIMP **3** A2
Crinnick's Hill PL31. . . . . . .**109** E4
Crinnis Cl PL25 . . . .**115** B3
Crinnis Rd PL25. . . . .**115** B3
Crinnis Wood PL25 . . . .**115** E3
Crinnis Wood Ave PL25 . . . .**115** D3
CRIPPLESEASE **77** A3
CROANFORD **34** C6
Crocker's Row PL18 . . . .**41** A6
Crockers Way PL15 . . . .**13** F1
Crockwell St PL31 . . . .**109** E5
Croft Comm TR14. . . . .**79** E5
Croft Farm Park ★ PL30 . . . .**59** F7
CROFTHANDY **68** E1
Croftlands PL27 . . . .**21** E3
CROFT MITCHELL **79** E4

Croft Parc TR12 . . . .**102** F2
Croft Pascoe
Goonhilly Downs TR12. . . . .**100** D2
Gwente TR12 . . . .**103** B8
Penhale TR12. . . . .**99** F1
Croft Pk PL6. . . . .**125** C7
Croft Rd TR18 . . . .**143** C4
Croft Row TR16. . . . .**80** F8
Crofty Cl TR15. . . . .**139** C5
Crohans Ct TR2 . . . .**84** B4
Cromartie Rd PL4 . . . .**129** B1
Cromer Cl PL6. . . . .**125** A7
Cromer Wlk PL6. . . . .**125** A7
Cromwell Gate PL6 . . . .**125** C7
Cromwell Rd Plymouth PL4 **149** C3
St Austell PL25. . . . .**114** F3
Crookeder Cl PL6. . . . .**136** A5
Crookedor La PL11. . . . .**65** D5
Crooklets EX23 . . . .**104** C7
Crooklets Rd EX23 . . . .**104** D6
Cross PL30 . . . .**47** F1
Cross Cl TR7 . . . .**111** C7
Cross Comm TR12. . . . .**102** F2
Crossfields TR19 . . . .**96** E4
CROSSGATE **19** A7
Cross Gn PL15 . . . .**19** F7
Cross Hill PL2 . . . .**127** E4
Cross La Bodmin PL31. . . . . .**109** E5
7 St Austell PL25 . . . .**114** C3
CROSS LANES **99** C4
Cross Lanes Chacewater TR4 **69** B1
Cross Lanes TR12. . . . .**99** C4
Launceston PL15 . . . .**106** C8
Stratton EX23 . . . .**4** F1
Crossmount TR7. . . . .**111** D7
Cross Park Ave PL6 . . . .**124** F1
Cross Park Rd PL6 . . . .**124** F1
Cross Park Terr PL26 . . . .**73** C4
Cross Park Way PL6 . . . .**124** F1
Cross Pk
Buckland Monachorum PL20 . .**42** A3
Crafthole PL11. . . . .**65** B5
Cross Roads Halgoss TR14 . . .**67** D3
Saveock TR4 . . . .**69** A3
Trevenson Moor TR14 . . . . .**139** A7
Crossroads Cl PL28. . . . .**31** F8
Cross St Camborne TR14. . . .**138** D2
Hayle TR27 . . . .**142** D6
Helston TR13 . . . .**146** B6
Padstow PL28 . . . .**107** D5
13 Penzance TR18 . . . .**143** E4
3 Penzance TR18. . . . .**143** E4
Wadebridge PL27 . . . .**108** B5
Cross Terr PL18 . . . .**40** F5
Cross The Camborne TR14 . .**138** C2
St Dominick PL12. . . . .**40** D2
St Newlyn East TR8. . . . .**56** B7
CROSSTOWN **2** B1
Crosswalla Fields TR13 . . . .**146** C7
Crosswater EX23 . . . .**2** C1
Crossway PL7 . . . .**130** D7
Crossway Ave PL4 . . . .**129** B3
Crossways 5 TR11 . . . .**144** F2
Crosswyn Hill PL26 . . . .**72** F4
CROWAN **79** C1
Crowan Prim Sch TR14. . . . . .**79** C2
Crow Hill PL26. . . . .**58** A4
CROWLAS **89** C8
Crowlas Ind Est TR20. . . . . . .**89** C8
Crowllas La TR20 . . . .**89** B8
Crown Cl TR7. . . . .**111** A6
Crown Cres TR18 . . . .**56** B7
Crowndale Ave PL3. . . . . . .**129** A6
Crowndale Rd PL19 . . . .**147** A2
Crown Gdns PL6 . . . .**125** A1
CROWNHILL **124** F2
Crownhill Ct PL6 . . . .**124** F2
Crownhill Fort ★ PL6. . . . . . .**124** F3
Crownhill Fort Rd PL6 . . . . .**124** F3
Crownhill Rd PL5. . . . .**124** C3
Crown Rd PL26 . . . .**58** D8
Crown Terr PL26 . . . .**58** D8
CROWNTOWN **91** B5
Crowntown TR13 . . . .**91** B5
Crow Pk PL3 . . . .**128** F5
Crows-an-Eglos 5 TR26 . . . .**77** A6
CROWS-AN-WRA **96** F8
CROW'S NEST **38** B4
Crows Nest View 6 TR18 . .**143** D6
Croydon Gdns PL5. . . . .**123** E4
Crozier Rd 6 PL4. . . . .**128** F4
CRUGMEER **107** A7
CRUMPLEHORN **62** D2
Crun-Melyn Parc TR27 . . . .**142** B4
Crusoe Flats 48 TR26 . . . . .**141** B6
Cryben PL12 . . . .**92** C1
Cryon View TR1 . . . .**69** E3
CUBERT **55** D8
Cubert C P School TR8. . . . . .**43** D1
Cuby Cl TR2 . . . .**72** A3
Cuby Rd TR2 . . . .**71** F4
Cuckoo La TR20 . . . .**77** A3
Cuddenbeake Terr PL12 . . . . .**65** B8
Cuddra Rd PL25 . . . .**115** C4
Cudna La TR13 . . . .**91** B5
Cuffe Rd PL3 . . . .**128** C4
Culbin Gn PL6 . . . .**129** D7
Culdrose Airfield TR12. . . . .**146** E1
Culdrose Cl PL5 . . . .**123** E4
Culdrose Rd
Goonhusband TR12 . . . .**98** F8
Goonhusband TR12 . . . .**146** C2
Rosevear TR12 . . . .**99** A7
Cullen View TR2. . . . .**71** C6
Culme Rd PL3 . . . .**129** A5
Cul-Rian PL26. . . . .**58** D7
Culver Cl PL6 . . . .**129** A8
Culver Ct PL12. . . . .**122** F2

Culverland Pk PL14 . . . .**113** C7
Culverland Rd PL14. . . . .**113** B8
Culver Rd PL12 . . . .**122** F2
Culvers Mdw PL15 . . . .**106** B8
Culver Way PL6. . . . .**129** A7
Culverwood Cl PL7 . . . .**131** C6
Culvery The PL27 . . . .**108** B4
Cumberland Rd PL1 . . . .**127** F1
Cumberland St PL1 . . . .**127** E2
Cumble Tor La PL12 . . . .**53** D2
Cundy Cl PL7. . . . .**130** A7
Cundy's La PL26. . . . .**58** D4
Cunliffe Ave PL9. . . . .**135** A6
Cunnack Cl TR13 . . . .**146** C7
Cunningham Pk TR10 . . . .**81** C1
Cunningham Rd PL5 . . . . . .**124** C8
Cunningham Way PL12 . . . .**122** D3
CURGURRELL **83** C4
Curlew Cl TR7 . . . .**110** B5
Curlew Mews PL3 . . . .**129** C4
Curlew Pk Ind Est TR4 . . . . . .**69** C3
Curlew Rd 4 EX23 . . . .**7** B8
Curlews TR8. . . . .**43** B1
Curnow Sch TR15. . . . .**140** B6
Curnows Rd TR27 . . . .**142** C5
Currian Hill PL26 . . . .**58** D8
Currian Rd PL26 . . . .**58** D7
CURRIAN VALE **58** D8
CURRY LANE **12** E4
Currys Hill PL15 . . . .**16** A6
Curtice Cl PL25 . . . .**114** E7
Curtis St PL1 . . . .**127** E1
Curtis VC Cl TR8. . . . .**56** B7
CURY **99** B4
Cury Colvennor TR12 . . . .**99** A5
Poldhu Cove TR12 . . . .**98** F3
Cury CE Prim Sch TR12. . . . . .**99** A4
Cury Cross La Nantithet TR12 **99** C4
Tregaddra TR12. . . . .**100** A4
CUSGARNE **81** B7
Cusgarne Comm Prim Sch
TR4. . . . .**81** C7
Cusgarne Hill TR4, TR16 . . . .**81** B8
Custom House Ct TR18. . . . .**143** F5
Custom House La
16 Penzance TR18. . . . . . .**143** E5
Plymouth PL1. . . . .**148** C3
Customs House Hill PL23 . .**116** D4
CUSVEORTH COOMBES. **69** B2
Cutcrew La PL12. . . . .**52** E3
Cuth Avallon TR1 . . . .**137** C4
Cutmere Hill PL12 . . . .**52** D3
Cutmere La PL12 . . . .**52** D3
Cuttings Hill Coombe TR14 . . .**66** F3
Kehelland TR14 . . . .**79** B7
Reskadinnick TR14 . . . .**138** A6
CUTTIVETT **53** B5
Cuxhaven Way TR20 . . . .**88** F6
Cuxton Mdws PL20 . . . .**41** F3
Cygnus Mews 4 PL9 . . . . . .**136** E8
Cypress Ave PL25. . . . .**115** F4
Cypress Cl 6 PL7. . . . .**131** C5
Cyril Rd TR1 . . . .**137** C5

D

Dabryn Way PL26 . . . .**58** B4
Dacum La TR13. . . . .**92** C8
DADBROOK **132** E4
Daglands Hill PL23. . . . .**116** C4
Daglands Rd PL23 . . . .**116** C4
DairyLand Farm World ★
TR8. . . . .**44** F1
Daisymount Dr PL28 . . . .**31** F7
Dale Ave PL6 . . . .**129** C7
Dale Cl TR7 . . . .**111** A4
Dale Gdns PL4. . . . .**128** D4
Dale Rd Newquay TR7 . . . . .**111** A4
Plymouth PL4. . . . .**128** D4
Daleswood Rd PL19 . . . .**147** A4
Dallard PL27 . . . .**22** E3
Dalton Gdns PL5. . . . .**123** E3
Damerel Cl PL1 . . . .**127** E2
Dandre Apartments TR7 . . .**111** A7
Dane Rd TR7 . . . .**110** D7
Daniel Cl PL25 . . . .**115** A4
Daniel Ct TR1. . . . .**137** C3
Daniell Gdns TR1 . . . .**137** C3
Daniell Rd TR1 . . . .**137** B3
Daniell St TR1 . . . .**137** C3
Daniel Pl TR18. . . . .**143** E4
Daniels La PL25. . . . .**115** B4
Daniels Sail Loft TR10 . . . . .**144** D7
Danmore Cl PL34 . . . .**14** C7
Danum Dr PL7 . . . .**131** B3
DARITE **38** B4
Darite Prim Sch PL14 . . . .**38** A4
Darke La PL12 . . . .**30** E1
Darkey La PL16 . . . .**19** F4
Dark La Camelford PL32 . . . .**105** C4
Liskeard PL14 . . . .**113** D6
Lostwithiel PL22 . . . .**112** C1
Trevillador PL27. . . . .**32** D5
Darklake Cl PL6 . . . .**125** E5
Darklake Pk PL6. . . . .**125** E5
Darklake View PL6 . . . .**125** E5
Dark Street La PL7. . . . .**130** E4
Darley Oak ★ **17** PL31. . . . . .**109** A5
Darlington Rd TR20. . . . .**88** F6
Darloe La PL13 . . . .**117** C3
DARRACCOTT **2** D4
Darracott Hill EX39 . . . .**2** E3
Dart Cl Plymouth PL3. . . . . .**129** D7

Dart Cl *continued*
St Giles on the Heath PL15 . . . . **13** F1
Dartington Wlk PL6. . . . . **129** E8
Dartmeet Ave PL3 . . . . **129** B6
Dartmoor View
Plymouth PL4. . . . . **129** C3
Saltash PL12 . . . . **122** E4
Dartmouth Wlk PL6. . . . . . . **129** E8
Darwin Cres PL3. . . . . **129** D5
Darwin Dr TR11 . . . . **144** F2
Dashwood Ho TR11. . . . . . . **145** A6
Daubuz Cl TR1. . . . . **137** C6
Daubuz Ct TR1 . . . . **137** D5
Daucus Cl PL19 . . . . **147** B4
Davenham Cl PL6. . . . . **125** B6
Davey's Cl TR11 . . . . **144** E1
David Cl PL7. . . . . **130** F6
David Penhaligon Way
TR1. . . . . **137** D3
David Southgate Ct PL1. . . . **148** A2
DAVIDSTOW **16** A6
Davidstow Aerodrome
PL32 . . . . **15** F4
Davidstow Airfield & Cornwall at War Mus PI32 . . . . **15** F5
Davy Cl Torpoint PL11 . . . . **126** F3
Tremar PL14 . . . . **38** A3
Davy Rd PL6. . . . . **125** C4
Davys Row PL14 . . . . **37** E4
Dawe Cres PL31 . . . . **109** C3
Dawes Cl PL14 . . . . **50** E7
Dawes La Millbrook PL10 . . **132** E5
Plymouth PL9. . . . . **136** D7
Dawlish Wlk PL6 . . . . **129** E8
Dawney Terr PL11 . . . . **65** B5
Dawn Rd PL13. . . . . **117** D2
Daws Ct PL12. . . . . **123** A2
DAW'S HOUSE. **18** E1
Daw's Mdw PL32. . . . . **105** E4
Dawson Cl PL3 . . . . **123** E1
Daymans Denzell Downs TR8 . . **32** A2
Trevilledon TR8. . . . . **31** F2
Daymer La PL27 . . . . **21** D4
Daymond Rd PL5 . . . . **123** D2
Dayton Cl PL1. . . . . **124** E3
Deacon Dr PL12 . . . . **122** F1
Deacons Gn PL19 . . . . **147** A3
Dean Cross PL9 . . . . **135** F7
Dean Cross Rd PL9 . . . . **135** E7
Dean Hill Liskeard PL14 . . . **113** D4
Plymouth PL9. . . . . **135** E7
Dean La PL14. . . . . **113** B6
Dean Park Rd PL9 . . . . **135** D7
Dean Rd PL7 . . . . **130** D6
Dean St PL14 . . . . **113** B5
Dean Terr PL14. . . . . **113** B6
Debden Cl PL5 . . . . **123** D4
Deeble Cl Plymouth PL7 . . . **130** E4
Threemilestone TR3 . . . . . . **69** C3
Deeble Dr **20** PL24. . . . . **60** B4
Deep La PL7. . . . . **131** C3
Deer La EX22 . . . . **13** A8
Deer Leap PL19. . . . . **147** D4
Deer Park Cl PL19 . . . . **147** C5
Deer Park Cres PL19 . . . . . . **147** C5
Deer Park Dr PL3 . . . . **129** D7
Deerpark Forest Trail
PL14 . . . . **50** C3
Deer Park La PL19 . . . . **147** C5
Deer Park Rd PL19 . . . . **147** C5
Deer Pk Newquay TR7 . . . . . **110** D6
Saltash PL12 . . . . **122** F3
Defoe Cl PL5 . . . . **124** C1
Degibna La TR12, TR13 . . . . **146** C2
DELABOLE **14** D3
Delabole Comm Prim Sch
PL33. . . . . **14** D2
Delacombe Cl PL7. . . . . **130** F7
De-la-Hay Ave PL3 . . . . **148** A4
Delamere Holiday Village
PL33 . . . . **14** D2
Delamere Rd PL6. . . . . **129** D7
Delavue Terr PL32. . . . . **105** C3
Delaware Com Prim Sch
PL18 . . . . **40** F6
Delaware Cotts PL18 . . . . . . **40** F6
Delaware Ct PL18. . . . . **40** F5
Delaware Gdns PL2. . . . . . . **127** F7
Delaware Rd
11 Gunnislake PL18. . . . . . . **40** F5
Gunnislake PL18 . . . . **40** F6
Delgany Dr PL6. . . . . **125** A5
Dell Cl TR18 . . . . **143** C3
Dell Mdw PL15 . . . . **18** B8
Dell The Plymouth PL7 . . . . **130** B6
Tavistock PL19. . . . . **147** B6
Truro TR1. . . . . **137** C5
DEMELZA **46** E6
Demelza Rd PL30. . . . . **46** E7
Denas Water TR2. . . . . **71** A5
Dengie Cl PL7. . . . . **131** B5
Denham Cl PL5 . . . . **124** C2
Dennis Cl PL5 . . . . **127** C2
Dennis Gdns PL15 . . . . **18** C2
Dennis La PL28 . . . . **107** D4
Dennison Ave PL25 . . . . **115** A4
Dennison Rd PL31 . . . . **109** D5
Dennis Rd Liskeard PL14 . . **113** D6
Padstow PL28 . . . . **107** D5
Dennybowl La PL12. . . . . **52** E3
Dens Meadow PL12. . . . . **52** F6
Denyer Ct TR1. . . . . **145** A6
Denys View TR9 . . . . **45** F2
De Pass Gdns TR11. . . . . . . **145** C3
De Pass Rd TR11. . . . . **145** C2

Deptford Pl PL4. . . . . **149** A4
Derby Rd PL5. . . . . **124** C4
Derby's La PL26. . . . . **85** C5
Dereham Terr **6** TR1. . . . . . **137** B4
Derowen Dr TR2. . . . . **142** B3
DERRIFORD **125** B4
Derriford Bsns Pk PL6 . . . . **125** A4
Derriford Health & L Ctr
PL6. . . . . **125** B3
Derriford Hospl PL6 . . . . . . **125** B4
Derriford Pk PL6 . . . . **125** A3
Derriford Rd PL6 . . . . **125** B4
DERRIL **8** D6
Derriton Rd EX22 . . . . **8** F6
Derry Ave PL4 . . . . **148** C4
Derry's Cross PL1 . . . . **148** B2
Derwent Ave PL3 . . . . **129** C5
Desborough La PL4. . . . . . . **149** C3
Desborough Rd PL4. . . . . . . **149** C3
Deva Ho TR7 . . . . **111** A6
DEVERAL. **78** D2
Deveral Rd TR27. . . . . **78** D2
Deveron Ct PL7. . . . . **131** A5
Devington Ct TR11. . . . . **145** C2
Devington Hall TR1. . . . . . . **137** E5
Deviock Hill PL11. . . . . **64** C5
Devonia Cl PL7 . . . . **130** E7
Devon Oaks PL20 . . . . **42** B5
DEVONPORT **127** D4
Devonport High Sch for Boys
PL1. . . . . **128** C6
Devonport High Sch for Girls
PL2. . . . . **128** C6
Devonport Hill
Kingsand PL10. . . . . **133** A2
Plymouth PL1. . . . . **127** F1
Devonport Leat PL6 . . . . . . **121** B5
Devonport Rd PL3 . . . . **127** F3
Devonport Sta PL1 . . . . **127** F3
Devon Progressive Sch
PL19 . . . . **42** A5
Devonshire Ct PL11. . . . . . . **127** B3
Devonshire Ho
Plymouth PL1. . . . . **148** B2
2 Tavistock PL19. . . . . **147** B5
Devonshire St PL4. . . . . **149** A3
Devon Terr PL3. . . . . **128** E5
Devon Tors Rd **9** PL20. . . . . **42** C3
DEVORAN **81** F6
Devoran La TR3 . . . . **81** F6
Devoran Sch TR3. . . . . **81** F6
Diamond Ave PL4. . . . . **149** B4
Diana Cl TR11 . . . . **144** E2
Dickens Rd PL5. . . . . **124** B1
Dickiemoor La PL5 . . . . **124** C2
Dickna St PL15. . . . . **13** F1
Dicky La TR3 . . . . **82** D6
Diddies La PL14 . . . . **4** E1
Diddies Rd EX23. . . . . **4** E1
Dieppe Cl PL1. . . . . **127** F2
Digby Gr PL5 . . . . **123** F5
Digey Flats **49** TR26. . . . . . . **141** B6
Digey The **25** TR26. . . . . **141** B6
Diggory's Field **4** PL14. . . . . **38** A5
Dinas Cl PL11 . . . . **64** C5
Dinas Rd **1** TR9 . . . . **45** D6
Dingle Cl PL17. . . . . **28** D1
Dingle Rd
Plymouth, North Prospect
PL2. . . . . **128** A6
Plymouth, Plympton PL7 . . **130** C6
Dingles Cl TR3 . . . . **81** B4
Dingle's Folly PL13 . . . . **117** C3
Dingles Way PL27 . . . . **21** E3
Dingwall Ave PL5. . . . . **124** E3
Dinham La Haywood PL30 . . **34** C8
Leeches PL30 . . . . **23** A1
DINWORTHY **3** F2
Dipper Cl EX23 . . . . **5** A6
Dipper Dr PL19 . . . . **147** D2
Dipper La EX23 . . . . **5** A7
Dirty La PL12 . . . . **122** B5
Discovery Wharf **20** PL4. . . . **149** A3
Distine Cl PL3. . . . . **129** B7
Dithmarschen Way PL25 . . **114** B2
Dittisham Wlk PL6. . . . . **129** E8
Ditton Ct PL6. . . . . **129** A8
Dixon Pl PL1 . . . . **127** F4
DIZZARD **6** B1
Dobbin Cl PL28 . . . . **20** F2
Dobbin La PL28. . . . . **20** F2
Dobbin Rd PL28 . . . . **20** F2
Dobbs La TR1 . . . . **137** A4
Dobell Rd PL25 . . . . **114** E4
DOBWALLS **50** E8
Dobwalls Prim Sch PL14 . . . **50** E7
Dockacre Rd PL15 . . . . **106** C6
Dockey **1** PL15. . . . . **106** C5
Dock La TR18 . . . . **143** F5
Dockray Cl PL6. . . . . **125** D4
Dockyard Sta PL2 . . . . **127** E4
DOCTON **2** F8
Doctors Hill **8** Boscastle PL35 **9** C1
5 St Keverne TR12. . . . . . . **101** C4
Doctors La PL12. . . . . **65** A8
Doctor's La PL14 . . . . **113** C6
Doctors Lane TR11 . . . . **92** F4
Doddridge Cl PL14 . . . . **50** E8
Dodson's Gap TR12. . . . . . . **99** B7
Doidges Farm Cl PL6 . . . . . **129** B8
Dola La TR20 . . . . **89** E5
Dolcoath Ave TR14 . . . . **138** F3
Dolcoath Ct TR14. . . . . **138** F3
Dolcoath Ind Pk TR14 . . . . **139** A4
Dolcoath Rd TR14 . . . . **138** F3
Dolgey Post PL27. . . . . **32** A4
Dolphin PL29. . . . . **22** D7
Dolphin Cl PL9. . . . . **135** F6

Dolphin Court Rd PL9. . . . . **135** F6
Dolphin Ho **18** PL4. . . . . . . **149** A2
Dolphin Sq PL1. . . . . **135** F6
Dolphin St PL29 . . . . **22** D7
Dolvin Rd PL19 . . . . **147** C5
Domellick Cnr PL26 . . . . **46** B1
Domellick Hill PL26. . . . . . . **46** B1
Doneys Mdw PL15 . . . . **17** F1
Doniert's Cl **11** PL14 . . . . . . **113** B5
Donkey La Millbrook PL10 . . **132** C4
Portwrinkle PL11. . . . . **65** A4
Donnington Dr PL3 . . . . **129** C7
Donnington Rd PL18. . . . . . **143** C3
Donovan Way PL31 . . . . **109** B4
Dopps Terr PL15 . . . . **140** C5
Dorchester Ave PL5 . . . . . . **124** D4
Dorchester Ct TR14. . . . . . . **138** E4
Doreena Rd PL9. . . . . **136** C7
Dorminack Cl PL26 . . . . **58** D8
Dormy Ave PL3. . . . . **128** F5
Dor Priweythor **2** TR7. . . . . **111** E6
Dorset Pk PL15. . . . . **13** A2
Dorsmouth Terr PL7. . . . . . **130** E4
DOUBLEBOIS **50** C8
Doublebois Ind Est PL14 . . . **50** D7
Doubletrees PL24 . . . . **60** B4
Doubletrees Ct **2** PL24. . . . . **60** B4
Doubletrees Sch **21** PL24. . . **60** B4
Double White Rise **1** PL18. . **40** E5
Douglas Cl PL26 . . . . **47** A3
Douglas Dr PL9. . . . . **136** A6
Douglass Rd PL3 . . . . **129** C6
Doulton Rd PL25. . . . . **115** A4
DOUSLAND **42** F3
Dousland Ho PL20. . . . . **42** E3
Dousland Rd PL20 . . . . **42** D3
Dousland Terr PL20 . . . . **42** E3
Dovedale Rd PL2. . . . . **128** A7
Dove Gdns PL3 . . . . **129** D7
Dover Rd PL6. . . . . **125** E3
Dove St **15** TR16. . . . . **141** B5
Dower's Terr TR16. . . . . **80** B5
Down Cl PL12 . . . . **122** C2
DOWNDERRY **64** C5
Downfield Dr PL7. . . . . **130** F5
Downfield Way PL7. . . . . . . **130** F5
Downfield Wlk PL7 . . . . **130** F5
DOWNGATE Kelly Bray. **40** A7
Pensilva **38** D5
Downgate Gdns PL2. . . . . . **128** D8
Downham Gdns PL5 . . . . . . **124** C7
Downhorne Pk PL5. . . . . . . **135** F6
Downlea PL11 . . . . **147** D4
Down Ln PL15. . . . . **17** E2
Down Park Dr PL19 . . . . **147** D4
Down Parks EX23. . . . . **5** B7
Down Rd Plymouth PL7. . . . **131** C5
Tavistock PL19. . . . . **147** D4
Downs Cl PL26 . . . . **58** C8
Downs Hill PL23 . . . . **61** B5
Downside Ave PL6. . . . . **129** C7
Downside Cl TR7 . . . . **111** A4
Downs La Looe PL13. . . . . . **117** B3
Polmenna PL14 . . . . **36** E1
Downs Lane Pk PL13. . . . . . **117** B3
Downs Rd PL13. . . . . **117** C4
Downs The PL13. . . . . **117** C3
Downstream Cl PL28 . . . . . . **107** C5
Downs View Bude EX23 . . . **104** D7
Looe PL13. . . . . **117** C3
Down The PL20. . . . . **41** C1
DOWN THOMAS. **135** C1
Downton Cl PL1 . . . . **148** A4
Dowren Ho TR27 . . . . **142** B5
Dozmere TR3. . . . . **82** C5
Dozmere Cl TR3 . . . . **82** C5
Dracaena Ave
Falmouth TR11. . . . . **144** F5
Hayle TR27. . . . . **142** E6
Dracaena Cres TR27 . . . . . . **142** E6
Dracaena Pl TR11 . . . . **144** F4
Dracaena View TR11. . . . . . **144** F5
Dragon L Ctr The PI31. . . . . **109** F1
Drake Cir PL1, PL4 . . . . **149** A3
Drakecircus Sh Ctr PL1 . . . **149** A3
Drake Ct
Plymouth, Ernesettle PL5 . . **123** E4
Plymouth, St Jude's PL4 . . . **149** B3
Drakefield Dr PL2 . . . . **123** A3
Drake Gdns PL19 . . . . **147** C4
Drake Prim Sch PL2 . . . . . . **127** E6
Drake Rd Padstow PL28 . . . **107** C5
Tavistock PL19. . . . . **147** C6
Drakes Cl PL6 . . . . **124** F4
Drake's Pk **3** PL20 . . . . **41** B1
Drake Villas PL19 . . . . **147** A4
Drakewalls Gdns PL18 . . . . . **40** F5
Drakewalls Pl PL18 . . . . **40** F5
Drake Way PL9 . . . . **135** E7
Drang The TR9 . . . . **45** E1
Drannack La TR27 . . . . **78** D4
Drannack Mill Lane TR27 . . **78** F2
Draper Terr **3** PL19 . . . . . . **147** B5
DRAWBRIDGE **49** F8
Drax Gdns PL6. . . . . **128** E8
Draycott Terr PL26 . . . . **141** C4
Drayton Rd PL5. . . . . **124** C1
Dreysen Cl TR15 . . . . **139** C8
DRIFT **87** F3
Drift Cl TR20. . . . . **87** F3
Drift La PL14 . . . . **49** C4
Drillfield La **9** TR26 . . . . . . **141** B5
Drina Cl PL5 . . . . **123** E4
Drinnick Hill PL15 . . . . **27** E6
Drinnick Rd PL26 . . . . **58** C6
Drinnick Terr PL26 . . . . **58** D6
Drive The Helston TR13 . . . **146** D7

Drive The *continued*
Plymouth PL3. . . . . **128** E7
Driving La PL24. . . . . **60** C6
Drogeada Cl
Coad's Green PL15 . . . . **27** D3
6 Landreyne PL15 . . . . **27** D3
Drop Stamp Rd **4** TR14. . . . **138** F3
Droskyn Castle **19** TR6 . . . . . **55** A5
Droskyn Cl **22** TR6 . . . . **55** A5
Droskyn House Villas TR6. . . **55** A5
Droskyn Way TR6. . . . . **55** A5
Druckham Pl PL15. . . . . **106** D5
Druckham Terr PL15. . . . . . **106** D5
Druid's Lodge TR15. . . . . . . **139** D5
Druid's Rd Camborne TR15 . **139** D5
Redruth TR15. . . . . **139** D6
Drummer's Hill PL26. . . . . . **114** C8
Drummond Cl PL2 . . . . **127** F7
Drummond Pl PL1 . . . . **127** F3
Drummond Way PL20. . . . . **119** E4
Drump Rd TR15. . . . . **140** C5
Drunkards La TR13 . . . . **90** F4
Drunken Bridge PL26 . . . . . . **72** E4
Drunken Bridge Hill PL7. . . **130** D4
Dryburgh Cres PL2 . . . . **128** A8
Dryden Ave PL5 . . . . **124** C1
Dry La PL30 . . . . **24** A4
Dry Wlk PL10. . . . . **133** E6
DRYM **91** A8
Drym La Leedstown TR14 . . . **78** F1
Nancegollan TR14 . . . . **91** A8
Drym Rd TR13 . . . . **91** B7
Dry Wlk PL10 . . . . **133** E6
Dualstone Cross EX22 . . . . . . **8** D3
Ducane Wlk PL6. . . . . **125** B1
Duchy Ave TR7 . . . . **111** C7
Duchy Cl Launceston PL15 . **106** C7
St Austell PL25. . . . . **114** F3
Duchy Coll St Breock PL27. . **33** C7
Stoke Climsland PL17. . . . . **28** D1
Duchy Coll Rosewarne
TR14. . . . . **138** D5
Duchy Cotts PL17. . . . . **28** D1
Duchy Hospl TR1 . . . . **69** E4
Duchy Terr Minions PL14 . . **38** B6
Upton Cross PL14. . . . . **38** D7
Duck La PL12. . . . . **53** E2
Duck St **9** Mousehole TR19. . **88** C1
St Austell PL25. . . . . **115** B2
Duckworth St **3** PL2 . . . . . . **128** A4
Ducky La PL12. . . . . **53** C3
Ducky Row PL17. . . . . **40** D4
Dudley Gdns PL6. . . . . **129** B8
Dudley Rd PL7. . . . . **130** B5
Dudman Rd TR1 . . . . **69** F3
Dudnance La TR15. . . . . **139** B4
Duke's Ct PL26 . . . . **46** F3
Dukes Dr PL19. . . . . **41** B4
Duke's Dr PL17 . . . . **28** F4
Dukes Ryde The **1** PL9 . . . . **135** F7
Duke St Launceston PL15 . . **106** C5
Lostwithiel PL22 . . . . **112** C2
Padstow PL28 . . . . **107** D5
Plymouth PL1. . . . . **127** D5
St Austell PL25. . . . . **115** B2
Tavistock PL19. . . . . **147** C6
11 Truro TR1 . . . . **137** D4
Duke's Way TR7. . . . . **111** A5
DULOE **51** A1
Duloe CE VA Jun & Inf Sch
PL14 . . . . **51** A1
Duloe Gdns PL2 . . . . **128** C8
Duloe Rd PL14. . . . . **50** E7
Dumbarton Terr **7** TR19. . . . **88** C1
Dumfries Ave PL5 . . . . **124** D3
Duncannon Dr TR11 . . . . . . **144** F4
Duncan St PL1. . . . . **127** E1
Dunclair Pk PL3. . . . . **129** D5
Duncombe Ave PL5. . . . . . . **124** A2
Dundas St **4** PL2. . . . . **128** A4
Dunders Hill PL27 . . . . **21** D5
Dundonald St PL2 . . . . **127** F4
Dungarth Gn PL14 . . . . **113** D6
Dungarth Rd PL14 . . . . **113** D6
Dunhead View PL15. . . . . . . **28** B6
Dunheved Fields PL15 . . . . **106** C4
Dunheved Rd
Launceston PL15. . . . . **106** C5
Saltash PL12 . . . . **122** F2
Dunkeswell Cl PL2. . . . . **127** E8
Dunley Wlk PL6 . . . . **125** C1
DUNMERE **34** D2
Dunmere Cl **1** PL24 . . . . **60** C4
Dunmere Rd PL31. . . . . **109** B5
Dunnet Rd PL6 . . . . **124** D7
Dunn St **10** PL35 . . . . **9** C1
Dunraven Dr PL6. . . . . **125** A6
Dunsdon Cross EX22. . . . . . . **5** F3
DUNSLEY **38** C6
Dunstable Cl PL26. . . . . **58** D6
Dunstan Cl TR10. . . . . **144** C8
Dunstan La St Mellion PL12 . **40** A1
Sewergan TR10 . . . . **92** C6
Dunstanville Terr
12 Falmouth TR11. . . . . . . **145** A5
Falmouth TR11. . . . . **145** B5
Dunster Cl PL7. . . . . **131** C4
Dunstone Cl PL26. . . . . **58** C8
Dunstone Ave PL9 . . . . **136** A7
Dunstone Cl PL9. . . . . **135** F7
Dunstone Dr PL9 . . . . **135** F7
Dunstone La PL9 . . . . **136** A7
Dunstone Prim Sch PL9. . . **136** A8
Dunstone Rd
Plymouth, Plymstock PL9 . . **135** F7
Plymouth, St Budeaux PL5. . **123** F3
Dunstone View PL9. . . . . . . **136** A7
DUNTERTON **28** F6
Duntz Hill PL16. . . . . **19** F4

Dunvegan Rd TR10 . . . . **144** B8
Dunveth Bsns Pk PL27. . . . . **33** C7
Dunveth Industrial Estate
PL27. . . . . **33** C7
Dunveth Rd PL27. . . . . **108** A5
Dupath La PL17. . . . . **40** A4
DUPORTH. **115** A1
Duporth Bay PL26. . . . . **115** A1
Duporth Rd PL24, PL26 . . . **115** A2
Dural Cross EX22. . . . . **3** E3
Durban Rd PL3. . . . . **128** D5
DURGAN **93** D2
Durgan Crossroads TR11 . . . **93** D2
Durgan La TR10 . . . . **144** C8
Durham Ave PL4. . . . . **149** C4
Durley Dene TR26 . . . . **77** E4
Durnford St PL1. . . . . **128** A1
Durnford Street Ope PL1 . . **128** A1
Durning Rd TR5 . . . . **54** C1
Durrant Cl PL1. . . . . **127** E3
Durris Cl PL6. . . . . **125** D4
Durris Gdns PL6 . . . . **125** D4
Durston Rd EX23 . . . . **104** E7
Durwent Cl PL9. . . . . **135** A6
DUTSON **106** E8
Dutson Rd PL15. . . . . **106** C7
Dutson Terr PL15 . . . . **106** C7
Dux Cross EX22. . . . . **8** C6
Duxford Cl PL5. . . . . **123** E5
Dye House Cotts PL14 . . . . . **36** F2
Dymond Cl PL32 . . . . **105** B2
Dymond Ct PL31. . . . . **109** C6
Dymond Ct (Kingdom Pl)
PL12 . . . . **122** F2
Dynas-la Rd TR26. . . . . **141** B4
Dynevor Cl PL3 . . . . **128** F7

E

Eagle Cl PL7. . . . . **131** C4
Eagle Rd PL7. . . . . **131** C4
Earle's Retreat TR11. . . . . . **145** B3
Earl's Acre PL3. . . . . **128** C4
Earls Dr PL10. . . . . **133** B3
Earl's Dr The Cawsand PL10 **133** A1
Kingsand PL10. . . . . **133** B3
Earls Mill Rd PL7 . . . . **130** E6
Earls Rise TR7 . . . . **111** B5
Earls Wood Cl PL6. . . . . . . **125** F3
Earls Wood Dr PL6 . . . . **125** F3
Eastbourne Cl PL25. . . . . . . **114** E3
Eastbourne Rd PL25 . . . . . . **114** D3
East Bridge **4** TR4 . . . . **69** A3
Eastbury Ave PL5 . . . . **124** A2
East Camps Bay PL11. . . . . . **64** D4
East Charles St TR14. . . . . . **138** E2
East Cl TR13. . . . . **146** D7
East Cliff PL13. . . . . **117** D3
Eastcliff Ave TR4. . . . . **68** A7
Eastcliff Avenue No 2 TR4 . **68** A7
Eastcliffe Rd PL24 . . . . **60** C5
East Cliff La TR17. . . . . **89** C5
Eastcote Cl PL6. . . . . **125** B6
EASTCOTT **3** A3
Eastcott Cross EX23 . . . . **3** A2
East Dr Braddock PL22 . . . . . **49** F5
Penhole PL14. . . . . **50** A5
Eastella Rd PL20. . . . . **42** D2
East End
Easterdown Cl PL9. . . . . . . **135** F7
Eastern Ave PL14. . . . . **113** D6
Eastern Gn Gulval TR18 . . . **88** E6
Penzance TR18 . . . . **143** F7
Eastern Green Pk TR18. . . . **88** E6
Redruth TR15. . . . . **140** D6
Eastern La TR14 . . . . **138** D4
East Fairholme Rd EX23 . . **104** F7
Eastfield Ave PL9. . . . . **135** C6
Eastfield Cres PL3 . . . . **129** A6
Eastfield Way PL25 . . . . **114** F5
East Hill Camborne TR14. . . **139** A5
St Austell PL25. . . . . **114** D3
EAST LOOE **117** D3
EAST PANSON **13** F3
East Park Ave PL4. . . . . **148** C4
East Park Cl EX23 . . . . **5** B2
East Pk Pensilva PL14 . . . . . **38** D4
Redruth TR15. . . . . **140** D6
Tregadillett PL15 . . . . **18** C2
East Pool Pk TR15. . . . . **139** D6
EAST PORTHOLLAND **84** E5
East Quay TR27. . . . . **142** B6
East Quay Ho PL13. . . . . . . **117** D3
East Rd Kilkhampton EX23. . . **5** A6
Menheniot PL14 . . . . **52** A5
Quintrell Downs TR8 . . . . . . **44** E3
Stithians TR3 . . . . **80** F3
East Rise TR11. . . . . **144** F3
East Rosewin Row **10** TR1 . **130** D6
East St Newquay TR7. . . . . **110** E6
Plymouth PL1. . . . . **148** A2
Polruan PL23. . . . . **116** D3
1 St Columb Major TR9 . . . **45** E6
EAST TAPHOUSE **50** B6
East Terr TR27. . . . . **142** B6
East View PL14. . . . . **51** F5
East Wharf PL26. . . . . **73** C3
East Wheel Rose Sta TR8 . **56** C6
Eastwood Park Ind Est
TR10. . . . . **144** D7
Eastwood Rd TR10. . . . . . . **144** D7
EAST YOULSTONE **3** C2
East Youlstone Cross EX23. . **3** C2
Eathorne TR11 . . . . **93** A6

Eathorne Ct [9] TR13 ....146 C5
Ebenezer PL26 ....47 E3
Ebenezer Pl [12] TR18 ...143 C1
Ebenezer Rd
  St Helena TR12 ....102 F5
  Treveddon TR12 ....103 A5
Ebrington St PL4 ....149 A3
Echo Cres PL5 ....124 D2
Eco Way PL6 ....125 C8
Eddystone Cl PL3 ....129 C6
Eddystone Ct PL13 ....117 D2
Eddystone Pl [3] PL27 ...108 B5
Eddystone Rd
  Down Thomas PL9 .....135 C1
  St Austell PL25 ....114 E5
  Wadebridge PL27 ......108 B6
Eddystone Rise PL14 .....113 D7
Eddystone Terr
  Plymouth PL1 ....148 B1
  [2] Wadebridge PL27 ..108 B5
Eden Cl [11] PL24 ....60 B4
Eden Gdns [14] TR18 ....143 C1
Eden Project★ PL24, PL26 ...115 D8
Edenside PL3 ....128 F6
Eden Terr [13] TR18 .....143 C1
Eden Way [16] PL26 .....59 D7
Edgar Rd Jacobstow PL15 ...11 A6
  Wainhouse Corner EX23 ...10 F6
Edgar Terr PL4 ....129 A4
Edgcumbe Ave
  Newquay TR7 ....110 F5
  Plymouth PL1 ....148 A3
Edgcumbe Cl PL18 ....41 A6
Edgcumbe Cres PL10 ....132 F6
Edgcumbe Ct [3] PL3 ...128 A3
Edgcumbe Dr PL19 ......147 B6
Edgcumbe Gdns TR7 ....110 F6
Edgcumbe Gn PL25 .....114 A3
Edgcumbe Ho PL1 ......148 B2
Edgcumbe Park Rd PL3 ..128 D6
Edgcumbe Rd
  [3] Edgcumbe PL19 ...29 C6
  Lostwithiel PL22 ......112 B1
  Roche PL26 ....46 F3
  St Austell PL25 ....114 A3
  St Dominick PL12 ....40 D2
  Saltash PL12 ....122 C5
Edgcumbe St PL1 ....128 A1
Edgcumbe Terr [1] PL24 ...60 B4
Edgecombe Way PL18 ...40 E5
Edgecumbe Terr [14] PL20 ...41 B1
Edgemoor Cl PL14 ......38 A3
Edinburgh Cl PL25 ......115 C3
Edinburgh St PL1 ....127 E1
EDISTONE 2 F8
Edith Ave PL4 ....149 C4
Edith St PL5 ....123 D1
EDMONTON 33 B7
Edmund Rd TR15 ....140 B6
Edna Terr PL4 ....149 C3
Ednovean La TR20 ......89 E4
Edward Hain Com Hospl
  TR26 ....141 B5
Edwards Cl PL7 ....131 B4
Edwards Cres PL12 .....122 C2
Edwards Dr PL7 ....131 B5
Edwards Rd Devoran TR3 ...81 F6
  St Giles on the Heath PL15 ...13 F1
Edward St Camborne TR14 ...138 F4
  Truro TR1 ....137 C4
Edymeade Cl PL15 ......106 C5
Edymeade Gdn [11] PL15 ...106 C5
  [9] Launceston PL15 ...106 C5
Edyvean Pl [3] PL25 ...114 F2
Effingham Cres PL3 ....128 D7
EFFORD 129 C5
Efford Cres PL3 ....129 B6
Efford Down Pk EX23 ...104 C4
Efford Farm Bsns Pk EX23 ...104 C4
Efford Farm Cotts EX23 ...104 C4
Efford Fort PL3 ....129 E6
Efford La PL3 ....129 B5
Efford Pathway PL3 ....129 C6
Efford Rd PL3 ....129 B6
Efford Wlk PL3 ....129 B6
Egerton Cres PL4 ......149 C3
Egerton Pl PL4 ....149 C3
Egerton Rd Padstow PL28 ...107 E4
  Plymouth PL4 ....149 C3
EGGBEARE 19 A7
EGGBUCKLAND 129 C8
Eggbuckland Rd PL3 ...129 C7
Eggbuckland Vale Prim Sch
  PL6 ....129 A8
Eglos Ct PL30 ....23 E7
Egloshayle Rd Hayle TR27 ...142 E6
  Wadebridge PL27 ....108 D5
EGLOSKERRY 18 A5
Egloskerry Sch PL15 ...18 A5
Eglos Mdw TR11 ....82 A3
Eglos Parc Mullion TR12 ...99 A2
  Wadebridge PL27 ....108 D5
Eglos Rd Ludgvan TR20 ...89 A7
  St Erme TR4 ....70 D8
  Shortlanesend TR4 ....69 F6
Eglos View [2] PL35 ...9 C1
EGOSHAYLE 108 D6
Egret Cl PL10 ....133 A6
Eider Wlk TR27 ....77 E3
Eight Acre Cl [1] PL7 ..131 C5
Elaine Cl PL7 ....130 B5
Elbow La PL19 ....147 C6
ELBURTON 136 C6
Elburton Prim Sch PL9 ...136 C7
Elburton Rd PL9 ....136 B8
Eldad Hill PL1 ....148 A3

Elder Cl [2] PL7 ....131 B5
Elderfield Cl [7] PL24 ...60 D5
Eleanor Rd PL1 ....148 A2
Electra Way [20] PL9 ...136 E8
Eleni Cl Carn Towan TR19 ...86 E1
  Sennen Cove TR19 ....96 C7
Elerkey Cl TR2 ....83 F6
Elerkey La TR2 ....83 F6
Eleven Doors PL25 ....115 B2
Elford Cres PL7 ....130 E7
Elford Dr PL9 ....135 C7
Elford Pk PL20 ....42 D2
Elgin Cres PL5 ....124 E3
Elim Ct PL3 ....128 E5
Elim Terr PL3 ....128 E5
Eliot Cl PL15 ....18 C2
Eliot Ct TR7 ....110 F6
Eliot Dr PL12 ....65 B8
Eliot Gdns TR7 ....110 F6
Eliot Rd St Austell PL25 ...114 C4
  Truro TR1 ....137 C5
Eliot St PL5 ....127 E8
Elizabeth Cl Bodmin PL31 ...109 D4
  Threemilestone TR3 ...69 C3
Elizabeth Ct Bugle PL26 ...47 C1
  [2] Plymouth PL1 .....128 F5
Elizabeth House Mus & Arts
  Gall★ PL4 ....149 A2
Elizabeth Pl PL4 ......149 A4
Elizabeth Rd Bude EX23 ...104 F5
  St Austell PL25 ....114 E3
Elizabeth Terr TR17 ...89 B5
Ellbridge La PL12 .....118 A3
Ellen Cl TR4 ....68 C6
Ellenglaze Ct TR8 ....55 D8
Ellenglaze La TR8 ....55 D8
Ellenglaze Mdw TR8 ..55 D8
Elliot Sq PL11 ....127 B3
Elliot St PL1 ....148 B1
Elliott Cl PL12 ....122 D2
Elliot Terr PL1 ....148 C1
Elliot Terrace La PL1 ..148 C1
Elliott Rd PL4 ....129 B1
Elliott's Store★ PL12 ...123 A2
Ellis Cl TR27 ....142 C5
Elliston Gdns [3] TR13 ...98 C8
Ellis Way TR27 ....142 C5
Elm Cl Callington PL17 ...39 F4
  Camborne TR15 ......139 D6
  Newquay TR7 ....110 F4
  Tavistock PL19 ....147 C3
Elm Cotts PL12 ......122 C3
Elm Court Gdns TR1 ..137 D5
Elm Cres PL3, PL4 ....129 A4
Elm Croft PL2 ....128 B7
Elm Ct TR1 ....137 D5
Elm Dr Bude EX23 ....104 F5
  [8] St Columb Major TR9 ...45 D6
Elmgate Crossways PL12 ...65 E8
Elm Gr Feock TR3 .....82 B8
  Plymouth, Eggbuckland PL6 ...129 B8
  Plymouth, Plympton PL7 ...130 E5
Elm Grove Cotts TR10 ...93 C6
Elmlea EX23 ....104 F5
Elm Mdw TR3 ....82 C5
Elm Meadow Dr PL13 ...117 D4
Elm Pk PL10 ....133 B6
Elm Rd
  Plymouth, Glenholt PL6 ...125 D6
  Plymouth, Mannamead PL4 ...128 F4
Elms Close Terr [25] TR18 ...143 C2
ELMSCOTT 2 E8
Elmsleigh PL25 ....114 B3
Elmsleigh Rd PL17 ....108 B6
Elms The Perranuthnoe TR20 ...89 D4
  Plymouth PL3 ....128 A3
Elm Terr [8] Mullion TR12 ...99 A2
  [1] Plymouth PL3 .....128 F5
  St Austell PL25 ....114 C4
Elm Terrace [21] PL26 ...85 D8
Elm Tree Rd PL13 .....117 D4
Elm Villas TR11 ......144 E1
Elmwood Cl PL6 ......125 D5
Elowen Cl TR11 ......144 E2
Elphinstone Rd PL2 ...128 C7
Elspeth Sitters Ho [11] PL4 ...149 A2
Elwell Rd PL12 ....123 A2
Elwick Gdns PL3 .....129 B5
Embankment La PL4 ...129 B2
Embankment Rd PL4 ...129 B2
Embankment Road Lane N
  PL4 ....129 B2
Emily Gdns PL4 ......149 B4
Emlyn Fields PL25 ....114 F6
Emma Pl [1] PL1 .....128 A1
Emma Place Ope PL1 ...128 A1
EMPACOMBE 133 D6
Empire Way TR11 ....144 E4
Empress Ave [23] TR18 ...143 E6
Empty La PL14 ....37 B2
Emslie Rd TR11 ......145 C2
Endeavour Ct PL1 ....128 A3
Endsleigh Dr
  Dunterton PL15, PL19 ...28 F5
  Endsleigh PL19 ....29 A5
Endsleigh Gdns [2] PL4 ..149 A4
Endsleigh Gdns Nursery★
  PL19 ....29 B5
Endsleigh Park Rd PL3 ...128 D6
Endsleigh Pk EX23 ....7 B6
Endsleigh Pl PL4 .....149 A4
Endsleigh Rd PL9 .....135 C7
Endsleigh Terr PL14 ...113 C6
Engelly Rd TR4 ......55 E4
Eningdale Rd PL19 ...147 A4
Ennerdale Gdns PL6 ...124 E5
ENNISCAVEN 46 D2

Ennis Rd TR4 ....56 D1
Ennor's Rd TR7 ....110 D6
Ensign Cl PL9 ....124 C3
Ensign Way [7] TR20 ...88 B7
Enterprise Dr PL5 ....124 D2
Enys Cl Carbis Bay TR26 ...141 D1
  Truro TR1 ....137 B5
Enys Cl TR19 ....75 A2
Enys Cotts TR19 ......75 A2
Enys Quay [5] PL1 ....137 D4
Enys Rd Camborne TR14 ...138 D4
  Truro TR1 ....137 B5
Enys Redenek TR14 ...138 F5
Epping Cres PL6 ......129 D7
Epworth Cl TR1 ......137 E4
Epworth Terr [4] PL2 ...127 F5
Erddison Ct PL12 .....65 B8
Ergue-Gaberic Way EX23 ...104 D5
Eric Rd Calstock PL18 ...41 B3
  Plymouth PL4 ....149 C3
Erisey Terr TR11 .....145 B4
Erith Ave PL2 ....127 E7
Erle Gdns PL7 ....130 F3
Erlstoke Cl PL6 ......125 D1
Erme Gdns PL3 ......129 C5
Ermington Terr PL4 ...128 E4
ERNESETTLE 123 E3
Ernesettle Cres PL5 ...123 E3
Ernesettle Gn PL5 ....123 E4
Ernesettle La PL5 .....123 D4
Ernesettle Prim Sch PL5 ...123 F4
Ernesettle Rd PL5 ....123 E3
Erow Glas TR10 ......144 C8
Esmonde Gdns PL5 ...127 B6
Esmonde Rd TR13 ....146 D4
Esperanza Ct TR11 ...144 F6
Esplanade PL23 ......116 C3
Esplanade Rd TR7 ....110 A6
Esplanade The PL1 ...148 C1
Essa Rd PL12 ....122 F2
Essex Dr TR15 ....139 B8
Essex St PL1 ....148 B4
Esso Wharf Rd PL4 ...149 C1
Eston Cl TR10 ....93 C8
ESTOVER 125 E4
Estover Cl PL6 ....125 F5
  Plymouth PL6 ....125 F5
Estover Ind Est PL6 ...125 E4
Estover Rd PL6 ......125 F4
Estuary View
  [2] Falmouth TR11 ...145 B5
  Lelant TR26 ....77 E3
  Newquay TR7 ....110 D5
  [12] Tremough TR10 ...81 C1
Estuary Way PL5 .....127 C7
Eton Ave PL1 ....148 C4
Eton Pl PL1 ....148 C4
Eton St PL1 ....148 C4
Eton Terr [3] PL1 ....148 B3
Euny Cl TR15 ....140 A4
Eureka Vale [7] TR6 ...55 A5
Europa Ct TR8 ....31 C2
Evans Ct PL1 ....148 A3
Evans Pl PL2 ....128 B5
Evans Way TR20 ....90 C4
Evea Cl TR1 ....69 F3
Evely Ct PL14 ....113 D7
Evelyn Pl PL4 ....149 A4
Evelyn St PL5 ....123 D1
Evenden Cl PL1 .....127 A3
Example Cross PL15 ...27 B6
Exchange (Gall) The★ [37]
  TR18 ....143 E5
Exchange St PL4 ....149 A2
Exe Gdns PL3 ....129 C7
Exeter Cl PL5 ....123 D4
Exeter Ct [6] PL15 ...106 C6
Exeter St Launceston PL15 ...106 C6
  Plymouth, Barbican PL4 ...149 A3
  Plymouth, St Jude's PL4 ...149 B2
Exmouth Ct PL1 ....127 F3
Exmouth Rd PL1 ....127 F3
Explorer Ct PL2 ....128 B5

F

Factory Cotts PL14 ...51 F5
Fairbourne Rd PL25 ...114 F4
Fair Cl TR8 ....56 F5
Fair Cross TR2 ......72 C6
Fairfax Rd TR2 ......70 F5
Fairfax Terr [5] PL2 ...127 F4
Fairfield Plymouth PL7 ...130 E7
  St Germans PL12 .....65 A8
Fair Field TR20 ......89 B8
Fairfield Ave PL2 ....128 C2
Fairfield Cl Lelant TR26 ...77 E4
  St Austell PL25 ......115 A4
Fairfield Pk PL15 ....26 C7
Fairfield Rd Bude EX23 ...104 E5
  Falmouth TR11 ......144 F4
Fairfields PL13 ......117 D5
Fairing Cl [12] PL31 ...109 A5
Fairlight PL14 ....113 D5
Fairmantle St TR1 ...137 D4
Fairmead Cl PL12 ....53 E4
Fairmead Mews PL12 ...122 C3
Fairmeadow TR10 ....144 B7
Fairpark Rd Liskeard PL14 ...113 C5
  Wadebridge PL27 ....108 B5
Fair Park View TR8 ...56 F5
Fair Pk Cl [10] PL15 ...106 C5
Fair View Bodmin PL31 ...109 B4
  Lanivet PL26 ....47 E4
Fairview Ave PL3 ....129 D5

Fairview Pk [5] TR9 ...45 E2
Fairview Pl TR11 ....145 B4
Fairview Terr TR7 ....110 E6
Fair View Terr TR4 ...55 D8
Fairview Way PL3 ...129 E5
Fairway St Austell PL25 ...115 D3
  Saltash PL12 ....122 C2
Fairways The PL30 ...48 C7
Fairway The TR11 ....93 C2
FAIRY CROSS 49 B5
Falcon Terr EX23 ....104 D5
FALMOUTH 145 B4
Falmouth Art Gall★ TR11 ...145 B4
Falmouth Bsns Pk TR11 ...144 E3
Falmouth Docks Sta TR11 ...145 D3
Falmouth Hospl TR11 ...144 F4
Falmouth Marine Sch [17]
  TR11 ....145 A4
Falmouth Pl [1] TR19 ...86 F8
Falmouth Prim Sch TR11 ...145 A5
Falmouth Rd Helston TR13 ...146 D7
  Penryn TR10 ....144 E7
  Redruth TR15 ....140 C4
  Truro TR1 ....137 C3
Falmouth Road TR13 ...146 E2
Falmouth Sch TR11 ...144 D5
Falmouth Town Sta TR11 ...145 C3
Falmouth University (Penryn
  Campus) TR10 ....144 A8
Falmouth University
  (Wellington Annexe)
  TR11 ....145 B4
Falmouth University
  (Woodlane Campus)
  TR11 ....145 B3
Falmouth Watersports Ctr [15]
  TR11 ....145 C3
Falmouth Wharves TR11 ...145 A6
Fanshawe Way PL9 ...135 C6
Faraday Mill Bsns Pk PL4 ...129 B1
Faraday Rd PL4 .....129 B1
Farfield Pl TR7 ......110 B5
Faringdon Rd PL4 ...129 B3
Farley Cl TR1 ....137 C3
Farm Cl PL7 ....130 C7
Farmers Cl PL14 ....50 B6
Farmers Ct TR20 ....89 B8
Farmer's La PL14 ...50 B6
Farmers Mdw [8] PL18 ...143 C2
Farmhouse La PL27 ...21 E5
Farm La Gwealmayowe TR13 ...146 C7
  Plymouth PL5 ....124 B2
  Saltash PL12 ....122 D1
FARMS COMMON 79 F1
Farm Town TR15 ....140 C3
Farnley Cl PL6 ......125 B6
Farrar Cl PL1 ....129 B1
Farriers Cotts PL7 ...130 E7
Farriers Gn PL32 ....105 B2
Farriers The PL19 ...30 A3
Farrow Fordh PL26 ...46 F3
Faugan La TR18 .....143 B1
Faugan Rd TR18 ....143 B1
Faukener Cl TR11 ...144 E4
Fayre View PL12 ....122 B1
Fearnside Way PL12 ...122 C3
Federation Rd PL3 ...129 C4
Feeding Field Cl [7] TR27 ...142 D6
Fegan Rd PL5 ....123 B1
Feliskirk La TR17 ....89 B6
Felixstowe Ave TR7 ...111 E7
Fellowes La [4] PL4 ...148 A4
Fellowes Pl PL1 .....128 A2
Fenten Cl EX23 .....104 E7
Fenten Pk PL12 .....122 F3
Fenteroon Rd PL32 ...105 C2
FENTONADLE 24 A5
Fentonluna La PL28 ...107 D6
Fenwick Rd TR11 ....145 B2
FEOCK 82 C5
Feock Rd TR3 ....82 B8
Fern Cl PL7 ....131 C5
Ferndale Ave PL2 ...127 E7
Ferndale Cl PL5 .....125 D8
Ferndale Rd Falmouth TR11 ...145 A2
  Plymouth PL2 ....127 F7
Ferndale Terr PL14 ...113 B6
Fern Glen [18] TR26 ...141 A5
Fernhill Rd TR7 .....110 D6
Fern Lee Terr [19] TR26 ...141 B5
Fernleigh Cres PL27 ...108 C4
Fernleigh Gdns PL27 ...108 C4
Fernleigh La PL27 ...108 C4
Fernleigh Rd Plymouth PL3 ...128 F5
  Wadebridge PL27 ....108 C5
Fernleigh Terr
  Gunnislake PL18 .....40 E5
  Nanpean PL26 ....58 C6
Fern Mdw PL19 .....147 D6
Fernside Pk PL14 ...38 A3
Fernside Rd TR14 ...138 B1
FERNSPLATT 81 C8
Ferrers Rd PL5 ......123 E1
Ferretts Cross EX23 ...11 A6
Ferris Town TR1 ....137 C4
Ferris Way PL23 ....116 E2
Ferry La PL11 ......126 D5
Ferry Rd Braunder PL20 ...41 A2
  Plymouth PL1 ....127 E3
Ferry St PL11 ......127 E3
Festival Villas TR3 ...69 D3
Fettling Lane [3] PL25 ...115 A3
Feversham Cl PL27 ...131 B6
FIDDLERS GREEN 56 B5
Field Pl TR11 ....93 D3
Field The TR20 .....76 F2
Fifield Ho PL26 .....58 B4

Fillace La [10] PL20 ...42 C4
Fillace Pk PL20 .....42 C4
Filtrick La TR16 ....139 E1
Finch Cl PL3 ....129 C4
Finches Cl PL9 ......136 C7
Findon Gdns PL6 ...125 D4
Finewell St PL1 .....148 C2
Finnigan Rd PL4 ...129 B1
Finn Vc Est [18] PL31 ...109 D5
Finnygook La PL11 ...65 A4
Finsbury Rise PL26 ...46 F3
Fir Cl Goonhavern TR4 ...55 D4
  Helston TR13 ....146 B7
  St Austell PL25 ......114 B3
Fir Cres PL26 ....58 D5
Fircroft Rd PL2 .....128 B7
Firebeacon Cross EX39 ...2 F7
Firestone Cl PL6 ...125 C1
Fir Gr [8] TR3 ......81 F7
Firsleigh Pk PL26 ...46 F3
First Ave
  Plymouth, Billacombe PL9 ...135 F8
  Plymouth, Stoke PL1 ...128 A2
Firs The PL6 ....58 E8
Fisgard Way PL11 ...126 D3
Fisher Cl PL27 .....108 D6
Fisher Rd PL2 ......128 A5
Fish Mkt PL4 ....149 B2
Fish Quay PL4 .....149 A2
Fish St [9] TR26 ...141 B6
Fish Strand Hill TR11 ...145 B4
Fish Strand Quay TR11 ...145 B4
Fistral Cl PL11 .....126 F4
Fistral Cres TR7 ....110 A5
Fistral Ct TR7 ......110 A5
Fistral Sands Apartments
  TR7 ....110 D7
Fitch La PL15 ......27 C4
Fitzford Cott PL19 ...147 A4
Fitzroy Rd PL1 .....128 A3
Fitzroy Terr [7] PL1 ...128 A3
Fitzsimmons Cl [7] TR13 ...146 C5
Five Fields La TR11 ...145 A4
Five Wells La TR13 ...146 B5
Flamank Pk PL31 ...109 C4
Flambards Experience The★
  TR13 ....146 E4
Flamborough Rd PL6 ...125 A7
Flamenco Way PL6 ...125 A6
Flamsteed Cres PL5 ...123 E1
Flaxmoor Terr [17] PL31 ...109 D5
Fleet St PL2 ....127 E6
Fleetwood Gdns PL6 ...125 A7
Fletcher Cres PL9 ...136 B6
FLETCHERSBRIDGE 48 F8
Fletchersbridge Hill
  Fletchersbridge PL30 ...35 C1
  Tawnamoor PL30 .....35 E1
Fletcher Way PL9 ...136 A6
Fletemoor Rd PL5 ...123 E1
Fletewood Sch PL4 ...148 C4
FLEXBURY 104 E6
Flexbury Ave EX23 ...104 E7
Flexbury Mews EX23 ...104 E7
Flexbury Park Ct EX23 ...104 E7
Flexbury Park Rd EX23 ...104 E6
Flexbury Pk EX23 ...104 E7
Flocksford PL30 ....35 D4
Flora Cotts PL1 ....148 B2
Flora Ct PL1 ....148 B3
Flora Gdns [5] TR13 ...146 C6
Flora St PL1 ....148 B2
Florence Hill PL17 ...39 F5
Florence Pl Falmouth TR11 ...145 B3
  Newlyn TR18 ....143 C3
  Plymouth PL4 ....149 C3
Florence Rd PL17 ...39 F5
Florence Road Bsns Pk
  PL17 ....39 F6
Florence Road Ind Est PL17 ...39 F6
Florence St PL5 ....123 C1
Florence Terr TR11 ...145 B3
Florida Gdns PL3 ...129 C6
Floyd Cl PL2 ....127 F7
FLUSHING Manaccan ...101 B8
  Penryn 145 C6
Flushing CE Prim Sch
  TR11 ....145 B6
Flushing Cove TR12 ...101 B8
Focus Sch - Plymouth Campus
  PL5 ....123 B1
Folders La PL30 ....23 F6
Foliot Ave PL2 .....128 A6
Foliot Rd PL2 ......128 A6
Folkstone Cl PL26 ...58 E6
FONSTON 11 C2
Forbes Cl TR18 ....143 B1
Forbes Rd TR18 ....143 B1
FORD 128 A5
Ford PL22 ....49 E3
Fordbrook La PL9 ...136 D4
Ford Cl PL14 ....39 A2
FORDER Cawsand ...132 F1
  Saltash 122 C1
Forder Hill PL10 ...132 F1
Forder Hts PL6 .....125 B1
Forder La PL10 .....132 F1
Forder Valley Rd PL6 ...129 D8
Fordh An Bal TR15 ...139 B5
Ford Hill PL2 ....128 A5
Fordh Talgarrek TR1 ...137 B2
Fordh Tobmen [9] TR5 ...54 C1
FORD PARK 128 D4
Ford Park La PL4 ...128 E4
Ford Park Rd PL4 ...128 D4

Ford Pk PL4 . . . . .128 E4
Ford Prim Sch PL2 . . . . . . .127 F5
Fords Hill TR12 . . . . .100 D7
Ford's Row TR15 . . . . .140 B5
Ford St PL19 . . . . .147 B5
Foredown Pk PL14 . . . . .38 C3
Forest TR16 . . . . .80 A4
Fore St Ashton TR13 . . . . . . .90 E3
   Barripper TR13 . . . . .79 B5
   Bere Alston PL20 . . . . .41 B1
   Bere Ferrers PL20 . . . . .119 F3
   Bodmin PL31 . . . . .109 D5
   Boscastle PL35 . . . . .9 C1
   Bugle PL26 . . . . .47 C1
   6 Callington PL17 . . . . . . .39 E4
   Calstock PL18 . . . . .41 A3
   Camborne TR15 . . . . .139 B6
   Camelford PL32 . . . . .105 D4
   Cargreen PL12 . . . . .119 A2
   Carharrack TR16 . . . . .80 F8
   Chacewater TR4 . . . . .69 A3
   Constantine TR11 . . . . .92 F4
   Crumplehorn PL13 . . . . .62 D1
   Fowey PL23 . . . . .116 D4
   Golant PL23 . . . . .61 B5
   Goldsithney TR20 . . . . .89 E5
   Grampound TR2 . . . . .72 A7
   Grampound Road TR2 . . . . . . .57 E1
   Gunnislake PL18 . . . . .40 F5
   Hayle TR27 . . . . .142 D6
   Herodsfoot PL14 . . . . .50 E3
   Kingsand PL10 . . . . .133 A2
   Lelant TR26 . . . . .77 E4
   Lerryn PL22 . . . . .61 C7
   Lifton PL16 . . . . .19 F4
   Liskeard PL14 . . . . .113 C6
   Looe PL13 . . . . .117 C3
   Lostwithiel PL22 . . . . .112 C2
   Madron TR20 . . . . .88 B7
   Marazion TR17 . . . . .89 C5
   Mevagissey PL26 . . . . .73 C3
   Millbrook PL10 . . . . .132 E5
   Milton Abbot PL19 . . . . .29 C6
   Mount Hawke TR4 . . . . .68 C6
   13 Mousehole TR19 . . . . . . .88 C1
   Nanpean PL26 . . . . .58 D7
   Newlyn TR18 . . . . .143 C1
   Newquay TR7 . . . . .110 D6
   Par PL24 . . . . .60 B5
   Penponds TR14 . . . . .138 B1
   Pensilva PL14 . . . . .38 E4
   Plymouth, Devonport PL1 . . .127 F2
   Plymouth, Plympton PL7 . . . .130 E4
   Plymouth, Tamerton Foliot
      PL5 . . . . .124 B6
   Polgooth PL26 . . . . .59 A1
   Polruan PL23 . . . . .116 D2
   4 Porthleven TR13 . . . . . . .98 B8
   Port Isaac PL29 . . . . .22 D7
   Praze-an-Beeble TR14 . . . . . .79 B2
   Probus TR2 . . . . .71 C6
   Redruth TR15 . . . . .140 B5
   Roche PL26 . . . . .46 F2
   St Austell PL25 . . . . .114 C3
   St Cleer PL14 . . . . .37 F3
   St Columb Major TR9 . . . . . . .45 E6
   St Day TR16 . . . . .68 D1
   St Dennis PL26 . . . . .58 C8
   St Erth TR27 . . . . .142 A1
   St Germans PL12 . . . . .65 A8
   St Ives TR26 . . . . .141 B6
   St Just TR19 . . . . .86 F6
   St Stephen PL26 . . . . .58 B4
   St Teath PL30 . . . . .23 E7
   Saltash PL12 . . . . .122 F2
   Sticker PL26 . . . . .58 E1
   7 Stratton EX23 . . . . .4 E1
   Tintagel PL34 . . . . .14 C7
   Torpoint PL11 . . . . .127 B3
   Tregony TR2 . . . . .71 F3
   Troon TR14 . . . . .79 E5
   9 Tywardreath PL24 . . . . . . .60 D5
Forest Ave PL2 . . . . .128 C7
Foresters Rd PL9 . . . . .135 D7
Forest Hos TR4 . . . . .70 D8
Forest View PL6 . . . . .125 D7
FORGE 68 A4
Forge Ind Pk TR14 . . . . . . .138 E5
Forge La PL12 . . . . .122 C4
Forge The TR3 . . . . .82 A7
Forge Way TR4 . . . . .69 F6
Forlaze Rd PL27 . . . . .21 D2
Formal Ind Pk TR14 . . . . . .138 B4
FORRABURY 9 C2
Forrabury Hill PL35 . . . . .9 C1
Forreglos Dr **10** TR17 . . . . . . .89 C5
Forresters Dr PL6 . . . . .125 D7
Forsters Ct TR2 . . . . .72 A7
Forsythia Dr PL12 . . . . .122 C3
Fort Austin Ave PL6 . . . . . .125 C1
Fortescue Cl PL26 . . . . .58 D6
Fortescue Pl
   Lostwithiel PL22 . . . . .112 D3
   Plymouth PL3 . . . . .129 A6
Fortescue Terr PL17 . . . . . .147 A6
Fortesque Ct **3** PL19 . . . . . . .30 A3
Forth an Cos TR3 . . . . .81 B4
Forth-an-Eglas TR16 . . . . . .68 D1
Forth-an-Nance TR16 . . . . . .67 C6
Forth-an-Praze
   Illogan TR15 . . . . .139 D8
   St Day TR16 . . . . .68 D1
Forth-an-Ryn TR15 . . . . . . .140 D4
Forth an Streth TR27 . . . . . .142 E7
Forth an Tewennow TR27 . .142 D7

Forth-an-Tre TR27 . . . . . . .142 D7
Forth an Ula TR27 . . . . .142 E7
Forth an Venegh PL31 . . . . .109 E3
Forth an Vre TR14 . . . . .139 A3
Forth Coth TR3 . . . . .82 A7
Forthcrom PL12 . . . . .92 C1
Forth Dall **21** TR16 . . . . .67 E4
Forth Gdns PL3 . . . . .129 D6
Forth Gwedhen TR13 . . . . .146 D8
Forth Kegyn TR15 . . . . .139 B4
Forthnoweth TR15 . . . . .140 B5
Forth Noweth **4** TR3 . . . . . . .81 F7
Forth Scol Camborne TR15 . .139 D7
   6 Porthleven TR13 . . . . . . .98 C8
Forthvean Camborne TR14 . .138 D1
   Portreath TR16 . . . . .67 C5
Forth Vean TR15 . . . . .90 E6
Forthvean Cres TR4 . . . . . . .68 A6
Forthvean Rd TR4, TR16 . . . .67 F7
Forth Veor TR15 . . . . .140 E7
Forthvras TR15 . . . . .139 B8
Fort Picklecombe PL10 . . . .133 F4
Fort Terr PL6 . . . . .124 F3
Fort The PL10 . . . . .133 A1
Fosbrooke Ct **10** PL3 . . . . . .128 F6
FOSS 133 A5
Foster Dr PL31 . . . . .109 C3
Fosters La PL34 . . . . .14 C7
Fosters Mdw PL18 . . . . .40 D6
Fosters Way EX23 . . . . .104 F6
Foulston Ave PL5 . . . . .127 B8
Foulston Way PL31 . . . . . . .109 B4
FOUNDRY 142 B5
Foundry Cl **2** TR14 . . . . . . .138 E5
Foundry Dr PL25 . . . . .115 B3
Foundry Flats TR27 . . . . . . .142 B5
Foundry Gdns PL15 . . . . . . .106 B6
Foundry Hill Hayle TR27 . . . .142 B4
   Stithians TR3 . . . . .80 F3
Foundry Ho **3** TR27 . . . . . . .142 B5
Foundry La Hayle TR27 . . . . .142 B5
   Newlyn TR18 . . . . .143 C2
Foundry Mews PL19 . . . . . .147 D6
Foundry Rd Camborne TR14 .138 E3
   Kennall Vale TR3 . . . . .81 A4
Foundry Row
   Marhamchurch EX23 . . . . .7 B6
   5 Redruth TR15 . . . . .140 B5
Foundry Sq TR27 . . . . .142 B5
Foundry St **6** PL27 . . . . . . .108 B5
Foundry Terr **14** PL27 . . . . .108 B5
Fountain Ct **26** TR18 . . . . . .143 E6
Fountains Cres PL2 . . . . . . .128 C8
Four Acres Rd TR2 . . . . .83 F6
Four Cross TR10 . . . . .81 C2
Fourgates PL14 . . . . .51 F5
FOUR LANES 80 A5
Four Lanes TR16 . . . . .80 B5
Four Lanes' End TR19 . . . . . .97 F6
Fourlanesend Com Prim Sch
   PL10 . . . . .132 F3
Four Turnings PL23 . . . . .60 F3
Fowenn Ct **12** PL14 . . . . . . .113 B6
FOWEY 116 B4
Fowey Com Coll PL23 . . . . .116 B4
Fowey Com L Ctr PL23 . . . . .116 B4
Fowey Cres **27** PL17 . . . . . . .39 F4
Fowey Gdns PL3 . . . . .129 D6
Fowey Hospl PL23 . . . . .116 C5
Fowey Mus * PL23 . . . . .116 B4
Fowlfield Row TR13 . . . . . . .90 F3
Foxdown PL27 . . . . .108 D5
Foxes Field TR18 . . . . .88 E6
Foxes La **5** TR19 . . . . .88 C1
Foxes Row TR16 . . . . .80 E8
Fox Field Cl PL3 . . . . .129 C5
Foxglove Cl PL26 . . . . .46 F3
Foxglove Cres PL28 . . . . . . .31 F7
Foxglove End **3** PL20 . . . . . .42 A2
Foxglove Rd **15** PL31 . . . . . .109 A5
Foxglove Way PL12 . . . . . . .122 B3
FOXHOLE 58 D5
Foxhole La PL26 . . . . .85 D5
Foxhole Prim Sch PL26 . . . . .58 D5
Fox's La TR11 . . . . .145 B3
Foxstanton Dr TR10 . . . . . . .144 D7
Foxs Yd TR10 . . . . .144 D7
Foxtor Cl PL15 . . . . .124 B3
Foxwood Gdns
   Plymouth, Plymstock PL9 . . . .135 F5
   Plymouth, Southway PL6 . . . .124 E5
Foyle Cl PL7 . . . . .131 A5
FRADDAM 78 D1
Fraddam Rd TR27 . . . . .78 D1
FRADDON 45 E1
Fradgan Pl TR18 . . . . .143 C2
Fradgan The **12** TR18 . . . . . .143 C2
Frances St TR1 . . . . .137 C4
Francis La PL27 . . . . .21 D5
Francis Rd PL27 . . . . .21 D5
Francis St PL1 . . . . .148 A3
Frankfort Gate **9** PL1 . . . . .148 B3
Frankland Cl TR11 . . . . .144 F3
Franklin Cl PL27 . . . . .108 D4
Franklyn Cl PL15 . . . . .114 F5
Franklyns' Pl PL6 . . . . .125 A4
Franklyns Cl PL6 . . . . .125 A4
Franwill Terr **16** TR18 . . . . .143 C1
Fraser Pl PL5 . . . . .124 C7
Fraser Rd PL5 . . . . .124 C7
Fraser Sq PL5 . . . . .124 C7
FREATHY 65 E3
Frederick Street E PL1 . . . . .148 A3
Frederick Street W **6** PL1 . .148 B3
Fredington Gr PL2 . . . . .128 B6

Freedom Sq PL4 . . . . .149 B4
Freeman Collins Dr TR11 . . .144 F4
Freemans Wharf PL1 . . . . . .134 A8
Fremantle Gdns **4** PL2 . . . .127 F4
Fremantle Pl PL2 . . . . .127 F4
Frenchman's La PL12 . . . . . . .53 C4
Frensham Ave PL6 . . . . .125 C7
Frensham Gdns PL6 . . . . . . .125 C7
Freshbrook Cl TR18 . . . . .88 E6
Freshford Cl PL6 . . . . .125 C1
Freshford Wlk PL6 . . . . .125 C1
Freshwater La TR2 . . . . .95 B6
Frewin Gdns PL6 . . . . .125 B6
Friars La TR12 . . . . .103 A6
Friars La TR12 . . . . .102 F6
Friars' La PL1 . . . . .149 A2
Friar's La TR12 . . . . .103 B5
Friars Wlk PL19 . . . . .147 E2
Friary Pk PL4 . . . . .149 B3
Friary St PL4 . . . . .149 B3
Frith Rd PL12 . . . . .122 D3
Frobisher App PL5 . . . . .124 D2
Frobisher Dr PL12 . . . . .122 E2
Frobisher Terr **9** TR11 . . . . .145 A5
Frobisher Way
   Tavistock PL19 . . . . .147 B5
   Torpoint PL11 . . . . .126 D3
Frog La TR2 . . . . .71 F3
Frogmore Ave PL6 . . . . .129 B7
Frogmore Ct PL6 . . . . .129 B7
FROGPOOL 81 C7
Frogwell Rd PL17 . . . . .39 E4
Frome Cl PL7 . . . . .131 A4
Frontfield Cres PL6 . . . . . . .124 E5
Front Rd TR11 . . . . .64 C4
Frost Ct TR11 . . . . .144 E5
Fuggoe Croft TR26 . . . . . . .141 C3
Fuggoe La TR26 . . . . .141 C3
Fullaford Rd PL17 . . . . .40 A4
Fuller Rd TR6 . . . . .55 A5
Fullerton Rd PL2 . . . . .128 A5
Fuller-Tre Cl TR26 . . . . .46 F3
Fulmar Rd **10** EX23 . . . . .7 B8
Furland Cl PL9 . . . . .135 C5
Furneaux Ave PL2 . . . . .128 B5
Furneaux Rd PL2 . . . . .128 B6
Furniss Cl **6** TR1 . . . . .137 D4
Furry The TR13 . . . . .146 B5
Furry Way TR13 . . . . .146 B5
Fursdon Cl PL9 . . . . .136 C6
Furse Pk PL5 . . . . .127 C7
Fursey La PL15 . . . . .27 B6
Furzeacre Cl PL7 . . . . .131 A7
Furze Gdns EX23 . . . . .2 D1
Furzedown Terr PL13 . . . . . .117 C4
Furzehatt Ave PL9 . . . . .136 A6
Furzehatt Park Rd PL9 . . . . .136 A6
Furzehatt Rd PL9 . . . . .135 F6
Furzehatt Rise PL9 . . . . .135 F6
Furzehatt Villas PL9 . . . . . . .135 F6
Furzehatt Way PL9 . . . . . . .136 A6
Furze Hill PL31 . . . . .109 E5
Furzehill Rd PL4 . . . . .128 F4
Furze Park Dr PL12 . . . . .52 F1
Furze Pk Polruan PL23 . . . . .116 D2
   St Issey PL27 . . . . .32 D5
   Trelights PL29 . . . . .22 D6
Furze Pk Dr PL12 . . . . .53 A1
Furze Vale PL25 . . . . .114 F2
FutureWorld@Goonhilly *
   TR12 . . . . .99 F4

G

Gabriel St **5** TR26 . . . . .141 B5
Gadiwall Rise TR27 . . . . .77 E3
Gainsborough Ct TR7 . . . . . .110 D5
Gainsborough Ho PL19 . . . .147 B6
Gains Cross EX22 . . . . .9 F5
Galgeth Rd PL30 . . . . .36 B2
Galileo Cl PL7 . . . . .130 E6
Galingale Dr **4** TR14 . . . . . .138 E5
Gallacher Way PL12 . . . . . . .122 B3
Galland Rd TR1 . . . . .69 F4
Gallant's Dr PL23 . . . . .116 B3
Galleon Ct TR7 . . . . .110 D4
Galleries The **48** TR26 . . . . .141 B6
Gallery La Landrake PL12 . . . .53 A1
   St Germans PL12 . . . . .65 A8
Galligan Cl TR19 . . . . .97 A6
Galligan La TR19 . . . . .97 A6
Gallopine La PL26 . . . . .73 B5
Gallops The PL12 . . . . .122 D4
Galsworthy Cl PL5 . . . . .124 C2
Galva Rd PL7 . . . . .131 D5
GAM 24 A4
Gander La TR13 . . . . .146 B6
GANG 38 F3
Ganges Cl TR11 . . . . .82 C2
Ganges Rd PL2 . . . . .128 A5
Ganna Park Rd PL3 . . . . . . .128 D6
Gannel Rd TR7 . . . . .110 E4
Gannel View Cl TR8 . . . . . . .111 B3
Gannet Dr PL25 . . . . .114 F4
Garage Field Pk EX23 . . . . . . .5 A6
Garby La TR15 . . . . .140 C3
Garcia Terr PL15 . . . . .106 D4
Garden Cl PL7 . . . . .131 D5
Garden Cres PL1 . . . . .148 B1
Gardeners Way PL27 . . . . . . .32 E6
Garden House The * PL20 . . . .42 A3
Garden La PL19 . . . . .147 B5
Garden Mdw TR11 . . . . .144 E3
Garden Park Cl PL9 . . . . . . .136 C7

Garden St PL2 . . . . .127 E4
Garden Village PL9 . . . . . . .135 F8
Garden Way TR8 . . . . .111 F3
Garden Wk PL26 . . . . .115 A1
Gards La PL5 . . . . .123 E2
Garfield Terr PL1, PL3 . . . . .128 A3
Garland Pl TR14 . . . . .138 D4
Garlidna **24** TR18 . . . . .143 E6
GARRAS 99 D6
Garras Com Prim Sch
   TR12 . . . . .100 A7
Garras Wharf TR1 . . . . .137 D3
Garrett St PL10 . . . . .133 A1
Garrick Cl PL5 . . . . .124 C2
Garris Cotts TR20 . . . . .88 E8
Garrison Cl PL1 . . . . .127 E1
Garro La TR12 . . . . .99 A1
Garston Cl PL9 . . . . .136 A8
Garth-an-Creet TR26 . . . . . . .77 A7
Garth Besydhyans **6** TR8 .111 D5
Garth Esels **3** TR8 . . . . .111 D5
Garth Glasneth **2** TR1 . . . . .137 B2
Garth Marhas TR14 . . . . . . .138 C3
Garth Mengleudh **6** TR7 . .111 E5
Garth Morcom PL14 . . . . . . .113 B5
Garth Rd TR18 . . . . .143 B3
Garth Woryan **7** TR7 . . . . .111 E5
Gartland Dr **3** PL31 . . . . . . .109 A5
Gascoyne Ct PL4 . . . . .149 A3
Gascoyne Pl PL4 . . . . .149 A3
Gas Hill TR1 . . . . .137 E2
Gashouse La PL4 . . . . .149 B2
Gasking St PL4 . . . . .149 A3
Gas La **8** TR15 . . . . .140 B4
Gas St TR14 . . . . .138 D3
Gateway St TR27 . . . . .77 E2
GATHERLEY 19 E1
Gavercoombe Pk **2** PL34 . .14 C7
Gawton Way **5** PL19 . . . . . .147 B7
Gay's Hill TR12, TR13 . . . . . .146 E4
Gdynia Way PL4 . . . . .149 C2
GEAR 99 F7
Gear Hill Madron TR20 . . . . . .88 C8
   Mawgan TR12 . . . . .99 E8
Gear La TR20 . . . . .88 B8
Gears La TR17, TR20 . . . . . . .89 D6
Geasons La PL7 . . . . .130 E5
Gedon Way PL31 . . . . .109 A5
Geevor Cotts TR19 . . . . .86 F8
Geevor Tin Mine Mus *
   TR19 . . . . .74 F1
Geffery Cl PL12 . . . . .53 C3
Gemini Dr PL14 . . . . .113 E7
Gemini Rd PL9 . . . . .136 E8
Gems Bolitho Sch TR18 . . . .143 C5
Gendalls Way PL15 . . . . . . .106 B8
Gennys Cl PL18 . . . . .40 E6
George Ave PL7 . . . . .130 F6
George Cross PL7 . . . . .130 F5
George Downing Ho PL6 . . .125 A1
George Fox Cl PL15 . . . . . . .106 A4
George La PL7 . . . . .130 F5
George Pl PL1 . . . . .148 A2
Georges La PL11 . . . . .65 C6
Georges Paddock PL15 . . . . .27 B3
George Sq PL1 . . . . .127 F1
George St Plymouth PL1 . . . .127 F1
   Truro TR1 . . . . .137 C4
GEORGIA 76 E3
Georgia Cres PL3 . . . . .129 C6
Georgia Hill TR20 . . . . .76 E3
Geraldine Terr PL12 . . . . . . .122 C1
GERMOE 90 C4
Germoe TR27 . . . . .90 C4
Germoe Com Prim Sch
   TR20 . . . . .90 C4
GERMOE CROSS ROADS 90 C3
Germoe La TR15 . . . . .90 C4
Gernick La TR14 . . . . .79 B3
GERRANS 83 B2
Gerrans Cl PL25 . . . . .115 B5
Gerrans Hill TR2 . . . . .83 B2
Gerrans Parish Her Ctr *
   TR2 . . . . .83 B2
Gerrans Sch TR2 . . . . .95 D7
Gerrans Sq TR2 . . . . .83 B2
Gewans Mdw PL25 . . . . . . .114 E2
Ghost Hill TR12 . . . . .99 A1
Gibbon La PL4 . . . . .149 A3
Gibbons Fields **9** TR12 . . . . .99 A2
Gibbon St PL4 . . . . .149 A3
Gibbs La PL35 . . . . .9 C1
Gibraltar Terr **6** TR2 . . . . . . .95 A6
Gibralter Sq **8** EX23 . . . . .4 E1
Gibson Way TR13 . . . . .91 B1
Gifford Pl PL3 . . . . .128 C4
Gifford Terrace Rd PL3 . . . . .128 E5
Gig La TR3 . . . . .82 A7
Gilbert Cl PL26 . . . . .58 B4
Gilbert Ct PL7 . . . . .131 B6
Gilbert La PL2 . . . . .128 C5
Gilbert Rd PL31 . . . . .109 F4
GILBERT'S COOMBE 140 A8
GILLAN 101 C8
Gillan Cove TR12 . . . . .101 C7
Gill-an-Creet TR26 . . . . .77 A7
Gillbard Centenary Flats
   PL15 . . . . .106 B5
Gillbard Centenary Homes
   PL15 . . . . .106 B5
Gilley La PL26 . . . . .73 A4
Gilliflower Cres **4** PL31 . . . .109 A5
Gilliflower Pl **5** PL14 . . . . . .113 D7
Gill Pk PL3 . . . . .129 B5
Gills Cl TR10 . . . . .144 B6
Gilly Fields TR15 . . . . .140 B3
Gilly Gabben Ind Est TR12 . .99 B7
Gilly Hill Cury TR12 . . . . .99 B5

Gilly Hill continued
   Redruth TR15 . . . . .140 C3
   Rosevear TR12 . . . . .99 B6
Gilly La TR26 . . . . .77 C1
Gilston Rd PL12 . . . . .122 D4
Gilwell Ave PL9 . . . . .136 B7
Gilwell Pl PL4 . . . . .149 A4
Gilwell St PL4 . . . . .149 A3
Gipsy La PL14 . . . . .113 A3
Gitchell La Crowlas TR20 . . . .89 C8
   St Erth TR26 . . . . .77 C1
Glade Cl PL6 . . . . .125 A4
Glade The Crapstone PL20 . . .42 B2
   St Minver PL27 . . . . .22 A3
Gladstone Rd PL30 . . . . .109 C2
Gladstone Terr
   Longrock TR20 . . . . .88 F6
   3 Redruth TR15 . . . . .140 C5
Gladwell Gdns **10** EX23 . . . . .4 D1
Glamis Rd TR7 . . . . .111 B6
Glantis Cres TR9 . . . . .45 E2
Glanville Rd
   1 Higher Rosewarne
      TR14 . . . . .138 D5
   Tavistock PL19 . . . . .147 B6
Glanville St PL1, PL4 . . . . . .148 C3
Glanville Terr PL12 . . . . . . .122 F3
Glasney Parc TR10 . . . . .144 A8
Glasney Pl TR10 . . . . .144 C7
Glasney Rd TR11 . . . . .145 A5
Glasney Terr TR10 . . . . .144 D7
Glasney View **2** TR10 . . . . .144 A8
Gleaner Cl **1** PL5 . . . . .124 D1
Glebe Ave PL2 . . . . .122 F3
Glebe Cl Mawgan TR12 . . . . .99 D3
   Pelynt PL13 . . . . .62 D5
   6 St Columb Major TR9 . . . .45 E6
Glebe Cres PL27 . . . . .32 D6
Glebe Dr PL26 . . . . .46 F3
Glebe Est PL14 . . . . .38 F2
Glebe Row PL27 . . . . .142 D7
Glebe Terr Constantine TR11 . .92 F4
   Ruan Minor TR12 . . . . .103 B5
Glebe The Camborne TR14 . .138 C3
   Cubert TR8 . . . . .55 D8
   St Mellion PL12 . . . . .53 D8
   Tregony TR2 . . . . .71 F4
   Week St Mary EX22 . . . . . . .11 E8
Glenavon Rd PL3 . . . . .128 E5
Glenburn Cl PL3 . . . . .128 E7
Glencross Ct **3** PL14 . . . . . .113 C6
Glen-Dale Cl **3** PL25 . . . . . .115 A5
Glendale Cres TR4 . . . . .68 C6
Glen Dale Cres TR15 . . . . . .140 D4
Glen-Dale Cres PL25 . . . . . .115 A5
Glendorgal Rd **13** PL18 . . . . .40 F5
Glendower Rd PL3 . . . . .128 C5
Gleneagle Ave **4** PL3 . . . . . .128 F6
Gleneagle Rd PL3 . . . . .128 F6
Gleneagle Villas **5** PL3 . . . . .128 F6
Glenfeadon Terr TR16 . . . . . .67 C6
Glenfield Cl PL6 . . . . .125 D6
Glenfield Rd PL6 . . . . .125 D6
Glenfield Way PL6 . . . . .125 D6
GLENHOLT 125 D6
Glenholt Cl PL6 . . . . .125 D6
Glenholt Rd PL6 . . . . .125 D6
Glenhurst Rd **5** PL3 . . . . . . .128 E6
Glen Leigh TR15 . . . . .140 A6
Glenleigh Pk PL26 . . . . .58 E7
Glenmoor La TR12 . . . . .99 A1
Glenmore Ave PL2 . . . . .127 F5
Glenmore Terr
   7 Liskeard PL14 . . . . .113 C6
   Mabe Burnthouse TR10 . . . . .81 A1
Glennaven Cl PL7 . . . . .131 C6
Glen Park Ave PL4 . . . . .148 C4
Glen Park Prim Sch
   Plymouth PL7 . . . . .130 E4
   6 Plymouth PL7 . . . . .131 B5
Glen Pk PL14 . . . . .38 D4
Glen Rd
   Plymouth, Mannamead PL3 . .128 F5
   Plymouth, Plympton PL7 . . . .130 F4
   Wadebridge PL27 . . . . .108 B5
Glenside Rise PL7 . . . . .130 E6
Glenthorne Rd TR3 . . . . .69 C3
Glentor Rd PL3 . . . . .128 E7
Glentowan Rd PL26 . . . . . . .73 C6
Glen Vale TR15 . . . . .139 E6
Glenview PL25 . . . . .114 B3
Glen View Callington PL17 . . .39 E5
   Penryn TR10 . . . . .144 B8
   Tywardreath PL24 . . . . .60 D5
   Wadebridge PL27 . . . . .108 B4
Glenwood Rd PL3 . . . . .128 E6
Glew Hill TR26 . . . . .77 A4
Globerdon Rd PL14 . . . . .38 E4
Globe Sq TR16 . . . . .139 F2
Gloucester Ave PL25 . . . . . .115 C3
Gloucester Cres TR18 . . . . . .143 C5
Gloucester Ct PL1 . . . . .148 C4
Gloucester Pl
   27 Newlyn TR18 . . . . .143 C2
   Plymouth PL1 . . . . .148 C4
Gloucester Rd TR18 . . . . . . .143 C2
GLOWETH 69 E3
Gloweth View TR1 . . . . .69 E3
Gloweth Villas TR1 . . . . .69 E3
Glubhole La PL15 . . . . .27 E4
GLUVIAN 45 E7
Gluyas The TR11 . . . . .144 E1

Glynn Ave 8 TR13 . . . . 146 C5
Glynn Rd Liskeard PL14 . . . . 113 A5
Padstow PL28 . . . . 107 D5
Glynn Valley La 9 PL9 . . . 129 D1
Glyn Way TR3 . . . . 69 D3
Goad Ave Plymouth PL4 . . . . 149 C2
Torpoint PL11 . . . . 126 E3
Goad Cl PL11 . . . . 126 F3
Godding Gdns PL6 . . . . 124 E6
Godolphin Ave TR17 . . . . 89 B5
Godolphin Bridge TR27 . . . . 90 D7
Godolphin Cl TR17 . . . . 89 B6
Godolphin Cres TR13 . . . . . . 90 E6
GODOLPHIN CROSS 90 E6
Godolphin Cross TR13 . . . . . 90 E6
Godolphin Ct 5 TR14 . . . . . 138 D3
Godolphin Dr TR17 . . . . 89 B5
Godolphin Est TR13 . . . . 90 D6
Godolphin Ho ★ TR13 . . . . . . 90 E6
Godolphin Ho PL19 . . . . 147 C5
Godolphin Pk 11 PL17 . . . . . . 39 E4
Godolphin Pl TR17 . . . . 89 B5
Godolphin Prim Sch TR13 . 90 E6
Godolphin Rd
Falmouth TR11 . . . . 144 F5
Helston TR13 . . . . 146 C6
Longrock TR20 . . . . 88 F6
Pengwedna TR13 . . . . 91 B6
Godolphin Terr TR17 . . . . 89 B5
Godolphin View TR14 . . . . . 138 D1
Godolphin Way TR7 . . . . . . 111 B7
Godrevy Ct TR26 . . . . 141 B7
Godrevy Dr TR27 . . . . 142 E6
Godrevy Ho TR1 . . . . 69 E4
Godrevy Terr 28 TR26 . . . . . 141 B6
GODREVY TOWANS 66 B3
GOLANT 61 A5
GOLBERDON 39 C6
Golberdon Rd PL17 . . . . 39 A5
Goldbank Bglws PL30 . . . . . . 34 C2
Golden Bank Pk TR11 . . . . . 144 E1
Golden Sands 11 TR6 . . . . . . 55 A5
Goldfinch Cl PL15 . . . . 106 E4
Goldfinch Gdns PL19 . . . . . 147 D2
Goldfinch Gr PL12 . . . . 122 D4
Goldmartin Cl TR11 . . . . 93 D3
Goldmartin Sq TR11 . . . . . . 93 D3
GOLDSITHNEY 89 D5
Goldsmith Gdns PL5 . . . . . . 124 D3
Goldsworthy Dr EX23 . . . . . 104 E5
Goldsworthy Way PL27 . . . . 108 B5
Golf Course Hill PL27 . . . . . 21 D2
Golf House Rd EX23 . . . . . . 104 D6
Golf Links Rd PL20 . . . . 42 A1
Golf Terr TR7 . . . . 110 C6
Golf View TR14 . . . . 79 B2
Golitha Falls National Nature
Reserve ★ PL14 . . . . 37 D3
Golitha Rise PL14 . . . . 113 E6
GOLLAWATER 55 A1
Golva Cl TR13 . . . . 91 E4
GONAMENA 38 B5
GONVENA 108 C6
Gonvena Hill PL27 . . . . 108 D6
Gonvena Ho PL27 . . . . 108 C6
Gonwin Manor Dr TR26 . . . 141 E1
Goodern Drive TR1 . . . . TR3 69
Goodeve Cl PL9 . . . . 135 E6
Goodmans La PL14 . . . . 38 D4
Goodwin Ave PL6 . . . . 125 A6
Goodwin Cres PL12 . . . . . . 128 A6
Goonabarn Cotts PL26 . . . . 58 C5
Goonabarn Rd PL26 . . . . . . 58 C5
Goonamarris PL26 . . . . 58 C6
Goonavean Pk PL26 . . . . . . 58 D5
Goonbarrow Mdw PL26 . . . 47 C1
GOONBELL 68 D8
GOON GUMPAS 68 F1
Goongumpas La TR16 . . . . . 68 E1
GOONHAVERN 55 E4
Goonhavern Ind Est TR4 . . 55 D4
Goonhavern Prim Sch TR4 . 55 D4
Goonhilly Cl TR4 . . . . 55 D4
Goonhilly Downs
Trevassack TR12 . . . . 99 F4
Trezise TR12 . . . . 100 C4
GOONHUSBAND 146 C1
Goonlaze TR5 . . . . 54 D1
Goonlaze Terr TR3 . . . . 80 D4
GOONOWN 54 D1
Goonown La TR5 . . . . 54 D1
Goonown Rd Goonbell TR5 . 68 D8
St Agnes TR5 . . . . 54 D1
Goonrawe TR16 . . . . 67 F4
Goonrea PL13 . . . . 117 B4
Goonreeve TR10 . . . . 81 D3
Goonvean Hill PL26 . . . . 58 B5
Goonvean La TR12 . . . . 103 C7
GOONVREA 68 B8
Goonvrea TR3 . . . . 81 D5
Goonvrea Cl TR7 . . . . 110 F4
Goonvrea Ct TR7 . . . . 110 F4
Goonvrea Rd TR5 . . . . 54 C1
Goonwartha Cl PL13 . . . . . . 117 C4
Goonwartha Rd PL13 . . . . . 117 B3
Gooseberry La Pensilva PL14 38 E4
Plymouth PL1 . . . . 148 B2
Gooseford La PL11 . . . . 132 C8
GOOSEHAM 2 C3
Goosewell Hill PL6 . . . . 135 F6
Goosewell Park Rd PL9 . . . 135 F6
Goosewell Prim Sch PL9 . . 135 F6
Goosewell Rd PL9 . . . . 135 F6
Goosewell Terr PL9 . . . . 135 F6
Gorbut Gdns PL19 . . . . 147 D4
Gordon Ct PL12 . . . . 122 D2
Gordon Pl 8 TR9 . . . . 45 E6
Gordons Cl TR3 . . . . 80 F3

Gordon Terr PL4 . . . . 128 E4
GORRAN CHURCHTOWN . . . 73 B1
GORRAN HAVEN 85 D5
GORRAN HIGH LANES 72 F2
Gorran Sch PL26 . . . . 85 B5
Gorse Cl TR7 . . . . 111 A4
Gorsey Cl PL5 . . . . 124 E2
Gorvin Cross EX39 . . . . 3 E6
Goss Moor National Nature
Reserve ★ PL26 . . . . 46 B2
Goswela Cl PL26 . . . . 135 F5
Goswela Gdns PL9 . . . . 135 F5
Gotch Gdns PL14 . . . . 50 B6
GOTHERS 46 D1
Gothers Hill Hendra PL26 . . 58 C8
St Dennis PL26 . . . . 46 D1
Gothers Rd PL26 . . . . 46 D1
Goudges La PL26 . . . . 58 E8
Gounce The 14 TR6 . . . . 55 A5
Gover Cl TR4 . . . . 68 C6
Gover Hill TR4 . . . . 68 C6
Gover La TR7 . . . . 110 D6
Gover Rd PL25 . . . . 114 B4
Goverseth Hill PL26 . . . . 58 D6
Goverseth Rd PL26 . . . . 58 D6
Goverseth Terr PL26 . . . . . . 58 D6
GOVER VALLEY 59 A4
Govetts Field 5 PL15 . . . . 106 D4
Gower Ridge Rd PL9 . . . . . 135 D6
Goyne's Field TR4 . . . . 68 A7
Gracca Terr PL26 . . . . 47 C1
Grade Rd TR12 . . . . 102 C4
Grade-Ruan CE Prim Sch
TR12 . . . . 103 B5
Grafton Rd PL4 . . . . 128 E4
Graham Ave PL25 . . . . 114 E4
Graham Rd TR15 . . . . 140 C5
Grainge Rd PL6 . . . . 125 A1
Grammers Park PL15 . . . . . 106 A5
GRAMPOUND 72 B7
Grampound Hill TR2 . . . . . . 72 B7
GRAMPOUND ROAD 57 E1
Grampound Road Ind Est
TR2 . . . . 57 E1
Grampound Road Village CE
Sch TR2 . . . . 57 E1
Grampound-with-Creed CE
Sch TR2 . . . . 72 A7
Granby Ct PL1 . . . . 127 E2
Granby Gn PL1 . . . . 127 E2
Granby Pl PL1 . . . . 127 E2
Granby St PL1 . . . . 127 E2
Granby Way PL1 . . . . 127 E2
Grand Hotel Rd PL1 . . . . . . 148 B1
Grand Par PL1 . . . . 148 B1
Grange Rd Helston TR13 . . 146 B5
Plymouth PL7 . . . . 131 A4
Yelverton PL20 . . . . 42 C3
Grange The PL14 . . . . 38 E1
Granite Way Callington PL17 . 39 F4
Trembraze PL14 . . . . 113 D8
Grannery Ct EX23 . . . . 104 D5
Granny Polly La TR13 . . . . . . 90 E5
Granny's Gn PL31 . . . . 109 E3
Granny's La TR6 . . . . 55 A4
Grantham Cl PL7 . . . . 130 B4
Grantley Gdns PL3 . . . . 129 A5
Grant's Cl PL25 . . . . 114 C3
Grant's Wlk 4 PL25 . . . . . . 114 C3
Granville Terr EX23 . . . . 104 D5
Grasmere Cl PL6 . . . . 124 E5
Grasmere La PL14 . . . . 38 B5
Grassendale Ave PL2 . . . . . 127 F7
Grass La PL2 . . . . 128 C4
Grassmere Way PL12 . . . . . 122 D4
Grass Valley Pk PL31 . . . . . 109 F1
Grassy La PL14 . . . . 36 E1
Gratton Cross PL20 . . . . 42 D2
Gratton La PL20 . . . . 42 D2
Gratton Pl PL6 . . . . 125 A1
Gravellings La PL30 . . . . 22 F5
Gravesend Gdns PL11 . . . . 127 B3
Gravesend Wlk PL11 . . . . . 123 D4
Graybridge Rd
12 Horrabridge PL20 . . . . . 42 C4
Horrabridge PL20 . . . . 42 C4
Gray Cres PL5 . . . . 127 C8
Great Berry Rd PL6 . . . . 124 F1
GREAT BOSULLOW 87 D8
Great Charles Cl PL26 . . . . . 58 B4
Great Churchway PL9 . . . . . 136 A7
Greatfield Rd PL3 . . . . 129 B7
Greatlands Cres PL2 . . . . . . 128 A6
Greatlands Pl 5 PL2 . . . . . . 128 A5
Great Mdw PL14 . . . . 36 F2
Great Mills Ind Parc PL25 . 115 E4
Great Mis Tor Cl 5 PL20 . . 42 C3
Great Orchard Cl PL9 . . . . . 135 E5
Great Park Cl 4 PL7 . . . . . 131 C5
Great Western Commercial
Village PL22 . . . . 112 D2
Great Western Rd PL1 . . . . 148 B1
Great Wheal Seton TR14 . . 138 F6
Greatwood TR11 . . . . 82 C3
Great Woodford Dr PL7 . . . 130 B6
Great Work TR13 . . . . 90 E5
Grebe Cl PL7 . . . . 130 F5
Greeb Way TR20 . . . . 89 D4
Green Acre PL15 . . . . 28 A5
Greenacres Bodmin PL30 . . 34 C2
Plymouth PL9 . . . . 135 F8
Greenbank
Connor Downs TR27 . . . . . . 78 D6
1 Penzance TR18 . . . . . . 143 D5
Plymouth PL4 . . . . 149 B4
Polruan PL23 . . . . 116 D2
Whitehill TR13 . . . . 146 C4
Greenbank Ave PL4 . . . . . . 149 B3

Greenbank Cl TR2 . . . . 57 E1
Greenbank Cottages PL4 . 149 B4
Greenbank Cres TR7 . . . . . 111 C7
Greenbank La PL14 . . . . . . 113 C6
Greenbank Rd Devoran TR3 . 81 F6
Liskeard PL14 . . . . 113 C6
Plymouth PL4 . . . . 149 B4
Greenbanks Rd PL26 . . . . . 21 E2
Greenbank Terr
1 Callington PL17 . . . . 39 F4
Plymouth PL4 . . . . 149 B4
GREEN BOTTOM 69 B4
Greenbury TR20 . . . . 90 A4
Green Cl Feock TR3 . . . . 82 C5
Truro TR1 . . . . 137 B3
Green Cres TR13 . . . . 146 D7
Greendale Rd PL2 . . . . 128 A7
Green Field Cl TR12 . . . . . . 102 F2
Greenfield Rd PL12 . . . . 122 D2
Greenfields Cl TR11 . . . . 93 D3
Greenfield Terr TR16 . . . . . . 67 D6
Greenfinch Cres PL12 . . . . 122 E4
Green Hill Lamerton PL19 . . 30 A3
St Martin PL18 . . . . 100 D6
Tavistock PL19 . . . . 147 D5
Wadebridge PL27 . . . . 108 E5
Greenhill Cl PL9 . . . . 135 F5
Greenhill Rd PL9 . . . . 136 A5
Greenhills PL32 . . . . 105 C5
Green Hill Terr TR11 . . . . . 100 D4
Green Hill Villas PL27 . . . . 108 E5
Greenla Treator PL28 . . . . . . 21 A2
Treator PL28 . . . . 107 A3
Green La Bodmin PL31 . . . 109 F2
Boscastle PL35 . . . . 9 C1
Crantock TR8 . . . . 43 D3
Fowey PL23 . . . . 116 C5
Gwithian TR27 . . . . 66 B2
Kingsand PL10 . . . . 133 A2
Lelant TR26 . . . . 77 E4
Lizard TR12 . . . . 103 A2
Marazion TR17 . . . . 89 B6
Penryn TR10 . . . . 144 B8
Porthleven TR13 . . . . 91 B1
Portreath TR16 . . . . 67 C6
Redruth, Plain-an-Gwarry
TR15 . . . . 140 B5
Redruth, Wheal Rose TR16 . 68 C4
Rock PL27 . . . . 21 D2
Tavistock PL19 . . . . 30 F1
Tavistock PL19 . . . . 147 E5
Tremough TR10 . . . . 81 D1
Truro TR1 . . . . 137 B3
Veryan TR2 . . . . 83 F6
Yelverton PL20 . . . . 42 C1
Greenland PL10 . . . . 132 F5
Greenlands Est PL19 . . . . . 147 D5
Green Lane EX39 . . . . 3 A7
Green Lane Cl TR10 . . . . . . 144 B8
Green Lane Hill TR18 . . . . . 143 F8
Green Lane Vean TR15 . . . . 140 B5
Green La The W TR17 . . . . . 89 B6
Green Lees Dr PL7 . . . . 131 B3
Greenmarket The 26 TR18 143 E5
Green Mdws PL32 . . . . 105 C4
Green Parc Rd TR27 . . . . . . 142 D5
Green Park Ave PL4 . . . . . . 128 D4
Green Park Rd PL9 . . . . 135 E5
Green Pk PL10 . . . . 133 A2
Greenscoombe La PL17 . . . 40 C8
GREENSPLAT 59 A6
Greensplat Rd PL25 . . . . . . 114 A6
Green St Penzance TR18 . . 143 F4
Truro TR1 . . . . 137 D4
Greens The TR19 . . . . 96 C7
Greensway Rd PL19 . . . . . . 147 A4
Green The Bridgerule EX22 . . 8 A5
5 Horrabridge PL20 . . . . . 42 C5
Kingsand PL10 . . . . 133 A2
Liskeard PL14 . . . . 113 B5
Meavy PL20 . . . . 42 F2
Milton Combe PL20 . . . . . 120 F8
Nancegollan TR13 . . . . 91 B7
Plymouth, Ernesettle PL5 . 123 E3
Plymouth, Hooe PL9 . . . . 135 B6
Probus TR2 . . . . 71 C6
St Buryan TR19 . . . . 97 A4
St Martin TR12 . . . . 100 D6
Saltash PL12 . . . . 122 C3
6 Trewoon PL25 . . . . 59 A3
Greenvalley Rd PL31 . . . . . 109 A5
Greenway Ave PL7 . . . . 130 B6
Greenway Cl 2 PL20 . . . . . 42 C5
Greenwich Pl PL12 . . . . 122 F3
Greenwith Cl TR3 . . . . 137 B3
Greenwith Cres TR3 . . . . . . 81 D6
Greenwith Hill TR3 . . . . 81 D6
Greenwith Rd TR3 . . . . 81 D6
Greenwix Parc PL30 . . . . . . 34 D8
Greenwood Cres TR10 . . . . 144 A8
Greenwood Park Cl PL7 . . . 131 B6
Greenwood Park Rd PL7 . . 131 B6
Greenwood Rd TR10 . . . . . 144 A8
Gregor Rd TR1 . . . . 137 F5
Gregory's Ct 10 PL31 . . . . 109 D5
Gregory's Mdw PL15 . . . . . 106 F3
Grenfell Ave PL12 . . . . 122 D3
Grenfell Gdns PL12 . . . . . . 122 C3
Grenfell St 19 TR19 . . . . . . 88 C1
Grenifer Rd TR15 . . . . 139 D7
Grenna La TR3 . . . . 81 D7
GRENOFEN 42 A6
Grenofen Cl PL19 . . . . 42 A6
Grenville Cl Callington PL17 . 39 F4
Nanpean PL26 . . . . 58 D6
Grenville Cres TR11 . . . . . . 144 F5
Grenville Ct Plymouth PL7 . 131 C6

Grenville Ct continued
2 St Austell PL25 . . . . . . 114 C3
Grenville Dr 6 St Agnes TR5 54 D1
Tavistock PL19 . . . . 147 B3
Grenville Gdns TR14 . . . . . . 79 E5
Grenville Mdws
Lostwithiel PL22 . . . . 112 E2
St Austell PL25 . . . . 58 D7
Grenville Meadow PL19 . . 147 B3
Grenville Pk PL26 . . . . 47 C5
Grenville Rd Falmouth TR11 145 A5
Helston TR13 . . . . 146 D5
Lostwithiel PL22 . . . . 112 E2
Padstow PL28 . . . . 107 C4
Plymouth PL4 . . . . 149 C3
Truro TR1 . . . . 137 B5
Grenville Road Lane S PL4 129 B2
Grenville Wlk PL13 . . . . 62 D2
Gresham Ct Newquay TR7 . 110 F7
Plymouth PL5 . . . . 124 C7
Greyfriars TR11 . . . . 145 C2
Grey Mare Hill PL22 . . . . . . 49 B7
Greys Terr 1 TR16 . . . . 140 F1
Greystoke Ave PL6 . . . . 129 D7
Greystone Ave PL26 . . . . . . 58 E5
Greystones TR9 . . . . 57 E8
Gribbas Cl TR3 . . . . 80 F3
Gribbas Cnr TR3 . . . . 80 F3
Gribben Cl PL25 . . . . 114 E6
Gribben Rd PL25 . . . . 114 E6
Gribbon Way PL24 . . . . 60 C4
Griffins The PL14 . . . . 113 D6
Griffin Way PL9 . . . . 136 C6
Griggs Cl PL7 . . . . 131 B4
Griggs Hill TR27 . . . . 77 E3
GRIMSCOTT 5 A2
Grimscott Est EX23 . . . . 5 B2
Grimspound Cl PL6 . . . . 129 E8
Grimstone Terr PL20 . . . . . . 42 B2
Grist La TR27 . . . . 78 C5
Grizedale Rd PL6 . . . . 129 D7
Grose Hill Cres 11 PL26 . . 59 D7
Grose Mdws PL26 . . . . 58 B8
Grosvenor Ave TR7 . . . . . . 110 E6
Grosvenor Cotts 1 PL4 . . 128 F5
Grosvenor Pl PL25 . . . . 114 B4
Grosvenor Rd PL6 . . . . 124 F2
Grove Cl 2 PL6 . . . . 124 C6
Grove Cotts TR2 . . . . 57 C1
Grove Dr 4 PL14 . . . . 51 A7
Grove Hill
Mawnan Smith TR11 . . . . . 93 D3
St Mawes TR2 . . . . 95 A6
Grovehill Cres TR11 . . . . . . 145 C3
Grovehill Dr TR11 . . . . 145 C3
Grovehill Ho TR11 . . . . 145 C3
Grove La TR20 . . . . 89 F5
Grove Park Ct PL14 . . . . . . 113 B4
Grove Pk PL24 . . . . 60 C6
Tavistock PL19 . . . . 147 D5
Torpoint PL11 . . . . 126 E3
Grove Pl 3 PL25 . . . . 145 C3
Grove Rd Par PL24 . . . . 115 F6
St Austell PL25 . . . . 114 B4
Grove The
Plymouth, Plymstock PL9 . 135 D8
Plymouth, Stoke PL3 . . . . 128 A4
Grovewood Ct TR9 . . . . 45 E1
Growan Rd PL25 . . . . 115 A6
GRUMBLA 87 C6
Grylls Parc TR13 . . . . 146 B6
Grylls Pk PL13 . . . . 62 A7
Guardian Ct 6 PL31 . . . . . 109 E5
Guelder Way 4 PL6 . . . . . . 124 C6
Gue The 2 TR13 . . . . 98 C8
GUILDFORD 142 E6
Guildford Cl Foxhole PL26 . 58 D6
Plymouth PL5 . . . . 124 E3
Guildford Rd PL27 . . . . 142 E7
Guildford Road Ind Est
TR27 . . . . 142 E6
Guildford St PL4 . . . . 149 A3
Guildhall La PL12 . . . . 122 C2
Guildhall Sq PL1 . . . . 148 C2
Guineaport Parc PL27 . . . . 108 C5
Guineaport Rd PL27 . . . . . . 108 C5
Guipavas Rd PL17 . . . . 39 F4
Guisseny Pl TR13 . . . . 91 B1
Gulland Rd PL21 . . . . 21 D6
Gull Rock Newquay TR7 . . . 110 A5
Wadebridge PL27 . . . . 21 D2
GULVAL 88 E6
Gulval Almshouses TR18 . 143 F8
Gulval Comm Prim Sch
TR18 . . . . 88 E6
Gulval Cross TR18 . . . . 143 F8
GULWORTHY 41 B8
Gulworthy Cotts PL19 . . . . 41 B7
Gulworthy Cross PL19 . . . . 41 B7
Gulworthy Prim Sch PL19 . 41 B7
Gun Hill Rd TR8 . . . . 43 B1
GUNNISLAKE 40 F5
Gunnislake Prim Sch PL18 . 40 F6
Gunnislake Sta PL18 . . . . . 40 F5
Gunnislake Rural Workshops
PL18 . . . . 40 F6
Gunpool La 9 PL35 . . . . 9 C1
Gunver PL28 . . . . 31 F7
GUNWALLOE 98 E5
Gunwalloe Rd TR12 . . . . . . 99 A7
Gunwin Cl PL26 . . . . 58 D8
Gurlyn Hill TR20 . . . . 90 A7
Gurnard Wlk PL3 . . . . 129 C6
Gurney Cl TR9 Bude EX23 . 104 E7
Torpoint PL11 . . . . 126 F3
Gurney's La 2 PL14 . . . . . . 138 D3
Gurneys Mews 6 TR14 . . . 138 D3

Gly–Gwi 161

Gurnick Est TR18 . . . . 143 B2
Gurnick Rd TR18 . . . . 143 B1
Gurnick St 24 TR19 . . . . . . 88 C1
Gustavus Rd TR14 . . . . 138 D3
Guttry Rd TR8 . . . . 43 D3
Gutt Rd PL27 . . . . 22 C7
Guy Miles Way PL5 . . . . . . 124 B3
GWALLON 89 C6
Gwallon La TR17 . . . . 89 C6
Gwallon Rd PL25 . . . . 114 E5
Gwarak Agravayn 1 TR7 . 111 E6
Gwarak An Warak TR1 . . . . 137 B2
Gwarak Esels TR8 . . . . 111 D5
Gwarak Gwel An Mor
Portscatho TR2 . . . . 83 B2
9 Portscatho TR20 . . . . . . 95 D8
Gwarak Nansavalen 1
TR1 . . . . 137 B2
Gwarak Tewdar TR1 . . . . . . 137 B2
Gwarak Trystan 1 TR7 . . . 111 D6
Gwarder Pl 2 TR14 . . . . . . 138 D4
Gwarnick Rd TR1 . . . . 137 B4
Gwartha Cl PL25 . . . . 115 C4
Gwarth an Drae TR13 . . . . 146 C8
Gwarth an Dre TR27 . . . . . 142 E8
GWAVAS 91 D4
Gwavas Bglws 4 TR18 . . . 143 C1
Gwavas La TR18 . . . . 88 C2
Gwavas Quay 7 TR18 . . . . 143 C2
Gwavas Rd TR18 . . . . 143 C1
Gwavas St 9 TR18 . . . . 143 E6
Gweal-an-Top TR15 . . . . . . 140 D5
Gweal Darras TR10 . . . . 81 C1
Gwealdues TR13 . . . . 146 D7
Gwealdues Ct TR13 . . . . . . 146 D7
GWEALFOLDS 146 C7
Gwealfolds Rd TR13 . . . . . 146 C7
Gweal Gollas TR27 . . . . 142 E8
Gwealhellis Warren TR13 146 B7
Gwealmayowe Pk TR13 . . 146 D6
Gweal Mellin TR11 . . . . 93 A3
Gweal Pawl TR15 . . . . 140 A4
Gweal Wartha TR13 . . . . . . 146 B8
Gweal Wollas Fields 3
TR12 . . . . 99 A4
Gwedhennek TR18 . . . . 143 F7
GWEDNA TR13 . . . . 90 F7
GWEEK 92 C1
Gweek Downs TR12 . . . . . . 92 B2
Gweek Dr Gweek TR12 . . . . 92 C1
Mawgan TR12 . . . . 99 D8
Gweek La TR13 . . . . 92 A3
Gweek Quay TR12 . . . . 92 A1
Gwel an Garrek 2 TR12 . . . 99 A1
Gwel-an-amor
1 Marazion TR17 . . . . 89 C5
St Austell PL25 . . . . 115 A5
Trenance TR8 . . . . 31 C2
Gwel-an-amor Apartments
TR26 . . . . 141 C4
Gwelanmor Cl TR26 . . . . . . 141 D2
Gwelanmor Rd TR26 . . . . . 141 D2
Gwel-an-Nans Cl 2 PL14 113 B5
Gwel-an-Scol TR3 . . . . 82 C5
Gwel-an-Skol TR14 . . . . . . 138 E5
Gwel an Wheal TR26 . . . . . 141 A4
Gwel an Wheal Cres TR26 141 A4
Gwel An Woon 5 TR4 . . . . 55 B4
Gwel Avon Bsns Pk PL12 . 122 D4
Gwelavon Cl PL27 . . . . 108 D5
Gwelenys Rd 3 TR19 . . . . . 88 C1
Gwel Eryon 3 TR14 . . . . . . 138 F2
Gwel Gwarthe TR16 . . . . . . 68 C3
Gwel Kann TR15 . . . . 139 C8
Gwel Ke 3 TR1 . . . . 137 B2
Gwell-an-Nans TR2 . . . . 71 C6
Gwel Lowern TR18 . . . . 88 E6
Gwel Marten Flats TR26 . . 141 C4
Gwelmeneth TR13 . . . . 146 B4
Gwelmeneth Pk 8 PL14 . . 38 A3
Gwel Mengleth PL27 . . . . . 108 D5
Gwelmor TR14 . . . . 138 E2
Gwel-Mor 9 TR19 . . . . 75 A1
Gwel-Tek TR27 . . . . 142 D8
Gwel Trencrom TR27 . . . . . 142 E3
Gwendra La PL25 . . . . 58 E8
Gwendreath Gwente TR12 . 103 C7
Trelan TR12 . . . . 100 C1
Gwendroc Cl TR1 . . . . 137 D3
Gwendroc Ho TR1 . . . . 137 D3
Gwendroc House Mews
TR1 . . . . 137 D3
Gwendrona Cl TR13 . . . . . 146 D8
Gwendrona Way TR13 . . . 146 D8
GWENNAP 80 F7
Gwennap Pit ★ TR16 . . . . . 140 F4
Gwenter Rd TR12 . . . . 103 D7
Gwindra Ind Est PL26 . . . . 58 C3
Gwindra Rd PL26 . . . . 58 B4
GWINEAR 78 E4
Gwinear Com Prim Sch
TR27 . . . . 78 E4
Gwinear La TR27 . . . . 78 E4
Gwinear Rd TR27 . . . . 78 E4
GWITHIAN 66 B2
Gwithian Cl St Austell PL25 114 E7
Torpoint PL11 . . . . 126 F4
Gwithian Green Nature
Reserve ★ TR27 . . . . 78 C8
Gwithian La 1 TR10 . . . . . 144 A8
Gwithian Rd PL25 . . . . 114 E7
Connor Downs TR27 . . . . . 78 D6
Gwithian Sands Chalet Pk
TR27 . . . . 66 B1
GWITHIAN TOWANS 66 A2

Gwithian Towans TR27 . . . .78 C7
Gwithian Towers Nature
  Reserve★ TR27 . . . . .78 B8
Gwyn Rd PL4 . . . . .149 C4
Gwythian Way TR6 . . . . .55 A4
Gyllyng Hall TR11. . . . . . . .145 B3
Gyllyng St TR11. . . . . .145 B4
Gyllyngvase Hill TR11. . . . .145 B2
Gyllyngvase Rd TR11. . . . . .145 C2
Gyllyngvase Terr TR11. . . . .145 C2
Gypsy Corner Rd PL30 . . . . . .46 D7
Gypsy La Delabole PL33 . . . . .14 C1
  St Elvan TR13. . . . . .91 C2

H

Haddington Rd PL2. . . . . . . .127 F4
Haddon Way PL25 . . . . .115 D3
Haddy's Row PL14. . . . . .39 A2
Haig Pl 6 TR18. . . . . .143 C7
Hain Wlk TR26. . . . . .141 C4
Halabezack TR13 . . . . .92 C8
HALAMANNING 90 A6
Halbullock View TR1 . . . . . . .69 E3
Halcyon Ct PL2 . . . . .128 A6
Halcyon Rd PL2 . . . . .128 A6
Haldon Pl PL5 . . . . .124 A3
Halecombe Rd 10 PL9 . . . . .129 D1
HALE MILLS 69 A1
Haley Barton 4 PL2 . . . . . .128 A5
HALGABRON 14 E7
Halgavor La Bodmin PL31 . . .109 E2
  Little Kirland PL31. . . . . . . .48 C8
Halgavor Pk PL31. . . . . .109 F1
Halgavor Rd PL30, PL31. . . . .109 D2
Halgavor View PL31 . . . . . . .109 F2
Halifax Rd PL27. . . . . .31 F3
Halimote Rd PL26 . . . . .58 C8
Hallane Rd PL25 . . . . .115 A6
Hallaze Rd PL26 . . . . .59 D7
Hallerton Cl PL6. . . . . .125 E2
Hallett Cl PL12 . . . . .122 B3
Hallett Way EX23 . . . . .104 F7
HALLEW 47 C2
Hallew Rd PL26. . . . . .58 C7
Halley Gdns PL5. . . . . .123 E1
Hall for Cornwall (Theatre)
  The★ 21 TR1 . . . . .137 D4
HALLIVICK 58 A4
Halloon Ave 9 TR9 . . . . .45 E2
Hall Rd PL26. . . . . .58 C8
Hall Terr PL23 . . . . .116 E5
HALLWORTHY 16 D6
HALSETOWN 77 A5
Halsetown Rd TR26 . . . . .77 A5
Halter Cl 2 PL5 . . . . .124 C8
Halton Quay
  Bohetherick PL18 . . . . .40 E1
  Greenbank PL20 . . . . .118 D8
Halt Rd Goonhavern TR4 . . . .55 D4
  St Newlyn East TR8 . . . . . . .56 B7
Halvana TR15. . . . . .140 D3
Halvarras Pk TR3 . . . . .82 B8
Halvarras Rd TR3 . . . . .82 B8
Halvasso Herniss TR10 . . . . . .80 F1
  3 Longdowns TR10 . . . . . .81 A1
Halveor Cl 5 TR9. . . . . .45 E6
Halveor Ct TR6 . . . . .55 B5
Halveor La TR9 . . . . .45 D6
HALVOSSO 93 A8
HALWIN 92 B8
Halwin TR13. . . . . .00 C1
Halwin Cres TR13. . . . . .92 B8
Halwin La TR13. . . . . .92 B8
Halwin Sch TR13. . . . . .92 B8
Halwyn Ave Crantock TR8 . . .110 A3
  Trevella TR8. . . . . .43 E3
Halwyn Cl 12 TR3 . . . . .81 F7
Halwyn Hill TR8 . . . . .110 A3
Halwyn Pl TR11. . . . . .137 B4
Halwyn Rd TR8 . . . . .110 A3
Halwyn Terr TR1 . . . . .137 B3
Halye Vw PL27. . . . . .108 A6
HAM. 128 A8
Hamble Cl PL3 . . . . .129 D7
Ham Cl PL2. . . . . .128 B8
Ham Dr PL2 . . . . .128 B8
Ham Field PL27. . . . . .21 D5
Ham Gn PL2. . . . . .128 A7
Ham Green Ct PL2. . . . . . . .128 A7
Ham Green La PL2. . . . . . . .128 A7
Ham Ho PL2 . . . . .128 A8
Hamilton Cl TR27. . . . . .142 B4
Hamilton Gdns PL4. . . . . . . .128 A7
Hamilton Pl TR11. . . . . .145 D3
Ham La PL2 . . . . .128 A8
Hammer Dr PL25 . . . . .114 E7
Hammill's Cl 13 TR13. . . . . . .98 C8
Hammills Dr 12 TR13 . . . . . . .98 C8
Hamoaze Ave PL5 . . . . .127 D8
Hamoaze Pl PL11. . . . . .127 D2
Hamoaze Rd PL11. . . . . .127 B2
Hampton Cl TR7. . . . . .110 D6
Hampton St PL4. . . . . .149 A3
Hancock Cl PL6 . . . . .124 D6
Hancock La 14 TR2 . . . . .95 A6
Hangar La PL6 . . . . .125 B5
Hangmans Hill TR14. . . . . . . .79 F3
Hangmans La 32 PL17. . . . . . .39 F4
Hangmans Wlk TR11. . . . . . .145 A1
Hannaford Rd PL16. . . . . .19 F3
HANNAFORE 117 C2
Hannafore Rd PL13. . . . . . . .117 C3

Hannafore La PL13 . . . . . . .117 D2
Hannafore Rd PL13 . . . . . . .117 D2
Hanover Cl
  17 Perranporth TR6. . . . . . .55 A5
  Plymouth PL3. . . . . .129 B5
Hanover Ct Camborne TR14 . .138 E4
  10 Penzance TR18 . . . . . . .143 E5
  16 Penzance TR18 . . . . . . .143 E5
Hanover Ho EX23 . . . . .4 D4
Hanover Parc TR9 . . . . .45 F2
Hanover Pk TR9 . . . . .45 F2
Hanover Rd PL3 . . . . .129 C4
Hanson Dr PL23 . . . . .116 C3
Hanson Rd PL14 . . . . .113 D6
Harbour Ave Plymouth PL4 . .149 A2
  Plymouth, Camels Head PL5 .127 E8
Harbour Ct Falmouth TR11. . .145 B4
  15 Penzance TR18. . . . . . .143 E5
  Portreath TR16 . . . . .67 C6
Harbour Lights 11 TR18 . . . .143 C1
Harbour Mews
  2 Carn Towan TR19 . . . . . .86 D1
  Sennen Cove TR19 . . . . . . .96 B7
Harbour Rd Par PL24 . . . . . . .60 C4
  Wadebridge PL27 . . . . . . .108 C5
Harbourside 12 TR13 . . . . . . .98 B8
Harbour Side PL13 . . . . .117 C3
Harbour St PL11 . . . . .127 B3
Harbour Terr
  Falmouth TR11. . . . . .145 B5
  Portreath TR16 . . . . .67 C6
Harbour View Fowey PL23 . .116 C4
  Hayle TR27. . . . . .142 B5
  Marazion TR17. . . . . .89 B5
  Penryn TR10 . . . . .144 B8
  Plymouth PL9. . . . . .135 A7
  5 Porthleven TR13 . . . . . . .98 B8
  Saltash PL12 . . . . .122 E2
  Truro TR1. . . . . .137 E3
Harbour View Cres TR18. . . .143 E6
HARCOURT. 82 B4
Harcourt Cl TR1. . . . . .69 F3
Harcourt La TR3 . . . . .82 B5
Harding Mdw PL2 . . . . .63 F8
Hardings Cl PL12 . . . . .122 E3
HARDISWORTHY 2 D7
Hardisworthy Cross EX39 . . . .2 E7
Hardwick Farm PL7 . . . . . . .130 C3
Hardy Cres PL5 . . . . .124 E1
Hardy Ho TR3 . . . . .80 F3
Harebell Cl PL12. . . . . .122 D4
Harefield Cres TR14 . . . . . . .138 D4
Hareston Cl PL7 . . . . .131 B3
Harewood Cl PL7. . . . . .130 E5
Harewood Cres PL5 . . . . . . .124 B2
Harewood Rd PL18 . . . . .41 A3
Hargood Terr 6 PL2 . . . . . . .127 F4
Hargreaves Cl PL5. . . . . .123 F2
Harlech Cl PL3 . . . . .129 A7
Harleigh Rd PL31 . . . . .109 E3
Harleigh Terr PL31 . . . . .109 E3
Harlequins 27 TR26 . . . . . . .141 B5
HARLYN 20 D2
Harlyn Barton PL28. . . . . . . .20 D2
Harlyn Cotts PL28 . . . . .20 D2
Harlyn Drive PL2 . . . . .128 D8
Harlyn Rd PL28 . . . . .20 D1
Harmer Pl PL31. . . . . .109 D6
Harmony Cl Redruth TR15 . . .140 B6
  Roche PL26. . . . . .46 F3
Harmony Mdw PL26 . . . . .46 F3
Harmony Rd PL26 . . . . .46 F3
Harmony Terr
  4 Illogan TR16. . . . . .67 E4
  Truro TR1. . . . . .137 E2
Harnorlen Rd PL2 . . . . .128 D7
Haroldsleigh Ave PL5. . . . . .124 E2
Harpers Mdw PL15 . . . . .27 B7
Harriet Gdns PL7 . . . . .130 B6
Harriet Pl TR11 . . . . .145 A5
Harris Cl 1 Penryn TR10 . . .144 C7
  Plymouth PL9. . . . . .135 B6
Harris Mill TR16 . . . . .67 F4
Harrison Gdns TR15 . . . . . . .139 D7
Harrison St 7 PL2. . . . . . . .127 F4
Harrison Terr TR1 . . . . .137 B4
Harriss Hill TR3 . . . . .82 A7
HARROWBARROW 40 D5
Harrowbarrow Sch PL17. . . . .40 D4
Harrowbeer La PL20. . . . . . . .42 C3
Hartland Cl PL6 . . . . .125 A7
Hartland Forest Golf & Leisure
  Parc EX39 . . . . .3 E6
Hartland Rd PL29. . . . . .22 E7
Hartland Terr EX23 . . . . .104 D6
HARTLEY. 128 E7
Hartley Ave PL3 . . . . .129 A6
Hartley Cl PL3 . . . . .129 A6
Hartley Park Gdns PL3. . . . . .128 F6
Hartley Rd PL3 . . . . .128 E6
HARTLEY VALE 129 A8
Hartmeade PL14. . . . . .52 A5
Hartwell Ave PL9 . . . . .136 D7
Harvenna Cl TR9 . . . . .45 E1
Harvenna Hts TR9 . . . . .45 E1
Harvest Cl 1 PL5 . . . . .124 C8
Harvest Moon TR7. . . . . .110 D7
Harvey Ave PL4 . . . . .129 B1
Harvey Rd TR1. . . . . .137 D2
Harvey St PL11 . . . . .127 B3
Harvey's Towans TR27. . . . . .142 A7
Harvey's Way TR27 . . . . .142 C5
Harwell Ct 6 PL1. . . . . .148 B3
Harwell St PL1 . . . . .148 B3
Harwood Ave PL5 . . . . .124 C7
Hastings St PL1 . . . . .148 B3
Hastings Terr PL1. . . . . .148 B3

Haswell Cl PL6 . . . . .129 A8
Hatch's Hill TR27 . . . . .78 C5
Hatchel Cres TR7. . . . . .110 B5
Hat La PL10 . . . . .132 F2
HATT 53 E4
Havelock Terr PL2. . . . . .127 F3
Haven Ct TR27 . . . . .142 C5
Haven Pk PL14 . . . . .39 A2
Haven Rd EX23 . . . . .10 C6
Havett Cl PL14. . . . . .50 E8
Havett Rd Dobwalls PL14. . . .50 E8
  Dobwalls PL14 . . . . .50 E8
Haviland Rd PL14 . . . . .113 E4
Hawarden Cotts PL4. . . . . . .129 B1
Haweswater Cl PL6. . . . . . . .124 E4
Hawke Cl TR7 . . . . .110 D6
Hawken Way 9 TR9 . . . . .45 D6
Hawke Rd TR13. . . . . .146 D4
Hawkers Ave PL4. . . . . .149 A2
Hawkers Ct EX23 . . . . .104 D7
Hawkers La PL3 . . . . .128 E5
Hawkeys Mews TR15 . . . . . .140 D2
Hawkinge Gdns PL5 . . . . . . .123 E4
Hawkins Cl PL6. . . . . .125 A5
Hawkins Ct 2 TR18. . . . . . .143 D5
Hawkins Rd Newquay TR7 . . .110 E5
  Padstow PL28 . . . . .107 C5
  Penzance TR18 . . . . .143 D5
Hawkins Way
  12 Falmouth TR11. . . . . . .145 A4
  Helston TR13. . . . . .146 D6
Hawks Pk PL12 . . . . .122 C2
Hawk's Tor Dr PL15. . . . . . . .27 B7
Hawthorn Ave Bude EX23. . .104 E4
  Torpoint PL11 . . . . .126 F3
Hawthorn Cl Bude EX23. . . .104 E4
  Camelford PL32. . . . . .105 D4
  Plymouth, Hooe PL9 . . . . .135 D7
  Plymouth, Woolwell PL6 . . .125 D7
  St Austell PL25. . . . . .114 F6
  7 St Columb Major TR9 . . . .45 D6
Hawthorn Gr PL2 . . . . .128 C7
Hawthorn Rd PL19. . . . . .147 C2
Hawthorns PL12. . . . . .122 C2
Hawthorn Way
  Plymouth PL3. . . . . .129 B7
  Threemilestone TR3 . . . . . .69 C3
Haxter Cl PL6. . . . . .121 B1
Haydon Gr PL5 . . . . .123 C1
Haydown Cl PL30 . . . . .24 B4
HAYE 40 A5
Haye Common Dr PL15 . . . .106 D3
Haye La PL17 . . . . .39 E5
Haye Rd Callington PL17 . . . .39 D4
  Plymouth PL7, PL9. . . . . . .130 C1
Haye Rd S PL9 . . . . .136 C7
Hayes Pl PL6. . . . . .129 B8
Hayes Rd PL9 . . . . .135 C7
Hay La Looe PL13. . . . . .117 E4
  Sheviock PL11 . . . . .65 B6
HAYLE 142 C6
Hayle Community School
  TR27. . . . . .142 D5
Hayle Ind Pk TR27 . . . . .142 F7
Hayle Rd Crowntown TR13 . . .91 A6
  Fraddam TR27 . . . . .78 C1
Hayle Sta TR27 . . . . .142 B5
Hayle Terr TR27 . . . . .142 C6
Hayman Way TR11. . . . . . . .144 E5
Hayne Corfe Cres TR1 . . . . .137 A4
Hayne Corfe Gdns TR1 . . . . .137 A4
Haystone Pl PL1. . . . . .148 B4
Haytor Cl PL5. . . . . .124 B3
Hazel Cl Plymouth PL6. . . . . .125 B6
  St Austell PL25. . . . . .115 A6
Hazel Dr PL9 . . . . .136 C7
Hazel Gr Plymouth PL9 . . . . .136 C7
  Yelverton PL20 . . . . .42 D3
Hazelmead PL14. . . . . .113 B5
Hazelmere Dr PL25 . . . . .115 B4
Hazel Rd PL19 . . . . .147 C2
Hazelwood Cres PL9. . . . . . .136 D7
Hazelwood Dr PL6. . . . . .125 D8
Hazelwood Rd PL17 . . . . .39 F4
Heabrook Parc 2 TR18. . . . .143 C7
Hea Cl TR18 . . . . .143 C7
Hea Cotts 5 TR18 . . . . .143 C7
Head La TR5. . . . . .68 D8
Headland Cl TR26 . . . . .141 E2
Headland Cotts
  Coverack TR12. . . . . .103 H7
  Newquay TR7. . . . . .110 C8
Headland Ct TR26 . . . . .141 E2
Headland Pk PL4 . . . . .149 A4
Headland Point TR7 . . . . . . .110 C7
Headland Rd
  Carbis Bay TR26. . . . . .141 E2
  Newquay TR7. . . . . .110 C7
Headlands The TR6. . . . . .55 A5
Headleigh Rd TR7 . . . . .110 F5
Headon Cross EX23. . . . . .11 A5
Healy Cl 9 PL2. . . . . .127 F4
Healy Pl PL2. . . . . .127 F4
HEAMOOR 143 B7
Heamoor Com Prim Sch
  Heamoor TR18. . . . . .88 B5
  Heamoor TR18. . . . . .143 B6
Heanton Terr
  Millbrook PL10. . . . . .132 E6
  Redruth TR15. . . . . .140 C4
Heanton Villas TR15. . . . . . .140 C4
Hea Rd TR18. . . . . .143 C7
Hearl Rd PL12. . . . . .122 B4
Heatherbell Gdns TR18. . . . .143 B7
  Tavistock PL19. . . . . .147 D4
Heather Gdns 16 PL31 . . . . .109 A5

Heather La TR27 . . . . .77 D2
Heather Mdw TR9 . . . . .45 E1
Heathers The Foxhole PL26. . .58 E5
  Plymouth PL6. . . . . .125 D7
Heather Vean TR3 . . . . .69 D4
Heather Way TR20. . . . . .89 F4
Heathfield Gdns TR15. . . . . .140 E7
Heathfield Pk PL20 . . . . .42 D3
Heathfield Rd PL4 . . . . .129 B3
Heathlands Bsns Pk PL14 . . .113 C5
Heathlands Ind Est 9
  PL14. . . . . .113 C5
Heathlands Rd PL14 . . . . . . .113 C5
Heath Terr PL18. . . . . .40 F5
Heavitree Rd PL10. . . . . .133 A2
Hedgerow Cl PL6. . . . . .125 E8
Hedgerow La PL26. . . . . .58 B4
Hedgerows The PL12 . . . . . .122 B3
Hedingham Cl PL7. . . . . .131 C4
Hedingham Gdns PL6. . . . . .125 B7
Hedra Dr TR26 . . . . .141 C3
HELE 13 C2
HELEBRIDGE 7 A6
Helebridge Rd EX23 . . . . .7 B6
Hele Cross PL15 . . . . .13 C3
Hele Gdns PL7. . . . . .131 A4
Hele La PL6 . . . . .121 F2
Helena Ct 7 PL26 . . . . .59 D7
Hele Rd Bude EX23 . . . . . . .104 F1
  Marhamchurch EX23 . . . . . . .7 A6
Hele's Sch PL7 . . . . .130 C6
Hele's Terr PL4. . . . . .129 B2
HELFORD 93 B1
HELFORD PASSAGE 93 C2
Heligan Ho PL26. . . . . .73 A5
Heligan La PL30 . . . . .34 F7
HELLAND 35 A5
Helland TR10. . . . . .93 B6
HELLANDBRIDGE 34 F6
Helland Rd PL31. . . . . .109 E6
Hellescoth Way
  Helston TR13. . . . . .146 D8
  13 Tremenheere TR13 . . . .146 D8
Hellescott Rd PL15 . . . . .18 B7
Hellesvean 2 TR26 . . . . .77 A6
Hellesvean Cl 3 TR26 . . . . . .77 A6
HELLESVEOR 77 A7
Helleur Cl 4 PL24 . . . . .60 B4
Hellis Wartha TR13 . . . . .146 D5
Helman Tor View PL31. . . . .109 E2
Helnoweth Cotts TR18 . . . . .143 F8
Helnoweth Gdns TR18 . . . . .143 F8
Helnoweth Hill TR18. . . . . . .143 F8
Helscott Rd EX23 . . . . .7 A6
HELSTON 146 D6
Helston Business Pk TR13 . .146 D5
Helston Com Coll TR13. . . . .146 C7
Helston Com Hospl TR13. . . .146 D3
HELSTONE 24 B8
Helston Folk Mus★ TR13 . . .146 B5
Helston Rd Penryn TR10. . . .144 C8
  Porkellis TR13. . . . . .92 A8
Helston Relief Rd TR13 . . . . .146 E6
Helston Sp Ctr TR13 . . . . . . .146 C7
Hemball Cl 5 PL25. . . . . .59 A3
Hemball La PL25 . . . . .59 A3
Hembal Rd Burngullow PL26 . .58 F3
  4 Trewoon PL25 . . . . .59 A3
HEMERDON. 131 D7
Hemerdon House★ PL7 . . . .131 E7
Hemerdon Hts PL7 . . . . .131 A6
Hemerdon La PL7 . . . . .131 C3
Hemerdon Way PL7 . . . . . . .130 D6
HENAFORD. 2 D7
Hendergulling PL13 . . . . .62 F4
Henders Cnr 6 PL5. . . . . . . .128 F6
Henderson Pl PL2 . . . . .127 F6
HENDRA Bodmin. 46 F7
  Camelford. 105 A4
  Mullion. 102 F7
  St Dennis 58 C8
Hendra Barton TR1. . . . . . . .137 B8
Hendraburnick Down PL32 . .15 E6
Hendra Cl Ashton TR13. . . . . .90 E3
  Liskeard PL14 . . . . .38 A4
  Stithians TR3 . . . . .80 E4
  5 Truro TR1 . . . . .137 C5
Hendra Garth PL15. . . . . .17 C6
Hendra Gdns PL15. . . . . . . .106 B5
Hendra Hts PL26. . . . . .58 C8
Hendra La Ashton TR13. . . . . .90 D2
  Botathan PL15. . . . . .27 E1
  Hendra PL30. . . . . .23 A2
  Trewethern PL27 . . . . .22 F2
Hendra Parc PL14 . . . . .113 E7
Hendra Pk PL15 . . . . .106 C5
Hendra Prazey PL26 . . . . .58 B8
Hendra Rd St Dennis PL26. . .58 C8
  Stithians TR3 . . . . .80 E4
  Truro TR1. . . . . .137 C5
Hendras Ct TR26. . . . . .141 E2
Hendras Parc TR26 . . . . .141 D2
Hendra Terr TR3 . . . . .80 E4
Hendra Tor View PL15 . . . . . .26 C7
Hendra Vale PL15 . . . . .106 B4
Hendra Vean
  Carbis Bay TR26. . . . . .141 E1
  Truro TR1. . . . . .137 B5
Hendrawna La TR6 . . . . .55 A4
Hendrawna Mdws 1 TR6. . . .55 A4
Hendwell Cl PL6. . . . . .124 E6
Henfor Cl 12 TR17 . . . . .89 C5
HENFORD 13 F5
Henfordh Grange PL14 . . . . .113 A6
Henfor Mews 6 TR17. . . . . . .89 C5
Henfor Terr 13 TR17 . . . . . . .89 C5

Hengar La PL30. . . . . .23 F3
Henley Cl TR4 . . . . .68 C6
Henley Cres TR4. . . . . .68 C6
Henley Dr Mount Hawke TR4. .68 C6
  Plymouth PL5. . . . . .124 C7
Henliston Dr TR13 . . . . .146 C4
Henry Avent Gdns PL9 . . . . .136 C5
Henry Scott Tuke Ho 5
  TR11. . . . . .145 A4
Henrys Croft 18 TR12 . . . . .102 F2
Hensbarrow Hill PL26. . . . . . .59 A7
Hensbarrow Mdws PL26 . . . . .58 D5
Hensbury La PL20 . . . . .119 F4
Henscol TR16 . . . . .80 D6
Henscol Praze TR16 . . . . .80 D6
Henscol Vale PL14. . . . . .113 A6
Henshorn Ct TR13 . . . . .146 C7
Hental 3 TR6 . . . . .55 A4
Henver Cl TR27 . . . . .78 E3
Henver Ct TR27 . . . . .111 C7
Henver Gdns TR27. . . . . .78 E3
Henver La TR4. . . . . .56 A3
Henver Rd TR7 . . . . .111 B7
Henvor Cl TR15. . . . . .140 D6
Henvor Terr TR15. . . . . .140 E7
HENWOOD 38 B8
Henwood Cres TR7 . . . . .111 D7
Hen Wythva TR14. . . . . .138 E2
Herbert Pl PL2 . . . . .127 E4
Herbert St PL2 . . . . .127 E4
Hercules Rd Plymouth PL9. . .130 E1
  Plymouth PL9. . . . . .136 D8
Hereford Rd PL5. . . . . .124 B5
Heritage Cl PL12 . . . . .122 C3
Heritage Pk PL19. . . . . .147 D6
Herland Hill TR27. . . . . .78 D4
Herland Pk TR13. . . . . .90 D5
Herland Rd TR13 . . . . .90 E6
Hermes Cl TR13 . . . . .146 C5
Hermes Rd TR13. . . . . .146 C4
Hermitage Ct 1 PL4. . . . . . .128 E4
Hermitage Rd
  Plymouth PL3. . . . . .128 C5
  Roche PL26. . . . . .46 F3
HERNISS. 80 F1
Herniss La TR10 . . . . .80 F1
HERODSFOOT 50 E3
Heron La Millbrook PL10 . . . .132 F6
  Tresillian TR2. . . . . .70 C5
Heron Rd 9 PL18. . . . . .40 F5
Herons Ct 13 TR6 . . . . .55 A5
Heron Way TR1. . . . . .137 E1
Herring Cl PL14 . . . . .113 D7
Herring Rd PL14. . . . . .113 D7
Herschel Gdns PL5 . . . . .123 E1
Hersham Cross EX23. . . . . . . .5 B2
Hertland Wlk PL2. . . . . .128 A7
Heskyn View 3 PL12 . . . . . . .52 F2
Hessary Dr PL6. . . . . .121 C1
Hessary Ho 1 PL14. . . . . . . .113 D6
Hessary View Saltash PL12 . .122 E4
  Tavistock PL19. . . . . .147 B6
HESSENFORD 64 C8
Hessenford Rd PL13, PL11. . .64 B6
Hetling Cl PL15. . . . . .148 B3
HEWAS WATER 72 D8
Hewer's Row PL4. . . . . .149 A3
Hewitt Cl PL12. . . . . .122 C1
Hexham Pl PL2. . . . . .128 A8
Hexton Hill Rd PL9. . . . . . . .135 B4
Hexton Quay PL9 . . . . .135 C6
Heybrook Ave PL5 . . . . .123 D1
Heybrook Mews TR7 . . . . . . .110 D6
Hibernia Rd TR13. . . . . .146 D4
Hibernia Terr PL5 . . . . .127 E8
Hichens La TR11. . . . . .145 A5
Hichens Rd TR13 . . . . .146 D4
Hickory Dr PL7 . . . . .131 B5
Hicks Cl TR2. . . . . .71 C6
Hick's La PL4. . . . . .149 A2
Hidden Valley Discovery Pk★
  PL15. . . . . .18 A3
Hidderley Park TR14. . . . . . .138 E5
High Atlantic TR8. . . . . .44 C6
Highbridge Ct PL7. . . . . .130 E5
Highburrow 24 TR13. . . . . . . .98 C8
Highburrow Ct TR15. . . . . . .139 C5
Highburrow La TR15. . . . . . .139 C5
Highbury PL17 . . . . .38 E8
Highbury Cres PL7 . . . . .130 D7
Highclere Gdns PL6 . . . . . . .125 B8
Highcliff PL27 . . . . .21 D5
Highcliffe PL27. . . . . .21 D5
Highcombe La PL9 . . . . .135 C4
High Cross Lanivet PL30. . . . .47 F5
  Porth Navas TR11 . . . . .93 A4
  12 St Columb Major TR9 . . .45 D6
  Treviades TR11 . . . . .93 A4
  Truro TR1. . . . . .137 D4
High Cross St PL25 . . . . .114 C4
Higher Albion Row TR16. . . . .80 F8
Higher Anderton Rd PL10 . . .132 F5
HIGHER BAL 54 B2
Higher Beech Terr PL13 . . . .117 C4
Higher Besore Rd TR3 . . . . . .69 C4
Higher Bodiniel Rd PL31 . . . .109 C7
Higher Bojewyan TR19 . . . . . .75 B3
Higher Bolenna 14 TR6 . . . . .55 A4
Higher Bore St PL31 . . . . . . .109 C4
HIGHER BOSCASWELL. 75 A1
Higher Boskerris TR26 . . . . .141 C1
HIGHER BREA 139 B3
Higher Bridge Pk PL27. . . . .108 D5
Higher Broad La TR15 . . . . . .139 D7
Higher Bugle Bugle PL26 . . . .47 C1
  Stenalees PL26. . . . . .59 C8
Higher Burrow Cl TR26 . . . . .141 A4
HIGHER CARNKIE 139 F2

Higher Chapel St PL13 . . . . . .117 D3
Higher Church St 3 TR27 .142 D6
Higher Churchway PL9 . . . .136 A7
Higher Cl PL27 . . . . .108 E4
HIGHERCLIFF. 63 B8
HIGHER COMPTON 129 A6
Higher Compton Rd PL3 . .128 F6
HIGHER CONDURROW 139 A1
Higher Condurrow TR14 . .139 A1
Higher Cotts TR2 . . . . .57 C1
HIGHER CRACKINGTON. 10 C6
Higher Crill TR11 . . . . .144 E3
Higher Croft Parc 17 TR12 102 F2
Higher Cross La PL32 . . . . .105 E4
Higher Daws La PL15 . . . . . . .18 E2
HIGHER DOWNS 89 F5
Higher Drym TR27 . . . . .90 F8
Higher East St 9 TR9. . . . . .45 E6
Higher Efford Rd PL3 . . . . .129 B5
Higher Elms PL27. . . . . .21 F3
Higher Fernleigh Rd PL27 108 C4
Higher Fore St
  Marazion TR17. . . . . .89 C5
  Redruth TR15. . . . . .140 C5
Higher Glen Pk PL14. . . . . . .38 D4
Higher Goongumpas La
  TR16 . . . . .68 F1
Higher Green St TR18. . . . .143 D1
Higher Grumbla TR20. . . . . .87 C4
Higher Gwavas Rd 3
  TR18 . . . . .143 C1
Higher Kehelland
  Kehelland TR14 . . . . .79 A7
  Nancemellin TR14 . . . . .66 E1
  Nancemellin TR14 . . . . .79 A7
Higher Kelly Calstock PL18 . .41 A3
  Trehill PL18 . . . . .40 F4
Higher Kenneggy TR20 . . . .90 A3
Higher La Ashton TR13. . . . .90 E3
  Clapper PL27. . . . . .108 E5
  Mawgan TR12. . . . . .99 D7
  Plymouth PL1. . . . . .148 C2
  Wadebridge PL27 . . . . .108 C4
Higher Lariggan TR18 . . . .143 D4
HIGHER LARRICK 27 E5
Higher Lavorrick PL26 . . . . .73 C4
Higher Lidden Rd TR18 . . . .143 C3
Higher Lux St PL14 . . . . . . .113 C6
Higher Market St
  Looe PL13 . . . . .117 D3
  Penryn TR10 . . . . .144 C7
Higher Mdw PL14. . . . . .50 E7
Higher Medrose PL33. . . . . .14 E3
Higher Middle Hill PL14. . . .38 D4
Higher Moor TR12 . . . . .103 A5
Highermoor Cross EX22 . . . . .5 E1
Higher Mount Ambrose La
  TR15 . . . . .140 D6
Higher Mowles PL3. . . . . . .129 B6
Higher Newham La TR1. . .137 D2
Higher Ninnis TR16 . . . . . .140 F4
Higher Park Cl PL7. . . . . . .131 B3
Higher Park Stenak TR16 . .80 F8
Higher Pengegon TR14 . . .138 F2
Higher Penponds Rd TR14 .79 B5
Higher Pentire TR12. . . . . .146 A1
Higher Pentreath 4 TR20. . .90 B3
Higher Peverell Rd TR18. .143 E7
Higher Polladras 3 TR13 . .90 F5
Higher Polsue Way TR2. . . .70 F5
HIGHER PORTHPEAN. 59 D1
Higher Port Veer PL12. . . .122 F2
Higher Pumpfield Row
  TR15 . . . . .139 B6
Higher Railway Terr TR16. .80 F8
Higher Rd Breage TR13 . . . .90 F3
  Pensilva PL14 . . . . .38 D4
  Polmenna PL14 . . . . .36 E1
Higher Redannick TR1. . . .137 B3
HIGHER ROSEWARNE 138 D5
Higher Row Ashton TR13. . . .90 E3
  Kingsand PL10. . . . . .133 A2
Higher Silver Hill TR13. . . .146 C6
Higher Stennack TR26 . . . .141 A5
Higher Stert Terr PL4. . . . .149 C3
Higher Tamar Terr PL18 . . .41 A7
Higher Terr TR3 . . . . .81 B4
HIGHER TOLCARNE 45 B8
Higher Tower Rd TR7. . . . .110 C6
HIGHERTOWN Camelford 24 E8
  Truro 69 F3
Highertown Portscatho TR2 .83 B2
  Truro TR1. . . . . .69 F3
Highertown Pk PL12. . . . . . .53 C2
Higher Tregajorran TR15 .139 C3
Higher Tregenna Rd TR26 141 B3
Higher Treglyn PL27. . . . . . .22 B3
Higher Trehaverne PL1. . .137 C6
Higher Treluswell TR10. . . .81 D2
Higher Tremena PL25 . . . . .114 C4
Higher Trenant Rd PL27 . .108 D6
Higher Trengr TR11. . . . . . . .92 D6
Higher Trerank La PL26. . . .46 F2
Higher Tresavean Terr
  TR16 . . . . .80 C6
Higher Trevithick TR27 . . .142 D5
Higher Trevorian Barns
  TR19 . . . . .97 D7
Higher Trewidden Rd
  TR26 . . . . .141 B4
HIGHER TREWINCE 44 E6
Higher Trezaise PL26. . . . . .47 A1
Higher Tristram PL27. . . . . .21 D5
Higher Vicarage La 7
  TR12. . . . . .99 A1
Higherwell Cl TR7. . . . . . . .111 A4
Higher Well La TR13. . . . . .146 C6

Higher Well Pk PL26. . . . . . .73 C3
Higher West End PL26 . . . . .73 C6
Higher Wharf EX23. . . . . . .104 D4
Higher Whiterock PL27 . . .108 B5
Higher Woodford La PL7. .130 C7
Higher Woodside PL25 . . . .114 A4
Highfield Ave
  St Austell PL25. . . . . .114 D3
  13 St Columb Major TR9 . . . .45 D6
Highfield Cl Plymouth PL3 .129 C5
  St Austell PL25. . . . . .114 D3
Highfield Ct 9 TR5. . . . . . . .54 D1
Highfield Est 9 PL14 . . . . . .38 E4
Highfield Park Rd PL15 . . .106 A5
Highfield Pk PL12 . . . . .122 B3
Highfield Rd
  Camelford PL32. . . . . .105 C3
  Falmouth TR11. . . . . .144 F4
  Mount Hawke TR4 . . . . .68 C6
Highfield Rd Ind Est PL32 105 C3
Highfields 19 TR18. . . . . . . .143 C2
Highfield View 3 PL5 . . . .124 C8
Highgate Hill 11 TR9. . . . . .45 E1
Highglen Dr PL7. . . . . .131 B7
High La Higher Treslea PL30. . .36 A3
  Tregonwell TR12 . . . . .100 F7
  Trezance PL30. . . . . .35 F4
  Trudgwell TR12 . . . . .101 A8
Highland Pk Penryn TR10 .144 B8
  Redruth TR15. . . . . .140 C5
Highlands PL9. . . . . .136 B3
HIGHLANES 32 B7
HIGH LANES 142 D5
High Lanes Cubert TR8. . . . .55 E8
  Hayle TR27. . . . . .142 D5
High Lanes Rd
  Leedstown TR27 . . . . .78 F1
  Tremayne TR14 . . . . .79 A2
Highmoor PL15. . . . . .12 B4
High Pk PL12. . . . . .52 F6
High Rd PL27. . . . . .32 C6
High St 14 PL15 . . . . .106 C6
  Boscastle PL35 . . . . .9 D1
  Camelford PL32. . . . . .105 C3
  Chacewater TR4 . . . . .68 F3
  Delabole PL33. . . . . .14 D3
  Falmouth TR11. . . . . .145 B5
  Launceston PL15. . . . . .106 C6
  Padstow PL28 . . . . .107 D5
  Penzance TR18 . . . . .143 E5
  3 Plymouth PL1. . . . . .149 A2
  Plymouth, Stonehouse PL1 .128 A2
  Probus TR2. . . . . .71 C6
  St Ives TR26. . . . . .141 B6
  St Keverne TR12 . . . . .101 C4
HIGH STREET. 58 D4
High Street Hill PL26 . . . . . .58 D2
High Street Ind Est PL26 . . .58 D3
High Street Prim Sch PL1 .128 A2
High Street & Waterloo Street
  Flats PL1 . . . . .128 A1
Hightrip La PL17. . . . . .39 F7
High Trip La PL17. . . . . .40 A8
Highview TR4 . . . . .68 E5
Highview Cl PL14. . . . . .38 A2
Highview Ct PL7 . . . . .130 B6
Highview Cres TR4 . . . . .68 E5
High View Prim Sch PL3 . .129 D6
Highway PL14. . . . . .50 B6
Highway La TR15 . . . . .140 D7
Highwood Pk PL14 . . . . .50 E7
Higman Cl PL14 . . . . .50 E7
Hilda Row PL25. . . . . .114 E7
Hilgrove Rd TR7. . . . . .111 A6
HILL 10 B5
Hill Bunkers PL30. . . . . .47 E2
Hill Church TR4 . . . . .68 F2
Hill Cl Heamoor TR18. . . . . .143 B7
  Plymouth PL7. . . . . .130 D4
  St Breward PL30. . . . . .24 B3
Hillcrest Helston TR13 . . . .146 C7
  Shortlanesend TR4 . . . . .69 F6
Hill Crest PL3 . . . . .128 E5
Hillcrest Ave TR1. . . . . .137 A5
Hillcrest Cl Plymouth PL7. .131 A5
  14 St Columb Major TR9 . . . .45 E6
Hillcrest Dr PL7 . . . . .131 A4
Hillcrest Gdns 3 TR13 . . . .146 C6
Hillcrest Rd TR27 . . . . .142 D5
Hilldale Rd PL9. . . . . .135 E6
Hilldean Cl PL5. . . . . .124 C7
Hill Gdns PL12. . . . . .119 A2
Hill Hay Cl PL23. . . . . .116 A4
Hillhead Gdns PL32. . . . . . .105 D4
Hillhead Rd TR11 . . . . .144 C5
Hillhead Rise TR11 . . . . . . .144 C4
Hill La PL3 . . . . .128 F7
Hillocks The PL13 . . . . .117 D4
Hillpark Cotts PL15 . . . . . .106 D6
Hill Park Cres
  Plymouth PL4. . . . . .149 A4
  St Austell PL25. . . . . .114 A4
Hillpark La PL30. . . . . .35 E3
Hill Park Mews PL4. . . . . . .149 B4
Hill Path PL5 . . . . .123 F5
Hill Pk PL27. . . . . .108 D6
Hill Rd Hill EX23. . . . . .10 B5
  Wadebridge PL27 . . . . .108 C5
  Welltown PL30. . . . . .36 B2
Hillsborough 2 PL4. . . . . . .128 F4
Hillsborough Cross EX22 . . .8 D7
Hillsdale Bglws TR13 . . . . . .90 F5
Hillsdunne Rd PL3. . . . . . . .128 E6
Hillside Grampound Road TR2. 57 E1
  Lanivet PL30 . . . . .47 C3
  Portreath TR16 . . . . .67 C6

Hillside continued
  St Austell PL25. . . . . .115 B3
  Trewellard TR19. . . . . .86 F8
Hillside Ave Par PL24. . . . . .60 B4
  Plymouth PL4. . . . . .128 D4
  Saltash PL12 . . . . .122 F3
Hillside Cres PL9. . . . . .135 F8
Hillside Ct Angarrack TR27 . .78 C5
  21 Yelverton PL20 . . . . .41 B1
Hillside Gdns PL22. . . . . . . .112 C2
Hillside Ind Est TR16 . . . . .140 E8
Hillside Mdw TR10. . . . . . . .144 D7
Hillside Mdws PL26. . . . . . . .58 D5
Hillside Parc TR20. . . . . .88 B7
Hillside Pk PL31. . . . . .109 D5
Hillside Rd Boslowick TR11 .144 F2
  Falmouth TR11. . . . . .144 F2
  St Austell PL25. . . . . .114 D5
  Saltash PL12 . . . . .122 E3
Hillside Terr
  Carharrack TR16 . . . . .80 E8
  Downderry PL11. . . . . .64 C5
  22 Newlyn TR18. . . . . .143 C2
  2 Redruth TR15. . . . . .140 C5
Hillside Villas PL13 . . . . . . .117 F5
Hillson Cl PL29 . . . . .22 E7
Hill St Padstow PL28 . . . . . .107 D5
  Plymouth PL4. . . . . .149 A3
Hillsview PL13. . . . . .62 D2
Hilltop Cotts PL8 . . . . .136 F5
Hill View PL20. . . . . .41 F3
Hilton Ave PL5 . . . . .124 D1
Hilton Rd EX23 . . . . .7 B6
Hingston Ct PL6. . . . . .129 A8
HINGSTON DOWN. 40 B6
Hinton Ct PL6 . . . . .125 C1
Hirmandale Rd PL5. . . . . . .123 F3
Hirst Ho TR14 . . . . .139 A4
Hobart St PL1 . . . . .148 A2
Hobbacott La EX23 . . . . .7 B6
Hobbacott Rise EX23 . . . . . . .7 B6
Hobbs Cres PL12 . . . . .122 C3
Hockens La PL23 . . . . .116 C2
Hockin Cl PL17. . . . . .39 E6
Hockings Gn 7 PL14. . . . . .113 D7
Hockings Ho PL14 . . . . .37 F3
Hodders Way PL12. . . . . . . .119 A2
Hodge Cl PL12. . . . . .122 C2
Hoe App PL1 . . . . .148 C2
Hoe Ct PL1 . . . . .148 C2
Hoegate Ct PL1. . . . . .148 C2
Hoegate Pl PL1. . . . . .148 C2
Hoegate St PL1. . . . . .149 A2
Hoe Gdns PL1 . . . . .148 C2
Hoe Rd PL1. . . . . .148 C1
Hoe St PL1 . . . . .148 C2
Hoe The PL1. . . . . .148 C1
Hogarth Cl PL9. . . . . .136 B6
Hogarth Ho 2 PL19. . . . . . .147 B6
Hogarth Wlk PL9 . . . . .136 B6
Holberton La PL25. . . . . . . .114 F7
Holberton Gdns 3 PL28 . . .107 C4
Holborn Pl PL7 . . . . .130 E6
Holborn St PL4. . . . . .149 B2
Holcombe Dr PL9. . . . . .135 F5
Holcroft Cl PL12. . . . . .122 D2
Holdsworth St PL4. . . . . . . .148 B4
Holebay Cl PL9. . . . . .136 A5
Hole Cross PL20 . . . . .119 E7
Hole La PL14 . . . . .36 E1
Hole Rd PL20 . . . . .120 A5
HOLESTROW 102 E2
Hollabury Rd EX23. . . . . . . .104 F7
Hollacombe Brake PL9 . . . .136 C1
HOLLACOMBE HILL 136 A2
Holland Rd
  Plymouth, Chaddlewood
    PL7. . . . . .131 D5
  Plymouth, Peverell PL3 . . . .128 E6
  Plymouth, Plymstock PL9 . . .135 F6
  Widegates PL13 . . . . .63 E7
Hollies Cl PL15 . . . . .106 B7
Hollies Rd PL15. . . . . .106 A7
Hollies The TR27 . . . . .142 B4
Hollong Pk PL11. . . . . .65 E5
Holloway Gdns PL9. . . . . . .136 A5
Hollowell Ho 1 PL35 . . . . . . .9 C2
Hollow Hayes PL6. . . . . . . .129 B8
Hollow's Terr TR27 . . . . . . .142 E7
Hollows The PL9 . . . . .136 B8
Holly Cl PL3 . . . . .69 C3
Hollycroft Rd PL3. . . . . .129 A7
Holly Ct PL6 . . . . .129 E7
Holly Park Cl PL5 . . . . .124 A5
Holly Park Dr PL5. . . . . . . .124 A5
Holly Terr 9 PL18. . . . . .41 A7
Hollywood Head PL30. . . . . .35 C8
Hollywood Terr PL1 . . . . . . .148 A3
Holman Ave TR14. . . . . .138 C4
Holman Ct PL2. . . . . .128 C8
Holman Rd PL14. . . . . .113 E6
Holmans Bldgs PL11. . . . . .127 D2
Holmans Mdw PL15. . . . . . . .19 C1
Holmans Moor Rd TR26. . . .76 E4
Holman's Pl 1 TR13 . . . . . . .98 C8
Holman's Terr TR16. . . . . . . .80 B5
HOLMBUSH 115 B4
Holmbush Arch Rd PL25 . . .115 B3
Holmbush Hill PL17. . . . . . . .39 F7
Holmbush Ind Est PL25 . . .115 B4
Holmbush Rd PL25 . . . . . . .115 C4
Holmer Down PL6. . . . . . . .125 D7
Holmes Ave PL3. . . . . .129 B5
Holmes Way 4 PL31. . . . . .109 F3
Holmwood Ave PL9. . . . . . .135 E5

Holne Chase PL6 . . . . .125 B7
Holnicote Rd EX23. . . . . . . .104 E5
Holt 7 PL7. . . . . .42 D3
Holt Cres TR7 . . . . .110 D5
Holtwood Rd PL6. . . . . .125 D6
Holwell Cl PL9. . . . . .136 A5
Holy Cross RC Prim Sch
  PL4 .149 A3
Holyrood La PL1. . . . . .148 C2
Holyrood Pl PL1 . . . . .148 C2
Holyway Cross PL15 . . . . . . .18 A1
HOLYWELL 43 B2
Holywell Bay Fun Pk ★ TR8 .43 C1
Holywell Cl TR3 . . . . .82 B8
Holywell Rd Cubert TR8. . . . .55 D8
  Holywell TR8. . . . . .43 C1
  Liskeard PL14 . . . . .113 E6
  Newquay TR7. . . . . .110 F6
  Playing Place TR3 . . . . .82 B8
Home Farm La TR14. . . . . .138 D8
Home Farm Rd PL9. . . . . . .135 E8
Homefield Pk PL31. . . . . . . .109 F3
Home Park Ave PL3. . . . . . .128 E6
Home Park (Plymouth Argyle
  FC) PL2 . . . . .128 C5
Home Park Rd PL12. . . . . . .123 A3
Home Pk Kilkhampton EX23 . .5 A6
  Landrake PL12. . . . . .53 C3
  Plymouth PL2. . . . . .127 F4
Homer Park Lane S PL9 . . .135 C5
Homer Park Rd PL28. . . . . . .20 F2
Homer Pk Plymouth PL9 . . .135 C5
  Saltash PL12 . . . . .122 D3
Homer Rise PL9. . . . . .136 B7
Homer Water Pk PL26 . . . . .58 B4
Homestead Ct TR11. . . . . . .144 F6
Home Sweet Home Terr
  PL4 .149 C2
Homeyard Homes The TR2. 83 F6
Honcray PL9 . . . . .135 D8
Honeypin Gr 8 PL14. . . . . .113 D7
Honeysuckle Cl
  Plymouth PL6. . . . . .125 C1
  Saltash PL12 . . . . .122 D4
Honeysuckle Gdns PL15 . . .106 E4
HONICKNOWLE 124 B2
Honicknowle PL5. . . . . .124 B2
Honicknowle Gn PL5 . . . . .124 B2
Honicknowle La PL5. . . . . .124 B1
Honicombe Cnr PL17. . . . . . .40 E5
Honicombe Pk PL17. . . . . . . .40 E5
Honiton Cl PL5. . . . . .124 B3
Honiton La PL15 . . . . .27 E7
Honiton Wlk PL5. . . . . .124 B4
Hood Hill TR14 . . . . .79 A6
HOOE. 135 C5
Hooe Hill PL9. . . . . .135 C5
Hooe La PL9. . . . . .135 D3
Hooe Lake La PL10 . . . . . . .133 C4
Hooe Manor PL9. . . . . .135 C5
Hooe Prim Sch PL9 . . . . . . .135 B5
Hooe Rd PL9 . . . . .135 C5
Hooksbury Ave PL7. . . . . . .131 B3
Hooper Ct PL14 . . . . .113 C8
Hooper La TR14 . . . . .138 D2
Hoopers Cl PL12. . . . . .53 C3
Hoopers La PL18 . . . . .40 F6
Hooper St PL11. . . . . .127 C3
Hope Terr TR7. . . . . .110 D6
Hopton Cl Bude EX23 . . . . .104 F5
  Plymouth PL6. . . . . .128 F7
Hornapark Cl PL16. . . . . .19 E3
Hornbrook Gdns PL6. . . . . .124 D6
Hornby Ct PL1. . . . . .148 A3
Hornby St 2 PL2. . . . . .127 F4
Hornchurch La PL5. . . . . . .123 E4
Hornchurch Rd PL5. . . . . . .123 E5
Horn Cross PL9. . . . . .135 F7
Horn Cross Rd PL9. . . . . . . .135 F7
Hornick Hill PL26. . . . . .58 E4
HORNINGTOPS 51 E3
Horn La Liskeard PL14. . . . . .113 B6
  Plymouth PL9. . . . . .135 F7
Horn Lane Flats 4 PL9 . . . .135 F7
HORRABRIDGE 42 C5
Horrabridge Com Prim Sch
  PL20. . . . . .42 C4
HORSEBRIDGE 29 C1
HORSEDOWNS 78 F1
Horsedowns Rd TR27. . . . . .78 F1
Horse & Jockey La 2
  TR13 . . . . .146 C5
Horsepool La PL11. . . . . .65 B6
Horsepool Rd
  Connor Downs TR27 . . . . . . .78 E6
  Sheviock PL11. . . . . .65 B6
Horse Rd EX23. . . . . .2 C1
Horseshoe Cl PL26 . . . . .47 A3
Horsewhim Dr PL17 . . . . . . .39 E6
Horse Whim Dr PL25. . . . . .115 B5
Horsham La
  Plymouth, Honicknowle
    PL5. . . . . .124 C2
  Plymouth, Tamerton Foliot
    PL5. . . . . .124 C2
Horslett Hill EX22. . . . . .13 B8
Horsley Rise PL25 . . . . .114 D3
Horswell Cl PL7. . . . . .131 B5
Horton Cross EX22 . . . . .3 F3
Horwell Dr TR7. . . . . .142 E6
Hosford Cl PL9 . . . . .136 A4
Hosken's Mdw TR19. . . . . . .97 A6
Hosking's Row TR15. . . . . .140 B4
Hospital Rd Plymouth PL4 . .149 B4
  Stratton EX23 . . . . .4 D1
Hotham Pl PL1. . . . . .148 A4
Houldsworth Rd PL9. . . . . .135 C7

Houndiscombe Rd PL4 . . .128 E4
Hounster Dr PL10. . . . . . . .132 D4
Hounster Hill PL10. . . . . . .132 D4
House Field Mdw 6 PL15 106 D4
Housel Bay Rd
  Church Cove TR12 . . . . .103 A2
  Lizard TR12. . . . . .102 F2
Housman Cl PL5. . . . . .124 D3
Howard Cl Plymouth PL5 . .123 F7
  Saltash PL12 . . . . .122 D3
  Tavistock PL19. . . . . .147 A5
Howard La EX23 . . . . .7 C8
Howard Rd PL9. . . . . .135 E8
Howards Way EX23 . . . . . . .104 D5
Howe Downs TR14. . . . . .79 A2
Howell's Rd 10 EX23 . . . . . . .4 E1
Howeson La PL6. . . . . .125 A4
How St PL4. . . . . .149 A2
HTP Apartments TR1 . . . . .137 E4
Hts The PL19 . . . . .147 A6
HUDDISFORD 3 F6
Hudson Cross EX22. . . . . .5 E4
Hudson Rd PL27. . . . . .31 F3
Hughville St TR14 . . . . .138 D4
Hugus Rd TR3 . . . . .69 D3
Hull Rd TR14 . . . . .138 F3
Hull's La TR11. . . . . .145 C3
Humber Cl PL3 . . . . .129 D6
Humphrey's Cl PL14 . . . . . . .37 F3
Humphry Davy La TR27 . . .142 D5
Humphry Davy Sch TR18 . .143 E6
Hungerford Rd PL2. . . . . . .128 B5
Hunkin Cl TR1. . . . . .137 C5
Hunter Cl PL6 . . . . .124 F2
Huntersfield TR14. . . . . . . .138 F7
Hunters Oak PL20. . . . . .41 D2
Huntfield Gdns 15 EX23. . . . .4 E1
Huntingdon Gdns PL5 . . . .124 D4
Huntley Pl PL3. . . . . .129 C4
Hunts Crossing Sta ★ PL15 .18 E4
Hurdon Rd Landlake PL15 . . .28 B8
  Launceston PL15. . . . . .106 D2
Hurdon Way PL15 . . . . .106 C3
Hurdwick Rd PL19. . . . . . . .147 A5
Hurland Rd TR1 . . . . .137 D3
Hurlers Ct 11 PL14. . . . . . . .113 C5
Hurlers The ★ TR14. . . . . . . .38 A6
Hurlings The TR9. . . . . .45 E5
Hurling Way 5 TR9. . . . . . . .45 E5
Hurrabrook Cl PL6. . . . . . . .125 E2
Hurrabrook Gdns PL6. . . . .125 E2
Hurrell Cl PL6 . . . . .124 D6
Hurrell Ct PL3 . . . . .129 C5
Hursley Bsns Pk PL6. . . . . .121 D1
Hurst Cl PL9 . . . . .135 F5
Hustyns PL27. . . . . .33 D3
Hutchings Cl PL6. . . . . .124 D6
Huthnance Cl TR1. . . . . . . .137 F5
Hutton Hts TR1 . . . . .135 E6
Huxham Cl PL6 . . . . .129 A8
Huxley Cl PL7. . . . . .130 F7
Hyde Park Inf School 1
  PL3. . . . . .128 E5
Hyde Park Junior School 2
  PL33. . . . . .128 E5
Hyde Park Rd PL3 . . . . .128 E5

I

IDLESS 70 B6
Idless La TR4. . . . . .69 F6
Idless Wood Forest Walk ★
  TR4. .70 B6
Ilbert Cotts PL7. . . . . .130 E4
Ilbert St PL1 . . . . .148 B4
Illand Rd PL15 . . . . .27 C5
ILLOGAN 67 E4
Illogan Churchtown TR16. .67 D4
Illogan Downs TR15 . . . . . .139 B8
ILLOGAN HIGHWAY 139 C6
Illogan Pk 8 TR16. . . . . .67 E4
Illogan Sch TR16. . . . . .67 D5
Imperial Ct TR1. . . . . .145 D3
Impham Cl 4 PL19 . . . . . . .147 B7
Ince Cl PL11. . . . . .126 F4
Inchkeith Rd PL6 . . . . .124 F7
INDIAN QUEENS 45 E1
Indian Queens Ind Est TR9 .45 F2
Indian Queens Prim Sch
  TR9. .45 E1
Indus Pl 3 PL9 . . . . .136 B6
Industrial Est The TR6. . . . . .55 B4
Infirmary Hill TR1 . . . . .137 C4
Ingra Rd PL3 . . . . .129 A6
Ingra Tor Cl 2 PL20 . . . . . . .42 C3
Ingra Wlk PL6 . . . . .125 B8
Inner Tide La TR7. . . . . .110 F4
Innes Ho PL1 . . . . .148 B3
Inney Cl PL17. . . . . .39 F4
Inow Terr TR11. . . . . .93 A2
Institute Hill TR13. . . . . .98 B8
Institute La PL30. . . . . .34 C2
Instow Wlk PL5. . . . . .124 A3
Inswell Ct PL19. . . . . .147 A6
INSWORKE 132 F6
Insworke Cl PL10. . . . . .133 A6
Insworke Cres PL10. . . . . . .132 F6
Insworke Pl PL10. . . . . .133 A6
Inverdene PL3. . . . . .129 B5
Ipswich Cl PL5. . . . . .124 C4
Iron Bars PL22. . . . . .48 D2
Iron Mine La PL20. . . . . .42 E3
Isacombe Oaks PL17. . . . . . .39 F6
Isambard Brunel Way PL1 148 A2

Island Cres TR7. . . . . .110 E6
Island Ct PL13 . . . . .117 D2
Island Lanes PL31 . . . . .109 F1
Island Point TR8. . . . . .44 C6
Island Rd **4** TR26. . . . . .141 B6
Island Sq **8** TR26. . . . . .141 B6
Islington Wharf TR10 . . . . . .144 D8
Ivanhoe **6** TR7 . . . . .110 F6
Ivanhoe Rd PL5. . . . . .123 D2
Ivey Terr PL14 . . . . .113 D7
Ivy Cl PL28 . . . . .31 F8
Ivy Cotts PL18 . . . . .40 F6
Ivydale PL15. . . . . .106 B6
Ivydale Rd PL4. . . . . .128 F4
Ivydene Flats TR7. . . . . .111 D7
Ivy Ho TR16. . . . . .80 C6
Ivy La TR18 . . . . .143 C5
Ivyleaf Hill EX23. . . . . .4 E3
Ivyleaf Holiday Pk EX23 . . . . . .4 F3

J

Jack Bice Cl PL14. . . . . .113 E5
Jackett's Steps **6** TR11. . . . .145 B5
Jack La TR18 . . . . .143 C2
Jackman's Mdw PL10. . . . . . .133 A3
Jacks Cl TR10 . . . . .144 D7
Jack's La PL11. . . . . .132 B8
Jackson Cl PL5. . . . . .127 F8
Jackson Pl PL2. . . . . .127 F4
Jackson Way PL12. . . . . .122 E3
Jack Stephens Est TR18. . . . .143 D6
Jacob's Ladder TR11 . . . . . . .145 B4
JACOBSTOW 11 B6
Jacobstow Com Prim Sch
EX23. . . . . .11 A6
Jago Ave PL11. . . . . .127 B3
Jago Cl PL31 . . . . .109 B3
Jago's Slip TR11. . . . . .145 B5
Jake's La TR4. . . . . .69 A3
Jamaica Inn Mus *★* PL15 . . .25 E3
Jamaica Pl **14** TR18. . . . . . .143 C7
Jamaica Terr **13** TR18. . . . .143 C7
James Cl PL9. . . . . .136 B6
James Pl TR1. . . . . .137 D4
James Rd PL19 . . . . .147 E2
James's Cross EX23 . . . . .2 C2
James St Plymouth PL4. . . . . .148 C4
  Plymouth, Mount Wise PL1 . .127 E1
Jane's Ct **9** TR1. . . . . .137 C4
Jan Luke Way **1** TR14. . . . . .138 F3
Jasmine Gdns
  Plymouth, Chaddlewood
  PL7. . . . . .131 B5
  Plymouth, Glenholt PL6. . . . .125 E6
Jasmine Pl **7** TR14. . . . . . . .138 E5
Jasmine Way St Merryn PL28 .31 F7
  18 Tregolds PL28. . . . . .31 F7
Jasper Parc PL14. . . . . .37 F3
Jays Cross PL15 . . . . .19 C6
Jean Cres PL3. . . . . .128 A8
Jeanne Rees Ct **9** PL14. . . . .113 B5
Jedburgh Cres PL2. . . . . .128 A8
Jeffery Cl PL4. . . . . .124 D6
Jelbert Way PL18. . . . . .88 E6
Jellicoe Rd PL5. . . . . .124 E1
Jenkins Cl PL9. . . . . .136 A5
Jenkins Terr **5** TR15. . . . . . .140 C5
Jenner Gdns TR9. . . . . .45 D6
Jenner Parc TR9. . . . . .45 D6
Jennings Rd TR10 . . . . .144 A6
Jennings St TR18. . . . . .143 E5
Jenns Cross EX22. . . . . .5 F7
Jennycliff La PL9. . . . . .135 A6
Jennys Combe Cl PL9. . . . . . .135 F4
Jephson Rd PL4 . . . . .129 B3
Jericho La Polhilsa PL17 . . . . . .39 D7
  St Erth TR27. . . . . .142 D1
Jeryon Cl PL25 . . . . .114 E6
Jessops PL7. . . . . .130 D7
Jethan Dr TR14. . . . . .138 B4
Jetty St PL26 . . . . .73 C3
Jewell's Terr TR16. . . . . .80 B5
JEWEL'S CROSS. 7 F6
Jinkin Ave PL4 . . . . .149 B4
Jobs Water Treverva TR10. . . .93 A6
  Treworvack TR10. . . . . .92 F6
Jodel Cl **1** PL6. . . . . .125 B5
John Ellis Ct TR27 . . . . .142 C5
John La PL4. . . . . .148 C4
John's Cnr TR20. . . . . .89 F5
Johnson Cl **2** PL20. . . . . . . .41 B1
John Sparke Ho **17** PL1 . . . .149 A2
Johns Pk TR15 . . . . .140 B6
John St Plymouth PL1. . . . . . .127 E3
  Truro TR1. . . . . .137 C4
JOLLY'S BOTTOM. 69 A4
Jon Davey Dr TR16 . . . . .140 C7
Jopes Cl **2** PL14. . . . . .38 A3
JOPPA Hayle. 142 E4
  St Just. 87 A4
Jordan La PL20. . . . . .42 C5
Jorys Mdw PL30. . . . . .23 E3
Joseph's Ct **27** TR6. . . . . . . .55 A5
Joseph's La TR18. . . . . .143 C8
Jubilee Bglws **20** TR18. . . . .143 C1
Jubilee Cl Cubert TR4. . . . . . . .55 D8
  Duloe PL14 . . . . .51 A1
  8 Kilkhampton EX23. . . . . . . .5 A6
  Saltash PL12 . . . . .122 C1
Jubilee Cotts Landrake PL12. .53 C3
  Saltash PL12 . . . . .122 C1
Jubilee Ct **15** TR26. . . . . . . .77 A6

Jubilee Hill PL13 . . . . .62 D5
Jubilee Mdw PL25. . . . . .115 C5
Jubilee Pl Camborne TR14. . . .138 E3
  Plymouth PL3. . . . . .129 C4
Jubilee Poll PL18. . . . . .143 F4
Jubilee Rd Falmouth TR11 . . .145 A5
  Pensilva PL14 . . . . .38 D4
  Plymouth PL5. . . . . .123 F3
  Threemilestone TR3. . . . . .69 C3
  Wadebridge PL27 . . . . .108 C5
Jubilee St TR7. . . . . .110 D6
Jubilee Terr Bodmin PL31. . . .109 B5
  3 Camborne TR14. . . . . . . .138 E2
  Goonhavern TR4. . . . . .55 D5
  Helston TR13. . . . . .146 C4
  Plymouth PL4. . . . . .129 B2
Julian St PL4. . . . . .149 C2
Julian Wlk PL6. . . . . .125 E6
Jump Cl PL6. . . . . .121 C1
Junction Gdns PL4 . . . . .149 C3
Juniper Cl **14** PL31. . . . . . . .109 A5
Juniper Gdns **2** PL14. . . . . . .50 D7
Juniper Way PL7 . . . . .131 B5
Juniper Wlk **6** PL14. . . . . . . .113 D8

K

Kailem Cl TR9 . . . . .45 D5
Kaolin Hts PL25. . . . . .114 E8
Karenza Ct TR26. . . . . .141 E2
Kargel Gdns TR11 . . . . .144 D1
Kathleaven St PL5. . . . . .123 D1
Kay Cl PL7. . . . . .130 F7
Kay Cres PL31 . . . . .109 B3
Kay Gdns PL27. . . . . .108 E5
Kays Mews **7** PL34. . . . . .14 C7
Kea Com Prim Sch TR3. . . . . . .70 A1
Keason Est PL14. . . . . .39 A2
Keason Hill PL12 . . . . .53 C8
Keast Cl **2** TR9. . . . . .45 E1
Keat St PL2. . . . . .127 E4
Keay Heights PL25. . . . . .114 E6
Kedlestone Ave PL5 . . . . .124 A3
Keeble Pk TR3. . . . . .81 E6
Keep The PL12 . . . . .122 C2
KEHELLAND 66 F2
Kehelland Village Prim Sch
  TR14. . . . . .66 F1
Keigwen Pl TR19 . . . . .88 C1
Keiro La Pityme PL27. . . . . . . .21 F3
  St Minver PL27. . . . . .22 A3
Kel Avon Cl TR1 . . . . .137 F5
Kellaway Pk TR13. . . . . .146 D6
Kelley Rd TR11 . . . . .144 E5
Kelliwith TR3. . . . . .82 B6
Kellow Hill PL13 . . . . .62 D2
Kellow Pk PL11. . . . . .65 A7
Kellow Rd PL26. . . . . .58 C8
KELLY 29 B8
KELLY BRAY 39 F6
Kelly Cl PL5. . . . . .127 C7
Kelly Coll PL19 . . . . .147 D7
Kelly Coll Prep Sch PL19 . . . .147 D7
Kelly Pk PL30. . . . . .34 C8
Kelvin Ave PL4 . . . . .149 C4
Kelwyn Ct TR26. . . . . .141 C2
KELYNACK 86 F4
Kemp Cl TR1 . . . . .137 D4
Kempe Cl PL2. . . . . .127 F6
Kemp's Cl **7** TR5. . . . . .54 C1
Kemyell Pl PL2 . . . . .127 E4
Kendal Gn TR2 . . . . .57 C1
Kendall Park PL23 . . . . .61 B1
Kendall Pk PL23 . . . . .116 D2
Kendal Pl PL5. . . . . .124 E4
Kenidjack Ct TR26. . . . . .141 E1
Kenilworth Rd PL2. . . . . .128 B7
Kenilworth Way PL26. . . . . . . .58 E5
Kenley Gdns PL5. . . . . .123 F4
Kenmare Dr PL7. . . . . .131 A5
Kennack Sands TR12 . . . . . . .103 C6
Kennall Pk TR3. . . . . .81 B4
Kennall Vale TR3. . . . . .81 B4
Kennall Vale Sch TR3. . . . . . . .81 B4
Kennall Valley TR3. . . . . .81 A4
Kenna Pk TR1 . . . . .69 F3
KENNARDS HOUSE. 18 B2
Kenn Cl PL5. . . . . .124 B3
Kennedy Cl TR15 . . . . .139 B8
KENNEGGY. 90 A3
KENNEGGY DOWNS. 90 B4
Kennel Hill Carwen PL30. . . . . .35 D8
  Plymouth PL7. . . . . .130 D4
Kennel Hill Cl PL7 . . . . .130 C4
Kennerley Terr **16** TR2. . . . . .95 A6
Kennet Cl PL3. . . . . .129 B6
Kenneth Launder Ct **10**
  PL14. . . . . .113 B5
Kensa Way TR27 . . . . .78 E6
Kensey Ct PL15. . . . . .106 C6
Kensey Pl **3** PL15. . . . . .106 C6
Kensey Valley Mdw PL15. . . . .106 D6
Kensey View PL15. . . . . .106 D5
Kensington Pl **8** PL4. . . . . . .128 F4
Kensington Rd PL4 . . . . .149 B4
Kenstella Rd TR18 . . . . .143 C2
Kent Ave PL25. . . . . .115 D3
Kent Cl PL26. . . . . .58 C8
Kent Rd PL2. . . . . .127 F5
KENTS. 10 F6
KENWYN 137 C6
Kenwyn Church Rd TR1. . . . . .137 B6
Kenwyn Cl Bude EX23. . . . . . .104 D7
  Truro TR1. . . . . .137 B6
Kenwyn Hill TR1. . . . . .137 B6
Kenwyn Mews TR1 . . . . .137 C4

Kenwyn Pk
  St Kew Highway PL30 . . . . . . .23 B2
  Truro TR1. . . . . .137 B6
Kenwyn Rd TR1. . . . . .137 C5
Kenwyn St TR1. . . . . .137 C4
Kenython La TR19 . . . . .86 F7
Keppel Pl PL2 . . . . .127 F4
Keppel St PL2. . . . . .127 F4
Keppel Terr **8** PL2. . . . . .127 F4
Kerensa Gdns **13** TR5 . . . . . .54 D1
  St Agnes TR5. . . . . .68 D8
Kerensa Gn TR11. . . . . .144 E5
Kergillack Cl TR11. . . . . .144 C4
Kergilliack Rd TR11. . . . . .144 D5
Kerhuon Ct PL31. . . . . .109 D5
Kerkin Cl **1** TR4. . . . . .55 E4
Kerley Gr TR1 . . . . .69 F3
Kerley Hill TR4 . . . . .69 A3
Kerley Vale TR4 . . . . .69 A3
Kernick Gdns TR10 . . . . .144 A6
Kernick Ind Est TR10 . . . . . . .144 A7
Kernick Pk TR10. . . . . .144 A7
Kernick Rd Penryn TR10 . . . . .144 B7
  Tregonetha PL30. . . . . .46 D6
Kernick Way TR27 . . . . .142 E8
Kernow Cl Bodmin PL31. . . . .109 F5
  Torpoint PL11. . . . . .126 E3
  Wadebridge PL27 . . . . .108 B5
Kernow Cres EX23. . . . . .104 E4
Kernow Ct Newquay TR7 . . . .110 E6
  Torpoint PL11. . . . . .126 E3
Kernow Mill *★* PL12. . . . . . . .52 E1
Kernyk Lowen TR14 . . . . .138 F5
Kernyk Parc **4** TR13. . . . . . .146 C6
Kerrier Way TR14. . . . . .138 E3
  Tuckingmill TR14 . . . . .139 A4
KERRIS. 97 E8
Kerris Gr TR1. . . . . .137 B5
Kerrow La PL26. . . . . .59 D8
KERROW MOOR. 59 D8
Ker St Ope PL1. . . . . .127 E2
Kersbrook Cross PL17 . . . . . . .27 F2
Kersey Cl TR27 . . . . .142 C5
Kersey Rd Flushing TR11 . . . .145 B7
  Flushing TR11 . . . . .145 C7
Ker St PL1. . . . . .127 E1
Keryor Cl PL25 . . . . .114 F3
Kestell Pk PL31. . . . . .109 E2
Kestenenn **16** PL31. . . . . . . .109 D5
KESTLE 73 A4
Kestle Ct PL31. . . . . .109 C5
Kestle Dr TR1 . . . . .69 F3
Kestle La PL15. . . . . .18 C2
KESTLE MILL. 111 F1
Kestle Rd PL26 . . . . .73 A4
Keston Gdns PL27 . . . . .108 A6
Kestor Cl PL2. . . . . .128 A7
Kestral Units PL5. . . . . .124 A1
Kestral Way **10** TR16. . . . . . .67 E4
Kestrel Cl **2** Guildford TR27 .142 E6
  Plymouth PL6. . . . . .125 D8
  7 Porthleven TR13. . . . . . . .98 B8
Kestrel Pk PL19. . . . . .147 D2
Keswick Cres PL6 . . . . .125 D2
Keveral La PL11. . . . . .64 B5
Kew Cl TR7. . . . . .111 A4
Kew Hal An Tow TR13. . . . . . .146 A6
Kew Klavji **11** PL31. . . . . . . .109 E5
Kew Lastanen TR1. . . . . .137 F5
Kew Noweth TR14 . . . . .138 D2
Kew Pendra TR19. . . . . .97 A6
Kew Pendra Cl TR19 . . . . .97 A6
Kew Vean TR26. . . . . .141 C3
KEYBRIDGE. 35 B8
Keyes Cl PL1. . . . . .127 F2
KEYHAM. 127 C5
Keyham Barton RC Prim Sch
  PL2. . . . . .127 C6
Keyham Ct PL2. . . . . .127 E6
Keyham Rd PL2. . . . . .127 C6
Keyham St PL5 . . . . .127 E8
Keyham Sta PL2 . . . . .127 C6
Khyber Pl PL11. . . . . .127 A3
Kibbiscombe Terr PL14 . . . . . .63 A8
Kidwelly Cl PL7. . . . . .131 C4
Kiel Pl PL3 . . . . .129 D5
Kiel Pla La PL3 . . . . .129 D5
Kilhallon PL24. . . . . .60 C5
Kilhallon Woodlands PL24 . . . .60 C5
KILKHAMPTON. 5 A6
Kilkhampton Junior and Infant
  Sch EX23. . . . . .5 A6
Killaganogue Rd PL30 . . . . . . .46 B8
KILLATOWN. 37 B1
Killatown Hill PL14 . . . . .37 B1
Killaton Cross EX22. . . . . .8 F7
Killerton La PL9. . . . . .129 D1
Killerton Rd EX23. . . . . .104 E5
Killicourt TR3. . . . . .82 A7
Killiers Ct TR15. . . . . .139 C7
Killiersfield TR15. . . . . .139 C6
Killigrew Ave PL12. . . . . .122 D1
Killigrew Gdns TR4. . . . . .70 D8
Killigrew Pl **9** TR11. . . . . . . .145 A4
Killigrew Rd PL14. . . . . .113 D6
Killigrew St TR11. . . . . .145 A4
KILLIVOSE. 138 C5
Killivose Beacon TR14. . . . . . .138 D1
  Shorts Hill TR14. . . . . .79 C5
Killivose Gdns TR14. . . . . .138 D1
Killivose Rd TR14. . . . . .138 D1
Killyvarder Way PL25. . . . . . . .115 B6
Kilmar Cl PL14. . . . . .37 F3
Kilmar Rd PL14. . . . . .113 D6
Kilmar St PL9. . . . . .129 D1
Kilmar Stkillerton La PL9 .129 D1
Kilmar Way PL14 . . . . .37 F3

Kilminorth Woods Nature
  Reserve *★* PL13. . . . . .117 A4
Kilna La PL12. . . . . .53 A2
Kiln Cl Cawsand PL10 . . . . . . .133 A1
  Mevagissey PL26. . . . . .73 C4
  Plymouth PL5. . . . . .127 C8
Kiln Mdws TR12. . . . . .92 C1
Kilnpark Wlk PL21. . . . . .126 E6
Kilworthy House Chelfham
  Senior Sch PL19. . . . . .30 E3
Kilworthy Hill PL19. . . . . .147 C6
Kilworthy Rd Tavistock PL19. .30 F3
  Tavistock PL19. . . . . .147 C6
Kimber Ct TR11. . . . . .145 B2
Kimberley Ct TR7. . . . . .110 D6
Kimberley Foster Cl PL11 . . . . .65 B5
Kimberley Park Rd TR11 . . . . .145 A4
Kimberley Pk PL14 . . . . .38 A3
Kimberley Pl TR11. . . . . .145 A4
Kimberley Rd PL27. . . . . .108 D5
Kimberly Cl TR7 . . . . .110 D6
Kimberly Dr PL6. . . . . .125 B1
Kimers Way PL13. . . . . .117 B8
Kiming EX23. . . . . .104 E4
Kimlers Way PL13. . . . . .117 B8
King Arthurs Terr **5** PL34. . . .14 C7
KINGBEARE 27 A1
King Charles Prim Sch
  TR11. . . . . .145 A3
King Charles St TR11 . . . . . . .144 F2
King Edward Cres TR7. . . . . . .110 D7
King Edward Mine Mus *★*
  TR14. . . . . .79 E5
King Edward Rd PL12. . . . . . .122 F2
Kingfisher Cl Plymouth PL6 .125 E6
  Tavistock PL19. . . . . .147 D2
Kingfisher Dr PL25 . . . . .115 A4
Kingfisher Way PL9. . . . . .135 C7
King George V Memorial Wlk
  TR27 . . . . .142 C6
KINGSAND. 133 A2
King's Ave Falmouth TR11 . . .144 F4
  St Austell PL25. . . . . .114 D3
Kingsbury Ho TR11 . . . . .145 A6
Kings Cross EX39. . . . . .2 E5
Kings Ct PL1 . . . . .128 A3
King's Hill EX23 . . . . .104 E3
Kings Hill Cl EX23. . . . . .104 E4
King's Hill Ind Est EX23 . . . . .104 F3
Kings Hill Mdw EX23. . . . . . . .104 E3
Kingsland Gardens Cl PL3 .128 B2
Kingsley Ave PL11. . . . . .127 B2
Kingsley Cl TR1. . . . . .69 E3
Kingsley Ct TR9. . . . . .57 E8
Kingsley Meade TR8. . . . . . . .111 B5
Kingsley Rd PL4. . . . . .128 E4
Kingsley Terr TR16 . . . . .67 C6
Kingsley Way TR13 . . . . .146 C5
Kingsmill Rd PL12. . . . . .122 C5
Kings Pippin PL26 . . . . .58 E5
Kings Rd Marazion TR17. . . . . .89 B5
  Plymouth, Devonport PL1. . . . .127 C3
  Plymouth, West Park PL5. . . . .123 F3
  4 St Mawes TR2. . . . . .95 B6
King's Rd Camborne TR14. . . .138 D4
  Penzance TR18 . . . . .143 D5
  Plymouth PL1. . . . . .128 A2
Kings Sch & Nur PL3. . . . . . . .128 E6
King's St PL22. . . . . .112 C2
King St Bude EX23. . . . . .104 C5
  Gunnislake PL18 . . . . .41 A6
  Millbrook PL10. . . . . .132 E5
  Newquay TR7. . . . . .110 D6
  Plymouth PL1. . . . . .148 B3
  Redruth PL15. . . . . .140 B5
  Tavistock PL19. . . . . .147 B6
  Torpoint PL11. . . . . .127 C3
  Truro TR1. . . . . .137 D4
KING'S TAMERTON. 123 F2
King's Tamerton Rd PL5 . . . . .123 F2
Kingston Cl PL7. . . . . .131 A5
Kingston Dr PL7. . . . . .131 B5
Kingston Rd PL7. . . . . .28 E1
Kingston Way **9** TR10. . . . . . .81 C1
Kingston Way Rd **10** TR10. . .81 C1
Kings Tor PL20. . . . . .42 E4
Kingsway PL10. . . . . .133 B2
Kingsway Gdns PL6. . . . . .124 F3
Kingswear Cres PL6. . . . . .125 B1
Kings Wood *★* PL26. . . . . . . .73 B7
Kingswood Est PL14. . . . . .38 C1
Kingswood Park Ave PL3 .128 D6
Kingswood Rd PL18. . . . . .41 A6
Kinnard Cres PL6. . . . . .124 F7
Kinross Ave PL4 . . . . .129 A4
Kinsale Rd PL5. . . . . .123 F3
Kinsman Est PL31. . . . . .109 C3
Kinterbury Rd PL5. . . . . .127 B8
Kinterbury St PL1. . . . . .149 A2
Kinterbury Terr PL5. . . . . .127 B8
Kinver Cl PL6. . . . . .125 D4
Kipling Gdns PL5. . . . . .124 D2
Kirby Rd TR1 . . . . .137 A4
Kirkby Pl PL4. . . . . .148 C4
Kirkby Terr PL4. . . . . .148 C4
Kirkdale Gdns PL2. . . . . .128 B7
Kirkland Cl PL20. . . . . .42 D2
Kirkland Ct PL20. . . . . .109 B7
Kirkstall Cl PL2. . . . . .128 A8
Kirkwall Rd PL5. . . . . .124 E3
Kirland Bower PL30. . . . . .48 B7
Kirland Rd PL30. . . . . .109 B2
Kirthen Wood TR27. . . . . .90 C8
Kirton Pl PL3. . . . . .129 B5
Kitchen Gdns TR11 . . . . .144 F5
Kit Hill Cres PL5. . . . . .127 C8
Kit Hill Ctry Pk *★* PL17. . . . . .40 A6
Kit Hill Rd PL17. . . . . .40 B6

Kit Hill Vw PL15. . . . . .106 D4
Kitley Way PL5 . . . . .123 D1
Kitter Dr PL9. . . . . .136 A5
Kittiwake Cl TR27. . . . . .77 E3
Kitts Ct **17** TR18. . . . . .143 E5
Kleinfontein Terr PL14. . . . . . . .38 D4
Knapmedown PL15. . . . . .11 B1
Knapps Cl PL9. . . . . .136 C6
Knave-Go-By TR14. . . . . .79 D5
Kneele Gdns PL3. . . . . .128 E8
Knighton Rd PL4. . . . . .149 C3
Knighton Terr **3** PL20. . . . . . .42 C5
Knightor Cl PL26. . . . . .59 E6
Knights Cl **1** PL34. . . . . .14 C7
Knights Ct PL22. . . . . .112 B3
Knights Hill TR1. . . . . .137 B6
Knights Mdw TR3. . . . . .81 F7
Knight's Mdws TR3. . . . . .81 F7
KNIGHTSMILL 23 F7
Knights Mill Hill
  St Teath PL30. . . . . .23 E7
  Tregreenwell PL30. . . . . .23 F7
Knights Way TR15 . . . . .140 D7
Knill Cl TR26 . . . . .141 C2
Knill Cross PL10. . . . . .132 E5
Knill Cross Cotts PL10 . . . . . .132 E5
Knoll Pk TR1. . . . . .137 F4
Knoll The PL7. . . . . .130 B6
Knowland Cl PL1. . . . . .127 F3
Knowle Ave PL2. . . . . .127 E6
Knowle Terr PL20 . . . . .42 E4
Koth Karrji PL30. . . . . .23 E7
KUGGAR. 103 B6
Kyl Cober Parc PL17. . . . . .28 E1
Kynance Cl PL11. . . . . .126 F4
Kynance Cove TR12. . . . . . . .102 E3
Kynance Ho TR1. . . . . .69 E4
Kynance Terr TR12 . . . . .102 F3

L

Labatt Cl PL6. . . . . .125 D3
Labernum Terr **1** EX23. . . . . . .5 A6
Labour In Vain TR19 . . . . .87 A5
Laburnum Cl TR11. . . . . .144 F5
Laburnum Cotts PL19. . . . . . .147 C6
Laburnum Ct TR11. . . . . .144 F6
Laburnum Dr TR11 . . . . .144 F5
Lacey Cl TR14 . . . . .79 E5
Ladder La PL30. . . . . .35 F2
LADOCK 57 C1
Ladock CE Sch TR2 . . . . .57 C2
Ladock Rd Ladock TR2. . . . . . .57 C1
  Probus TR2 . . . . .71 C7
Lady Beam Ct PL17. . . . . .39 F6
Ladybird La **6** PL20. . . . . .42 D3
Ladycross PL15. . . . . .18 F7
Ladyfern Rd PL6. . . . . .121 C1
Lady La **2** TR2 . . . . .84 A8
Lady Modiford's CE Prim Sch
  PL20. . . . . .42 E4
LADY NANCE. 44 F3
Ladysmith Cl PL4. . . . . .149 C4
Ladysmith Rd PL4. . . . . .129 B3
Lady St TR13 . . . . .146 B5
Ladywell PL28. . . . . .107 D5
Ladywell Pl PL4. . . . . .149 B3
Laflouder Fields TR12 . . . . . . .99 A2
Laflouder La TR12. . . . . .99 A2
Lafrowda Cl TR19. . . . . .86 E6
Lafrowda Terr TR19. . . . . .86 F6
Laguna Ct TR15. . . . . .140 B5
LAIRA. 129 C4
Laira Ave PL3. . . . . .129 C4
Laira Bridge Rd PL4 . . . . .129 B1
Laira Gdns PL3. . . . . .129 C4
Laira Green Prim Sch PL3 .129 C4
Laira Park Cres PL4. . . . . .129 B4
Laira Park Pl PL4. . . . . .129 B4
Laira Park Rd PL4. . . . . .129 B4
Laira Pl PL4. . . . . .149 C2
Laira St PL4. . . . . .149 C3
Laity TR13. . . . . .92 B5
Laity Dr TR14. . . . . .138 F3
Laity Fields TR14. . . . . .138 F3
Laity La Carbis Bay TR26. . . . .77 C4
  Withen TR26. . . . . .141 B1
Laity Moor Burnthouse TR3 . .81 B3
  Forge TR16. . . . . .68 A4
Laity Rd TR14. . . . . .79 C4
Laity Wlk PL6. . . . . .124 D6
LAKE. 42 E3
Lake La Dousland PL20. . . . . . .42 E3
  Liskeard PL14 . . . . .113 C5
Lake Mews PL10. . . . . .132 E5
Lake Rd PL9. . . . . .135 B6
Lakeside PL19. . . . . .147 B6
Lakeside Dr PL5. . . . . .123 E5
Lake View TR13. . . . . .53 C8
Lake View TR15. . . . . .124 B6
Lakeview Dr PL5. . . . . .124 B5
Lalebrick Rd PL9. . . . . .135 B5
LAMANVA. 93 C6
Lamanva Cl **16** TR16. . . . . . . .67 E4
Lamanva Rd **17** TR16. . . . . . .67 E4
Lambert Rd PL5. . . . . .124 E6
Lambert Terr **4** TR11. . . . . . .145 A5
Lambhay Hill PL1. . . . . .149 A1
Lambhay St PL1. . . . . .149 A1
LAMBOURNE. 55 B2
Lambourne Ave **7** TR5 . . . . . .54 D1
Lamb Pk **5** PL24 . . . . .60 C4
Lambs Cl TR11. . . . . .144 E5
LAMELLION. 113 A4
Lamellyn Dr TR1. . . . . .69 C5
Lamellyn Rd PL24. . . . . .60 B4
Lamerhooe Cross PL19 . . . . . .29 C1

Lamerhooe Dr
  Horsebridge PL19 . . . . .29 C1
  Luckett PL19 . . . . .40 C8
LAMERTON. 30 B3
Lamerton CE Prim Sch
  PL19 . . . . .30 B3
Lamerton Cl PL5. . . . . .124 E3
Lametton Gn PL14. . . . . .51 B4
Lamledra Hill PL26 . . . . .85 D5
Lamorak Cl PL26 . . . . .73 B3
LAMORICK 47 E7
LAMORNA 97 E5
Lamorna Cl TR27 . . . . .78 D6
Lamorna Ct TR16 . . . . .67 D6
Lamorna Dr [11] PL17. . . . . . .39 F4
Lamorna Parc [12] PL17 . . . . .39 F4
Lamorna Pk St Austell PL25 .114 E7
  Torpoint PL11 . . . . .126 C4
Lamorne Cl [4] TR6 . . . . .55 A4
LAMORRAN 83 C8
Lampen Rd PL14. . . . . .36 F2
Lampen Terr PL14 . . . . .36 F2
LANA 13 D7
Lana Cotts EX22 . . . . .13 C7
Lanadwell St PL28 . . . . .107 D5
Lanaton Rd TR10 . . . . .144 A8
Lancamshire La TR20. . . . . . .89 F5
Lancaster Cres PL27 . . . . . . .31 F3
Lancaster Gdns PL5 . . . . . . .124 D4
Lanchard La PL14. . . . . .113 B5
Lanchard Rd PL14 . . . . .113 B5
Lanchard Rise PL14. . . . . . . .113 B5
Landaviddy La PL13. . . . . . . .62 D2
Lander Ct TR1 . . . . .137 D3
Lander Rd PL12. . . . . .122 F3
Landers Hill PL27 . . . . .32 F5
Landerslake PL15 . . . . .27 B7
Landeryon Gdns PL18 . . . . .143 D5
Landewednack Com Prim Sch
  TR12 . . . . .102 F2
Landithy TR20 . . . . .143 A8
Landlake Cross PL15 . . . . . . .28 A8
Landlake Rd Landlake PL15. . .28 A8
  Launceston PL15 . . . . .106 B2
Landlooe La PL14 . . . . .51 C2
LANDRAKE 53 B3
Landrake Cl PL5. . . . . .127 C8
Landreath Pl PL24 . . . . .60 B5
Landrew Rd PL25. . . . . .114 F6
LANDREYNE. 27 C2
Land's End Airport TR19 . . . .86 F3
Lands End Rd TR19 . . . . .97 A6
Lands Pk PL9 . . . . .135 F7
LANDULPH. 123 A7
Landulph Cross PL12 . . . . . .118 F1
Landulph Gdns PL5 . . . . . . .127 C8
Landulph Sch PL12 . . . . . . .118 F1
LANE 111 B3
LANEAST 17 B2
Lane End Cross PL19. . . . . . .29 D2
Lanepark La EX39 . . . . .2 D5
Lane Reddin Terr [21] TR18 .143 C2
LANESCOT. 60 D6
Lane The PL7. . . . . .130 D6
Langage Cross PL7 . . . . . . .131 F6
Langage Ind Est PL7 . . . . . .131 D4
Langage Pk PL7 . . . . .131 C4
Langage Science Pk PL7. . . .131 D5
Langage S Rd PL7 . . . . .131 E4
Langarth Cl TR3 . . . . .69 D4
Langdale Cl PL6. . . . . .125 D1
Langdale Gdns PL6 . . . . . . .125 D1
LANGDON. 11 C3
Langdon Cross PL15 . . . . . . .18 D8
Langdon Ct PL9 . . . . .136 B6
Langdon Down Way PL11 . .136 B7
Lang Dr [1] PL27 . . . . .108 C5
Langerwell Cl PL12 . . . . . . .122 C3
Langerwell La PL12 . . . . . . .122 C3
Langford Pl [6] PL28 . . . . . .107 C4
Langfords Mdw [4] PL35. . . .9 C1
Lang Gdns PL18 . . . . .41 A3
Lang Gr Plymouth PL9 . . . . .136 C7
  Tavistock PL19 . . . . .147 D5
Langham Pl PL4 . . . . .149 C3
Langhill Rd PL3 . . . . .128 C5
Langley Cl PL6 . . . . .125 A7
Langley Cres PL6. . . . . .124 F7
Langman Ct [13] PL20 . . . . . .41 B1
Langmead Cl PL6. . . . . .129 C8
Langmead Rd PL6 . . . . .129 C8
Langmore Cl PL6. . . . . .129 A7
LANGORE 18 D5
Langore Rd PL15 . . . . .18 D5
Langorran Rd TR14 . . . . . . .138 B3
Langreek Bglws PL13 . . . . . .62 C2
Langreek Rd PL13 . . . . .62 C2
Langstone Rd PL2. . . . . .128 C7
Langstone Terr PL2. . . . . . . .128 C7
Langton Hiill PL15 . . . . .27 F7
Langton Rd Falmouth TR11 .145 A6
  [8] Yelverton PL20 . . . . . . .42 C3
Langton Terr [8] TR11 . . . . .145 A6
Langurrock Rd TR8. . . . . . . .110 A3
Langurtho Rd PL23 . . . . . . .116 B4
Langweath Est TR12 . . . . . . .99 D7
Langweath Gdns TR27 . . . . .77 E3
Langweath La TR12. . . . . . . .99 D7
Langwedh TR16 . . . . .67 D4
Lanhenvor Ave TR7. . . . . . .110 E5
Lanherne Ave TR8 . . . . .45 A8
Lanhydrock Parc [4] TR12 . .101 C4
Lanhydrock Ho & Gdns ★
  PL30. . . . . .48 D6
Lanhydrock Rd PL4. . . . . . . .129 B2
Lanhydrock View PL31. . . . .109 D3
Laninval Hl PL30. . . . . .47 F8

LANIVET 47 F6
Lanivet Prim Sch PL30. . . . . .47 E7
LANJETH 58 E3
LANJEW 46 F7
Lanjowan TR13 . . . . .146 B6
LANK 24 B2
Lankelly Cl PL23 . . . . .116 B4
Lankelly La PL23. . . . . .116 A4
LANLIVERY 48 C1
Lanlivery Prim Sch PL30 . . . .48 D2
Lanlovie Mdw TR8. . . . . .55 D8
Lanmoor Est TR16 . . . . .80 D6
Lannarth Glas TR16. . . . . . .140 E1
LANNER 80 D6
Lanner Gn TR16 . . . . .140 E1
Lanner Hill Redruth TR15. . .140 D2
  Redruth, Pennance TR16 . .140 E1
Lanner Moor Terr TR16 . . . . .80 E6
Lanner Prim Sch TR16 . . . . .80 D6
Lanner Sq TR16 . . . . .80 D6
Lannoweth Rd TR18 . . . . . .143 F6
Lanoweth TR10 . . . . .81 D2
Lanow La PL30 . . . . .23 A4
Lanoy Rd PL15. . . . . .27 D5
LANREATH 62 B7
LANSALLOS 62 A2
Lansallos St PL13. . . . . .62 D1
Lansdown Cl EX23 . . . . .104 D5
Lansdowne TR26 . . . . .141 B4
Lansdowne Cl TR18. . . . . . .143 C5
Lansdowne Ct TR18. . . . . . .143 B5
Lansdowne Pl TR18. . . . . . .143 C4
Lansdowne Rd
  Callington PL17 . . . . .39 E4
  Falmouth TR11. . . . . .145 C3
  Penzance TR18 . . . . .143 C5
  Plymouth PL6. . . . . .124 F2
Lansdown Rd Bude EX23. . .104 D5
  Wadebridge PL27 . . . . . . .108 B5
LANSTEPHAN 106 C8
Lansweden La EX23. . . . . . . .10 C6
Lantallack Cross PL12 . . . . . .53 A3
LANTEGLOS 14 F1
Lanteglos Highway 61 C8
Lantoom Way [8] PL14 . . . . .50 E7
Lanuthnoe Est TR27 . . . . . . .77 F1
Lanwithan Cl PL22 . . . . . . .112 D2
Lanwithan Rd PL22 . . . . . . .112 E1
Lanxon Cres PL30. . . . . .48 C2
Lanxon Rd PL30 . . . . .35 C8
Lanyon Ct PL14. . . . . .37 F3
Lanyon Rd Bosiliack TR20. . .87 F8
  Playing Place TR3 . . . . . . .82 B8
Lappa Valley Steam Railway ★
  TR8. . . . . .56 C7
Lapthorn Cl PL9 . . . . .135 C4
Larch Cl PL12. . . . . .122 C3
Larch Dr PL6 . . . . .125 E2
Larcombe Rd PL25. . . . . . . .115 A6
Laregan Hill PL18 . . . . .143 C3
Lariggan Cres PL18 . . . . . . .143 D4
Lariggan Rd PL18 . . . . .143 D4
Larkfield Cl PL26 . . . . .58 E5
Larkfield Rise [3] TR2 . . . . . .95 A6
Larkhall Rise PL3. . . . . .129 B5
Larkham Cl PL7 . . . . .130 C6
Larkham La PL7 . . . . .130 C6
Lark Hill PL2 . . . . .128 A6
LATCHLEY 40 D8
Latchley Plain PL18. . . . . . . .40 D7
Latham Cl PL6. . . . . .129 A7
Latimer Cl PL7 . . . . .131 B5
Latimer Wlk PL6. . . . . .124 E7
Launcells Cross EX23. . . . . . .5 B1
LAUNCESTON 106 D5
Launceston Castle ★ PL15 .106 C6
  Plymouth PL6. . . . . .125 B7
Launceston Coll PL15. . . . . .106 C4
Launceston Comm Prim Sch
  PL15. . . . . .106 C5
Launceston Community Hospl
  PL15. . . . . .106 C4
Launceston Rd Bodmin PL31 .35 B1
  Holton PL31. . . . . .35 B3
  Kelly Bray PL17 . . . . .39 E6
  Newtown PL15 . . . . .27 C5
  St Clether PL15 . . . . .17 A3
  Treraven PL15 . . . . .16 F3
Launceston Ret Pk PL15 . . .106 C4
Launceston Sta ★ PL15 . . . .106 B6
  PL15. . . . . .18 E3
Launceston Steam Rly ★
  PL15. . . . . .18 E3
Laura Cl PL34. . . . . .14 D7
Laura Dr PL25 . . . . .115 A5
Laurel Ct PL2. . . . . .128 A7
Laurel Dene PL2. . . . . .128 A7
Laurel Dr PL6 . . . . .125 E5
Laurel La PL17 . . . . .39 E6
Laurel Rd PL2 . . . . .128 A7
Laurels The PL18 . . . . .40 E6
La Vague TR3 . . . . .82 C5
Lavington Cl PL7 . . . . .131 B5
Lavinia Dr PL7. . . . . .130 C5
Lavorrick Orchs PL26 . . . . . .73 C4
Lawellan La PL30. . . . . .47 B8
LAWHITTON 19 C1
Lawn Cl [2] PL7 . . . . .131 C5
Lawn Steps TR11 . . . . .145 B4
Lawns The Plymouth PL5 . . .124 E1
  Torpoint PL11 . . . . .127 A4
Lawn The Par PL24 . . . . .60 B5
  Tavistock PL19 . . . . .147 D6
Lawrence House Mus ★
  PL15. . . . . .106 C6
Lawrence Rd Plymouth PL9 .135 A6
  St Agnes TR5 . . . . .54 C1
Lawry Cl [6] PL14. . . . . .113 B5

Lawson Gr PL9 . . . . .135 C7
Lawton Cl TR7. . . . . .110 B5
Law Wlk PL6. . . . . .124 D6
Leader Rd TR7. . . . . .111 E7
Leafield PL31. . . . . .35 B2
Leander Way PL5. . . . . .124 D2
Leanway PL12 . . . . .122 E2
Leap Pk TR3. . . . . .69 C3
Leas The TR1 . . . . .137 E5
Leat Cl PL20 . . . . .42 E3
Leatfield PL26 . . . . .73 C3
Leatherby Cl PL4. . . . . .124 E7
Leathern Bottle Hill PL30 . . .24 A5
Leather Tor Cl [4] PL20. . . . .42 C3
Leat Rd Lifton PL16 . . . . . . .19 F3
  Pentreath TR19 . . . . .75 A1
Leatside PL6. . . . . .121 C1
Leats The TR1 . . . . .137 C4
Leat The [9] EX23 . . . . .4 E1
Leat View PL12 . . . . .122 B3
Leat Wlk Plymouth PL3 . . . .128 E6
  Saltash PL12 . . . . .122 D4
Leaves Yd PL3 . . . . .129 B7
Lea Way EX23 . . . . .104 F6
Le Ball Hill Bellasize PL30 . . .49 B8
  Tawnamoor PL30. . . . . .35 F1
LEBURNICK 28 D8
Leburnick Cross PL15. . . . . . .28 D8
Lecudden Rd PL30. . . . . .34 F5
Ledgate La PL7 . . . . .131 F8
Ledra Cl TR12. . . . . .103 A4
Leigham Gdns PL25 . . . . . . .114 B3
Ledrah Rd PL25. . . . . .114 B3
LEEDSTOWN 78 E1
Leedstown Com Prim Sch
  TR27. . . . . .78 E1
Leeside Ct [7] PL2. . . . . . . .128 A4
Lefra Orch TR19 . . . . .97 B6
Legendry Land's End ★
  TR19. . . . . .96 A5
Leggos Ct [5] TR15. . . . . . .140 B5
Legion Hall La [12] PL18. . . .40 F5
Legion La [3] PL24 . . . . .60 D5
Legis Wlk PL6 . . . . .125 B8
Leg O Mutton Corner [13]
  PL20 . . . . .42 C3
Le Hayes Hill PL30. . . . . .35 F4
LEIGHAM 129 E8
Leigham Ct PL1 . . . . .148 B2
Leigham Manor Dr PL6 . . . .129 E8
Leigham Prim Sch PL6. . . . .125 E1
Leigham St PL1. . . . . .148 B1
Leigham Terrace La PL1 . . . .148 B2
Leigham Terr La W PL1 . . . .148 B2
Leight Ct PL6. . . . . .129 A8
Leigh La Hatt PL12 . . . . .53 D6
  Roborough PL6 . . . . .121 D2
Leighton Rd PL3. . . . . .128 F8
LELANT 77 E4
LELANT DOWNS 77 D2
Lelant Mdws TR26. . . . . .77 E4
Lelant Saltings Sta TR26 . . . .77 F3
Lelant Sta TR26. . . . . .77 E4
Lemellen Gdns PL30. . . . . . .23 A7
Lemin Parc TR27 . . . . .78 E3
Lemin's Ct TR15 . . . . .140 B5
Lemon Hill TR11. . . . . .82 A3
Lemon Mews Rd TR1 . . . . .137 D4
Lemon Quay TR1 . . . . .137 D4
Lemon Row TR1. . . . . .137 D4
Lemon St St Keverne TR12 . .101 D4
  [19] Truro TR1 . . . . .137 D4
Lender La [5] TR12 . . . . .99 A2
Lendra La PL17 . . . . .39 D4
Leo Ave [12] PL9 . . . . .136 E8
LERRYN 61 D8
Lerryn CE Prim Sch PL22. . . .61 D8
Lerryn Rd PL22 . . . . .49 A1
Lerryn View PL22. . . . . .61 C8
Lerwick Rd PL27. . . . . .31 F3
Lescudjack Cres TR18. . . . . .143 F6
Lescudjack Rd TR18 . . . . . .143 E6
Lescudjack Terr TR18. . . . . .143 F6
Lesingey La TR20. . . . . .88 A5
Leskinnick Pl [14] TR18. . . .143 E6
Leskinnick Terr TR18 . . . . . .143 E6
Leslie Ct TR13 . . . . .146 B6
LESNEWTH 10 A1
Lesnewth [18] PL24 . . . . . . .60 B4
Lester Cl PL3 . . . . .129 B6
Lestraynes La TR10 . . . . .92 E8
Lethlean Cl TR27 . . . . .142 D7
Lethlean La TR27 . . . . .142 D7
Lethlean Towans TR27. . . . .142 D8
LEVALSA MEOR 73 B8
Levant Cl TR19 . . . . .86 F8
Levant Mine & Beam Engine ★
  TR19. . . . . .74 E1
Levant Rd TR19. . . . . .86 F8
Leven Cotts EX23. . . . . .104 D5
Leverlake Rd EX23. . . . . .6 F4
Levine View TR11. . . . . .144 E1
LEWANNICK 27 B7
Lewannick Cl PL15 . . . . .27 B7
Lewannick Com Prim Sch
  PL15. . . . . .27 B7
Lewannick Rd TR8. . . . . .43 D1
Lewarne Cres TR7. . . . . . . .111 C7
Lewarne Hill PL14. . . . . .36 E5
Lewarne Rd TR7. . . . . .111 C8
Little Ash Gdns PL5. . . . . . .123 B1
Little Ash Rd PL5 . . . . .123 B1
LITTLE BOSULLOW 75 D1
Little Bridge Cross EX22 . . . .8 A5
Littlebridge Mdw EX22 . . . . .8 A5

Lewman Rd TR2 . . . . .71 C6
Leworthy Cross EX22 . . . . . . .8 E4
LEY. 36 E1
Leyford La PL9 . . . . .135 F3
Ley La PL20. . . . . .119 D6
Leypark Ct PL6 . . . . .125 E2
Leypark Dr PL6 . . . . .125 E2
Leypark Wlk PL6 . . . . .125 E2
Leys La TR17 . . . . .89 B5
LEZANT 28 B6
Libby Ct PL12. . . . . .122 C5
Liberator Row [4] PL27 . . . . .31 F3
Libra Ave [5] PL9. . . . . .136 E8
Lidden Cl TR18. . . . . .143 C3
Lidden Cres TR18. . . . . .143 C3
Lidden Rd TR18. . . . . .143 C3
Liddicoat Rd PL22 . . . . .112 D3
Liddle Way PL7. . . . . .131 B6
Lifeboat Hill [32] TR26. . . . .141 B6
LIFTON 19 F3
Lifton Comm Prim Sch
  PL16. . . . . .19 F4
LIFTONDOWN 19 D4
Liftondown Cross PL16 . . . . .19 D4
Liggars Dr [9] PL14. . . . . . . .50 E7
Liggars Farm Rd PL14 . . . . . .50 F5
Lighterage Hill TR1. . . . . . .137 E2
Lighthouse Hill TR16 . . . . . .67 C6
Lighthouse La PL26 . . . . .85 C5
Lighthouse Rd
  [19] Lizard TR12. . . . . . . .102 F2
  Lizard TR12. . . . . .102 F2
Lilac Cl PL9 . . . . .135 C5
Lily Way PL28 . . . . .31 F7
Lime Cl TR8 . . . . .44 F6
Limerick Pl PL4 . . . . .149 C3
Limes La Liskeard PL14. . . . .113 B5
Limes The PL6. . . . . .124 F2
Lime Tree Way PL15 . . . . . . .27 D4
Limmicks Rd PL13 . . . . .117 D6
Lincoln Ave PL4 . . . . .149 C4
Lincoln Row [6] PL27. . . . . . .31 F3
Linden Ave TR7. . . . . .110 E5
Linden Cres TR7. . . . . .110 E5
Linden Terr PL4. . . . . .149 C3
Lindsay Fields TR9 . . . . .45 E1
Lingard Cl PL14. . . . . .113 A6
Lingfield Ave PL26. . . . . .58 E1
Linhay Cl PL25. . . . . .115 D6
Linhay La [4] PL6. . . . . .129 D1
Linkadells PL7 . . . . .130 D6
Link Cl TR11. . . . . .144 F4
Linketty La E PL6. . . . . .125 A1
Linketty Lane E PL6. . . . . . .130 C5
Link Rd PL15 . . . . .106 B3
Links The Falmouth TR11 . . .144 F1
  Praa Sands TR20 . . . . .90 C4
Links View EX23 . . . . .104 F6
Linley Cl PL3 . . . . .69 D3
Linnet Ct PL12. . . . . .122 C2
Linton Cl PL5. . . . . .124 C8
Linton La EX39 . . . . .2 C1
Linton Rd PL5 . . . . .124 C7
Linton Sq PL5 . . . . .124 C8
Lippell Dr PL9 . . . . .135 E6
Lipson Co-operative Academy
  PL4. . . . . .129 A4
LIPSON 149 C4
Lipson Ave PL4 . . . . .149 C4
Lipson Ct PL4 . . . . .149 B3
Lipson Rd PL4 . . . . .149 B4
Lipson Sp Ctr PL4. . . . . .129 A4
Lipson Terr PL4 . . . . .149 C4
LIPSON VALE 129 A4
Lipson Vale PL4. . . . . .129 A4
Lipson Vale Prim Sch PL4 . .129 C4
Lipstone Cres PL4 . . . . .149 C4
Lisburn Ter PL11. . . . . .127 B3
Liscawn Terr PL11 . . . . .127 B3
Liscombe Cl PL18. . . . . .41 A7
Lishaperhill Cross EX22. . . . .5 E2
LISKEARD 113 E6
Liskeard Bsns Pk PL14 . . . . .113 E6
Liskeard Com Hospl PL14 . .113 E7
Liskeard & District Mus ★
  PL14 . . . . .113 C6
Liskeard Hill PL14 . . . . .36 F2
Liskeard Hillfort Prim Sch
  PL14 . . . . .113 A6
Liskeard Rd Callington PL17 .39 E4
  Newtown PL15 . . . . .27 C4
  Saltash PL12 . . . . .122 B3
  Trematon PL12 . . . . .53 E3
Liskeard Sch & Com Coll
  PL14 . . . . .113 C7
Liskeard Sta PL14. . . . . .113 B4
Liskerrett Rd PL14 . . . . .113 D5
Liskey TR6 . . . . .55 A4
Liskey Hill TR6 . . . . .55 A4
Liskey Hill Cres [1] TR6. . . . .55 A4
Liskey Tourist Pk TR3. . . . . . .69 C4
Lisson Gr PL4 . . . . .128 F4
Lister Cl PL7. . . . . .130 F6
Lister Hill [10] TR11. . . . . . .145 A4
Lister St TR11 . . . . .145 A3
Listowel Dr PL13 . . . . .117 D4
Listry Rd TR7. . . . . .110 E5
Litchaton Cres PL7 . . . . . . .130 B7
Litchaton Way PL7. . . . . . . .130 B7
Litchfield Cl PL7 . . . . .131 B6

Little Bridge Pk PL27 . . . . .108 D6
LITTLE BRYNN 46 E5
Little Butts PL9. . . . . .135 E6
Little Castle St [7] TR1 . . . .137 C4
LITTLE COMFORT 28 C7
Little Dean PL14. . . . . .113 A5
Little Dinas PL28 . . . . .107 E4
Little Dock La PL5 . . . . .124 B2
Little Down La PL6. . . . . . . .121 E3
Little Downs Pk TR7 . . . . . .111 A4
Little Downs PL30 . . . . .36 A2
LITTLE FALMOUTH 145 B7
Little Falmouth TR11 . . . . . .145 B7
Little Fancy Cl PL6 . . . . .125 C2
Little Field Ct PL19 . . . . . . .147 E5
Little Gilly Hill [3] TR15. . . .140 C4
Little Gn PL12 . . . . .62 D1
Little Gregwartha TR16. . . . .80 A5
Little-in-sight [19] TR26 . . .141 A5
LITTLE KIRLAND 109 C1
Little La Hayle TR27. . . . . . .142 E7
  Kingsand PL10. . . . . .133 A2
  Staddiscombe PL9. . . . . . .135 D3
Little Laney PL13 . . . . .62 D1
Little Mdw Bodmin PL31. . . .109 D5
  Pyworthy EX22 . . . . .8 E5
Little Mill La TR27 . . . . .77 E2
Little Nanteague TR4 . . . . . .69 E7
Little Oaks TR10 . . . . .144 B6
Little Orch PL12 . . . . .53 C3
LITTLE PETHERICK 32 C6
Little Point Cres PL10 . . . . .132 F5
LITTLE PRIDEAUX 60 B7
Little Sinns TR16 . . . . .68 A3
Little Stark Cl PL26 . . . . .58 B4
Little Trelower Pk PL26 . . . . .58 F1
Little Treloweth TR15. . . . . .139 B6
Little Trelyn PL27. . . . . .21 E2
Little Trenethick [15] TR13 .146 D8
Little Treslea Hill PL30. . . . . .36 A3
Little Trethewey Est TR19 . .96 E4
Little Trethiggey TR8 . . . . . .111 F2
Little Treverrow PL27. . . . . . .21 E2
Little Trethiggey TR8 . . . . . .111 F2
Little Treviscoe PL26. . . . . . .58 B7
Little Western Rly ★ TR7. . .110 F5
Little Woburn Cl PL15. . . . .106 C4
Littlewood Cl PL7. . . . . .131 A4
Littlewood Mill La PL30 . . . .23 C1
LIZARD 102 F2
Lizard Cl PL6 . . . . .124 F7
Lizard Head La TR12 . . . . . .102 F2
Lizard Lighthouse Her Ctr ★
  TR12. . . . . .102 F1
Lizard Nature Reserve The ★
  TR12. . . . . .100 F2
Lizard Point TR12 . . . . .102 F1
Lizard Point Holiday Park ★
  TR12. . . . . .102 F8
Lizard Point Holiday Pk ★
  TR12. . . . . .99 D1
Lizard Wlk PL6 . . . . .125 A7
Llantillio Dr PL2 . . . . .128 B8
Llawnroc Cl TR14. . . . . .138 E2
Llewellyn Cl PL32. . . . . .105 C3
Lloyds Rd TR12 . . . . .103 A2
Loatmead Cross EX22. . . . . . .3 E3
LOCKENGATE 47 E4
Lockeridge Rd PL20. . . . . . . .41 B3
Lockington Ave PL3 . . . . . . .128 F7
Locks Wlk PL1 . . . . .127 E1
Lockyer Ct PL1 . . . . .148 C2
Lockyer Mews PL19. . . . . . .147 C6
Lockyer Rd PL3. . . . . .128 E5
Lockyers Quay PL4 . . . . . . .149 B2
Lockyer St PL1 . . . . .148 C2
Lockyer Terr PL12. . . . . .123 A3
Lodenek Ave PL28 . . . . .107 D4
Lodge Dr TR1 . . . . .137 F6
Lodge Gdns PL6 . . . . .124 E3
Lodge Hill PL14. . . . . .113 A3
Lodge La PL8. . . . . .136 F5
Lodge Way TR9. . . . . .45 F2
Loe Bar Rd TR13 . . . . .98 C8
Loe Hill TR11. . . . . .82 C5
Loe Valley Rd TR13 . . . . . . .146 B3
Lofoten Cl PL1 . . . . .127 E2
Loftus Gdns PL5 . . . . .123 C2
Logans Cl TR26. . . . . .141 D2
Loggans Cl TR27 . . . . .142 E8
Loggans Rd TR27 . . . . .142 E8
Loggans Way TR27 . . . . . . .142 E8
Loggans Wlk TR27 . . . . . . .142 E8
Lollabury Rd PL12. . . . . . . .122 C3
Lomond Hall TR26 . . . . . . .141 D1
LONDON APPRENTICE 59 B1
Longacre
  Harrowbarrow PL17 . . . . . .40 C4
  Plymouth PL7. . . . . .130 B7
Long Acre PL12. . . . . .122 B4
Long-A-Row Cl EX23 . . . . . .10 C6
Long Barn The TR20 . . . . . . .89 D8
LONGBRIDGE 129 F7
Longbridge Cl PL6. . . . . . . .129 F6
Longbridge Rd
  Plymouth, Laira PL3. . . . . .129 C4
  Plymouth, Longbridge PL6. .129 E2
Longbrook Barton PL7. . . . .130 D5
Longbrook St PL7 . . . . .130 F4
Longcause PL7. . . . . .130 F4
Longcause Specl Sch PL7 . .130 F4
Longcoombe La PL13. . . . . . .62 D3
Long Croft Rd [11] TR27 . . .142 E8
LONGCROSS 29 F6
Long Cross PL29. . . . . .22 C6

Longcross Victorian Gdns★
PL29 . . . .**22** C6
Long Down Gdns PL6 . . . .**125** E3
LONGDOWNS **81** A1
Longdowns Ind Est 6 TR10 **81** A1
Longdowns Trad EstTR10 . .**81** A1
Longfield TR11 . . . .**144** E4
Longfield Cl 25 PL17 . . . . . .**39** F4
Longfield Dr PL32 . . . .**105** C3
Longfield Pl PL4. . . . .**149** B4
Longfield Rd PL32 . . . .**105** C3
Long Field Rd PL15 . . . . . .**106** D4
Longfield Villas PL9 . . . . . .**135** D8
Longhouse La PL27 . . . .**21** F3
Long La High Street PL26 . .**58** C4
Ludgvan TR20 . . . .**89** A7
St Erth TR20, TR7. . . . . . .**89** E8
Tregurrian TR8. . . . .**44** F8
LONGLANDS **122** A1
Longlands PL9 . . . .**135** D8
Longlands La PL12. . . . . . .**122** B1
Long Lanes TR20 . . . .**89** F7
Long Ley PL3 . . . .**129** B6
Longman's La 3 PL17 . . . . . .**39** E4
Long Mdw Chapel PL15 . . . .**106** A5
Plymouth PL7. . . . .**130** D7
Long Mdw La 1 TR11. . . . .**144** D5
Long Mdw View PL23 . . . .**116** B5
Longmeadow Cl PL7. . . . . .**130** E7
Longmeadow Rd PL12 . . . .**122** E3
Long Moor TR12. . . . .**103** A5
Long Orch PL20 . . . .**41** B1
Long Park Cl PL9 . . . .**135** F5
Long Park Dr PL6. . . . .**125** D7
Long Park Rd PL12 . . . .**122** D2
Longpark Way PL25 . . . . . .**114** F5
Long Pk PL15 . . . .**18** D2
LONGROCK **88** F6
Long Rock Business Park
TR20. . . . .**88** F6
Long Rock Industrial Estate
TR20 . . . .**88** F6
Long Row TR19 . . . .**97** F7
Long Rowden PL3 . . . .**128** E6
Long Steps SP23 . . . .**116** C4
LONGSTONE Carbis Bay . . .**141** E1
St Mabyn **34** F8
Longstone Ave PL6 . . . .**125** A6
Longstone Cl TR26. . . . .**141** E1
Longstone Downs TR13. . . . .**91** E6
Longstone Hill TR26 . . . . . .**141** E1
Longstone Rd PL30 . . . .**34** E8
Long Terrace Cl 5 PL7 . . . .**131** C5
Longview Rd PL12 . . . .**122** D3
Longview Terr PL3 . . . .**129** B7
Longwood Cl PL7. . . . .**131** A4
Longwool Mdw EX23 . . . .**7** B6
LOOE **117** D3
Looe Com Academy PL13 .**117** D6
Looe Hill Looe PL13. . . . .**63** F5
Seaton PL13, PL11. . . . .**64** A5
Looe Prim Sch PL13 . . . . . .**117** D4
Looe St PL4 . . . .**149** A2
Looe Sta PL13 . . . .**117** C4
Lookout The 7 TR11 . . . . . .**145** B5
Looseleigh Cl PL6 . . . .**125** A4
Looseleigh La PL6. . . . .**124** F5
Looseleigh Pk PL6. . . . .**124** E5
Lopes Dr PL6. . . . .**121** C1
Lopes Rd Dousland PL20. . . . .**42** E3
Plymouth PL2. . . . .**128** B6
Lopwell Cl PL6 . . . .**124** F5
Lord Louis Cres PL9 . . . . . .**134** F6
Lords Mdw TR2. . . . .**71** F3
Lorrimore Ave PL2 . . . .**127** F5
Loscombe Ct TR16. . . . .**80** A5
Loscombe La TR16. . . . .**80** A5
Lost Gdns of Heligan The★
PL26 . . . .**73** B5
LOSTWITHIEL **112** E1
Lostwithiel Mus★ PL22 . . .**112** C2
Lostwithiel Prim Sch PL22**112** C2
Lostwithiel Rd PL30, PL31. .**48** C7
Lostwithiel St PL23 . . . . . .**116** C4
Lostwithiel Sta PL22. . . . . .**112** D2
Lostwood Rd PL25 . . . .**114** E4
Lotherton Cl PL7 . . . .**131** B3
Loughboro Rd PL5. . . . .**123** C1
LOVATON **42** F1
Love La Bodmin PL31 . . . . . .**109** F5
Hayle TR27. . . . .**142** E7
Mousehole TR19 . . . .**88** C1
Penryn TR10 . . . .**144** D8
Penzance TR18 . . . .**143** C4
24 St Ives TR26 . . . .**141** B6
Saltash PL12 . . . .**122** E2
Lovell Rd PL3. . . . .**128** F6
Lovely La PL12 . . . .**65** A8
Loveny Cl 1 Bodmin PL31 . .**109** A4
St Neot PL14 . . . .**36** F2
Loveny Rd PL14. . . . .**36** F2
Lovering Rd PL25 . . . .**114** E6
Lovers La EX23 . . . .**10** B7
Lovibond Wlk PL27 . . . .**108** C5
Lowarth Cl TR13. . . . .**146** B6
Lowarth Elms 13 TR15 . . . .**140** B5
Lowarthow Marghas TR15**140** D5
Lowenac Cres TR27. . . . .**78** E6
Lowenac Gdns TR14 . . . . . .**138** C2
Lowen Bre TR1 . . . .**69** E3
Lowen Ct 7 TR1. . . . .**137** D4
Lowenek Cl TR11 . . . .**144** E5
Lowenna Fields TR11 . . . . . .**93** D4

Lowenna Gdns PL13 . . . . . .**117** C4
Lowenna La 3 TR6 . . . .**55** B4
Lowenna Manor PL27. . . . . .**21** E3
Lowen Way TR3 . . . .**69** C3
Lower Anderton Rd PL10. .**132** F5
Lower Balwest TR13 . . . .**90** D4
Lower Barncoose TR15 . . . .**139** F6
Lower Biteford Cross EX39. .**3** E6
Lower Bore St PL31. . . . . . .**109** D5
Lower Boscaswell Parc
TR19. . . . .**74** F1
LOWER BREA **139** A3
Lower Broad La TR15,
TR16. . . . .**139** C8
Lower Cardrew La TR15. . . .**140** B6
Lower Carnkie TR16 . . . .**140** A1
Lower Castle Rd TR2. . . . . . .**95** A5
Lower Chapel St PL13. . . . .**117** D3
Lower Church St 2 TR27 . .**142** D6
Lower Cleaverfield PL15 . .**106** C7
LOWER CLICKER **51** F4
Lower Clicker Rd PL14. . . . . .**51** F4
LOWER COMPTON **129** A5
Lower Compton Rd PL3. . . .**128** F5
Lower Condurrow TR14. . . .**139** A1
Lower Coronation Terr 9
PL17. . . . .**39** F4
Lower Eastcliff TR4. . . . .**68** A7
Lower East Street 1 TR9 . .**45** E6
Lower Elms PL27 . . . .**21** F3
Lower Fairfield PL12. . . . . . .**65** A8
Lower Farm Rd PL7. . . . . . .**131** A4
Lower Fore St PL12. . . . .**123** A2
Lower Glen Pk PL14 . . . .**38** D4
Lower Goongumpas La
TR16 . . . .**68** F1
Lower Goonrea PL13 . . . . . .**117** B4
LOWER GREEN **146** A5
Lower Green St TR18 . . . . . .**143** D1
Lower Greenbanks PL27 . . . .**21** E2
Lower Grumbla Rd TR20. . . .**87** C4
Lower Gurnick Rd TR18. . . .**143** B3
Lower Hill TR13 . . . .**146** C6
Lower Hillcrest
Helston TR13. . . . .**146** C6
9 Perranporth TR6. . . . . . .**55** A4
Lower Hillside PL14 . . . .**50** B6
Lower Hugus Rd TR3 . . . . . .**69** C3
Lower Kelly PL18 . . . .**41** A3
Lower Kennegy TR20 . . . .**90** A3
Lower La Mawgan TR12 . . . . .**99** D7
6 Plymouth PL1 . . . .**149** A2
Lower Lux St 5 PL14 . . . . . .**113** C6
Lower Market St
Looe PL13 . . . .**117** D3
Penryn TR10 . . . .**144** C7
Lower Mdw 5 TR4 . . . .**69** A3
Lower Merritts Hill 22 TR16 **67** E4
Lower Middle Hill PL14 . . . .**38** E4
Lower Molinnis PL26 . . . . . .**47** D2
LOWER NINNES **76** B1
Lower Ninnis TR16 . . . .**140** F5
Lower North Country TR16. **67** F4
Lower Parc TR12 . . . .**92** C2
Lower Park Dr PL9 . . . .**135** F4
Lower Pengegon TR14. . . . .**138** F3
Lower Pentreath 5 TR20 . . .**90** B3
Lower Peverell Rd TR18 . . .**143** E7
Lower Pk TR2 . . . .**70** F5
Lower Polstain Rd TR3. . . . .**69** D3
Lower Porkellis TR3 . . . .**92** A7
LOWER PORTHPEAN **59** E1
Lower Port View PL12 . . . . .**122** F2
LOWER PROSPIDNICK **91** C6
Lower Pumpfield Row
TR15 . . . .**139** B6
Lower Quay TR12 . . . .**92** C1
Lower Quay Rd TR3 . . . .**81** F6
Lower Rd Downderry PL11. . . .**64** C4
Welltown PL30 . . . .**36** A2
Lower Redannick TR1 . . . . .**137** C4
Lower Ridings PL7 . . . .**131** B7
LOWER ROSE **55** D5
LOWER ROSEWARNE **138** C4
Lower Rosewin Row 9
TR1 . . . .**137** D5
Lower Row PL10. . . . .**133** A2
Lower Rowes Terr PL26. . . . .**58** D5
Lower Saltram PL9 . . . .**135** C7
Lower Sheffield TR19. . . . . .**97** F7
Lowerside PL7 . . . .**128** A8
Lower Sladesmoor Cres
PL15 . . . .**13** F1
Lower Sq EX22 . . . .**11** E8
Lower St Looe PL13. . . . .**117** D3
Plymouth PL4. . . . .**149** A3
Lower Tamar Terr PL18 . . . .**41** A4
Lower Terr TR3 . . . .**81** B4
Lower Tokenbury Rd PL14 . .**38** E5
LOWERTOWN Helston **91** E4
Lostwithiel. **48** A4
Lowertown TR13 . . . .**146** C8
Lower Town PL17. . . . .**28** E1
Lowertown Cl PL12. . . . .**53** C3
Lowertown La TR13. . . . . . .**146** C7
LOWER TREBULLETT **28** A4
Lower Treculliacks TR11. . . .**92** D5
Lower Tregongeeves PL26. .**59** A1
Lower Trelowth Rd PL26. . . .**59** A1
Lower Treluswell TR10 . . . . .**81** D2
Lower Trevance Rd PL27. . . .**32** E7
Lower Tywarnhayle 18 TR6 **55** A5
Lower Well La TR13. . . . .**146** C6
Lower Well Pk PL26 . . . .**73** C3
Lower Wesley Terr PL14 . . . .**38** D4

Lower Woodside PL25 . . . .**114** A4
Lowery Cross PL20 . . . .**42** F4
Low Lee Rd TR19 . . . .**88** D1
Lowley Rd PL15. . . . .**18** E2
Lucas Cl PL31 . . . .**109** E3
Lucas La PL7 . . . .**130** D6
Lucas Terr PL4 . . . .**129** B2
LUCKETT **40** B8
Luckett Hill PL17 . . . .**40** B7
Lucknow Rd PL31. . . . .**48** D8
Lucknow Road S 2 PL31. . . .**48** D8
LUDGVAN **89** A7
Ludgvan Com Prim Sch
TR20. . . . .**89** B8
Ludlow Rd 2 PL3. . . . .**128** E6
LUFFINCOTT **13** C5
Lugful Cl PL13 . . . .**62** D6
Lugger The TR2 . . . .**83** B2
Lukes Cl TR1 . . . .**137** F5
Luke's La PL7 . . . .**89** F6
Lulworth Dr PL6. . . . .**125** B7
Lundy Cl PL6 . . . .**124** F7
Lundy Dr EX23. . . . .**10** C6
Lundy Rd PL29. . . . .**22** C6
Luney La PL26 . . . .**72** E8
Lusart Dr TR12 . . . .**102** F2
Luscombe Ave 1 PL19. . . . .**147** B7
Luson Cl 4 PL28 . . . .**107** C4
Lusty Glaze Adventure Ctr
TR7. . . . .**111** A8
Lusty Glaze Rd TR7 . . . .**111** A7
LUTSFORD **3** A6
Lutsford Cross EX39 . . . .**3** A6
Lutyens Fold PL29 . . . .**29** C6
Luxland View TR7 . . . .**110** F3
Luxmore Cl PL6 . . . .**125** E1
Luxon Dr TR7. . . . .**110** F4
Lux Park L Ctr PL14 . . . .**113** C7
Luxstowe Dr 1 PL14. . . . . .**113** C6
Luxstowe Gdns PL14. . . . . .**113** C6
LUXULYAN **48** A1
Luxulyan Rd PL24. . . . .**115** F7
Luxulyan Sch PL30. . . . .**48** A1
Luxulyan Sta PL30. . . . .**47** F1
Lych Cl PL9. . . . .**135** A6
Lychgate Dr TR1. . . . .**137** C6
Lydcott Cl PL13. . . . .**63** F8
Lydcott Cres PL13 . . . .**63** F8
Lydcott La PL13 . . . .**64** A8
Lydcot Wlk PL6 . . . .**125** A1
Lydford Park Rd PL3. . . . . .**128** D5
Lyd Gdns PL19 . . . .**147** D5
Lydia Way PL4. . . . .**149** B4
Lympne Ave PL5. . . . .**123** F5
Lynbridge Ct 5 PL19 . . . . . .**147** B5
Lyndhurst Ave PL25. . . . . . .**115** A4
Lyndhurst Cl PL12 . . . .**128** C6
Lyndhurst Rd PL2. . . . .**128** C6
Lyndon Ct PL12 . . . .**122** D4
Lyndrick Rd PL3 . . . .**128** E7
Lynes Cotts 2 PL14. . . . .**51** A7
Lynher Cl PL15 . . . .**27** B3
Lynher Ct PL12 . . . .**122** F1
Lynher Dr PL12 . . . .**122** F1
Lynher La PL15 . . . .**27** B2
Lynher St PL5 . . . .**123** D2
Lynher View 2 PL17. . . . . . .**38** E8
Lynher Way
28 Callington PL17 . . . .**39** F4
North Hill PL15 . . . .**27** A4
Lyn-Meynek TR15 . . . .**140** D4
Lynmouth Cl PL7 . . . .**130** C7
LYNSTONE **104** D3
Lynstone Cotts EX23 . . . . . .**104** D3
Lynstone Rd EX23 . . . .**104** D3
Lyn Terr 7 TR18. . . . .**143** C1
Lynwood Ave PL7. . . . .**130** B6
Lynwood Bungalows TR13 .**91** A1
Lynwood Cl PL31. . . . .**109** E4
Lynwood Cotts 1 TR19 . . . . .**88** C1
Lynwood Flats TR13 . . . .**91** A1
Lynx La 2 PL9. . . . .**136** E8
Lyons Rd PL25. . . . .**115** B4
Lysander La 2 PL6 . . . .**125** B5
Lytton Pl PL25 . . . .**114** F4

M

MABE BURNTHOUSE **93** C8
Mabena Cl PL30 . . . .**34** C8
Mabe Prim SchTR10. . . . . . .**81** C1
Macadam Rd PL4. . . . .**149** C1
Macaulay Cres PL5 . . . .**124** C1
Macey St PL11. . . . .**127** C3
Mackenzie Pl PL5 . . . .**123** C2
Mackerel Cl PL25. . . . .**114** E7
Madden Rd PL1 . . . .**127** F2
Maddever Cres PL14. . . . . . .**113** C5
Maddock Cl PL7 . . . .**131** A4
Maddock Dr PL7. . . . .**131** A4
Maddocks Cross EX22 . . . .**3** F2
Madeira Rd
Falmouth TR11 . . . .**145** A1
Plymouth PL1. . . . .**149** A1
Madeira Villas 1 PL20. . . . . .**42** C5
Madeira Wlk TR11 . . . .**145** A2
MADERS **39** D6
Madford La PL15 . . . .**106** C5
Madge Ct 3 PL19. . . . .**147** B6
Madge La PL19 . . . .**147** B6
Madison Terr TR27 . . . .**142** E7
Madison Vean TR27 . . . .**142** E7
MADRON **143** B8
Madron Rd TR18. . . . .**143** C7
MAENPORTH **93** F4
Maenporth Est TR11 . . . .**93** E4

Maenporth Rd
Maenporth TR11. . . . .**93** E4
Mawnan Smith TR11 . . . . .**93** E4
Tregedna TR11. . . . .**94** B3
Maen Valley Pk TR11 . . . . . .**93** E5
MAER. **104** D8
Maer Down Rd EX23 . . . . . .**104** C7
Maer La EX23 . . . .**104** D8
Magdalen Gdns PL7 . . . . . .**130** F3
Magistrates Gr PL14 . . . . . .**113** C8
Magnificent Music Machines
Mus★ PL14. . . . .**51** C3
Magnolia Cl 3 PL7 . . . .**131** B5
Magnolia Ct 3 PL9 . . . .**135** F7
Magor Ave PL14 . . . .**79** E5
Magor Hill TR14 . . . .**67** B3
Maida Vale Terr PL4 . . . . . .**128** F4
Maiden St 1 EX23 . . . .**4** E1
Maidenwell Rd PL7 . . . .**130** C5
Maidstone Pl PL5. . . . .**123** E4
Maine Gdns PL2 . . . .**127** F7
Mainlay TR12. . . . .**99** B7
Main Rd Crumplehorn PL13. . .**62** D2
Downderry PL11. . . . .**64** C5
Main St TR18 . . . .**143** C7
MAINSTONE. **125** F2
Mainstone Ave PL4 . . . .**149** C2
Maitland Dr PL3 . . . .**128** F8
Maker La PL10. . . . .**133** B4
Maker Rd PL11 . . . .**127** A2
Maker View TR1. . . . .**128** B4
Maker View Rd PL10. . . . . . .**133** A6
Malabar Ho TR1 . . . .**69** F3
Malabar Rd TR1 . . . .**69** F3
Mallard Cl PL7 . . . .**130** F5
Mallets Ct PL27 . . . .**108** C6
Malletts Hill PL14. . . . .**36** E2
Mallory Dr TR7 . . . .**111** B5
Malmesbury Cl PL2. . . . . . .**128** B8
Malory Cl PL5 . . . .**124** D2
MALPAS **70** D2
Malpas Ho TR1 . . . .**137** E4
Malpas Rd TR1 . . . .**137** E2
Malthouse Cl 16 TR3. . . . . . .**81** B4
Malt House Ct 1 TR27 . . . .**142** D6
Malt House Gdns 2 TR18 .**143** C2
Malthouse La TR17 . . . .**89** C5
Malt House The 3 TR18 . . .**143** C2
MANACCAN **101** A8
Manaccan TR12 . . . .**101** A8
Manaccan Prim SchTR12 .**101** A8
MANADON **124** D1
Manadon Cl PL5. . . . .**124** E1
Manadon Dr PL5 . . . .**124** E1
Manadon Football Ctr PL2**124** D2
Manadon Vale Prim Sch 1
PL5 . . . .**128** E8
Manaton Cl TR13 . . . .**146** D8
Manaton Dr PL15 . . . .**106** C5
Manby Gdns PL5. . . . .**123** F5
Mandalay Villas 8 TR9 . . . . .**45** E1
Mandeley Cl PL33 . . . .**14** D2
Maneley Wy PL17. . . . .**40** C4
Manely Way PL17. . . . .**40** C4
Manewas Way TR7 . . . .**111** B7
Manfield Way PL25 . . . .**115** C4
Manhay TR3. . . . .**92** B5
Manifold Gdns PL3 . . . .**129** D5
Manley Cl PL14 . . . .**113** B5
Manley Rd PL14 . . . .**113** B5
Manley Terr 5 PL14. . . . . . .**113** B5
MANNAMEAD **128** F5
Mannamead Ave PL3 . . . . . .**128** F5
Mannamead Ct 9 PL3 . . . . .**128** F6
Mannamead Rd PL3 . . . .**128** F6
Man of War View TR12 . . . .**102** F2
Manor Bourne Rd PL9 . . . . .**135** C1
Manor Cl Blisland PL30 . . . . . .**35** D8
Crackington Haven EX23. . . .**10** C6
Falmouth TR11. . . . .**144** E5
Heamoor TR18. . . . .**143** D7
Helston TR13. . . . .**146** D8
St Austell PL25. . . . .**114** F5
Tavistock PL19. . . . .**147** A6
Manor Cotts TR11 . . . .**145** D3
Manor Cres TR11 . . . .**144** E5
Manor Ct TR2. . . . .**95** A6
Manor Dr TR26 . . . .**141** C3
Manor Est PL20. . . . .**42** B4
Manor Farm PL20. . . . .**42** E3
Manor Farm Cl 7 TR20 . . . .**89** E5
Manor Farm Rd PL26 . . . . . .**115** A1
Manor Gdns
Camelford PL32. . . . .**105** D4
Horrabridge PL20 . . . .**42** B4
Millbrook PL10. . . . .**132** F6
Plymouth PL1. . . . .**148** B2
Redruth PL15 . . . .**140** B6
St Erth TR27. . . . .**142** A1
Truro TR1 . . . .**137** E5
Manor La PL3 . . . .**129** D5
Manor Park Cl PL7. . . . .**130** F5
Manor Park Dr PL7 . . . .**131** A4
MANOR PARSLEY **68** B5
Manor Pk Dousland PL20 . . . .**42** E3
Duloe PL14 . . . .**51** A1
Saltash PL12 . . . .**122** D2
Manor Pl TR18. . . . .**143** D7
Manor Rd Bude EX23 . . . . . .**104** E4
Camborne TR14. . . . .**138** C2
Carharrack TR16 . . . .**80** E8
Falmouth TR11. . . . .**144** E5
Newquay TR7. . . . .**110** D6
Plymouth PL9. . . . .**135** B8
Tavistock PL19. . . . .**147** A6
Manor St PL1. . . . .**148** A3

Manor View PL24. . . . .**60** B4
Manor Way Heamoor TR18. .**143** D7
Helston TR13. . . . .**146** D8
Tavistock PL19. . . . .**147** B6
Manse Rd 6 TR3 . . . .**81** F7
Mansion Ho The PL1. . . . . .**134** A8
Manson Pl PL26 . . . .**58** C8
Manston Cl PL5. . . . .**123** E5
Mantle Gdns PL5 . . . .**127** D8
Maple Ave Camelford PL32. .**105** E5
Torpoint PL11 . . . .**127** A3
Maple Cl Bodmin PL31 . . . . .**109** B4
23 Callington PL17 . . . .**39** F4
Plymouth PL6. . . . .**125** E6
5 St Columb Major TR9 . . .**45** D6
St Dennis PL26. . . . .**58** B8
Tavistock PL19. . . . .**147** C3
Maple Ct 2 PL9 . . . .**135** F7
Maple Gr
Plymouth, Mutley PL4 . . . .**128** A4
Plymouth, Plympton PL7 . . .**130** B5
Maple Leaf Dr PL27 . . . .**108** C7
Maple Way PL6. . . . .**125** E7
MARAZION **89** B6
Marazion Mus★ TR17. . . . . .**89** B5
Marazion SchTR17. . . . .**89** C5
Marazion Way PL2. . . . .**128** D8
Marchant's Cross PL20 . . . . .**42** F1
Marchant's Way PL20. . . . . .**42** F2
Marconi Centre (Mus)★
TR13. . . . .**98** F2
Marconi Cl TR13. . . . .**146** B6
Marcus Hill TR7 . . . .**110** E6
Marcwheal 6 TR19. . . . .**88** C1
Mardon Cl PL6 . . . .**125** D4
Marett Rd PL5. . . . .**123** F3
Margaret Ave PL25 . . . .**114** E3
Margaret Cnr PL31. . . . .**109** C4
Margaret Cres PL31 . . . .**109** C4
Margaret Gdns PL27 . . . . . .**108** D5
Margaret Pk PL3 . . . .**128** E8
Margaret Pl TR11. . . . .**144** F3
Margate La PL10. . . . .**35** C1
MARHAMCHURCH **7** B6
Marhamchurch CE Prim Sch
EX23. . . . .**7** B6
Maria's La TR19 . . . .**96** B7
Maribuc Ct PL28. . . . .**31** F7
Marina Ct TR16 . . . .**67** C5
Marina Rd PL5. . . . .**123** F3
Marina Terr 7 PL4 . . . .**128** F4
Marine Academy PL5 . . . . . .**123** E1
Marine Cres 5 TR11. . . . . . .**145** C3
Marine Ct Falmouth TR11. . .**145** D3
26 Perranporth TR6. . . . . . .**55** A5
Torpoint PL11 . . . .**127** B2
Marine Dr Looe PL13. . . . . . .**117** C1
Torpoint PL11 . . . .**127** B2
Widemouth Bay EX23 . . . . . .**6** E4
Widemouth Bay EX23 . . . . . .**6** E5
Marine Par TR2. . . . .**95** A5
Marine Rd PL9 . . . .**135** C8
Marine Terr Boscastle PL35. . .**9** C2
7 Penzance TR18 . . . .**143** E4
Maristow Ave PL2 . . . .**127** F5
Maristow Cl PL6 . . . .**124** F5
Maristow La PL12. . . . .**122** F3
Maritime House Discovery
Quay 16 TR11 . . . .**145** C3
Marjorie Ct PL12 . . . .**122** C4
Market Ave PL1 . . . .**148** B3
Market Cl PL1 . . . .**128** A1
Market Ct 4 Hayle TR27 . . .**142** D6
9 Launceston PL15 . . . . . .**106** C6
Market Hill PL25. . . . .**114** C4
Market House Arc
3 Bodmin PL31 . . . .**109** E5
10 Launceston PL15 . . . . .**106** C6
Market Inn PL24. . . . .**60** B5
Market Jew St TR18 . . . . . .**143** E5
Market Pl Camelford PL32. . .**105** D4
Helston TR13. . . . .**146** B5
Marazion TR17. . . . .**89** B5
Padstow PL28 . . . .**107** D5
25 Penzance TR18 . . . . . .**143** E5
St Columb Major TR9 . . . . .**45** E6
33 St Ives TR26 . . . .**141** B6
Week St Mary EX22 . . . . . .**11** E8
Market Rd Plymouth PL7 . . .**130** D5
Tavistock PL19. . . . .**147** C5
Market Sq 18 Callington PL17 **39** E4
Hayle TR27. . . . .**142** D6
Plymouth PL1. . . . .**148** C3
St Day TR16 . . . .**68** D1
St Just TR19. . . . .**86** F6
Market St Bodmin PL31 . . . .**109** E5
Devoran TR3 . . . .**81** F6
Falmouth TR11. . . . .**145** B4
Fowey PL23 . . . .**116** D4
Hayle TR27. . . . .**142** D6
Kingsand PL10. . . . .**133** A1
11 Launceston PL15 . . . . .**106** C6
Liskeard PL14 . . . .**113** C6
Plymouth PL1. . . . .**128** A1
6 St Austell PL25 . . . .**114** C3
St Just TR19. . . . .**86** F6
3 Stratton EX23 . . . .**4** E1
Tavistock PL19. . . . .**147** C5
Market Strand
Falmouth TR11. . . . .**145** B4
Padstow PL28 . . . .**107** D5
2 Redruth TR15 . . . .**140** B5
8 St Ives TR26 . . . .**141** B6
Market Way Plymouth PL1. .**148** C3
4 Redruth TR15 . . . .**140** B4
Marks Dr PL31. . . . .**109** E3
Mark's Way TR7 . . . .**110** D4
Markwell La PL12. . . . .**53** C1

Marlborough Ave TR11 ....145 A3
Marlborough Cl
 1 Falmouth TR11 ....145 A3
 Saltash PL12 ....122 F1
Marlborough Cres TR11 ...145 A3
Marlborough Ct **5** TR11 ..145 A3
Marlborough Gr **2** TR11 ..145 A3
Marlborough Prim Sch
 PL1 ....127 E2
Marlborough Rd
 Falmouth TR11 ....145 B3
 Plymouth PL4 ....149 A4
Marlborough Row PL1 ....127 E2
Marlborough Sch TR11 ...145 A3
Marlborough St PL1 .....127 E2
Marlborough Way PL26 ...58 E1
Marldon Cl PL5 ....124 B3
Marlow Cres PL16 ....29 F8
Marlow Gdns PL9 ....135 F5
Marriotts Ave TR14 .....138 B4
Marrowbone Slip PL4 ....149 B2
Marryat Gdns PL5 ....124 E1
Marshall Ave PL27 ......108 C5
Marshall Cl Roche PL26 ..46 F3
 Tavistock PL19 ....147 D2
Marshallen Rd TR4 ......68 C6
Marshall Rd Bodmin PL31 ..109 D3
 Bodmin, Nanstallon PL30 ...34 C2
 Plymouth PL7 ....130 A5
 Tavistock PL19 ....147 D2
Marshalls Way PL29 .....22 D6
Marsh Cl PL6 ....129 F6
Marshfield Cl **4** TR4 ....55 D4
Marshfield View PL11 ...64 B5
MARSHGATE 10 C2
Marsh La Angarrack TR27 ..142 F7
 Calstock PL18 ....41 A3
 Hayle TR27 ....142 F7
Marshlands PL27 ....34 A6
Marsh Lane Ind Est TR27 ..142 F7
MARSH MILLS 130 A6
Marsh Mills PL6 ....129 F7
Marsh Mills Pk PL6 .....129 F6
Marsh Mills Ret Pk PL6 ..129 F7
Marsh Mills Sta ✱ PL7 ..130 A7
Marthas Mdw TR9 ....45 E1
Marthus Ct **10** PL14 ....113 C5
Martin Cl TR15 ....140 D5
Martin Ho **11** TR15 .....140 B4
Martin La PL4 ....149 A2
Martins Cl PL14 ....113 E7
Martin's Ct **2** PL31 ....109 D5
Martin's La TR15 ....139 C8
Martin Sq **6** PL17 .....39 F4
Martin St PL1 ....148 B2
Martinvale Ave TR15 ....140 E7
Martinvale Parc TR15 ...140 E7
Martlesham Pl PL5 ......123 F4
Martyn's Cl TR4 ....55 D4
Mary Dean Ave PL5 .....124 C7
Mary Dean Cl PL5 ....124 C7
Mary Dean's CE Prim Sch
 PL5 ....124 C7
Maryland Gdns PL2 .....127 F7
Mary Moon Cl PL12 .....53 B7
Mary Newman's Cottage ✱
 PL12 ....123 A2
Mary Seacole Rd PL1 ...148 A3
Marys Well TR16 ....67 D4
Marythorne Rd **15** PL20 ..41 B1
Masefield Gdns PL5 .....124 B1
Masons Row PL18 ....40 F6
Masterman Rd PL2 ......127 F4
Matela Cl **10** TR13 .....98 C3
Matthews Way PL14 .....51 F6
Maudlin Cl PL14 ....113 D5
Maudlins La PL19 ....147 A5
Maudlins Pk **7** PL19 ...147 A5
Maunsell Cl PL2 ....127 F7
Mavisdale PL2 ....127 F6
Mawes Ct PL18 ....40 D5
Mawgan Garras TR12 ....100 A6
 Mawgan TR12 ....99 D6
Mawgan Cross TR12 .....99 D7
Mawgan-in-Pydar Com Prim
 Sch TR8 ....45 A8
MAWGAN PORTH 31 B2
Mawgan Porth Hill TR8 ..31 C1
Mawgan Vu TR9 ....57 E8
MAWLA 68 B4
MAWNAN 93 E2
Mawnan Church of England
 (Voluntary Aided) Primary
 School TR11 ....93 D3
MAWNAN SMITH 93 E3
Maxwell Rd PL4 ....135 B8
MAXWORTHY 12 B3
Maxworthy Cross PL15 ..12 B4
Maxworthy Rd PL15 .....12 B4
Maybank Rd PL4 ....149 C3
Maybrook Dr PL12 ......122 D2
Mayers Way PL9 ....135 D6
Mayfair Cres PL6 ....125 B1
Mayfair Ho PL4 ....149 A3
Mayfield Cl Bodmin PL31 ..35 B2
 Port Isaac PL29 ....22 D7
 St Austell PL25 ....115 A4
Mayfield Cres TR7 ......110 E5
Mayfield Dr
 Port Isaac PL29 ....22 E7
 Roche PL26 ....47 A3
Mayfield Rd
 Falmouth TR11 ....144 F4
 Newquay TR7 ....110 E5
 Port Isaac PL29 ....22 D7
Mayflower Cl
 18 Bere Alston PL20 ....41 B1
 Plymouth PL9 ....135 F7

Mayflower Community
 Academy & Nursery **1**
 PL2 ....128 A7
Mayflower Dr PL2 ....128 B5
Mayflower L Ctr PL2 ....128 C5
Mayflower St PL1 ....148 C3
May Gdns TR16 ....80 D6
May La PL13 ....117 F5
Maymear Terr PL30 .....23 E3
Mayna Parc PL15 ....18 B8
Maynarde Cl PL7 ....131 B5
Mayne Cl PL15 ....106 B7
Maynes Row TR14 ......139 A5
MAYON 96 B6
Mayon Farm TR19 ......96 B6
Mayon Green Cres TR19 ..96 B7
May Terr PL4 ....149 B3
McCarthy Dr PL26 ......58 B4
Mclean Dr PL26 ....58 B4
MEAD 2 D4
Mead Cnr EX39 ....2 D4
Meadfoot Terr **2** PL4 ..128 F5
Mead Gdns **11** PL31 ....109 A5
Mead Hos The TR18 ....143 F8
Meadowbank TR11 .....82 A3
Meadowbank Rd TR11 ..145 A6
Meadow Brook PL19 ....147 A4
Meadow Cl Gloweth TR1 ..69 E3
 Newquay TR7 ....111 A4
 Plymouth PL7 ....131 D4
 Polruan PL23 ....116 D2
 St Austell PL25 ....114 F6
 St Stephen PL26 ....58 B4
 Saltash PL12 ....122 F3
Meadow Ct Mevagissey PL26 ..73 C3
 Padstow PL28 ....107 B4
 St Mabyn PL30 ....34 C8
 Stithians TR3 ....80 E4
Meadowfield Pl PL7 ....131 B3
Meadow Flats **27** TR26 ..141 B6
Meadowhead PL27 ......108 C4
Meadow La TR1 ....137 D3
Meadowlands PL6 ....125 D7
Meadowlands Leisure Pool
 PL19 ....147 B5
Meadow Pk
 7 Liskeard PL14 ......113 B5
 Plymouth PL9 ....135 C5
 Trewoon PL25 ....59 A3
Meadow Pl PL31 ....109 D4
Meadow Plash PL30 .....35 C8
Meadow Rd PL12 ....62 A7
Meadow Rise Foxhole PL26 ..58 D6
 1 Penwithick PL26 .....59 D7
 12 St Columb Major TR9 ..45 E6
Meadowside
 Launceston PL15 ....106 A4
 Newquay TR7 ....111 A4
 Plymouth PL9 ....135 F7
 St Austell PL25 ....115 C6
 Whitstone EX22 ....12 B8
Meadowside Cl Hayle TR27 ..142 A3
 St Kew Highway PL30 ....23 B2
Meadow St TR11 ....144 F2
Meadow St PL26 ....73 C3
Meadows The
 St Dennis PL26 ....58 C8
 St Dominick PL12 ....40 D2
 St Teath PL30 ....23 E7
 Torpoint PL11 ....126 E4
Meadowsweet Cl **5** PL14 ..113 D8
Meadowsweet Pk PL12 ..122 C2
Meadow Terr PL14 ......37 F3
Meadow The Illogan TR16 ..67 D4
 Polgooth PL26 ....59 A1
 47 St Ives TR26 ....141 B6
 Truro TR1 ....137 B5
Meadow View
 Camborne TR14 ....138 E1
 8 Goldsithney TR20 ...89 E5
 St Minver PL27 ....21 F3
 St Tudy PL30 ....23 E3
Meadow View Rd PL7 ...130 D5
Meadow Villas **8** TR18 ..143 C1
Meadow Way Plymouth PL7 ..130 D7
 St Issey PL27 ....32 E6
Meadow Wlk PL23 ......116 D2
Mead The PL7 ....130 D7
Meadway Looe PL13 ....117 E4
 St Austell PL25 ....114 F5
 Saltash PL12 ....122 E1
MEADWELL 29 C8
Mearwood La TR11 .....144 F4
Meaver La **3** TR12 .....99 B2
Meaver Rd TR12 ....99 B1
MEAVY 42 F2
Meavy Ave PL5 ....124 E2
Meavy Bourne PL20 ....42 D2
Meavy CE Prim Sch PL20 ..42 F2
Meavy La PL20 ....42 D2
Meavy Villas PL20 .....42 D2
Meavy Way Plymouth PL5 ..124 E2
 Tavistock PL19 ....147 D5
MEDDON 3 C4
Meddon Cross Edistone EX39 ..3 C5
 Welcombe EX39 ....3 C4
Medland Cres PL6 ......124 D6
Medland Gdns PL25 ....114 C4
Medlyn Carnkie TR13 ...80 C1
 Halwin TR13 ....92 C8
Medlyn Ct **3** TR13 .....146 B5

Medrose PL27 ....21 D2
Medrose St PL33 ....14 E3
Medrose Terr **21** TR18 ..143 E6
Medrow PL15 ....27 A8
Medway Pl PL3 ....129 D6
Melbourne Cotts PL1 ...148 B3
Melbourne Gn **2** PL1 ...148 B3
Melbourne Pl PL1 ......148 B4
Melbourne Rd PL14 ....113 B5
Melbourne St PL1 ......148 B3
Melbourne Terr **17** TR18 ..143 C7
MELBUR 57 F5
Melin Dr TR1 ....137 B6
Mellanear Cl TR27 .....142 B4
Mellanear Ct TR27 .....142 B4
Mellanear Rd TR27 .....142 B3
Mellangoose TR13 .....146 A8
Melliars Way EX23 .....104 F6
MELLINGEY 32 D6
Mellingey Rd PL27 .....32 D6
Mellingey Valley **5** TR3 ..81 D6
Melrose Ave PL2 ....128 C8
Melrose Terr **6** TR9 ....45 E1
Melvill Cres TR11 ......145 B3
Melvill Ct TR11 ....145 B2
Melville Pl **1** PL1 ......128 A5
 Threemilestone TR3 .....69 D3
Melville Terr PL22 ......112 C2
Melville Terrace La PL2 ..128 A5
Melvill La TR11 ....145 B2
Melvill Rd TR11 ....145 A2
Melyn Cl TR27 ....142 E8
Memory La PL9 ....135 E7
Menabilly Cl PL17 ......39 E3
Menabilly Rd PL25 .....114 E6
Mena Chinowyth **3** TR11 ..144 F2
Menacuddle Hill PL25 ..114 C4
Menacuddle La PL25 ...114 C4
MENADARVA 66 E2
Menadue Ct TR27 ......78 E3
Menage St TR13 ....146 C5
MENAGISSEY 68 C5
Menague PL27 ....21 E3
Menakarne TR16 ....80 F8
Menallack Cheese Farm ✱
 TR10 ....93 A6
Mena Park Cl PL9 ......136 B7
Mena Park Rd PL9 .....136 B7
MENDENNICK 132 C7
Mendennick Hill
 Freathy PL11 ....65 F4
 Mendennick PL11 ....132 B7
Meneage Cotts **3** TR13 ..146 C5
Meneage Ho **4** TR13 ...146 C5
Meneage Parc TR13 ....146 C5
Meneage Rd TR13 .....146 C5
Meneage St TR13 ......146 C5
Meneage Villas PL25 ...114 B3
Menear Rd PL25 ....115 A6
Menefreda Way PL27 ...22 A4
Menerdue La TR16 .....80 E1
Meneth Rd TR14 ....138 F2
Menhay Gdns TR15 ....139 D7
Menhay View TR11 ....144 C3
MENHENIOT 52 A5
Menheniot Cres PL15 ..18 D5
Menheniot Prim Sch PL14 ..52 A5
Menheniot Sta PL14 ...51 F4
Menhinick Cl PL12 .....53 C3
Menhyr Dr TR26 ....141 C2
Menhyr Pk TR26 ....141 C2
Menna La Ladock TR2 ...57 E5
 St Dennis PL26 ....46 C1
Mennaye Ct TR18 ......143 D4
Mennaye Rd TR18 .....143 D4
Merafield Cl PL7 ....130 B5
Merafield Dr PL7 ......130 C4
Merafield Farm Cotts PL7 ..130 B4
Merafield Rd PL7 ......130 B5
Merafield Rise PL7 ....130 A5
Merbein Cotts TR8 .....44 E8
Merchant's House (Mus) ✱
 PL1 ....148 C2
Merchants Quay PL15 ..18 E2
Meredith Rd PL2 ....128 C6
Meres Valley TR12 .....99 A2
Meridian Ho PL4 ....149 A3
Merlin Cl PL6 ....125 E8
Merlin Pl TR20 ....88 D1
Merlins Way PL34 .....14 D7
Mermaid Ct TR7 ....111 C8
Merrick Ave TR1 ....137 E6
MERRIFIELD 7 F4
Merrifield Cl TR1 ......137 B5
Merrifield Cross EX22 ..7 F4
Merrill Pl TR1 ....145 A3
Merritts Hill TR16 .....67 E4
Merritts Way TR15 .....139 C7
Merrivale Rd
 Plymouth, Ham PL2 .....128 B7
 Plymouth, Honicknowle PL5 ..124 B3
Merrivale View Rd PL20 ..42 E3
MERRYMEET 38 C1
Merry Meeting TR4 ....78 F6
Merry Meet La TR11 ...144 C3
Merry Mit Mdw TR11 ..144 C3
Merryn Hts **20** PL28 ...31 F7
Mersey Cl PL3 ....129 D6
Merthen TR11 ....92 E2
MERTHER 70 F3
Merther Cl TR13 ....91 B3
Merther Collyn TR2 ....83 B3
Merther La TR13 ......91 B3
MERTHER LANE 70 F1

Messack Cl TR11 ......144 E2
Metha Pk TR8 ....56 C9
Metha Rd TR8 ....56 C7
METHERELL 40 D4
Metherell Cl PL18 .....40 D4
Methleigh Bottoms TR13 ..91 A1
Methleigh Parc TR13 ..91 A1
MEVAGISSEY 73 D3
Mevagissey Aquarium ✱
 PL26 ....73 C3
Mevagissey Com Prim Sch
 PL26 ....73 C4
Mevagissey Ho TR1 ....69 E4
Mevagissey Mus ✱ PL26 ..73 C3
Mews Ct PL14 ....51 F6
Mews The Launceston PL15 ..106 C4
 Par PL24 ....60 B5
 3 Penzance TR18 .....143 E6
 Plymouth, Devonport PL1 ..128 A3
 Plymouth, Stonehouse PL1 ..148 A3
Mexico La TR27 ....142 C7
Mexico Terr TR27 .....142 C8
Michael Rd PL3 ....129 A5
MICHAELSTOW 24 A5
Michell Ave TR7 ....110 E6
Michell Ct TR7 ....110 D6
Michigan Way PL3 .....129 C6
Mid Churchway PL9 ....136 A7
Mid Cornwall Bsns Ctr
 PL25 ....115 E4
MIDDLE CRACKINGTON ..10 B6
Middle Down Cl PL9 ...136 A5
Middlefield Rd PL6 ....124 D6
Middlefield Ct PL12 ...122 B2
Middlegates **5** TR5 ...54 D1
MIDDLE GREADOW 48 B1
MIDDLEHILL 38 D3
Middle Market St PL13 ..117 D3
MIDDLEMOOR 147 F2
Middle Rd TR15 ....140 E7
Middle Rosewin Row **8**
 TR1 ....137 D5
Middle Row TR13 ......90 E3
Middle St Padstow PL28 ..107 D5
 Port Isaac PL29 ....22 D7
Middle Stennack Cotts **13**
 TR26 ....141 A5
Middleton Cres TR7 ...110 F4
Middletons Row **6** TR15 ..140 C5
Middleton Wlk PL5 ....123 D4
Middleway PL24 ....60 B5
Middlewell Parc PL27 ..108 B4
Middle Wharf PL26 ....73 C3
Middle Wlk **1** PL26 ....115 A1
MIDDLEWOOD 27 B2
Midella Rd PL20 ....42 D2
Mid Moor PL14 ....38 B6
Midway Dr TR1 ....137 E5
Midway Rd PL31 ......109 A5
Miers Cl PL5 ....127 C8
Miers Ct PL5 ....127 C8
Milch Pk PL12 ....122 C2
MILCOMBE 62 F6
Mildmay St PL4 ....149 A4
Mile End Grochall TR12 ..102 F4
 Lizard TR12 ....102 F4
Mile Hill TR4 ....68 A5
Milehouse Rd PL2 .....128 A5
Miles Mitchell Ave PL6 ..125 A1
Milestone Ct TR3 ......69 D4
Milford La PL5 ....124 B5
Military Rd Millbrook PL10 ..132 C3
 Plymouth PL3 ....129 C6
 Rame PL10 ....64 C2
 St Mawes TR2 ....95 B4
Milladon La PL12 ......64 D8
Mill Ball Hill EX23 .....10 B7
Millbank Mdw TR27 ...78 E1
MILLBAY 148 B2
Millbay Rd PL1 ....148 A2
Mill Bridge PL1 ....148 A3
MILLBROOK 132 E5
Millbrook Bsns Ctr PL11 ..132 C6
Millbrook CE VA Prim Sch
 PL10 ....132 E5
Mill Cl Porthleven TR13 ..91 A1
 Wadebridge PL27 ....108 E5
Mill Cotts TR13 ....146 A6
Millefleur TR11 ....144 F3
MILLENDREATH 117 F5
Millennium Appartments
 TR10 ....81 D2
Millennium Way TR13 ..146 D8
Miller Bsns Pk PL14 ...113 B4
Miller Ct Liskeard PL14 ..113 B4
 Plymouth PL1 ....148 A2
Miller Way PL6 ....125 E3
Millet Cl TR17 ....89 D5
Millfield TR18 ....88 E6
Millfields TR17 ....89 B6
Mill Flats TR13 ....146 B6
Mill Ford Sch PL5 .....123 F4
Mill Gdns PL22 ....112 C2
Millham La PL22 ......112 E3
MILLHILL 30 B1
Mill Hill Crumplehorn PL13 ..62 D1
 Lelant TR27 ....77 E3
 Lostwithiel PL22 ....112 D2
Mill Hill Cotts PL19 ...30 B1
 St Just in Roseland TR2 ..82 F3
Millhouse Pk PL11 ....127 A2
Mill La Camelford PL32 ..105 D5
 Coad's Green PL15 .....27 C1
 Grampound TR2 ....72 A7
 Helston TR13 ....146 B6
 Middlewood PL15 ......27 B2

Mill La continued
 20 Mousehole TR19 ....88 C1
 Porthleven TR13 ....91 A1
 St Breward PL30 ....24 B3
 St Germans PL12 ......65 A8
 St Kew PL30 ....23 A4
 Torpoint PL11 ....127 A2
 Tregony TR2 ....71 F3
 Truro TR3 ....137 C1
MILLOOK 6 D2
Millpond Ave TR27 ....142 B4
MILLPOOL Cardinham ...35 F5
 Praa Sands 90 B5
Millpool Lostwithiel PL22 ..112 F3
 Newtown TR20 ....90 B4
 Rilla Mill PL14 ....38 E8
Millpool Head PL10 ...132 E4
Millpool Hill PL30 .....35 F5
Millpool Rd PL10 .....133 A6
Mill Rd Millbrook PL10 ..133 A5
 Otterham Mill PL32 ....10 E1
 Padstow PL28 ....107 D5
 Penhallick PL12 ....101 C1
 Penponds TR14 ....79 B5
 Perranporth TR6 ......55 B4
 Tideford PL12 ....52 F2
Mill Rd Est PL12 ......52 F2
Mill Rise PL27 ....108 E5
Mills Gdns TR16 ......68 E1
Mills Rd PL1 ....127 F2
Mills' St TR16 ....68 E1
Mill St PL31 ....109 C5
MILLTOWN Cardinham ..35 E3
 Lostwithiel 60 F8
Milltown Gdns PL15 ...18 E6
Milltown La PL14 .....36 F2
Mill View Gdns PL10 ..132 F5
Mill View Rd PL10 ....132 F5
Millway PL9 ....135 D8
Millwood Dr PL6 ......125 E1
Mill Yard **17** TR3 ....81 B4
Milne PL1 ....127 F3
MILTON ABBOT 29 D6
Milton Abbot Sch PL19 ..29 D5
Milton Cl PL5 ....124 D2
MILTON COMBE 120 F8
Milton Cres PL17 .....147 D5
Milton Ct
 Plymouth, Cattedown PL4 ..149 C2
 Plymouth, Prince Rock PL4 ..129 B1
MILTON GREEN 29 D5
Minack Open Air Theatre ✱
 TR19 ....96 E2
Mine Hill PL14 ....51 F6
Mine La PL30 ....47 E7
Miners Cl Perranporth TR6 ..55 A4
 Redruth TR15 ....140 C5
Miners Row TR15 .....140 C5
Miners Way **12** TR5 ...54 D1
 Liskeard PL14 ....113 D7
Minerva Cl PL7 ....131 A6
MINGOOSE 68 C7
Miniatura Park ✱ TR4 ..55 E4
MINIONS 38 B6
Minions Heritage Ctr ✱
 PL14 ....38 B6
Minions Row PL14 .....38 B6
Minnie Pl TR11 ....145 B3
Minorca La PL26 ......47 D2
Minses Cl PL9 ....136 C7
Minster Ave EX23 .....104 F4
Minster Mdw TR12 ....101 A8
Minster Rd PL35 ......9 E1
Minster Terr TR12 ....101 A8
Minton Cl PL25 ....115 A4
Mirador Pl PL4 ....129 C3
Mission The TR18 .....143 F4
Misterton Cl PL9 .....136 B8
MITCHELL 56 F5
Mitchell Cl Lizard TR12 ..102 F2
 Plymouth PL5 ....135 D5
Mitchell Ct **11** TR1 ...137 D5
Mitchell Hill TR1 ......137 D5
Mitchell Hill Terr **4** TR1 ..137 D5
Mitchell La Camborne TR14 ..138 E3
 Mitchell TR8 ....56 E5
Mitchell Mews **17** TR1 ..137 D4
Mitchell Rd Camborne TR14 ..138 E3
 St Austell PL25 ....114 F4
Mitchell's Boatyard PL26 ..73 C2
Mitchells Cnr **24** TR6 ..55 A5
MITHIAN 54 F1
MITHIAN DOWNS 68 F8
Mithian Prim Sch TR5 ..54 E1
Mitre Cl PL19 ....147 A3
Mitre Ct **15** PL1 ......149 A2
MIXTOW 116 D7
Moat Pk PL6 ....125 C1
Mob La PL14 ....37 B2
Modbury Cl PL5 ....124 B3
Modus La PL26 ....58 E1
Modyford Wlk PL20 ...41 F3
Mohun's Cl PL19 .....147 C4
Mohun's Pk PL19 .....147 C3
Molenick La PL12 .....52 E3
Molesworth Cl **4** PL27 ..108 B5
Molesworth Rd
 Plymouth, Plympton PL7 ..130 C6
 Plymouth, Stoke PL1 ..128 A3
 Wadebridge PL27 ....108 B5
Molesworth St Tintagel PL34 ..14 C7
Molesworth Terr PL10 ..132 F5
MOLINNIS 47 C2
Molinnis PL26 ....47 C2

Molinnis Rd PL26 47 C2
Mollison Rd PL5 123 E2
Molyneaux Pl 10 PL1 127 F3
Monastery Cl TR12 101 D4
MONGLEATH 144 E4
Mongleath Ave TR11 144 E3
Mongleath Cl TR11 144 E3
Mongleath Rd TR11 144 E3
Monica Wlk PL4 149 B4
Monkey Sanctuary The★ PL13 63 F5
Monks Hill PL15 28 C4
Monksmead PL19 147 A4
Monks Park Cotts PL15 106 D6
Monmouth Gdns PL5 124 C4
Monmouth La PL22 112 D2
Monroe Gdns PL4 148 B4
Montacute Ave PL5 124 B2
Montague Ave TR15 140 A6
Monterey Cl EX23 104 E4
Monterey Gdns TR1 137 E5
Montgomery Cl PL12 122 D3
Montgomery Dr PL19 147 A6
Montgomery Rd 2 PL26 59 D7
Montpelier Prim Sch PL2 128 B6
Montpelier Rd PL2 128 C7
Montrose Way 2 PL5 124 D2
Monument Rd TR13 146 B5
Monument St PL1 127 E1
Monument Way PL31 109 C4
Moonrakers TR26 141 D2
Moonsfield 5 PL17 39 F4
Moon St PL4 149 A3
Moorcroft Cl PL9 136 A7
Moor Cross EX22 8 D3
Moor Cross Cotts EX23 4 C3
Moorfield PL16 19 F4
Moorfield Ave 4 PL6 129 C7
Moorfield Rd
Camborne TR15 139 C6
St Giles on the Heath PL15 13 F1
Moor Hill PL15 26 E4
Moor La PL5 123 E1
Moorland Ave PL7 130 F6
Moorland Cl Liskeard PL14 113 D7
Pendeen TR19 74 F1
Yelverton PL20 121 D8
Moorland Ct
1 St Austell PL25 114 C3
Yelverton PL20 42 C2
Moorland Dr PL7 130 E6
Moorland Gdns PL7 130 F6
Moorland Rd
Indian Queens TR9 45 F2
Launceston PL15 106 A4
Plymouth PL7 130 E5
St Austell PL25 114 C3
Tywardreath PL24 60 C4
Moorland Road Ind Est TR9 45 F2
Moorlands La PL12 122 C4
Moorlands Trad Est PL12 122 C4
Moorland View
Golberdon PL17 39 B6
Liskeard PL14 113 D7
Plymouth, Derriford PL6 125 A5
Plymouth, Plymstock PL9 136 B7
Saltash PL12 122 F4
Moorland Villas 18 PL20 42 D2
Moorland Way PL18 40 F5
Moorlan Mdws PL26 47 A3
Moor Parc TR12 100 D6
Moor St TR14 138 D3
Moors The PL22 112 C1
Moorstone Pl 15 PL26 59 D7
Moorswater Ind Est PL14 51 A7
Moor The TR11 145 B4
MOORTOWN Tavistock 42 D8
Tetcott 13 C7
Moor View Bodmin PL31 109 F2
Plymouth PL9 135 D7
Plymouth, Keyham PL2 127 F5
Plymouth, Laira PL3 129 C4
Torpoint PL11 127 B3
Moorview Ct PL6 125 F5
Moorview Terr PL14 38 D7
Moor View Terr
Plymouth PL4 128 E4
Yelverton PL20 42 D2
Morcom Cl PL25 115 A5
Moresk Cl TR1 137 D5
Moresk Gdns TR1 137 D5
Moresk Rd TR1 137 D5
Moreton Ave PL6 124 F1
Moreton La EX23 5 B2
Morice Sq PL1 127 E2
Morice St PL1 127 E2
MORICE TOWN 127 D3
Morice Town Prim Sch PL2 127 E4
Morlaix Ave TR1 137 D3
Morlaix Dr PL6 125 B4
Morla La TR15 140 A6
Morleigh Cl PL25 114 F3
Morley Cl PL7 130 A5
Morley Ct PL1 148 B3
Morley Dr PL20 42 A2
Morley View Rd PL7 130 C6
MORNICK 39 B7
Morrab Ct 8 TR7 110 F6
Morrab Gdns 40 TR18 143 E5
Morrab Pl 34 TR18 143 E5
Morrab Rd Camborne TR14 138 C3
Penzance TR18 143 E5
Morrab Terr 35 TR18 143 E5
Morris Gdns TR7 110 D4
Morrish Pk PL9 135 F6
Morshead Rd PL6 124 F2
Mortain Rd PL12 122 D4
Mortimore Cl PL12 122 D2
MORVAH 75 C2
Morvah Hill TR20 75 C2
MORVAL 63 D7
Morvan Trad Est PL25 114 F3
Morven Rd PL25 114 F3
Morview Rd PL13 63 F8
Morwell Gdns PL2 128 A6
MORWELLHAM 41 B4
Morwellham Cl PL5 127 C8
Morwellham Quay★ PL19 41 B4
Morwenna Gdns TR6 55 B5
Morwenna Pk EX23 5 A6
Morwenna Rd EX23 2 D1
Morwenna Terr EX23 104 D6
MORWENSTOW 2 B2
Morweth Cotts PL11 64 C5
Morweth Ct PL11 64 C5
Moses Cl PL6 124 E7
Moses Ct PL6 124 E7
Mosquito Cres 3 PL27 31 F3
Moss Side Ind Est 30 PL17 39 F4
Moss Terr PL23 116 D3
Mostyn Ave PL4 129 A4
Mote Pk PL12 122 C3
Mothecombe Wlk PL6 125 E1
Moulton Cl PL7 131 B5
Moulton Wlk PL7 131 B4
MOUNT Cardinham 36 B2
Cubert 55 C7
Mount Agar Rd TR3 81 F7
MOUNT AMBROSE 140 E7
Mount Ambrose TR15 140 E7
Mountbatten Cl
Plymouth PL9 135 D6
St Columb Minor TR7 111 E7
Mount Batten Ctr★ PL9 134 F7
Mountbatten Rd 5 PL26 59 D7
Mountbatten Way PL9 135 E6
Mount Bennett Rd 5 PL24 60 D5
Mount Bennett Terr 4
PL24 60 D5
Mount Camel PL32 105 C4
Mount Carbis Gdns TR15 140 C3
Mount Carbis Rd TR15 140 D3
MOUNT CHARLES 114 E4
Mount Charles Prim Sch PL25 114 F3
Mount Charles Rd PL25 114 F3
Mount Cres PL24 60 C4
Mount Edgcumbe House & Country Pk★ PL10 133 E6
Mount Edgcumbe Terr TR11 145 B4
Mountfield Terr 6 PL24 60 C4
Mount Folly TR27 142 C6
Mount Folly Sq PL31 109 E4
Mount Ford PL19 147 A5
Mount George Rd TR3 82 B7
MOUNT GOULD 129 B3
Mount Gould Ave PL4 129 B2
Mount Gould Cres PL4 129 B3
Mount Gould Hospl PL4 129 B3
Mount Gould Rd PL4 129 B3
Mount Gould Way PL4 129 B3
MOUNT HAWKE 68 C6
Mount Hawke Academy TR4 68 C6
Mount Ho PL11 64 C5
Mount House Sch PL19 147 E7
MOUNTJOY 45 A3
MOUNT LANE 13 E6
Mountlea Dr 9 PL24 60 C4
Mount Lidden TR18 143 C4
Mount Pleasant
Bodmin PL31 109 E5
Boscastle PL35 9 D1
Falmouth TR11 144 E1
Hayle TR27 142 C6
Lelant TR26 77 E3
Millbrook PL10 132 E5
Newlyn TR18 143 C4
Par PL24 60 B6
Plymouth PL5 124 B2
39 St Ives TR26 141 B6
Mount Pleasant Cl TR14 138 E1
Mount Pleasant Gdns TR27 142 C6
Mount Pleasant Pl PL22 112 C3
Mount Pleasant Rd
Camborne TR14 138 D1
11 Porthleven TR13 98 B8
Threemilestone TR3 69 D3
Mount Pleasant Terr PL2 128 A4
Mousehole TR19 88 C1
Redruth TR15 140 E7
Mount Pleasure TR14 138 E1
Mount Prospect Terr TR18 143 C3
Mount Rant Hill PL14 50 A8
Mount Rd Mount PL30 36 A3
Par PL24 60 C4
Mount Royal Cl TR18 143 F6
Mount's Bay Academy TR18 143 B7
Mounts Bay Rd TR18 143 C4
Mounts Bay Terr TR13 90 E3
Mount's Bay Terr 21 TR13 98 C8
Mount's Rd 20 TR13 98 C8
Mount St Mevagissey PL26 73 C3
Penzance TR18 143 E6
Plymouth, Mount Wise PL1 127 E1
Plymouth, Mutley PL4 149 A4
Mount Stamper Rd PL25 114 D7
Mountstephen Cl PL25 114 B3
Mount Stephens La TR11 144 F4
Mount Stone Rd PL1 134 A8
Mount Street Prim Sch PL4 149 A4
Mount Tamar Cl PL5 123 E2
Mount Tamar Sch PL5 123 E2
Mount Tavy Rd PL19 147 E6
Mount Terr 9 PL24 60 B4
Mount View Lane TR8 111 B3
Madron TR20 88 A7
Mount View Cl 15 TR2 83 B2
Mount View Cotts TR20 89 A7
Mount View Terr
5 Marazion TR17 89 C5
24 Newlyn TR18 143 C2
Mount Whistle Rd TR14 138 F7
MOUNT WISE 127 F1
Mount Wise
Launceston PL15 106 C5
Newquay TR7 110 D5
Mount Wise Com Prim Sch PL1 127 E1
Mount Wise Cotts TR7 110 E5
Mount Wise Ct PL1 127 F1
Mount Zion 52 TR26 141 B6
Mourne Villas PL9 135 F8
MOUSEHOLE 88 D1
Mousehole Com Prim Sch TR19 88 C1
Mousehole La TR19 88 C1
Mowbray Mews PL32 10 B2
Mowhay Cl TR7 111 A4
Mowhay Cotts PL26 85 C5
Mowhay La 1 PL17 39 E4
Mowhay Mdw TR9 45 E1
St John PL11 132 B8
Wadebridge PL27 108 B4
Mowhay Rd PL5 124 A2
Mowie The 13 TR9 45 E2
Moyle Rd PL28 107 E4
MUCHLARNICK 62 E7
Mudgeon TR12 100 D7
Mudgeon Vean TR12 100 D8
Mudges Terr PL18 41 A6
Mudge Way PL7 130 E5
Mulberry Cl PL6 125 E7
Mulberry Ct 12 TR11 145 B5
Mulberry Gr PL19 147 C2
Mulberry Quay 11 TR11 145 B5
Mulberry Rd PL12 122 E1
MULFRA 76 B1
Mulgrave St PL1 148 C2
Mullet Ave PL3 129 C4
Mullet Cl PL3 129 C4
Mullet Rd PL3 129 C4
MULLION 99 A1
Mullion Cl PL25 114 E7
Torpoint PL11 126 F4
Mullion Cove Mullion TR12 98 F1
Mullion TR12 102 B7
Mullion Junior & Infant Sch TR12 99 A1
Mullion Rural Workshops TR12 99 A1
Mullion Sch TR12 99 B1
Mundys Field TR12 103 A5
Muralto Ho PL19 147 A4
Murdoch Cl Redruth TR15 140 B6
Truro TR1 137 E6
Murdoch Flyer The★ 12 TR15 140 B4
Murdoch House & St Rumon's Gdn★ 13 TR15 140 B4
Murdock Rd PL11 126 F3
Murhill La 1 PL9 129 D1
Murray Villas TR19 86 E6
Murtons Terr TR16 80 E7
Mus of Witchcraft★ PL35 9 C2
MUTLEY 128 F4
Mutley Ct PL4 149 A4
Mutley Plain PL4 128 E4
Mutley Plain La PL4 128 E4
Mutley Rd PL3 128 E5
Mutton Hill TR27 78 D6
Mutton Row TR10 144 C8
MYLER CHURCHTOWN 82 C2
MYLOR BRIDGE 82 A3
Mylor Bridge Prim Sch TR11 82 A3
Mylor Cl PL2 128 D8
My Lords Rd TR9 57 E8
Mylor Yacht Harbour TR11 145 D8
Myrtle Cl PL20 42 E3
Myrtle Ct PL26 73 C3
Myrtles Ct PL12 122 D4
Myrtle Terr 10 PL18 40 F5
Myrtleville PL2 128 A6
Mythyon Ct 4 TR18 143 C7

N

Nailzee Ho PL13 117 D2
Nailzee Point PL13 117 D2
Nalder's Ct 10 TR1 137 C4
Nampara Cl TR26 141 E2
Nampara Ct 7 TR6 55 A4
Nampara Row 21 TR6 55 A4
Nampara Way TR1 137 F4
Nancarrow Ct 6 PL25 114 F2
Nancarrows PL12 122 C2
Nancealverne Specl Sch TR20 143 C6
Nancedden Farm TR20 89 A8
NANCEGOLLAN 91 C7
Nancegollan Ind Est TR13 91 B7
Nancekuke Cambrose TR16 67 F6
Nancekuke *continued*
Porthtowan TR16 68 A5
NANCEMELLIN 66 D1
Nancemellin Cl 3 TR3 81 D6
Nancemere Rd TR1 137 D6
Nancevallon TR14 139 B3
Nancherrow Hill TR19 86 F6
Nancherrow Row TR19 86 F6
NANCLEDRA 76 F2
Nancledra Bottoms TR20 76 F2
Nancledra Hill TR20 76 F2
Nancledra Prim Sch TR26 76 F3
Nangitha Cl TR11 144 C3
Nangitha Terr TR11 144 C3
Nanhayes Row TR8 56 B7
Nanjivey Pl 8 TR26 141 A5
Nanjivey Terr 9 TR26 141 A5
NANPEAN 58 D7
Nanpean Com Prim Sch PL26 58 D6
Nanpusker Cl TR27 142 E6
Nanpusker Rd TR27 78 C4
Nansalsa Ct TR7 111 A6
Nansavallon Rd TR1 69 F3
Nanscober Pl TR13 146 B8
Nanscothan 10 TR15 140 B4
Nanseglos Hill Madron TR20 88 B6
Madron TR20 143 A8
Nans Kestenen TR13 146 B5
NANSLADRON 73 B7
Nansloe Academy TR13 146 C4
Nansloe Cl TR13 146 D4
Nansmellyon Rd
Henscath TR12 102 B7
Mullion TR12 99 A1
Nanstallo Com Prim Sch PL30 34 C1
NANSTALLON 34 C1
Nanterrow Dr 6 PL31 109 A5
Nanterrow La TR27 66 D1
NANTITHET 99 B5
Nanturras Parc TR20 89 F5
Nanturras Row TR20 89 E5
Nanturras Way TR20 89 F5
Napier St PL1 127 F3
Napier Terr PL4 128 E4
Napps La PL15 17 A4
NARKURS 64 D6
Narkurs Cross PL11 64 D7
Narrowcliff TR7 111 A7
Narrow La
Botusfleming PL12 122 C7
Davidstow PL15 16 A6
Summercourt TR8 57 C8
Nash Cl PL7 131 A5
Nathan Cl TR7 111 B5
National Lobster Hatchery★ PL28 107 E5
National Marine Aquarium★ PL4 149 A2
National Maritime Mus Cornwall★ TR11 145 C3
National Seal Sanctuary The★ TR12 92 C1
NAVARINO 18 B8
Navy Inn Ct 10 TR18 143 C1
Neal Cl PL7 131 B4
Neath Rd PL4 149 C4
Neeham Rd TR8 56 B7
Negus Gdns 5 PL31 109 A5
Nelson Ave PL1 127 F3
Nelson Gdns 5 PL1 127 F3
Nelson St PL4 149 A4
Nelson Terr PL6 125 E6
Nepean St 1 PL2 127 F3
Neptune Ave PL27 31 F3
Neptune Pk PL9 135 B8
Neswick St PL1 148 B3
Neswick Street Ope PL1 148 A3
NETHERCOTT 13 E7
Nethercott Cross EX21 13 F7
NETHERTON 38 D7
Netherton Est PL20 42 A3
Netherton Rd PL28 107 D4
Netley Mdw PL26 47 C1
Nettell's Hill TR15 140 B5
Nettlehayes PL9 136 D7
Netton Cl PL9 136 B6
Nevada Cl PL3 129 D6
Nevada Pl 16 TR18 143 C7
Nevada St TR18 143 C7
Nevada Villas 8 PL24 60 C4
Newacott Cross EX22 7 F5
New Barn Hill PL7 130 F5
New Bglws PL30 36 B3
NEWBRIDGE Callington 39 D2
Penzance 87 E6
Truro 69 F3
Newbridge Hill PL18 41 A6
Newbridge La TR1, TR3 69 F3
New Bridge St 9 TR1 137 D4
Newbridge Vw TR1 69 E3
Newbridge Way TR1 69 F3
Newbury Cl PL5 124 B4
Newcastle Gdns PL5 124 B5
New Connection St 4 TR14 138 D3
New Cotts Gunnislake PL18 41 A6
2 Kilkhampton EX23 5 A6
New Ct TR11 145 B4
New Cut TR15 140 B5
New Dairy La TR17 89 B6
NEW DOWNS St Agnes 54 B2
St Just 86 E6
New George St PL1 148 C3
Newham Est TR1 137 D3
Newham Ind Est TR1 137 D2
Newham La Helston TR13 146 A7
Newham La *continued*
Lostwithiel PL22 49 A1
Newham Rd TR1 137 E2
Newhams La PL15 27 B4
New Hill Est TR2 72 A7
New Hos TR14 139 B3
Newhouses 3 PL17 38 E8
New La TR15 140 E7
New Launceston Rd PL19 147 A5
NEWLYN 143 D2
Newlyn Art Gall★ TR18 143 C3
Newlyn Halt Sta★ TR8 56 C6
Newlyn Rd TR19 97 B6
Newlyn Sch TR18 143 C3
Newman Rd Plymouth PL5 123 E2
Saltash PL12 122 F3
NEWMILL Penzance 76 B1
Poundstock 7 A1
Newmills Cl TR1 137 B6
New Mills Farm Pk★ PL15 18 D4
Newmills Hill PL15 18 C4
New Mills La TR1, TR4 137 A6
Newmills Sta★ PL15 18 D4
New Molinnis PL26 47 C2
Newnham Ind Est PL7 130 F6
Newnham Rd PL7 130 F7
Newnham Way PL7 130 F6
New Northernmaye 2 PL15 106 C6
New Park Rd Plymouth PL7 131 A4
Wadebridge PL27 108 C5
New Passage Hill PL1 127 E3
New Pk Horrabridge PL20 42 C4
Wadebridge PL27 108 C4
NEW POLZEATH 21 E6
NEWPORT 106 B7
Newport Callington PL17 39 E4
St Germans PL12 65 A8
Newport Cl 8 PL17 39 F4
Newport Ind Est PL15 106 C6
Newport Industrial Est PL15 106 C6
New Portreath Rd
Illogan TR16 67 F5
Redruth TR16 140 A7
Newport Sq PL15 106 B7
Newport St Millbrook PL10 132 E5
Plymouth PL1 128 A1
Newport Terr 3 PL17 39 F4
NEWQUAY 110 E7
Newquay Adult Ed Ctr TR7 110 F6
Newquay Airport TR8 44 F8
Newquay Hospl TR7 110 F5
Newquay Junior Academy TR7 110 F6
Newquay Rd
Goonhavern TR4 55 D4
Roche PL26 46 F3
St Columb Major TR9 45 D6
Truro TR1 137 F7
Newquay Sports & Com Ctr TR7 111 B6
Newquay Sta TR7 110 F6
Newquay Tretherras Sch TR7 111 B6
Newquay Zoo TR7 111 A5
New Rd Barripper TR14 79 B5
Bere Alston PL20 41 B2
Bodelva PL24 60 A6
Boscastle PL35 9 C2
Cadgwith TR12 103 A4
Callington PL17 39 E4
Camborne TR14 139 B3
Cawsand PL10 133 A1
Coldvreath PL26 46 F1
Kingsand PL10 133 B2
Lifton PL16 19 F4
Liskeard PL14 113 B5
Newlyn TR18 143 C3
Perranporth TR6 55 B4
Port Isaac PL29 22 D7
Portscatho TR2 83 B2
Roborough PL6 121 D2
St Columb Major TR9 45 E6
St Hilary TR20 89 F6
St Just TR19 86 F6
Saltash PL12 122 E3
Stithians TR3 80 F3
Stratton EX23 4 D1
Summercourt TR8 57 D7
Tregony TR2 71 F3
Tregurrian TR8 44 F8
Troon TR14 79 E4
New Road Cl PL10 133 A2
New Road Hill PL23 116 C4
New Road Terr PL12 53 C3
New Row Gweek TR12 92 C1
Mylor Bridge TR11 82 A3
Nancledra TR20 76 F2
Redruth TR16 139 D1
Summercourt TR8 57 B6
New St Bugle PL26 47 C1
Falmouth TR11 145 B4
Millbrook PL10 132 E5
Padstow PL28 107 D5
Penryn TR10 144 D7
Penzance TR18 143 E5
Plymouth PL1 149 A2
Troon TR14 79 E4
Newtake Rd PL19 147 E2
Newton Ave PL5 123 E2
Newton Ct Dobwalls PL14 50 E8
Redruth TR15 140 B6
Newton Farm Cotts PL13 62 E3
Newton Gdns PL5 123 F2
Newton Moor Tolcarne TR14 79 E5
Treskillard TR14 139 B1
Newton Pk 12 TR2 95 A6

Newton Rd Newton PL30 . . . . 35 F8
  St Mawes TR2 . . . . .95 A6
  Treswigga PL30 . . . . .24 E1
  Troon TR14. . . . . .79 E5
Newton's Margate Ind Est
  PL31 . . . . 35 B1
NEWTOWN Coad's Green. 27 D5
  Praa Sands 90 B4
Newtown Fowey PL23. . . . . . .60 F3
  Newtown TR20 . . . . .90 B4
  Tregidden TR12 . . . . 100 E5
  Trevegean TR19. . . . . .86 F4
NEWTOWN-IN-ST
  MARTIN 100 E6
Newtown La TR17, TR20 . . . . .89 A7
Newtown Rd PL15 . . . . .27 D5
New Windsor Terr 11
  TR11 . . . . 145 A4
New Wood Cl PL6 . . . . .125 E8
New Zealand Ho PL3. . . . . . .128 B4
Nicholas Ave TR16. . . . . .80 A5
Nicholas Holman Rd 2
  TR14 . . . . 138 E3
Nicholas Mdw PL17. . . . . .40 E4
Nicholas Parc 3 PL18 . . . . .143 C7
Nicholson Rd PL5 . . . . .124 E2
Nicolls Flats PL15 . . . . .106 B5
Nightingale Cl PL9 . . . . .136 C8
Nine Maidens TR16. . . . . .80 A4
Nine Maidens Short Stay Sch
  TR16. . . . . .80 A4
Nine Oaks Est PL20 . . . . .42 F3
Ninnesbridge Rd TR27. . . . . .77 B3
NINNIS BRIDGE 77 B2
No Go By Hill TR19. . . . . .86 F7
NO MAN'S LAND 63 E7
No Mans' Land Rd TR11 . . . . .93 D5
Nook The PL19 . . . . .147 D6
NOONVARES 90 E7
Noonvares La TR13. . . . . .90 D7
Norfolk Cl PL3. . . . . .129 C5
Norfolk Rd Falmouth TR11 . .145 B4
  Plymouth PL3. . . . . .129 C4
Norman Cotts PL15 . . . . . . .106 C7
Normandy Hill PL5 . . . . .123 B2
Normandy Way
  Bodmin PL31 . . . . .109 F2
  Plymouth PL5. . . . . .123 C2
Norman's Way PL30 . . . . .23 E3
NORRIS GREEN 40 E4
Northampton Cl PL5. . . . . . .124 B5
NORTH BEER 12 F3
NORTH BRENTOR 30 E8
North Carnmarth
  Busveal TR16. . . . . .80 D8
  Busveal TR16. . . . . .140 E3
North Cl EX23 . . . . .5 A6
North Cliff 12 TR18 . . . . .88 C1
North Cliffs Churchtown TR14 67 B5
  Coombe TR14. . . . . .66 F3
North Cnr 1 TR18 . . . . .143 C7
NORTH CORNER 101 C4
North Cornwall Mus & Gall *
  PL32 . . . . .105 C4
NORTHCOTT Bude 4 C3
  St Giles on the Heath 13 D3
Northcott Mouth Rd EX23 104 F8
NORTH COUNTRY 140 B8
NORTH DARLEY 38 D8
North Dimson PL18 . . . . .40 F6
North Down Cres PL2. . . . . .127 C6
North Down Gdns PL2 . . . . .127 F6
North Down Rd PL2. . . . . . . .128 B6
Northesk St PL2. . . . . .128 A4
Northey Cl TR4 . . . . .69 F6
Northey Rd Bodmin PL31 . . .109 D4
  Bodmin PL31. . . . . .109 D4
Northfield Cl TR16. . . . . .68 E1
Northfield Dr TR1 . . . . .137 D3
Northgate Pl 1 PL15 . . . . .106 C6
North Grange Ind Est TR3 . .81 F6
NORTH HILL 27 B3
North Hill Blackwater TR4 . . .68 E5
  Carharrack TR16. . . . . .80 F8
  Chacewater TR4 . . . . .68 F3
  6 Plymouth PL4 . . . . .149 A4
North Hill Pk PL25 . . . . .114 C4
North La PL14 . . . . .49 E7
NORTHMOOR. 3 F3
North Moor Cross EX22. . . . . .3 F3
Northolt Ave PL5 . . . . .123 D4
North Orchard Ct 1 TR20. . .89 E5
North Par Camborne TR14 . .138 E3
  Falmouth TR11. . . . . .145 A6
  Penzance TR18 . . . . .143 E5
  Portscatho TR2. . . . . .83 B2
North Parade Rear TR14. . . .138 D3
North Park Villas PL12 . . . . .122 C4
NORTH PETHERWIN 18 A8
North Petherwin Ind Est
  PL15. . . . . .18 A8
North Petherwin Prim Sch
  PL15. . . . . .12 B1
North Pier TR18 . . . . .143 C2
North Pl 15 TR26. . . . . .141 B6
North Pool Cl TR15 . . . . . . .139 C7
North Pool Rd TR15. . . . . . .139 C7
NORTH PROSPECT 128 A6
North Prospect Rd PL2 . . . .128 A6
North Quay Hayle TR27 . . . .142 B6
  Padstow PL28. . . . . .107 D6
North Quay Hill TR7 . . . . . . .110 D7
North Quay Par PL28. . . . . . .107 D6
North Rd Camborne TR14 . . .138 D3
  Goldsithney TR20. . . . . .89 E5
  Landrake PL12. . . . . .53 C3

North Rd continued
  Lifton PL16. . . . . .19 F4
  Looe PL13. . . . . .117 C3
  Pentewan PL26 . . . . .73 C6
  Plymouth PL12. . . . . .123 A2
  Redruth TR16. . . . . .140 E1
  St Teath PL30 . . . . .23 E7
  Saltash PL12 . . . . .122 F3
  Torpoint PL11 . . . . .127 B3
  Whitemoor PL26 . . . . .58 E8
  Yelverton PL20 . . . . .42 C3
North Road E PL4. . . . . .148 C4
North Road W PL1. . . . . .148 B4
North Roskear TR14 . . . . . . .138 F5
North Roskear Mdw TR14 138 E5
North Roskear Rd TR14 . . . .138 F5
North Row TR19 . . . . .86 F6
North Terr
  2 Penzance TR18 . . . . . . .143 E4
  12 St Ives TR26 . . . . .141 B5
  Whitemoor PL26. . . . . .58 E8
Northumberland St PL5 . . . .127 E8
Northumberland Terr PL1 148 B1
North View PL13. . . . . .117 D4
North Way TR8 . . . . .111 F4
North Weald Gdns PL5. . . . .123 E5
Norton Ave PL4. . . . . .149 C4
Norton Ct 2 PL31 . . . . .109 E5
Norway La TR3 . . . . .81 D5
Norwich Ave PL5 . . . . .124 B5
Notley Gdns PL2. . . . . .128 A8
Notre Dame Cl PL6 . . . . . . .124 E5
Notre Dame Ho PL1 . . . . . . .148 B3
Notre Dame RC Sch PL6 . .124 F5
Notte St PL1. . . . . .148 C2
Novorossisk Rd PL6 . . . . . . .125 E2
Noweth Pl TR11 . . . . .144 E5
N Polmenor Downs TR14 . . 78 F5
Nuffield Health Plymouth
  Hospl PL6. . . . . .125 B4
NUMPHRA 87 A4
Nunnery Hill PL26 . . . . .72 F7
Nurseries The TR11. . . . . . . .144 D5
Nursery Cl Plymouth PL5 . . .124 B7
  Truro TR1. . . . . .137 D5
  11 Tywardreath PL24 . . . . . .60 D5
Nut La TR27 . . . . .77 E3
Nut Tree Hill PL12 . . . . .65 B8
Nutwell Cl 2 PL28. . . . . . . .107 C4

O

Oakapple Cl PL7. . . . . .130 B7
Oak Apple Cl PL12. . . . . . . .122 D4
Oak Ave PL12. . . . . .40 A1
Oakcroft Rd PL2. . . . . .128 B6
Oakdene Rise PL9 . . . . .135 F6
Oakdene Villas 7 TR9 . . . . . .45 E1
Oak Dr 8 Liskeard PL14 . . . .113 B5
  Plymouth PL6. . . . . .124 F3
Oakey Orch PL17 . . . . .40 D4
Oakfield PL15 . . . . .27 D3
Oakfield Cl PL7. . . . . .131 C6
Oakfield Dr PL15 . . . . .106 D3
Oakfield Pl PL4. . . . . .129 B1
Oakfield Rd Falmouth TR11 144 F5
  Plymouth PL7. . . . . .130 C6
Oakfield Terrace Rd PL4. . .129 B1
Oak Ford PL30. . . . . .48 C7
Oakham Rd PL5 . . . . .124 B5
Oakhill PL30. . . . . .47 C6
Oak La Truro TR1. . . . . .69 E4
  Whitstone EX22. . . . . .7 F1
Oakland Pk PL11 . . . . .144 D5
Oaklands PL19 . . . . .147 A4
Oaklands Bsns Pk PL13 . . . .63 D8
Oaklands Cl PL6. . . . . .125 C7
Oaklands Ct TR9. . . . . .45 E6
Oaklands Dr PL12. . . . . .122 C3
Oaklands Ind Est PL14. . . .113 E6
Oaklands Rd PL14 . . . . .113 E6
Oakleigh Terr TR7. . . . . .110 F6
Oak Moor Dr PL15 . . . . .106 D3
Oak Park Terr PL14. . . . . . . .113 A6
Oak Pk PL30. . . . . .23 E3
Oak Rd PL19. . . . . .147 C2
Oakridge PL12. . . . . .53 C7
Oak Ridge PL16. . . . . .19 F4
Oaks The 12 Par PL24. . . . . .60 C4
  Quintrell Downs TR8 . . . . . . .111 F3
  St Austell PL25. . . . . .114 B3
Oak Tree Cl PL25 . . . . .115 B3
Oaktree Ct PL14. . . . . .124 F1
Oak Tree La
  Godolphin Hill TR27 . . . . .90 C6
  Tavistock PL19. . . . . .147 C1
Oak Tree Pk PL15. . . . . .125 D6
Oak Tree School 9 TR4 . . . .69 C3
Oak Vale TR2. . . . . .72 A7
Oak Way TR1. . . . . .137 E4
Oakwood Cl PL6. . . . . .125 D7
Oakwood Pk PL31 . . . . .109 F4
Oakwood Prim Sch PL6. . . .125 A6
Oakwood Rise PL32 . . . . . . .105 E5
  Camelford PL32. . . . . .105 E5

Oates Rd Helston TR13 . . . .146 C6
  Marazion TR17. . . . . .89 C5
  Plymouth PL2. . . . . .128 B5
Observer Cl TR1. . . . . .137 C3
Ocean Cres 22 TR13. . . . . . .98 C8
Ocean Ct Plymouth PL1. . . .133 F8
  Porthtowan TR4. . . . . .68 A7
Ocean St PL2. . . . . .127 E6
Ocean View
  Indian Queens TR9 . . . . .45 E1
  Newquay TR7. . . . . .110 B5
  Polruan PL23. . . . . .116 D2
  St Austell PL25. . . . . .114 E7
Ocean View Rd EX23. . . . . . .104 D7
Ocean View Terr TR26 . . . . .141 A6
Octagon St PL1. . . . . .148 B3
Octagon The PL1 . . . . .148 B2
Octans Way 6 PL9 . . . . . . .136 E8
Okehampton Cl PL7 . . . . . . .131 B4
Old Bakehouse Flats The
  TR18 . . . . .143 F6
Old Barn Ct TR7. . . . . .110 D4
Old Barns The TR14. . . . . . . .66 F2
Old Boat Yard The PL28. . .107 E6
Old Boys School TR16. . . . . .67 E5
Old Brewery Yd 4 TR18 . . .143 E5
Old Bridge St TR1 . . . . .137 D4
Old Butchers Shop The
  TR20 . . . . .89 B8
Old Cable La TR19 . . . . .96 E3
Old Callywith Rd PL31 . . . . .35 B2
Old Canal Cl EX23 . . . . .7 B6
Old Cardinham La PL30 . . .35 F2
Old Carnon Hill TR3 . . . . .81 F6
Old Chapel The TR4 . . . . .68 F5
Old Chapel Way PL10 . . . . .132 F6
Old Chough Flats TR7. . . . . .111 B7
Old Church Rd TR11 . . . . .93 E2
Old Church The TR18 . . . . . .143 D4
Old Coach Rd
  Lanivet PL26, PL30 . . . . .47 D6
  Playing Place TR3 . . . . .82 B8
  Truro TR3. . . . . .70 A1
Old Coastguard Cotts PL11 65 A4
Old Coastguard Row TR19 . 96 B7
Old Corn Mill The TR12 . . . .92 C1
Old Cottage La PL7 . . . . .22 F1
Old Dairy The Plymouth PL3 129 B6
  Sancreed TR20 . . . . .87 E4
Old Drovers Way EX23. . . . . .4 E1
Old English Ind Est PL20 . . .42 E3
Old Exeter Rd PL19 . . . . . . .147 D7
Old Falmouth Rd TR1. . . . . .137 C1
Old Farm Rd PL5. . . . . .127 C8
Old Ferry Rd PL12. . . . . .123 A3
Old Foundry Cl TR19 . . . . . . .86 F6
Old Foundry The
  Menheniot PL14 . . . . .51 E6
  Tavistock PL19. . . . . .147 D6
Old George St PL1. . . . . . . .148 C2
Old Grammar School Ct
  PL22 . . . . .112 C2
Old Grammar School, The
  PL32. . . . . .105 D4
Old Greystone Hill PL15,
  PL19 . . . . .28 F6
Old Guildhall Mus * PL13. .117 D3
Old Hill Falmouth TR11 . . . .144 F6
  Grampound TR2. . . . . .72 A7
  Helston TR13 . . . . .146 A6
  Lewannick PL15. . . . . .27 B7
  Trethevey PL30 . . . . .34 C8
Old Hill Cres TR11 . . . . .144 F5
OLD KEA 82 E8
Old La PL16. . . . . .46 F3
Old Laira Rd PL3. . . . . .129 C4
Oldlands Cl PL6. . . . . .125 B6
Old Launceston Rd PL19 . .147 B6
Old Laundry The PL1 . . . . . .148 A3
Old Lawn School La PL25 .114 A3
Old Market Pl PL31 . . . . . . .109 C4
Old Mill Ct PL7 . . . . .130 E5
Old Mill Herbary The *
  PL30. . . . . .34 F6
Old Mill La Camborne TR14 . .78 F6
  Penponds TR14. . . . . .79 A6
Old Mill The
  3 Boscastle PL35. . . . . .9 C2
  Lerryn PL22. . . . . .61 D8
Old Mine La PL18. . . . . .40 E6
Old Nursery Cl TR13 . . . . . . .91 A1
Old Orchard Ct EX23. . . . . . .7 B6
Old Park Rd PL3. . . . . .128 D6
Old Paul Hill TR18 . . . . .143 C2
Old Plymouth Rd PL3 . . . . .129 E5
Old Portreath Rd
  Illogan TR16. . . . . .67 F5
  Redruth TR15. . . . . .67 F4
Old Post Office Hill 8 EX23. 4 E1
Old Pound PL26 . . . . .58 E6
Old Priory PL7. . . . . .130 D5
Old Priory Jun Sch PL7 . . . .130 D5
Old Quarry Rd PL20. . . . . . . .42 A3
Old Quay La PL12 . . . . .65 B8
Old Rail Rd TR14. . . . . .79 C2
Old Rd Boscastle PL35. . . . . . .9 C2
  Liskeard PL14. . . . . .113 A6
Old Rectory Dr TR9. . . . . . . .45 E6
Old Rosclyn Cres PL24. . . . .60 D5
Old Roselyn Rd PL24. . . . . . .60 C4
Old Sandy La TR16. . . . . . . .140 D3
Old School Cl PL27 . . . . .21 F3
Old School The
  Padstow PL28. . . . . .107 D5
  Wadebridge PL27 . . . . .108 B5
Old School Ho The PL10 . .133 A1
Old Schoolhouse The
  TR11 . . . . .145 B4

Old School La PL30 . . . . .34 D4
Old School Rd Pityme PL27. .21 F3
  Plymouth PL5. . . . . .127 C8
Old School The 10 TR5 . . . . .54 D1
Old Smithy Cl TR17 . . . . .89 C5
Old Smithy Cotts EX39 . . . . . .2 E4
Old Sta La TR17. . . . . .89 A6
Old Station Rd
  Horrabridge PL20 . . . . .42 C4
  1 Plymouth PL4. . . . . .51 A7
Old Station The PL20 . . . . . .42 B4
Old Tannery Bsns Pk The 4
  PL4. . . . . .149 A4
Old Tannery La TR2. . . . . . . .72 A7
Old Temple Rd
  Merrifield PL30 . . . . .36 B8
  Sprey Moor PL14. . . . . .25 C1
Old Town St PL1. . . . . .148 C3
Old Tram Rd
  Carnon Downs TR3 . . . . .82 A5
  Devoran TR3 . . . . .81 F6
  Stencoose TR16. . . . . .68 B4
Old Truro Rd TR14 . . . . .55 E3
Old Vicarage Cl TR3 . . . . . . .80 F4
Old Vicarage Pl 11 PL15. . .114 C3
Old Vicarage The TR26. . . . . .76 E5
Old Warleigh La PL5. . . . . . .124 B7
Old Well Gdns TR10. . . . . . .144 C8
Old Wharf The PL9 . . . . .135 C7
Old Wheel Rd PL30. . . . . . . .23 C1
Old Woodlands Rd PL5 . . . .124 D3
Old Workhouses The TR15 140 B8
Oliver Ct Liskeard PL14. . . . .50 E8
  St Mellion PL12. . . . . .40 A1
Oliver's Terr TR13 . . . . .146 C5
Olive Villas TR3. . . . . .81 F6
Olivey Pl TR11. . . . . .82 A3
Olivia Ct PL4. . . . . .149 B4
Oll An Gwella 10 PL18. . . . . .40 D6
Olympic Way PL6. . . . . .125 C6
Omaha Rd PL31. . . . . .109 F3
Onslow Rd PL2 . . . . .128 C7
Ope's Ct 13 TR11. . . . . .145 B5
Opies La PL31 . . . . .109 C5
Opie's Row TR16 . . . . .80 B5
Opie's Terr TR16 . . . . .80 A5
Orange La TR26 . . . . .141 A6
Orchard Ave PL6 . . . . .129 B7
Orchard Cl PL15. . . . . .106 B7
  Helston TR13 . . . . .146 B7
  3 Plymouth PL7. . . . . .131 C5
  Poughill EX23 . . . . .4 D2
  St Austell PL25. . . . . .114 E4
  St Giles on the Heath PL15 . .13 F1
  St Mellion PL12. . . . . .53 C8
  Tavistock PL19. . . . . .41 D8
  Tideford PL12 . . . . .52 F2
  Truro TR1. . . . . .69 F3
Orchard Cotts
  Lamerton PL19 . . . . .30 B3
  St Austell PL25. . . . . .114 F5
Orchard Cres PL9. . . . . .135 C7
Orchard Ct Lamerton PL19. . .30 A3
  Penzance TR18 . . . . .143 C5
Orchard Gr PL25. . . . . .114 B4
Orchard Ho 11 TR18 . . . . . .143 C2
Orchard La Helford TR12 . . . .93 B1
  Plymouth PL7. . . . . .130 E6
  Tregonhaye TR11. . . . . .144 C5
Orchard Mdw 4 PL12 . . . . .53 E4
Orchard Pk PL26 . . . . .47 C2
Orchard Pl 10 TR18 . . . . . .143 C2
Orchard Pl PL2. . . . . .128 B7
Orchard Terr 20 TR18 . . . . .143 C2
Orchard The Gunnislake PL18 41 A6
  Lerryn PL22. . . . . .61 D8
  Newquay TR7. . . . . .111 B7
  North Petherwin PL15 . . . . . .18 B8
  St Erth TR27. . . . . .77 E2
Orchardton Terr 2 PL9. . . . .135 F5
Orchard Vale TR11 . . . . .145 C7
Orchard Way
  6 Goldsithney TR20. . . . . . .89 E5
  2 St Austell PL25. . . . . . . .115 A1
Orchard Wlk 13 PL27 . . . . .108 B5
Orchard Wy EX23. . . . . .104 E5
Orch The PL13. . . . . .117 D4
Ordnance St PL1 . . . . .127 E2
Ordulf Rd PL19 . . . . .147 A5
Oregon Way PL3. . . . . .129 D6
ORESTON 135 C2
Oreston Com Academy
  PL9 . . . . .135 C7
Oreston Rd PL9. . . . . .135 E4
Orion Dr PL7. . . . . .31 F3
Osborne Ct PL1. . . . . .148 C2
Osborne Parc TR13 . . . . . . .146 B7
Osborne Pl PL1. . . . . .148 C2
Osborne Rd PL3 . . . . .128 A3
Osborne Villas
  10 Falmouth TR11 . . . . .145 C3
  2 Plymouth PL3 . . . . .128 A3
Osprey Gdns PL9 . . . . .136 C7
OTTERHAM 10 D1
Otterham Com Prim Sch
  PL32. . . . . .10 C2
Otterham Pk PL32 . . . . .16 A8
Otterham Sta PL32. . . . . .16 A8
OTTERIIAM STATION. 16 A8
OTTERY. 30 A2
Ottery Cotts PL19. . . . . .30 A2
Ottery Park Ind Est PL19 . . .30 A2
Outer Down PL19. . . . . .30 A3
Outland Rd PL2. . . . . .128 C2
Outta Sight Ct 7 PL31. . . . .109 A5
Overcliff PL29 . . . . .22 D8
Overton Gdns 3 PL3 . . . . . .128 F5

New – Par 169

Overton Villas 6 PL15. . . . .106 C5
Owen Dr PL7. . . . . .130 C7
Owen Sivell Cl PL14. . . . . . .113 E6
Oxford Ave PL3. . . . . .128 E5
Oxford Gdns PL3 . . . . .128 E5
Oxford Pl PL1 . . . . .148 C3
Oxford St PL1. . . . . .148 B3
Oxford Terr 4 PL1 . . . . .148 B3
Ox La TR8 . . . . .31 E1
Oxland Rd TR16 . . . . .67 E5
Oxley Vale TR7 . . . . .111 B5

P

Paardeburg Rd 1 PL31 . . . . .48 D8
Packet La TR20 . . . . .89 F5
Packington St PL2. . . . . .128 A4
Packsaddle 3 TR10 . . . . .81 D2
Packsaddle Cl TR10. . . . . . . .81 D2
Paddock Cl Plymouth PL9 . .135 E5
  Saltash PL12 . . . . .122 D4
Paddock The Helston TR13 146 C7
  Redruth TR15. . . . . .140 D4
  Sticker PL26 . . . . .58 E1
Paddons Row PL19 . . . . .147 C6
Padnover Terr 22 TR26. . . . .141 B5
PADSTOW 107 C4
Padstow Harbour Ind Est
  PL28. . . . . .107 C4
Padstow Mus * PL28. . . . . .107 D5
Padstow Sch PL28. . . . . .107 C4
Padstow Workshop Units
  PL28. . . . . .107 B4
Page's Cross PL15. . . . . .106 D4
Pagoda Dr PL26. . . . . .115 A1
Paiges Farm PL9 . . . . .135 C1
Painton Water EX39. . . . . .3 A8
Palace Rd PL25 . . . . .114 D4
Palace St PL1 . . . . .149 A2
Palm Ct TR1. . . . . .137 D3
Palm Dr PL28. . . . . .31 F7
PALMERSBRIDGE 25 C4
Palmers Terr PL34. . . . . .14 C6
Palmerston St PL1. . . . . .148 A4
Palmers Way PL27 . . . . .108 D6
PANCRASWEEK. 8 C8
Pannier La TR26 . . . . .141 C2
Pannier Mkt PL19. . . . . .147 C5
Panson Cross PL15 . . . . .13 E3
PANTERSBRIDGE 36 D3
PAR. 60 C4
Parade PL1. . . . . .149 A2
Parade Bsns Pk 4 PL19. . .147 B4
Parade Hill TR19 . . . . .88 D1
Parade Ope PL1. . . . . .149 A2
Parade Pass 29 TR18. . . . . .143 E5
Parade Rd PL5 . . . . .124 A3
Parade Sq PL22. . . . . .112 D2
Parade St TR18 . . . . .146 C5
Parade The Helston TR13 . . .113 C6
  Liskeard PL14. . . . . .113 C6
  Lostwithiel PL22 . . . . .112 D2
  Millbrook PL10. . . . . .132 E5
  Milton Abbot PL19 . . . . .29 C6
  Mousehole TR19 . . . . .88 D1
  Truro TR1. . . . . .137 E4
Paradise Park & The World
  Parrot Trust * TR27. . . . . .142 A4
Paradise Pk EX22. . . . . .7 F1
Paradise Pl PL1 . . . . .128 A2
Paradise Rd Boscastle PL35. . .9 C1
  Plymouth PL1. . . . . .128 A2
PARAMOOR 72 E8
Par Beach & St Andrews Rd
  Nature Reserve * PL24. . . . .60 D4
Parc-Abnac TR20. . . . . .88 B7
Parc-an-Bal Ct TR14. . . . . . .138 E4
Parc-an-Bre Dr PL26 . . . . . . .58 E3
Parc-an-Cady Est TR19. . . . .97 A6
Parc-an-Challow TR10 . . . . .144 B8
Parc-an-Creet TR26. . . . . . . .77 A7
Parc-an-Dillon Rd TR2. . . . . .83 B2
Parc-an-Dix La TR27 . . . . . .142 C7
Parc-an-Dower TR13. . . . . . .146 C6
Parcandowr TR7 . . . . .57 E1
Parc-an-Forth 6 TR26 . . . . .77 A6
Parc An Gew TR13 . . . . .146 C8
Parc-an-Gwarry 7 TR3. . . . .81 F7
Parc-an-Ithan TR12 . . . . . . .102 F2
Parc-an-Maen 11 TR13. . . . .98 C8
Parc an Manns TR1. . . . . . . .93 D3
Parc-an-Peath TR19 . . . . . . .97 A6
Parc-an-Stamps 4 TR26. . . .77 A6
Parc an Yorth TR19 . . . . . . .86 F8
Parc-Askell Cl TR12. . . . . . . .98 E5
Parc Bean Terr TR26. . . . . . .141 A6
Parc Behan TR2. . . . . .83 F6
Parc Bottom TR12 . . . . .92 C1
Parc Bowen TR13. . . . . .92 A3
Parc-Bracket St TR14. . . . . .138 D3
Parc Brawse TR12 . . . . .102 F2
Parc Briwer TR10. . . . . .144 D7
Parc Eglos Helston TR13 . . .146 B8
  St Merryn PL28 . . . . .31 F8
Parc Eglos Sch TR13 . . . . . .146 C6
Parc Enys TR12. . . . . .99 B4
PARC ERISSEY. 68 A3
Parc Erissey Ind Est TR16. . .68 A3
Parc Fer Cl EX23. . . . . .4 E1
Parc Garland 15 TR12. . . . .102 F2
Parc Godrevy TR7. . . . . .110 C5
Parc Holland TR13. . . . . . . .146 D8

Parc Ledden TR13 .... 146 C6
Parc Ledrak TR13 .... 146 B8
Parc Letta TR18 .... 143 C7
Parc Mellan TR18 .... 143 D7
Parc Merys TR2 .... 83 B2
Parc Monga Dr TR11 ... 92 F3
Parc Monga Rd TR11 ... 92 F3
Parc Morrep TR20 .... 90 B3
Parc Owles TR26 .... 141 D2
Parc Peneglos TR11 ... 82 A3
Parc Pennkarn PL33 ... 14 C3
Parc Pordic TR27 .... 142 D5
Parc Shady TR26 .... 77 C1
Parc Stephney TR11 .... 144 C2
Parc Terr 19 TR18 .... 143 C1
Parc Trenance TR28 .... 31 F7
Parc Trethias PL28 .... 31 F7
Parc Vean TR30 .... 34 C1
Parc Venton Cl 2 TR14 ... 138 F2
Parc Villas 17 TR18 .... 143 C1
Parc Wartha Ave TR18 .... 143 D6
Parc Wartha Cres TR18 ... 143 D6
Par Gn PL24 .... 60 C4
Pargolla Rd TR7 .... 110 F6
Parka Cl 12 TR9 .... 45 E2
Park-an-Bans TR14 .... 138 E1
Parkancreeg 3 TR2 .... 81 F7
Park An Dreas 4 TR2 .... 83 F6
Park An Fenten TR13 .... 146 E7
Park an Gonwyn TR26 .... 141 E2
Park an Gorsaf TR14 .... 138 D2
Park An Gwarry 7 TR3 ... 81 F7
Park an Harvey TR13 .... 146 C6
Park An Keres PL14 .... 52 A5
Park-an-Mengleth TR15 .. 140 D4
Park-an-Pyth 2 TR19 ... 75 A1
Park-an-Tansys TR14 .... 138 F2
Parka Rd Indian Queens TR9 .. 45 E1
  8 St Columb Road TR9 ... 45 E2
Park Ave
  Plymouth, Devonport PL1 ... 127 C3
  Plymouth, Plymstock PL9 ... 135 D7
  St Ives TR26 .... 141 B5
PARK BOTTOM 139 B8
Park Bottom TR15 .... 67 D3
Park Cl Illogan TR15 .... 139 B8
  Nancegollan TR13 .... 91 B7
  Plymouth PL7 .... 130 B7
Park Cnr TR18 .... 143 E6
Park Cres Falmouth TR11 ... 145 A4
  Helston TR13 .... 146 B5
  Plymouth PL9 .... 135 C7
  Ponsanooth TR3 .... 81 B4
Park Ct Chillaton PL16 ... 29 F8
  28 Penzance TR18 .... 143 E5
Park Dr PL31 .... 109 B4
Parkenbutts TR7 .... 111 D7
Parkengear Vean TR2 ... 71 D6
Parkengue TR10 .... 144 A7
Parkenhead La PL28 ... 20 F2
Park Enskellaw 6 TR12 ... 99 A4
Park en Venton TR12 .... 99 A2
Park-en-Vine PL27 .... 32 C6
Park En Vine PL27 .... 32 D7
Parker Cl PL7 .... 130 B5
Parker Rd PL2 .... 128 B6
Parkers Cross PL13 .... 63 A4
Parker's Gn PL18 .... 40 F6
Parkesway PL12 .... 122 D2
Park Fenton PL14 .... 113 D5
PARKFIELD 39 A2
Parkfield Dr PL6 .... 125 F1
Park Gwyn PL26 .... 58 B4
Park Hill TR11 .... 145 A4
Park Ho PL25 .... 114 B3
Park Holly TR14 .... 138 B3
Parkins Terr 7 TR1 .... 137 D5
Park La 8 Bere Alston PL20... 41 B1
  Bugle PL26 .... 47 C1
  Camborne TR14 .... 138 E2
  Plymouth PL5 .... 135 C7
Parklands 14 TR5 .... 54 D1
  Nanpean PL26 .... 58 C7
Parklands Cl TR7 .... 111 D6
Park Leder TR16 .... 68 C3
Park Leven TR16 .... 139 C8
Park Lowen TR26 .... 141 C2
Parknoweth TR12 .... 99 A4
Parknoweth Cl TR8 .... 56 B6
Park Pl Grampound Road TR2 . 57 E1
  Wadebridge PL27 .... 108 B5
Park Place La 12 PL3 .... 128 A4
Park Rd Camborne TR14 ... 138 E4
  Fowey PL23 .... 116 C4
  Illogan TR15 .... 139 B7
  Lifton PL16 .... 19 F3
  Liskeard PL14 .... 113 C6
  18 Newlyn TR18 .... 143 C1
  Plymouth PL3 .... 129 A6
  Ponsanooth TR3 .... 81 B4
  Redruth TR15 .... 140 C4
  St Austell PL25 .... 114 C3
  St Dominick PL12 .... 40 D2
  Torpoint PL11 .... 127 B3
  Wadebridge PL27 .... 108 B5
  Whitemoor PL26 .... 58 E8
Park Rd Hos PL22 .... 112 C2
Park Rise TR11 .... 145 A4
Parkryn Rd 4 TR19 .... 88 C1
Parkside PL3 .... 127 F5
Park St PL3 .... 128 A4
Park Stenak TR16 .... 80 F8
Parkstone La PL7 .... 130 F6
Park Street Ope PL3 .... 128 A4

Park Terr Falmouth TR11 ...145 A4
  Truro TR1 .... 70 D1
Park The Penryn TR10 ...144 B7
  Tregony TR2 .... 71 F4
Parkvedras Ho 5 TR1 ...137 B4
Parkvedras Terr 4 TR1 ...137 B4
Parkventon PL26 .... 47 C2
Park View Lifton PL16 .... 19 F4
  Liskeard PL14 .... 113 C6
  Perranworthal TR3 .... 81 E6
  Plymouth PL4 .... 149 C3
  Summercourt TR8 .... 57 B7
  Truro TR1 .... 137 C3
Parkview Apartments TR7 110 F5
Park View Rd TR13 .... 146 B5
Park View Terr TR27 ...108 B5
Park Villas TR3 .... 81 B4
Park Way PL25 .... 114 F5
Parkway Ct TR1 .... 129 E7
Parkway Ind Est The PL6 ...129 E7
Parkway The PL3, PL5, PL6 ..128 F1
Park Wise Penryn TR10 ...144 C7
  Penryn TR10 .... 144 C8
Parkwood Cl PL6 .... 121 B2
Parkwood Ct PL19 .... 147 D6
Parkwood Rd PL19 .... 147 D6
Park Wood Rise PL16 ... 19 F4
Parkwoon Cl PL26 .... 46 F3
Par La PL24 .... 60 B4
Par Moor Rd Par PL24, PL25 .60 B3
  St Austell PL24, PL25 ...115 F4
PARNACOTT 8 E8
Parnell Cl PL6 .... 129 A8
Parr La PL4 .... 149 B2
Parr St PL4 .... 149 B2
Parsonage Ct PL16 .... 19 F4
Parsonage Way PL4 .... 149 B2
Parsons Cl PL9 .... 136 A4
Parsons Ct PL10 .... 132 F6
Parsons Gn PL17 .... 39 E6
Partwayes PL19 .... 30 A3
Pascoe Cl TR3 .... 69 D4
Pasley St E PL2 .... 127 F4
Pasley St PL2 .... 127 E4
Pasmore Road TR13 ...146 D6
Passage Hill TR11 .... 82 A3
Passage La PL23 .... 116 B5
Passage St PL23 .... 116 B5
Passmore Cl Blackwater TR4.68 E5
  Liskeard PL14 .... 113 D6
Pathfields EX23 .... 104 C5
Pathway Fields The TR27 .142 C5
Patience Cl PL27 .... 31 C4
Patna Pl PL1 .... 148 B4
Pato Point PL11 .... 127 A5
Patterdale Cl PL6 .... 125 D3
Patterdale Wlk PL6 ...125 D3
Pattern Cl 1 PL25 ...115 A3
Pattinson Ct PL6 .... 125 E2
Pattinson Cl PL6 .... 125 E2
Pattinson Dr PL6 .... 125 F2
PAUL 88 C2
Paull Rd PL31 .... 109 B4
Paulls Row 4 TR15 ...140 C5
PAUL'S GREEN 90 E8
Paul's Row TR1 .... 137 D5
Paul's Terr TR1 .... 137 D5
Paviland Grange 6 PL1..128 A3
Pavilion Pk TR14 .... 138 F4
Pavilion Rise 5 PL26 ...115 A1
Pavlova Cl PL14 .... 113 C5
Pavlova Ct 6 PL14 ...113 C5
Pavo St 10 PL9 .... 136 E8
Paynter's Cross PL12 ... 53 E7
Paynter's Cross Cotts PL12 53 E7
Paynters La TR1 .... 67 E4
PAYNTER'S LANE END ... 67 E4
Paynter's Lane End Est
  TR16 .... 67 D4
Paynter Wlk 5 PL7 ...131 B5
Peachys Hill PL30 .... 35 E3
Peachys Rd PL30 .... 35 F3
Peacock Ave PL11 .... 127 A3
Peacock Cl PL7 .... 130 F7
Peacock La PL4 .... 149 A2
Pearce's La 12 TR26 ...141 A5
Pearce's Row 3 PL24 ... 60 C4
Pearn Cotts 2 PL3 ...128 F6
Pearn Gdns PL3 .... 129 A7
Pearn Rd PL3 .... 129 A7
Pearn Ridge PL3 .... 129 A7
Pearson Ave 9 PL4 ...128 F4
Pearson Rd PL4 .... 128 F4
Pebble Ct PL7 .... 111 C7
Pedlars Cl PL15 .... 18 B8
Pedlars Orchard PL15 ... 18 A8
Pedna Carne TR9 .... 57 E8
Pedna Carne Mobile Home Pk
  TR9 .... 57 E8
Pednandrea TR19 .... 86 E6
Pednavounder PL7 ...103 F7
Pedn-m'n-du TR19 .... 96 A7
Pedn-Moran TR2 .... 95 B6
Pedn-y-ke 1 TR12 .... 99 A1
Peek Moor Cross EX22... 13 E4
Peeks Ave PL9 .... 135 F7
Peel St PL1 .... 128 A1
Pegasus Pl PL9 .... 136 E8
Peguarra Cl PL28 .... 20 E1
Peguarra Ct PL28 .... 20 E1
Pelean Cross
  Ponsanooth TR3 .... 81 B5
  Trebost TR3 .... 81 A5
Pelham Ct 11 TR11 ...145 C3
Pellew Cl 7 Falmouth TR11 145 A5
  Padstow PL28 .... 107 C5

Pellew Cres TR13 .... 146 C4
Pellew Pl PL2 .... 127 F4
Pellew Rd TR11 .... 145 A5
Pellor Fields TR13 .... 90 F3
Pellor Rd TR13 .... 90 F3
Pellymounter Rd PL25 ...114 F2
PELYNT 62 D5
Pelynt Sch PL13 .... 62 D6
Pemboa La Tregarrick TR13 146 F4
  Trewennack TR13 .... 92 A2
  Whitehill TR13 .... 91 F1
Pembrey Wlk PL5 .... 123 E4
Pembroke Cl 7 PL24 ... 60 C4
Pembroke La PL1 .... 127 E1
Pembroke Rd TR7 .... 111 E7
Pembroke St PL1 .... 127 E1
Pemros Rd PL5 .... 123 C1
Penair Cres TR1 .... 137 F6
Penair Sch TR1 .... 70 D4
Penair View TR1 .... 137 F4
Penally Ct PL35 .... 9 D2
Penally Hill PL35 .... 9 D2
Penally Terr PL35 .... 9 C2
Penalverne Ave TR18 ...143 D5
Penalverne Cres TR18 ...143 D5
Penalverne Dr TR18 ...143 D5
Penalverne Pl TR18 ...143 D5
Penameyne Ct 5 TR26 ...141 B6
Pen-an-Gwel TR26 ...141 A4
Pen-An-Vre 11 TR10 ... 81 C1
Penare Gdns 2 TR18 ...143 E6
Penare TR18 .... 143 E6
Penare Terr TR18 .... 143 E6
Penarrow Cl TR11 .... 144 E2
Penarrow Rd TR11 ...145 C8
Penarth PL13 .... 117 B3
Penarth Rd TR11 .... 145 A5
Penarvon TR12 .... 93 B1
Penarwyn Cres TR18 ...143 B7
Penarwyn Rd PL24 .... 60 B4
Penarwyn Woods 6 PL24..60 B4
PENBERTH 97 A3
Penberthy Cross TR27 ... 89 F7
Penberthy Rd Helston TR13 146 C5
  Portreath TR16 .... 67 D6
Penbothidno TR11 .... 92 F3
Pen Brea Cl TR2 .... 95 B6
Penbrea Rd TR18 .... 143 E7
Penbro Way 4 TR13 ... 91 A3
Penbugle La PL31 .... 109 E7
Pencair Ave PL11 .... 126 E2
Pencalenick Sch TR1 ... 70 E4
Pencarn Parc TR16 .... 80 A5
Pencarrick Cl TR1 .... 137 B6
PENCARROW 105 D1
Pencarrow* PL30 .... 34 C6
Pencarrow Cl PL17 ... 39 E3
Pencarrow Rd 13 TR16... 67 E4
Pencavo Hill TR12 .... 53 A3
Pencoys Prim Sch TR16 ... 80 A5
Pencrebar La PL17 .... 39 E3
Pencreber Rd 3 PL20 ... 42 C4
PENCUKE 10 D5
Pencuke La EX23 .... 10 D5
Pendale Sq TR1 .... 137 B4
Pendarves St Merryn PL28 ... 31 F7
  Tresillian TR2 .... 70 F5
Pendarves Est TR14 ... 79 C5
Pendarves Rd
  Camborne TR14 .... 138 C1
  Falmouth TR11 .... 144 F6
  Penzance TR18 .... 143 D6
  Truro TR1 .... 137 C6
Pendarves St
  Camborne, Beacon TR14 ...138 F1
  Troon TR14 .... 79 E4
Pendarves View TR14 ...138 C1
Pendean Ave PL14 .... 113 B6
Pendean Cl PL14 .... 113 B6
Pendean Ct PL14 .... 113 B6
Pendean Dr PL14 .... 113 B6
PENDEEN 75 A1
Pendeen Cl Plymouth PL6 ..124 F6
  Threemilestone TR3 .... 69 D3
Pendeen Cres
  Plymouth PL6 .... 125 A6
  Threemilestone TR3 .... 69 D3
Pendeen Ho TR1 .... 69 E4
Pendeen Pk TR13 .... 146 C8
Pendeen Pl TR7 .... 110 F6
Pendeen Rd Porthleven TR13 91 B1
  Threemilestone TR3 .... 69 D3
  Truro TR1 .... 137 E3
Pendeen Sch TR19 .... 75 A1
Pendennis Castle* TR11 .145 E2
Pendennis Cl
  Penzance TR18 .... 143 E7
  Plymouth PL3 .... 128 F8
  Torpoint PL11 .... 126 F3
Pendennis Ct TR11 .... 145 D3
Pendennis Pl TR18 .... 143 E7
Pendennis Rd
  Falmouth TR11 .... 145 D3
  Looe PL13 .... 117 D5
  Penzance TR18 .... 143 E7
Pendennis Rise TR11 ...145 D3
Pender's La TR15 .... 140 B5
Pendilly Ave PL11 .... 126 F2
Pendilly Dr PL25 .... 114 F2
Pendinnes Gdns PL15...106 B8

PENDOGGETT 23 A6
Pendoggett Rd
  Treharrock PL30 .... 23 A6
  Trewiggett PL30 .... 22 F5
Pendola Wlk TR26 ...141 B5
Pendour Pk PL22 .... 112 C2
Pendower Ct TR2 .... 83 D5
Pendower Rd Looe PL13 ...117 E4
  Veryan TR2 .... 83 F6
Pendower Terr TR14 ...138 E1
Pendragon Cres TR7 ...111 A4
Pendragon Ho TR11 ...145 D3
Pendragon Rd 8 PL14...113 D6
Pendra Loweth TR11 ...144 D1
Pendray Gdns PL14 ... 50 E2
Pendrea Cl TR18 .... 143 F7
Pendrea Pk TR14 .... 138 F5
Pendrea Rd TR18 .... 143 F7
Pendrea Rd TR18 .... 143 F7
Pendrea Wood TR1 ... 69 F3
PENDRIFT 24 B1
Pendrim Rd PL13 .... 117 D4
Pendruccombe Ct PL15 .106 D5
Pen-Eglos 8 TR2 .... 95 A6
PENELEWEY 82 C7
Penforth TR14 .... 138 E2
Penfound Gdns EX23 ...104 F5
Pengannel Cl TR7 .... 110 D4
Pengarrock Hill TR12 ...101 D5
Pengarth 1 TR5 .... 54 D1
Pengarth Cl TR1 .... 137 C2
Pengarth Rd TR11 .... 145 A3
Pengarth Rise TR11 .... 145 A3
PENGEGON 138 F2
Pengegon Moor TR14... 138 F2
Pengegon Parc
  Camborne TR14 .... 138 F2
  Pengegon TR14 .... 138 F2
Pengegon Way TR14 ...138 F2
PENGELLY 14 E2
  Delabole PL33 .... 14 E2
Pengelly Cl PL11 .... 126 F5
Pengelly Cross
  Godolphin Cross TR27 ... 90 F7
  Wadebridge PL27 .... 108 C1
Pengelly Hill Pengelly PL14.. 50 B8
  Torpoint PL11 .... 127 A5
Pengelly Pk PL11 .... 126 F5
Pengelly Pl TR11 .... 144 E5
Pengellys Row TR14 ...139 A5
Pengelly Way TR3 ... 69 D3
Pengeron Ave 1 TR14 ...138 F7
Pengersick Est TR20 ... 90 C3
Pengersick La TR20 ... 90 C3
Pengersick Parc TR20 ... 90 C3
Pengliddon PL27 .... 33 B7
PENGOLD 10 A5
Pengover Cl PL14 .... 113 D6
Pengover Gn PL14 ... 51 E8
Pengover Hts PL14 .... 113 D6
Pengover Parc PL14 ...140 C6
Pengover Pk PL14 .... 113 D6
Pengover Rd PL14 .... 113 E6
Pengrowyn PL26 .... 59 D6
Pengwarras Rd TR14 ...138 C3
Pengwel 16 TR18 .... 143 C2
PENHALE Indian Queens ... 57 D8
  Millbrook 132 D7
  Mullion 99 D1
Penhale Crowntown TR13 ... 91 A5
  1 Perranporth TR6 .... 55 A5
Penhale Cl 10 Dobwalls PL14 50 E7
  St Cleer PL14 .... 37 F3
Penhale Cotts TR15 .... 82 D6
Penhale Est TR15 .... 140 B6
Penhale Gdns TR9 .... 57 D8
Penhale La St Cleer PL14 ... 38 F3
  Treworrick PL14 .... 37 F3
Penhale Mdw PL14 ... 37 F3
Penhale Rd Barripper TR14 ... 79 A4
  Carnhell Green TR14 .... 78 F4
  Falmouth TR11 .... 144 F1
  Penhale PL32 .... 10 D2
  Penwithick PL26 .... 59 D7
PENHALLICK 139 C4
Penhallick TR12 .... 101 A2
Penhall La TR4 .... 68 C6
PENHALLOW 55 B2
Penhallow TR15 .... 139 B8
Penhallow Cl
  Mount Hawke TR4 .... 68 C6
  Veryan TR2 .... 83 C5
Penhallow Ct TR7 .... 111 C7
Penhallow Parc PL33 ... 14 D2
Penhallow Rd TR7 .... 111 C7
Penhalls Way TR3 .... 82 B8
PENHALVEAN 80 C4
Penharget Cl PL14 ... 38 D5
Penhaven Cl TR8 .... 56 B7
Penhaven Ct TR7 .... 110 E6
Penhellaz Hill TR13 ...146 B6
Penhellaz Rd TR13 ...146 B6
Penhole Cl PL15 .... 27 D3
Penhole Dr PL15 .... 106 D3
Penhole Rd PL15 .... 27 C3
Penina Ave TR7 .... 110 F4
Peninsula Coll PL2 .... 127 E4
Peninsular Pk PL12 ...122 C4
Penisker PL25 .... 58 F4
Penjerrick Gdns* TR11 ... 93 D5
Penjerrick Hill
  Budock Water TR11 ...144 C1
  Falmouth TR11 .... 93 E5
Penkenna Cl EX23 .... 10 C6

Penkernick Cl TR18 ...143 B1
Penkernick Way TR9 ... 45 E6
Penknight La PL22 .... 112 A2
Penlea Cl TR15 .... 140 D7
Penlea Rd TR10 .... 144 B8
Penlee Apartments PL23 .116 C3
Penlee Cl 13 Callington PL17 . 39 F4
  Praa Sands TR20 .... 90 C3
  Tregony TR2 .... 71 F4
Penlee Cotts PL10 .... 64 C2
Penlee Gdns PL3 .... 128 A4
Penlee Ho TR1 .... 69 E4
Penlee House Gall & Mus*
  TR18 .... 143 E5
Penlee Manor Dr TR18 ...143 E4
Penlee Pk PL11 .... 126 E4
Penlee Pl 4 PL4 .... 128 F4
Penlee Rd PL3 .... 128 A4
Penlee St 10 TR18 ...143 E6
Penlee View Terr 3 TR18 143 E4
Penlee Villas TR3 .... 82 B8
Penlee Way PL3 .... 128 B4
Penlu TR14 .... 138 F5
Penlu Ho TR14 .... 138 F5
Penluke Cl TR16 .... 80 A5
Penmare Ct TR27 .... 142 E7
Penmare Ct TR27 .... 142 E7
Penmare Terr TR27 ...142 E7
PENMARTH 80 C2
Penmayne Parc TR16 ...140 F1
Penmayne Villas PL27 ... 21 E3
Penmead Rd PL33 .... 14 E2
Penmelen PL32 .... 105 C4
Penmenner Est 7 TR12..101 C4
Penmenner Gdns 14 TR12 102 F2
Penmenner Rd TR12 ...102 F2
Penmere Cl Helston TR13 ...146 B7
Penmere Cres TR11 ...144 F3
Penmere Ct 4 TR11 ...145 A3
Penmere Dr Newquay TR7..110 C5
  Swanvale TR11 .... 144 F3
Penmere Hill 7 TR11 ...145 A3
Penmere Pl
  3 Falmouth TR11 ...145 A3
  Penzance TR18 .... 143 E7
Penmere Rd Penzance TR18 143 E7
  St Austell PL25 .... 115 A4
Penmere Sta TR11 .... 144 F3
Penmerrin Ct TR7 .... 110 E5
Penmeva View PL26 ... 73 C3
Penmorvah TR11 .... 82 A2
Penmorvah Pl TR14 ...138 E2
Penmorvah Rd TR1 .... 137 F6
PENNANCE 140 F1
Pennance Field TR11 ... 94 B3
Pennance Ho TR11 .... 145 A2
Pennance La TR16 .... 140 F1
Pennance Parc TR16 ...140 F1
Pennance Rd
  Falmouth TR11 .... 145 A2
  Falmouth TR11 .... 145 B2
  Lanner TR16 .... 80 E7
  Redruth TR16 .... 140 F1
Pennance Terr TR11 ...145 A2
Penn an Drea Helston TR13 146 D8
  14 Tremenheere TR13 ...146 D8
Pennant Farm PL29 ... 22 E6
Pennant Hill PL30 ... 48 C2
Pennard Villas PL27 ... 33 B5
Pennare TR12 .... 101 C7
Penn Kernow PL15 .... 106 E4
Pennor Dr PL25 .... 114 D3
Pennoweth Prim Sch
  TR15 .... 140 C5
PENNYCOMEQUICK ...148 B4
Pennycomequick Hill PL4 148 B4
PENNYCROSS 128 C8
Pennycross Cl PL2 ...128 C8
Pennycross Park Rd PL2..128 C7
Pennycross Prim Sch PL2 128 C8
Pennygillam Ind Est PL15 106 A4
Pennygillam Way PL15 ... 18 E2
Pennys La PL24 .... 115 F5
Penny's La PL9 .... 136 D6
PENNYTINNEY 23 A4
Penoweth TR11 .... 82 A2
PENPETHY 14 F5
PENPILLICK 60 D7
PENPOL 82 B6
Penpol Ave TR27 .... 142 C5
Penpol Hill Crantock TR8 ...110 B4
  Devoran TR3 .... 82 B6
PENPOLL 61 D5
Penpol Prim Sch TR27 ...142 C5
Penpol Rd TR27 .... 142 B5
Penpol Terr TR27 .... 142 B5
Penpol Vean TR27 .... 142 C5
PENPONDS 138 B1
Penponds Prim Sch TR14 .. 79 B5
Penponds Rd TR13 .... 91 A1
Penpons Cl TR18 .... 143 C4
PENPONT 24 A1
Penpont TR8 .... 31 E1
Penpont Rd TR15 .... 140 D6
Penpont View PL15 ... 26 C7
Pen Porth Ave TR26 ... 77 A7
Penpraze TR16 .... 67 C5
Penquite Dr PL31 .... 109 F5
Penreath La PL22 .... 112 A6
Penrice Com Coll PL25 ..115 A3
Penrice Parc PL25 .... 115 A3
Penrith Cl PL6 .... 125 D3
Penrith Gdns PL6 .... 125 D3
Penrith Wlk PL6 .... 125 D3

PENROSE St Breward........24 A3
St Eval.............31 E5
Penrose Ct Penzance TR18 ..143 F6
2 South Tehidy TR14.....138 F7
Penrose Est Degibna TR13...98 D8
Nansloe TR12.............146 A3
Whitehill TR13.............91 E1
Penrose La Penrose PL15 ...17 E8
Penrose PL27.............31 F5
Trevengenow PL27........32 A4
Penrose Mdws **3** TR4 ...55 E4
Penrose Parc TR13......91 B1
Penrose Rd Falmouth TR11 .145 A4
Helston TR13.............146 C6
Penrose St PL1...........148 B3
Penrose Terr TR18........143 F6
Penrose Villas **5** PL4...128 F4
Penrose Walks ★ TR12,TR13 98 D8
PENRYN.................144 B7
Penryn Campus TR10....144 A8
Penryn Coll TR10.........144 B7
Penryn Com Inf Sch TR10 144 B7
Penryn Jun Sch TR10 ....144 B8
Penryn Mus ★ TR10......144 C7
Penryn St TR15..........144 B4
Penryn Sta TR10.........144 B8
Pensans Com Prim Sch
TR18.................143 D6
Penscombe Cross PL15 ...28 C3
Penscott La PL26.........114 C1
Penscowen Rd **5** TR14 ..138 D4
PENSILVA...............38 E5
Pensilva TR6.............55 A4
Pensilva Ind Est PL14......38 E4
Pensilva Prim Sch PL14....38 E5
Pensilva Rd TR1..........137 E6
Penstowe Pk EX23........4 F6
Penstowe Rd **5** EX23 ...5 A6
Penstrasse Pl **1** PL24 ...60 D5
PENSTRAZE.............69 A4
Penstraze Bsns Ctr TR4 ...69 A5
Penstraze La PL26........69 A4
Penstruthal Carvannel TR16 .80 C6
Pennance TR16...........80 C6
Pennance TR16...........140 D1
Pensylva PL25...........114 E3
Pentalek Rd TR14.........138 D1
Pentamar St PL2.........127 E4
Pentargon Rd **1** PL35 ..9 C1
PENTEWAN..............73 C6
Pentewan Hill PL26........73 D6
Pentewan Rd
St Austell PL24, PL26.......59 C1
Tregorrick PL26...........114 C1
Pentidna La TR27.........66 B2
Pentillie PL26.............73 C4
Pentillie Cl **22** PL20 ....41 B1
Pentillie Cres PL4........128 D4
Pentillie Gdns
14 Callington PL17......39 E4
St Austell PL25...........114 C1
Pentillie Rd Bere Alston PL20 41 B1
Plymouth PL4.............128 E4
Pentillie View **23** PL20 ..41 B1
Pentillie Way PL26........73 C4
PENTIRE...............43 D4
Pentire **15** PL28........31 F7
Pentire Ave TR7.........110 A4
Pentire Cres TR7........110 B5
Pentire Ct TR7...........110 B6
Pentire Gn TR8..........43 D3
Pentire Hts TR7.........110 A5
Pentire Rd Newquay TR7...110 C5
Penryn TR10.............144 B8
Torpoint PL11............126 F3
Pentland Cl PL6..........124 F7
Pen Tor PL30............35 C8
Pentor Ct PL30..........35 C8
Pentour **3** PL24.......60 B4
Pentowan Ct TR26.......141 E2
Pentowan Gdns TR27....142 E8
Pentowan Rd TR27.......142 E8
Pentreath Cl Fowey PL23 ..116 B5
Lanner TR16.............80 E7
Penzance TR18..........143 D7
Pentreath La Lizard TR12 ..102 F2
Praa Sands TR20.........90 B3
Pentreath Terr TR16......80 E7
Pentre Cl PL26...........46 F3
Pentre Ct EX23...........4 D4
Pentrevah Ct TR7.......110 D6
Pentrevah Rd **8** PL26...59 D7
Pen-Tye TR27...........78 E3
Pentyre Ct PL4..........149 C4
Pentyre Terr PL4........149 C4
Penvale **3** Pensilva PL14 ...38 E4
Treluswell TR10..........81 D3
Penvale Cl TR14.........79 B5
Penvale Cres TR10......144 B8
Penvale Ct **8** TR11 ....145 A4
Penvale Villas TR10......81 D3
Penvean Cl TR10.........93 C8
Penvean La TR11.......144 E5
Penvenen **2** TR6.......55 A5
Penventinnie La TR1......69 E4
Penventinue La PL23....116 B7
Penventon TR16..........80 B6
Penventon Terr
Four Lanes TR16.........80 B6
Redruth TR15............140 A4
Penventon View TR13....146 B5
Penverne Cres TR13.....146 B5
Penvorder Cotts PL30....24 B2
Penvorder La PL30.......24 B2
Penvose La TR10.........81 C2
Penware Parc TR14......138 C1
Penwarne Cl Penjerrick TR11 93 D5

Penwarne Cl continued
South Tehidy TR14........138 F7
Sparnon TR11...........144 A1
Penwarne La PL26........73 C3
Penwarne Rd TR11.......93 D5
Penwartha TR12.........101 B2
Penwartha Cl
Constantine TR11.........92 F3
St Columb Minor TR7.....111 D7
PENWARTHA COOMBE ...55 B3
Penwartha Ct TR11.......92 F3
Penwartha Rd
15 Illogan TR16.......67 E4
Perranporth TR6..........55 B4
Penwartha Vean **14** TR16 ..67 E4
PENWEATHERS.........69 E2
Penwerris Ct TR11.......145 A6
Penwerris Farm TR11.....144 F5
Penwerris La TR11.......145 A6
Penwerris Rd TR1........69 F3
Penwerris Rise TR20......90 B3
Penwerris Terr
Falmouth TR11..........145 A5
10 Falmouth TR11.....145 A5
Penwethers La TR1.......69 F3
Penwinnick Cl **9** TR5....54 C1
Penwinnick Parc **4** TR5 ..54 D1
Penwinnick Rd St Agnes TR5 68 D8
St Austell PL25..........114 B3
Penwith Bsns Ctr TR20 ...88 F6
Penwith Cl TR26.........141 A4
Penwithick Rd PL26......59 D7
Penwithian Ct TR27......142 E6
PENWITHICK............59 E7
Penwithick Pk **6** PL26...59 D7
Penwith Rd TR26.........141 A4
Penwith St **11** TR18....143 E6
Penworth Cl PL15.......106 C5
Penwyth TR12...........92 C1
Pen y Bryn PL27.........108 D6
Pen Y Morfa Cl TR8......45 A8
Penyoke La PL12........119 A2
PENZANCE.............143 F5
Penzance L Ctr TR18....143 D6
Penzance Rd Helston TR13 146 A6
St Buryan TR19...........97 C7
Penzance School of Art
TR18.................143 E5
Penzance Sta TR18......143 F6
Pepo La TR19............72 A7
Pepper Cl PL12...........40 C2
Pepper La PL9...........136 D7
Peppers Ct PL12.........40 C2
Peppers Hill Cl PL15......18 F7
Peppers Park Rd PL14....113 C8
Pepper St PL19..........147 C6
Pepys Pl PL5...........124 E1
PERCUIL................83 A1
Percy Davy Cl TR6........55 A5
Percymews PL28........107 C4
Percy Mews PL28........107 C4
Percy St PL5............123 D1
Percy Terr PL4..........129 A4
Pergolla Ct **9** TR7.....110 F6
Perhaver Pk PL26........85 D5
Perhaver Way PL26......85 D5
Periwinkle Dr PL7........131 C5
Periwinkle Gr **7** PL14 ..113 D8
Per Kithen TR12.........102 F2
Permain Rd TR10........144 C8
PERRANARWORTHAL....81 D6
Perran-ar-Worthal Comm
Prim Sch TR3...........81 D6
Perran Cl Devoran TR3....81 F6
Perran Downs TR20.......89 F5
Perrancombe Garden Ct
TR6.................55 A4
PERRANCOOMBE........55 A4
Perran Crossroads TR20...89 E5
PERRAN DOWNS.........89 E5
Perran Downs Lane TR20 ..89 F5
Perran Foundry TR3......81 D5
Perran La TR20..........89 E4
PERRANPORTH.........55 B5
Perranporth Cl
3 Penryn TR10.......144 A8
Plymouth PL5...........123 E4
Perranporth Com Prim Sch **18**
TR6.................55 A4
PERRANUTHNOE.........89 D4
PERRANWELL Goonhavern..55 C3
Perranarworthal..........81 C6
Perranwell Rd TR4.......55 B4
Perranwell Sta TR3.......81 E6
PERRANZABULOE.......55 B3
Perrily Mount EX23......104 E4
Perry Cl PL9............147 B6
Perryfield Pl PL9........129 D1
Perryman Cl PL7........130 E7
Perseus Cres **17** PL7...136 E7
Perseverance Cotts **1**
PL7.................130 E7
Peryn Rd PL19..........130 E7
Peter Hopper's Hill PL5...120 C2
Peter's Cl PL9...........136 C7
Petersfield Cl PL3.......129 B6
PETER'S FINGER.........19 C7
Peters Hill PL26..........58 E4
Peters Park Cl PL5.......123 E1
Peter's Park La PL5......123 E1
Peters Row **1** TR19....75 A1
PETERVILLE............54 D1
Petes Pl **24** TR26......141 B5
Petherick Rd EX23.......104 E7
PETHERWIN GATE........18 B7
Pethick Cl PL6..........124 D6
Pethill Cl PL6...........125 F2

Pethybridge Dr PL31......109 B3
Petroc Ct PL18...........40 D6
PEVERELL..............128 D6
Peverell Park Rd PL3.....128 D6
Peverell Rd Penzance TR18 143 E7
7 Porthleven TR13.....98 C8
Peverell Terr Plymouth PL3 128 D5
Porthleven TR13..........98 B8
Pew Tor Cl **3** PL20.....42 C3
Phernyssick Rd PL25.....114 F6
Philgray CT TR7..........142 E7
Philip Cl PL9............136 A6
Philip Gdns PL9..........135 F6
PHILLACK.............142 D7
Phillack Hill TR27........142 D7
PHILLEIGH..............83 B6
Phillimore Ct PL26........58 D5
Phillimore St **3** PL2.....127 F4
Philpott La PL19.........147 B2
Phoebe Cl **2** PL18......40 E5
Phoenix Bsns Pk PL6....125 F4
Phoenix Cl **8** PL20......42 C4
Phoenix L Ctr PL1.......106 C4
Phoenix St PL1.........148 A2
Piala Pl TR27...........142 E7
Piazza **14** TR26........141 B6
Piazza The **5** PL31.....109 E5
Pickard Way EX23.......104 D7
Pickering Villas TR4......69 A3
Picketts Yd TR10........144 D7
Pickle Cl **1** TR11......144 F2
Picklecombe Dr PL5.....124 E4
Pick Pie Dr PL6.........125 E4
PIECE................139 D2
Pier La PL10............133 A1
Pier St PL1.............148 B1
Pigmeadow La PL14.....113 C6
Pike Rd PL3............129 D5
Pikes Hill PL23..........116 C4
Pike's Hill TR11..........145 B3
Pike St TR14............113 C6
Pilchard Works The ★
TR18.................143 C3
Pilgrim Cl PL2..........128 B6
Pilgrim Ct **11** PL20.....41 B1
Pilgrim Dr PL20..........41 B1
Pilgrim Prim Sch PL1.....148 B3
Pilgrims Way TR27.......78 C1
Pillars Cl TR8...........56 F5
Pillars Rd Flushing TR11 ..145 B8
Mylor Bridge TR11.......82 A2
Pillar Wlk PL6...........124 E7
PILLATON..............53 B6
PILLATONMILL...........53 B6
Pill La Saltash PL12......122 E4
Trevilla TR3.............82 C5
Pillmere Dr PL12........122 D4
Pilot Cotts PL28.........21 B4
Pinch Hill Bude EX23.....104 F2
Marhamchurch EX23......7 B7
Pinder Ct PL19..........147 B5
Pine Cl TR13...........146 D5
Pine Ct Par PL24........115 F6
Perranarworthal TR3......81 D6
Pinehurst Cl PL31.......109 E3
Pine Lodge Gdns ★ PL25 ..115 D4
Pine Rd PL18............40 D6
Pine Trees on the Lizard ★
TR12.................99 F5
Pine View Gunnislake PL18 ..41 A6
St Dennis PL26...........46 D1
Pinewood Cl PL7........130 E6
Pinewood Dr PL6........125 C4
Pinewood Flats PL27.....21 D5
Pinkhams Cotts PL12....122 B6
Pink Moors TR16.........68 D1
Pin La PL1.............149 A2
Pinnacle Quay PL4......149 B2
Pinsla Garden & Nursery ★
PL30.................35 L1
Pinslow Cross PL15.......19 C8
Pintail Ave TR27.........77 E3
Pintail Way PL6.........125 B2
Pipers Cl PL15...........18 E2
Pipers Ct TR8...........56 F5
PIPERS POOL...........17 F3
Pipers Pool Rd PL15......17 F4
Piper St PL6............125 B5
Pipit Cl TR27...........142 E6
Pippin Ave Saltash PL14 ..113 D7
Addington PL14.........113 D7
Piran Cl PL18............40 D6
Piran Hts EX23..........104 C2
Piran View **2** TR6......55 B4
Pitick Terr TR13.........145 B6
Pitland Cnr PL19.........30 D4
Pit Mdw TR11...........144 E3
Pits La PL10............64 B2
Pitts Cleave Ind Est PL19 ..30 F3
Pittsmingle Hill PL26......46 E2
PITYME...............21 F3
Pityme PL27.............21 F3
Pityme Bsns Ctr PL27.....21 F3
Pityme Farm Rd PL27.....21 F3
Pityme Ind Est PL27.......21 F3
Pixie's Hall ★ TR11......92 E4
Pixon La PL19...........147 B4
Pixon Trad Ctr **2** PL19 ..147 B4
Place de Brest PL1.......148 C3
Place Hill PL28..........107 C5
Place Parc TR7..........111 D7
Place Rd PL23...........116 C4
Place Stables PL23.......116 C4
Place View Rd **15** TR2...95 A6
PLAIDY................117 E5
Plaidy La PL13..........117 E4
Looe PL13.............117 E4

Plaidy Park Rd PL13......117 E4
PLAIN-AN-GWARRY......140 B6
Plain-an-Gwarry TR15 ...140 B5
Plain St PL27............22 B5
Plaistow Cl PL5.........123 E2
Plaistow Cres PL5.......123 E2
Plaistow Hill Inf & Nur Sch
PL5.................123 E2
Planet Pk PL33..........14 D2
Plantation TR14..........79 D3
Plantation La TR27......142 B5
Plantings Sch PL3.......128 E6
Plashford Bridge PL13....63 B8
Plas Jowan PL26..........46 F2
Platt The PL27..........108 C5
PLAYING PLACE.........82 B8
Pleasant Pl **18** TR18...143 C7
Pleasure Hill Cl PL9......135 D8
Plestin Cl PL15.........106 C7
Pleyber Christ Way PL22..112 C2
Pleydon Cl **13** PL2.....62 E2
Plintona View PL7.......130 E7
Plougastel Dr PL12......122 C3
Plough Ct TR10..........81 C2
Plough Gn PL12.........122 C3
Plover Avenue TR13.....146 D6
Plovers Field TR13.......91 B5
Plumer Rd PL6.........124 F2
PLUSHABRIDGE.........38 F7
Plymbridge Gdns PL7....130 C7
Plymbridge La PL6......125 B4
Plymbridge Rd
Plymouth, Eggbuckland
PL6.................125 C1
Plymouth, Estover PL6....125 C1
Plymouth, Mainstone PL6 ..125 F2
Plymouth, Plympton PL7 ..130 C7
Plym Cres PL19.........147 D5
PLYMOUTH.............148 C1
Plymouth Arts Ctr ★ PL4...149 A2
Plymouth Athenaeum &
Theatre ★ PL1.........148 B2
Plymouth Business Sch
PL4.................149 A3
Plymouth City Mkt PL1...148 A3
Plymouth City Mus & Art Gal ★
PL4.................149 A3
Plymouth Coll PL4.......128 E4
Plymouth Coll Inf Sch **1**
PL3.................128 E5
Plymouth Coll of Art & Design
PL4.................149 A3
Plymouth Coll of Art & Design
(Sutton Annexe) PL4.....149 A3
Plymouth Coll Prep Sch
PL1.................148 A3
Plymouth Discovery Ctr ★
PL3.................129 F6
Plymouth Eggbuckland Com
Coll PL6.............129 A8
Plymouth Girls High Sch
PL4.................149 A4
Plymouth Knowle Prim Sch
PL5.................124 A4
Plymouth Medical & Tech Pk
PL6.................125 A3
Plymouth Pavilions PL1...148 B2
Plymouth Rd
Bolitho PL14...........113 D4
Horrabridge PL20........42 B4
Liskeard PL14..........113 D5
Plymouth PL7...........130 B6
Tavistock PL19.........147 B4
Plymouth Road Ind Est
PL19.................147 C3
Plymouth St Joseph's RC Prim
Sch PL1.............127 E2
Plymouth Sch of Creative Arts
PL1.................148 A2
Plymouth Sta PL4.......148 C4
Plymouth Sta PL4.......148 C4
Plymouth Trade Pk PL4 ..149 C1
Plymouth Univ Marine Station
PL4.................149 B1
PLYMPTON.............130 E5
Plympton Hill PL7........130 D5
Plympton St Mary CE Inf Sch
PL7.................130 D5
PLYMPTON ST MAURICE...130 E4
Plympton St Maurice Prim Sch
PL7.................130 D3
Plym St PL4............149 A3
PLYMSTOCK............135 E6
Plymstock Rd PL9.......135 D7
Plymstock Sch PL9......135 F8
Plymstock Sp Ctr PL9....135 F8
Plymtree Dr PL7.........130 C7
Plym Valley Rly ★ PL7....130 A7
Poadsmill Hill PL15.......27 B8
Poad's Trust PL14........51 F5
Pochin Ho PL25.........114 F7
Pocklington Rise PL7.....130 E5
Pocohontas Cres **4** TR9 ..45 E1
Pode Dr PL7............131 B4
Poets Corner **1** PL5....124 C1
POINT.................82 B5
Point Neptune PL23......116 B3
Point Rd TR3............82 A6
Polapit Tamar PL15.......19 A8
Polaris Mews **2** PL9....136 E7
POLBATHIC.............64 F8
Polbathic Rd TR15.......140 C6
POLBORDER............53 D7
Polbreen Ave **12** TR5...54 C1
Polbreen La **11** TR5....54 C1
POLBROCK.............34 A4

Polcoverack
Penhallick TR12.........101 A2
Penhallick TR12.........103 F8
Poldark Gdns **7** PL24...60 B4
Poldark Mine ★ TR13.....92 A6
Poldark Rd **12** TR16....67 E4
Poldark Way **2** TR14...138 F3
Poldhu Cl TR26.........141 D1
Poldhu Rd Liskeard PL14...113 D6
Mullion TR12............99 A2
Poldice La TR16..........68 E1
Poldice Terr TR16.......68 E1
Poldory TR13............91 A4
Poldown TR13...........91 A4
Poldrea PL24............60 D5
Poldrissick Hill PL12.......53 C2
Poldrissick La PL12.......53 C2
Poldue Cl TR15.........140 D6
Polean La PL13.........117 B4
Polean Trad Est PL13.....117 B4
Polecoverack La TR12....101 C1
Polgarth **1** Camborne TR15 139 C6
Newlyn TR18............143 B3
Polgarth TR16..........141 D1
Polgaver Ho PL25.......115 E3
Polgear PL26............80 A4
POLGIGGA.............96 D4
Polgine Cl TR14.........79 E5
Polgine La TR14.........79 E5
Polglase Wlk TR4........70 D8
Polglaze Ct TR18........143 D7
Polglist PL26............58 D5
Polgoon Cl TR18........143 C5
POLGOOTH.............59 A1
Polgooth Cl TR15........140 D6
Polgover Way **5** PL24...60 B4
Polgrain Hill PL30........46 C7
Polgrain Rd TR14........138 F6
Polgrean Pl PL24........60 B5
Polhigey TR16............80 C1
Polhigey Terr TR16.......80 C2
Polhorman La TR12......99 A2
Police Ho TR11..........145 B4
Polisken Way TR4........56 D1
Polkanugga
Lesneague TR12........101 A4
Tregeague TR12........100 F4
Polkanuggo La TR10......80 F1
POLKERRIS.............60 E3
Polkerris Pk PL24........60 C4
Polkerris Rd TR16........80 F8
Polkirt Hill
Gorran Haven PL26.......73 B1
Mevagissey PL26........73 C3
Polkirt Hts PL26.........73 C3
Polkyth L Ctr PL25......114 E4
Polkyth Par PL25........114 E4
Polkyth Rd PL25........114 F4
POLLADRAS.............90 F5
Pollard Cl Plymouth PL9...135 B5
Saltash PL12...........122 B2
Pollard Rd **7** PL17......39 F4
Pollards Ct Goonhavern TR4 ..55 D4
Pensilva PL14..........38 E4
Pollards Way PL12......122 E3
Polmark Dr PL28........20 D2
Polmarth Cl PL25.......114 F6
POLMASSICK...........72 E4
Polmassick Vineyard ★
PL26.................72 E4
POLMEAR.............60 E4
Polmear Ct **9** PL27....108 B5
Polmear Hill PL24.......60 E4
Polmear Parc PL24......60 D4
Polmear Rd St Austell PL25 114 F3
Tywardreath PL24........60 D4
Polmeere Ho TR18.......143 E7
Polmeere Rd TR18.......143 E7
Polmena La PL12........112 E1
Polmenna Hill PL14......36 F1
Polmenna La PL14.......36 E1
Polmennor Dr TR26......141 D1
Polmennor Rd
Falmouth TR11.........144 F1
Heamoor TR18..........143 C8
Polmenor Downs N TR14,
TR27.................78 F5
Polmenor Downs S TR14...78 F4
Polmeor Cl TR26.........141 D1
Polmewan Flats PL26.....59 A1
POLMORLA.............108 A4
Polmorla Mews **10** PL27 108 B5
Polmorla Rd PL27........108 B5
Polmorla Wlk PL27......108 B5
Polmor Rd TR20.........89 B8
Polpennic Dr PL28......107 C4
POLPEOR..............77 B3
Polpeor La TR12........102 F1
Polpeor Row TR27.......77 A3
POLPERRO.............62 E2
Polperro Com Prim Sch
PL13.................62 E2
Polperro Heritage Mus of
Smuggling & Fishing ★
PL13.................62 E2
Polperro Model Village ★
PL13.................62 D1
Polperro Pl PL2.........128 D8
Polperro Rd PL13........117 B4
Polpey La PL24..........60 D5
POLRUAN..............116 C2
Polruan Cl TR26.........77 C4
Polruan Ct TR1..........137 E2
Polruan Prim Sch PL23 ..116 D2

Polruan Rd Redruth TR15. . .140 D6
  Truro TR1. . . . . .137 E2
Polruan Terr PL1. . . . . .148 A3
POLSCOE. 112 E3
Polscoe Rd PL22. . . . . .112 F3
Polsethow Penryn TR10. . .144 B7
  Tremough TR10. . . . . .81 D1
Polsethow Vale TR10. . . . .144 B7
Polstain Cres TR3. . . . . .69 D3
Polstain Rd TR3. . . . . .69 D3
Polstain Villas TR3. . . . . . .69 D3
Polstrong Kehelland TR14. .66 F1
  Treswithian TR14. . . . . .79 B7
  Treswithian TR14. . . . . .138 A3
Polsue Way TR2. . . . . .70 F5
Poltair Ave PL25. . . . . .114 E4
Poltair Cl TR18. . . . . .143 C7
Poltair Cres PL25. . . . . . . .114 D4
Poltair Ct PL25. . . . . .114 E4
Poltair Dr TR10. . . . . .144 B7
Poltair Rd Penryn TR10. . .144 B7
  St Austell PL25. . . . . .114 D4
Poltair School PL25. . . . . .114 D4
Poltair Terr 17 TR18. . . . . .143 C7
Poltamar PL15. . . . . .106 D5
Pol-Tec Lane PL23. . . . . . . .61 D3
POLTESCO. 103 B5
Poltesco La TR12. . . . . . . .103 B5
Poltisco Cl TR1. . . . . .137 E3
Poltisco Wharf TR1. . . . . .137 E4
Poltisko Rd TR10. . . . . . . .144 B7
Poltisko Terr TR10. . . . . . .144 B7
Poltreen Cl TR26. . . . . . . .141 D1
Polurrian Cliffs
  3 Henscath TR12. . . . . .98 F1
  Mullion TR12. . . . . .102 B8
Polurrian Rd TR12. . . . . . . .99 A1
Polvarth Es 3 TR2. . . . . . .95 B6
Polvarth La 4 TR2. . . . . . . .95 B6
Polvarth Rd TR2. . . . . .95 A6
Polvean Cross PL14. . . . . . .51 A1
Polvean Terr PL14. . . . . . . .51 A1
Polvella Cl TR7. . . . . .110 B5
Polvellan Manor PL13. . . .117 C4
Polvellan Terr PL13. . . . . .117 C4
Polvelyn Parc TR27. . . . . .142 E7
Polventon 17 PL28. . . . . . . .31 F7
Polventon Cl
  Falmouth TR11. . . . . .144 E4
  Heamoor TR18. . . . . .143 C7
Polventon Hill PL14. . . . . . .37 A1
Polventon Parc 6 TR12. . .101 C4
Polvillion Rd PL23. . . . . . .116 B4
Polweath Cl TR18. . . . . . . .143 E7
Polweath Rd TR18. . . . . . .143 E7
Polwhaveral Terr 6 TR11 145 A5
Polwheal Rd TR14. . . . . . .138 F6
Polwhele House Sch TR4 . .70 C6
Polwhele Rd Newquay TR7.111 A3
  Truro TR1. . . . . .137 F6
Polwithen Ct TR26. . . . . . .141 C2
Polwithen Dr TR26. . . . . . .141 C1
Polwithen Gdns TR26. . . .141 C1
Polwithen Rd
  Falmouth TR11. . . . . .145 A4
  Penryn TR10. . . . . .144 B7
  Penzance TR18. . . . . .143 D5
Polwrath Terr PL14. . . . . . .38 A3
Polwyn Cl TR18. . . . . .143 B7
Poly Arts & Science TR11 .145 B4
Polyear Ct PL25. . . . . .59 A1
Polyne Cotts PL13. . . . . . . .62 F3
POLYPHANT. 17 F1
POLZEATH. 21 E5
Polzeath Ct PL27. . . . . .21 D6
Polzeath Gdns PL2. . . . . . .128 D8
Pomarine Ct 1 EX23. . . . . . .7 B8
POMPHLETT. 135 E8
Pomphlett Cl PL9. . . . . . . .135 D8
Pomphlett Farm Ind Est
  PL9. . . . . .129 E1
Pomphlett Gdns PL9. . . . .135 D8
Pomphlett Prim Sch PL9. .135 E8
Pomphlett Rd PL9. . . . . . .135 E8
Ponchin Dr PL25. . . . . . . .114 E7
  St Austell PL25. . . . . .114 E7
Pondbridge Hill 1 PL14. .113 C5
Pondfield Rd PL12. . . . . . .122 B3
Pondhu Cres PL25. . . . . . .114 B3
Pondhu Prim Sch PL25 . . .114 B2
Pondhu Rd PL25. . . . . .114 C3
Pond La TR15. . . . . .140 A6
Pond Lanes End TR15. . . .140 B6
Ponds Hill TR19. . . . . .75 B1
Pond View Terr PL26. . . . . .58 D5
Pond Wlk TR27. . . . . .142 D7
PONIOU. 76 A5
Poniou La TR20. . . . . .88 F6
Poniou Rd TR20. . . . . .88 F6
Poniou Way TR20. . . . . .88 F6
Ponsandane Farm Mews
  TR18. . . . . .143 F7
PONSANOOTH. 81 B5
PONSHARDEN. 144 E7
Ponsharden Cotts TR11. . .144 E6
Ponsharden Ind Est TR11. .144 E6
Ponsmere Ct 9 TR6. . . . . . .55 A5
Ponsmere Rd TR6. . . . . . . .55 A5
Ponsonby Rd PL3. . . . . . . .128 B4
PONSONGATH. 103 C2
Ponsongath
  Penhallick TR12. . . . . .101 A1
  Trelan TR12. . . . . .100 F1
Ponstantual Hill TR12. . . . .99 D7

Ponsvale TR3. . . . . .81 B4
PONT. 61 D3
Pont Bottom PL23. . . . . . . .61 D3
Pontsmill Rd PL24. . . . . . . .60 C6
POOL. 139 B5
Pool Academy TR15. . . . . .139 B6
Pool Bsns Pk TR15. . . . . . .139 B4
Pool Hall PL14. . . . . .51 F5
Pool Ind Est TR15. . . . . . . .139 C5
Pool La Milltown PL30. . . . .35 F2
  Welltown PL30. . . . . .36 A2
Pool Rd PL15. . . . . .17 E2
Pool's Ct TR27. . . . . .142 D6
Pool St PL31. . . . . .109 E5
Poorhouse Hill PL15. . . . . .12 B2
Poor House Hill TR10. . . . . .81 E3
Poplar Cl PL7. . . . . .131 B5
Poplars Ct 16 TR6. . . . . . . .55 A5
Poplar Terr TR11. . . . . . . .145 B7
Popplestone Pk PL8. . . . . .136 F5
Porcupine Rd PL24. . . . . . .60 C6
Pordenack Cl TR26. . . . . . .141 E2
Porfell Wildlife Park &
  Sanctuary* PL14. . . . . . .50 A2
Porhan Gn TR11. . . . . .144 E6
PORKELLIS. 92 B8
Pork St TR12. . . . . .100 D6
Porsham Cl PL6. . . . . .121 B1
Porsham La PL5. . . . . .124 E8
Porspoder Pl PL10. . . . . . .133 A2
Portbigham PL13. . . . . . . .117 C3
Portbyhan Rd PL13. . . . . .117 C3
PORTEATH. 22 A6
Porteath Bee Ctr* PL27. . .22 A6
Porteath Rd PL27. . . . . . . .21 F6
Porteous Cl PL1. . . . . .127 F3
Porter Way PL12. . . . . . . .122 C3
PORT GAVERNE. 22 E7
PORTH. 111 C8
PORTHALLOW Looe. 62 F2
  St Keverne. 101 D6
Porth Beach Rd TR7. . . . . .111 B8
Porth Bean Ct TR7. . . . . . .111 C7
Porth Bean Rd TR7. . . . . . .111 C7
Porthcollum La TR27. . . . . .78 A1
PORTHCOTHAN. 31 C6
PORTHCURNO. 96 E3
Porthcurno Telegraph Mus*
  TR19. . . . . .96 E3
Portheast Cl PL26. . . . . . . .85 C5
Portheast Way PL26. . . . . .85 C5
Portherras Cross TR19. . . .75 A1
Portherras Terr 11 TR19 . . .75 A1
Portherras Villas 10 TR19 . .75 A1
Porthgwidden TR3. . . . . . . .82 C4
Porthgwidden Studios
  TR26. . . . . .141 C6
Porthia TR26. . . . . .141 A4
Porthia Cres TR26. . . . . . .141 A4
Porthia Rd 12 TR26. . . . . . .77 A6
PORTHILLY. 21 D2
Porthilly Cvn Site PL27. . . .21 D2
Porthilly La PL27. . . . . .21 D2
Porthilly View PL28. . . . . .107 E4
PORTH KEA. 70 B1
Porthkerris TR12. . . . . . . .101 E5
Porthkerris Divers* TR12 .101 E5
PORTHLEVEN. 98 B8
Porthleven Com Prim Sch
  TR13. . . . . .91 B1
Porthleven Rd TR13 . . . . .146 A5
Porthmellon Gdns PL17. . .39 F4
PORTHMEOR. 75 F4
Porthmeor Ct 51 TR26. . . .141 B6
Porthmeor Hill TR26. . . . .141 A6
Porthmeor Rd
  St Austell PL25. . . . . .115 B3
  6 St Ives TR26. . . . . .141 B6
Porthmeor Sq 21 TR26. . .141 B6
Porthmeor Studios 50
  TR26. . . . . .141 B6
Porthminster Terr 23
  TR26. . . . . .141 B5
Porthmissen 16 PL28. . . . . .31 F7
PORTH NAVAS. 93 B2
PORTHOUSTOCK. 101 E4
Porth Par TR7. . . . . .111 C8
Porthpean Beach Rd
  PL26. . . . . .59 E1
Porthpean Rd PL24, PL26 .114 F2
Porthrepta Rd TR26. . . . . .141 E1
Porth Sawle Flats TR2. . . . .83 B2
PORTHTOWAN. 68 A6
Porth View TR2. . . . . .95 B6
Porth Way TR7. . . . . .111 B7
PORTINGTON. 29 E3
PORT ISAAC. 22 D8
Port Isaac Prim Sch PL29. .22 E7
Port La PL15. . . . . .27 B2
Portland Cl PL14. . . . . . . .113 D7
Portland Ct 9 PL1. . . . . . .127 F3
Portland Gdns TR11. . . . . .144 F4
Portland Pl 23 TR19. . . . . . .88 C1
Portland Rd PL1. . . . . .127 F3
Portland Sq PL4. . . . . .148 C4
Portland Square Lane N
  PL4. . . . . .149 A4
Portland Terr PL14. . . . . . .113 C4
Portland Villas PL4. . . . . . .148 C4
PORTLOE. 84 B3
PORTLOOE. 117 A2
PORTMELLON. 73 C3
Portmellon Pk PL26. . . . . . .73 C3
Portmellon Rd PL26. . . . . . .73 C3
PORT QUIN. 22 B7
PORTREATH. 67 C6

Portreath Com Prim Sch
  TR16. . . . . .67 D6
PORTSCATHO. 83 B2
Portuan Rd PL13. . . . . .117 D1
Portway Cl PL9. . . . . .136 D7
PORTWRINKLE. 65 B4
Posses La PL18. . . . . .88 E6
Possession La PL12. . . . . . .53 C3
Post Box Row TR14. . . . . . .139 B3
Potters La PL35. . . . . .9 C1
Potters Mews TR4. . . . . . . .55 D4
Potters Way PL7. . . . . .130 D5
Pottery Est PL10. . . . . .132 E6
Pottery Rd PL1. . . . . .127 D3
POUGHILL. 4 D2
Poughill Rd EX23. . . . . . . .104 F7
Poultney Cl PL7. . . . . .131 A5
Pounda PL14. . . . . .51 B4
Pound Dean PL14. . . . . . . .113 A5
Poundfield Cl 2 EX23. . . . . .4 D1
Poundfield Hill 1 EX23. . . . .4 D1
Poundfield La EX23. . . . . . . .4 D1
Pound Hill PL12. . . . . .53 C3
Pound La Bodmin PL31. . . .109 E5
  Stoke Climsland PL17. . . . . .28 E1
  Threemilestone TR3. . . . . . .69 E1
Pound Pk PL14. . . . . .51 F5
Pound Rd PL20. . . . . .42 B3
Pound's Cross PL6. . . . . . .120 E5
Pounds Park Rd
  1 Bere Alston PL20. . . . . . . .41 B3
  Plymouth PL3. . . . . .128 D7
Pounds Pk PL12. . . . . .122 F3
Pound St Liskeard PL14 . . .113 C6
  Plymouth PL1. . . . . .134 A8
POUNDSTOCK. 6 E2
Poundstock Cl PL30. . . . . . .35 F3
Powderham Rd PL3. . . . . .128 F7
Powis Gdns PL5. . . . . .124 B2
Powisland Dr PL6. . . . . . . .125 A5
PRAA SANDS. 90 C3
Praa Sands Holiday Pk 6
  TR20. . . . . .90 B3
Praed Pl TR26. . . . . .77 E4
Praed's La TR17. . . . . .89 C5
Pras An Fer La 4 PL32. . . .105 C3
Pras Coth TR16. . . . . .68 C3
Pras Gwartha 5 PL14. . . . .51 A1
Pras Meynek TR12. . . . . . . .99 A2
PRAZE-AN-BEEBLE. 79 C2
Praze-an-Creet TR26. . . . . .77 A7
Praze-an-Cronor TR9. . . . . .45 E5
Praze Bsns Pk TR14. . . . . . .79 B2
Prazegooth La TR12. . . . . .103 A4
Praze La PL30. . . . . .35 E5
Praze Mdw TR10. . . . . . . .144 C8
Praze Rd Leedstown TR27 . .78 E1
  Newquay TR7. . . . . .111 B7
  Porthleven TR13. . . . . .91 B1
  Praze-an-Beeble TR14. . . . . .79 A2
Praze The TR10. . . . . .144 C8
Prednannack PL12. . . . . . .102 B7
Predannack Airfield*
  TR12. . . . . .102 D6
Predannack Holiday Village
  TR12. . . . . .102 E6
Predannack Rd
  Henscath TR12. . . . . .102 C7
  4 Mullion TR12. . . . . .99 A1
Preeze Cross PL30. . . . . . . .35 M4
Prestonbury Cl PL6. . . . . .125 B7
Prevenna Rd 2 TR19. . . . . .88 C1
Prickly Post La PL23. . . . . .116 A5
Primarce Cl PL12. . . . . . . .122 C5
Prideaux Cl PL12. . . . . . . .122 C5
Prideaux Place* PL28. . . .107 C6
Prideaux Rd PL24. . . . . . . .60 B6
Pridham La PL2. . . . . .128 D7
Pridmouth Rd PL25. . . . . .114 E6
Priestacott Pk 6 EX23. . . . .5 A6
Priesthood Terr PL10. . . . .132 E5
Priestley Ave PL5. . . . . . . .123 E2
Primelin Pl 8 TR10. . . . . . .81 C1
Primitive Row PL14. . . . . . .37 A5
Primrose Cl Camborne TR14 138 B4
  9 Goldsithney TR20. . . . . . .89 E5
  Roche PL26. . . . . .47 A3
  Torpoint PL11. . . . . .126 E4
Primrose Cotts TR2. . . . . . .71 C6
Primrose Ct TR26. . . . . . . .141 B4
Primrose Dr PL28. . . . . . . .31 F7
Primrose Gdns Illogan TR16 67 D4
  Tavistock PL19. . . . . .147 E4
Primrose Hill TR20. . . . . . . .89 E5
Primrose La 4 TR20. . . . . . .89 E5
Primrose Rd EX23. . . . . . . .104 F5
Primrose Terr
  Newlyn TR18. . . . . .143 D1
  Portreath TR16. . . . . .67 D6
  Tresillian TR2. . . . . .70 F5
Primrose Valley TR26. . . . .141 C4
Primrose Wlk PL12. . . . . . .122 D4
Prince Charles Cl PL15. . . .106 C7
Prince Charles Ho PL25. . .114 E5
Prince Charles Pk PL25. . . .114 E5
Prince Charles Rd PL25. . . .114 E5
Prince Maurice Ct PL4. . . .149 B3
Prince Maurice Rd PL4. . . .128 F4
Prince of Wales Quarry Trail*
  PL34. . . . . .14 C5
Prince Park Rd PL30. . . . . .46 F7
Prince Philip Rd PL15. . . . .106 C7
PRINCE ROCK. 129 B1
Prince Rock Prim Sch PL4 129 B2
Princes Rd PL6. . . . . .125 E6
Princes Row PL14. . . . . . . .38 B6
Princess Ave
  Plymouth, Plymstock PL9 . . .135 E6
  Plymouth, West Park PL5. . .124 A3

Princess Cres PL9. . . . . . . .135 E6
Princess Ct 12 TR18. . . . . .143 E5
Princess Parc TR9. . . . . . . .45 E1
Princes Sq PL13. . . . . .117 C3
Princess Rd PL14. . . . . .38 E4
Princess St PL1. . . . . .148 C2
Princess Street Ope PL1. . .148 C2
Princes St Bude EX23. . . . .104 D6
  Looe PL13. . . . . .117 C3
  Penzance TR18. . . . . .143 E5
  Plymouth PL1. . . . . .127 E2
Prince's St TR1. . . . . .137 D4
Princess Terr 7 PL14. . . . . .38 E4
Princess Villas PL17. . . . . . .28 B1
Princess Way PL1. . . . . . . .148 C2
Princetown Rd PL20. . . . . . .42 E3
Prior's Barn PL31. . . . . . . .109 F4
Priors Cl 10 TR26. . . . . . . .77 A6
Priors Row TR13. . . . . .90 E3
Priory Cl Par PL24. . . . . . . .60 C5
  Tavistock PL19. . . . . .147 D3
Priory Cotts PL15. . . . . . . .106 B6
Priory Dr PL7. . . . . .130 D5
Priory Gdns PL19. . . . . . . .147 D3
Priory La PL15. . . . . .106 B7
Priory Lawn Terr PL3. . . . .129 A6
Priory Mews PL15. . . . . . . .106 B7
Priory Mill PL7. . . . . .130 D5
Priory Park Rd PL15. . . . . .106 B6
Priory Rd Bodmin PL31. . . .109 F4
  Plymouth PL3. . . . . .129 A6
  St Austell PL25. . . . . .114 C4
  St Columb Minor TR7, TR8 . . .111 E7
Priory Ridge PL7. . . . . .130 D5
Prislow Cl TR11. . . . . .144 E2
Prislow Fields TR11. . . . . .144 E2
Prislow La TR11. . . . . .144 E2
Proad La PL30. . . . . .23 F6
PROBUS. 71 C6
Probus Com Prim Sch TR2 .71 C6
Promised Land TR5. . . . . . .54 D1
Prospect Bldgs TR7. . . . . .110 E6
Prospect Cl 5 TR27. . . . . .142 D6
Prospect Gdns TR1. . . . . . .137 E6
Prospect La PL12. . . . . . . .122 C3
Prospect Pl Ashton TR13 . . .90 E3
  3 Falmouth TR11. . . . . . . .145 B5
  Hayle TR27. . . . . .142 D6
  Helston TR13. . . . . .146 C5
  Mevagissey PL26. . . . . .73 C4
  25 Penzance TR18. . . . . . . .143 E5
  Plymouth PL1. . . . . .148 B2
  St Blazey PL24. . . . . .60 D5
  5 Truro TR1. . . . . .137 D5
Prospect Row PL1. . . . . . .127 E1
Prospect St PL4. . . . . .149 A3
Prospect Terr Bodmin PL31 109 E4
  Gunnislake PL18. . . . . .41 A6
  Gunnislake, St Ann's Chapel
    PL18. . . . . .40 E5
  Mevagissey PL26. . . . . .73 C4
Prospect Wlk PL12. . . . . . .122 C3
Prosper Hill TR27. . . . . . . .66 B1
Prosper Rd Roche PL26. . . .47 A2
  Trezaise PL26. . . . . .47 A2
Protector Rd 1 PL5. . . . . .124 D2
Prouse Cres PL2. . . . . .128 C8
Prouse Rise PL12. . . . . . . .122 E2
Prouts Ct 4 PL15. . . . . . . .106 C6
Prout's La TR27. . . . . .78 D6
Prouts Mews 5 PL15. . . . .106 C6
Prouts Way PL15. . . . . .106 B6
Providence Pl Calstock PL18 41 A3
  Plymouth PL1. . . . . .128 A3
Providence St PL4. . . . . . . .149 A4
Provis Rd PL25. . . . . .143 C4
Prussia Cove TR20. . . . . . . .89 F4
Prussia Cove Rd TR20. . . . .89 F4
Prynne Cl PL1. . . . . .148 B3
Puckator La PL14. . . . . .38 C2
Puffin Close EX23. . . . . . . .104 F5
Puggis Hill PL14. . . . . .138 A5
Pulla Cross TR4. . . . . .81 B6
Pulsack TR27. . . . . .78 C6
Pump La TR20. . . . . .88 A5
Putnam Cl PL14. . . . . .113 D5
Pydar Cl TR7. . . . . .111 B5
Pydar Mews 8 TR1. . . . . . .137 C4
Pydar St TR1. . . . . .137 C5
Pym St Plymouth PL1. . . . .127 F3
  Tavistock PL19. . . . . .147 C6
Pyramid Cl PL25. . . . . .58 F4
Pyrite Gdns 4 PL14. . . . . .113 D8
PYWORTHY. 8 E5
Pyworthy CE Prim Sch EX22. 8 E5
PZ Gall* TR18. . . . . .143 F4

Q

Quakers Rd Polzeath PL27 . . .21 F5
  Ponsanooth TR4, TR3. . . . . .81 B6
Quant Pk PL19. . . . . .147 C6
Quarry Cl EX23. . . . . .104 E7
Quarry Cl Rd PL26. . . . . . . .58 C7
Quarry Cnr PL20. . . . . .41 C2
Quarry Cotts Plymouth PL1 148 A3
  Plymouth, Honicknowle PL5 .124 B2
Quarry Cres PL15. . . . . . . .106 A3
Quarry Ct TR11. . . . . .145 B4
Quarry Gdns TR18. . . . . . .143 D5
Quarry Hill Falmouth TR11. 145 B4
  Gulval TR18. . . . . .88 E7
  Landreyne PL15. . . . . .27 C2
  Tregellist PL30. . . . . .22 F3
Quarry House Flats TR1. . .137 E4
Quarry La Gunnislake PL18. . .40 F6

Quarry La continued
  Landrake PL12. . . . . .53 D3
  Launceston PL15. . . . . .18 E2
  11 Pensilva PL14. . . . . .38 E4
  St Germans PL12. . . . . .65 A8
  Sheffield TR19. . . . . .97 F7
Quarrymans Cotts PL27. . . .33 B7
Quarry Park Ave PL9. . . . .135 D7
Quarry Park Rd
  Newquay TR7. . . . . .110 F5
  Plymouth, Peverell PL3. . . . .128 D5
  Plymouth, Plymstock PL9. . .135 D7
Quarry Park Terr PL31. . . .109 C4
Quarry Pk 6 TR13. . . . . . .146 B5
Quarry Rd Pensilva PL14 . . .38 E4
  Perranporth TR6. . . . . .55 B4
Quarry St St Germans PL12 .65 A8
  Torpoint PL11. . . . . .127 C3
Quarterdeck The PL1. . . . .134 A8
Quartz Ct PL14. . . . . .113 D8
Quay Hill Falmouth TR11. . .145 C4
  Penryn TR10. . . . . .144 D7
Quay La PL12. . . . . .53 D1
Quay Mews 8 TR1. . . . . . .137 D4
Quay Rd Crumplehorn PL13. . .62 D1
  Devoran TR3. . . . . .81 F6
  Landrake PL12. . . . . .53 A2
  Looe PL13. . . . . .117 C3
  Mylor Bridge TR11. . . . . .82 B4
  St Agnes TR5. . . . . .54 D2
  St Austell PL25. . . . . .115 B2
  St Germans PL12. . . . . .65 B8
  Tideford PL12. . . . . .52 F2
  Trenarth TR11. . . . . .93 B2
Quayside TR19. . . . . .147 B5
Quay St Falmouth TR11. . .145 C4
  Looe PL13. . . . . .117 C3
  Lostwithiel PL22. . . . . .112 C2
  11 Mousehole TR19. . . . . . .88 C1
  Penzance TR18. . . . . .143 F4
  St Ives TR26. . . . . .141 C6
  20 Truro TR1. . . . . .137 D4
Quay The Pentewan PL26. . .73 C6
  Penzance TR18. . . . . .143 F5
  Plymouth PL9. . . . . .135 C7
  Polruan PL23. . . . . .116 D3
  Portscatho TR2. . . . . .83 B2
  St Germans PL12. . . . . .65 B8
  St Mawes TR2. . . . . .95 B5
Queen Anne Gdns TR11. . .144 E3
Queen Anne's Quay PL4. . .149 B2
Queen Elizabeth Rd PL15 .106 C7
Queenie Dr 2 PL14. . . . . .113 D8
Queen Mary Cl TR11. . . . .145 B2
Queen Mary Rd TR11. . . . .145 B2
Queens Cl
  5 Indian Queens TR9. . . . . .45 E1
  Plymouth PL6. . . . . .125 E6
  St Austell PL26. . . . . .46 F3
Queen's Cres PL31. . . . . . .109 B3
Queen's Ct 6 TR18. . . . . . .143 E4
Queen's Gate
  Plymouth, Lipson PL4. . . . . .149 B4
  Plymouth, Stoke PL3. . . . . . .148 A4
Queen's Gate Mews PL4. . .149 B4
Queen's Gate Villas PL4. . .149 B4
Queen's Gate Villas Rd
  PL4. . . . . .149 B4
Queens Pk PL27. . . . . .108 C4
Queens Rd Plymouth PL5. . .123 F3
  St Austell PL25. . . . . .114 E3
Queen's Rd PL4. . . . . .149 B4
Queen's Sq 24 TR18. . . . . .143 E5
Queen St Bude EX23. . . . .104 D6
  Goldsithney TR20. . . . . .89 E5
  Lostwithiel PL22. . . . . .112 C2
  Penzance TR18. . . . . .143 E5
  St Just TR19. . . . . .86 E6
Queen's Way
  2 Goldsithney TR20. . . . . . .89 E5
  Plymouth PL3. . . . . .129 A6
Queen Terr PL17. . . . . .40 C4
Quenchwell Rd TR3. . . . . . .81 F7
QUETHIOCK. 52 C7
Quethiock La Parkfield PL14 39 A1
  Quethiock PL14. . . . . .52 C8
Quethiock Prim Sch PL14. . .52 C7
Quilkin Av TR15. . . . . .139 B5
Quillet Cl PL26. . . . . .114 F2
Quillet Rd TR18. . . . . .143 B3
Quilver Cl PL26. . . . . .85 D5
Quimperle Way PL14. . . . .113 E6
Quintrell Cl TR8. . . . . .44 E3
QUINTRELL DOWNS. 44 E3
Quintrell Downs Sta TR8. .111 F3
Quintrell Gdns TR8. . . . . . .44 E3
Quintrell Rd TR7, TR8. . . . .111 E5
QUITHER. 30 A8
QUOIT. 45 F4

R

Rabys Row TR16. . . . . .140 F8
Race Course Rd PL31. . . . . .35 A4
Race Hill Launceston PL15. .106 C5
  Truro TR4. . . . . .81 C8
Race Hill Terr PL15. . . . . . .106 C5
Rachel's Way 17 TR9. . . . . .45 E6
Radar Rd PL6. . . . . .125 B5
Radcliffe Cl PL26. . . . . . . .124 E6
Radford Ave PL4. . . . . .129 B1
Radford La PL10. . . . . .132 D4
Radford Park Dr PL9. . . . . .135 D6
Radford Park Rd PL9. . . . . .135 D6
Radford Rd PL1. . . . . .148 B1

Radford View PL9 . . . . 135 D6
Radiant Ho PL1 . . . . 148 B2
Radland Cross PL12 . . . . . . 40 C3
Radnor Cl PL31 . . . . 109 F4
Radnor Hall PL4 . . . . 149 A3
Radnor Pl PL4 . . . . 149 A3
Radnor Rd
  Redruth, North Country
  TR16 . . . . 140 C8
  Redruth, Scorrier TR16 . . . . 68 D3
Radnor St PL4 . . . . 149 A3
Raginnis Hill 25 TR19 . . . . . 88 C1
Raglan Ct PL1 . . . . 127 F2
Raglan Gdns PL1 . . . . 127 F2
Raglan Rd PL1 . . . . 127 F2
Rail Way PL15 . . . . 17 F5
Railway Cotts
  Camborne TR14 . . . . 139 A4
  Falmouth TR11 . . . . 145 D3
  6 Plymouth, Ford PL2 . . . 127 F5
  Plymouth, Plymstock PL9 . 135 D7
  Tavistock PL19 . . . . 147 B6
Railway Cres PL14 . . . . 38 A4
Railway Terr Bodmin PL31 . 109 D5
  Carharrack TR16 . . . . 80 F8
Railway Villas TR15 . . . . . . 139 F6
Rainham Cl TR15 . . . . 139 C8
Rainyfields PL28 . . . . 107 D5
Rainy Fields Cl PL28 . . . . . 107 D5
Raleigh Cl PL28 . . . . 107 C4
Raleigh Ct PL7 . . . . 131 B6
Raleigh Gdns 5 PL31 . . . . 109 F3
Raleigh Rd PL28 . . . . 107 C5
Raleigh Pl 13 TR11 . . . . . . 145 A4
Raleigh Rd PL28 . . . . 107 C5
Ralph's Ct PL19 . . . . 147 B5
Ramage Cl PL6 . . . . 125 F3
RAME Cawsand 64 B2
  Stithians 92 E8
Rame Comm TR13 . . . . 80 E1
Rame Croft TR10 . . . . 80 E1
Ramehead Cotts PL10 . . . . . 64 B1
Ramehead La PL10 . . . . 64 B1
Rame La Cawsand PL10 . . . 132 F1
  Rame PL10 . . . . 64 B2
Rame Terr PL10 . . . . 80 E1
Rame View PL13 . . . . 117 E5
Ramillies Ave PL5 . . . . 124 A4
Ramoth Way TR6 . . . . 55 B5
Ramsey Gdns PL5 . . . . 124 D1
Ramsgate TR14 . . . . 79 B5
Ranch View PL15 . . . . 106 A5
Randwick Park Rd PL9 . . . . 135 D7
Ranelagh Ct TR7 . . . . 111 C7
Ranelagh Mews PL31 . . . . 109 D5
Ranelagh Rd PL25 . . . . 114 F4
Range Rd PL30 . . . . 35 F4
Ranneys Cl PL13 . . . . 117 C6
Ransum Way PL19 . . . . 147 B4
Raphael Cl PL9 . . . . 136 B5
Raphael Dr PL9 . . . . 136 A6
Raphael Rd PL13 . . . . 62 C1
Rapson Rd PL14 . . . . 113 D6
Rashleigh Ave
  Plymouth PL7 . . . . 130 F4
  Saltash PL12 . . . . 122 D1
Rashleigh Ct PL25 . . . . 115 C3
Rashleigh La PL23 . . . . 116 A4
Rashleigh Mews PL25 . . . . 115 A3
Rashleigh Pl PL25 . . . . 114 F4
Rashleigh Road 6 PL26 . . 115 A1
Rashleigh Vale TR17 . . . . . 137 E4
Ratcliffes La TR13 . . . . 146 A5
Rattle St PL26 . . . . 85 D5
Rawley Rd TR7 . . . . 110 E5
Rawley La TR7 . . . . 110 E5
Rawlin Cl PL6 . . . . 129 C8
Rawlings La PL23 . . . . 116 D5
Raymond Rd TR15 . . . . 140 C4
Raymond Way PL7 . . . . 130 D6
Raynham Rd PL3 . . . . 128 B4
Read Cl TR10 . . . . 144 B7
Reading Wlk PL5 . . . . 124 C4
READYMONEY 116 B3
Readymoney Rd PL23 . . . . 116 B3
REAWLA 78 E3
Reawla La TR27 . . . . 78 E3
Rebecca Cl PL24 . . . . 60 B6
Recreation Rd PL2 . . . . 128 C7
Recreation Road Ind Est
  PL2 . . . . 128 C7
Rectory Gdns
  Camborne TR14 . . . . 138 C2
  Lanreath PL13 . . . . 62 B8
  St Stephen PL26 . . . . 58 B4
Rectory La PL30 . . . . 34 D7
Rectory Rd Camborne TR14 138 C2
  Lanivet PL30 . . . . 47 F6
  Plymouth PL1 . . . . 128 A2
  St Buryan TR19 . . . . 97 B6
  St Dennis PL26 . . . . 46 B1
  St Stephen PL26 . . . . 58 B4
Rectory The TR1 . . . . 137 C5
Redannack Est 11 TR12 . . . 99 A1
Redannack N 1 TR12 . . . . . 99 A2
Redannack Cres TR1 . . . . . 137 B3
Redannick La TR1 . . . . 137 B4
Redbrooke Rd TR14 . . . . . . 138 E2
Redbrooke Terr TR14 . . . . . 138 C2
Red Cove Cl 10 PL27 . . . . . 31 F3
Reddicliff Cl PL9 . . . . 135 E5
Reddicliff Rd PL9 . . . . 135 D5
Reddington Rd PL3 . . . . . . 129 B7
Red Down Ct PL15 . . . . 17 F5
Redfern Ct 2 TR26 . . . . . . 141 B6
Redhill Cl PL5 . . . . 123 E4
Redinnick Gdns 4 TR18 . . 143 E4
Redinnick Terr TR18 . . . . . 143 D4
Redinnick Terr 1 TR18 . . . 143 E4
Red La Bugle PL26 . . . . 47 C2
  Rosudgeon TR20 . . . . 89 F5
REDMONSFORD 3 F2
Redmoor Cl PL19 . . . . 147 A7
Redmoor Rd PL17 . . . . 39 E6
Redmore Cl PL17 . . . . 39 E6
RED POST 7 F8
Red River Valley Nature
  Reserve ★ TR27 . . . . 66 D2
REDRUTH 140 D5
Redruth Cl PL5 . . . . 124 A5
Redruth Highway TR15 . . . 140 E5
Redruth Old Cornwall Society
  Mus ★ TR16 . . . . 67 F5
Redruth Rd Helston TR13 . . 146 D2
  Lowertown TR13 . . . . 91 E4
Redruth Sch & Tech Coll
  TR15 . . . . 140 A5
Redruth Sta TR15 . . . . 140 C5
Redvale Rd PL30 . . . . 23 E3
Redvers Gr PL7 . . . . 130 E4
Redvers Hts TR15 . . . . 140 B3
Redwing Dr PL6 . . . . 125 D8
Redwood Dr PL7 . . . . 131 B5
Redwood Gr EX23 . . . . 104 E5
Reeds Pk PL22 . . . . 112 D2
Reeds Way TR7 . . . . 110 D5
Reen Cross Rd TR4 . . . . . . 55 D4
Reen Hill TR6 . . . . 55 B4
Reen La TR6 . . . . 55 B5
Reens Cres TR18 . . . . 143 D7
Reens Rd TR18 . . . . 143 C7
Reeshill Rd PL26 . . . . 46 F2
Reeves Ct TR13 . . . . 91 B1
Regal Ct PL12 . . . . 122 F2
Regal Theatre ★ 11 TR15 . 140 B5
Regan Ct TR10 . . . . 144 A7
Regency Rd PL25 . . . . 115 E3
Regent Bldgs 36 TR18 . . . 143 E5
Regent Ct PL4 . . . . 149 A3
Regent Sq 21 TR18 . . . . . . 143 E5
Regent St PL4 . . . . 149 A3
Regent Terr Penzance TR18 143 E4
  St Just TR19 . . . . 86 E5
Regulator Rd PL30 . . . . 23 A5
Reigate Rd PL7 . . . . 130 E8
Rejarden TR27 . . . . 90 B5
REJERRAH 55 F7
Relistian La TR27 . . . . 78 E3
Relistian Pk TR27 . . . . 78 E3
RELUBBUS 90 A7
Relubbus Hill TR20 . . . . . . 90 A7
Relubbus La TR20 . . . . 90 A6
Renaissance Gdns PL2 . . . 128 C7
Rendlesham Gdns PL6 . . . 125 E3
Rendle St Delabole PL33 . . . 14 E3
  Plymouth PL1 . . . . 148 B3
Renney Rd PL9 . . . . 135 C1
Rennie Ave PL5 . . . . 124 C1
Renoir Cl PL9 . . . . 136 A6
Renown St PL2 . . . . 127 E6
Reperry Cross PL30 . . . . . . 47 F6
Reppersfield Row TR13 . . . 90 F3
RESCASSA 72 F1
RESCORLA 59 D8
Rescorla Ct TR27 . . . . 142 C5
Research Way PL6 . . . . 125 D4
Reservoir Cres PL9 . . . . . . 136 B7
Reservoir La 1 PL3 . . . . . . 128 F6
Reservoir Rd
  Plymouth, Hartley PL3 . . . 128 F6
  Plymouth, Plymstock PL9 . 136 B7
  Reservoir Way PL9 . . . . . . 136 B7
RESKADINNICK 138 B5
Reskadinnick Rd TR14 . . . 138 B4
Reskadinnick Streams
  TR14 . . . . 138 B6
RESKIVERS 71 F3
Resolution Ho PL4 . . . . 149 B3
Respryn Cl PL14 . . . . 113 D6
Respryn Rd PL31 . . . . 48 D8
RESTORMEL 112 C5
Restormel Ind Est PL22 . . . 112 D2
Restormel Rd Looe PL13 . . 117 D4
  Lostwithiel PL22 . . . . 112 C4
  Newlyn TR18 . . . . 143 C3
  Plymouth PL4 . . . . 148 C4
Restormel Terr
  Falmouth TR11 . . . . 145 B3
  Plymouth PL4 . . . . 148 C4
Restronguet TR11 . . . . 82 B3
Restronguet Barton TR11 . . 82 B3
Restronguet Hill TR11 . . . . 82 B4
RESTRONGUET PASSAGE . . 82 A4
RESUGGA GREEN 59 D8
Resugga Green La 18 PL26 59 D7
Resugga Green Residential
  Homes Pk 59 D7
Reswythen Wlk PL14 . . . . . 38 F7
Retallack Gdns 3 TR20 . . . 89 E5
Retallick Mdws PL25 . . . . . 115 B5
Retanning La PL26 . . . . 58 E1
Retreat The
  8 Chacewater TR4 . . . . . 69 A3
  Plymouth PL3 . . . . 129 D7
  St Columb Major TR9 . . . . 45 E6
Revell Park Rd PL7 . . . . . . 130 D6
Revel Rd PL3 . . . . 129 A6
Reynolds Gr PL5 . . . . 127 C8
Reynolds Rd PL7 . . . . 130 C6
REZARE 28 E4
Rheola Gdns PL6 . . . . 125 D3
Rhind St PL31 . . . . 109 E5
Rhodes Cl PL7 . . . . 130 E7
Rhubarb Hill TR8 . . . . 43 B1
Rhude Cross EX23 . . . . 5 B3
Rialton Hts TR7 . . . . 111 E7
Rialton Rd TR7, TR8 . . . . . . 111 E6
Ribble Gdns PL3 . . . . 129 D7
Rice La PL26 . . . . 85 C5
Richard Lander Sch TR3 . . . 69 D3
Richards Cres TR1 . . . . 69 F3
Richards La TR16 . . . . 67 E4
Richards Row PL3 . . . . 128 F7
Richards Terr PL10 . . . . . . 132 E5
Richmond Hill TR1 . . . . 137 B4
Richmond Pl
  40 St Ives TR26 . . . . 141 B6
  3 Truro TR1 . . . . 137 B4
Richmond Rd Pelynt PL13 . . 62 D6
  Plymouth PL6 . . . . 125 A2
Richmond St
  Heamoor TR18 . . . . 143 C7
  Penzance TR18 . . . . 143 E6
Richmond Terr
  Buckland Monachorum PL20 . 41 F3
  Truro TR1 . . . . 137 B4
Richmond Way TR16 . . . . . 141 D1
Richmond Wlk PL1 . . . . 127 F1
Ricketts Rd PL26 . . . . 59 A1
Rick Mdw PL15 . . . . 18 E6
Ride The PL7, PL9 . . . . 129 D2
Ridge Cross PL9 . . . . 136 A3
Ridgegrove Hill PL15 . . . . . 106 D6
Ridgegrove La PL15 . . . . . . 106 C7
Ridge Ho PL4 . . . . 129 A4
Ridgeley Cl 2 PL27 . . . . . . 108 C5
Ridge Park Ave PL4 . . . . . . 128 D4
Ridge Park Rd PL7 . . . . 130 F5
Ridge Pk PL7 . . . . 130 E5
Ridge Rd PL7 . . . . 130 E3
Ridgevale Cl TR18 . . . . 143 F8
Ridgevale La TR18 . . . . 143 F8
Ridgeway
  28 Perranporth TR6 . . . . . 55 A5
  Plymouth, Plympton PL7 . 130 D5
  Plymouth, Plympton St Maurice
  PL7 . . . . 130 F5
  Probus TR2 . . . . 71 C6
  Saltash PL12 . . . . 122 D1
Ridgeway Sch PL7 . . . . 130 E5
Ridgeway Sp Ctr PL7 . . . . . 130 E5
Ridgewell Terr TR9 . . . . . . 57 E8
Ridgewood Cl PL26 . . . . . . 114 F1
Riflemans Walk PL6 . . . . . . 125 B7
Riga Terr PL3 . . . . 129 C4
Rigdale Cl PL6 . . . . 129 A7
RILLA MILL 38 E8
Ringmore Way PL5 . . . . 124 B3
Ringway Flats 8 PL31 . . . . 109 D5
Ringwell Hill TR3 . . . . 81 E7
RINSEY 90 D2
Rinsey La TR13 . . . . 90 D2
Risdon Ave PL4 . . . . 129 B1
Rivendell PL27 . . . . 108 C4
River Ct Saltash PL12 . . . . 122 D5
  Tavistock PL19 . . . . 147 D6
Riverford Cl PL6 . . . . 125 C5
River Pk 11 PL20 . . . . 42 C4
Riversdale Pl 8 PL27 . . . . 108 B5
RIVERSIDE 123 A1
Riverside Angarrack TR27 . . 78 C4
  3 Chacewater TR4 . . . . . 69 A3
  Lelant TR26 . . . . 77 E4
  Padstow PL28 . . . . 107 E5
Riverside Ave TR7 . . . . 110 A5
Riverside Bsns Pk PL1 . . . 127 E3
Riverside Cl 1 PL20 . . . . . 42 C4
Riverside Com Prim Sch
  PL5 . . . . 127 C8
Riverside Cott PL12 . . . . . . 122 C1
Riverside Cres TR7 . . . . . . 110 A5
Riverside Ct PL22 . . . . 112 C2
Riverside Ho TR1 . . . . 137 D1
Riverside Mews
  Angarrack TR27 . . . . 78 C5
  Saltash PL12 . . . . 123 A3
Riverside Mills
  Launceston PL15 . . . . . . 106 B7
  6 Newport PL15 . . . . . . 106 A7
Riverside Pl PL1 . . . . 127 D2
Riverside View TR1 . . . . . . 137 E3
Riverside Wlk PL5 . . . . 124 B6
River St Mevagissey PL26 . 73 C3
  Portscatho TR2 . . . . 83 B2
  Truro TR1 . . . . 137 C4
Rivers The PL12 . . . . 122 E1
Riverview TR11 . . . . 145 A6
River View Flushing TR11 . 145 B7
  Gunnislake PL18 . . . . 40 E5
  Lerryn PL22 . . . . 61 C7
  Plymouth PL4 . . . . 129 B1
  Saltash PL12 . . . . 122 F3
  Tresillian PL22 . . . . 70 E4
River View La PL4 . . . . 129 B1
River Wlk PL25 . . . . 114 B3
Riviera Apartments TR26 .141 D2
Riviera Cl
  8 Helston TR12 . . . . 99 A1
  3 Mullion TR12 . . . . 99 A1
Riviera Est TR12 . . . . 70 D1
Riviera La TR2 . . . . 95 A6
RIVIERE TOWANS 142 B7
Riviere Towans TR27 . . . . . 142 B7
Rix Hill PL19 . . . . 41 F6
Roach's Ct TR26 . . . . 141 E1
Roach's Row TR15 . . . . 140 B5
Road From Prazegooth La To
  Ingewidden TR12 . . . . . . 103 A4
Robartes Ace Acad PL31 . . 109 D4
Robartes Ct 13 TR1 . . . . . . 137 C4
Robartes Gardens Flats
  PL25 . . . . 114 E4
Robartes Gdns PL25 . . . . . 114 E4
Robartes Pl PL25 . . . . 114 E5
Robartes Rd Bodmin PL31 . 109 C4
  Newquay TR7 . . . . 110 F5
  St Dennis PL26 . . . . 58 C8
Robartes Terr
  3 Illogan TR16 . . . . 67 E4
  Lostwithiel PL22 . . . . 112 C3
Robert Adams Cl PL7 . . . . 130 B5
Robert Eliot Ct PL25 . . . . . 114 B3
Robert Hichens Rd TR11 . . 145 A5
Roberts Ave PL11 . . . . 127 B3
Roberts Rd PL5 . . . . 127 D8
Robin Dr PL15 . . . . 106 E4
Robins Cl 13 PL24 . . . . 60 B4
Robinsons Av PL5 . . . . 139 B5
Robins Way PL9 . . . . 135 E8
ROBOROUGH 121 D1
Roborough Ave PL6 . . . . . . 125 B5
Roborough Cl PL6 . . . . 125 B5
Roborough Down La PL6 . 121 C5
Roborough La PL5 . . . . 124 D8
Robyns Cl PL7 . . . . 131 B5
ROCHE 46 F3
Roche Com Prim Sch PL26 . 46 F2
Roche Rd Bugle PL26 . . . . . 47 C2
  Stenalees PL26 . . . . 59 C7
  Trezaise PL26 . . . . 47 A2
Roche Rural Workshops
  PL26 . . . . 47 A4
Roche Sta PL26 . . . . 47 A4
Rochester Rd
  3 Plymouth PL4 . . . . 128 F4
  7 Plymouth PL4 . . . . 149 A4
Rochford Cres PL5 . . . . . . 123 F5
ROCK 21 D2
Rock Cl 1 TR14 . . . . 138 F2
Rock Close Ho TR27 . . . . . 142 A1
Rockfield Ave PL6 . . . . 124 F6
Rock Gdns PL9 . . . . 129 D1
Rockhaven Gdns PL27 . . . . 21 F3
ROCKHEAD 14 E3
Rockhead St PL33 . . . . 14 E3
Rock Hill PL5 . . . . 124 C7
Rockingham Rd PL3 . . . . . 129 A5
Rock La PL31 . . . . 109 C4
Rock Rd Newlyn TR18 . . . . 143 C3
  St Minver PL27 . . . . 21 E2
Rock Terr Heamoor TR18 . . 143 C7
  Plymouth PL7 . . . . 130 D4
Rock Twrs PL13 . . . . 117 D2
Rock View Parc PL26 . . . . . 47 A3
  Tregony TR2 . . . . 71 F3
Rock Villas PL27 . . . . 21 D2
Rockville Pk PL9 . . . . 135 E8
Rockwood Rd PL6 . . . . 125 E8
Rocky Hill PL19 . . . . 147 B5
Rocky La Gweek TR12 . . . . . 92 A1
  Praa Sands TR20 . . . . 90 C6
  St Agnes TR5 . . . . 54 C2
  Veryan TR2 . . . . 83 D5
Rocky Park Ave PL9 . . . . . . 135 E8
Rocky Park Rd PL9 . . . . . . 135 E8
Rodda Cl PL18 . . . . 41 A7
Rodda's Rd TR14 . . . . 68 C6
Rock Rd Newlyn TR18 . . . . 143 C3
Roddick Way 8 PL7 . . . . . 131 C5
Rodings The PL14 . . . . 51 F5
Rodney St PL5 . . . . 127 D8
Rodwell Cl TR15 . . . . 140 D5
Rodwill Cl TR27 . . . . 78 E1
Roebuck Villas TR11 . . . . . 145 B4
Roekindale Cl TR15 . . . . . . 139 D6
Roeselare Ave PL11 . . . . . . 127 A3
Roeselare Cl PL11 . . . . 127 A3
Rogate Dr PL6 . . . . 125 D4
Rogate Wlk PL6 . . . . 125 D4
Rogers Dr PL12 . . . . 122 D4
Roland Bailey Gdns PL19 . 147 A6
Rollis Park Cl PL9 . . . . 135 C8
Rollis Park Rd PL9 . . . . 135 C8
Rolston Cl PL6 . . . . 124 D6
Roma Cl TR7 . . . . 111 C7
Roma Ct TR27 . . . . 142 B5
Roman Bridge PL13 . . . . . . 62 D1
Roman Dr PL31 . . . . 109 F2
Roman Rd PL5 . . . . 123 E2
Roman Way PL5 . . . . 123 E2
Romilly Gdns PL7 . . . . 130 B5
Romney Cl PL5 . . . . 124 B1
Ronald Terr PL2 . . . . 127 F5
Ronsdale Cl PL9 . . . . 135 D8
Rooke Rd PL27 . . . . 22 D5
Roope Cl PL5 . . . . 127 C7
Ropehaven Cl PL25 . . . . . . 114 E6
Ropehaven Rd PL25 . . . . . 114 E6
Roper Ave PL9 . . . . 135 D5
Ropewalk 9 TR2 . . . . 95 A6
Ropewalk Ct 2 TR11 . . . . 145 C3
Ropewalk Rd TR3 . . . . 137 C1
Ropewalk The TR18 . . . . . 143 C4
Rope Wlk Mount Hawke TR4 . 68 C6
  Padstow PL28 . . . . 107 D5
  3 St Austell PL26 . . . . . . 115 A1
Rope Wlk The 3 TR26 . . . 141 B6
Rorkes Cl PL5 . . . . 123 E2
Roscadghill Parc 1 TR18 . 143 C7
Roscadghill Rd TR18 . . . . . 143 C6
Roscarrack Cl TR11 . . . . . . 144 E2
Roscarrack Rd TR11 . . . . . 144 E3
Roscarrack Villas TR11 . . . 93 D3
Roscarrock Hill PL29 . . . . . 22 C7
ROSCROGGAN 138 D7
Roscrow Dr 1 TR14 . . . . . 138 D4
ROSE 55 C5
Rose Acre Dr 8 TR15 . . . . 140 C5
ROSE-AN-GROUSE 77 D2
Roseannon TR11 . . . . 93 D3
Rosebery Ave PL4 . . . . 149 C4
Rosebery La PL4 . . . . 149 C4
Rosebery Rd PL4 . . . . 149 C4
ROSECARE 10 C6
Roseclave Cl PL7 . . . . 131 C6
Rose Cottage TR27 . . . . . . 21 F5
Rosecott Pk 4 EX23 . . . . . 5 A6
Rose Cotts Camborne TR14 . 138 C4
  Plymouth PL6 . . . . 129 B8
  Stithians TR3 . . . . 80 F3
Rosecraddoc View PL14 . . . 38 A2
Rose Ct PL25 . . . . 115 A5
Rosedale Ave PL2 . . . . 128 D7
Rosedale Gdns PL31 . . . . . 35 B2
Rosedale Rd TR1 . . . . 137 C5
Rosedene Farm TR3 . . . . . . 69 C4
ROSEDINNICK 45 E8
Rosedown Ave PL2 . . . . . . 128 A7
Rose Eglos TR11 . . . . 144 C2
Rose Eglos Cl TR11 . . . . . 144 C2
Rose Gdns PL6 . . . . 125 E6
ROSEHILL Goonhavern 55 D5
  Lostwithiel 112 C1
Rosehill Heamoor TR20 . . . 88 A5
  Ladock TR2 . . . . 57 C1
  Lanivet PL30 . . . . 47 C6
  Marazion TR17 . . . . 89 B5
  Mylor Bridge TR11 . . . . . . 82 A2
  Tregolds PL27 . . . . 32 C6
Rose Hill Altarnun PL15 . . . 26 F7
  Fowey PL23 . . . . 116 C4
  Par PL24 . . . . 60 B5
  Porthtowan TR4 . . . . 68 A6
  Port Isaac PL29 . . . . 22 D7
  Redruth TR15 . . . . 140 B5
  Sticker PL26 . . . . 58 F1
Rose Hill Cl PL22 . . . . 112 C2
Rosehill Gdns TR18 . . . . . 143 B6
Rosehill Mdw TR18 . . . . . . 143 B6
Rose Hill Terr PL17 . . . . . . 41 A3
Rosehip Cl PL6 . . . . 125 E7
Rose In The Bush PL12 . . . 99 B8
Rose In The Bush Pk PL12 . 99 B8
Rose La 23 TR26 . . . . 141 B6
Roseladden TR13 . . . . 91 A3
ROSELAND 51 E6
Roseland Cres
  6 Chacewater TR4 . . . . . 69 A3
  Tregony TR2 . . . . 71 F3
Roseland Flats TR2 . . . . . . 82 E1
Roseland Gdns
  Bodmin PL31 . . . . 109 E6
  Redruth TR15 . . . . 140 D6
  Veryan TR2 . . . . 83 F6
Roseland Parc 8 TR2 . . . . 84 A8
Roseland Rd TR14 . . . . 138 D4
Roselands La PL31 . . . . . . 35 A2
Roselands Rd PL31 . . . . . . 109 F6
Roseland Terr TR4 . . . . 55 F2
Roselare Cl 5 PL25 . . . . . 114 E7
Roselidden Parc TR13 . . . . 146 B7
Roseline Est TR13 . . . . 80 D1
Roselyon Pl PL24 . . . . 60 C5
Roselyon Preparatory School
  PL24 . . . . 60 C4
Rosemaber TR13 . . . . 90 F4
Rose Mdw TR3 . . . . 80 F3
Rose Mdws TR4 . . . . 55 D4
Rosemellen Terr PL14 . . . . 113 B4
Rosemellin TR14 . . . . 138 E4
Rosemellin Com Prim Sch
  TR14 . . . . 138 E4
ROSEMELLING 59 F8
ROSEMERGY 75 D3
Rosemerryn Bareppa TR11 . 93 E4
  Carlidnack TR11 . . . . 94 A2
Rosemorran 28 TR26 . . . . . 141 B5
Rosemullion 4 TR6 . . . . . . 55 A5
Rosemullion Gdns 3
  TR14 . . . . 138 F7
Rose Mullion Gdns PL17 . . 39 F5
Rosemullion Ho TR1 . . . . . 69 E4
Rosemundy TR5 . . . . 54 D1
ROSENANNON 33 A1
Rosenannon La TR15 . . . . . 139 B8
Rosenannon Rd TR15 . . . . 139 B8
Rose Row TR15 . . . . 140 B5
ROSERROW 21 E5
Rose Terr Gunnislake PL18 . 40 E5
  Mitchell TR8 . . . . 56 F5
  22 Penzance TR18 . . . . . 143 E6
Rosevale TR18 . . . . 143 D4
Rosevale Cres TR14 . . . . . 138 C4
Rosevale Gdns PL30 . . . . . 59 F8
Rosevalley TR3 . . . . 69 D3
Rose Valley TR19 . . . . 75 B2
Rosevallen La PL31 . . . . . . 109 C5
ROSEVEAN 47 D1
Rosevean Ave TR14 . . . . . . 138 E3
Rosevean Cl TR14 . . . . 138 E3
Rosevean Ct 8 PL3 . . . . . . 128 F6
Rosevean Gdns PL3 . . . . . 128 F6
Rosevean Ho 7 PL3 . . . . . 128 F6
Rosevean Rd TR18 . . . . . . 143 E6
Rosevean Terr TR18 . . . . . 143 E6
ROSEVEAR 99 C7
Roseveare Dr PL26 . . . . . . 46 D1
Roseveare Mobile Home Pk
  PL26 . . . . 46 D1
Rosevear Hill TR12 . . . . . . 99 C7
Rosevear Rd PL26 . . . . 47 C1

ROSEVINE. 83 B3
Rosevine Way 4 TR14 . . . . . 138 D4
Rosewall Cotts 16 TR26 . . . 141 A5
Rosewall Terr 17 TR26 . . . . 141 A5
ROSEWARNE 78 F3
Rosewarne TR13 . . . . 91 A1
Rosewarne Cl TR14 . . . . . . 138 D4
Rosewarne Downs
  Reskadinnick TR14 . . . . 79 C8
  Reskadinnick TR14 . . . . . 138 D5
Rosewarne Gdns TR14 . . . 138 D3
Rosewarne Mews TR14 . . 138 D4
Rosewarne Pk TR14 . . . . . 138 E4
Rosewarne Rd
  1 Camborne TR14 . . . . . . 138 D3
  Carnhell Green TR27 . . . . . 78 F4
Rosewarne Terr TR14. . . . 138 D5
Rosewarne (Trng Ctr)
  TR14. . . . . 138 D5
Rosewin Bridge Rd PL27 . . . 22 A4
Rosewin Mews 3 TR9 . . . . 45 E6
Rosewin Row
  2 St Columb Major TR9 . . . 45 E6
  Truro TR1 . . . . 137 D5
Rosewithian Cl TR27. . . . . . 78 E6
Rosewood Cl PL9 . . . . 135 F5
ROSEWORTHY Camborne . . 78 F6
  Shortlanesend. 69 E6
ROSEWORTHY BARTON . . . 78 F6
Roseworthy Hill TR14 . . . . . 78 F6
Rosina Way PL26 . . . . 59 D7
Roskear TR14 . . . . 138 E4
ROSKEAR CROFT 138 E6
Roskear Croft TR14. . . . . . 138 E6
Roskear Fields TR14. . . . . 138 E4
Roskear Parc TR14 . . . . . . 138 F5
Roskear Prim & Nur Sch
  PL9. . . . . 135 B5
Roskear Rd TR14 . . . . 138 E3
Roskear Sch TR14 . . . . . . 138 F3
Roskilling TR13. . . . . 146 D7
Roskilling Wartha TR13 . . 146 D7
Roskilly Cotts TR19. . . . . . . 88 C2
Roskilly La TR14 . . . . 138 E4
Roskilly's Ice Cream & Organic
  Farm ★ TR12. . . . . 101 D3
Roskrow TR10 . . . . 81 C2
Roskrow Cl TR16. . . . . 80 A5
Roskruge Cl TR13. . . . . . . 146 D8
Ros Lyn TR26 . . . . 141 C1
Roslyn Cl St Austell PL25 . . 114 F5
  2 St Austell PL25 . . . . . . 115 A5
Rosparc TR2 . . . . 71 D6
Rosparvah Gdns TR18 . . . 143 C7
Rospeath Cres PL2 . . . . . . 128 D8
Rospeath La TR20 . . . . 89 C7
Rossett Gdns PL31 . . . . 35 B5
Rossiter Ho TR19 . . . . 96 B6
Rosslyn Park Rd PL3. . . . . 128 D5
Ross St PL2 . . . . 127 E4
Rossventon TR4 . . . . 69 A1
Rostalek PL30. . . . . 24 B2
Rostigan Hill PL30. . . . . 46 E7
ROSUDGEON 89 F4
Rosudgeon Downs 3 TR20 89 F4
Rosva Morgowr TR11 . . . . 144 F2
Rotair Rd 1 TR14. . . . . 138 E3
Rothbury Cl PL6 . . . . 125 E4
Rothbury Gdns PL6. . . . . . 125 D4
Rothesay Gdns PL5 . . . . . 124 D3
Rougemont Cl PL3. . . . . . . 129 B7
Rough La PL3 . . . . 81 B4
Rough St TR16. . . . . 80 D6
Roughtor Dr PL32 . . . . 105 C3
Roughtor Rd PL32 . . . . 15 D1
Roughtor View PL33 . . . . . . 14 D2
Rounders Rise 10 TR27 . . 142 D6
Roundhayes Farm Cotts
  EX23 . . . . 10 C5
Roundhouse Way TR13 . . 146 B4
Round Ring TR10 . . . . 144 D8
Round Ring Gdns 3 TR10. 94 A8
Round's La PL34. . . . . 14 D7
Rous Rd PL12 . . . . 40 C2
ROW. 24 B3
Rowan Cl Bodmin PL31 . . . 109 B4
  Plymouth PL7. . . . . 131 B5
  Tavistock PL19. . . . . 147 C3
Rowan Ct PL12 . . . . 122 C2
Rowan La 6 Lamellion PL14 . 51 A7
  Lamellion PL14 . . . . 113 A6
Rowans The Bude EX23 . . 104 E4
  Lifton PL16. . . . . 19 F4
  St Mellion PL12 . . . . 53 C8
Rowan Way PL6 . . . . 125 E7
Rowan Wood Rd PL19 . . . . . 30 F3
Rowden St PL3 . . . . 128 E5
Rowdown Cl PL7 . . . . 131 D4
Rowe Ct PL14. . . . . 50 E8
Rowe's La TR13. . . . . 146 E8
Rowe St PL11. . . . . 127 B3
Rowes Terr PL26 . . . . 58 D5
Row La PL5. . . . . 123 E2
Rowland Cl PL9 . . . . 135 E5
Rowse Gdns PL18. . . . . 41 A3
Row The Launceston PL15 . . 17 F1
  Pillaton PL12. . . . . 53 B7
  Portloe TR2. . . . . 84 A4
Royal Cornwall Hospl TR1. . 69 E4
Royal Cornwall Mus ★ TR1 137 C4
Royal Cornwall Showground ★
  Pl27 . . . . 33 C6
Royalist Ct 14 TR11 . . . . . 145 C3
Royal Navy Ave PL2. . . . . 127 F6
Royal Par PL1 . . . . 148 C2

Royal Talbot PL22 . . . . 112 C2
Royal William Rd PL1. . . . 134 A8
Royal William Yard PL1. . 134 A8
Roydon Cl PL15. . . . . 106 B8
Roydon La PL15. . . . . 106 B8
Roydon Rd PL15. . . . . 106 B8
Royffe Way PL31. . . . . 109 F3
RUAN HIGH LANES 83 E6
RUAN LANIHORNE 83 E8
RUAN MAJOR 102 F6
RUAN MINOR 103 B5
Ruan Minor Treleague TR12 103 A5
  6 Treleague TR12. . . . . . 103 B4
Rubble La TR7. . . . . 110 B5
Ruby Terr TR13. . . . . 92 B8
RUDDLEMOOR. 59 B6
Rudyerd Wlk PL3 . . . . 129 D6
Rufford Cl PL2. . . . . 128 A7
Rule Cross EX23 . . . . 2 E2
RUMFORD 32 A5
Ruminella View TR12. . . . 103 A4
Rumours Apartments TR7 111 B7
Rundle Ct PL14. . . . . 113 B4
Rundles Ct TR1. . . . . 137 E3
Runnymede Ct PL6 . . . . . 125 E2
Ruscullion La PL27 . . . . 32 B6
Ruses Mill La PL15 . . . . 27 D4
RUSHFORD. 30 A3
Rush Park Terr PL18 . . . . . . 40 F7
Ruskin Cres PL5 . . . . 124 C2
Ruskin Ct TR9 . . . . 45 D5
Russell Ave PL3 . . . . 128 F7
Russell Cl Gunnislake PL18. . 41 A7
  Plymouth PL9. . . . . 136 B7
  Saltash PL12 . . . . 122 C3
Russell Court Gdns PL19. . 147 B6
Russell Ct Plymouth PL1. . 148 C2
  Saltash PL12 . . . . 122 C3
  Tavistock PL19. . . . . 147 B6
Russell Mews PL31 . . . . . 109 C5
Russell Pl PL1. . . . . 148 B4
Russell St 7 Liskeard PL14 113 C5
  Tavistock PL19. . . . . 147 C5
Russell Way 4 TR10 . . . . 144 C7
Russet Wood PL5. . . . . . . 123 F4
Rutger Pl PL1 . . . . 148 A4
Ruthdower TR13 . . . . 90 F7
RUTHERNBRIDGE 34 A1
Ruthern Valley PL30 . . . . . . 34 A1
Ruthven Cl PL6 . . . . 128 F8
Ruthy's La PL28 . . . . 107 D5
RUTHVOES. 45 F3
Rutland Rd PL4. . . . . 128 F4
Rydal Cl PL6. . . . . 125 D2
Ryder Rd PL2. . . . . 127 F4
Rydon La EX22. . . . . 8 F7
Rye Hill Ponsanooth TR3 . . 81 B4
  Saltash PL12 . . . . 122 C2
Rylands Terr PL30 . . . . 24 B3

S

Saffron Cl PL23. . . . . 116 C4
Safron La PL23 . . . . 61 D2
Sail Loft Flats 2 TR26 . . . 141 B6
ST AGNES 54 D1
ST AGNES BEACON. 54 B1
St AgneS Mus ★ TR5. . . . . 54 C1
St AgneS Sch TR5. . . . . 54 C1
St Albans Pk PL20 . . . . 42 D2
ST ALLEN 56 B1
St Ambrusca Rd TR8. . . . 110 A3
St Andrew's CE Prim Sch
  PL20 . . . . 41 F3
St Andrew's CE VA Prim Sch
  PL1. . . . . 148 B2
St Andrews Cl
  12 Bere Alston PL20 . . . . . . 41 B1
  Ponsanooth TR3. . . . . 81 B4
  Saltash PL12 . . . . 122 C2
St Andrew's Cl PL18 . . . . . 41 A3
St Andrew's Cross 1 PL1 149 A2
St Andrews Rd PL19 . . . . 147 D2
St Andrew's Rd Par PL24 . . 60 C5
  12 Stratton EX23. . . . . 4 D1
St Andrew's St
  Cawsand PL10. . . . . 133 A1
  1 St Ives TR26 . . . . 141 B5
St Andrew St
  Millbrook PL10. . . . . 132 E5
  Plymouth PL1. . . . . 148 C2
St Andrews Terr TR3. . . . . 81 B4
St Andrew's Terr PL24 . . . . 60 C5
St Annes TR11 . . . . 93 D3
St Annes Cl Lelant TR26 . . . 77 E4
  Whitstone EX22. . . . . 7 F1
St Annes Rd 17 PL24 . . . . . 60 B4
St Anne's Rd Newquay TR7 111 A7
  Plymouth PL6. . . . . 125 D6
  Saltash PL12 . . . . 122 E3
  3 Trewoon PL25. . . . . 59 A3
ST ANN'S CHAPEL 40 E6
St Ann's Hill EX23. . . . . . . 104 F3
St Anta Rd TR26 . . . . 141 E1
ST ANTHONY 95 B5
St Anthony TR12. . . . . 101 B8
ST ANTHONY-IN-
  MENEAGE 101 C8
St Anthony Rd TR12. . . . . 101 B8
St Anthony Way TR11 . . . 145 A2
St Aubyn TR16. . . . . 140 E5
St Aubyn Ave PL2. . . . . . . 127 F5
St Aubyn Cres TR7 . . . . . 111 A6
St Aubyn Est TR14 . . . . . . 79 B3
St Aubyn Rd PL1. . . . . 127 E3
St Aubyns TR20. . . . . 89 E5

St Aubyn's Rd TR1. . . . . . 137 D3
St Aubyn St PL1 . . . . 127 E2
St Aubyn's Vean TR1. . . . 137 D3
ST AUSTELL 114 B5
St Austell Bay Bsns Pk
  PL25. . . . . 115 E4
St Austell Brewery Visitor
  Ctr ★ PL25. . . . . 114 B4
St Austell Com Hospl PL26 114 F1
St Austell Rd PL24 . . . . . . 115 F5
St Austell Row 2 TR2. . . . . 95 A6
St Austell St
  Summercourt TR8 . . . . 57 C6
  Truro TR1. . . . . 137 D4
St Austell Sta PL25 . . . . . 114 D4
St Barnabas Ct PL1 . . . . . 148 A4
St Barnabas Hospl PL1. . . 122 F2
St Barnabas Terr PL1 . . . . 148 A4
St Benedicts 13 PL24 . . . . 60 D5
St Benets Cl PL30. . . . . 47 E6
ST BLAZEY. 60 B5
ST BLAZEY GATE. 115 F6
St Blazey Rd PL24. . . . . 60 C4
St Boniface Cl PL2. . . . . . 128 C7
St Boniface Dr PL2 . . . . . 128 C7
St Boniface RC Coll PL5. . 124 E1
St Breaca Cl TR13 . . . . 91 A3
ST BREOCK 33 C6
St Breock Prim Sch PL27 . 108 B5
ST BREWARD 24 B3
St Breward Prim Sch PL30 . 24 B3
St Bridget Ave PL6. . . . . . 124 F1
ST BUDEAUX 123 D2
St Budeaux Bypass
  Honicknowle PL5. . . . . . . 124 A1
  St Budeaux PL5 . . . . 123 F2
St Budeaux Ferry Rd Sta
  PL5 . . . . 127 D8
St Budeaux Foundation CE (A)
  Jun Sch PL5. . . . . 123 F2
St Budeaux Victoria Rd Sta
  PL5. . . . . 123 D1
ST BURYAN 97 B6
St Buryan Hill TR19 . . . . . . 96 F4
St Buryan Prim Sch TR19 . . 97 B6
St Cadocs PL28. . . . . 31 F7
St Carantoc Way TR8 . . . . . 43 D3
St Catherine's Castle ★
  PL23. . . . . 116 B2
St Catherine's CE Prim Sch
  PL15. . . . . 106 A4
St Catherines Ct PL23. . . 116 C3
St Catherine's Parade
  PL23 . . . . 116 B4
St Clare Flats TR18 . . . . . 143 D6
St Clare St Heamoor TR20 . . 88 C5
  Penzance TR18 . . . . 143 D6
  2 Rosehill TR18 . . . . 143 D6
ST CLEER 37 F2
St Cleer Dr PL27. . . . . 108 D6
St Cleer Prim Sch PL14 . . . 38 A3
St Cleer Rd PL14. . . . . 113 C7
ST CLEMENT 70 D2
St Clement's Cl TR1 . . . . . 137 E4
St Clement's Hill TR1. . . . 137 E4
St Clements Parc TR1 . . . 137 E4
St Clement Sch TR1 . . . . 137 D5
St Clement's Terr 3 TR1 . 137 D5
St Clement Vean TR1 . . . 137 F6
ST CLETHER 17 A3
St Columb Bsns Ctr TR9. . . 45 E6
ST COLUMB MAJOR 45 E6
St Columb Major Academy
  TR9 . . . . 45 D6
St Columb Major Bsns Pk
  TR9. . . . . 45 E5
St Columb Major Ind Est
  TR9. . . . . 45 D5
ST COLUMB MINOR 111 E7
St Columb Minor Academy
  TR7. . . . . 111 D7
ST COLUMB ROAD 45 D2
St Columb Road Ind
  Workshops TR9 . . . . 45 D2
St Columb Road Sta TR9. . . 45 D2
St Crewenna Terr TR27. . . . 78 E1
St Cuthbert Cl PL15. . . . . 106 B7
St Cuthbert's Rd TR7 . . . 110 C6
St Cyriac PL28. . . . . 47 F1
St Davids Cl EX23. . . . . 4 C8
St David's Rd PL19. . . . . . 147 E5
ST DAY 68 E1
St Day & Carharrack Com Sch
  TR16. . . . . 68 E1
St Day Rd TR15 . . . . 140 C5
ST DENNIS 58 C8
St Dennis Com Prim Sch
  PL26 . . . . 58 C8
St Dennis Ind Est PL26 . . . 58 B8
St Dominic Cl PL31 . . . . . 109 C5
ST DOMINICK 40 D3
St Dominick CE Prim Sch
  PL12 . . . . 40 D2
St Dominic Pk PL17. . . . . . . 40 C4
St Dominic Sq 4 TR1 . . . . 137 C4
St Dominic St
  8 Penzance TR18. . . . . . . 143 E6
  5 Truro TR1. . . . . 137 C4
St Dunstan's Terr PL4 . . . 149 C3
St Edmunds La PL28 . . . . 107 D5
St Edward Gdns PL6 . . . . 125 B1
St Edward's CE Prim Sch
  PL6. . . . . 125 C1
St Eia St TR26 . . . . 141 C6
St Elizabeth Cl PL7 . . . . . 130 F3
St Elvan Cres TR13. . . . . . . 91 A1
St Elwyns Rise TR27 . . . . 142 B6
ST ENDELLION 22 D5

St Endellion Rd PL30. . . . . . 22 E5
ST ENODER 57 B7
St Enodoc Cl PL27 . . . . . . 108 D6
ST ERME 70 E8
St Erme with Trispen Com
  Prim Sch TR4. . . . . 70 D8
ST ERNEY 53 B2
ST ERTH 142 A1
St Erth Com Prim Sch
  TR27. . . . . 142 A1
St Erth Hill TR27 . . . . 77 F1
St Erth Ind Est TR27. . . . . . 77 E2
ST ERTH PRAZE 142 F1
St Erth Rd PL2. . . . . 128 D7
St Erth Sta TR27 . . . . 77 E2
St Eval Hayle TR27 . . . . 31 F3
St Eval Pl PL5. . . . . 123 E4
St Eval Rd TR8. . . . . 31 C2
ST EWE 72 E5
St Fimbarrus Rd PL23. . . . 116 C3
St Francis CE Sch TR11 . . 144 E3
St Francis Ct PL5 . . . . 124 B3
St Francis Mdw TR8 . . . . . 56 F5
St Francis Rd TR9 . . . . 45 E2
St Francis St 5 TR18. . . . . 143 E6
St Gabriel's Ave PL3 . . . . 128 D5
ST GENNYS 10 C8
St George's Arc TR11. . . . 145 B4
St George's Ave PL2 . . . . 128 C7
St George's CE Prim Acad
  PL1 . . . . 148 A1
St George's Cres PL31 . . . 109 C4
St Georges Ct Looe PL13 . . 117 D2
  1 Plymouth PL2. . . . . 127 F4
St George's Hill TR6. . . . . . 55 A4
St Georges Hill 13 TR6 . . . 55 A4
St George's Pk PL22 . . . . 112 C3
St Georges Rd
  Nanpean PL26 . . . . 58 D6
  Saltash PL12 . . . . 122 D3
St George's Rd Hayle TR27 142 C5
  Looe PL13 . . . . 117 D2
  Newquay TR7. . . . . 110 D5
  Saltash PL12 . . . . 122 E3
  Truro TR1. . . . . 137 B5
St George's Terr
  Perranporth TR6 . . . . 54 F4
  Plymouth PL2. . . . . 127 F4
ST GERMANS 65 A8
St Germans Prim Sch PL12. . 65 A8
St Germans Rd PL17 . . . . . 39 F3
St Germans Sta PL12 . . . . . 65 B8
St Giles Dr PL27. . . . . 108 C6
St Giles Mews PL27 . . . . . 108 C6
ST GILES ON THE HEATH. . . 13 E1
St Giles-on-the-Heath Com
  Sch PL15 . . . . 13 F1
ST GLUVIAS 144 D8
St Gluvias Parc PL14. . . . 144 D8
St Gluvias St TR10 . . . . . 144 D7
St Golder Rd TR18 . . . . . . 143 B3
St Gothian Sands Nature
  Reserve ★ TR27. . . . . 66 B2
St Grace's Ct TR2 . . . . 71 C6
St Helens Wlk PL5 . . . . . . 124 C5
St Henry St 4 TR18. . . . . . 143 E6
ST HILARY 89 E6
St Hilary Sch TR20 . . . . 89 F6
St Hilary Terr PL4 . . . . 149 C3
St Ia Sch TR26 . . . . 141 D1
St Ingunger La PL30 . . . . . 48 B6
ST ISSEY 32 E6
St Issey CE Prim Sch PL27. . 32 D6
St Issey Hill PL27. . . . . 32 D7
ST IVE 38 F2
ST IVE CROSS 39 A1
St Ive Rd PL14. . . . . 38 E4
ST IVES 141 C6
St Ives Jun & Inf Schs
  TR26. . . . . 141 A5
St Ives La TR27 . . . . 66 B1
St Ives L Ctr TR26. . . . . . 141 A5
St Ives Mus ★ TR26 . . . . . 141 C6
St Ives Mushroom Farm
  TR26. . . . . 77 A5
St Ives Rd Carbis Bay TR26 . 141 D1
  Pendeen TR19 . . . . 75 A1
  St Ives Sch TR26 . . . . 141 B3
  St Ives Sta TR26. . . . . . . 141 B5
St James Ct Delabole PL33 . . 14 E2
  Plymouth PL1. . . . . 148 B2
  Torpoint PL11. . . . . 127 B3
St James Mews PL1 . . . . . 148 B2
St James' Place E PL1 . . . 148 B2
St James' Place W PL1. . . 148 B2
St James's Rd PL11. . . . . . 127 B2
St James's St TR18 . . . . . 143 E5
St James View TR9 . . . . . . 57 D8
ST JIDGEY 32 F4
ST JOHN 132 C8
ST JOHNS 146 A6
St Johns PL19 . . . . 147 C5
St John's Bridge Rd PL4 . . 149 B2
St Johns Bsns Pk TR13 . . 146 B6
St John's Catholic Prim Sch 4
  TR14. . . . . 138 E2
St Johns Cl PL6. . . . . 125 D4
St John's Cl Helston TR13 . . 146 A6
  Millbrook PL10. . . . . 132 E5
St Johns Ct 7 TR18. . . . . 143 E5
St John's Ct
  7 Falmouth TR11 . . . . . . 145 A4
  Hayle TR27. . . . . 142 D6
St John's Dr PL9. . . . . 135 B6
St Johns Gdns TR11 . . . . 145 B6
St Johns La PL11 . . . . 132 B8
St Johns Rd PL15 . . . . . . 106 B4

St John's Rd Helston TR13 . 146 B6
  Horrabridge PL20. . . . . . . 42 C4
  Millbrook PL10. . . . . 132 F5
  Newquay TR7. . . . . 110 D5
  Plymouth PL4. . . . . 149 B2
  Plymouth, Turnchapel PL9 . 135 A6
St John's St Hayle TR27. . 142 D6
  Plymouth PL4. . . . . 149 B2
St John's Terr 8 TR19 . . . 75 A1
St Johns Wlk TR26. . . . . . . 77 A7
St Joseph's Cl PL6. . . . . . 124 F1
St Joseph's Rd PL15 . . . . 106 B8
St Joseph's Sch PL15 . . . 106 B7
ST JUDE'S 149 B3
St Jude's Rd PL4 . . . . 149 B2
St Julians Cres PL10 . . . . 133 E7
ST JULITTA 48 A1
ST JUST 86 E6
ST JUST IN ROSELAND . . . 82 F7
St Just Prim Sch TR19 . . . . 86 E6
St Keri Ct PL15 . . . . 18 A5
ST KEVERNE 101 C4
St Keverne Com Prim Sch
  TR12. . . . . 101 D4
St Keverne Pl PL2 . . . . . . 128 D8
St Keverne Rd TR12. . . . . . 99 D7
St Keverne Rural Workshops
  TR12. . . . . 101 C3
ST KEW 23 A4
ST KEW HIGHWAY 23 A2
St Kew Prim Sch PL30 . . . . 22 F3
St Kew Rd PL30. . . . . 23 A2
ST KEYNE 51 A3
St Keyne Cl TR1 . . . . 137 C6
St Keyne Wishing Well Halt
  PL14. . . . . 51 C3
ST LAWRENCE 34 D1
St Lawrence Mews PL4 . . 149 A4
St Lawrence Rd
  Bodmin PL30, PL31. . . . . 109 A4
  Plymouth PL4. . . . . 149 A4
St Leonards PL31 . . . . 109 C5
St Leonard's Rd
  Launceston PL15 . . . . 106 B8
  Plymouth PL4. . . . . 149 C2
St Leonards Terr PL31 . . . 109 C5
St Leo Pl PL2 . . . . 127 E4
ST LEVAN 96 D3
St Levan Cl 8 TR17. . . . . . 89 C5
St Levan Prim Sch TR19 . . 96 E5
St Levan Rd
  7 Marazion TR17. . . . . . . 89 C5
  Plymouth PL2. . . . . 127 F5
ST MABYN 34 C8
St Mabyn CE Prim Sch
  PL30. . . . . 34 D8
St Mabyn Hill PL27. . . . . . . 34 A6
St Madderns CE Sch TR20 143 A8
St Margarets La PL26 . . . . 59 A1
St Margarets Rd PL7. . . . 130 B7
St Mark's CE Prim Sch EX23. 2 E2
St Marks Rd PL6. . . . . 125 D5
St Marnarch's PL13. . . . . . 62 B8
St Marnarch's Rd PL13. . . 62 B8
ST MARTIN Looe 117 D7
  Mawgan 100 D6
St Martin-in-Meneage Com
  Prim Sch TR12. . . . . 100 D6
St Martin's Ave PL3. . . . . 128 D7
St Martin's CE Prim Sch
  PL14. . . . . 113 D5
St Martins Cl Lewannick PL15 27 B7
  Looe PL13 . . . . 117 D5
St Martin's Cl 2 TR14. . . . 138 C2
St Martin's Cres TR14. . . . 138 C3
St Martins Cl PL14. . . . . . 113 E5
St Martins Green 4 TR12 100 D6
St Martins Rd EX23 . . . . . . 7 B8
St Martin's Rd PL13. . . . . 117 D6
St Martin's Terr TR14. . . . 138 C4
St Marwenne Cl EX23. . . . . 7 B6
St Maryhaye PL19 . . . . . . 147 A5
St Mary's PL13 . . . . 117 D3
St Mary's CE Prim Sch
  TR18. . . . . 143 E4
St Mary's CE Sch TR1 . . . 137 C6
St Marys Cl PL7. . . . . 130 D5
St Mary's Cl PL31 . . . . . . 109 C4
St Marys Ct PL7 . . . . 130 D5
St Mary's Ct 2 TR7. . . . . . 110 C5
St Mary's Gdns PL31. . . . 109 C4
St Mary's RC Prim Sch
  Bodmin PL31. . . . . 109 C4
  Falmouth TR11. . . . . 144 E3
St Mary's RC Sch TR18. . . 143 E7
St Marys Rd Callington PL17 . 39 F5
  Par PL24 . . . . 60 B4
St Mary's Rd Bodmin PL31. . 109 B3
  Launceston PL15 . . . . 106 C8
  Newquay TR7. . . . . 110 D5
  Plymouth PL7. . . . . 130 D5
St Mary's St Penzance TR18 143 E6
  12 Truro TR1. . . . . 137 D4
St Mary's Street Mews 10
  TR1 . . . . 137 D4
St Mary St PL1 . . . . 148 A2
St Mary's Terr
  Penzance TR18 . . . . 143 E5
  4 Truro TR1. . . . . 137 C5
St Matthews Hill PL27 . . . 108 D5
St Maurice Ct PL7 . . . . . . 130 F4
St Maurice Mews PL7. . . . 130 E4
St Maurice Rd PL7 . . . . . . 130 F3
St Maurice View PL7. . . . . 131 B4
ST MAWES 95 B6
St Mawes Castle ★ TR2 . . . 95 A5

St Mawes Prim Sch TR2......95 A6
St Mawes Terr **8** PL2......127 F5
ST MAWGAN......45 A8
St Mawgan Cl PL31......109 F5
St Mellans Terr **5** TR12......99 A1
ST MELLION......53 E8
St Mellion CE School PL12..53 D8
ST MELLION PK......53 C8
St Meriadoc CE Infant
  Academy TR14......138 C2
St Meriadoc CE VA Junior
  Academy TR14......138 B2
St Meriadoc Rd TR14......138 C3
ST MERRYN......31 F8
St Merryn Airfield PL28....31 F6
St Merryn Sch PL28......31 E8
ST MEWAN......59 A2
St Mewan Com Prim Sch
  PL26......59 A2
St Mewan La PL24, PL26....59 A3
St Michael Ave PL2......127 F5
ST MICHAEL CAERHAYS......72 D1
ST MICHAEL PENKEVIL......70 F1
St Michael's CE Prim Sch
  TR13......146 C5
St Michaels Cl PL15......19 C1
St Michael's Cl Hayle TR27 142 B4
  Plymouth PL1......127 E1
St Michael's Cotts **11** TR18 143 E5
St Michaels Ct
  Mawnan Smith TR11......93 D3
  18 Penzance TR18......143 E5
St Michael's Ct **7** PL1......127 F3
St Michael's Hospl TR27..142 B4
St Michael's Mount ★ TR17..89 B4
St Michael's RC Small Sch **17**
  TR1......137 C4
St Michaels Rd TR3......81 B4
St Michael's Rd
  Newquay TR7......110 D5
  Perranporth TR6......55 A4
  3 Ponsanooth TR3......81 C4
  3 Stratton EX23......4 D1
St Michael's St TR18......143 E6
St Michael's Terr
  Penzance TR18......143 D6
  Plymouth PL4......148 C4
  8 Plymouth, Devonport PL1 127 F3
St Michaels Way
  Marazion TR17......89 C5
  St Austell PL26......47 A2
St Michaels Wy PL26......46 F2
ST MINVER......22 A4
St Minver Sch PL27......21 F3
St Modwen Rd PL6......129 F7
St Moritz Ct PL27......21 D5
St Moritz Villas PL27......21 D5
St Nazaire App PL1......127 F2
St Nazaire Cl
  3 Boslowick TR11......144 F1
  Plymouth PL1......127 E2
ST NEOT......36 F2
St Neot Com Prim Sch PL14 36 F2
ST NEWLYN EAST......56 C7
St Newlyn East Prim Sch
  TR8......56 B7
St Nicholas' CE Prim Sch
  PL11......64 C4
St Nicholas Cl TR27......78 C6
St Nicholas Ct **1** TR26......141 B6
St Nicholas Pk PL22......112 B3
St Nicholas St Bodmin PL31 109 E4
  14 Truro TR1......137 D4
St Nonna's Cl PL15......26 C8
St Olaf's Rd **13** EX23......4 F1
St Pancras Ave PL2......128 D8
St Paternus Cl PL15......27 E8
St Pauls Cl PL3......129 C5
St Paul's RC Prim Sch PL5 123 D1
St Paul St PL1......134 A8
St Peter Cl PL7......130 F4
St Peters CE VA Prim Sch &
  Nur PL1......148 B3
St Peters Ct PL1......148 A3
St Peter's Hill TR18......143 C1
St Peter's RC Prim Sch
  PL5......124 B5
St Peters Rd
  Plymouth PL5......124 C2
  11 Stratton EX23......4 D1
St Peter's Rd TR11......145 B7
St Peters St **16** TR26......141 B6
St Peters Way TR13......98 C8
St Petrocs CE VA Prim Sch
  PL31......109 E4
St Petrocs Cl PL31......109 E4
St Petrocs Mdw PL28......107 C5
St Petroc's Sch EX23......104 D7
St Petry TR20......89 C5
St Philip St **7** TR18......143 E6
ST PINNOCK......50 D6
St Piran Cl PL31......109 B4
St Pirans Cl **2** TR1......137 D4
St Piran's Cl PL25......114 C4
St Pirans Ct
  Camborne TR14......138 D3
  13 Penzance TR18......143 E5
  Tintagel PL34......14 E8
St Pirans Hill TR3......81 D6
St Pirans Ho **15** TR6......55 A5
St Pirans Par **10** TR6......55 A5
St Pirans Parc **14** TR13......98 C8
St Pirans Rd TR6......55 A5
St Piran's Rd TR7......110 C6
St Piran's Sch TR27......142 B4
St Pirans Way TR20......89 D4
St Pol de Leon View TR19...88 C2
ST RUAN......103 A4

St Rumon's CE Inf Sch
  PL19......147 C6
St Sampsons Cl **6** PL24....60 D5
St Sampson's Terr PL23....61 B5
St Saviour's Hill PL23......116 D2
St Saviour's La PL28......107 D6
St Simon's La PL4......129 B3
St Smithwick Way TR11....145 C3
ST STEPHEN......58 B4
St Stephen Churchtown Prim
  Sch PL26......58 B4
St Stephen Rd PL7......130 F3
ST STEPHENS Launceston..106 A8
  Saltash......122 D2
St Stephens Community Prim
  Sch
  Launceston PL15......106 B8
  Saltash PL12......122 E2
St Stephens Ct PL15......106 B7
St Stephen's Hill
  Launceston PL15......106 B7
  Saltash PL12......122 C1
St Stephens Rd PL26......58 E1
St Stephen's Rd PL12......122 E2
St Stephen St PL1......127 F1
St Sulien PL30......48 A1
ST TEATH......23 E7
St Teath Com Prim Sch
  PL30......23 E7
St Teresa Ho PL4......149 A3
St Therese Cl **20** PL17......39 F4
St Therese's Ct PL1......127 F2
ST THOMAS......106 B6
St Thomas Cl Plymouth PL7 130 F3
  Truro TR1......69 F3
St Thomas Hill PL15......106 B6
St Thomas Rd PL15......106 B6
St Thomas' Rd TR7......110 F5
St Thomas St TR10......144 D7
St Tinney Farm PL32......10 D1
ST TUDY......23 E3
St Tudy CE Prim Sch PL30..23 E3
St Tudy Rd Cross Hill PL30..23 F1
  Treveglos PL30......34 D8
St Uny CE Sch TR26......141 D1
St Uny Cl TR26......77 E3
St Uny Cres TR15......139 F5
ST VEEP......61 C6
St Vincent St PL2......127 E4
St Warren St **6** TR18......143 E6
ST WENN......46 D7
St Wenn Sch PL30......46 D7
St Winnolls Pk PL13......117 D4
ST WINNOW......61 C6
St Winnow Barton Farm Mus ★
  PL22......61 A8
St Winnow CE Prim Sch
  PL22......112 F2
Salamanca St PL11......127 B3
Salcombe Rd PL4......149 C4
SALEM......68 F3
Salisbury Ope PL3......128 B5
Salisbury Rd Plymouth PL4 149 C4
  Truro TR1......137 B4
Salisbury Road Jun Sch
  PL4......149 C3
Salmon Row **3** TR1......137 D4
SALTASH......122 B1
Saltash Bsns Pk PL12......122 A1
Saltash Com Sch PL12......122 E1
Saltash Her Mus ★ PL12....123 A2
Saltash Ind Est PL12......122 D4
Saltash L Ctr PL12......122 E3
Saltash Parkway Ind Est
  PL12......122 B3
Saltash Rd Callington PL17...39 F4
  Plymouth PL3......148 C4
  Plymouth, Keyham PL2....127 E6
Saltash Sta PL12......123 A2
Saltbox Cl TR11......82 A2
Saltbox Rd TR11......82 A2
Saltburn Rd PL5......123 C1
Salt Cellar Hill **10** TR13....98 B8
Saltings Cl TR26......77 E3
Saltings Reach TR26......77 E3
Saltings The TR26......77 E4
Salt Mill PL12......122 F4
Saltmill Cl PL12......122 F3
Saltponds **27** TR19......88 C1
Salts Mdw PL14......50 B6
Sam Bonds Nip PL4......22 E3
Sampford Gdns PL20......42 D5
SAMPFORD SPINEY......42 E7
Sampford Terr **6** PL20....42 C5
Sampson Cl PL18......40 D6
Sampson Gdns TR3......81 B4
Sampson's Ct TR27......78 D6
Sampson Way TR3......69 D3
Sampys Hill TR11......93 D3
Sams La PL24......60 C5
Samuel Bassett Ave PL6..125 B4
Samuel Bone Cl PL14......113 D6
SANCREED......87 E4
Sancreed La TR20......87 D6
Sancreed Rd TR20......87 E4
Sanctuary Cl TR14......138 C2
Sanctuary La Helston TR13 146 C6
  12 Stratton EX23......4 E1
Sanctuary Lane Flats
  TR13......146 C6
Sand Bay TR11......145 C2
Sandercock Cl PL17......39 F7
Sanderling Cl **7** EX23......7 B8
Sanders Hill Rosken PL28...32 A8
  Tregolds PL28......31 F7
Sandfield Cres **3** TR14...138 C2
Sandford Rd PL9......135 F8

Sand Hill PL18......41 A6
Sand Hill Pk PL18......40 F5
Sandhole Cross EX39......2 D8
Sandhurst Terr **1** TR1....137 C5
Sand La PL18......41 A3
Sandon Wlk PL6......125 A1
Sandows La **18** TR26......141 A5
Sandpiper Rd
  9 Binhamy EX23......7 B8
  Plymouth PL6......125 B2
Sandpiper Road EX23......104 F5
SANDPLACE......63 C7
Sandplace Rd Looe PL13...117 C6
  Looe, Sandplace PL13......63 B7
Sandplace Sta PL13......63 B8
Sandra Way PL31......109 C5
Sandyacres TR27......78 B6
Sandy Acres TR27......142 E8
SANDY BOTTOM......114 F4
Sandy Cl TR4......51 B3
Sandy Cove TR4......68 A7
Sandy Ct TR8......31 B2
Sandy Hill PL25......114 F4
Sandy Hill Academy PL25..114 F4
Sandyhills PL27......21 E2
Sandy La Harlyn PL28......20 D2
  Redruth TR15, TR16......140 D5
  Trevone PL28......20 F2
Sandylake La PL22......112 F3
Sandymoor TR14......139 B3
Sandy Rd Plymouth PL7....131 C4
  Porthtowan TR4......68 A7
Sandy Way Colcerrow PL24..60 C8
  Kerrow PL30......24 C1
Sango Ct PL10......132 F6
Sango Rd PL11......127 A2
San Sebastian Sq PL1....148 C2
Saracen Cl TR10......144 C7
Saracen Cres TR10......144 C7
Saracen Ho **5** TR10......144 C7
Saracen Pl TR10......144 C7
Saracen Way TR10......144 C7
Sarah Cl PL21......81 B1
Sarahs Cl PL28......107 D4
Sarah's Ct PL28......107 D4
Sarah's Gate PL27......32 C7
Sarah's La PL28......107 D4
Sarah's Mdw PL28......107 D4
Sarah's View PL28......107 D4
Sargents Mdw EX23......2 D1
Sarum Cl PL3......128 F7
Saud La PL17......40 B7
Saunders Cl PL11......65 A5
Saunders Wlk PL6......124 D6
Savage Rd PL5......127 D7
Savath La PL26......47 D4
SAVEOCK......69 B3
Savery Terr PL4......129 A4
Savoy Bldg **3** PL25......114 C3
Sawles Rd PL25......114 B2
Sawmills Cl **8** PL31......109 A5
Sawmills La TR16......68 D3
Sawrey St PL1......148 A2
Sawyers Ct TR13......92 A6
Saxon Rd PL19......147 A6
Scannell Cl PL12......122 D1
SCARCEWATER......57 E5
Scarletts Well Pk PL31....109 C6
Scarletts Well Rd PL31....109 C5
Scarlett's Well Rd PL31....109 B5
Scarne Ind Est PL15......106 C3
Scarne Lake Gdns PL15...106 C3
Scarne Mill Ind Est PL15..106 C3
Scarne Side Gr PL15......106 D3
Scawns Cl **11** PL14......50 E7
Scholars Cl PL14......38 F2
Scholar's La TR13......91 C3
School Cl Par PL24......60 B4
  Plymouth PL7......130 D7
  St Columb Minor TR7......111 E6
  Tavistock PL19......147 D5
School Dr PL6......125 D7
School Hill Golant PL23.....61 B5
  Herodsfoot PL14......50 E3
  Lanjeth PL26......58 E4
  Mevagissey PL26......73 C4
  Padstow PL28......107 D5
  Penhallick TR12......101 C1
  Perranarworthal TR3......81 D6
  St Buryan TR19......96 E5
  St Keverne TR12......101 D4
  St Keverne, Porthallow TR12 101 D6
  St Neot PL14......36 F2
  Shortlanesend TR4......69 F6
  South Petherwin PL15......27 E8
School La
  Budock Water TR11......144 C3
  Gulval TR18......88 E6
  Harrowbarrow PL17......40 C4
  Jacobstow EX23......11 A6
  Marazion TR17......89 C5
  Plymouth PL7......130 E4
  Polruan PL23......116 D2
  Redruth TR15......140 D5
  St Austell PL25......115 C6
  St Erth TR27......142 A1
  St Hilary TR20......89 F6
  Summercourt TR8......57 C7
  Tregclliot PL30......22 F4
  Troon TR14......79 E4
  Truro TR1......137 C5
School Rd
  Harrowbarrow PL17......40 D4
  Landrake PL12......53 C3
  Pensilva PL14......38 E5
  Summercourt TR8......57 B7
  Tavistock PL19......147 D2
School Wlk PL27......108 D6

Sclerder La PL13......62 E4
Scoble's Terr TR1......70 D1
Sconner Rd PL11......127 A3
Scoria Cl TR16......68 D3
SCORRIER......68 D2
Scorrier House Workshops
  TR16......68 D2
Scorrier Rd Treleigh TR16..140 F8
  Treleigh TR16......140 F8
Scorrier St TR16......68 E1
Scott Ave PL5......127 C8
Scott Bsns Pk PL2......128 A6
Scott Cl **2** PL14......38 E4
Scott Hospl PL2......128 A6
Scott Rd PL2......128 A6
Scowbuds TR14......138 F5
Scrations La PL22......112 C2
SCREDDA......114 D8
Screech Owl Sanctuary ★
  TR9......46 A3
Sculptor Way **11** PL9......136 E8
Seabank TR11......145 B2
Sea Breeze Cl PL34......14 C6
Seacroft Rd PL5......123 C2
Sea Front PL13......117 D3
Seaholme Ct TR11......145 A5
Sea La TR27......142 D6
Sea Pt PL25......115 D2
SEATON......64 B5
Seaton Ave PL4......128 E4
Seaton Bsns Pk PL6......125 B3
Seaton La PL4......128 E4
Seaton Pk PL11......64 B5
Seaton Pl PL2......127 F5
Seaton Valley North Nature
  Reserve ★ PL13, PL13...64 B6
Seaton Way PL20......42 A2
Sea Urchin TR26......141 E2
Seaureaugh TR3......80 F4
Sea View
  Crackington Haven EX23...10 C6
  Gunnislake PL18......40 E5
Sea View Ave PL4......149 C4
Sea View Cl EX23......5 A6
Seaview Cotts **10** TR11...145 B5
Sea View Cotts PL26......73 C3
Sea View Cres **11** TR2....95 A6
Sea View Ct TR11......145 B3
Sea View La TR8......43 C1
Sea View Pl TR26......141 C6
Sea View Rd Falmouth TR11 145 B2
  St Mawes TR2......95 A6
Seaview Terr TR8......57 E6
Sea View Terr
  Camborne TR14......138 E2
  Carn Towan TR19......96 C7
  Helston TR13......146 B6
  6 Newlyn TR18......143 C1
  Par PL24......60 B6
  Penwithick PL26......59 D7
  Plymouth PL4......149 B4
  Redruth TR15......140 C5
  20 St Ives TR26......141 B5
Seawell Rd EX23......104 F7
Second Ave
  Plymouth, Billacombe PL9..130 A1
  Plymouth, Devonport PL1...128 A2
  Plymouth, Weston Mill PL2 127 E7
Sedley Way PL5......124 D3
Sefton Ave PL4......129 B3
Sefton Cl PL4......149 C4
Segrave Rd PL2......128 B6
Seiners Ct **10** TR6......55 A4
Seleggan Hill Carnkie TR16..80 B7
  Pennance TR16......140 A1
Selkirk Ho **5** PL9......135 F7
Selkirk Pl PL5......124 E2
SELLAN......87 E5
Selsden Cl PL9......136 C6
Sendall's Way PL6......124 F4
Seneschall Pk TR13......146 D8
SENNEN......96 B6
Sennen Cl PL11......126 F4
SENNEN COVE......96 B7
Sennen Cty Prim Sch TR19 86 E1
Sennen Hts TR19......96 B7
Sennen Pl PL2......127 E5
Sentry Cl PL27......32 C6
Sergeants Hill TR4......68 F3
Serpell Cl PL6......124 E6
Serpells Mdw PL15......17 F1
Serpens Vale **1** PL9......136 E7
Sethnoe Way TR13......91 A3
Seton Gdns TR14......138 B4
Setons The **8** TR14......138 F7
Seven Stars La PL5......124 C6
Seven Trees Ct PL4......149 B4
Severn Pl PL3......129 C5
Sewell Ct PL3......128 E5
SEWORGAN......92 C6
Seymour Ave Newquay TR7 110 C6
  Plymouth PL4......149 B4
Seymour Cl TR3......69 C3
Seymour Dr PL3......128 F5
Seymour Mews PL4......149 C4
Seymour Pk PL3......129 A5
Seymour Pl PL1......148 A4
Seymour Rd
  Plymouth, Mannamead PL3..128 F5
  Plymouth Plympton PL7....130 C6
Seymour St PL4......149 A3

Shakespeare Prim Sch
  PL5......124 B2
Shakespeare Rd PL5......124 C2
Shaldon Cres PL5......124 B3
Shallowford Cl PL6......129 C8
Shallowford Rd PL6......129 C8
Shapleys Gdns PL9......136 A5
Shapters Rd PL4......149 C2
Shapters Way PL4......135 B8
Sharaman Cl PL25......115 A5
Sharlands Rd EX23......7 B6
Sharon Way PL6......125 A5
Sharpitor Gdns PL2......128 A7
Sharpitor Row PL20......42 E4
Sharrose Rd PL9......135 B5
Shaw Way PL9......135 A7
Shearwater Dr **11** EX23....7 B8
Shearwood Cl PL7......130 C6
Sheep Fair Mdw **14** PL17...39 F4
Sheepsbor Rd PL6......125 D1
SHEFFIELD......97 F7
Sheila's Ct TR26......141 D1
Shelburne Ct TR11......144 F3
Shelburne Rd TR11......144 F3
Shell Cl PL25......125 E1
Shellduck Cl **5** EX23......7 B8
Shelley Ave PL19......147 D5
Shelley Rd PL25......115 A4
Shelley Way PL5......123 D1
Shepherds Hill PL30......34 C5
Shepherds La PL4......149 B2
Sherborne Cl PL9......136 C6
Sherford Cres
  Plymouth, Elburton PL9.....136 C7
  Plymouth, West Park PL5...124 A3
Sherford Rd PL9......136 D7
Sherford Wlk PL9......136 F2
Sheridan Rd PL5......124 C1
Sherrell Pk PL20......41 B1
Sherril Cl PL7......135 F4
Sherwell La PL4......149 A4
Sherwood Dr PL31......109 C5
SHEVIOCK......65 B6
Sheviock La PL11......65 B5
Shilla Pk PL32......24 A8
Shilson Terr **7** PL15......106 C5
Shipbuilder Cl PL26......73 C4
Shipley Wlk PL6......125 A1
Shippen Wlk **5** PL25......114 F2
Ships & Castles L Ctr TR11 145 E3
Shirburn Rd PL6......129 B8
Shire Horse Farm & Carriage
  Mus The ★ TR16......79 F5
Shires Way PL6......46 F3
Shirley Gdns PL5......124 C1
Shoemaker's La PL12......122 E2
Shoemakers Row PL13.....63 B7
Shoot Row TR15......140 C5
SHOP Morwenstow......2 D1
  St Merryn......31 E8
Shop Hill **3** TR17......89 C5
Shop La PL30......35 F3
Shop Pk PL14......38 A2
Shoreline TR7......111 B8
Shores La PL27......21 E3
Shore View TR11......145 A1
Short Cotts PL11......127 A3
Short Cross Mews TR4......68 C6
Short Cross Rd TR4......68 C6
Shortlands PL22......8 E5
SHORTLANESEND......69 F6
Shortlanesend Com Prim Sch
  TR4......69 F6
Short Park Rd PL3......128 D5
Short Stone Rd PL30......34 C7
Shortwood Cres PL9......136 A7
Shrewsbury Rd PL5......124 C4
Shrubberies Hill TR13......98 C8
Shuffley TR15......139 E8
Shute Hill Breage TR13......90 F3
  Carharrack TR16......80 E8
  Lostwithiel PL22......112 C2
  Mawnan Smith TR11......93 D3
  Pelynt PL13......62 D5
Shute La Penryn TR10......144 C4
  Pensilva PL14......38 E4
  6 Porthleven TR13......98 B8
Shute Mdw TR10......144 C7
Shute Park Rd PL9......135 F6
SHUTTA......117 C4
Shutta Rd PL13......117 C4
Siding Rd PL4......148 C4
Sidings The Bugle PL26.....47 C2
  Delabole PL33......14 E2
Sidmouth Cotts **9** PL4....128 F4
Sidney Terr **17** TR15......140 C5
Sika Dr TR13......146 D6
Silvanus Jenkin Ave PL14 113 E5
Silver Birch Cl PL6......125 C7
Silver Birch Cres **13** PL3 109 A5
Silver Ct **1** TR15......140 B4
Silverdale Ct TR7......110 E6
Silverdale Rd TR11......145 A2
Silver Hill
  Perranarworthal TR3......81 D6
  Trebarvah TR11......92 C5
Silvershell Rd PL29......22 D7
Silvershell View PL29......22 D7
Silver St Bere Ferrers PL20..120 A3
  Saltash PL12......123 A2
Silver Terr PL10......133 A6
Silverton Ct PL23......104 E5
Silverton Rd EX23......104 E5
Silver Way TR3......69 C3
SILVERWELL......68 F7

Simms Terr PL18 . . . . **41** A6
Simon Cl PL9 . . . . **135** E6
Simpsons Ct **30** TR18 . . . . **143** E5
Sina Hill PL30 . . . . **36** B1
Singlerose Rd PL26 . . . . **59** C7
Sinns Common TR16 . . . . . . **68** B4
Sir James Smith's Com Sch
PL32 . . . . **105** C4
Sir John Hunt Com Sports Coll
PL5 . . . . **124** D4
Sir Robert Geffery's CE Prim
Sch PL12 . . . . **53** C3
Sir Williams Morles
Almshouses PL12 . . . . . . **65** A8
Sisna Park Rd PL6 . . . . **125** E5
SITHNEY **91** B3
SITHNEY COMMON **91** C3
Sithney Common Hill TR13 . . **91** C2
Sithney Com Prim Sch
TR13 . . . . **91** B5
SITHNEY GREEN **91** C4
Sithney Old Hill
Helston TR13 . . . . **146** A6
St Elvan TR13 . . . . **91** C2
Sithney St PL5 . . . . **123** C1
Six O Clock La PL7 . . . . **130** E3
Six Turnings TR11 . . . . **82** A2
Skardale Gdns PL6 . . . . **129** D8
Skardon Pl PL4 . . . . **149** A4
Skerries Rd PL6 . . . . **124** F7
Skewes Rd PL30 . . . . **46** E8
Skidden Hill **18** TR26 . . . . . **141** B5
Skimmel Hill TR20 . . . . **87** E5
Skinnard La PL18 . . . . **40** F5
SKINNERS BOTTOM **68** D5
Skitches Cnr EX23 . . . . **4** D1
Skitta Cl PL17 . . . . **39** F5
Skyburriowe Burnoon TR12 **100** A5
Trevassack TR12 . . . . **99** D5
Trevassack TR12 . . . . **100** A5
Skyburriowe La TR12 . . . . . . **99** C6
Skyburriowe Hill TR12 . . . . . **99** C5
Skylark Rise Plymouth PL6 . **125** E8
Tavistock PL19 . . . . **147** D1
Slade Cl PL9 . . . . **136** A5
Slade Park Rd PL14 . . . . **38** E5
SLADESBRIDGE **34** A6
Slades La **2** TR10 . . . . **144** C7
Slades Rd PL25 . . . . **114** E5
Slate Ave **3** PL14 . . . . **113** D8
Slate Cl PL33 . . . . **14** D2
Slate La PL1 . . . . **148** A2
Slatelands Cl PL7 . . . . **131** B3
SLAUGHTERBRIDGE **105** D7
Slemans La Milland PL30 . . . **36** A4
Trezance PL30 . . . . **35** F4
Slipway PL27 . . . . **21** D2
Slipway Quay PL12 . . . . **119** B2
Smallack Cl PL6 . . . . **124** F2
Smallack Dr PL6 . . . . **124** F2
Smallridge Cl PL9 . . . . **135** F5
Smallridge La EX23 . . . . **4** F1
Small Side **8** TR27 . . . . . . **142** D6
Smeaton Sq PL3 . . . . **129** D6
Smeaton's Twr ★ PL1 . . . . . **148** C1
Smithfield Ct TR8 . . . . **111** B3
Smithfield Dr PL12 . . . . **122** B3
Smithick Hill TR11 . . . . **145** B4
Smiths Way PL12 . . . . **122** B3
Smithy Cl PL12 . . . . **122** C4
Smithy Ct PL32 . . . . **105** D3
Smithy La TR3 . . . . **81** F7
Smugglers Ct **2** TR18 . . . . **143** D6
Smugglers Row **8** TR11 . . **145** B5
Snell Dr PL12 . . . . **122** B3
Snowdrop Cres PL15 . . . . . . **106** E4
Snow Hill Lanlivery PL30 . . . **48** C2
Trelill PL30 . . . . **23** C5
Snow's Pas TR11 . . . . **145** B4
Soap St Ferryport PL1 . . . . . **134** C8
Millbay PL1 . . . . **148** A2
Socotra Dr **7** PL25 . . . . **59** A3
Solar Row **6** TR1 . . . . **137** D5
Soldon Cl PL28 . . . . **107** C4
Somer Ct TR11 . . . . **145** B4
Somerset Cotts **10** PL3 . . . **128** A4
Somerset Pl PL3 . . . . **128** A4
Somerset Place La **11** PL3 **128** A4
Somerville Rd TR6 . . . . **55** A4
Sona Merg Cl TR18 . . . . **143** C7
Sonnet Cl PL5 . . . . **124** C2
Sopers Hill PL6 . . . . **121** A2
Soper's Hill PL5 . . . . **120** E1
Sorrell St **3** TR27 . . . . **142** E6
Sortridge Cl **8** PL19 . . . . . **147** B7
Sourton Sq **8** PL9 . . . . **129** D1
South Albany Rd TR1 . . . . . **140** C3
Southbourne Cl PL26 . . . . . . **58** E6
Southbourne Rd PL25 . . . . . **114** E2
South Calvadnack TR16 . . . . **80** B2
South Carn Brea
Bosleake TR16 . . . . **67** F1
Carnkie TR16 . . . . **80** A7
Carnkie TR16 . . . . **139** F3
Pennance TR16 . . . . **140** A1
Southcliff TR11 . . . . **145** C2
South Cliff **18** TR19 . . . . . . **88** C1
South Coombe La PL17 . . . . **39** F8
SOUTHCOTT **11** A6
Southcott Mdws EX23 . . . . . **11** A6
South Crofty Way TR15 . . . **139** A5
SOUTHDOWN **133** B6
Southdown Cl PL26 . . . . **58** E1
Southdown Cotts PL10 . . . **133** B6

Southdown Quay PL10 . . . . **133** B6
Southdown Rd
Millbrook PL10 . . . . **133** A6
Sticker PL26 . . . . **58** E1
South Down Rd PL2 . . . . . . **128** B6
South Downs TR15 . . . . **140** D2
Southdown Terr PL10 . . . . . **133** A6
South Dr Redruth TR15 . . . . **140** D2
South Tehidy TR14 . . . . . . **138** E8
Southella Rd PL20 . . . . **42** D2
Southern Cl PL2 . . . . **127** F7
Southernhaye **21** PL15 . . . **106** C5
Southern Rd **81** PL17 . . . . . **39** F4
Southern Terr PL4 . . . . **128** F4
Southernway PL9 . . . . **136** A8
Southern Way PL27 . . . . . . **108** C5
Southfield PL12 . . . . **122** C3
Southfield Rd EX23 . . . . . . **104** E5
Southfields EX22 . . . . **8** A5
Southfields Pl **3** TR26 . . . . **141** A5
Southgate Ave PL9 . . . . **135** E4
Southgate Cl PL9 . . . . **135** E4
Southgate Pl **4** PL15 . . . . . **106** C5
Southgate St
Launceston PL15 . . . . **106** C5
Redruth TR15 . . . . **140** C3
South Harbour TR10 . . . . . **144** D7
SOUTH HILL **39** C7
South Hill
Plymouth, Hooe PL9 . . . . . **135** C5
Plymouth, Stoke PL1 . . . . . **128** A3
South Hill Rd PL17 . . . . **39** E5
SOUTH HOLE **2** D7
Southlea Terr TR3 . . . . **80** F3
Southleigh Ho **15** TR1 . . . **137** C4
Southleigh Mews **14** TR1 . **137** C4
South Milton St PL4 . . . . . . **149** C2
South Par **33** TR18 . . . . . . **143** E5
South Park Cl TR15 . . . . . . **140** A4
Southpark Rd PL24 . . . . **60** C5
SOUTH PETHERWIN **27** E8
South Petherwin Prim Sch
PL15 . . . . **27** E8
SOUTH PILL **122** C3
South Pk Jacobstow EX23 . . **11** A6
Redruth TR15 . . . . **139** F6
16 St Columb Major TR9 . . . **45** E6
South Pl TR19 . . . . **86** E4
South Place Folly **5** PL18 **143** E4
South Place Gdns TR19 . . . . **86** E6
South Quay PL28 . . . . **107** D5
South Quay Hill TR7 . . . . . **110** D6
South Rd Goldsithney TR20 . **89** C5
Stithians TR3 . . . . **80** F3
South Roskear Terr TR14 . . **138** F4
Southside Ope **14** PL1 . . . **149** A2
Southside St PL1 . . . . **149** A2
South St Fowey PL23 . . . . . **116** C4
Grampound Road TR2 . . . . **57** E1
Lostwithiel PL22 . . . . **112** C2
St Austell PL25 . . . . **114** C3
SOUTH TEHIDY **138** E7
South Terr Camborne TR14 . **138** D2
12 Penzance TR18 . . . . . . **143** E4
South Towan TR4 . . . . **68** A6
Southview PL10 . . . . **133** A6
South View
9 Horrabridge PL20 . . . . . **42** C4
Liskeard PL14 . . . . **113** D7
Penryn TR10 . . . . **144** C8
Plymouth, Crownhill PL5 . . **124** E2
Plymouth, Elburton PL9 . . **136** B6
Porthleven TR13 . . . . **91** A1
South View Cl PL7 . . . . **130** D7
Southview Dr PL31 . . . . **109** E5
South View Parc TR4 . . . . . . **68** A6
South View Pk PL7 . . . . **130** D7
Southview Rd **15** PL24 . . . . **60** B4
Southview Terr **8** TR19 . . . **88** C1
South View Terr
Nancegollan TR13 . . . . **91** B7
Plymouth PL4 . . . . **149** C3
SOUTHWAY **124** F6
Southway PL28 . . . . **20** F2
South Way TR9 . . . . **111** F3
Southway Dr PL6 . . . . **124** E6
Southway La
Plymouth, Southway PL6 . . **125** B6
Plymouth, Tamerton Foliot
PL6 . . . . **124** C6
Southwell Rd PL6 . . . . **124** E1
SOUTH WHEATLEY **11** F3
Sovereign Ct PL7 . . . . **130** C5
Sowton Rd PL20 . . . . **121** D8
Spargo Ct TR10 . . . . **93** C8
Spargo's La TR1 . . . . **137** E5
Sparkatown La PL20 . . . . . . **42** E3
SPARKWELL **131** F8
Spar La TR15 . . . . **67** D4
Sparnock Grove TR1 . . . . . . **69** E3
SPARNON **96** F5
Sparnon Cl Redruth TR15 . . **140** C4
St Austell PL25 . . . . **114** B4
Sparnon Cross TR13 . . . . . . **90** F5
Sparnon Ct TR15 . . . . **140** C4
SPARNON GATE **67** F4
Sparnon Gate TR16 . . . . **67** F4
Sparnon Hill **1** TR15 . . . . **140** C4
Sparnon Terr **2** TR15 . . . . **140** C4
Sparrow Cl **1** TR27 . . . . . . **142** E6
Sparry La TR16 . . . . **80** F8
Spaven Mor TR14 . . . . **138** F5
Speares The PL12 . . . . **122** B2
Spear's Terr TR11 . . . . **144** F1
Speech La TR3 . . . . **81** C4
Speedwell Cl Bude EX23 . . . **104** F5
Millbrook PL10 . . . . **132** F5

Speedwell Cres PL6 . . . . . . **129** B7
Speedwell Wlk PL6 . . . . . . **129** B7
Spencer Gdns PL12 . . . . . . **122** F1
Spencer Rd PL9 . . . . **135** E8
Spernen Cl TR26 . . . . **141** C2
Spernen Wyn Rd TR11 . . . . **145** B2
Spicers La **11** EX23 . . . . **4** E1
Spindrift TR8 . . . . **44** C6
Spinnaker Dr TR2 . . . . **95** A6
Spinnaker Quay PL7 . . . . . **134** F7
Spinney The PL7 . . . . **131** A4
Spire Cl PL3 . . . . **129** B5
Spire Hill Pk PL12 . . . . **122** C2
Spires The TR1 . . . . **137** C6
Spitfire Row PL27 . . . . **31** F3
Splash Pool EX23 . . . . **104** F5
SPLATT Rock. **21** E3
Warbstow Cross **17** B7
Sportmans Cl PL15 . . . . **28** C4
Sportmans PL32 . . . . **105** C3
Sportmans Rd PL32 . . . . . . **105** C3
Sprey Rd **2** PL31 . . . . **109** A4
SPRIDDLESTONE **136** C4
Springfield Horrabridge PL20 **42** C4
Portscatho TR2 . . . . **83** B2
12 Yelverton PL20 . . . . . . **42** C4
Springfield Ave PL9 . . . . . . **136** B6
Springfield Bsns Pk PL15 . . **18** E2
Springfield Cl Dobwalls PL14 **50** E7
Lostwithiel PL22 . . . . **112** C2
Phillack TR27 . . . . **142** D7
Plymouth PL9 . . . . **136** B7
Polgooth PL26 . . . . **59** A1
St Austell PL25 . . . . **114** F5
Springfield Dr PL3 . . . . **128** A4
Springfield Gate PL13 . . . . **117** D5
Springfield La PL9 . . . . **136** B7
Springfield Pk
Barripper TR14 . . . . **79** B5
Mylor Bridge TR11 . . . . . . **82** A3
Widegates PL13 . . . . **63** E7
Springfield Pl **15** TR9 . . . . . **45** E6
Springfield Rd
Falmouth TR11 . . . . **144** E5
Goldsithney TR20 . . . . **89** C5
Liskeard PL14 . . . . **113** E6
Looe PL13 . . . . **117** D5
Newquay TR7 . . . . **110** F6
Plymouth PL9 . . . . **136** B6
Springfield Rise PL9 . . . . . **136** B7
Springfields PL26 . . . . **47** C2
Springfields Fun Pk & Pony
Ctr ★ TR9 . . . . **45** E4
Springfield Way Roche PL26 **46** F3
St Day TR16 . . . . **68** D1
Threemilestone TR3 . . . . . . **69** C3
Springhill PL2 . . . . **128** C8
Spring Hill PL19 . . . . **147** B5
Springhill Gn PL2 . . . . **128** C8
Spring Pk PL6 . . . . **125** E7
Springwell View PL31 . . . . **109** F5
Springwood Cl PL7 . . . . . . **131** A3
Spurway Rd PL14 . . . . **113** D5
Square The
16 Bere Alston PL20 . . . . . **41** B1
Cawsand PL10 . . . . **133** A1
2 Chacewater TR4 . . . . . . **69** A3
Grampound Road TR2 . . . . **57** E1
Gunnislake, St Ann's Chapel
PL18 . . . . **40** E5
3 Kilkhampton EX23 . . . . . **5** A6
Landrake PL12 . . . . **53** C3
Lizard TR12 . . . . **102** F2
Ludgvan TR20 . . . . **89** A8
Manaccan TR12 . . . . **101** A7
Marazion TR17 . . . . **89** B5
7 Pendeen TR19 . . . . **75** A1
Penryn TR10 . . . . **144** D7
Pentewan PL26 . . . . **73** C6
Plymouth, Stonehouse PL1 . **128** A2
Portreath TR16 . . . . **67** C4
Portscatho TR2 . . . . **83** B2
Praze-an-Beeble TR14 . . . . **79** B2
Probus TR2 . . . . **71** C6
Redruth TR16 . . . . **80** B5
St Keverne TR12 . . . . **101** D4
3 St Mawes TR2 . . . . **95** A6
St Stephen PL26 . . . . **58** B4
St Teath PL30 . . . . **23** E7
Saltash PL12 . . . . **122** C3
Tregony TR2 . . . . **71** F3
Veryan TR2 . . . . **83** F6
Week St Mary EX22 . . . . . . **11** E8
Squire La TR16 . . . . **80** F8
Squires La TR13 . . . . **91** C2
Stable Cotts PL7 . . . . **130** F5
Stable Ct PL27 . . . . **108** C6
Stable Hobba TR20 . . . . . . **142** A6
Stable Hobba Ind Est TR18 **143** B3
Stables The TR14 . . . . **78** B4
STADDISCOMBE **135** F3
Staddiscombe Rd PL9 . . . . **135** F4
Staddon Cres PL9 . . . . **135** E6
Staddon Gn PL9 . . . . **135** D6
Staddon La PL9 . . . . **135** E4
Staddon Park Rd PL9 . . . . . **135** E6
Staddon Terrace La PL1 . . . **148** B4
Stafford Cl PL19 . . . . **111** D6
Staggy La TR3 . . . . **81** F7
Stag La
Plymouth, Elburton PL9 . . **136** B8
Plymouth, Plympton PL7 . . **135** A6
Stamford Cl PL9 . . . . **135** A6
Stamford Fort Cotts PL9 . . **135** A6
Stamford Hill EX23 . . . . **4** D1
Stamford La PL9 . . . . **135** A6
Stamps Hill Fraddon PL26 . . **57** F8

Stamps Hill continued
Indian Queens TR9 . . . . **45** F1
Stamps La TR15 . . . . **139** D6
Stamps The PL17 . . . . **40** D5
Stanborough Cross PL9. . . . **136** C7
Stanborough Rd PL9. . . . . . **136** B7
Stanbury Ave PL6. . . . . **124** F1
Stanbury Cl PL15 . . . . **13** F1
Stanbury Cross EX23 . . . . . . **2** C1
Stanbury Hill PL15. . . . . **27** B6
Stancombe La PL15. . . . . . . **12** B2
Standarhay Cl PL9 . . . . **136** C7
Standarhay Villas PL9 . . . . **136** C7
Stanford Cl **5** TR18. . . . . . **143** D5
Stanford Mews TR9. . . . . . . **45** E6
Stanford Terr TR18 . . . . . . **143** D5
Stangray Ave PL4. . . . . **128** D4
Stanharver Cl TR7 . . . . **111** E6
Stanhope Rd PL5 . . . . **123** C1
Stanley Ct **4** PL31 . . . . . . **109** D5
Stanley Pl PL4. . . . . **129** B2
Stanley Terr **1** TR15. . . . . **140** B5
Stanley Way PL15 . . . . **140** C6
Stannary Bridge Rd PL19 . . **147** D6
Stannary La PL7 . . . . **130** C5
Stannary Rd Pengegon TR14 **138** F3
Stenalees PL26 . . . . **59** C8
Stantons Row PL14 . . . . **38** A3
Stanways Rd TR7 . . . . **111** D7
Staple Cl PL6. . . . . **121** C1
Stapleford Gdns PL5. . . . . . **123** F5
Stapleton Rd EX23 . . . . **104** F4
Star Pk PL18. . . . . **41** A6
START **77** E3
Statham Rd PL31 . . . . **109** D4
Station App
3 Newquay TR7 . . . . **110** F6
3 St Columb Road TR9 . . . **45** E2
St Erth TR27 . . . . **77** E2
Station Hill Badharlick PL15 . **17** F5
Hayle TR27 . . . . **142** B5
Lelant TR26 . . . . **77** E4
Praze-an-Beeble TR14 . . . . **79** B2
Redruth TR15 . . . . **140** B4
Station La PL18 . . . . **41** A3
Station Par TR7 . . . . **110** F6
Station Rd
20 Bere Alston PL20 . . . . . **41** B1
Bere Ferrers PL20 . . . . . . **119** E3
Bugle PL26 . . . . **47** C2
Camborne TR15 . . . . **139** C5
Carnhell Green TR14 . . . . . **78** F4
Chacewater TR4 . . . . **68** F4
Fowey PL23 . . . . **116** D5
Grampound Road TR2 . . . . **57** E1
Gunnislake PL18 . . . . **40** F6
Helston TR13 . . . . **146** C7
Horrabridge PL20 . . . . **42** C4
Kelly Bray PL17 . . . . **39** F6
Launceston PL15 . . . . **106** C6
Liskeard PL14 . . . . **113** B4
Looe PL13 . . . . **117** C4
Marazion TR17 . . . . **89** A6
Mary Tavy PL19 . . . . **30** F5
North Brentor PL19 . . . . . . **30** E8
Padstow PL28 . . . . **107** D5
Par PL24 . . . . **60** C5
Penryn TR10 . . . . **144** B8
Penzance TR18 . . . . **143** F5
Perranarworthal TR3. . . . . . **81** E6
Perranporth TR6 . . . . **55** B5
Plymouth, Elburton PL9 . . **136** C7
Plymouth, Keyham PL2 . . . **127** E5
Plymouth, Plympton PL7 . . **130** E5
Plymouth, Tamerton Foliot
PL5 . . . . **124** A6
Redruth TR15 . . . . **140** C5
St Columb Major TR9 . . . . . **45** E5
St Mabyn PL30 . . . . **34** C8
St Newlyn East TR8 . . . . . . **56** B7
Saltash PL12 . . . . **123** A2
Truro TR1 . . . . **137** B4
Yelverton PL20 . . . . **42** D2
Station View PL19 . . . . **30** E8
Station Yd **6** PL31 . . . . . . **109** D4
Steamers Hill TR27 . . . . **78** C5
Steamers Mdw TR27 . . . . . . **78** C5
Steeple Cl Plymouth PL9. . . **135** F4
St Ives TR26 . . . . **141** B4
Steeple La TR26 . . . . **141** B3
Steeple View Ct TR26 . . . . **141** C1
Steeple Woodland Nature
Reserve ★ TR26 . . . . **141** B3
Steer Park Rd PL7 . . . . **131** C5
Steer Point Cotts PL8. . . . . **136** F2
Steer Point Rd PL8 . . . . **136** F3
Stefan Cl PL9 . . . . **135** B5
STENALEES **59** B8
Stenalees Hill PL26 . . . . **59** C7
Stenhill Hill PL15 . . . . **18** C8
Stenlake Pl PL4 . . . . **129** B2
Stenlake Terr PL4 . . . . **129** B2
STENNACK **79** D4
Stennack Gdns **14** TR26 . . **141** A5
Stennack Parc TR19 . . . . . . **86** F8
Stennack Rd PL25 . . . . **115** B4
Stennack The TR26 . . . . . . **141** B5
Stentaway Cl PL9 . . . . **135** F8
Stentaway Dr PL9 . . . . **136** A8
Stentaway Rd PL9 . . . . **135** F8
STEPASIDE **58** B5
Stephens Rd PL14 . . . . **113** E7
Stephney Cl TR11 . . . . **144** D3
Steppy Downs Rd TR27 . . . . **78** A1
Sterts Theatre ★ PL14 . . . . . **38** D7
Stewart Ct **2** TR11 . . . . . . **144** F1
Stewarts Rd Kiltleigh EX23 . . **7** D2

Stewarts Rd continued
Week St Mary EX22 . . . . . . **11** E8
STIBB **4** D5
STICKER **58** E1
Stiles The TR8 . . . . **56** B7
Stillman Ct **7** PL4. . . . . . . **149** A2
Stillman St PL4. . . . . **149** A4
Stippy Stappy **11** TR5 . . . . **54** D1
Stirling Cl PL5 . . . . **123** C1
Stirling Rd PL5 . . . . **123** C1
STITHIANS **80** F3
Stithians Com Prim Sch
TR3. . . . . **80** F4
Stithians Row TR16 . . . . **80** B5
Stockadon Farm Barns
PL12 . . . . **118** B4
Stocks La PL30 . . . . **24** A5
Stoggy La PL7 . . . . **131** A6
STOKE **128** A3
Stoke Climsland **28** E1
Stoke Climsland Sch PL17 . . **28** D1
Stoke Damerel Bsns Ctr **9**
PL3. . . . . **128** A4
Stoke Damerel Com Coll
PL3. . . . . **128** A4
Stoke Damerel Prim Sch
PL1. . . . . **128** A3
Stoke Hill PL17. . . . . **28** D1
Stoke Hill La PL20 . . . . **42** B2
Stoke Rd Bray Shop PL17 . . . **28** A1
Kelly Bray PL17 . . . . **39** E6
Linkinhorne PL17. . . . . **39** A8
Plymouth PL1. . . . . **148** A3
Stokesay Ave PL6. . . . . **125** A5
Stokes La PL15 . . . . **149** A2
Stokes Rd TR1. . . . . **137** C5
Stoke Terr PL17 . . . . **39** E6
Stokingway Cl PL9 . . . . **135** E5
Stonebarton Cl PL7. . . . . . . **130** C6
Stonebarton Rd PL7 . . . . . . **130** C6
Stone Chair La TR19 . . . . . . **96** B7
Stone Cross PL16. . . . . **19** F5
Stonehall Flats PL1. . . . . . . **128** A1
Stone Hill EX23. . . . . **4** E2
STONEHOUSE **128** A1
Stonehouse Bridge PL1. . . . **128** A1
Stonehouse St PL1 . . . . **148** A2
Stonerock Flats PL13 . . . . . **117** C1
Stones Ct **30** TR26 . . . . . . **141** B4
Stonewood Ct **4** TR9 . . . . . **45** E6
Stoney Hill PL25 . . . . **59** A4
Stoney La
3 Goonhavern TR4 . . . . . . **55** F4
Illand PL15 . . . . **27** C6
Polgooth PL26 . . . . **59** A1
St Austell PL25. . . . . **114** C4
Stoney Lands PL12 . . . . **53** C3
Stony La Bodmin PL31. . . . . **34** D1
Gunnislake PL18 . . . . **40** F5
Stopford Pl PL1 . . . . **127** F3
STOPTIDE. **21** E2
Stott Cl PL3. . . . . **129** D5
Stour Cl PL3. . . . . **129** D6
STOURSCOMBE. **106** F4
Stourscombe PL15 . . . . **106** F3
Stourscombe Wood PL15 . . **106** F4
Stowe Gdns PL5 . . . . **124** B2
STOWFORD **5** E8
Stowford Cl PL20. . . . . **42** E3
Stowford Cross EX22 . . . . . . **5** F8
Stracey Rd TR11 . . . . **145** B2
Strafford Cl EX23 . . . . **104** C3
Strand TR18 . . . . **143** C2
Strand Sh Ctr The EX23 . . . **104** D5
Strand St Padstow PL28 . . . **107** D5
Plymouth PL1. . . . . **134** A8
Strand The Bude EX23 . . . . **104** D5
Falmouth TR11 . . . . **145** C2
Padstow PL28 . . . . **107** D5
Strangways Terr TR1 . . . . . **137** D3
Strangways Villas TR1 . . . . **137** D3
STRATTON **4** E1
Stratton Hospl EX23 . . . . **4** D1
Stratton Pl TR11 . . . . **145** A6
Stratton Prim Sch EX23 . . . . **4** D1
Stratton Rd Bude EX23 . . . **104** F4
Stratton EX23 . . . . **4** D1
Stratton Ter TR11 . . . . **94** C6
Stratton Terr
Falmouth TR11 . . . . **145** A6
Flushing TR11 . . . . **145** A6
Truro TR7 . . . . **137** B4
Stratton Wlk PL2 . . . . **128** D8
Strawberry Cl TR15 . . . . . . **140** B6
Strawberry Cres TR15 . . . . **140** B6
Strawberry Fields
Crowlas TR20 . . . . **89** D4
Mitchell TR8 . . . . **56** F5
Redruth TR11 . . . . **140** E1
Strawberry Gdns TR16 . . . . **140** E6
Strawberry La Hayle TR27 . . **142** D4
Lelant TR26 . . . . **77** E4
Redruth TR15 . . . . **140** B6
Stray Park Ct TR14. . . . . . . **138** F2
Stray Park Rd TR14 . . . . . . **138** E2
Stray Park Way TR14 . . . . . **138** F2
Street-an-Garrow **17**
TR26 . . . . **141** B5
Street-an-Pol **3** TR26. . . . **141** B5
Stret Caradoc TR7 . . . . **110** D5
Stret Constantine TR7 . . . . **110** C5
Stret Dor Wartha **3** TR7 . . **111** D5
Stret Euther Penndragon **1**
TR7 . . . . **111** D5
Stret Goryan
Trencreek TR8. . . . . **111** D5
5 Trencreek TR8 . . . . **111** D5
Stret Grifles TR7 . . . . **111** E5

Stret Kosti Veur Woles
  TR7 . . . . .111 D6
Stret Lugan TR7 . . . . .111 E5
Stret Myghtern Arthur
  TR8 . . . . .111 D5
Stret Rosemelin TR1 . . . .137 F6
Stret Trystan TR7 . . . . . . .111 E5
Stretyn 5 PL6 . . . . .81 F7
Strickland Cotts 6 TR18 . .143 C2
Stringers Hill TR20 . . . . . .88 A5
Strode Rd PL7 . . . . .130 F6
Stroma Cl PL6 . . . . .124 F7
Stroud Park Rd PL2 . . . . .128 C2
Stuart House Arts & Heritage
  Ctr ★ PL14 . . . . .113 C5
Stuart Rd PL3 . . . . .148 A4
Stuart Road Prim Sch PL1 148 A4
Stuarts Way PL12 . . . . . . .53 E5
Stucley Rd EX23 . . . . .4 D1
Sturdee Rd PL2 . . . . .128 A5
Stursdon Cross EX23 . . . . .5 A8
Sturta La PL30 . . . . .48 D4
Sugar Mill Bsns Pk PL9 . .129 C1
SUMMERCOURT 57 C7
Summercourt TR10 . . . . .144 D7
Summercourt Prim Sch
  TR8 . . . . .57 C7
Summerfield Cl PL26 . . . . .73 B3
Summerfields PL12 . . . . .122 D1
Summer Gn 2 PL19 . . . . .30 A3
Summerheath TR10 . . . . .81 C1
Summerhill Rd PL15 . . . . .106 A5
Summer La PL13 . . . . .62 D6
Summerlands Cl PL7 . . . .131 C5
Summerlands Gdns PL7 . .131 C5
Summerlane Pk PL13 . . . . .62 D6
Summerleaze Ave EX23 . .104 D7
Summerleaze Cres EX23 .104 D6
Summers Cl PL6 . . . . . . .129 B7
Summers La PL24 . . . . . . .60 B8
Summers St PL22 . . . . . .112 C2
Summerville Cross EX39 . . .3 C6
Suncrest PL14 . . . . .38 A4
Suncrest Est TR9 . . . . . . .45 E1
Sunderland Cl PL9 . . . . . .135 A6
Sunderland Rd PL27 . . . . .31 F3
Sun Girt La PL14 . . . . . . .113 C5
Sunningdale TR1 . . . . . . .137 A4
Sunningdale Rd PL12 . . . .122 C2
Sunnybank 2 TR13 . . . . . .98 C8
Sunny Bank Bodmin PL30 . .48 E8
  Liskeard PL14 . . . . .113 A4
Sunnybanks PL12 . . . . . . .53 E4
Sunny Cnr Goldsithney TR20 . 89 F5
  Truro TR4 . . . . .81 B7
Sunny Corner La TR19 . . . .96 C7
Sunnycroft PL13 . . . . . . .117 C3
Sunny Dene PL5 . . . . . . .123 D1
Sunnyside PL11 . . . . .64 F7
  Carnkie TR13 . . . . .80 D1
  Crantock TR8 . . . . .110 A3
  Menheniot PL14 . . . . . . .51 F5
  Menheniot PL14 . . . . . . .52 B5
  2 Perranporth TR6 . . . . .55 A4
  Portscatho TR2 . . . . .83 B2
  7 Redruth TR15 . . . . . . .140 B4
Sunnyside Mdw PL32 . . . .105 D4
Sunnyside Parc TR15 . . . .139 C8
Sunnyside Rd PL4 . . . . . .129 B2
Sunny Terr TR18 . . . . . . .143 B2
Sunnyvale Cl TR16 . . . . . .67 C6
Sunnyvale Rd TR16 . . . . . .67 D6
Sunrise Hill TR16 . . . . . . .80 E8
Sunrising Est PL13 . . . . . .117 D5
Sunset Dr 8 TR13 . . . . . . .98 C8
Sunset Gdns 9 TR13 . . . . .98 C8
Sun Valley Pk TR9 . . . . . . .45 E6
Sunway Cl PL19 . . . . .147 A6
Sunwell La Antony PL11 . . .65 E4
  St John PL11 . . . . .132 A8
Surf View TR7 . . . . .110 A6
Sussex Pl PL1 . . . . .148 C2
Sussex Rd PL2 . . . . .127 F5
Sussex St PL1 . . . . .148 C2
Sussex Terr 5 PL2 . . . . .127 F5
Sutherland Rd PL4 . . . . . .149 A4
Sutton Ct PL1 . . . . .127 F1
Sutton Mews 22 PL4 . . . .149 A2
Sutton Pl PL4 . . . . .149 B2
Sutton Rd PL4 . . . . .149 B2
Sutton Wharf PL4 . . . . . .149 A2
Swaindale Rd 3 PL3 . . . .128 E6
Swale Cl PL3 . . . . .129 B6
Swallow Cl PL3 . . . . .104 C1
Swallowfield Cl PL24 . . . . .60 D5
Swallows End PL9 . . . . . .135 E8
Swan Cl PL10 . . . . .133 A6
Swan Gdns PL7 . . . . .130 F5
Swanpool Ave TR10 . . . . .144 A8
Swanpool Ct TR11 . . . . . .145 A1
Swanpool Hill TR11 . . . . .145 A2
Swanpool Nature Reserve ★
  TR11 . . . . .145 A2
Swanpool Rd TR11 . . . . .144 F1
Swanpool St TR11 . . . . . .145 C3
Swans Reach 1 TR11 . . . .144 F1
SWANVALE 144 F3
Swanvale Rd TR11 . . . . . .144 F3
Sweet Briar Cres TR7 . . . .111 A4
Sweetshouse Rd PL22 . . . .112 A2
Swift Gdns PL5 . . . . .124 C2
Swinburne Gdns PL5 . . . .124 C1
Swingate Cross EX22 . . . .13 E8
Sycamore Ave
  Plymouth PL4 . . . . .149 C2
  St Austell PL25 . . . . . . .114 E5
  Tavistock PL19 . . . . .147 C2

Sycamore Cl Bodmin PL31 .109 B4
  Polgooth PL26 . . . . .59 A1
  Praze-an-Beeble TR14 . . .79 B2
  Rock PL27 . . . . .21 E3
Sycamore Dr Illogan TR15 .139 D7
  Plymouth PL6 . . . . .125 C7
  Redruth TR15 . . . . .140 D5
  Torpoint PL11 . . . . .127 A3
  Trispen TR4 . . . . .56 D1
Sycamore Gdns TR8 . . . . .57 B7
Sycamore Rd PL12 . . . . . .122 B3
Sycamores The PL25 . . . .114 C4
Sycamore Way PL6 . . . . .125 E6
Sydenham Cross PL19 . . . .29 C2
SYDENHAM DAMEREL 29 D2
Sydney Cl Plymouth PL7 . .130 E4
  St Austell PL25 . . . . . . .114 C3
Sydney Rd Newquay TR7 . .110 D6
  Torpoint PL11 . . . . .127 B3
Sydney St PL1 . . . . .148 B4
Sylvan Cl PL25 . . . . .114 E6
Sylvan Ct PL11 . . . . .128 A3
Sylverton Pl 12 TR18 . . . .143 C7
Symons Cl Blackwater TR4 . .68 E5
  St Austell PL25 . . . . . . .115 A5
Symons Hill TR11 . . . . . .145 A5
Symons Rd PL2 . . . . .122 F2
Symons Row PL14 . . . . . . .37 F3
Symons Terr TR15 . . . . . .140 B5
Syra Cl PL30 . . . . .23 B2

T

Tabernacle St TR1 . . . . . .137 D4
Tackbear Rd EX22, EX23 . . .7 E4
Tailyour Rd PL6 . . . . .124 F2
Talbot Gdns PL5 . . . . . . .127 D7
Talexandra Terr PL15 . . . .106 D5
Talgarrek Wartha 4 TR1 .137 B2
Talgos Cl TR16 . . . . .140 E8
TALLAND 62 F2
Talland Ct 28 TR26 . . . . .141 B5
Talland Hill PL13 . . . . .62 E2
Talland Rd TR26 . . . . . . .141 B5
Talland St PL13 . . . . .62 D1
Tall Ships Cl 2 TR11 . . . .144 F2
Tally Ho 6 TR20 . . . . .88 B7
Talmena Ave PL27 . . . . . .108 A5
TALSKIDDY 45 E8
Talveneth Camborne TR14 .138 F3
  Pendeen TR19 . . . . .75 A1
  Redruth TR15 . . . . .140 C6
Talvenydh Ct PL31 . . . . . .109 D5
Tamar Ave Plymouth PL2 .127 E5
  Tavistock PL19 . . . . .147 D5
Tamar Bridge PL5 . . . . . .123 A2
Tamar Bsns Pk PL15 . . . . .18 E2
Tamar Cl 18 Bere Alston PL20 41 B1
  29 Callington PL17 . . . . .39 F4
Tamar Ho PL1 . . . . .127 E1
Tamarisk Cl PL28 . . . . . . .31 F7
Tamarisk La TR7 . . . . . . .111 A4
Tamar Otter & Wildlife Ctr ★
  PL15 . . . . .18 B8
Tamar Science Pk PL6 . . .125 C4
Tamarside Sp Complex
  PL5 . . . . .123 F2
Tamar St Plymouth PL1 . . .127 E3
  Saltash PL12 . . . . .123 A2
  Torpoint PL11 . . . . .127 C3
Tamar Terr Calstock PL17 . .41 A3
  Horsebridge PL19 . . . . . .29 C1
  Launceston PL15 . . . . . .106 C1
  Saltash PL12 . . . . .123 A3
Tamar Valley Ctr ★ PL18 . .40 F5
Tamar Valley Discovery Trail ★
  PL20 . . . . .41 C1
Tamar Valley Donkey Pk ★
  PL18 . . . . .40 D7
Tamar View
  Launceston PL15 . . . . . .106 D5
  Milton Abbot PL19 . . . . . .29 C6
  St Dominick PL12 . . . . . . .40 D2
Tamar View Ind Est PL12 .122 D5
Tamar Villas PL9 . . . . . . .135 D7
Tamar Way PL18 . . . . .41 A6
Tamar Wharf PL1 . . . . . . .127 D3
Tamblin Ave PL14 . . . . . . .50 E7
Tamerton Ave PL5 . . . . . .123 D1
Tamerton Cl PL5 . . . . . . .124 A6
TAMERTON FOLIOT 124 A6
Tamerton Foliot Rd PL6 . .124 D5
Tamerton Hill EX22 . . . . . .13 A8
Tamerton Rd PL6 . . . . . . .121 B2
Ta Mill Rd PL15 . . . . .16 D4
Tangmere Ave PL5 . . . . . .123 E5
Tangye Cl TR16 . . . . .67 E5
Tangye Rd TR15 . . . . .139 C6
Tanhouse Rd PL22 . . . . . .112 C2
Tanners La TR3 . . . . .81 C6
Tanwood La Bodmin PL31 . .34 E2
  Bodmin PL31 . . . . .109 A6
Tanwood View TR11 . . . . .109 C5
Tanyard La 19 PL17 . . . . . .39 E4
Tapson Dr PL9 . . . . .135 A6
Taranto Rd TR13 . . . . . . .146 D4
Taroveor Rd TR18 . . . . . .143 E6
Taroveor Terr 3 TR18 . . .143 E5
Tarr PL22 . . . . .49 E3
Tarrandean La TR3 . . . . . .81 E6
Tarten Cross PL12 . . . . . . .53 B4
Taunton Ave PL5 . . . . . . .124 B5
Taunton Pl PL5 . . . . .124 B5
Taurus St PL9 . . . . .136 E8
Tavern Barn PL23 . . . . . .116 C5
TAVISTOCK 147 E5

Tavistock Coll PL19 . . . . . .147 A3
Tavistock Community Hospital
  PL19 . . . . .147 B5
Tavistock Com Prim Sch
  PL19 . . . . .147 B4
Tavistock Cross PL20 . . . . .41 C2
Tavistock Mus ★ PL19 . . . .147 C5
Tavistock Pl PL4 . . . . .149 A3
Tavistock Rd Callington PL17 39 F4
  Launceston PL15 . . . . . .106 D5
  Launceston, Stourscombe
    PL15 . . . . .106 E3
  Plymouth PL6 . . . . .125 B5
  Plymouth Manadon PL5 . .124 E1
  Yelverton PL20 . . . . .42 C3
Tavistock St Peter's CE Jun
  Sch PL19 . . . . .147 D5
Tavy Pl PL4 . . . . .128 F4
Tavy Rd Saltash PL12 . . . .123 A3
  Tavistock PL19 . . . . .147 D5
Taw Cl PL3 . . . . .129 D6
Tawna La PL30 . . . . .36 B2
Tayberry Dr TR16 . . . . . .140 F1
Tay Gdns PL3 . . . . .129 D7
Taylor Cl PL12 . . . . .122 C3
Taylor Rd PL12 . . . . .122 C4
Taylor's Cross EX23 . . . . . .5 B7
Taylors La Legonna TR8 . . .44 C2
  Legonna TR8 . . . . .111 C2
Taylor Sq PL19 . . . . .147 B6
Teason Hill Trezance PL30. .35 F4
  Trezance PL30 . . . . .35 F4
Teats Hill Flats PL4 . . . . .149 B1
Teats Hill Rd PL4 . . . . . . .149 B1
Tedder Rd 4 PL26 . . . . . .59 D7
Tees Cl PL3 . . . . .129 C7
Teetotal St TR26 . . . . . . .141 C6
Tehidy Cl TR14 . . . . .138 F7
Tehidy Copse TR14 . . . . . .67 B4
Tehidy Country Park ★
  TR14 . . . . .67 B4
Tehidy Gdns TR14 . . . . . .138 F7
Tehidy Hill TR14 . . . . . . .138 F7
Tehidy Rd Camborne TR14 .138 D4
  Tywardreath PL24 . . . . . .60 D5
Tehidy Terr TR11 . . . . . . .145 A6
Teign Rd PL3 . . . . .129 B6
Telcarne Ct TR27 . . . . .78 D6
Telegraph Hill TR16 . . . . . .68 E1
Telegraph St TR16 . . . . . . .68 D1
Telegraph Wharf PL1 . . . .134 A8
Telephone La PL26 . . . . . .59 C8
Telford Cres PL5 . . . . . . .123 F2
Temeraire Rd PL5 . . . . . .124 D2
TEMPLE 36 B8
Tenacres La PL14 . . . . . . .38 E4
Tenby Rd PL5 . . . . .123 C1
TENCREEK 63 A3
Tencreek Ave TR18 . . . . . .143 E5
Tenderah Ct TR13 . . . . . .146 C7
Tenderah Rd TR13 . . . . . .146 C6
Tennyson Gdns PL5 . . . . .124 B1
Tern Gdns PL7 . . . . .130 F5
Terrace The Chacewater TR4 68 F3
  Crafthole PL11 . . . . .65 B5
  Dobwalls PL14 . . . . .50 D7
  Downderry PL11 . . . . .64 C5
  East Portholland PL26 . . . .84 E5
  Harrowbarrow PL17 . . . . .40 D5
  Penryn TR10 . . . . .144 C7
  Pentewan PL26 . . . . .73 D6
  Port Isaac PL29 . . . . .22 E7
  Portwrinkle PL11 . . . . . . .65 A4
  Rock PL27 . . . . .21 D2
  St Ives TR26 . . . . .141 B5
  Yeolmbridge PL15 . . . . . .18 E6
Terra Nova Gn PL2 . . . . . .128 B5
TERRAS 58 A4
Terras Hill PL22 . . . . .112 C3
Terras Rd PL26 . . . . .58 A4
TETCOTT 13 C7
Tethadene PL30 . . . . .23 E7
Tewedh Pl 4 PL27 . . . . . .21 E3
Tewington Pl PL25 . . . . . .114 C4
Tewkesbury Cl PL2 . . . . . .128 A8
Tewynn Ct TR27 . . . . .142 E8
Teyla Tor Rd TR26 . . . . . .141 D1
Thackeray Gdns PL5 . . . . .124 B1
Thames Gdns PL3 . . . . . .129 D5
Thanckes Cl PL11 . . . . . . .127 A3
Thanckes Dr PL11 . . . . . . .127 A4
The All Saints CE Academy
  PL5 . . . . .124 B1
Theatre Ope PL1 . . . . . . .127 F1
Theatre Royal Plymouth
  PL1 . . . . .148 C2
The Bank PL27 . . . . .71 C6
The Bay Holiday Complex ★
  PL13 . . . . .63 A2
The Beeches PL18 . . . . . . .40 D5
The Bishops CE Prim Sch
  TR7 . . . . .110 F4
The Carn TR14 . . . . .79 D1
The Coach Ho 14 TR10 . . .144 D7
The Crescent PL25 . . . . . .114 E4
The Cross 10 PL14 . . . . . .38 E4
The Drive PL14 . . . . .114 F1
The Glebe 11 PL14 . . . . . .37 F3
The Hayes TR1 . . . . .137 E6
The Level Ponjeravah TR11 .92 F4
  Treviades TR11 . . . . .93 A4
The Lizard TR12 . . . . .102 F3
The Meadow TR3 . . . . . . .81 D5
The Moors TR13 . . . . .98 B8
The Oaks 8 PL15 . . . . . . .27 B7
The Quarry 13 TR2 . . . . . .83 B2
The Quay TR5 . . . . .54 D2
Therlow Rd PL3 . . . . .129 B6

The Roseland Com Coll
  TR2 . . . . .72 A4
The Shrubberies 26 TR13 .98 C8
The Sidings PL25 . . . . . . .114 E3
  Nancegollan TR13 . . . . . .91 B7
The Straight Billacott PL15 .12 C1
  Navarino PL15 . . . . .18 A8
Thetford Gdns PL6 . . . . . .129 D8
The Village PL19 . . . . .29 C6
The Wharf EX23 . . . . .104 D5
Theydon Rd TR11 . . . . . . .144 F3
Third Ave
  Plymouth, Billacombe PL9 .130 A1
  Plymouth, Camels Head PL2 .127 E7
  Plymouth, Stoke PL1 . . . .128 A2
Thirlmere Gdns PL6 . . . . .124 F4
Thistle Cl PL5 . . . . .124 D2
Thomas Bullock Cl PL30 . .48 C2
Thomas Johnson Ct 6
  TR1 . . . . .137 C4
Thomas La PL4 . . . . .149 B4
Thomas St 4 TR13 . . . . . .98 C8
Thomas Terr 5 TR13 . . . . .98 C8
Thornberry Terr TR16 . . . .143 F6
Thornbury Park Ave PL3 . .128 D6
Thornbury Prim Sch PL6 . .125 C4
Thornbury Rd PL6 . . . . . .125 E4
Thorn Cl PL15 . . . . .26 C7
Thorndon Cross EX22 . . . . .8 F5
Thorne Cross EX23 . . . . . . .4 F2
THORNE MOOR 19 F8
Thorney Wlk 1 PL27 . . . .108 C6
Thornhill Rd PL3 . . . . . . .128 E6
Thornhill Way PL3 . . . . . .128 E6
Thorn La PL12 . . . . .122 C3
Thorn Moor Cross PL15 . . .19 F7
Thornpark Rd PL25 . . . . . .114 C5
Thorn Pk PL3 . . . . .128 F5
Thornton Ave PL4 . . . . . .149 B4
Thornton Cl PL26 . . . . . . .46 F3
Thornville Terr PL9 . . . . . .135 C7
Thornwell La PL12 . . . . . . .53 E2
Thornyville Cl PL9 . . . . . .135 C8
Thornyville Dr PL9 . . . . . .135 C8
Thornyville Villas PL9 . . . .135 C8
Three Bridges Specl Sch 1
  TR10 . . . . .144 C8
THREE BURROWS 68 F5
Three Corners Cl TR32 . . . .95 E8
Three Cross TR13 . . . . . . .91 F5
THREE HAMMERS 17 C6
Three Holes Cross PL27. . .34 A8
THREEMILESTONE 69 D4
Threemilestone Ind Est
  TR4 . . . . .69 C3
Threemilestone Ret Pk TR3 69 C4
Threemilestone Sch TR3 . .69 D3
THREEWATERS 34 C1
THURDON 5 D5
Thurlestone Wlk PL6 . . . .129 D8
Tichbarrow Rd
  Davidstow PL15 . . . . . . .16 A6
  Hendra PL32 . . . . .15 F7
Tiddy Brook Rd
  Tavistock PL19 . . . . .147 E2
  Whitchurch PL19 . . . . . .147 E2
Tiddy Cl St Germans PL12 . .65 B8
  Tavistock PL19 . . . . .147 B3
TIDEFORD 52 F2
Tideford Cross La PL12 . . . .52 F3
Tideford Dr Landrake PL12 .53 A2
  St Germans PL12 . . . . . . .65 B8
Tideford Rd PL12 . . . . . . .53 C3
Tidemill Ho TR11 . . . . . . .145 C3
Tides Reach TR7 . . . . . . .111 B7
Tillard Cl PL7 . . . . .131 C5
Tillie St 5 PL17 . . . . .39 E4
Tilly Cl PL9 . . . . .135 F4
Timber Cl PL25 . . . . .114 B4
Tincombe PL12 . . . . .122 C2
Tincroft Rd TR15 . . . . . . .139 B4
Tin Hut La EX23 . . . . .10 E7
Tin La PL4 . . . . .149 A2
Tinners Croft TR8 . . . . . . .56 B7
  Callington PL17 . . . . .39 F5
  New Polzeath PL27 . . . . .21 D6
  16 St Ives TR26 . . . . . . .77 A6
Tinners Dr PL27 . . . . .21 D6
Tinners La PL14 . . . . .36 F3
Tinners Way
  Boslowick TR11 . . . . . . .144 F2
  Callington PL17 . . . . .39 F5
Tinners Wlk TR11 . . . . . . .145 D3
Tinney Dr TR1 . . . . .137 F5
Tinney Hall La PL15 . . . . . .27 B7
Tinside Lido PL1 . . . . .148 C1
TINTAGEL 14 D7
Tintagel Castle ★ PL34 . . .14 B8
Tintagel Cres PL2 . . . . . . .128 C8
Tintagel Hts PL34 . . . . . . .14 D6
Tintagel Old Post Office ★
  PL34 . . . . .14 C7
Tintagel Prim Sch PL34 . . .14 C6
Tintagel Rd PL35 . . . . .9 C1
Tintagel Terr PL29 . . . . . . .22 D7
Tintagel Toy Mus ★ PL34 . .14 C7
Tintagel Visitor Ctr ★ PL34. .14 C7
Tintern Ave PL4 . . . . .149 C2
Tiny Mdws Launceston PL15 .18 E1
  South Petherwin PL15 . . .27 F8
Tipple Cross PL15 . . . . . . .19 C6
Titan Ave 19 PL9 . . . . . . .136 E8
Titchborough Hill PL15 . . .16 A8
Tithe Rd PL7 . . . . .130 B7
TITSON 9 F4
Tiverton Cl PL6 . . . . .125 D8
Toads Hole PL26 . . . . .46 D2
Tobruk Rd PL12 . . . . .122 E3

Toby Way TR7 . . . . .110 D7
Todda Cl PL15 . . . . .25 E3
Toddington Lea PL26 . . . . .58 E5
TODPOOL 68 F2
TOLBOROUGH 25 E4
TOLCARNE Camborne 79 D5
  Newlyn 143 C3
Tolcarne TR16 . . . . .80 E8
Tolcarne Cl PL25 . . . . . . .114 E3
Tolcarne La Tolcarne TR13 . .80 A1
  Tregurrian TR8 . . . . .44 E8
  Trevarrian TR8 . . . . .31 C1
Tolcarne Mews 7 TR7 . . .110 F6
Tolcarne Rd Camborne TR14 79 D5
  Newquay TR7 . . . . .110 F6
  St Day TR16 . . . . .68 D1
  Tolcarne PL15 . . . . .26 F5
Tolcarne St TR14 . . . . . . .138 D2
Tolcarne Terr TR18 . . . . . .143 C3
Tolcrows Ct TR7 . . . . .111 C7
TOLDISH 45 F2
Toldish La TR9 . . . . .45 F2
Tolgarrick Rd TR14 . . . . . .138 F5
Tolgus Illogan TR15 . . . . . .67 F3
  Tolskithy TR15 . . . . .139 F8
Tolgus Hill TR15 . . . . . . .140 A5
TOLGUS MOUNT 139 E8
Tolgus Mount TR15 . . . . . .139 F8
Tolgus Pl TR15 . . . . .140 A6
Tolgus Tin ★ TR16 . . . . . . .67 F5
Tolgus Vean TR15 . . . . . . .140 A5
Tolgus Wartha TR15 . . . . .140 A6
Tollgate Cl PL14 . . . . .113 B4
Tollgate Rd PL31 . . . . .35 B1
Tollox Pl PL3 . . . . .129 B4
Tolponds Rd TR13 . . . . . . .91 A1
Tolroy Rd TR27 . . . . .142 D1
TOLSKITHY 139 E7
Tolskithy La TR15 . . . . . . .139 E6
Tolticken Hill TR16 . . . . . . .67 E6
Toltuff Cres TR18 . . . . . . .143 C4
Toltuff Rd TR18 . . . . .143 C4
TOLVADDON 138 F6
Tolvaddon Reskadinnick TR14 79 D8
  Tolvaddon TR15 . . . . . . .138 F6
Tolvaddon Bsns Pk TR14 .139 A7
TOLVADDON DOWNS 139 A7
Tolvaddon Energy Pk
  TR14 . . . . .138 F7
Tolvaddon Rd TR15 . . . . .139 A5
Tolvan Cross TR12 . . . . . . .92 C2
Tolver Pl TR18 . . . . .143 E6
Tolver Rd TR18 . . . . .143 E6
Tolverth Terr TR20 . . . . . . .88 F6
Tolview Terr TR27 . . . . . . .142 B4
Tom Lyon Rd PL14 . . . . . .113 E5
Tom Nicolls Cl 7 PL14 . . . .38 A3
Tom Putt Mews 6 PL14 . .113 D7
Top Hill TR2 . . . . .57 E1
Top of the Town Ctyd
  PL12 . . . . .122 F2
Top Rd PL11 . . . . .64 C5
Torbridge Cl PL12 . . . . . .122 D2
Tor Bridge High PL6 . . . . .125 D2
Tor Bridge Prim Sch PL6 . .125 D2
Torbridge Rd
  6 Horrabridge PL20 . . . .42 C4
  Plymouth PL7 . . . . .130 E6
Torbryan Cl PL6 . . . . .130 E6
Tor Cl Plymouth, Hartley PL3 128 E7
  Porthleven TR13 . . . . . . .91 B1
Tor Cres PL3 . . . . .128 E7
Torland Rd PL3 . . . . .128 E7
Torleven Rd TR13 . . . . . . .91 B2
TORPOINT 127 C3
Torpoint Com Coll PL11 . .127 A4
Torpoint Nur & Inf Sch
  PL11 . . . . .127 B3
Tor Rd Newquay TR7 . . . . .110 E6
  Plymouth PL3 . . . . .128 E7
Torridge Cl PL7 . . . . .131 A6
Torridge Rd PL7 . . . . .130 F6
Torridge Way PL3 . . . . . . .129 C5
Torr La PL3 . . . . .128 E7
Torr Rd PL3 . . . . .128 D7
Torr View Ave PL3 . . . . . .128 D7
Tors View Cl PL17 . . . . . . .39 F4
Torver Cl PL6 . . . . .125 D2
Tor View Bugle PL26 . . . . .47 C2
  Camelford PL32 . . . . . . .105 C2
  7 Horrabridge PL20 . . . .42 C4
Torwood Cl PL31 . . . . . . .109 D4
Tregadillett PL15 . . . . .18 C2
Tory TR3 . . . . .81 A3
Tory Brook Ave PL7 . . . . .130 E6
Tory Brook Ct PL7 . . . . . .130 E6
Tory Way PL7 . . . . .130 D6
TOSBERRY 3 B8
Tosberry Cross EX39 . . . . . .3 B8
Tothill Ave PL4 . . . . .149 B3
Tothill Rd PL4 . . . . .149 B3
Totnes Cl PL7 . . . . .131 A4
Tottentown La Lampen PL14 .36 F2
  Polventon PL14 . . . . .37 A1
Touch Me Pipes TR12 . . . .101 D3
Tovey Cres PL5 . . . . .124 D2
Towan Blystra Rd TR7 . . . .111 A5
TOWAN CROSS 68 B7
Towan Ct PL28 . . . . .31 E8
Towan Rd Pentewan PL26 . .73 D8
  Porthtowan TR4 . . . . .68 A7
Trevear PL28 . . . . .31 E8

Towans The PL28 . . . . 20 D1
Towans View TR27 . . . . . . 78 D6
TOWEDNACK 76 E5
Towednack Rd TR26 . . . . . 77 A6
Tower Cl Pelynt PL13 . . . . . 62 D6
  Sennen TR19 . . . . 96 B6
Tower Ct PL12 . . . . 122 C2
Towerfield Dr PL6 . . . . . . 125 C8
Tower Hill Looe PL13 . . . . 117 D3
  Wadebridge PL27 . . . . 108 E5
Tower Hill Gdns 12 PL31 . 109 E5
Tower Hill Rd PL15 . . . . . . 13 F1
Tower Mdws TR19 . . . . 97 A6
Tower Park Est TR13 . . . . . 62 D6
Tower Park Rd PL13 . . . . . 62 C6
Tower Pk Fowey PL23 . . . 116 B3
  Lanivet PL30 . . . . 47 E7
  Pelynt PL13 . . . . 62 D6
Tower Rd Newquay TR7 . . 110 D6
  St Erme TR4 . . . . 70 D8
Towers Cl PL6 . . . . 125 F2
Tower St PL15 . . . . 106 C6
Tower View PL12 . . . . 122 D1
Town Arms Pas PL31 . . . . 109 E5
Town End PL31 . . . . 109 C5
Town Farm TR15 . . . . 140 C3
Town Farm Cl 5 PL20 . . . 42 C4
Townfield PL15 . . . . 139 C6
Town Hill TR5 . . . . 54 D1
TOWNLAKE 29 C1
Town Mill Gdns PL19 . . . 147 C6
Town Mills Cl 7 PL15 . . . 106 A7
Town Mills Flats PL15 . . 106 B7
Town Quay TR1 . . . . 137 D4
Townsend Polruan PL23 . 116 D2
  14 Stratton EX23 . . . . 4 E1
TOWNSHEND 90 D7
Townshend Ave PL2 . . . . 127 C5
Townswell Cl PL12 . . . . . . 53 E2
Townswell La PL12 . . . . . . 53 E2
TRABOE 100 E4
Traboe Cross TR12 . . . . . 100 D3
Tracey Ct PL1 . . . . 148 B3
Track Pot Rd PL30 . . . . . . 22 E4
Tradewinds Cl 10 PL31 . 109 A5
Trafalar Fields TR20 . . . . . 88 B7
Trafalgar Pl PL5 . . . . 127 D8
Trafalgar Fields TR20 . . . . 88 B7
Trafalgar Pl 3 PL1 . . . . . 127 F3
Trafalgar Place La PL1 . . 127 F3
Trafalgar Sq TR1 . . . . . . 137 D4
Trafalgar St PL4 . . . . 149 A3
Traine Brake PL9 . . . . . . 136 C1
Traine Rd PL9 . . . . 136 B1
Traly Cl EX23 . . . . 104 F4
TRAMAGENNA 105 A1
Tram Cross La TR16 . . . . 140 D1
Tram La TR16 . . . . 140 E1
Tramway Rd PL6 . . . . . . 125 E7
TRANNACK 91 D5
Trannack Com Prim Sch
  TR13 . . . . 91 E5
Trannack Mill Ind Est TR13 . 91 E5
Trannack Rd TR20 . . . . . . 87 D5
Trannack Terr TR18 . . . . 143 E2
Tranquil La PL31 . . . . 109 C5
Transit Way PL5 . . . . 124 C3
Trasdeves Orch 16 PL17 . . 39 F4
Travers Cl TR11 . . . . 113 A6
Treago Gdns PL6 . . . . . . 125 C8
Treago Rd TR8 . . . . 43 D3
TREAL 103 A6
Trease 3 TR19 . . . . 75 A1
Treassowe Mews TR20 . . 88 F8
Treassowe Rd TR18 . . . . 143 E6
Treassowe Riding TR20 . . 88 F8
TREATH 93 C1
TREATOR 107 A5
Treator Cotts PL28 . . . . . 107 A5
Trebah TR11 . . . . 93 D2
Trebah Gdns ★ TR11 . . . . 93 C2
Treban Rd TR18 . . . . 143 C4
TREBARBER 44 F5
TREBARTHA 27 A4
Trebartha Cl PL17 . . . . . . 39 E3
Trebartha Rd TR1 . . . . . . 137 F5
Trebarthen Terr TR4 . . . . 55 D5
Trebarva Ct TR15 . . . . . . 140 A4
TREBARVAH 89 E4
Trebarvah Cl 1 TR11 . . . . 92 E4
Trebarvah Ct 2 TR11 . . . . 92 E4
Trebarvah La TR11 . . . . . . 92 E4
  3 PL11 . . . . 92 E4
  Rosudgeon TR20 . . . . 89 E4
Trebarvah Rd TR11 . . . . . . 92 E4
Trebarvah Woon TR11 . . . 92 C4
TREBARWITH 14 C5
Trebarwith Cres TR7 . . . 110 E6
Trebarwith Rd PL33 . . . . . 14 D4
TREBEATH 17 F6
Trebeath Ln PL15 . . . . 17 E6
Treberran Gdns TR14 . . . 138 F6
TREBETHERICK 21 D4
Trebost La Trebost TR3 . . 81 A5
  Trembrooath TR16 . . . . 80 F5
Treboul Cross PL12 . . . . . 64 F8
Treboul Way PL12 . . . . . . 65 B8
Trebray Rd PL15 . . . . 16 E1
TREBUDANNON 45 C4
TREBULLETT 28 A5
Treburdon Dr PL26 . . . . . 46 F3
TREBURGETT 23 D6
Treburgie Water PL14 . . . 50 D7
Treburick La PL27 . . . . . . 32 B7
TREBURLEY 28 C4

Treburley Cl PL15 . . . . . . 28 C4
Treburley Ind Est PL15 . . 28 C4
TREBURSYE 31 D5
Trebursye Rd PL15 . . . . . 18 E3
TREBYAN 48 C6
Trebyan Bsns Pk PL30 . . . 48 C6
Trebyhan Parc TR3 . . . . . 80 F3
Treby Rd PL7 . . . . 130 F4
Trecarn Cl PL15 . . . . 106 B5
Trecarne TR11 . . . . 144 E5
Trecarne Cl Polgooth PL26 . 59 A1
  St Austell PL25 . . . . 115 B5
Trecarne La 10 PL14 . . . . 38 A3
Trecarne View PL14 . . . . . 37 F3
Trecarrack Rd TR14 . . . . 138 F3
Trecarrell Launceston PL15 106 C4
  1 Scarne PL25 . . . . 106 D4
Trecerus Ind Est PL28 . . 107 B4
Treclago View PL32 . . . . 105 C2
Trecombe TR11 . . . . 93 C4
TRECROGO 27 E7
Treculliacks TR11 . . . . 92 D6
Tredanek Cl PL31 . . . . . . 109 B5
Tredannick Hill PL27 . . . . 34 A6
Tredarrup Cross PL15 . . . . 11 A1
Tredarvah Dr TR18 . . . . . 143 C5
Tredarvah Rd TR18 . . . . . 143 C5
TREDAVOE 143 A4
Tredavoe La TR18 . . . . . . 143 B1
Tredenham Cl 4 PL24 . . . 60 C4
Tredenham Rd TR2 . . . . . . 95 B6
TREDETHY 34 D6
Tredethy Hill PL30 . . . . . . 34 E6
Tredethy Rd PL30 . . . . . . 34 F6
TREDINNICK Looe 63 A8
  Penzance 76 A1
  St Issey 32 D5
Tredinnick Cotts TR20 . . . 76 A1
Tredinnick La PL12 . . . . . . 53 B2
Tredinnick Rd PL27 . . . . . 32 E4
Tredinnick Way 12 TR6 . . 55 A4
Tredinnick Wood CI TR13 146 D8
Tredis Vw PL11 . . . . 65 B5
Tredore La PL27 . . . . 32 D7
Tredour Rd TR7 . . . . 110 E4
Tredova Cres TR11 . . . . . 145 B2
TREDOWN 2 E5
Tredragon Cl TR8 . . . . 31 C2
Tredragon Rd TR8 . . . . . . 31 C2
Tredrea Gdns TR3 . . . . . . 81 D5
Tredrea La TR2 . . . . 77 E2
Tredrea Manor TR3 . . . . . 81 D5
TREDRIZZICK 21 F4
Tredrizzick Cl PL27 . . . . . 21 F3
Tredruston Rd PL27 . . . . . 33 B6
Tredydan Rd PL15 . . . . . 106 B6
Tredynas Rd TR11 . . . . . 145 D3
Tredyson Pl TR11 . . . . . . 145 A3
Tre-el-Verne Cl TR1 . . . . 137 A4
TREEN Porthcurno 96 F3
  Zennor 75 F4
Treen Cotts TR26 . . . . 75 F4
Treen Flats TR14 . . . . . . 138 F3
Treen Hill TR19 . . . . 96 F4
TREESMILL 60 D6
Treetop Cl PL12 . . . . 122 D4
Treetops Hill PL13 . . . . . 117 A3
Treeve La TR27 . . . . 78 C6
TREFANNY HILL 62 D8
Treffry Ct TR7 . . . . 110 E6
Treffry La PL30 . . . . 48 C6
Treffry Rd TR1 . . . . 137 E7
Treffry Way 12 PL24 . . . . 60 B4
Trefinnick Rd PL17 . . . . . . 39 B8
Trefleur Cl 3 PL35 . . . . . . 9 C1
Trefloyd Cl PL17 . . . . 39 E6
TREFODFA 24 A8
Treforda Rd PL7 . . . . 110 F4
Treforest Rd PL27 . . . . . 108 A6
Treforthlan 7 TR16 . . . . . 67 E4
Treforthlan Cl 6 TR16 . . . 67 E4
Trefrank Rd PL15 . . . . 16 F4
TREFREW 105 D6
Trefrew Rd PL32 . . . . 105 D5
TREFRIZE 27 E3
Trefrize La PL15 . . . . 27 E3
Trefula Redruth TR16 . . . . 68 C1
  Trefula TR16 . . . . 140 E5
Trefusis Terr
  Millbrook PL10 . . . . 132 E6
  Redruth TR15 . . . . 140 C4
Tregaddock La PL30 . . . . . 34 E8
TREGADILLETT 18 C2
Tregadillett Comm Prim Sch
  PL15 . . . . 18 C2
Tregaer TR1 . . . . 137 E5
Tregainlands Pk PL30 . . . . 34 D3
TREGAJORRAN 139 D4
Tregalister Gdns PL12 . . . 65 B8
Tregaller La PL15 . . . . 28 A2
Tregallon Rd PL30 . . . . . . 34 C7
TREGAMERE 45 F7
Treganoon Rd TR15 . . . . 140 D7
Tregargus View PL26 . . . . 58 B4
TREGARLAND 63 C8
TREGARLANDBRIDGE 63 B8
Tregarland Cl
  Camborne TR14 . . . . 138 E2

Tregarland Cl continued
  Coad's Green PL15 . . . . 27 D4
Tregarne Terr TR15 . . . . 114 C4
Tregarrian Rd TR14 . . . . 138 F7
Tregarrick PL13 . . . . 117 B3
Tregarrick Cl PL13 . . . . . 146 B7
Tregarrick Ct PL13 . . . . . 117 B3
Tregarrick La PL13 . . . . . . 62 D6
TREGARRICK MILL 62 D7
Tregarrick Rd PL26 . . . . . 46 F3
Tregarrick View TR13 . . . 146 D6
Tregarrick Way PL13 . . . . 62 D6
Tregarth 12 PL26 . . . . . . 59 D7
Tregartha Way PL14 . . . . 113 D6
Tregarthen 2 St Ives TR26 141 A5
  Tregarthen TR20 . . . . 88 F7
  Varfell TR20 . . . . 89 A7
Tregarth Pl TR18 . . . . . . 143 C4
Tregaskes Parc EX23 . . . 104 F5
Tregaskis Rd TR20 . . . . . . 88 F7
Tregassack Rd TR2 . . . . . 83 B1
Tregastick La PL13 . . . . . . 51 F2
TREGASWITH 45 C5
Tregaswith Rd TR8 . . . . . 45 C5
Tregatherall La PL35 . . . . 15 C7
TREGATTA 14 C6
Tregavarras 85 A5
Tregavarras Row PL26 . . . 85 A5
Tregavethan View TR3 . . . 69 C4
Tregay La PL14 . . . . 113 C7
Tregeagle Rd PL26 . . . . . 47 A2
Tregea Hill TR16 . . . . 67 C6
Tregear Cl TR12 . . . . 99 D6
TREGEARE 17 D5
Tregeare Rd PL15 . . . . . . 17 E5
Tregear Gdns TR1 . . . . . 137 C4
Tregear Hill Polmassick PL26 72 F4
  Treworrick TR2 . . . . 84 F8
Tregea Terr TR16 . . . . 67 C6
Tregeath La PL34 . . . . 14 D6
Tregella La Tregella PL28 . 32 A8
  Tregella PL28 . . . . 107 A2
Tregellas Cl TR5 . . . . 54 C1
Tregellas Rd TR12 . . . . . . 99 B1
Tregellas Tapestry The ★ 12
  TR15 . . . . 140 B4
Tregellast Cl TR12 . . . . . 101 D4
Tregellast Parc TR12 . . . 101 D4
Tregellast Rd TR12 . . . . . 101 D3
TREGELLIST 22 E4
Tregellist Rd PL30 . . . . . . 22 F4
Tregembo Hill TR20 . . . . . 90 A7
Tregender La TR20 . . . . . . 89 B8
Tregender Rd TR20 . . . . . 89 B8
Tregenna Cl Plymouth PL7 . 131 C4
  Wainhouse Corner EX23 . . 10 F6
Tregenna Ct
  Camborne TR14 . . . . 138 C2
  Falmouth TR11 . . . . 145 C3
Tregenna Fields TR14 . . . 138 C2
Tregenna Hill 16 TR26 . . 141 B5
Tregenna La TR14 . . . . . 138 C2
Tregenna Parc TR26 . . . . 141 C3
Tregenna Pl 4 TR26 . . . . 141 B5
Tregenna Rd PL30 . . . . . . 35 C8
Tregenna Terr TR26 . . . . 141 B5
Tregenver La TR11 . . . . . 144 F4
Tregenver Rd TR11 . . . . . 144 F4
Tregenver Terr TR11 . . . . 144 F4
Tregenver Villas TR11 . . 144 F4
TREGESEAL 86 F7
Tregeseal Hill TR19 . . . . . 86 F7
Tregeseal Row TR19 . . . . 86 F6
Tregeseal Terr TR19 . . . . 86 F6
TREGEW 145 B8
Tregew Cl TR11 . . . . 145 B7
Tregew Ct 3 TR14 . . . . . 138 D4
Tregew Rd Flushing TR11 . 145 B8
  Penryn TR10,TR11 . . . . . . 81 F2
Treggodick Cotts TR20 . . 143 A8
Tregian Cl TR1 . . . . 137 F5
Tregidden TR12 . . . . 100 E5
Tregidden Hill
  Lesneague TR12 . . . . 101 A5
  St Martin TR12 . . . . 100 F5
Tregie TR18 . . . . 143 B3
Tregildry La TR12 . . . . . . 101 D4
Tregirls La Trethellick PL28 . 21 B3
  Trethillick PL28 . . . . 107 C6
TREGISKEY 73 C5
Tregiskey Cotts PL26 . . . . 73 C5
Tregisky La TR12 . . . . . . 101 C1
Treglenwith Rd TR14 . . . 138 C4
Treglines La Gunvenna PL27 22 A6
  Polzeath PL27 . . . . 21 F5
Treglisson Rural Workshops
  TR27 . . . . 78 C3
Tregloan Cl TR18 . . . . . . 143 B1
Treglyn Farm Cotts PL27 . 22 B3
Tregoddick Cl TR20 . . . . . 88 B7
Tregoide La PL30 . . . . 23 A8
Tregolds La St Merryn PL28 . 31 F7
  Tregolds PL27 . . . . 32 C6
  Tregolds PL28 . . . . 31 F7
TREGOLE 6 E1
TREGOLLS 80 F3
Tregolls Cl TR1 . . . . 137 E5
Tregolls Hill PL30 . . . . . . 33 C2
Tregolls Rd Tregustick PL30 33 D1
  Truro TR1 . . . . 137 E5
Tregolls Sch TR1 . . . . . . 137 E5
TREGONCE 107 F2
TREGONETHA 46 C6
Tregoney Ct 13 PL26 . . . . 85 D8
Tregoney Hill PL26 . . . . . 73 C3
Tregongeeves La PL26 . . . 59 A2

TREGONHAWKE 132 B4
Tregonhay PL14 . . . . 38 C7
Tregonhayne TR1 . . . . 72 A4
Tregoniggie Ind Est TR11 . 144 D4
Tregoning Rd PL11 . . . . . 126 F2
Tregonissey Cl PL25 . . . . 114 D5
Tregonissey Rd PL25 . . . 114 E5
Tregonissey La End PL25 . 114 E6
TREGONNA 32 C7
Tregonna Hill Tregonna PL27 . 32 C7
  Tregonna PL27 . . . . 32 C7
Tregonnett La PL17 . . . . . 39 B5
Tregonning Ct 8 TR6 . . . . 55 A5
Tregonning Hill TR13 . . . . 90 E4
Tregonning La TR13 . . . . . 90 F5
Tregonning Parc 10 PL12 . 101 C4
Tregonning Rd TR3 . . . . . 80 F3
Tregonning Terr TR13 . . . 90 F5
Tregonning View 17 TR13 . 98 C8
TREGONY 71 F4
Tregony Com Prim Sch TR2 71 F3
Tregony Hill TR2 . . . . 71 F3
Tregony Ind Est TR2 . . . . 71 E3
Tregony Rd TR2 . . . . 71 D6
TREGOODWELL 105 F4
Tregorden La Bodieve PL27 . 33 F8
  Tregorden PL27 . . . . 22 E1
  Trevarner PL27 . . . . 108 E8
Tregorden Mine La
  Bodieve PL27 . . . . 33 F8
  Trevarner PL27 . . . . 108 E8
TREGORRICK 114 D1
Tregorrick Pk (St Austell RFC)
  PL26 . . . . 114 E1
Tregorrick Rd PL26 . . . . . 114 E1
Tregos Rd TR26 . . . . 141 C2
TREGOSS 46 D3
Tregoss Moor PL26 . . . . . 46 E3
Tregoss Rd TR7 . . . . 110 F6
Tregothnan Rd
  Falmouth TR11 . . . . 145 A5
  Truro TR1 . . . . 137 E3
Tregowris Court Cotts
  TR12 . . . . 101 B5
Tregrea TR14 . . . . 138 E1
TREGREENWELL 23 F7
Tregreenwell Hill PL30 . . . 23 F7
Tregrehan Gdns ★ PL24 . 115 E6
TREGREHAN MILLS 115 D6
Tregudda Cl PL15 . . . . . . 18 A1
Treguddock Dr PL27 . . . 108 D5
Tregue PL15 . . . . 16 E2
Tregullan TR15 . . . . 139 C8
Tregulland Rd PL15 . . . . . 16 E5
Tregullan View PL31 . . . 109 D3
Tregullon La PL30 . . . . . . 48 A7
Tregullow Rd TR11 . . . . . 144 F5
Tregundy Cl 21 TR6 . . . . . 55 A5
Tregundy Ct 20 TR6 . . . . . 55 A5
Tregundy La TR6 . . . . 55 A5
Tregundy Rd TR6 . . . . 55 A5
TREGUNE 10 F4
TREGUNNA 33 B8
Tregunna Cl TR13 . . . . . . 91 B1
Tregunnel Hill TR7 . . . . . 110 D4
Tregunnick La PL11 . . . . . 64 B6
Tregunnus La PL11 . . . . . 64 D5
Tregunter Mews TR11 . . 145 D3
Tregunwith TR11 . . . . 82 A4
Tregurra La TR1 . . . . 137 E6
TREGURRIAN 44 E8
Tregurrian Hill TR8 . . . . . 44 E8
Tregurtha Farm Cotts TR17 89 D6
Tregurtha View TR20 . . . . 89 E5
Tregurthen Cl TR14 . . . . 138 C2
Tregurthen Rd TR14 . . . . 138 C2
TREGUSTICK 33 D1
Tregustick Rd PL30 . . . . . 33 E1
Treguth Cl TR8 . . . . 43 B1
Tregwary Rd TR26 . . . . . 141 A5
Tregwina La PL27 . . . . . . 32 A3
Tregye Rd TR3 . . . . 82 A7
Trehaddle TR4 . . . . 81 B7
TREHAN 122 A1
Trehane Rd TR14 . . . . . . 138 B3
Trehannick Cl PL30 . . . . . 23 E7
Trehannick Rd PL30 . . . . . 23 E6
Trehaverne Cl TR1 . . . . . 137 C5
Trehaverne La TR1 . . . . . 137 C5
Trehaverne Terr 3 TR1 . . 137 C5
Trehaverne Vean TR1 . . . 137 C5
Trehawke La PL14 . . . . . . 38 C1
Trehayes Mdw TR27 . . . . 77 E2
Trehayes Parc TR27 . . . . 142 E7
Trehaze-Na Cl TR32 . . . . . 10 C3
Treheath Rd PL14 . . . . . . 50 E7
Trehill Cross PL12 . . . . . . 40 C2
Trehill La Newbridge PL17 . 39 E3
  Rame PL10 . . . . 64 B2
TREHUNIST 52 C6
Trehunsey Cl TR11 . . . . . 93 C2
Trehurst TR18 . . . . 143 D4
Trekeek Rd PL32 . . . . 15 C6
Trekee La PL30 . . . . 23 C7
Trekeen Rd TR10 . . . . . . 144 B8
TREKEIVESTEPS 37 E4
TREKENNER 28 B5
Trekenner Com Prim Sch
  PL15 . . . . 28 C5
TREKENNING 45 D5
Trekenning Rd TR9 . . . . . 45 D5
Trekernell Rd Tolcarne PL15 . 26 F5
  Trebartha PL15 . . . . 27 A5
Trekestle Pk PL15 . . . . . . 18 C2
TREKNOW 14 C5
Trekye Cl TR16 . . . . 80 B5
Trelake La PL34 . . . . 14 D5

Trelake Rd PL25 . . . . 114 B4
TRELAN 100 E1
Trelan TR14 . . . . 138 F3
Trelander Barton TR1 . . . 137 E5
Trelander E TR1 . . . . 137 F4
Trelander Highway TR1 . . 137 E4
Trelander N TR1 . . . . 137 F5
Trelander S TR1 . . . . 137 F4
Trelander Vean TR1 . . . . 137 F5
Trelantis PL28 . . . . 20 E1
Trelantis Est 4 PL28 . . . . 31 D4
TRELASH 10 E1
Trelaske La Lewannick PL15 . 27 C7
  Pelynt PL13 . . . . 62 F4
Trelavour Prazey PL26 . . . 58 B8
Trelavour Rd PL26 . . . . . . 58 C8
Trelavour Sq PL26 . . . . . . 58 C8
Trelawne 10 TR3 . . . . 81 F7
Trelawne Cottage Gdns
  PL13 . . . . 62 E4
Trelawne Gdns PL13 . . . . 62 E5
Trelawne Rd TR3 . . . . 81 F7
Trelawney Apartments
  TR7 . . . . 110 F6
Trelawney Ave
  Falmouth TR11 . . . . 145 B3
  Plymouth PL5 . . . . 123 C1
  Poughill EX23 . . . . 4 C3
  Redruth TR15 . . . . 140 E7
  St Ives TR26 . . . . 141 A5
Trelawney Cl Bodmin PL31 109 C4
  Maenporth TR11 . . . . 93 E3
  Torpoint PL11 . . . . 126 E3
  Warbstow Cross PL15 . . . . 11 B1
Trelawney Cotts PL15 . . . 106 C5
Trelawney Ct PL27 . . . . . . 21 E3
Trelawney Est
  Madron TR20 . . . . 143 A8
  Ponsanooth TR4 . . . . 81 B7
Trelawney Gdns PL14 . . . 38 D4
Trelawney Hts 19 PL17 . . 39 F4
Trelawney Parc
  St Columb Major TR9 . . . . 45 D5
  Warbstow Cross PL15 . . . . 11 B1
Trelawney Pl Hayle TR27 . 142 C6
  Penryn TR10 . . . . 144 C8
  Plymouth PL5 . . . . 123 D1
Trelawney Rd
  Bodmin PL31 . . . . 109 C3
  Callington PL17 . . . . 39 F4
  Camborne TR14 . . . . 138 D3
  Chacewater TR4 . . . . 69 A3
  Helston TR13 . . . . 146 C5
  Newquay TR7 . . . . 110 E5
  Padstow PL28 . . . . 107 D4
  Plymouth PL3 . . . . 128 D5
  Ponsanooth TR3 . . . . 81 B4
  St Austell PL25 . . . . 114 C5
  St Ives TR26 . . . . 141 A5
  St Mawes TR2 . . . . 95 A4
  Saltash PL12 . . . . 122 E2
  Truro TR1 . . . . 137 E5
Trelawney Rise
  18 Callington PL17 . . . . . . 39 F4
  Torpoint PL11 . . . . 126 E3
Trelawney Terr Cury TR12 . 99 B4
  Looe PL13 . . . . 117 C4
Trelawney Way Hayle TR27 142 C6
  Torpoint PL11 . . . . 126 E3
Trelawny Ct TR14 . . . . . . 138 C3
Trelawny Rd Falmouth TR11 145 B4
  Menheniot PL14 . . . . 52 A6
  Plymouth PL7 . . . . 130 C6
  St Agnes TR5 . . . . 54 C1
  Tavistock PL19 . . . . 147 C6
Treleague TR12 . . . . 101 C2
Treleague Crossroads
  TR12 . . . . 103 A5
Trelean Vean PL26 . . . . . . 72 F4
Treleaver Way TR1 . . . . . . 69 F3
Trelee Cl TR27 . . . . 142 E7
TRELEIGH 140 D8
Treleigh Ave TR15 . . . . . 140 B6
Treleigh Com Prim Sch
  TR16 . . . . 140 C8
Treleigh Downs TR16 . . . 140 C8
Treleigh Ind Est TR16 . . . 140 C7
Treleigh Terr TR15 . . . . . 140 C5
Trelevan Cl PL25 . . . . . . 114 C3
Treleven Rd EX23 . . . . . . 104 F4
TRELEW 82 B2
Treliddon La PL11 . . . . . . 64 C5
Treliever Cl TR10 . . . . 81 D2
Treliever Cross TR10 . . . . 81 C1
Treliever Layby TR10 . . . . 81 C2
Treliever Rd
  Mabe Burnthouse TR10 . . . 81 D1
  Penryn TR10 . . . . 144 B8
TRELIGGA 14 C3
Treligga Downs Rd PL33 . 14 D2
Treligga Rd PL33 . . . . 14 C2
Treliggon Bottoms PL30 . 48 A7
TRELIGHTS 22 C6
Trelil Cvn Site TR13 . . . . 146 E7
TRELILL 23 C5
Trelill La TR1 . . . . 144 C2
Trelindon PL15 . . . . 27 E8
Trelill Rd PL30 . . . . 23 C4
Trelinnoe Cl PL15 . . . . . . 27 E8
Trelinnoe Gdns PL15 . . . . 27 E8
Treliske Ind Est TR1 . . . . 69 E4
Treliske La TR1, TR4 . . . . 69 F4
Treliske Rd TR5 . . . . 140 D6
Trelispen Park Dr PL26 . . 85 C5
Trelispen Pk PL26 . . . . . . 85 C5
Trelissick Fields TR27 . . . 142 E3
Trelissick Gdns PL17 . . . . 39 E3
Trelissick Gdns ★ TR3 . . . 82 D6

Trelissick Rd
  Falmouth TR11 . . . . 144 F5
  Hayle TR27 . . . . 142 B3
Trelissick Woodland Wlk★
  TR3 . . . . 82 D6
TRELIVER 46 E8
Treliver Hill PL30 . . . . . . 46 F8
Treloan La TR2 . . . . 83 B1
Treloar Terr PL15 . . . . . . 106 B6
Treloggan Ind Est TR7 . . 111 B4
Treloggan Rd TR7 . . . . . . 111 A4
Trelorrin Gdns PL3 . . . . . 128 E5
Trelowarren★ TR12 . . . . . 99 F6
Trelowarren Ct 13 PL17 . . 39 E4
Trelowarren Est
  Garras TR12 . . . . 100 A7
  Halligey TR12 . . . . 99 E6
Trelowarren St TR14 . . . . 138 D3
Treloweck TR14 . . . . 79 A4
Trelowen Dr TR10 . . . . . . 144 A6
Treloweth Cl Plymouth PL2 128 D8
  St Erth TR27 . . . . 77 E2
Treloweth Com Prim Sch
  TR15 . . . . 139 D6
Treloweth Gdns TR15 . . . 139 C6
Treloweth La TR27 . . . . . . 77 E2
Treloweth Rd TR15 . . . . . 139 C6
Treloweth Terr TR15 . . . . 139 B7
Treloweth Way TR15 . . . . 139 C7
Trelowth Rd PL26 . . . . . . 59 A1
Treloyan TR12 . . . . 101 E4
Treloyhan Cl TR26 . . . . . . 141 C3
Treloyhan Manor Dr TR26 141 C3
Treloyhan Park Rd TR26 . 141 C3
Treluswell Roundabout
  TR10 . . . . 81 D3
Trelyn PL27 . . . . 21 E3
Trelyn Rd TR12 . . . . 101 D4
TRELYON 141 B3
Trelyon TR2 . . . . 57 F3
Trelyon Ave TR26 . . . . . . 141 C4
Trelyon Cl TR19 . . . . 97 B6
Tremabe La Dobwalls PL14 . 38 A2
  Tremabe PL14 . . . . 38 A2
Tremabe Pk PL14 . . . . . . 50 E7
Tremadart Cl PL14 . . . . . . 51 A1
Tremadart Farm Barns
  PL14 . . . . 51 A1
Tremaddock Cotts PL14 . 36 F3
Tremaddock Council Hos
  PL14 . . . . 36 F3
TREMAIL 16 B5
Tremaine Cl TR18 . . . . . . 143 C7
Tremalic PL13 . . . . 117 B3
Tremall Parc TR3 . . . . . . 80 F3
Tremanor Way TR11 . . . . 144 D5
TREMAR 38 A2
Tremar Cl PL14 . . . . 38 A2
Tremar La St Cleer PL14 . . 37 F3
  Tremar PL14 . . . . 38 A3
Tremarle Home Pk TR14 . 138 F5
Tremarne Cl TR3 . . . . 82 C5
Tremar Rd TR26 . . . . 77 A7
Tremarren Rd PL27 . . . . . 108 B5
TREMATON 53 E2
Trematon Cl PL11 . . . . . . 126 E4
Trematon Terr PL4 . . . . . 128 E4
TREMAYNE 79 C2
Tremayne TR14 . . . . 79 C2
Tremayne Cl TR3 . . . . 81 F6
Tremayne Ho PL31 . . . . . 109 B4
Tremayne Pk TR14 . . . . . 138 F2
Tremayne Rd
  Carharrack TR16 . . . . . . 80 F8
  St Austell PL25 . . . . 114 E4
  Truro TR1 . . . . 137 C5
Tremayne Rise PL19 . . . . 147 B5
Tremayne Terr PL13 . . . . 63 F8
Trembath Cres TR7 . . . . . 110 E5
Trembear Rd PL25 . . . . . 114 A4
Trembel La Mullion PL12 . . 99 B1
  Mullion TR12 . . . . 102 D8
Trembel Rd TR12 . . . . . . 99 B2
Trembleath Rd TR9 . . . . . 45 B8
Trembrase TR19 . . . . 96 C7
TREMBRAZE 113 D8
Trembraze La PL14 . . . . . 113 D7
Tremeadow Terr
  Hayle TR27 . . . . 142 B4
  Liskeard PL14 . . . . 113 D7
Tremeale PL15 . . . . 18 E2
Tremear Gn 6 TR9 . . . . . 45 E2
Tremearne Rd 16 TR13 . . 98 C8
Tremeddan Ct 2 PL14 . . . 113 C6
Tremeddan La PL14 . . . . . 113 C6
Tremeddan Rd PL14 . . . . 113 B4
Tremeer La PL30 . . . . 23 E3
Tremellin La TR27 . . . . . . 77 F1
Tremena Gdns PL25 . . . . 114 C4
Tremena Rd PL25 . . . . . . 114 C4
Tremenheere Ave TR13 . . 146 D8
Tremenheere Ct TR13 . . . 146 E4
Tremenheere Rd TR18 . . . 143 E6
Tremenva Ct 1 TR13 . . . . 146 C5
TREMETHICK CROSS 88 A5
Tremewan 1 PL25 . . . . . . 59 A3
Tremodrett La PL26 . . . . . 47 B4
Tremodrett Rd
  Dowdens PL26 . . . . 47 D4
  Roche PL26 . . . . 46 F3
Tremoh Ct TR2 . . . . 71 C6
TREMOLLETT 27 D2
Tremollett Cotts PL17 . . . 28 B1
Tremollett Rd PL15 . . . . . 27 D3
TREMORE 47 C7
Tremore Rd TR15 . . . . . . 140 D6
Tremorva TR27 . . . . 142 C6
Tremorvah Barton TR1 . . 137 E5

Tremorvah Cres TR1 . . . . 137 E5
Tremorvah Ct
  Falmouth TR11 . . . . 144 F1
  Truro TR1 . . . . 137 E5
Tremorvah Pk TR11 . . . . . 144 F1
Tremorvah Way 4 TR11 . 144 F1
Tremorvah Wood La TR1 . 137 E5
Tremough Barton Cotts
  TR10 . . . . 81 C1
Tremoughdale
  Penryn TR10 . . . . 144 B8
  Treliever TR10 . . . . 81 D2
Trenale La PL34 . . . . 14 D7
Trenalt Terr TR1 . . . . 137 B5
TRENANCE Newquay 110 E5
  Roche 46 F7
  St Issey 32 D5
  Tregurrian 31 C2
Trenance Ave TR7 . . . . . . 110 F5
Trenance Cl TR13 . . . . . . 146 B7
Trenance Ct TR7 . . . . 110 E4
Trenance Dr PL19 . . . . . . 30 A3
Trenance Hill PL25 . . . . . 114 A5
Trenance La TR7 . . . . 110 E4
Trenance Learning Academy
  TR7 . . . . 110 E5
Trenance Leisure Park &
  Gdns★ TR7 . . . . 111 A5
Trenance Pl PL25 . . . . . . 114 B4
Trenance Rd
  Camborne TR14 . . . . 138 E4
  Newquay TR7 . . . . 110 E5
  St Austell PL25 . . . . 114 B4
  Tregurrian TR27 . . . . . . 32 D5
TRENANT 37 C3
Trenant TR16 . . . . 68 D1
Trenant Cl PL27 . . . . 21 E5
Trenant Cross PL14 . . . . . 63 A6
TRENANT GIRT 108 C3
Trenant Ind Est PL27 . . . 108 D6
Trenant Rd Looe PL13 . . . 117 D5
  2 Tywardreath PL24 . . . 60 D5
Trenant Vale PL27 . . . . . . 108 D6
TRENARREN 73 E7
Trenarren View PL25 . . . . 115 A6
Trenarth TR10 . . . . 144 C8
Trenarth Rd TR7 . . . . 110 E5
Trenawin La TR27 . . . . . . 78 E5
TRENCREEK 111 C4
Trencreek Cl TR4 . . . . . . 56 D1
Trencreek La TR8 . . . . . . 111 B4
Trencreek Rd TR7, TR8 . . 111 B4
TRENCROM 77 B3
Trencrom La TR26 . . . . . . 141 D1
Trencrom Rd TR27 . . . . . 77 C3
Trencrom Row TR20 . . . . 77 B3
TRENDEAL 57 C3
Trendeal Gdns 1 TR18 . . 143 E5
Trendeal La TR8 . . . . 57 C5
Trendlewood Rd PL6 . . . . 125 D7
Trendreath CE Prim Sch
  PL27 . . . . 77 E3
Treneague Pk PL27 . . . . . 108 B4
TRENEAR 92 A6
Trenear Trenear TR13 . . . 92 A7
  Wendron TR13 . . . . 91 F6
Trenear Ct TR15 . . . . 140 D6
TRENEERE 143 E7
Treneere La TR18 . . . . . . 143 D7
Treneere Rd TR18 . . . . . . 143 D6
TRENEGLOS 16 F7
Treneglos TR4 . . . . 56 D1
Treneglos Terr Gulval TR18 88 E6
  Newlyn TR18 . . . . 143 C3
Trenerry Cl TR1 . . . . 137 D6
TRENERTH 78 D2
Trenerth Rd TR27 . . . . . . 78 E2
Trenethick Ave TR13 . . . . 146 D8
Trenethick Bsns Pk TR13 . 146 C8
Trenethick Cl TR13 . . . . . 146 D7
Trenethick Farm TR13 . . . 146 B8
Trenethick Parc TR13 . . . 146 B8
TRENEWAN 62 A4
TRENGALE 37 C2
Trengove PL26 . . . . 47 C1
Trengove Cross TR11 . . . 92 D5
Trengrouse Ave PL11 . . . 126 F3
Trengrouse Way TR13 . . . 146 C5
TRENGUNE 11 A4
Trenhaile Terr TR1 . . . . . 70 D1
Trenhayle La TR27 . . . . . 142 B3
Treniffle La
  Stourscombe PL15 . . . . . 106 F3
  Treniffle PL15 . . . . 19 C2
Treningle Hill PL30 . . . . . 47 F7
Treningle View PL31 . . . . 109 C3
TRENINNICK 111 A4
Treninnick Hill TR7 . . . . . 110 F5
Treninnow & Wiggle Chalets
  PL10 . . . . 132 C2
Trenithick Mdw TR4 . . . . 68 C6
Trenithon La TR8 . . . . . . 57 C6
Trennal La TR2 . . . . 90 C5
Trennance Ct 6 TR12 . . . 99 A1
Trennick La TR1 . . . . 137 E3
Trennick Row TR1 . . . . . . 137 E3
Trennick Villas Ct TR1 . . . 137 E3
Trenode CE Prim Sch PL13 51 F1
Trenouth Cl 5 PL14 . . . . 30 A3
Trenouth La PL27 . . . . . . 32 B5
Trenovissick Rd PL24 . . . 60 B4
Trenowah Rd PL25 . . . . . 115 C5
Trenower La PL26 . . . . . . 47 B4
TRENOWETH 93 B8
Trenoweth TR14 . . . . 79 B3
Trenoweth Ave TR14 . . . . 138 B3
Trenoweth Cres TR18 . . . 143 B4
Trenoweth Est TR12 . . . . 102 F2

Trenoweth Est TR15 . . . . 140 A8
Trenoweth La TR10 . . . . . 93 B8
Trenoweth Mdw TR12 . . . 102 F2
Trenoweth Rd
  Falmouth TR11 . . . . 144 F2
  Penzance TR18 . . . . 143 B5
Trenoweth Terr TR10 . . . . 93 B8
Trenoweth Vean TR10 . . . 81 B1
Trenow La TR20 . . . . 89 D5
Trenowth Terr TR2 . . . . . . 57 E1
Trent Cl PL3 . . . . 129 B6
Trentham Cl PL6 . . . . 125 B6
Trentworthy Cross EX22 . . 3 E2
TRENWHEAL 90 F7
Trenwheal TR13 . . . . 90 F7
Trenwith La PL26 . . . . . . 141 A4
Trenwith Pl 14 TR26 . . . . 141 B5
Trenwith Rd TR14 . . . . . . 138 B3
Trenwith Sq TR26 . . . . . . 141 A5
Trenwith Terr 11 TR26 . . 141 B5
Trenython Rd 10 PL24 . . 60 B4
Treore Cl PL30 . . . . 23 A6
Treore La Hendra PL29 . . . 23 A7
  Tregaverne PL29 . . . . . . 22 F7
Treovis Cross PL14 . . . . . 38 C8
Tre-Pol PL26 . . . . 58 F1
TREQUITE 23 B3
Treraven La PL27 . . . . . . 108 C3
Treraven Rd PL15 . . . . . . 16 E2
Trereife Pk TR20 . . . . 143 A4
Trerew Rd TR18 . . . . 143 C4
Trerice★ TR8 . . . . 44 D1
Trerice Cl 15 PL17 . . . . . 39 E4
Trerice Dr TR7 . . . . 111 B5
Trerice Fields TR14 . . . . . 79 B2
Trerice Holdings TR8 . . . . 44 C1
Trerice Pl TR26 . . . . 141 A5
Trerice Rd 6 TR26 . . . . . 141 A5
Trerice Terr PL26 . . . . . . 58 A8
Trerieve PL11 . . . . 64 C5
TRERISE 103 A7
Trerise Rd TR14 . . . . 138 C3
Treroosel Rd PL30 . . . . . 23 D8
Trerose Coombe PL11 . . . 64 C5
Treruffe Hill TR15 . . . . . . 140 B4
Treruffe Terr 9 TR15 . . . 140 B4
TRERULEFOOT 52 D2
Treryn Cl PL24 . . . . 60 B5
Tresaderns Rd TR15 . . . . 140 A6
Tresahor Rd TR11 . . . . . . 145 A3
Tresahor Treverva TR11 . . 93 A5
  Trewardreva TR11 . . . . . 92 F5
Tresamble Hill TR4, TR3 . 81 B6
TRESARRETT 35 B8
Tresavean Est TR16 . . . . . 80 E6
Tresavean Hill TR16 . . . . 80 E6
Tresavean Terr TR16 . . . . 80 E6
Tresawla Ct TR14 . . . . . . 138 F6
TRESAWLE 71 C5
Tresawle Rd TR11 . . . . . . 145 A4
Tresawls Ave TR1 . . . . . . 69 F3
Tresawls Rd TR1, TR4 . . . 69 E4
Tresawna Terr TR11 . . . . 145 B4
Tresawya Dr TR1 . . . . . . 137 C4
Trescobeas Rd
  Falmouth TR11 . . . . 144 E5
  4 Mongleath TR11 . . . . 144 D5
  Mongleath TR11 . . . . . . 144 E4
Trescoe Rd TR20 . . . . . . 88 F6
Tresco Gdns PL6 . . . . . . 124 F7
Tresco Pl TR11 . . . . 144 F4
Trescore PL28 . . . . 31 F7
TRESCOWE 90 B5
Trescowe TR27 . . . . 90 B5
Trescowe Comm TR27 . . 90 C6
Trescowe Rd TR20 . . . . . 89 F5
Tresdale Parc TR27 . . . . . 78 D6
Treseder's Gdns TR1 . . . 137 D5
Tresevern Cl TR3 . . . . . . 80 D4
Tresevern Hill TR3 . . . . . 80 D4
Tresidder CE Prim Sch
  TR11 . . . . 144 E4
TRESILLIAN 70 F5
Tresillian Ho TR1 . . . . . . 69 E4
Tresillian Rd TR11 . . . . . 144 F6
Tresillian St PL4 . . . . 149 C2
TRESINNEY 24 C8
Tresithney Rd TR16 . . . . 80 F8
Treskerby TR16 . . . . 140 F7
Treskewes Est 1 TR12 . . 101 C4
Treskewes Ind Est 1
  TR12 . . . . 101 C3
TRESKILLARD 139 C1
Treskilling PL30 . . . . 59 F8
TRESKINNICK CROSS 6 F1
TRESLOTHAN 79 D4
Treslothan Rd TR14 . . . . 79 D4
Tresluggan Rd PL5 . . . . . 123 D1
Tresooth Ct TR10 . . . . . . 144 D7
Tresooth La TR10 . . . . . . 144 C8
Tresooth Terr TR10 . . . . . 144 D7
Tresowes TR13 . . . . 90 D4
TRESOWES GREEN 90 D4
Tresowes Hill TR13 . . . . . 90 E4
Tresowgar La TR2 . . . . . . 71 B6
TRESPARRETT 10 B2
TRESPARRETT POSTS . . . 10 C4
Trespison Tregarrick TR13 146 E5
  Whitehill TR13 . . . . 91 F2
Trespison Ct TR13 . . . . . 146 E5
Tressa Dowr La TR1 . . . . 137 F5
Tressvennack TR20 . . . . . 88 C5
Treswigga Rd PL30 . . . . . 24 E1
TRESWITHIAN 138 A4
Treswithian Barns TR14 . 138 A3
Treswithian Downs
  Kehelland TR14 . . . . 66 F1

Treswithian Downs continued
  Kehelland TR14 . . . . 79 A7
  Reskadinnick TR14 . . . . . 138 A5
Treswithian Park Rd TR14 138 B3
Treswithian Rd TR14 . . . . 138 B3
Tretawn Cl PL30 . . . . 23 B2
Trethannas Gdns TR14 . . 79 B2
Tretharrup TR16 . . . . 80 D6
TRETHELLAN 110 C6
Trethellan TR16 . . . . 80 D5
Trethellan Hill TR7 . . . . . 110 C6
Trethern Cl TR14 . . . . . . 79 E4
Tretherras Cl TR7 . . . . . . 111 A6
Tretherras Rd TR7 . . . . . 111 A6
TRETHEVEY 14 F8
Trethevy Cl PL14 . . . . . . 37 F3
Trethevy Quoit★ PL14 . . 38 A3
TRETHEWEY 96 E4
Trethewey Cl 10 TR9 . . . 45 E6
Trethewey Way TR7 . . . . 110 D5
Trethew Gdns TR14 . . . . 138 D5
Trethiggey Cres TR8 . . . . 111 F3
Trethillick La
  Trethellick PL28 . . . . 21 B2
  Trethillick PL28 . . . . 107 C6
Trethill La PL11 . . . . 65 C5
Trethorne Leisure Farm★
  PL15 . . . . 18 B2
Trethorns Ct TR20 . . . . . 89 A8
TRETHOSA 58 A5
Trethosa Downs PL26 . . . 58 B5
Trethosa Hill PL26 . . . . . 58 A5
Trethosa Rd PL26 . . . . . . 58 B4
Trethowan Hts TR1 . . . . . 69 F3
TRETHOWEL 114 C6
Trethurffe TR2 . . . . 57 C1
Trethurffe Terr TR9 . . . . . 45 E5
Trethurffe Villas TR2 . . . . 57 C1
TRETHURGY 59 F6
Trethurgy Gdns 17 PL17 . 39 E4
Tretoil Hill PL30 . . . . 48 B7
Tretoil View PL31 . . . . . . 109 E2
Tretorvic TR18 . . . . 143 C8
Tretower Cl PL6 . . . . 124 F5
TREVADLOCK 27 A6
Trevadlock Hall Pk PL15 . 27 A6
TREVAIL 43 D1
Trevail Cotts TR8 . . . . . . 43 D1
Trevail Way PL25 . . . . . . 114 E4
Trevale TR18 . . . . 143 C5
Trevales TR3 . . . . 81 A2
TREVALGA 9 B1
Trevalga Cl 5 TR6 . . . . . 55 A4
Trevalga Hill PL35 . . . . . 14 F8
Trevalga Rd PL35 . . . . . . 15 A8
Trevallack Cl 9 TR12 . . . 101 C4
Trevallack Parc 3 TR12 . 101 C4
Trevallack View 2 TR12 . 101 C4
Trevallett La PL15 . . . . . . 18 A3
Trevallion Pk TR3 . . . . . . 82 B5
Trevallyn Rd PL15 . . . . . . 106 B4
TREVANCE 32 E6
Trevance TR10 . . . . 144 A8
Trevance Pk PL24 . . . . . . 60 D5
Trevance Rd PL27 . . . . . . 32 E6
Trevaney PL11 . . . . 93 A4
TREVANGER 21 F4
Trevanger La PL27 . . . . . 21 F4
Trevanion Cl PL27 . . . . . 108 B4
Trevanion Ct
  Mawnan Smith TR11 . . . 93 D3
  1 Newquay TR7 . . . . . . 110 F6
  Truro TR1 . . . . 69 F3
Trevanion La PL25 . . . . . 59 A3
Trevanion Pk PL27 . . . . . 108 C4
Trevanion Rd
  Liskeard PL14 . . . . 113 D5
  St Austell PL25 . . . . 114 D2
  2 Trewoon PL25 . . . . . 59 A3
  Wadebridge PL27 . . . . . 108 B4
Trevanion Terr PL27 . . . . 108 C4
Trevannion Cl PL6 . . . . . 129 A8
TREVANSON 33 C7
Trevanson Rd
  Wadebridge PL27 . . . . . 108 A5
  Whiterock PL27 . . . . 108 A5
Trevanson St PL27 . . . . . 108 B6
Trevanson Street PL27 . . 108 B6
Trevarner Mdw PL27 . . . 108 D6
Trevarner Way PL27 . . . . 108 D6
Trevarno TR13 . . . . 91 C4
Trevarno Estate & Gdns★
  TR13 . . . . 91 C5
TREVARNON 78 D6
Trevarnon Cl TR27 . . . . . 78 D6
Trevarnon La TR27 . . . . . 78 D6
Trevarnon Moor TR27 . . . 78 D6
Trevarrack Cl TR18 . . . . . 143 F8
Trevarrack La TR18 . . . . . 143 F8
Trevarrack Pl TR18 . . . . . 143 F8
Trevarrack Rd Gulval TR18 143 F8
  Trythogga TR18 . . . . . . 143 F8
Trevarrack Row TR18 . . . 88 E6
TREVARREN 45 E3
Trevarren Ave TR16 . . . . 80 A5
TREVARRIAN 31 C1
Trevarrian Hill TR8 . . . . . 44 D8
TREVARRICK 72 F2
Trevarrick Cl TR26 . . . . . 141 C1
Trevarrick Dr PL25 . . . . . 114 B4
Trevarrick Rd PL25 . . . . . 114 B3
TREVARTH 80 E7
Trevarth 22 PL26 . . . . . . 85 D8
Trevarthen Cl TR27 . . . . . 78 D6
Trevarth Est PL26 . . . . . . 73 C4
Trevarthian Ho TR17 . . . . 89 B5
Trevarthian Rd PL25 . . . . 114 C4

Trevarth Rd TR11 . . . . . . 144 F5
Trevarth Terr TR16 . . . . . 80 E7
Trevarweneth Rd 8 PL24 . 60 B4
Trevassack Ct TR27 . . . . 142 D6
Trevassack Hill TR27 . . . . 142 E6
Trevassack Manor Pk 6
  TR27 . . . . 142 D6
Trevassack Parc TR27 . . . 142 E6
Trevaunance Cl TR5 . . . . 54 C2
Trevaunance Cove★ TR5 . 54 D2
Trevaunance Rd TR5 . . . . 54 C2
Trevaylor Cl TR1 . . . . 137 E6
Trevaylor Rd TR11 . . . . . 144 F5
Trevean Cl TR14 . . . . 138 B3
Trevean Gdns 3 TR18 . . . 143 D5
Trevean La Rosudgeon TR20 . 89 F4
  Trevean PL27 . . . . 31 E7
Trevean Rd Penzance TR18 143 D5
  Truro TR1 . . . . 69 F3
Trevean Way Newquay TR7 110 C5
  Rosudgeon TR20 . . . . . . 89 F4
Trevear Cl PL25 . . . . 114 D3
Trevear Rd PL26 . . . . 58 B4
Trevease TR10 . . . . 92 D7
Trevecca Cotts PL14 . . . . 113 C8
Trevedras Rd TR8 . . . . . . 31 F1
Trevegean TR19 . . . . 86 E4
Treveglos TR27 . . . . 142 B6
Treveglos Rd TR11 . . . . . 144 E1
TREVEIGHAN 23 F6
Trevelga Ct TR7 . . . . 111 A7
Trevelgue Ct TR8 . . . . . . 44 C6
Trevelgue Rd TR7, TR8 . . 44 C6
Trevellance La TR6 . . . . . 55 B4
Trevellan Rd TR11 . . . . . 82 A3
Trevella Rd EX23 . . . . . . 104 E7
TREVELLAS 54 F2
Trevella Vean TR4 . . . . . . 70 D8
Trevell La PL15 . . . . 26 F7
TREVELMOND 50 D6
Trevelthan Rd 18 TR16 . . 67 E4
Trevelva Rd TR1 . . . . 137 E2
Trevelveth Rd TR8 . . . . . 110 B3
Trevelyan Cl 10 TR20 . . . 89 E5
Trevelyan Gr TR20 . . . . . 89 F5
Trevelyan Holiday Homes
  TR12 . . . . 102 E6
Trevelyan Rd TR16 . . . . . 67 E4
Trevelyan Way 5 TR20 . . 89 E5
TREVEMPER 110 E2
Trevemper Rd TR7, TR8 . . 110 F3
TREVEN 14 C6
Trevena Cl TR18 . . . . 143 C4
Trevena Cross Breage TR13 90 F3
  Trevena TR13 . . . . 90 F4
Trevena Dr 8 PL34 . . . . . 14 C7
Trevena Gdns TR11 . . . . 93 D3
Trevena La TR13 . . . . 90 F4
Trevena Lodge 6 PL34 . . 14 C7
Trevena Rd TR18 . . . . . . 143 C4
Trevena Terr TR7 . . . . . . 110 D6
Trevendon PL17 . . . . 28 D1
Treveneague Gdns PL2 . . 128 D8
Trevenen TR13 . . . . 92 A4
Trevenen Bal TR13 . . . . . 91 F4
Trevenen Rd TR13 . . . . . 146 C5
Treveneth Cres TR18 . . . 143 C1
Treveneth Pl 1 TR18 . . . 143 C1
Treven La TR27 . . . . 78 B1
Trevenna Cross TR8 . . . . 45 A8
Trevenner Ho 8 TR15 . . . 140 B5
Trevenner La TR17 . . . . . 89 C5
Trevenner Mews 6 TR15 . 140 B5
Trevenner Sq TR17 . . . . . 89 C5
TREVENNING 23 F5
Trevenn La PL15 . . . . 17 A3
Treven Noweth TR16 . . . . 68 C3
Trevenson Ct TR15 . . . . . 139 B6
Trevenson La
  Camborne TR14 . . . . 138 D2
  Camborne, Pool TR15 . . . 139 A6
Trevenson Moor TR14 . . . 139 A7
Trevenson Rd
  Camborne TR15 . . . . 139 B5
  Newquay TR7 . . . . 111 B6
Trevenson St TR14 . . . . . 138 D2
Treventon Cl
  Falmouth TR11 . . . . 144 E4
  Portscatho TR2 . . . . 83 B2
Treventon Rd TR2 . . . . . . 83 B2
Treventon Rise 11 TR9 . . 45 E6
TREVERBYN Penwithick . . 59 C7
  St Cleer 37 B2
Treverbyn Academy PL26 . 59 C8
Treverbyn Cl Liskeard PL14 113 E6
  Plymouth PL7 . . . . 130 D6
Treverbyn Gdns PL25 . . . 114 F4
Treverbyn Rd
  Falmouth TR11 . . . . 144 E1
  Padstow PL28 . . . . 107 E4
  Plymouth PL7 . . . . 130 D6
  St Austell PL25 . . . . 114 E7
  St Ives TR26 . . . . 141 A5
  Stenalees PL26 . . . . 59 C8
  Truro TR1 . . . . 137 E6
Treverbyn Rise TR10 . . . . 144 A8
Trevere Cl TR27 . . . . 78 C6
Treverno Rd TR14 . . . . . . 138 E6
Treverry La TR12 . . . . . . 99 B8
TREVERVA 93 B6
Treveryn Parc TR4 . . . . . 144 C2
TREVESCAN 96 B5
Trevessa Cl PL2 . . . . 128 D8
Trevethan Cl TR6 . . . . . . 55 B4

Trevethan Cl continued
Falmouth TR11 . . . . .145 A4
Trevethan Ct **2** TR11 . . . . . . .145 A5
Trevethan Gdns **2** TR11 . .145 A4
Trevethan Hill **1** TR11 . . .145 B5
Trevethan Pk PL20 . . . . .119 F4
Trevethan Rd
Falmouth TR11 . . . . .145 A4
Falmouth TR11 . . . . .145 A4
Trevethan Rise TR11 . . . . . . .145 A4
Trevethenick Rd TR1 . . . . . .137 E3
Treveth La TR13 . . . . .146 D8
TREVETHOE 77 D3
Treveth Tean TR9 . . . . .57 E8
Treveth Ylyn TR14 . . . . .138 F5
TREVIA 105 B4
TREVIADES 93 A3
Trevia La PL32 . . . . .105 B4
Trevian Cl **6** TR6 . . . . .55 A4
Trevia Pk Terr PL32 . . . . . . .105 C3
Treviglas Cl TR7 . . . . .111 D7
Treviglas Com Coll TR7 . .111 D7
Treviglas La TR2 . . . . .71 C6
Treviglas Rise TR2 . . . . .71 C6
TREVIGRO 39 C4
TREVILLA 82 C6
Trevilla Hill TR3 . . . . .82 C6
Trevilla Rd TR3 . . . . .82 C6
Trevillet Rd PL32 . . . . .15 A6
Trevilley La PL30, PL33 . . . . .23 E8
Trevillick La PL30. . . . . .23 F6
Trevilling Rd PL27 . . . . .108 B6
Trevillis Pk PL14 . . . . .113 B4
TREVILSON 56 D6
Trevilson Cl TR8. . . . . .56 C7
Trevince Parc TR16 . . . . .80 F8
Trevingey Cl TR15 . . . . .140 A3
Trevingey Cres TR15 . . . . . .140 A3
Trevingey Parc TR15 . . . . . .140 A4
Trevingey Rd TR15. . . . . . . .140 A3
Trevinnick Rd PL30 . . . . .22 F4
TREVISCOE 58 B7
Trevisker Com Prim Sch
PL27 . . . . .31 F3
Trevisker Dr TR13 . . . . .91 A1
Treviskey Hill TR2 . . . . .84 B3
Trevisquite La PL30. . . . . . . .23 D1
Trevissome Bissom TR11. . . .81 F1
Bissom TR11 . . . . .94 B7
Bissom TR11 . . . . .144 F8
Trevissome Ct TR11 . . . . . .144 F6
Trevithick Ave PL11 . . . . . .126 F4
Trevithick Cl Newquay TR7 110 F4
St Merryn PL28 . . . . .31 F8
1 St Merryn PL28. . . . . .31 F8
Truro TR1 . . . . .137 E6
Trevithick Cres TR27 . . . . . .142 D5
Trevithick Ct
Camborne TR14 . . . . .138 C3
3 Camborne, Illogan Highway
TR15 . . . . .139 C6
Truro TR1 . . . . .137 E6
Trevithick Est **7** PL28 . . . .31 F8
Trevithick Hill PL26 . . . . .72 D4
Trevithick Learning Academy
TR14 .138 D1
Trevithick Rd
Camborne TR14 . . . . .138 D3
Camborne, Illogan Highway
TR15 . . . . .139 C6
Chacewater TR4 . . . . .69 A3
Falmouth TR11 . . . . .144 E5
Plymouth PL5 . . . . .123 E2
St Austell PL25 . . . . .114 E3
Truro TR1 . . . . .137 E5
Trevitho La **4** TR12 . . . . . . .99 B2
Trevoarn TR27 . . . . .142 B5
Trevol Bsns Pk PL11 . . . . . .126 D3
TREVOLLARD 53 D1
Trevollard PL13 . . . . .61 F7
Trevollard La PL12. . . . . .53 D1
Trevol Pl PL11 . . . . .126 E3
Trevol Rd PL11 . . . . .126 E3
TREVONE 20 E2
Trevone TR10 . . . . .93 B7
Trevone Cres PL26. . . . . . . .114 A4
Trevone Gdns PL2 . . . . .128 D8
Trevone Rd PL28 . . . . .20 F2
Trevoney TR11 . . . . .144 C2
Trevonnen Cl TR13 . . . . .90 E3
Trevonnen Rd TR3. . . . . .81 B4
Trevorder Cl PL11 . . . . .126 F2
Trevorder Ct PL25 . . . . .114 E7
Trevorder Rd PL11. . . . . . . .126 F2
Trevorgans Cross TR19 . . . .96 F8
TREVORRICK 107 E1
Trevorrick Rd PL27 . . . . .32 D7
Trevose Ave TR7 . . . . .110 C4
Trevose Cl
Constantine Bay PL28 . . . . . .20 C1
St Agnes TR5 . . . . .54 C1
Trevose Ho TR1 . . . . .69 E4
Trevose Rd TR1 . . . . .69 F4
Trevose Way PL3 . . . . .129 C6
Trevothen Penhallick TR12. .101 A1
Penhallick TR12 . . . . .103 F8
Trevowah Mdws TR8 . . . . . .110 A3
Trevowah Rd TR8. . . . . .43 D3
TREVOWHAN 75 C2
Trevowhan Hill TR20 . . . . . .75 C2
Trevozah Cross PL15 . . . . . . .28 B8
Trevu Ho TR14 . . . . .138 E1
Trevu Rd TR14. . . . . .138 E2
Trevurvas La TR13 . . . . .90 C3
TREW 90 F4

Trew TR13 . . . . .90 F4
TREWALDER 14 E1
Trewalder Rd PL33 . . . . .14 D1
Trewall Hill PL11 . . . . .64 D5
Trewan Hall TR9 . . . . .45 E7
Trewans Terr TR15 . . . . .140 A6
Trewardreva Cross TR11. . . .92 E4
Trewarlett Cross PL15 . . . . . .28 A7
TREWARMETT 14 D5
Trewarmett La PL33 . . . . . . .14 D5
Trewarne La TR8 . . . . .111 F3
Trewartha Ct TR26. . . . . . . .141 D1
Trewartha Ct **4** PL14 . . . . .113 C6
Trewartha Est TR26. . . . . . .141 D1
Trewartha Flats TR26. . . . . .141 D1
Trewartha Rd TR20 . . . . .90 C3
Trewartha Terr **12** TR18. . .143 E6
Trewarton Rd TR10 . . . . .81 D2
Trewarveneth Farm Cotts
TR18 . . . . .88 C2
Trewarveneth St TR18 . . . .143 C2
TREWASSA 15 F5
Trewassa Flats PL32 . . . . . . .15 F5
Trewavas TR13 . . . . .90 D2
Trewavas Cres TR13 . . . . . .146 C5
Trewavas Rd TR18. . . . . . . .143 C1
Treweath TR16 . . . . .80 C2
Treweath Rd TR18. . . . . . . .143 D7
Trewedna La TR3. . . . . .81 C5
Treweeks Rd TR19. . . . . .75 A1
Treweese Cross PL14. . . . . . .52 B7
Treweese Rd Menheniot PL14 52 B7
Quethiock PL14 . . . . .52 B8
TREWELLARD 86 F8
Trewellard Hill TR19. . . . . . .87 A8
Trewellard Ind Est TR19 . . . .86 F8
Trewellard Rd TR19 . . . . .86 F8
Trewelloe Rd TR20 . . . . .90 C3
Trewelm La TR16 . . . . .68 E1
TREWEN 17 E2
Trewen Farm La
Menehay TR11 . . . . .144 C1
Sparnon TR11. . . . . .93 D6
Tregedna TR11. . . . . .94 A4
Trewen Hill PL15 . . . . .17 E1
TREWENNACK 146 F8
Trewennack
Treloquithack TR13 . . . . .92 A4
Tremenheere TR13 . . . . .91 F4
Trewennack TR13 . . . . .146 F8
TREWENNAN 23 E8
Trewennan Hill PL30 . . . . . . .23 E8
Trewen Rd TR11 . . . . .144 C2
Trewen Terr TR11 . . . . .144 C2
Trewern La TR20 . . . . .87 E6
TREWETHA 22 E7
Trewetha Farm Lodges
PL29 . . . . .22 E7
Trewetha La PL29 . . . . .22 D7
Trewethen La PL30 . . . . .23 C5
TREWETHERN 22 E3
TREWEY 76 B5
Trewey Hill TR26 . . . . .76 B4
Trewhella La TR20 . . . . .89 F7
Trewhiddle Rd PL25 . . . . . .114 C2
Trewidden Cl TR1 . . . . .137 E5
Trewidden Ct TR1 . . . . .137 E5
Trewidden Ct TR26 . . . . . . .141 B5
Trewidden Gdn * TR20 . . . .88 A4
TREWIDLAND 51 C2
Trewidland Prim Sch PL14 . .51 C2
Trewiggett La PL30 . . . . .23 B6
Trewince TR11 . . . . .93 B3
Trewince La
Grampound Road TR2 . . . . . . .57 E1
Lostwithiel PL22 . . . . .112 C3
Porth Navas TR11 . . . . .93 B3
Trewince Manor TR2 . . . . . .95 C6
Trewince Terr **2** TR18. . . .143 C1
Trewince Villas PL27 . . . . . . .32 E6
Trewinnard Ct TR1 . . . . . . .137 B6
Trewinnard Gr TR1. . . . . . . .137 B6
Trewinnard La TR27 . . . . . . .77 E1
Trewinnard Rd TR3. . . . . . . .81 D5
Trewinnick Council Hos
PL27 . . . . .32 A5
Trewinnick Rd PL27 . . . . .32 A5
Trewinnow Cross PL15 . . . . .27 D6
Trewin Rd **2** PL31. . . . . . . .109 A5
TREWINT 10 F8
Trewint Cres PL13 . . . . .117 D4
Trewint Est PL14 . . . . .52 A5
Trewint Hill PL27 . . . . .21 D4
Trewint La Landrake PL12 . . .53 B2
Rock PL27 . . . . .21 D3
Trewint Rd PL14. . . . . .52 A6
Trewirgie Gdns TR15 . . . . . .140 B4
Trewirgie Hill TR15 . . . . . . .140 B3
Trewirgie Jun & Inf Schs
TR15 .140 B4
Trewirgie Rd TR15. . . . . . . .140 B3
Trewirgie Vean TR15 . . . . . .140 B4
Trewiston La PL27 . . . . .21 E3
Trewithan Parc PL22 . . . . . .112 D2
Trewithen TR3 . . . . .80 E4
Trewithen Gdns * TR2. . . . . .71 E6
Trewithen La PL28 . . . . .32 A8
Trewithen Parc TR8 . . . . . . .56 B7
Trewithen Rd TR18 . . . . . . .143 D5
Trewithen Terr TR13. . . . . . .90 D5
Trewithey La PL15 . . . . .27 C4
TREWITHIAN 83 B4
Trewithick Hill PL15 . . . . . . .18 C4
Trewithick La PL15 . . . . .18 C4
Trewithick Rd TR13. . . . . . . .90 F2
Trewithy Ct PL6 . . . . .124 F1
Trewithy Dr PL6 . . . . .124 F1
TREWOLD 9 E1

Trewollack Rd St Wenn PL30 46 D8
Trewollack PL30 . . . . .33 B1
Trewollock Cl PL26 . . . . .85 C5
Trewollock La PL26. . . . . . . .85 C5
TREWOODLOE 39 B6
Trewoolsta Terr **5** PL14 . . .38 E4
TREWOON Mullion 99 B2
St Austell 59 A3
Trewoon Rd TR12. . . . . .99 B2
Trewoon Cl EX23 . . . . .4 E1
Trewoorder La
7 Treleague TR12 . . . . . . .103 B5
Wadebridge PL27 . . . . .108 F5
Trewoorder Rd TR1. . . . . . .137 B3
TREWORGA 83 D7
Treworgan View TR4 . . . . . . .56 D1
Treworgie La TR12 . . . . .100 F6
TREWORLAS 83 D5
Treworlis Cl TR13 . . . . .146 D8
TREWORNAN 22 C1
TREWORRICK 37 E3
TREWORTHAL 83 C5
Treworthal Rd TR3 . . . . .81 D5
Treworval TR11 . . . . .93 C4
Treworvenneth Dr **9** TR17.89 C5
Trewrickle La PL11 . . . . .65 A5
Trewyn Flats **41** TR26 . . . .141 B6
Treyarnon La PL28. . . . . .31 D8
Treyew Pl TR16. . . . . .80 F8
Treyew Prim Sch TR1 . . . . .137 A4
Treyew Rd TR1 . . . . .137 B3
TREZAISE 47 A2
Trezaise Cl PL26 . . . . .47 A2
Trezaise Cl PL26 . . . . .47 A2
Trezaise Rd PL26 . . . . .46 F2
Trezaise Sq PL26 . . . . .47 A2
Treza Rd TR13 . . . . .91 A1
Trezebel Hill TR12. . . . . . . .101 A6
Trezela Rd TR18 . . . . .143 D6
Triangle, The 16 TR12. . . .102 F2
Trillacott Rd Billacott PL15 . 12 B1
Navarino PL15. . . . . .18 A8
Trillacott PL15 . . . . .17 F8
Trinity Bldgs TR19 . . . . .96 B6
Trinity Cl Bere Alston PL20. . .41 B1
Carnkie TR16 . . . . .80 C2
Trinity Praze TR16. . . . . .80 C2
Trinity St PL25. . . . . .114 C3
Trinity Way PL19 . . . . .147 A4
Tripp Hill PL14 . . . . .36 F2
TRISPEN 56 D1
Trispen Hill TR4 . . . . .56 D1
Tristan Dr TR1 . . . . .137 F5
Triumphal Cres PL7 . . . . . . .130 A6
TROAN .57 C8
Trolver Hill TR3 . . . . .82 B6
Trolvis TR10. . . . . .81 A1
Trolvus Vean TR10. . . . . .81 A1
Troods Mill PL15 . . . . .106 B7
TROON .79 E5
Troon CP Sch TR14. . . . . . . .79 E4
Troon Moor TR14. . . . . .79 E4
Troon Row TR13 . . . . .90 F3
Trossell Rd PL15. . . . . .11 F1
Troswell Hill
Caudworthy Bridge PL15. . . . .11 A2
Webworthy PL15 . . . . .12 A3
Troubridge Rd TR13 . . . . . .146 C4
Trowan La TR26 . . . . .76 F7
Trowbridge Cl PL5 . . . . .124 C4
Troy Ct PL23. . . . . .116 C4
Truck Hill TR2. . . . . .71 B6
Trungle Parc **3** TR19 . . . . .88 C2
Trungle Terr TR19 . . . . .88 C2
TRURO 137 E3
Truro Bsns Pk TR3 . . . . .69 C3
Truro Dr PL5 . . . . .124 A5
Truro High Sch TR1 . . . . . . .137 C3
Truro Hill TR10 . . . . .144 C8
Truro La TR10 . . . . .144 C8
Truro L Ctr TR1 . . . . .69 E3
Truro & Penryn Coll
Truro TR1 . . . . .69 E3
22 Truro TR1 . . . . .137 D4
Truro Prep Sch TR1 . . . . .69 F4
Truro Rd Lanivet PL30 . . . . . .47 F7
St Austell PL25 . . . . .114 A2
Truro Sch TR1 . . . . .137 E3
Truro Sta TR1 . . . . .137 B4
Truro Vean Terr TR1 . . . . . .137 D5
TRURO VEAN 137 D5
TRUSCOTT 18 D4
Truscott La PL15 . . . . .18 C4
Trussall TR13. . . . . .92 B4
TRUTHAN 56 C2
Truthan View TR4 . . . . .56 D1
TRUTHWALL Marazion 89 D7
St Just .86 E7
Truthwall La TR19 . . . . .86 F7
Tryelyn PL13 . . . . .109 F2
Tryhornek TR26 . . . . .77 D4
Trythall Prim Sch TR20. . . . .76 B1
TRYTHOGGA 143 F3
Trythogga Hill TR18 . . . . . .143 F3
Trythogga Rd TR18 . . . . . . .143 F3
Tubbon Hill Ponsanooth TR3. 81 A4
Trebost TR3 . . . . .81 A4
TUBBS MILL 72 D2
Tucker Cl PL5 . . . . .127 F8
TUCKERMARSH 41 B2
Tuckers Cl TR8 . . . . .111 B4
TUCKINGMILL Camborne . .139 A4
St Breward 24 B4
Tuckingmill TR13. . . . . .91 D4
Tuckingmill Terr TR13 . . . . . .91 E4
Tucoyse Hill PL26 . . . . .72 D4
Tucoyse La TR11 . . . . .92 D4
Tudor Cl PL9 . . . . .135 E5
Tudor Ct PL12 . . . . .123 A2

Tudor Lodge Pk TR20 . . . . . .89 C7
Tuke Cl TR11 . . . . .144 E5
Tunnels Through Time ★
TR7 . . . . .110 D5
Turbill Gdns **4** PL7 . . . . . .131 B5
TURFDOWN 48 E8
Turfdown Rd PL30 . . . . .48 E8
Turf St PL31 . . . . .109 E5
Turnavean Rd PL25 . . . . . . .114 A5
Turnaware Rd TR11. . . . . . .144 E2
TURNCHAPEL 135 B7
Turnpike
Gunnislake/Calstock PL18 . . .40 E5
Helston TR13 . . . . .146 C7
Trebyan PL30 . . . . .48 D5
Turnpike Hill **2** TR17 . . . . .89 C5
Turnpike Pl PL14 . . . . .113 B4
Turnpike Rd
Connor Downs TR27 . . . . .78 D6
Marazion TR17. . . . . .89 C5
Turnpike The TR19 . . . . .86 F6
Turnquay PL9 . . . . .135 C7
Turnstone Way EX23. . . . . .104 F4
Turret Gr PL4. . . . . .128 F4
TUTWELL 29 A2
Tuxton Cl PL7 . . . . .131 C3
TWELVEHEADS 69 B1
Twelvewoods Bsns Pk 3
PL14 . . . . .50 D7
Twelvewoods Cl PL14. . . . . .50 E8
Twelvewoods Pl PL14. . . . . .50 E8
Twiggy La TR27 . . . . .90 C6
Twinbrook Pk TR11. . . . . . . .93 B3
TWO BURROWS 68 E5
Two Chimneys Caravan Pk 7
TR20 . . . . .90 B3
Two Hills Pk PL12 . . . . .122 C2
Two Trees PL27 . . . . .108 B4
Two Trees Rd PL22 . . . . .112 F1
Tyacke Rd TR13 . . . . .146 B5
Tybesta TR2. . . . . .72 A7
Grampound TR2. . . . . .72 A7
Tye Hill Cl PL25. . . . . .59 A3
Tyland Rd PL32 . . . . .105 F4
Tylney Cl PL6 . . . . .125 B6
Tyndale Cl PL5 . . . . .124 B1
Tyringham Pl TR26 . . . . .77 E4
Tyringham Rd TR26. . . . . . . .77 E4
Tyringham Row TR26 . . . . . .77 E4
Tyshute La PL26 . . . . .59 A1
Tything Wlk **4** PL3 . . . . . .128 E6
TYWARDREATH 60 D5
Tywardreath Highway PL24 60 C6
Tywardreath Hill PL24. . . . . .60 D5
Tywardreath Sch PL24 . . . . .60 D5
Tywarnhale Way TR4 . . . . . .68 A6
Tywarnhayle Rd TR6. . . . . . .55 A5
Tywarnhayle Sq **23** TR6 . . .55 A5

Uglow Cl TR14 . . . . .138 C3
Ualia Rd TR7. . . . . .110 F6
Ullswater Cres PL6 . . . . .124 E4
Umfulla Pl **18** TR26 . . . . . .141 B5
Under Chapel Yd TR18. . . . .143 F4
Undercliff TR27 . . . . .142 D7
Undercliff Rd PL9 . . . . .135 B7
Underhayes La PL15 . . . . . .106 A8
Underhill Rd PL3 . . . . .128 A4
Underhill Villas **1** PL3. . . .128 A3
Underla TR13. . . . . .92 D8
Under La Cross Hill PL30. . . .23 C1
Haywood PL30. . . . . .34 C8
Launceston PL15 . . . . .18 C3
Plymouth, Plympton PL7 . . .130 C5
Plymouth, Plymstock PL9 . .135 A6
Under Rd Boscastle PL35. . . . .9 C1
Bridgerule EX22 . . . . .8 A5
Gunnislake PL18 . . . . .41 A6
Underways PL20. . . . . .41 B1
UNDERWOOD 130 C5
Underwood Rd PL7. . . . . . . .130 D4
Unicorn Cl PL7 . . . . .130 B6
Union Cnr TR11. . . . . .144 D5
Union Hill
St Columb Major TR9 . . . . . . .45 E6
6 Stratton EX23. . . . . .4 D1
Truro TR1 . . . . .70 D5
Union Pl Fowey PL23. . . . . .116 D4
Plymouth PL1. . . . . .148 A2
Truro TR1 . . . . .137 D5
Union Rd TR11 . . . . .144 D6
Union Sq TR9 . . . . .45 E6
Union St Camborne TR14 . .138 D2
27 Penzance TR18. . . . . . .143 E5
Plymouth PL1. . . . . .148 A2
Truro TR1 . . . . .137 C5
UNITED DOWNS 81 A8
United Downs Ind Pk
Truro TR16 . . . . .81 A8
United Downs TR16 . . . . .81 A8
United Rd Carharrack TR16 . .80 F8
United Downs TR16 . . . . .81 A8
Unit Hos PL27 . . . . .33 B5
Unity Cl PL6. . . . . .125 D5
Unity Rd TR13 . . . . .98 C8
University of Plymouth Bsns
Sch PL4. . . . . .148 C4
University of Plymouth
(Cookworthy Bldg) PL4. .149 A3
Univ of St Mark & St John
PL6. . . . . .125 C4
UPCOTT 2 F4
Upcott Cross EX39. . . . . .2 F5

Upland Cl TR1 . . . . .137 F6
Upland Cres TR1 . . . . .137 E6
Upland Dr PL6. . . . . .125 A5
Uplands Lostwithiel PL22. . .112 B2
Saltash PL12 . . . . .122 E1
Tavistock PL19 . . . . .147 A4
Uplands Vean TR1. . . . . .137 F5
Upper Castle Rd TR2 . . . . . .95 A6
Upper Chapel PL15 . . . . . . .106 A4
Upper Dobbin PL28 . . . . . . .20 F2
Upper Dobbin La PL28 . . . . .20 F2
Upper Eastcliffe Rd PL24. . .60 D4
Upper Hillcrest **8** TR6. . . . .55 A4
Upper Knollys Terrace La
PL3 . . . . .128 C4
Upper Lemon Villas TR1. . .137 C3
Upper Ridings PL7. . . . . .131 B7
Upper School La TR1 . . . . . .137 C3
Upperton La PL6 . . . . .121 F3
Upper Tredrea TR3 . . . . .81 D5
UPTON Bude 104 C2
Upton Cross. 38 C7
Upton Cl PL3 . . . . .129 B7
UPTON CROSS. 38 D6
Upton Cross EX23 . . . . .104 C2
Upton Cross Prim Sch PL14 38 C7
Upton Mdws EX23 . . . . .104 C3
Upton Terr EX23 . . . . .104 C2
UPTON TOWANS. 78 B6
Upton Towans
Gwithian TR27. . . . . .66 B1
Upton Towans TR27. . . . . . . .78 C7
Upton Twrs Nature Reserve ★
TR27. . . . . .78 B6
Urban Terr PL17 . . . . .39 F5
Ursa Gdns **21** PL9 . . . . . . .136 E8
UTC Plymouth PL19 . . . . . .127 E3
Uxbridge Dr PL5 . . . . .123 E4
Uzella Pk PL22 . . . . .112 C2

V

Vaagso Cl PL1. . . . . .127 E2
Valency Row PL35 . . . . .9 C2
Valentine Row **4** PL17. . . . .39 E4
Valiant Ave PL5. . . . . .124 A4
Vallard's La PL12 . . . . .53 E4
Valletort Flats PL1. . . . . . . .128 A2
Valletort Ho PL1 . . . . .148 C3
Valletort La PL1 . . . . .128 A3
Valletort Pl PL1 . . . . .128 A2
Valletort Rd PL1, PL3 . . . . .128 A3
Valletort Terr PL1 . . . . .148 A4
Valley Bglws PL13 . . . . .117 F5
Valley Cl Goonhavern TR4. . .55 C3
Truro TR1 . . . . .69 F3
Valley Gdns **20** TR16 . . . . .67 E4
Valley Gr TR1 . . . . .81 F7
Valley Park La PL26 . . . . .73 C3
Valley Pk **20** PL26. . . . . . . .85 D8
Valley Rd Bude EX23 . . . . . .104 E5
Carbis Bay TR26 . . . . .141 C2
Mevagissey PL26. . . . . .73 C4
Plymouth PL7. . . . . .130 B5
Saltash PL12 . . . . .122 E2
Valley The TR19 . . . . .96 E3
VALLEY TRUCKLE 105 C2
Valley View Bodmin PL31. . .109 E3
19 Illogan TR16. . . . . .67 E4
Plymouth PL6. . . . . .125 D7
Redruth TR16. . . . . .140 E1
St Keyne PL14 . . . . .51 A4
St Teath PL30. . . . . .23 E7
Wadebridge PL27 . . . . .108 C4
Valley View Cl PL3. . . . . . . .129 B6
Valley View Dr TR1 . . . . .69 F3
Valley View Pk Bodmin PL31 34 C2
St Austell PL26. . . . . .47 C2
Valley View Rd PL3 . . . . . . .129 B7
Valley View Terr TR3 . . . . . . .81 B5
Valley Wlk PL6 . . . . .125 E6
Vanguard Cl PL5 . . . . .124 D1
Vapron Rd PL3 . . . . .128 F6
Varfell La TR20 . . . . .89 A7
Varley La PL14. . . . . .113 B5
Varley Terr **1** PL14 . . . . . . .113 B5
Vauban Pl PL2. . . . . .127 F4
Vaughan Cl PL2 . . . . .128 C7
Vauxhall Ct **10** PL4. . . . . . .149 A2
Vauxhall Quay PL4. . . . . . . .149 A2
Vauxhall St PL4. . . . . .149 A2
Vauxhall Street Flats 19
PL4 . . . . .149 A2
Vean Rd TR14 . . . . .138 E2
Vean Terr TR14 . . . . .138 E2
Vear Ho TR14 . . . . .138 D2
Vellan Cl TR14. . . . . .79 B5
Vellan Dreath TR19 . . . . .86 E1
Vellan Parc TR3. . . . . .80 F3
Vellanhoggan Mews TR18 . .88 E6
VELLANOWETH 89 A8
Vellan Parc Ave TR27 . . . . . .78 C5
Vellan Vrane TR27 . . . . .78 C5
Venetian Views TR9 . . . . . . .57 D8
Venland Cl **9** PL14 . . . . . . .38 A3
Venn Cl **6** PL3 . . . . .128 E6
Venn Cres PL3. . . . . .128 E6
Venn Ct PL3 . . . . .128 E6
Venn Gdns PL3 . . . . .128 E7
Venn Gr PL3. . . . . .128 E6
Venn Hill PL19. . . . . .29 C6
Venn La PL30. . . . . .36 A2
Venn Way PL3 . . . . .128 E7
Vensloose Hill PL14 . . . . . . .113 B7
VENTERDON 28 D2
Ventnor Terr TR26 . . . . .141 A6
Venton East Sq TR19. . . . . . .86 F6

VENTONGIMPS 55 C2
Venton Lace Rd TR2 . . . . . . .57 E1
VENTONLEAGUE 142 F7
Ventonleague Hill TR27. .142 E7
Ventonleague Row TR27. .142 E7
Ventonraze TR16 . . . . .67 E4
Ventonraze Terr **2** TR16. . .67 E4
Venton Rd Falmouth TR11 . .141 C3
St Ives TR26. . . . . .141 C3
Ventonvaise **5** TR6. . . . . .55 A5
Venton Vision Rise TR26 . . .77 A7
Veor Rd TR7. . . . . .111 C7
Verden Cl PL3 . . . . .128 E5
Verdun Terr PL14. . . . . .113 B5
Vermont Gdns PL2 . . . . . . .127 F7
Verna Pl PL5 . . . . .123 D2
Verna Rd PL5. . . . . .123 E2
Vcrnigo Cross PL12. . . . . . . .40 D1
Vernon Pl TR11. . . . . .145 B4
Vernon Villas PL24 . . . . .60 B4
Vernon Way TR10. . . . . . . .144 B7
VERYAN 83 F6
Veryan CE Prim Sch TR2 . . .83 F6
VERYAN GREEN. 83 F7
Viaduct Hill TR27. . . . . .142 E6
Viaduct La TR14 . . . . .138 A1
Vicarage Cl
  Budock Water TR11. . . . . .144 C3
  Menheniot PL14 . . . . .51 F5
Vicarage Gate TR27. . . . . . .142 A1
Vicarage Gdns
  Milton Abbot PL19 . . . . . . .29 C6
  Plymouth PL5. . . . . .123 B1
Vicarage Hill
  Budock Water TR11. . . . . .144 C3
  Mevagissey PL26. . . . . .73 C4
  10 St Austell PL25. . . . . .114 C4
  St Day TR16 . . . . .68 E1
  9 Tintagel PL34 . . . . .14 C7
Vicarage La Lelant TR26 . . .77 E4
  Manaccan TR12. . . . . .101 A8
  Poundstock EX23. . . . . .6 F2
Vicarage Mdw PL23 . . . . . .116 C4
Vicarage Rd Bude EX23 . . .104 D5
  Plymouth PL7. . . . . .130 C6
  Porthleven TR13. . . . . .91 A1
  St Agnes TR5 . . . . .54 D1
  Torpoint PL11 . . . . .127 B2
  Tywardreath PL24 . . . . .60 D5
Vicarage Row TR13. . . . . . . .90 F3
Vicarage Terr TR11. . . . . . . .92 F4
VICTORIA Lostwithiel 112 B2
  Roche 46 F4
Victoria Ave PL1. . . . . .148 A4
Victoria Bsns Pk PL26. . . . .47 A4
Victoria Cl PL14 . . . . .113 C6
Victoria Cotts
  Budock Water TR11. . . . . .144 C3
  Falmouth TR11. . . . . .145 B3
  Plymouth PL6. . . . . .129 B8
Victoria Ct **15** TR18 . . . . . .143 E6
Victoria Gdns
  2 St Columb Road TR9 . . .45 E2
  Threemilestone TR3 . . . . . .69 D3
Victoria La PL12 . . . . .122 F2
Victoria Mews **17** TR18. . .143 E6
Victoria Pk PL27. . . . . .108 D6
Victoria Pl
  31 Penzance TR18. . . . . . .143 E5
  Plymouth PL1. . . . . .148 A2
  Plymouth, Devonport PL2 . .127 F4
  Ponsanooth TR3. . . . . .81 B4
  9 St Austell PL25 . . . . . .114 C3
  12 St Ives TR26 . . . . .141 B6
Victoria Quay
  5 Falmouth TR11 . . . . . .145 B5
  Truro TR1 . . . . .70 D1
Victoria Rd Bude EX23 . . .104 D7
  Camelford PL32. . . . . .105 E4
  Plymouth PL5. . . . . .123 D2
  Roche PL26 . . . . .46 F3
  St Austell PL25. . . . . .114 F3
  11 St Ives TR26 . . . . .141 B6
  Saltash PL12 . . . . .122 F2
  Threemilestone TR3 . . . . . .69 D3
Victoria Road Prim Sch **1**
  PL5. . . . . .123 D1
Victoria Row TR19. . . . . . . .86 E6
Victoria Sq Bodmin PL31 . .109 F3
  16 Penzance TR18. . . . . .143 E6
  Truro TR1. . . . . .137 C4
Victoria St Camborne TR14 .138 D2
  St Columb Major TR9 . . . . .45 E6
  Torpoint PL11 . . . . .127 B3
Victoria Terr
  4 Liskeard PL14. . . . . . . .113 B5
  Plymouth PL4. . . . . .148 C4
  Portscatho TR2 . . . . .83 B2
  St Breward PL30 . . . . .24 B3
Victory Cl **8** TR20 . . . . . . .88 B7
Victory Rd EX22 . . . . .13 A8
Victory St PL2 . . . . .127 E6
Vigo Bridge Rd PL19 . . . . .147 C6
Vigo Mews PL19. . . . . .147 C6
Village Dr PL6. . . . . .121 C1
Village Farm Cl EX23 . . . . . .7 B6
Village The
  Buckland Monachorum PL20. .19 F2
  Duloe PL14 . . . . .51 A1
Villa Marina TR17. . . . . .89 B5
Villiers Cl PL9 . . . . .135 D7
Vincent Way PL12 . . . . .122 F2
Vine Ct PL2 . . . . .128 B6
Vine Gdns PL2. . . . . .128 B6
Vine Pl **10** PL4. . . . . .60 D5
Vinery La PL7, PL9. . . . . . . .130 E1
Vineyard The TR3 . . . . .80 F3
Vingoe's La TR20 . . . . .88 B7

West Porthmear Ct PL25...115 B2
WEST PORTHOLLAND 84 D5
West Quay PL10 ....132 E5
West Rd Looe PL13 ....117 C4
Quintrell Downs TR8 ....111 E3
West Rise TR11 ....144 F3
West Seton
Higher Rosewarne TR14 .....138 D5
Reskadinnick TR14 ....79 C8
West Seton Rd 6 TR14 ...138 E5
West St Grimscott EX23 ......5 B1
Liskeard PL14 ....113 B6
Millbrook PL10 ....132 C6
Penryn TR10 ....144 C8
Polruan PL23 ....116 C2
St Columb Major TR9 ......45 E6
Tavistock PL19 ....147 B5
Torpoint PL10 ....132 E4
WEST TAPHOUSE 49 E6
West Tehidy TR14 ....138 F7
West Terr Hayle TR27 .....142 B6
Newlyn TR18 ....143 C3
WEST TOLGUS 139 D8
West Tolgus TR15 ....139 D8
West Trevingey TR15 ......140 A3
West Trewirgie Rd TR15 ..140 B4
Westview TR6 ....55 B5
West View Porthleven TR13 ..91 A1
Tavistock PL19 ....147 E2
Trevone PL28 ....20 E2
West View Rd 5 PL20 .....41 B1
West Villas TR8 ....57 B7
Westward PL27 ....21 D5
Westward Rd TR26 ....141 A6
WEST WATERGATE 62 E4
Westway PL9 ....135 B5
West Week Cl EX22 ....11 E8
West Wharf PL26 ....73 C3
Westwinds PL32 ....16 A8
Westwood PL14 ....113 B6
Westwood Ave PL6 ......125 C6
WEST YOULSTONE 3 B2
Wetherham La PL30 ....23 E3
Wet La PL30 ....24 A5
Whalesborough Parc EX23104 F1
Wharf Rd Penzance TR18 ..143 F5
St Ives TR26 ....141 B6
Wharfside 8 TR18 ....143 E5
Wharfside Sh Ctr TR18 ...143 F5
Wharfside Village 9 TR18 143 E5
Wharf The
22 Mousehole TR19......88 C1
St Ives TR26...........141 B6
Wharf Theatre & Gall The*
PL19..................147 B5
Whatley Mews 3 PL9....129 D1
Wheal Agar 5 TR14 .....138 F7
Wheal Agar TR15 ....139 C6
WHEAL ALFRED..........142 F4
Wheal Alfred Rd TR27 ...142 F5
Wheal-an-Wens TR17 .....89 C5
Wheal Ayr Ct 1 TR26 ...141 A5
Wheal Boys TR16 ....140 E8
Whealbrake Lodge PL26 ...58 D6
Whealbrothers La PL17 ....40 C4
Wheal Bull PL26 ....58 D5
Wheal Buller Carnkie TR16 .80 C7
Pennance TR16 ....140 A1
WHEAL BUSY 68 F3
Wheal Busy La TR4 ....68 F3
Wheal Butson Rd TR5.....68 D8
Wheal Catherine Cl TR6 ...55 B5
Wheal Cl TR8 ....56 B7
Wheal Damsel Rd TR16 ....80 E8
Wheal Dance TR16 ......140 D3
Wheal Dream TR26 ......141 C6
Wheal Eliza Cl PL25.....115 B5
Wheal Fortune TR13 ......91 A3
Wheal Fortune La TR15 ..139 D6
WHEAL FRANCES 55 D3
Wheal Friendly La TR5....54 C2
Wheal Gerry TR14 ......138 E4
Wheal Golden Dr TR8.....43 C1
Wheal Gorland Rd TR16 ...68 D1
Wheal Harmony Terr TR15140 B7
Wheal Jane Mdws TR3....69 C3
Wheal Jewel (Gipsy Site)
TR16 ....68 E1
Wheal Kitty TR5 ....54 D1
Wheal Kitty La TR5 ....54 D2
Wheal Kitty Rd TR27......77 A3
Wheal Kitty Workshops
TR5....................54 D2
Wheal Leisure TR6 ....55 A5
Wheal Leisure Cl 25 TR6 ..55 A5
Wheal Margery TR26 ....141 C3
Wheal Maria PL19 ....29 D1
Wheal Maria Cotts PL19 ...29 D1
Wheal Martyn Mus* PL26..59 B6
Wheal Montague TR16....140 B7
Wheal Northey PL25.....115 B5
Wheal Oak TR13........146 D8
Wheal Prussia TR16 .....140 D8
Wheal Quoit Ave TR5....54 C1
Wheal Ramoth 3 TR6.....55 A5
Wheal Regent Pk PL25...115 D3
Wheal Rodney Holiday Pk*
TR20.....................89 C6
WHEAL ROSE 68 C3
Wheal Rose 19 TR13 ......98 C8
Wheal Silver TR15 ....140 B5
Wheal Speed Rd TR16....141 C2
Wheal Sperries Way TR1...69 E3
Wheal Tehidy La TR15 ...139 E6
Wheal Trefusis TR15.....140 D2

Wheal Trelawney TR16 ...140 D3
Wheal Venture Rd TR26...141 C3
Wheal View PL26 ....58 B4
Wheal Virgin Ho TR26 ....77 A6
WHEAL VOR 91 A5
Wheal Vor TR15 ....90 D3
Wheal Vrose Business Pk 12
TR13...................146 D8
Wheal Vyvyan TR11.......92 F4
Wheal Whidden TR26.....141 C2
Wheatfield Cl 3 PL15 ....106 D4
Wheatfield Cres TR7......111 A4
Wheatley Rd EX22 ....11 F4
Wheatridge PL7 ....130 B7
Wheel Ayr Terr TR26.....141 A6
Wheelgate House Sch TR8 .43 D2
Wheelwright Ct PL20 ......42 E4
Wherry Pl PL23 ....116 D2
WHERRY TOWN...........143 D4
Wherry Way PL14.........50 E7
Whieldon Rd PL25.......115 A4
Whimbrel Way PL9 ......136 C8
Whimple St PL1 ....148 C2
Whin Bank Rd PL5 ......124 E2
WHIPSIDERRY 44 C6
Whipsiderry Cl TR7.......44 C6
Whistley Down PL20......42 B2
Whitby Cres PL6.........125 A1
Whitby Rd PL6...........125 A1
WHITCHURCH 147 D3
Whitchurch Com Prim Sch
PL19...................147 D2
Whitchurch Rd
Horrabridge PL20 ....42 C5
Tavistock PL19 ....147 C3
Tavistock PL19 ....147 C4
Whitcross Hill TR15.....139 C3
Whitebarrow Cotts PL15 ..37 A4
Whitecroft Way EX23 ......5 A6
WHITECROSS Crowlas 77 C1
Wadebridge.............33 B7
Whitecross Blisland PL30...35 D7
Bodinnick PL23 ....116 F6
WHITE CROSS Mullion.....99 B4
St Columb Road 45 C2
White Cross Cury TR12 ....99 B4
Redruth TR16............68 D3
White Cross Ct PL4 .....149 A3
Whitecross Hill PL23 ......61 D3
Whitecross Ind Est TR8 ....45 B2
Whitefield Terr PL4 ......149 B4
Whiteford Cl 16 PL17 ....39 E4
Whiteford Rd PL3 ....128 E6
White Friars La PL4......149 B3
Whitegate PL26 ....58 B8
Whitegate Mdws PL26 ....58 B8
Whitegate Rd TR7 ....111 A6
Whitegate Sh Complex
TR7...................111 A7
Whitehall Dr
9 Bere Alston PL20 ......41 B1
Plymouth PL9...........136 B7
Whitehall Est PL30........23 B2
White Hart Arc The 3
PL15...................106 C5
Whitehaven Way PL6....125 A7
WHITEHILL 146 C4
Whitehill Cross PL15 .....19 C6
Whitehill Terr TR13......146 C4
White Horse
Crowntown TR13..........91 A6
Nancegollan TR13 ....91 A6
White House Cl TR26....141 C2
Whitehouse Villas 5
TR10 ....81 A1
White La Philleigh TR2 ....83 B6
Plymouth PL1............149 A2
White Lady Rd PL9......135 D5
White Lodge EX23 ....10 C7
WHITEMOOR 58 E8
Whitemoor Inf & Jun Sch
PL26....................58 E8
White River Pl TR13.....114 C3
White River Pl Sh Ctr
PL25...................114 C3
WHITEROCK.............108 A5
Whiterock Cl PL27 ....108 B5
Whiterock Rd PL27 ......108 B5
Whiterocks Pk PL18 ......40 D6
Whiterock Terr PL27......108 B5
White's Cl 3 TR5.........91 A6
White Smock Mdw 7 PL35 .9 C1
Whitestone Cres PL31....109 C3
Whitestone Rd PL31.....109 C3
White Walls Ct 16 TR6 ....55 A4
Whitewater Ct PL7 ......130 E6
WHITEWELL.............23 D7
Whitewell Rd PL30 ....23 D7
Whitham Pk PL19........147 C4
WHITLEIGH 124 C5
Whitleigh Ave PL5 ......124 E2
Whitleigh Com Prim Sch
PL5....................124 D4
Whitleigh Cotts PL5 .....124 E2
Whitleigh Ct PL5 ....124 D4
Whitleigh Gn PL5 ....124 C4
Whitleigh Villas PL5 .....124 E2
Whitleigh Way PL5 ......124 C4
Whitley Cl TR1 ....137 D4
Whitley Grange PL14.....113 A6
Whitlieburn Terr PL13.....117 C3
Whitpot Hill PL12.........64 F8
Whitsam Cross PL20......41 A1
Whitsand Bay View PL11...65 A4
Whitson Cross PL5.......124 C7
Whitsoncross La PL5......124 C7
WHITSTONE 7 F1

Whitstone Cty Prim Sch
EX22 ....7 F1
Whitstone Head Sch EX22 ..7 F1
Whittington St PL3 ......148 B4
Whitworth Cl TR5 ....54 C1
Whity Cross PL12.........44 A4
Whym Kibbal Crt TR15 ...140 C5
Widegate Nursery PL9....136 D8
WIDEMOUTH BAY..........6 F5
WIDEWELL 125 B7
Widewell La PL6.........125 C7
Widewell Prim Acad PL6...125 B7
Widewell Rd PL6.........125 B7
Widey Court Prim Sch PL6 124 F1
Widey Cross PL6.........124 F1
Widey Ct PL6............124 F1
Widey La PL6............124 F1
Widey View PL3..........128 F6
Widgeon Way TR27.......77 E3
Wigeon Rd 6 EX23 ....7 B8
Wilcove PL11............127 A6
Wilcove La PL11.........126 E5
Wildebeest Rd 7 PL27....31 F3
Wilderness Rd PL3.......128 E5
Wilderness Trail* PL30 ....48 C5
Wildflower La TR7.......111 A6
Wilkes Wlk TR1..........137 D4
Wilkinson Cl PL17 ....39 E6
Wilkinson Rd PL5........127 D8
Willapark View PL35 ......9 C1
Willas Rd PL16 ....19 F4
William Edwards Cl EX23 .104 E6
William Evans Cl PL6 ....124 D5
William Laundry Cl PL14...52 A5
William Prance Rd PL6 ...125 A3
Williams Ave PL4 ....129 B1
Williams St Camborne TR14.138 D4
Truro TR1...............137 D4
William Young Mews
PL14 ....113 E5
Willis Vean PL12 ....99 A1
Willoughby Pl PL17 ....39 E4
Willoughby Way TR27 .....78 D6
Willowby Pk PL20 ....42 D2
Willow Cl 22 Callington PL17 .39 F4
Mylor Bridge TR11........82 A3
Plymouth PL3...........129 C5
Quintrell Downs TR8 ......44 E3
Willow Cotts PL7 ....130 D4
Willow Ct PL6...........124 B4
Willow Dr TR14 ....138 B4
Willowfield TR18 ....143 C5
Willow Gn PL12..........122 D2
Willow Rd PL19..........147 C3
Willows The Bugle PL26 ...47 C1
Whipsiderry TR7..........44 C6
Willow Way PL14........113 B5
Willow Wlk PL6..........125 D5
Wills Cl PL6.............124 E7
Wills La TR26 ....141 B6
Wills Moor PL26 ....85 C5
Will's Row PL15 ....139 C8
Willsworthy Dr 2 PL19 ..147 B7
WILMINSTONE 30 F3
Wilminstone Ind Est PL19 147 E2
Wilmot Gdns PL5........124 D3
Wilsey View St Clether PL15 .17 B7
Splatt PL15 ....17 B7
Wilson Cres PL2.........128 B5
Wilson Way
Camborne TR15..........139 D5
14 Par PL24.............60 B4
Wilsworthy Cross EX22 ...12 C7
Wilton Rd PL11..........128 A3
Wilton St PL1...........148 A4
Wilton Terr PL13 ....62 D6
Wiltshire Cl PL4.........128 F4
Winchester Gdns PL5.....124 A5
Windermere Cres PL6 ....124 F4
Winding Terr TR10 ....81 A1
WINDMILL 20 F1
Windmill PL23...........116 C4
Windmill Hill TR2 ....57 E1
Launceston PL15.........106 C5
St Just in Roseland TR2 ....82 F2
Saltash PL12 ....122 E2
Windmill Hill Terr PL15 ..106 C5
Windmill Ho PL23 ....116 C4
Windmill Ind Est PL23.....116 C4
Windmill La PL15 ....106 C5
Windmill Park PL15......106 C5
Windmill Rd PL27........22 A5
Windsbatch La 7 PL9 ...129 D1
Windsor Ct Falmouth TR11 .145 B4
Newquay TR7...........110 D5
Windsor Dr PL25 ....115 C3
Windsor Gr PL31 ....109 F5
Windsor Hill 8 TR26 ....141 B5
Windsor Ho 9 PL31 ......109 E5
Windsor La Kelly Bray PL17 ..39 F6
Saltash PL12 ....122 E2
Windsor Mews PL31......109 E5
Windsor Pl Liskeard PL14 ..113 C5
28 Penzance TR18.......143 E6
Plymouth PL1...........148 C2
Windsor Rd PL3.........129 B7
Windsor Terr
Falmouth TR11..........145 B4
Penzance TR18 ....143 D6
4 St Ives TR26.........141 A5
Windsor Villas PL1 ......148 C2
Windsworth PL24........115 F7
Windy Ridge PL26 ....46 D1
Wingfield PL31 ....35 B2
Wingfield Mans PL3 .....128 A3
Wingfield Rd PL3........148 A4

Wingfield Way PL3 ......148 A4
Winifred Baker Ct 5 PL4 .149 A4
Winnard's Perch TR9......32 D1
Winnicott Cl PL6 ....124 E7
Winnow Cl PL9 ....135 F4
Winns Row
Gwealmayowe TR13 ......146 C6
Helston TR13 ....146 C6
Winsbury Ct PL6 ....125 A1
Winsor Cotts PL15.......106 B7
Winsor Est PL13 ....62 D5
Winsor La TR8 ....31 E1
Winstanley Wlk PL3 .....129 D6
Winston Ave PL4 ....148 C4
Winstowe Terr TR8 ......110 A3
Winwell Field PL27 ......108 D6
Wireless Rd PL26 ....87 B5
Wishing Well La TR20.....88 A7
Witham Gdns PL3 ....129 C5
WITHEVEN 11 D3
WITHIEL 47 A8
WITHIELGOOSE MILLS.....47 C8
Withies St 5 PL9........129 C1
WITHNOE 132 A4
Withnoe La PL10 ....132 B6
Withnoe Terr PL10 ....65 E3
Withnoe Way PL15 ......106 D3
Wixenford Ct PL9........135 F8
Woburn Rd PL15.........106 B4
Woburn Terr PL9 ....135 C7
Wodehouse Terr TR18 ....145 B4
Wolcocke Cl TR17 ....89 D5
Wollaton Gr PL5 ....123 F3
Wolrige Ave PL7 ....131 B5
Wolrige Way PL7 ....131 A5
Wolsdon Pl PL1 ....148 A3
Wolsdon St PL1 ....148 B3
Wolseley Bsns Pk 2 PL2...128 A5
Wolseley Cl PL2 ....128 A5
Wolseley Rd
Plymouth, Camels Head
PL5....................127 F6
Plymouth, St Budeaux PL5..123 C1
Wolseley Road Flats PL2..127 F6
Wolverwood Cl PL7 ......131 C3
Wolverwood La PL7 .....131 B3
Wombwell Cres PL2 .....127 E7
Wood Acre PL12 ....122 B4
Woodacre Ct PL12.......122 B4
Wooda La PL15..........106 B6
Wooda Rd PL15.........106 C6
Woodbine Cotts PL7 ....130 E4
Woodbine La TR16........67 D4
Woodbury Gdns PL5 .....124 A3
Woodchurch PL20........42 B3
Wood Cl
17 Resugga Green PL26 ...59 D7
Saltash PL12 ....122 B3
Woodcock Cl PL10.......133 A6
Woodend Rd PL6 ....125 D7
Woodfield Prim Sch PL5 ..124 C5
Woodfield Rd EX23......104 E7
Woodford Ave PL7 ......130 A7
Woodford Cl PL7 ....130 A7
Woodford Cres PL7.......130 A6
Woodford Cross EX23 ......2 C1
Woodford Gn PL7 ....130 B6
Woodford Prim Sch PL7 ..130 B6
Woodford Rd PL6........125 D6
Woodgate Rd PL14 ......113 A5
Woodgrove Pk PL26 ......59 A1
Woodhill TR10 ....81 B2
Wood La Landrake PL12 ...53 D2
Truro TR1...............137 D3
Tywardreath PL24 ....60 D5
Woodland Ave Penryn TR10 144 B7
Plymouth PL9...........136 A8
12 Tywardreath PL24 .....60 D5
Woodland Cl
Gunnislake PL18 ....40 F6
Lanivet PL30 ....47 E7
St Austell PL25..........114 E3
Woodland Ct TR1........137 E5
Woodland Dr PL7........130 B4
Woodland Glade PL30 ....47 E7
Woodland Hill
Doublebois PL14 ....50 B8
Polmenna PL14 ....36 F1
Woodland Hts TR1.......137 E5
Woodland Rd Plymouth PL7 130 C6
St Austell PL25..........114 E3
Woodland Rise
Penryn TR10 ....144 B7
Rilla Mill PL17 ....38 E8
Woodlands Dousland PL20 .42 E3
4 Mullion TR12..........99 A2
10 Par PL24.............60 C4
Plymouth PL9...........135 F6
Woodlands Ct PL5 ....124 A3
Woodlands End PL6......125 D5
Woodlands La Coombe PL26.58 C2
Plymouth PL6...........125 F1
Woodlands Sch PL5 .....124 B4
Woodlands Terr 3 TR16 ..140 F1
Woodlands The TR14 .....67 B4
Woodlands View PL13 ...117 B4
Woodland Terr
Plymouth PL4...........149 B4
4 St Columb Road TR9 ....45 E2
Woodland Terr La PL4 ...149 B4
Woodland View 7 PL26 ..115 A1
Coombe PL26............58 C2
Lanivet PL30 ....47 E6
Woodland Way
Gunnislake PL18 ....41 A7
Torpoint PL11 ....126 F3

Woodland Way Cl 2 PL18..40 F6
Woodlane TR11 ....145 B3
Woodlane TR11 ....145 B3
Woodlane Cres TR11 .....145 B3
Woodlane Dr TR11.......145 B3
Woodley Cl 8 EX23 ....4 D1
Woodman's Cnr PL20 .....42 D3
Woodpecker Way PL19 ..147 D2
Woods-Browning Ind Est
PL31...................109 F2
Woodside Penryn TR10 ..144 B7
Plymouth PL4...........149 B4
Woodside Ave PL9 ......135 C6
Woodside Ct PL7 ....130 E4
Woodside La PL4 ....149 B4
Woodstock Gdns PL5 ....123 D1
Woodvale Terr PL15......106 C5
Wood View TR10 ....144 B7
Woodview Pk PL9 ....136 A6
Woodville Cl PL2 ....127 F7
Woodville Rd
Morwenstow EX23 ....2 C1
Plymouth PL2...........127 F6
Woodford EX23 ....4 D8
Woodway Penryn TR10...144 B7
Plymouth PL9...........136 A7
Woolacombe Cross PL20 ..41 C1
Woolacombe Rd PL20 ....41 C1
Woollcombe Ave PL7 ....130 F4
WOOLLEY 3 A3
Woolster Ct 8 PL4 ......149 A2
WOOLSTON 38 E3
WOOLWELL 125 D7
Woolwell Cres PL6 ......125 C8
Woolwell Dr PL6 ....125 C7
Woolwell Rd PL6 ....125 D7
Woon La 3 TR3 ....81 F7
Worcester Rd PL25 .....115 A4
Wordsworth Cres PL2 ...127 F7
Wordsworth Rd PL2 .....127 F7
Worvas La TR12 ....102 F5
Wotton Cross PL12 ....53 B4
Wreford Cl 11 TR9 ....45 D6
Wren Gdns PL7 ....130 C6
Wren Ind Est TR1 ....69 E4
Wrens Gate PL9 ....135 E8
Wrey Ave PL14 ....113 C7
Wright Cl PL1 ....127 E3
WRINGSDOWN 18 E6
Wrinklets Rd PL30........23 A4
Wyatts La PL19 ....147 B6
Wych Hazel Way TR7 ....110 F4
Wycliffe Rd PL3 ....129 B4
Wye Gdns PL3 ....129 D7
Wykeham Dr PL2 ....128 A7
Wyndham La PL1 ....148 A3
Wyndham Mews PL1 ....148 A3
Wyndham Pl PL1 ....148 A3
Wyndham Sq PL1 ......148 A3
Wyndham Street E PL1 ..148 B3
Wyndham Street W PL1 ..148 B3
Wyndhurst Orch PL27 ...108 B4
Wyoming PL3 ....129 C6
Wythburn Gdns PL6 ....125 D3

Y

Yardley Gdns PL6........125 E3
Yarrow Mead PL9 ....136 D7
Yealmpstone Cl PL7 .....131 B4
Yealmpstone Dr PL7......131 B3
Yealmpstone Farm Prim Sch
PL7....................131 B3
Yeats Cl PL5............124 C2
Yellowmead Rd PL2......128 A7
Yellow Tor Ct PL12 ......122 C2
Yellow Tor La PL12 ......122 C2
Yellow Tor Rd PL12......122 B2
Yellow-Wort TR16.........80 C3
YELVERTON 42 D3
Yelverton Bsns Pk PL20...42 B2
Yelverton Cl PL5 ....123 E4
Yelverton Paperweight Mus*
PL20....................42 C2
Yelverton Terr
Tavistock PL19...........147 D6
Yelverton PL20 ....42 D2
Yeo Cl PL3 ....129 B5
Yeoland Down PL20......121 E8
Yeoland La PL20.........42 C1
YEOLMBRIDGE 18 F6
Yeomadon Cross EX22......8 E4
Yeomans Cl PL14........113 D5
Yeomans Way PL7.......131 A4
Yeoman Way TR8........44 B4
Yewdale Gdns PL6.......125 D2
Yew Tree Ct TR1.........137 F6
Yonder St PL9 ....135 B6
York Pl PL2 ....127 F4
York Rd Plymouth PL5....127 E8
Torpoint PL11 ....127 B3
York St Penzance TR18 ...143 D6
Plymouth PL1...........127 C6
York Terr 7 PL2.........127 F5
Youldon Way PL20........42 C4

Z

Zaggy La PL17 ....39 E4
ZELAH 56 A2
ZENNOR 76 B5
Zennor/Truro & Penwith Coll
TR18..................143 D7
Zion St PL1.............148 C2
Zodiac Ho TR19 ....96 E3